Communications in Computer and Information Science 560

Commenced Publication in 2007
Founding and Former Series Editors:
Alfredo Cuzzocrea, Dominik Ślęzak, and Xiaokang Yang

More information about this series at http://www.springer.com/series/7899

Tom H. Brown · Herman J. van der Merwe (Eds.)

The Mobile Learning Voyage - From Small Ripples to Massive Open Waters

14th World Conference
on Mobile and Contextual Learning, mLearn 2015
Venice, Italy, October 17–24, 2015
Proceedings

Springer

Editors
Tom H. Brown
University of South Africa
Pretoria
South Africa

Herman J. van der Merwe
North-West University: Vaal Triangle Campus
Vanderbijlpark
South Africa

ISSN 1865-0929 ISSN 1865-0937 (electronic)
Communications in Computer and Information Science
ISBN 978-3-319-25683-2 ISBN 978-3-319-25684-9 (eBook)
DOI 10.1007/978-3-319-25684-9

Library of Congress Control Number: 2015952041

Springer Cham Heidelberg New York Dordrecht London

Printed on acid-free paper

Springer International Publishing AG Switzerland is part of Springer Science+Business Media
(www.springer.com)

Preface

The international conference on mobile and contextual learning, mLearn 2015, took place during October 17–24, 2015. The conference was hosted on a Royal Caribbean International cruise ship called "Splendour of the Seas." The cruise departed from Venice for a round trip in the Adriatic and Mediterranean waters. This was the 14th annual conference on mobile and contextual learning with the relevant and suitable conference theme of "The Mobile Learning Voyage: From Small Ripples to Massive Open Waters."

This conference theme pays tribute to the developments that brought mobile learning from its infancy steps in the early 2000s to more maturity in 2015, while simultaneously paving the way for the broad and open waters ahead with new developments and progress in mobile learning and emerging ambient technologies. The conference provided an opportunity for researchers to share and present their work during the past year or two.

The International Association for Mobile Learning (IAmLearn; http://www.iamlearn.org) is the custodian of the mLearn conference series. The annual mLearn conference is a key research and networking event for researchers, strategists, educators, technologists, and industry practitioners from all over the world. mLearn attracts participants from more than 60 countries representing all continents, and is, therefore, the world's largest international conference on mobile and blended learning and emerging ambient technologies. It fulfils the need for stimulating critical debate on and research into theories, approaches, principles, applications, and the implementation of mobile learning. It provides an opportunity for professionals and practitioners to share their knowledge, experience, and research in the various areas in which mobile learning is applied.

The conference program made provision for two leading, invited keynote speakers, namely, Dr. Ernst Adams (founder of the International Game Developers Association, part-time senior lecturer at the University of Uppsala in Sweden, game design consultant and trainer) and Prof. Marcus Specht (Professor of Advanced Learning Technologies at Welten Institute, Research Center for Learning, Teaching and Technology, at the Open University of The Netherlands, and director of the Learning Innovation Labs). The program included pre-conference workshops, full and short papers, poster presentations, special interest groups (SIG), and practical events including technology, product, and service demonstrations. A doctoral consortium for active PhD students was among the five pre-conference workshops.

These proceedings comprise all the full and short papers that were accepted to be included in the conference program by the Program Committee and the international review panel. The call for papers resulted in a total of 81 paper submissions from 24 countries around the world. Every submission was subjected to a double-blind peer-review process. The first round of reviews focused on abstract submissions. Each abstract was reviewed by three reviewers (blind peer review). The authors received the blind reviews and feedback to use in preparation of their papers. Authors of successful abstract submissions with suitable reviews were notified to submit a full paper by August 1, 2015. The second round of reviews took place once the completed full paper submissions were received. Each full paper was reviewed by three reviewers (blind peer review). Out of the 81 original submissions, 23 were selected as full papers and six as short papers. The authors received the blind reviews and feedback and were requested to amend and revise their papers according to the reviewers' comments. The authors that received suitable reviews were requested to submit revised full papers in the required format to be included in the conference proceedings. All the revised full papers were then submitted to Springer for editing and processing.

The authors who have contributed to these proceedings are researchers, developers, and practitioners in both educational and commercial organizations from 21 countries: Australia, Brazil, Canada, Finland, Germany, India, Italy, Kazakhstan, The Netherlands, New Zealand, Qatar, Saudi Arabia, Singapore, South Africa, Sweden, Switzerland, Thailand, Turkey, United Arab Emirates, the UK, and the USA. Some of the papers detail the findings of mobile learning projects; some are based on desk research and attempts by the author(s) to identify and further develop theory relevant in mobile learning; and many report on work in progress. Work in progress includes both research and the development of mobile learning materials and systems.

We would like to thank all participants for their contributions to the conference program and for their contributions to these proceedings. A special thanks to the members of the Program Committee and international review panel for their commitments and dedicated assistance with the paper reviews and decisions. This amidst an already busy academic and research schedule.

We are looking forward to mLearn 2016.

mLearn 2015
International Mobile Learning Conference
From Small Ripples to Massive Open Waters

IAmLearn
International Association for Mobile Learning

September 2015

Tom H. Brown
Herman J. van der Merwe

Organization

Steering Committee

Herman J. van der Merwe (Conference Chair)
Tom H. Brown (Program Chair)
Johan Freysen (Operations Chair)
IAmLearn Executive Committee

Program Committee

Tom H. Brown, South Africa
Herman J. van der Merwe, South Africa
Johan Freysen, South Africa
Marcus Specht, The Netherlands
Mike Sharples, UK
Mohamed Ally, Canada
John Traxler, UK
Agnes Kukulska-Hulme, UK

International Review Panel and Scientific Committee

Mohamed Ally, Canada
Stamatina Anastopoulou, Greece
Inmaculada Arnedillo-Sánchez, Ireland
Phillip Benachour, UK
Seugnet Blignaut, South Africa
Tom H. Brown, South Africa
Peter Bruck, USA
Neil Butcher, South Africa
Inge de Waard, UK
Linda Du Plessis, South Africa
Johan Freysen, South Africa
Christian Glahn, Switzerland
Agnes Kukulska-Hulme, UK
Derek Law, UK
Verona Leedertz, South Africa
Jacobus Liebenberg, South Africa
Chee Kit Looi, Singapore
Cheri MacLeod, Qatar
Machdel Matthee, South Africa

Lydia Mbati, South Africa
Marcelo Milrad, Sweden
David Parsons, New Zealand
Rob Power, Qatar
Demetrios Sampson, Greece
Mike Sharples, UK
Marcus Specht, The Netherlands
Dolf Steyn, South Africa
Brendan Tangney, Ireland
Marian Theron, South Africa
John Traxler, UK
Maritza van den Heuvel, South Africa
Herman J. van der Merwe, South Africa
Linda van Ryneveld, South Africa
Steve Vosloo, South Africa
Jocelyn Wishart, UK
Hasnain Zafar Baloch, Malaysia
Olaf Zawacki-Richter, Germany

Contents

Using Mobile Devices in Supervision of Graduate Research in Distance Education: A Personal Journey

Mokholelana Ramukumba(✉)

Department of Health Studies, University of South Africa, Pretoria, South Africa
ramukmm@unisa.ac.za

Abstract. Supervision of research, especially during the proposal writing stage requires access to adequate intellectual resources, and can be a daunting task for master's students, more so, when they are supervised in an open distance learning context (ODL). The emergence of innovative technologies and smartphone applications has increased the potential of m-learning and therefore, m-supervision.

Purpose: The purpose of this paper is to describe my personal journey in supervising graduate students using personal mobile devices in (ODL) context.

Method: Autoethnography following Driscoll (2000) model of structured reflection guided my reflective narrative. Reflexivity provided the opportunity to challenge myself to explicitly examine my supervisory practices, assumptions, personal epistemologies, and emotions involved in mobile supervision. Strategies used to bridge the distance gap included instant communication (WhatsApp), Wikispaces as a repository for learning triggers, Dropbox for immediate and elaborate feedback, and Skype for individual, collaboration and incorporation of alternative perspectives. These strategies were embedded within various tenets of learning theories and supervision pedagogy.

The reflective data illuminated the potential of using a safe and informal communication space to enhance students' outcomes. The informal social environment offered means of blending affective domain, rationality and autonomy in supervision. Supervisory pedagogy for mobile devices is worthy of being explored and exploited.

Keywords: Graduate research · Interactivity · Mobile devices · Mobile supervision

1 Introduction

This paper aims to express and reveal my experiences and reflections on mobile devices that I used to create an authentic presence in the lives of my masters students doing research in open distance learning context (ODL). Moore (2007) transactional distance theory suggests that distance education students are removed from personal interaction with their mentors both by geographical space and a psychological distance, and this gap can be bridged through concerted efforts such as flexibility of the course structure, dialogue between educator and learner, and learner autonomy. It is a known fact that

T.H. Brown and H.J. van der Merwe (Eds.): mLearn 2015, CCIS 560, pp. 1–14, 2015.
DOI: 10.1007/978-3-319-25684-9_1

learning research, especially during the proposal writing stage requires access to adequate academic resources, and can be a daunting task for master's students more so, when they are geographically separated from the supervisor.

Besides theories and personal epistemologies, my style of research supervision is shaped by lived experiences of ODL, and an understanding of how lonely that road can be. The evolution of handheld portable devices and wireless technology (El-Hussein and Cronje 2010), and the variety of mobile devices that are part of my being, made me ponder the ways I could reach out to the students and bridge the distance gap. In this paper, I review literature on supervisory practices and the use of mobile devises in learning to identify possibilities of using same for supervision, secondly, I describe and analyze the applications that I use to create presence in my students' research journey, and lastly, I reflect on my experiences as a way of making sense of the journey, comparing and contrasting them with the extant literature to generate insights into this area of supervision (Ellis et al. 2011). This reflection culminates with suggestions and pertient questions on using mobile devices in supervision, working around issues of balancing academic demands, and re-thinking appropriate learning theories.

2 Research Supervision: A Complex Space

Supervision of higher degrees research is not only a complex teaching task, it is a joint endeavour in which both the supervisor and student have a scholarly interest (Bruce and Stoodley 2013). It is an evolving and dynamic partnership that is influenced by an array of intertwined social, cultural, emotional, and intellectual factors (Maritz 2013). It can also be an unknown terrain as the supervisor and the candidate bring unique experiences to the partnership/relationship. For this relationship to flourish, it is necessary for supervisors to utilise approaches based on empirical evidence to enhance student outcomes (Lee 2007). Blending technology with face-to-face approaches has been growing in recent years (Donnelly and Fitzmaurice 2013); it is up to supervisors to select technologies that are relevant and acceptable to students.

Complementary approaches to supervision are emerging and have different areas of focus: engagement, authenticity, relevance, resourcefulness, support, facilitation, co-learning, scholarship, transformation, multidimensionality, and scientific writing (Donnelly and Fitzmaurice 2013, Stanley 2015; Frith and Martens 2008; Lee 2007; Manathunga 2007). At the core of these approaches are the strengths, challenges, and contributions supervision brings to knowledge creation, as well as the need to transform learners, enabling them to achieve quality research. It is evident from various models in literature that supervision of graduate students is not free from the complex ideologies as well as institutional demands on both the student and the supervisor. Manathunga (2007) uses the center-periphery argument which focuses on the flow of power and control (center) to the supervisors (periphery), to describe the adverse effects of managerial overemphasis of accountability on academics. Lee (2007) concurs that the pressures within academia to produce high quality research and completion rates place high demands on supervisors. However, Frith and Martens (2008) believe that the entrenched institutional roles are important and necessary to foster an understanding of supervision as a specialist form of teaching. They acknowledged that many supervisors combine mentor and friend in their relationships with graduate students, but emphasize that power; desire and emotion exist in the realm of supervision. These arguments relate to my experience, as the decision to invest time in going an extra mile to reach out to the ODL students invariably places tensions in academic roles. I argue that the choices we make as supervisors are influenced by personal styles and anticipated outcomes.

The view of supervision as teaching acknowledges the role of the research candidates as leaners as well as contributors in knowledge generation (Bruce and Stoodley 2013). Vilkinas (2008) agrees that approaches that incorporate reflective, pedagogically sound, collegial activity where students are viewed as learners and contributors of knowledge tend to be more successful. The discussions within supervision literature made me acutely aware of the need to provide supervision based on empowerment thus, giving students the opportunity to take control of the research processes.

3 Mobile Learning: Opportunities for mSupervision

The portability, technical advancements, and immediacy of mobile devices offer opportunities to address geographic challenges in distance learning, give feedback on the go, and to enrich collaborative learning (Chen et al. 2006; Nassuora 2012; Fuegen 2012). It is against these advancements that I borrowed concepts from El-Hussein and Cronje (2010) to define mSupervision as the 'use of mobile technology, by a mobile supervisor to create authentic supervision pedagogy'. My interest in the social context of learning enabled me to develop a supervision pedagogy that guided the selection and implementation of mobile applications, so to create an informal space characterised by high forms of interactivity to promote research development. The desire to explore, learn, and abandon the constraints of habitual ways of thinking (El-Hussein and Cronje 2010) became the driving force.

I tend to lean towards the views of supervision as a higher form of teaching; from this stance, I regard myself as engaged in a process of 'becoming' as I learn from my experiences. Hence, this paper intergrates frameworks from transformational learning with mSupervision pedagogy. mlearning is not explored further, as it is not within the scope of this paper.

4 Autoethnography and Research Supervision Journey

Autoethnography is viewed as a qualitative research method that seeks to describe and systematically analyse personal experience. It generates data about the self, draws upon ethnographic attention to socio-cultural context (Ellis et al. 2011, Raab 2013), allows authors to write complex, meaningful phenomenon in a unique way, thus, communicating the self to the world (Custer 2014), provides the emotional truth of the story and enables readers to engage with personal stories as experienced by authors (Ngunjiri et al. 2010). "*The ontological foundation for truth in autoethnography is the self who was 'there'*" (Niamh 2014). Like any methods of research, autoethnography generates debates and critique. Much of the critique centres on subjectivity, criticality and selectivity in expressing the stories (Learmonth and Humphrey in Stanley 2015). The work of Anderson (2006) assists in addressing issues related to academic legitimacy, he recommends the theoretical oriented interpretation of autoethnography texts where others are consulted as part of the ethnographic process, but still focusing on the self. He proposes analytical reflexivity that includes awareness of the reciprocal influence of the context and the others.

On the other hand, other autoethnographers choose to remain true to the tenets of epistemology of the self (Ellis et al. 2011), some believe that the distinction between approaches of autoethnography is unnecessary, rather the distinction should be made between forms of autoethnographic practices that are oriented toward explicit analysis and those that are not (Vryan in Pace 2012). To overcome challenges of validity and reliability, authors need to be systematic, express experience in relation to literature, and identify patterns in the analysis (Raab 2013, Chatham-Carpenter 2010). Ngunjiri et al. (2010) suggest that research is an extension of researchers' lives and scholarship is inextricably connected to self-personal interest and experience. Therefore, subjectivity is an impossible task.

The epistemological complexities of autoethnography steered me towards reflexivity to construct data about the self within the context of research development. The essence of this paper is to articulate my experiences with mobile applications, assumptions, personal epistemologies, students, research development, and emotions involved in my supervisory practice. Driscoll (2000) model of structured reflection provides the framework for this paper. The main feature of my approach is self-exploration, and brief excerpts from students' discussions are included to give the narrative methodological transparency and legitimacy (Chatham-Carpenter 2010, Ellis et al. 2011). My story serves as a reflective account of my experiences and forms the basis of my findings. Ethical issues of informed consent and ethical clearance were adequately addressed.

5 Venturing into the Unknown Terrain

I joined the university 8 months before I was allocated my first batch of 7 master's students, and embraced the task with great anticipation and excitement, driven by personal epistemologies and assumptions about research and supervision. I had a good understanding of the isolation and helplessness that sometimes engulf distance learners as I walked that path many times before. I was new (but not new to research supervision), my students were new to doing research, the newness of communication patterns and systems were at best, overwhelming. I was from a high technology learning environment and could not comprehend the limited resources I had to contend with. Students were also taking a long time to respond to my emails. The slow response compelled me to turn focus to the content of my emails and realised that they were way too rigid and formal, and probably made students to think whether or not doing a master's degree was the right choice. I used the common language used in the university corridors because I needed to be 'academically correct'. The style of communication was alien to me, it created tensions which translated into a 'problem', I was compelled to bring the true self forward and change the communication style.

I could almost 'hear' the sigh of relief in students' correspondence. The change heralded what was to be a 'cordial dialogue' between us.

I needed communication tools that would create a safe space for the supervisory relationships to evolve, and recognised the fact that the students were also on a challenging journey of balancing multiple roles. I designed the supervisory pedagogical strategy based on Siemens (2004) theory of connectivism and Mezirow (2000) transformational learning that supports empathy, caring, autonomy, self-reflection, collaboration and self-directedness. The focus was on enhancing cognitive engagement with the research process, inculcating a sense of self-regulation, collaboration, and finding meaning and purpose in the supervision process (Fig. 1).

Fig. 1. Mobile application used. Source: www.printermedia.com

5.1 Bridging the Distance Gap and Creating a Presence

My teaching philosophy premises interactive dialogue, collaboration, autonomy, and connectivity. The immediate communication functionalities of my mobile devices were well suited to my core beliefs. I leveraged Web 2.0 technologies. My main proposition was to use a range of tools that allow reflection and complement different learning preferences. The profile of my students necessitated starting with the basics or the 'knowns'. WhatsApp, Dropbox, Skype, and Wikispaces became the preferred modes of communication.

5.1.1 WhatsApp

WhatsApp is a cross platform smartphone messenger that uses internet data plan for social networking; it provides an alternative to texting. It is available for Apple IOS, Google Android, Blackberry OS, Microsoft windows phones (WhatsApp 2010). Users can exchange text messages, images, videos, and voice notes. Students can interact socially with the supervisors to facilitate learning (Zengin et al. 2011). Its attractive user interface makes discussions rich (Bouhnik and Deshen 2014). I got students' mobile numbers and created a WhatsApp group for the 7 registered for the proposal module. The key aspect of the instant messaging was to broadcast important messages to the group and individually, it also became a good platform for collaboration as students supported each other on various issues. To give structure to the discussions, I developed a schedule for bi-weekly announcements for synchronous discussions, this was possible because all students were at the same stage/phase of the research process. Individual needs were addressed through anytime, on-the-go research conversations. This application also became the just-in-time way of introducing other technology tools. See texts below:

2015-07-10 10:23:20: Mags: Watch YouTube on how to probe to obtain in-depth info. U need quality data in order to have a winning research

2015-07-10 10:24:58: M1: Dr where to find YouTube?

I posted links, images, self created audio clips, and screenshots of any information related to their studies, especially during proposal writing stage. The short audio clips provided a useful platform when I could not express myself fast enough in writing. The texts were not mere chats, the tool was used as a form of teaching and learning, making students feel my involvement in their studies, listen to their struggles, and just be there when they needed me. For record keeping, I sent the chat history to my office email at the end of each month, after intense individual conversations, I printed the history to review and identify any gaps or misunderstandings in communication. The chat histories provided me the opportunity to reflect on the style of conversations and identify instances where I could have unintentionally used intimidating top-down approaches. I kept a diary of students' progress, summaries of our texts conversations including my reflections as a way of 'making sense of it all'.

5.1.2 Skype

Skype is a telecommunication software that can be used via the internet to create conference calls, share screen, make calls, send files and photos and texting (Skype 2003). To compensate for the sensory loss, I increased the audio-visual component of our interactions by encouraging students to sign up for Skype. I used the calendaring and scheduling functionalities on my Smartphone running on IOS 7 platform to draw up schedules for group video conferencing. Topics were jointly generated and the conversations were informal but serious. The initial focus was on students' presentations of their progress reports characterized by question and answer method to stimulate dialogue. However, I could only get 2 at a time due to time differences and constraints. Later, we resorted to individual video chats. Pre-planning was important to conserve students' internet resources and also, to provide structured and meaningful guidance. Sometimes, the calls were casual just to follow up on progress. Most of the video calls happened after hours to accommodate their working hours, that suited me very well because I tend to be more creative in the evenings. WhatsApp became the vehicle for scheduling meetings.

2015-06-30 17:37:27: M3: Dr, I'm conected. tnx

2015-06-30 17:25:13: Mags: Hello, need to Skype with u to discuss ch2.

5.1.3 Dropbox

Dropbox is a cloud-based file sharing system that can be installed on various devices and uses Bluetooth technology to synchronize data sending and receiving across devices (Dropbox 2012). Students were invited to share individual folders and were given editing functions. 5 students created accounts and used it fully. The more I shared files, the more storage space I got from dropbox. My nocturnal tendencies enabled me to create longer videos from the comfort of my home, and these were uploaded on shared folders to increase access to resarch resources. Examplary research reports by previous students, as well as screenshots on any relevant topic were also uploaded. File sharing saved time and eliminated the need to download, edit, upload documents, and send as attachments. It became the easiest form of retrieving work and giving quick feedback. I could read their work from anywhere, anytime using Word application on my IPad, the versatility of dropbox allowed me, as an administrator, to restore files that students deleted accidentally.

2015-07-14 07:06:32: M6: Good morning Dr, I created an outline for literature review, on dropbox new folder 2015 " LITERATURE REVIEW OUTLINE JULY 13", thank you.

2015-02-27 21:12:59: M3: Ok, Dr. tnk u, wid all my heart, I tnk u. u hav thot me so much. n u hav been so patient wid al my bad technology n al dat. God bles ♥

5.2 Wikispaces

Wiki is a website that works best on Google chrome, it can be built collaborately, students can add and grow content base. It can also be used as a reservoir of content and can link to other pages in a fast and efficient way (Maloney et al. 2013). I needed a bigger space for effective collaboration and monitoring of activities, and decided on this tool due to the limitations of the institution's online learning platforms for post-graduate students. Invites to join Wikispaces virtual space were sent through students' emails. The uptake was slow and I was beginning to sense some level of frustration with the new 'things'. My intention is to go slow on this one and not 'impose' since not all students accepted my invitation, only 4 students joined. Currently, I use Wikispaces mainly as a repository for learning material, personally created video clips, short notes and interactive tasks to trigger critical thinking and reflection (Fig. 2).

2015-03-17 13:16:15: M1: Thanx Dr I joined last week.

2015-03-17 13:12:40: Mags: Have u joined our virtual space on wiki?

2015-03-27 15:06:37: M3: Hi Dr. I am curently listening to d audio file

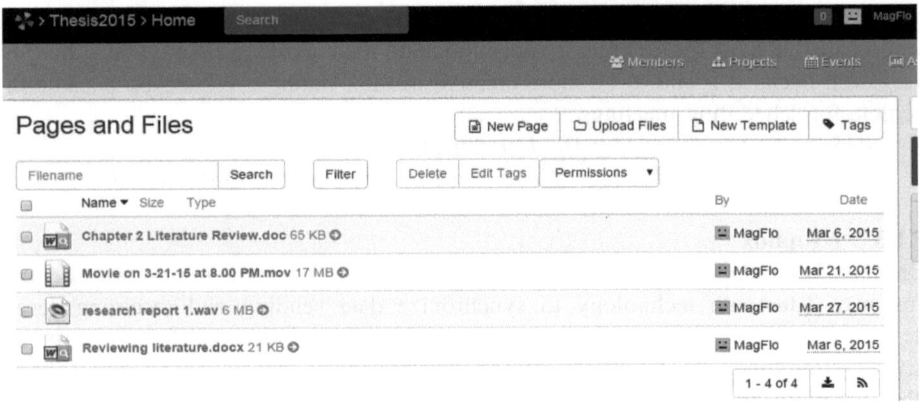

Fig. 2. Wikispaces group page. Source: http://www.wikispaces.com/user/my/MagFlo

6 Making Sense of It All

My main aim was to use my mobile devices to offer maximum support with emphasis on self-directed learning, reflection and reflexive dialogue. I aspired for a situation where students would not readily accept my feedback without scrutiny and questioning. Uppermost on my mind was the need for them to get into the habit of conversations and justifications of positions they were taking within a reasonable time frame (Leamnson 2000). I was aware that I was dealing with mature students who had their own set of rules and expectations regarding their studies. My selection of mobile applications was influenced by the conception that learning occurs when students think deeply and more frequently about something, and the supervisor needs to ensure that students hear and see this 'something' (Taylor 2000).

During the initial stages I fluctuated between frustration and despondency when I could not get the right combination of applications that appealed to my students. I started with various tools; the uptake was challenging and eventually selected what they felt comfortable with. There were times I could not tell exactly, whether it was the application or the very research supervision that left me feeling helpless. The distance prevented me from seeing their 'agony', I could only imagine their frustrations with the additional things they were asked to learn, over and above the complex research language. On hindsight, I realized that I did not have sufficient information about their technology readiness, internet connectivity and their expectations of my supervisory role. The push for me was to find ways of supporting those students who were still moving into self-directed mode, and find a structure that would help them grow. When they finally got into 'it', the immediacy, interactivity, and accessibility of WhatsApp messaging (Chen et al. 2006) supported the urgency of learning research. The students gained from my anytime availability, especially the instant feedback and opportunity to reflect. I allowed my private space to be invaded, but I did not mind as these were mature professionals who were 'taught' the strange language of 'download', 'icon', navigate by their children (some shared with me). The WhatsApp audio clips and screenshots became popular to some, but, for others a bit confusing, especially the audio clip on 'writing the research problem statement'. It was a 3 min clip where I provided a brief summary of the steps. Maybe, the timing was not appropriate, as the content assumed some form of existing knowledge.

Skype was new to the majority of students. However, the initiation and adoption was less stressful, only 5 students used it fully. The technology tools are not culturally neutral (Maritz 2013), the issue of coming 'face to face' with the supervisor might have been culturally intimidating or it could have been a simple matter of preference. I learned to travel this journey alongside my students and give them space to be, and to let go of things I did not have control over. The good moments exemplified by '*oh it is so good to see your face'*, were personally gratifying. I could sense their contentment at putting a face to a name and experiencing human caring and empathy within the intellectual space. The after hours video calls were an extra bonus to all, there was a sense of psychological comfort and satisfaction. I am aware that it would not be reasonable to expect any supervisor to do what I did. I had time, resources, passion for technology, and my biogical clock favoured their working hours.

The shift to one-to-one mentoring using WhatsApp and Skype increased individual spaces and provided personalised support. Skype supported a safe environment where students took responsibility, and where reflexive dialogue became a norm (Billington 2000). This provided me the opportunity to use scafolded supervision. The combination of media, involving maximum immediacy and personal interaction, combined with recording for later review, has been shown to yield the richest and most flexible supervision (Sussex in Donnelly and Fitzmaurice (2013). There were low moments too, Wikispaces did not gain traction with some, those who used it benefited from sharing and bigger and longer audio clips. Maloney et al. (2013) posit that digital repository is the most efficient and preferred source of learning. I also observed the relationship between the pace of technology uptake and the degree of conceptualization of the research process, my literature search to confirm or disprove the findings yielded no results. Those few students benefited from a temporary 'breathing space'. After this uphill journey, they gained the momentum and are now maximizing the benefits.

I had to content with the fact that adult learners learn well if they set own goals, discover needed resources on their own and choose methods by which they learn (Billington 2000). Knowles et al. (1998) concur and acknowledge that adults resent and resist situations in which they feel others are imposing their will on them. I was compelled to reassess my position in relation to blanket use of mobile applications.

7 Finding the Balance

The newness of the situation, eagerness for my students to succeed and many other academic demands threw me off balance for a while. Substantial time was spent on the design of the supervision strategies, initiation and motivation to use them. In the process, I 'neglected' some key performance areas such as research output. I experienced a great sense of helplessness, despair and failure. The journey was long – there were moments of helplessness where I went into my private space to question the wisdom of the 'extra burden' I created for myself. Most of the time I could not find answers, but, peeling off deeper layers from my consciousness revealed the nurturing aspect of the self, and there were moments that provided emotional gratification:

2015-03-23 12:52:40: M3: Tnx 4 everythin u hav done 4 me Dr. I apreciate u

The question that was uppermost on my mind was – how best can I maintain the balance, to be innovative in supervision, to enable my students to learn the 'how' of research and writing skills within the university proposal completion time, at the same time produce acceptable research output? I realized that my on-the-go availability needed some modifications. I grappled with my personal beliefs regarding my role as a supervisor and I asked myself if there was another way out there to become a scholar. Mine was a journey characterized by a strange form of loneliness, I did not have reference points, I could not share ideas, the dominant voices I heard in the corridors were all about manuscripts and publications. Despite all the hits and misses, I could only sit back and appreciate what emerged from my on-the-move supervision. All students obtained ethical clearance, considering the time at our disposal and the vigorous quality processes proposals are subjected to. Those were not the only factors; there was a noticeable growth in self-regulation and articulation of ideas.

2015-02-09 15:23:41: M4: Thanks Dr for the support. I truly appreciate it. There was time when I felt like giving up but your patience and support kept me going. God bless!

2015-02-27 08:44:20: M1: Thank you very much Dr. Your support is much appreciated. May you be blessed more abundantly□□

8 What Insights Emerged from This Journey?

It is evident that forms of teaching and learning, including research supervision, are being impacted by technology. The mobile applications used enabled productive and engaged supervisory relationship. The supervision pedagogy applied seemed to work for most students, the informal spaces offered gratifying learning experiences. Planning as well as supportive images and audio clips were made possible by the smartphone functionalities. Connectivism recognizes the significant trends in learning contexts that both include informal aspects and the influence of technology on thinking processes (Siemens 2004). However, there are no proven learning designs for mobile devices (Benyon et al. 2005). Technology becomes a tool, a means to an end when it is connected to a problem and the interface between content and pedagogy (Zhao 2003). The learning theories that guided this journey are for different contexts, however, some components are applicable to mobile supervision.

The ability to provide frequent feedback and to create an authentic presence in safe spaces, where students hear your empathic voice and read your supportive messages are all human tools that supervisors could use to remove the mask of rigidity that we sometimes wear. The good emerged out of the ordinary. The access to students' work anywhere, anytime, and in various formats has the potential to enhance deep student learning (Amry 2014, Keengwe et al. 2008). The web storage and synchronization of Dropbox was very convenient, there was no need to send large files and video through email, I could write comments on the files and students would easily access it. I also noticed that some shared folders among themselves for increased collaboration. The downside of it according to one student, is that Dropbox updates use a lot of data, something to consider when choosing applications.

It was also evident that when students were empowered, they take control and initiate contact. However, I learned that technology is not for everyone; I will never use it for the sake of being relevant or current, assessing students' technology disposition before embarking on any innovative ideas prevents unnecessary tensions.

2015-03-27 14:56:28: M6: Hi I'm now on the page which allows me to invite people, join code, pending members requests and I'm stuck I don't know where to go pls assist.

This experience has made me to question every move I take. Do I know what they want? Do I know what they don't know regarding mobile technology and research process? How am I going to use these devices to support them build the necessary skills to manage knowledge and complete their studies on time? Teaching philosophy, assumptions, personal epistemologies blended with selected tenets of multiple learning theories, and supervision pedagogy should form the framework in the selection of mobile applications. Whatever we do must suit the present.

I learned that the affective element is a very important part of learning and supervision processes. We need to hit the pause button frequently to reassess the truths that we hold, be receptive to all forms of knowing and develop appropriate strategies to manage this knowledge creation process. More importantly, to recognize that there a persona behind that name, student number and research title. I believe that the real self manifests and connects with students in safe and informal spaces, where it provides maximum guidance for intellectual processes to flourish. It is during students' 'dis-connected' times that these safe spaces become useful. A short message or an invite to Skype to follow up on progress provides an instant uplift.

8.1 What Now? Where Do We Go from Here?

This narrative integrates 4 complex issues, supervision pedagogy, mobile applications, adult students, and academic environment. What then can be concluded from this narrative? My findings show that we need to rethink the way we connect with students. The permanency, accessibility, immediacy, and interactivity offered by mobile device applications are worthy to be explored and exploited. I argue that we can relate this form of mobile supervision to mlearning. El-Hussein and Cronje (2010) describe mlearning components as mobile learner, mobile technology, and mobile pedagogy. Several questions come to the fore: How do we leverage existing mobile technologies to create an authentic presence in ODL contexts? What new learning frameworks/theories do we need, what should be the emphasis of these theories? How do we give students a real voice in our selection and initiation of moble technologies? How do we integrate mobile applications with web based learning systems to enehance ubiquitous supervision? How do we maintain balance between all competing demands?

If I had the time back, and if I could do things differently it would be to discuss the mobile learning possibilities with students before I initiate any application. Secondly, I would seek academics (university wide) who are using mobile applications or any form of technology to share ideas. Thirdly, I would discuss my reflections with interested colleagues within my department to deepen my insights, and lastly, seek formal support from the relevant departments within the university so to build on the existing technologies. Autoethnography supported this reflective journey as I attempted to utilize data about self and to gain understanding of the connectivity between the self and my students (Ngunjiri et al. 2010). This form of inquiry is believed to be shaping the future and face of science (Davidson in Custer 2014). I also acknowledge that the question of what constitutes knowledge is a contested terrain, perhaps one day researchers would combine quantitative, constructivism, and autoethnography to potentially add a new layer of depth and richness to data (Sell-Smith and Lax 2013 in Custer 2014).

I believe that these findings (critical reflections) are transferable to any ODL setting. Each research situation is unique and so, the supervision will be different each time. This journey is a never-ending process that stands to be perfected as new meanings emerge. Mine is an ongoing dialogue with the self as I search for appropriate learning theories and relevance in the world of ODL supervision.

Acknowledgments. I am thankful to my students who are making the journey of supervision bearable, no matter how hard I push them, their eagerness to learn new ways of communication is fulfilling. I appreciate the inputs from the critical reviewer.

References

Anderson, L.: Analytic autoethnography. J. Contemp. Ethnogr. **35**, 373–394 (2006)

Amry, A.B.: The impact of WhatsApp mobile social learning on the achievement and attitudes of female students compared with face to face learning in the classroom. Eur. Sci. J. **10**(22), 116–136 (2014). http://eujournal.org/index.php/esj/article/viewFile/3909/3700

Benyon, D., Turner, P., Turner, S.: Designing Interactive Systems: People, Activities, Context, Technologies. Addison Wesley, Pearson Education, New York (2005)

Billington, D.D.: Effective Adult Learning Programs. New Horizons, Seattle (2000)

Bouhnik, D., Deshen, M.: WhatsApp goes to school: mobile instant messaging between teachers and students. J. Inf. Technol. Educ. Res. **13**, 217–231 (2014). http://www.jite.org/documents/Vol13/JITEv13ResearchP217-231Bouhnik0601.pdf. Accessed 16 February 2014

Bruce, C., Stoodley, I.: Science and technology supervision resource and cases. Queensland University of Technology, Brisbane (2010)

Bruce, C., Stoodley, I.: Experiencing higher degree research supervision as teaching. Stud. High. Educ. **38**(2), 226–241 (2013)

Chatham-Carpenter, A.: 'Do thyself no harm': protecting ourselves as autobiographers. J. Res. Pract. **6**(1), 183–213 (2010). http://jrp.icaap.org/index.php/jrp/article/view/213/183. Accessed 26 March 2015

Chen, G.D., Chang, C.K., Wang, C.Y.: Ubiquitous learning website: scaffold learners by mobile devices with information-aware techniques. Comput. Educ. **50**, 77–90 (2006)

Custer, D.: Autoethnography as a transformative research method. Qual. Rep. **19**(21), 1–13 (2014). http://www.nova.edu/ssss/QR19/custer21.pdf. Accessed 23 February 2014

Donnelly, R., Fitzmaurice, M.: Development of a model for blended postgraduate research supervision in irish higher education. In: O'Farrell, C., Farrell, A. (eds.) Emerging Issues in Higher Education III, From Capacity Building to Sustainability, Dublin, Educational Developers in Ireland Network (EDIN) (2013)

Driscoll, J.: Practising Clinical Supervision: A Reflective Approach. Bailliere-Tindall, London (2000)

Dropbox (2012). www.dropbox.com

Ellis, C., Adams, T.E., Bochner, A.P.: Autoethnography: an overview. Forum Qual. Res. **12**(1), 1–18 (2011). http://www.qualitative-research.net/index.php/fqs/article/view/1589/3095. Accessed 18 August 2011

El-Hussein, M.O.M., Cronje, C.: Defining mobile learning in the higher education landscape. Educ. Technol. Soc. **13**(3), 12–21 (2010)

Firth, A., Martens, E.: Transforming supervisors? A critique of post-liberal approaches to research supervision. Teac. High. Educ. **13**(3), 279–289 (2008)

Fuegen, S.: The impact of mobile technologies on distant education. TechTrends **56**(6), 49–53 (2012)

Jacob, S.B., Isaac, B.: Mobile learning culture and effects in higher education. IEEE Multidiscip. Eng. Educ. Mag. **2**(2), 19–21 (2007)

Keengwe, J., Onchwari, G., Wachira, P.: Computer technology integration and student learning: barriers and promise. J. Sci. Educ. Technol. (JOST) **17**(6), 560–565 (2008)

Knowles, M., Holton, E., Swanson, R.A.: The Adult Learner. Gulf Publishing, Houston (1998)

Leamnson, R.: Learning as biological brain change. Change Mag. High. Learn. **32**(6), 34–40 (2000)

Lee, A.M.: Developing effective supervisors: concepts of research supervision. S. Afr. J. High. Educ. **21**(4), 680–693 (2007)

Maloney, S., Chamberlain, M., Morrison, S., Kotsanas, G., Keating, J.L., Ilic, D.: health professional learner attitudes and use of digital learning resources. J. Med. Internet Res. **15**(1), e7 (2013). doi:10.2196/jmir.2094

Manathunga, C.: Supervision as mentoring: the role of power and boundary crossing. Stud. Continuing Educ. **29**(2), 207–221 (2007)

Maritz, J.: A journey through currere: challenging hegemonies in research education and post graduate supervision on tertiary open distance learning. Progression **35**(2), 157–176 (2013)

Mezirow, J.: Learning to think like an adult: core concepts of transformative theory. In: Mezirow, J. (ed.) Learning as Transformation: Critical Perspectives on a Theory in Progress. Jossey-Bass Publishers, San Franscisco (2000)

Moore, M.G.: The theory of transactional distance. In: Moore, M.G. (ed.) Handbook of Distance Education, pp. 89–105. Erlbaum, Mahwah (2007)

Nassuora, A.B.: Students' acceptance of mobile learning for higher education in Saudi Arabia. Am. Acad. Sch. Res. J. **4**(2), 24–30 (2012)

Ngunjiri, F.W., Hernandez, K.C., Chang, L.L.: Living autoethnography: connecting life and research. J. Res. Pract. **6**(1), 1–17 (2010). http://jrp.icaap.org/index.php/jrp/article/view/241/186

Niamh, O.R.: Autoethnography: proposing a new method for information systems research. In: Twenty Second European Conference on Information Systems, Tel Aviv, September 2014

Pace, S.: Writing the self into research: using grounded theory analytical strategies in autoethnography. In: (eds.) Creativity: Cognitive, social and Cultural Perspectives (2012). http://www.textjournal.com.au/speciss/issue13/Pace.pdf

Raab, D.: Transpersonal approaches to autoethnography research and writing. Qual. Rep., 18, Article 42, 1–18 (2013). www.nova.edu/ssss/QR18/raab42.pdf. Accessed 14 August 2015

Siemens, G.: Connectivism: a learning theory for the digital age. Int. J. Instr. Technol. Distance Learn. (online) (2004). http://itdl.org/Journal/Jan_05/article01.htm. Accessed 12 March 2015

Skype (2003). www.skype.com

Stanley, P.: Writing the Ph.D. journey(s): an autoethnography of zine-writing, angst, embodiment, and backpacker travels. J. Contemp. Ethnogr. **44**(2), 143–168 (2015)

Taylor, E.W.: Analyzing research on transformative learning theory. In: Mezirow, J. (ed.) Learning as Transformation: Critical perspectives on a Theory in Progress, pp. 29–310. Jossey-Bass, San Francisco (2000)
Vilkinas, T.: An exploratory study of the supervision of Ph.D./Research students' Theses. Innov. High. Educ. **32**, 297–311 (2008)
WhatsApp (2010). www.whatsapp.com
Zengin, B., Arikan, A., Dogan, D.: Opinions of English major students about their departments' websites. Contemp. Educ. Technol. **2**(4), 294–307 (2011)
Zhao, F.: Transforming quality in research supervision: a knowledge-management approach. Qual. High. Educ. **9**, 187 (2003)

Technology Integration in Diverse Contexts: Models of Competency-Based Professional Learning in Three School Districts

Kathryn Martin[1(✉)], David Miyashiro[2], and Tim Baird[3]

[1] Director of Professional Learning, San Diego, USA
martin@sandiego.edu
[2] Superintendent Cajon Valley Union School District, El Cajon, USA
miyashirod@cajonvalley.netz
[3] Superintendent Encinitas Union School District, Encinitas, USA

Abstract. Innovation in education requires educators to develop new skills, knowledge, and mindsets. Reimagining professional learning approaches to provide educators with the time, space, and resources to develop the necessary competencies is critical to creating optimal learning environments. Three school district leaders from urban and suburban districts in the United States with high populations of second language learners will share their competency-based professional learning model. The district leaders will share their professional learning models and the impact in their unique context. The focus will be based on personalized professional learning to support powerful learning and teaching accelerated by technology. An emphasis will be on personalized professional learning and demonstrations of teacher development linked to student outcomes rather than seat time. Implications will be shared for designing an ecosystem, characterized by high expectations and high support, to impact a culture of learning and innovation.

Keywords: Professional learning · Leadership · Competency-based · Personalized learning

1 Introduction

Innovation in education requires educators to develop new skills, knowledge and mindsets. Reimagining professional learning approaches to provide educators with the time, space, and resources to develop the necessary competencies is critical to creating optimal learning environments. Meeting teachers where they are and helping them move forward requires a systematic approach to support personalized professional learning. It is critical to build an ecosystem of support, characterized by high expectations and high support to impact a culture of learning and innovation. Mobile Technology Learning Center (2015) research indicates that to authentically integrate technology, teachers desire to:

1. Build a shared understanding of the role of technology in the classroom.
2. Engage in personalized professional learning to develop confidence and competence at their own time, place and path

T.H. Brown and H.J. van der Merwe (Eds.): mLearn 2015, CCIS 560, pp. 15–30, 2015.
DOI: 10.1007/978-3-319-25684-9_2

3. Observe and experience models of desired teaching and learning
4. Receive feedback to develop their practice
5. Opportunities for structured collaboration to learn with peers teaching the same content

Traditional professional development manifests itself in the form of off campus workshops and typically little connection or implementation is generally made at the school level. Darling-Hammond and McLaughlin (1995) have long argued that professional development needs to shift from imposing knowledge and skills onto teachers, to providing opportunities for reflection on practice in order to develop their own understanding of content, pedagogy and learners. Quality teachers with experience and content knowledge exist in many schools and are often the most untapped resources. Establishing networks of support for teachers, both novice and veteran can serve as highly effective professional learning.

Revisiting the purpose and vision to support the fast pace of change in the growing information economy is critical to creating learning environments the meet the needs of today's learners. The work of district leaders is not to manage the resources, decisions or data, but to ensure the schools and teachers remain focused on the vision and are empowered to engage in the continuous learning required to achieve it. It is critical to facilitate the development of collaborative environments where learners develop content knowledge and skills that will prepare them for our globally competitive world.

2 Theoretical Framework

There are wide-ranging developmental influences that affect teachers' experiences. Experience is defined by Bronfenbrenner (2005) as subjective feelings that emerge in early childhood and continue through life. Experiences are "emotionally and motivationally loaded" (p. 5). Teachers are influenced by their beliefs, personal experiences, professional preparation and ongoing professional learning. To understand teachers' experiences, it is important to understand the influences that perpetuate their development and situate the teaching and learning in context.

Bandura's social learning theory (1977) explains how behaviors are learned through observation of behaviors, attitudes and emotional reactions of others. Social learning theory focuses on the learning that occurs within a social context. People learn from one another, through observation, imitation and modeling. When schools are organized to facilitate positive learning models, interactions promote learning and foster school wide achievement (Darling-Hammond and McLauglin 1995; Meier 2002).

In order for students to achieve high levels of success, administrators can organize schools in a way that supports teachers' development and understanding of how to teach students in that context (DuFour 2007; Mertens and Flowers 2004). Continuous professional discourse about powerful learning experiences and authentic technology integration, with regard to specific issues that school populations face such as motivation, developmental appropriateness, race, socio-economic status, specific learning needs, English proficiency and other challenges that exist in students' lives are important for teacher development.

3 Literature Review

There is wide agreement that as environments, resources and tools change to meet the needs of today's learners, the role of teachers must shift as well. The desire to "transform" learning and teaching is often expressed as a goal but the teacher's role in this change, or how to get there, is not often as clearly articulated. To help teachers develop the pedagogical, technological, and content expertise or TPACK (Mischra and Koehler 2006), it is critical that teachers engage in learning experiences that model the desired learning (Ottenbreit-Leftwich et al. 2010), have opportunities to collaborate and opportunities to personalize the learning for their own needs.

Research overwhelming identifies that effective professional learning is ongoing and situated within a community of learners (Darling-Hammond 1997; Garet et al. 2001; Stoll et al. 2006). Teachers are socialized in various ways including the observation of their previous teachers known as the *apprenticeship of observation* (Lortie 1975), during their preparation programs and especially on-the-job experiences. Seeing models of desired learning environments helps teachers deepen their understanding of how to organize instructional time and effectively teach. Observations and models of teaching practices impact teaching practices (Hughes 2013), especially when coupled with critical reflection to challenge assumptions and traditional practice (Antonacopoulou 2004; Boud and Walker 1998; Brockbank and McGill 2006; Brookfield, 2005; Katz et al. 2005). In addition, incorporating mentoring, coaching and critical dialogue in the tea cher's day can increase students' understanding and achievement, as well as teacher job satisfaction (Kardos 2004; Smith, and Ingersoll 2004). Establishing networks of support for teachers, both novice and veteran can serve as highly effective professional development. Although the research outlines effective characteristics of professional learning, a great disparity between research and practice still exists resulting in professional learning as episodic and didactic, separate from authentic work. (Gravani 2007; Hawley and Valli, 1999; Murrell 2001)

3.1 Visionary Leadership

Establishing a shared vision among stakeholders is imperative when trying to implement wide-scale change. Identifying and articulating a vision imply "practices aimed at identifying new opportunities for the school, and developing, articulating, and inspiring others with a vision of the future" (Ng 2008, p. 5). The literature has emphasized the importance of developing, articulating, and communicating a shared vision of the intended change in general (Fullan 2013; Tearle 2004) and school planning and vision with regard to technology in particular (Fishman and Pinkard 2001; Hall and Hord 2006; Lim and Khine 2006). Research suggests that the lack of technology integration may be caused by a misalignment between the leader's vision of technology integration and the teacher's vision of technology integration (Shattuck 2010). To ensure that there is a common understanding about the role of technology and innovation, Winschitl and Sahl (2005) suggest the institutional vision must encompass beliefs about learners, beliefs about what characterizes meaningful learning, and beliefs about the role of the teachers within the vision. The beliefs that teachers hold directly impact their actions and decision-making in the classroom. Moreover, how teachers understand the vision, based on their beliefs and experience can directly influence the way in which they design learning experiences.

3.2 Changing Role of the Teacher

Mobile technology can transform teaching and learning through strategic design and implementation. There is great potential to facilitate deeper learning experiences for all students; however, this type of instruction calls for a shift from the traditional norms in education. To facilitate this shift, school leaders can ensure teachers have access to high quality digital content and be supported to become designers of robust learning experiences for all students. According to Fullan and Langworthy (2013), in order to effectively integrate technology, the teachers need to shift from transmitters of knowledge to:

1. Designers of powerful learning experiences
2. Sources of human, social and decisional capital in the learning experience
3. Partners in learning with students, accelerated by technology

To feel confident in becoming designers of powerful learning experiences, however, many teachers express having to learn two things: how to operate the technology and how to integrate its use into learning and teaching. Teachers want to increase their effectiveness with technology integration through professional development, but recognize they also need the time and space to translate these skills into their classroom practice. For teachers, time to plan or strategize how they will incorporate what they learned into their instruction, needs to be embedded in ongoing collaboration to fully realize the potential of the technology. It takes time and support to internalize and implement the many uses of technology to enhance instruction in the classroom.

3.3 A Culture of Learning

To facilitate the changing role of the teachers, effective technology integration requires understanding the vision and the dynamic relationship between pedagogical, content, and technological knowledge, known as TPACK (Mishra and Koehler 2006) (See Fig. 2). Innovative Teaching and Learning (2011) research findings concluded that innovation flourished when teachers collaborated on best teaching practices, were provided opportunities to learn and practice new methods, and were guided by a common vision and continuous support. Transformational leaders create systems to embed this work into the school day and facilitate teachers of the same content in continuous planning, analyzing and reflecting on student learning through small collaborative learning communities (Joyce and Showers, 2002; Marzano, Waters, and McNulty, 2005). Such programs can be structured in ways that provide teachers with consistent and meaningful collaboration with colleagues, afford them opportunities for learning, and allow them to be learners alongside their students (Darling-Hammond and McLauglin, 1995; Lieberman and Miller 1999; Meier 2002).

Within the systems to support learning, effective professional learning actively engages teachers in authentic contexts (Elmore 2002), including time that teachers can plan lessons with their colleagues and be empowered to make decisions to improve their own professional practice. Project Discovery (Shulman and Armitage 2005), an urban middle school reform effort, utilized inquiry-based methods, interdisciplinary curriculum and invited teachers to take control of the learning in their classrooms. This program provides a model of professional development that yielded results in both student achievement and teacher satisfaction. A significant increase was found in the number of students meeting state standards on standardized tests in mathematics and English. Additionally teachers reported an improved school climate and a sense of empowerment (Shulman and Armitage 2005). Lessons and activities that teachers create and apply in their own classrooms, followed by more discussion and learning with their peers is an ideal form of professional learning.

3.4 Competency-Based Professional Learning

Teacher's beliefs, knowledge and use of technology were the strongest barriers preventing their use of it in the classroom (Ertmer and Ottenbreit-Leftwich 2010). It is essential that professional learning meet teachers where they are to increase knowledge and skills to increase their confidence while minimizing the fear associated with using technology. Given the diverse skill and comfort levels that teachers bring, there is a need for personalized support to build on their strengths and support areas of growth. Robust systems of support for teachers must embed opportunities for collaboration, coaching, and access to resources that allow teachers to chose their learning path based on their goals and needs. Effective leaders create job-embedded collaboration to ensure teachers share and learn about how to effectively leverage technology to meet their desired learning objectives. Guided by their belief that technology is not an add on, they prioritize resources to provide ubiquitous access for all students.

To shift from a traditional professional learning model to competency-based professional learning, a system that provides clear expectations and offers multiple pathways for teachers to learn is necessary to effectively support the diverse teaching force. A competency-based system allows teachers to demonstrate proficiency in areas where they excel and seek support and guidance for specific areas of growth (Cator et al. 2014). Similar to demonstrations of student learning linked to mastery, competency-based professional learning allows leaders to identify the expectations and allows for personalized paths to develop and demonstrate mastery of effective teaching practices. Valuing the differences in teachers and immersing them in transformative learning experiences is a key lever that will allow them to design similar learning experiences for the students they teach (Fig. 1).

This paper is critical because it provides specific examples of districts that are implementing competency-based professional learning systems to provide educators with high expectations and high support to help them develop the knowledge and skills aligned to the changing role of the teacher in three unique contexts. District leaders can model and support their vision through the type of professional learning opportunities they provide for their teachers. According to Baylor and Ritchie (2002), leaders who

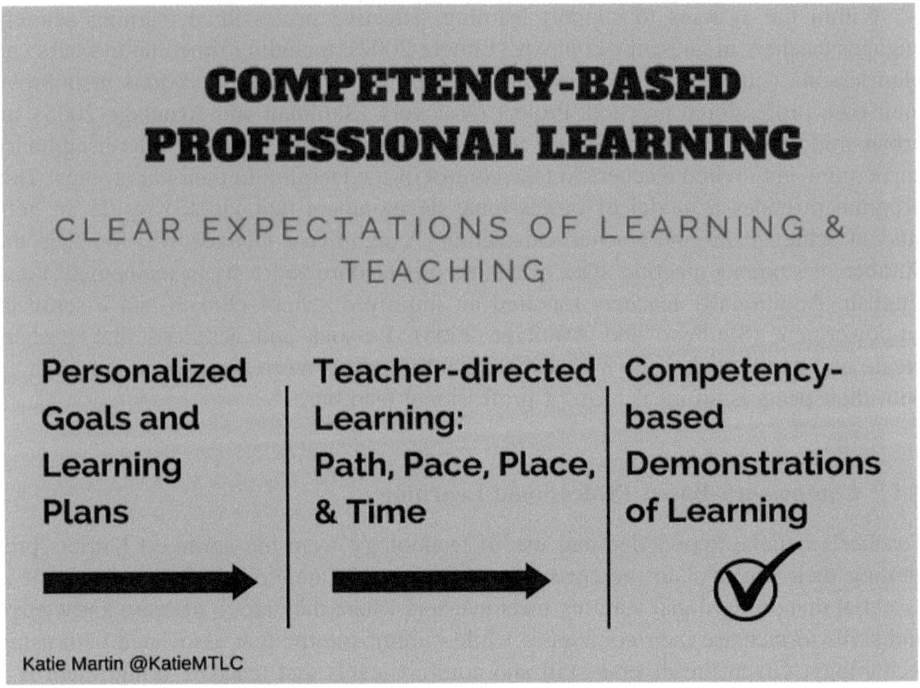

Fig. 1. Competency-based professional learning

promote the use of technology, not only in words but also in action, lend credence to a technology-rich culture. Moving away from assessing learning opportunities by seat time, a competency-based approach allows leaders to identify the expectations and allows for personalized paths to develop and demonstrate evidence aligned to effective teaching practices.

4 Case Study 1: Encinitas Union School District

A small coastal elementary district in Southern California has provided iPads for students across the district for the past seven years. To ensure technology is leveraged to innovate and drive powerful learning, EUSD has developed a system of support to meet the teachers' needs. The comprehensive plan provides robust support for teachers through district wide vision and alignment, site based learning and development, personalized learning, instructional coaching and communities of practice.

4.1 District Wide Vision and Alignment

In order to align the district priorities, there are five days of professional learning that the district provides for teachers. Once at the beginning of the school year and four additional times throughout the year to support district-wide priorities such as information literacy, math instruction, Next Generation science standards and English Language Development. These initial sessions are intended to set the expectations and teachers will follow up on integration of new knowledge in collaboration and planning time in their committee work as well as their personalized learning plans.

4.2 Site-Based Professional Learning

Hall (2010) found that the school principals had the most impact on teacher's technology integration. To allow for school leaders to strategically support teachers based on needs and context, sites determine their instructional goals and needs for professional learning. Each site has 6 "First Fridays" for site-based professional learning. To further support teacher development, each grade level meets weekly to allow for teachers to plan, collaborate and share strengths and challenges as they integrate new learning. Finally, each Friday is an early release day, which affords teacher the opportunity to plan. As teacher-driven curriculum is a priority, teachers also have two release days to draft curriculum maps.

4.3 Personalized Learning

To support diverse learning needs and styles, the district has created a personalized learning plan that provides teachers with a $500 stipend to pay for resources, workshops, or time while they work to meet their desired learning goal. EUSD also offers after school support for technology specific tools and Friday afternoon support in district programs such as DefinedSTEM, Hapara, Digital Library along with iTunesU courses that teachers can access based on their needs and goals. In addition there are district-wide instructional coaches that provide feedback to teachers based on their goals to help them improve their practice. The district has also created their own EdCamp, an un-conference driven by the needs of the learners attending rather than pre-determined sessions. This is an opportunity for teachers, principals and central office leaders to share and discuss their ideas that are relevant to them about how to meet the needs of their students, create powerful learning experiences, and develop a culture that supports and sustains powerful learning.

4.4 Communities of Practice

Extended learning opportunities are also provided for teachers that want to work in a cohort or community of practice to further their learning and engage with like-minded peers. In these summer and winter sessions, teachers focus on an in depth topic and through activities, readings, and modeling of the new ideas. Teachers have opportunities to work together to plan for how they might integrate new learning with colleagues from across the district.

5 Case Study 2: Cajon Valley Union School District

Cajon Valley Union School District (CVUSD) is a K-8 district of 24 schools in eastern San Diego that serves a high population of English language learners and has a high population of Title 1 students. In 2014 they began a 1:1 initiative to meet the needs of their diverse student population. In addition, to support their teachers, they have redesigned their professional learning approach to allow teachers and administrators to personalize their support to ensure teacher build confidence and competence in the new tools and resources as well as pedagogy to facilitate powerful learning.

5.1 Digital Academy

CVUSD minimized templates and structures to focus on competency-based demonstrations of learning. They have developed an online digital academy that provides teachers with the content and skills necessary to complete a Demonstration of Learning (DOL), which leads to the earning of a digital badge and corresponding stipend. Most professional development models pay teachers for their time to sit through a "training" or "workshop". This innovative approach to professional development makes time the variable and learning constant. Advanced teachers can skip through modules and go straight to the Demonstrations of Learning. Novice teachers on a given competency may go slow, work with a team, or have in person support if necessary as they complete their badges.

Cajon Valley's Digital Academy is an online platform for teachers to access tools, examples and learning modules to support their professional growth. With ample resources to explore, teachers can elect to participate in online professional development to develop the desired competence. Once teachers have applied the skill, they submit evidence of student work. As teachers learn new skills, gain knowledge and build expertise, integrating technology into the teaching and learning process, their accomplishments will be acknowledged with digital badges. Cajon Valley Digital Academy provides a framework, which allows teachers to learn about and apply digital tools in their instructional practice. This platform has been designed so educators have all the resources needed to master the digital-age skills embodied in the ISTE NETs Standards for Teachers.

5.2 Personalized Pathways

Based on the desired learning objectives (outlined by the Demonstrations of Learning), Cajon Valley has created modules and resources to guide learning. To meet these learning objectives, the various pathways honor teacher's learning style, time, and existing level of competence in the desired skill. Teachers can learn on their own, during the workday with release time, in self-selected communities of practice, intersession workgroup and grade level teams.

5.2.1 On Your Own

Teachers are given choice to use their own personal learning network, online resources, or face-to-face based on their needs and learning styles. Teachers are empowered to learn in a way that meets their needs. The focus is on how they have integrated their learning based on the clear expectations, rather than how they are learning.

5.2.2 Release Time

Many teachers do not have the opportunity to go to conferences or spend their personal time learning because of the many other responsibilities they have outside of their professional lives. The district has provided the option to pay for release time for teachers to take time during their workday to learn new skills or tools and plan for how to integrate them into their learning experiences.

5.2.3 Communities of Practice

Many teachers prefer to learn with like-minded peers in a community setting where they can share, discuss, and problem solve. The district has been the catalyst to convene groups of educators for this purpose but many communities of practice have also emerged organically to support emerging needs and learning goals.

5.2.4 Intersession Workgroups

For teachers who prefer a more guided learning experience CVUSD created professional learning workgroups during intersession breaks. These sessions are facilitated and help guide teachers through the learning experiences and provide opportunities to develop the desired skills and knowledge in a face-to-face setting.

5.2.5 Teacher Collaboration Teams

In addition to the Digital Academy that helps teachers develop skills and knowledge to more effectively leverage the Chromebooks to facilitate innovative learning environments, the district has modified their schedule to provide teachers time to plan and collaborate on a weekly basis. To delve deeper and engage in personalized professional learning teachers meet with their grade level team and receive customized professional learning based on their instructional goals and the needs of the team.

5.3 Apprenticeship Model

Beyond the pathways for teachers to learn, CVUSD has piloted a model to create meaningful learning experiences for both students and teachers. Opportunities for teachers to be immersed in authentic learning experiences with technology allows for increased technological proficiency and their approach to using technology in create authentic learning experiences for students (Shapley et al. 2010). CVUSD leveraged their summer school program to provide learning opportunities for students but also to model innovative approaches to learning for their teachers. Over 200 students from Kindergarten to seventh grade participated in the summer extension program. They selected eight “lead teachers” based on knowledge and expertise to design the summer school courses. Each teacher had six partner teachers and throughout the summer sessions these teachers collaborated, observed, learned, and had opportunities to practice new learning. Despite it's value, this apprenticeship model is rarely used outside of pre-service programs. As the needs of our students change, it is critical that teachers have opportunities to observe and experience new models of learning to change their practice and meet students where they are.

6 Case Study 3: Houston Independent School District

Houston Independent School District (HISD), a large urban school district has implemented PowerUp, a digital transformation initiative that provides each high school student a laptop to ensure students have the knowledge, skills, and resources to be globally competent and competitive. As the environments, resources and tools change to meet the needs of learners in our schools today, teachers' roles must shift (Storz and Hoffman 2013). To do this, it was necessary to identify the desired characteristics of a global graduate in order to identify what teachers need to know and do to support this development. To articulate these expectations, a diverse committee that had representatives across the district initiatives and included both school level and central office leaders, defined the desired teacher competencies to include: Life-long Learner, Deeper Learning Cultivator, Social and Emotional Learning Facilitator, Data Driven, Personalized Learning Architect, and Literacy Developer. Throughout the iterative process, there was feedback from site-based teams to ensure the competencies aligned with the vision of the global graduate, the district priorities, and teacher development and appraisal. To ensure that teachers not only had high expectations to but that there was a robust system of support, the Secondary Curriculum and Development reorganized the professional learning and curriculum development team to provide more personalized support for teachers and align their work to the desired teacher competencies. To build a shared vision, school leaders and teachers each engaged deeply in learning experiences that allowed them to become learners with the technology in order to envision their role in created the desired learning environments (Ottenbreit-Leftwich et al. 2010). Creating opportunities for teachers and leaders to leverage technology is instrumental in helping them to provide new and better learning experience for students.

6.1 Micro-credentials

To support teachers to develop the necessary skills and knowledge to facilitate optimal learning experiences, HISD and the University of San Diego (USD) have teamed up with Digital Promise to pilot a competency-based professional learning model that prioritizes learning pathways over seat time to support teacher development. Honoring teachers existing knowledge, interests and expertise allows for a diverse teachers to deepen knowledge and skills to maximize the potential of all learners. Based on the HISD teacher competencies, we have developed micro-credentials to identify specific skills, resources and evidence that support the optimal learning environment. Creating a system of micro-credentials redefines the traditional professional learning model and empowers educators to make decisions about their learning needs based on their unique context and learning goals aligned to a common vision.

Based on demonstrations of competence, teachers will submit artifacts that demonstrate their learning through authentic artifacts such as videos, student work, reflection, and observations to be assessed initially by the University of San Diego and eventually in a peer-review process by those who have also received the micro-credentials. Once teachers have demonstrated their competence, the micro-credentials are intended to create pathways for teachers to provide support for peers through professional learning, mentoring, collaboration and networks with and beyond schools. By moving recognition of professional learning away from seat time and towards competency, educators will become empowered to drive their learning and create networks of professional learning communities. These communities will, in turn, encourage system-level improvement.

6.2 Ecosystem of Support

To support sustained growth and impact student learning, there will be ongoing support for teachers to develop competencies to facilitate the digital transformation. A robust ecosystem of professional learning is necessary to support teachers and meet their unique needs, based on individual experiences, strengths and skill sets. To articulate the shared vision and communicate the desired competencies, the HISD summer professional learning institutes enables teachers to experience different learning environments specific to their content and grade level. Embedded in this is the opportunity to reimagine learning and implications for their own classrooms and plan for implementation. In addition to content development and instructional pedagogy, attendees had options to learn about the HUB, the district's learning management system, project-based learning, formative assessments for instructional planning, global communication and literacy, tools for classroom innovation and strategies facilitating deeper learning. These sessions were aligned to the teacher competencies to help make the teacher development explicitly tied to the vision.

To build on this work and ensure systemic impact, teachers will assess their current practice, develop a personal learning plan to determine next steps and align

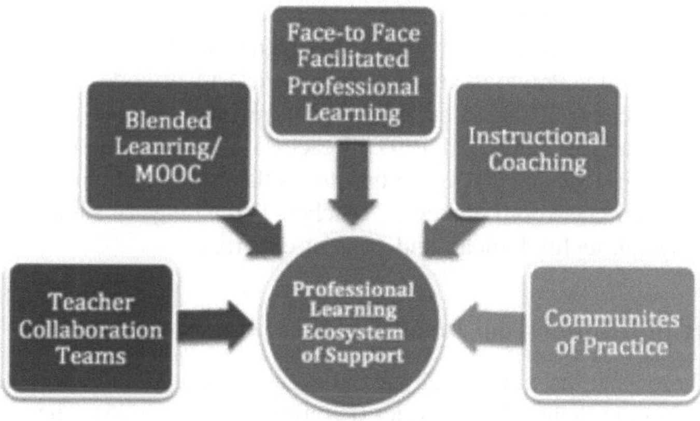

Fig. 2. Professional learning ecosystem of support

professional learning opportunities to support their growth. Ample opportunities for teachers to continue their professional learning and develop their teaching practice are provided throughout the year. In addition to professional learning sessions aligned to specific competencies and micro-credentials, each school has coaches and is designing systems to ensure that support and learning is systemic and sustainable. Teachers work with instructional coaches (CITs, District Curriculum Specialists, Teacher Leaders) as part of their work day and have access to online resources for learning, and regular face-to-face teacher collaboration teams meet to plan, collaborate and analyze the impact of their instructional practices.

7 Discussion

These three unique districts provide models for how to support teachers through competency-based professional learning. Each of these systems are designed to meet the unique needs of the district in service of all learners through the alignment of the vision, empowering teacher voice and choice, and creating a culture of learning and innovation.

7.1 Alignment of Vision

Research has indicated that leadership is a crucial aspect of innovation. District and school leaders have the ability to impact school culture, technology integration practices, the acceptance of a district-wide vision, teacher pedagogical beliefs, the effectiveness of professional development and even influence student content acquisition (Ertmer and Ottenbreit-Leftwich 2010; Hew and Brush 2007). To develop a new professional learning model each of the districts had to ensure there was a shared vision that was clear and articulate it to all stakeholders. This ongoing commitment to the shared vision helps everyone work together for a common purpose.

7.2 Teacher Voice and Choice

The extent to which teachers feel comfortable in the learning process influences their willingness and confidence in their ability to integrate technology into their teaching (Adiguzel et al. 2011). Previous attempts by districts to provide professional development for all teachers at the same time and pace have not met the vast range of teachers' needs (Darling-Hammond 1997). Teachers in each of the districts had voice and choice in their learning opportunities to build confidence in their abilities to integrate it into their classroom practices. Teachers had a range of support to meet their diverse pedagogical, technological, and content expertise.

7.3 Culture of Learning and Innovation

In each of these districts contextual factors were addressed to make the most that impact on teachers in their unique district (Bronfrenbrenner, 2005). The vision and the desired learning environments were explicitly communicated to facilitate teacher development and impact student learning. Each of the districts modeled new ways of learning resulting in new ways of teaching. By personalizing learning for teachers, they have been empowered to try new and innovative practices to leverage technology and other resources to meet the needs of their students.

7.4 Implications

Realizing professional learning needs to change is one thing but shifting a culture to make this systemic change is a challenge that plagues many schools and districts. These three case studies present models for shifting from traditional professional learning to one that prioritizes demonstrations of learning and addresses the strengths and challenges of diverse teachers to make the most impact on their students.

1. **Clear Expectations for Learning and Teaching -** Based on a shared vision, determine what you want teachers to be able to know and do to create the desired learning experiences for students. Without a common understanding many people guess and the shared vision can rarely materializes in the majority of classrooms.
2. **Learning Experiences and Models -** Providing learning experiences and models of authentic learning environments with 1:1 technology supports teachers to develop technological expertise and allows them to use design learning experiences for their students to leverage the technology
3. **Personalized Goals and Learning Plans -** Support teachers to self-assess their strengths and goals in respect to the desired learning environments in order to determine personal goals and craft a personalized learning plan based on the resources and support available.
4. **Teacher-Directed Learning (Path, Time, Place, and Pace) -** Teachers have diverse expertise and preferences about how and what they learn. Provide clear learning goals but allow for choice and voice to empower teachers to learn in a way that suits their needs and builds on their strengths to develop and apply new knowledge.
5. **Competency-Based Demonstrations of Learning -** To move from assessing professional development by the number of days or hours teachers have attended, prioritizing the application can help shift professional learning from something we do to educators to an improvement process that impacts learning for all.

7.5 Considerations for Further Investigation

Although the benefits of the three competency-based professional learning models provide each district with success, there are questions that they illuminate for further investigation as we move away from more traditional models.

8 Vision and Expectations

Each of the district models had varying levels of expectations for what teachers are expected to know and do. It is worth investigating the implications of these expectations and how they foster or hinder teacher development and integration of practices aligned with the vision. As these districts transition from a system that focus on attending mandated trainings and move towards empowering them to learn in more personalized ways, the model of accountability changes. The demonstrations of learning are the measure rather than the logged hours of training. As the goal is to empower others, not mandate, there is a balance that these districts are working to achieve. The question remains as to the best way to ensure that all teachers are moving forward and creating a system that remains focused on learning rather than external incentives.

8.1 Assessment and Accountability

Connected to the both vision and expectations, the assessment measures will drive the learning. Accountability helps ensure that we are meeting desired outcomes but can also be too stringent and limit creativity and innovation. It's a delicate balance to create a system that provides clear expectations yet enough autonomy to drive personalized learning for all.

9 Conclusion

In order to meet the needs of teachers, it is critical to reimagine professional learning to foster innovative teaching and learning. Taking into account the unique context and resources, each district must design professional learning systems to provide educators with the clear expectations, models, resources, and time to collaborate with peers to develop new skill sets aligned to the vision. The needs, capacities, and priorities of students, teachers, and leaders should guide resource allocation and learning opportunities so that technology integration and classroom application are effective. To realize the vision of powerful learning accelerated by technology, systems that foster personalized professional learning and robust support are necessary to fully integrate new learning into classrooms. Building and ecosystem that cultivates a culture of learning requires safe opportunities to practice, observations of models, time for reflection and revision, and capacity building collaboration. The power of professional learning comes from this continuous cycle that promotes and sustains new learning and innovation based on the needs and interests of the learners.

References

Adiguzel, T., Capraro, R., Willson, V.: An examination of teacher acceptance of handheld computers. Int. J. Spec. Educ. **26**(3), 12–27 (2011)

Antonacopoulou, E.: The dynamics of reflexive practice: the relationship between learning and changing (2004)

Baylor, L.A., Ritchie, D.: What factors facilitate teacher skill, teacher morale, and perceived student learning in technology-using classrooms? Comput. Educ. **39**, 395–414 (2002)

Boud, D., Walker, D.: Promoting reflection in professional courses: the challenge of context. Stud. High. Educ. **23**(2), 191–206 (1998)

Brockbank, A., McGill, I.: Facilitating and coaching. Kogan Page, Philadelphia (2006)

Bronfenbrenner, U.: The bioecological theory of human development. In: Bronfenbrenner, U. (ed.) Making Human Beings Human: Bioecological Perspectives on Human Development, pp. 3–15. Sage, Thousand Oaks (2005)

Cator, K., Schneider, C., Vander Ark, T.: Preparing teachers for deeper learning: competency-based teacher preparation and development (2014). http://cdno4.gettingsmart.com/wp-content/uploads/2014/01/FINAL-Preparing-Teachersfor-Deeper-Learning-Paper.pdf

Darling-Hammond, L.: The Right to Learn: A Blueprint for Creating Schools that Work. Jossey-Bass, San Francisco (1997)

Darling-Hammond, L., McLaughlin, M.W.: Policies that support professional development in an era of reform. Phi Delta Kaplan **76**(8), 597–604 (1995)

DuFour, R.: Professional learning communities: a bandwagon, an idea worth considering, or our best hope for high levels of learning? Middle Sch. J. **39**(1), 4–8 (2007)

Elmore, R.F.: Bridging the gap between standards and achievement: The imperative for professional development in education. Albert Shanker Institute, Washington DC (2002)

Ertmer, P.A.: Teacher pedagogical beliefs: the final frontier in our quest for technology integration? Educ. Technol. Res. Develop. **53**(4), 25–39 (2005)

Ertmer, P.A., Ottenbreit-Leftwich, A.T.: Teacher technology change: how knowledge, confidence, beliefs, and culture intersect. J. Res. Technol. Educ. **42**(3), 255–284 (2010)

Fishman, B.J., Pinkard, N.: Bringing urban schools into the Information age: planning for technology vs. technology planning. J. Educ. Comput. Res. **25**(1), 63–80 (2001)

Fullan, M.: The new pedagogy: students and teachers as learning partners. Learn. Landscapes **6** (2), 23–29 (2013)

Fullan, M., Langworthy, M.: Towards a new end: New Pedagogies for deep learning (2013). http://www.newpedagogies.org/Pages/assets/new-pedagogies-for-deep-learning—aninvitation-to-partner-2013-19-06.pdf

Garet, M., Porter, A., Desimone, L., Birman, B., Yoon, K.S.: What makes professional development effective? Results Nat. Am. Educ. Res. J. **38**(4), 915–945 (2001)

Gravani, M.: Unveiling professional learning: shifting from the delivery of courses to an understanding of the processes. Teach. Teach. Educ. **23**, 688–704 (2007)

Hall, G.: Technology's achilles heel: achieving high-quality implementation. J. Res. Technol. Educ. **42**(3), 231–253 (2010)

Hall, G., Hord, S.: Implementing Change: Patterns, Principles and Potholes, 2nd edn. Pearson Educational Inc, Boston (2006)

Hew, F.K., Brush, T.: Integrating technology into K-12 teaching and learning: current knowledge gaps and recommendations for future research. Educ. Tech Res. Develop. **55**, 223–252 (2007)

Hughes, J.E.: Descriptive indicators of future teachers' technology integration in the PK- 12 classroom: trends from a laptop-infused teacher education program. J. Educ. Comput. Res. **48** (4), 491–516 (2013)

ITL Research.: Innovative Teaching and Learning Research: 2011. Findings and Implications. Retrieved from ITL Research website (2011). http://www.itlresearch.com/research-a-reports/2011-itl-research-findings

Johnson, S.M., Birkeland, S.: Pursuing a "sense of success": new teachers explain t heir career decisions. Am. Educ. Res. J. **40**(3), 581–617 (2003)

Joyce, B., Showers, B.: Designing training and peer coaching: our needs for learning. In: Joyce, R., Showers, B. (eds.) Student Achievement Through Staff Development, 3rd edn. Association for Supervision and Curriculum Development, Alexandria (2002)

Kardos, S.M.: Supporting and Sustaining New Teachers in Schools: The Importance of Professional Culture and Mentoring. Harvard University, Cambridge (2004)

Katz, S., Sutherland, S., Earl, L.: Towards an evaluation habit of mind: mapping the journey. Teach. Coll. Rec. **107**(10), 2326–2350 (2005)

Lieberman, A., Miller, L.: Teachers—Transforming Their World and Their Work. Teachers College Press, New York (1999)

Lim, C.P., Khine, M.S.: Managing teacher' barriers to ICT integration in Singapore schools. J. Technol. Teach. Educ. **14**(1), 97–125 (2006)

Lortie, D.: Schoolteacher: A sociological study. University of Chicago Press, London (1975). Mapping the journey. Teachers College Record, 707(10), 2326-2350

Meier, D.: The power of their ideas: Lessons from a small school in Harlem. Beacon Press, Boston (2002)

Mertens, S.B., Flowers, N.: Research summary: interdisciplinary teaming. AMLE (2004)

Mishra, P., Koehler, M.J.: Technological pedagogical content knowledge: a framework for teacher knowledge. Teach. Coll. Rec. **108**(6), 1017–1054 (2006)

Murrell, P.C.: The Community Teacher. Teachers College Press, New York (2001)

Ng, W.: Transformational leadership and the integration of information and communications technology into teaching. Asia-Pac. Educ. Res. **17**(1), 1–14 (2008)

Ottenbreit-Leftwich, T.A., Glazewski, D.K., Newby, J.T., Ertmer, A.P.: Teacher value beliefs associated with using technology: addressing professional and student needs. Comput. Educ. **55**, 1321–1335 (2010)

Shapley, K., Sheehan, D., Maloney, C., Caranikas-Walker, F.: Effects of technology immersion on teachers' growth in technology competency, ideology, and practices. J. Educ. Comput. Res. **42**(1), 1–33 (2010)

Shattuck, G.: Understanding school leaders' role in teachers' adoption of technology integration classroom practices. In: Orey, M., Jones, S.A., Branch, R.M. (eds.) Educational Media and Technology Yearbook, vol. 35, pp. 7–28. Springer, New York (2010)

Shulman, V., Armitage, D.: Project discovery: an urban middle school reform effort. Educ. Urban Soc. **37**, 371–397 (2005)

Smith, T.M., Ingersoll, R.M.: What are the effects of induction and mentoring of beginning teacher turnover? Am. Educ. Res. Assoc. **42**(3), 681–715 (2004)

Stoll, L., Bolam, R., McMahon, A., Wallace, M., Thomas, S.: Professional learning communities: a review of the literature. J. Educ. Change **7**, 221–258 (2006)

Storz, M., Hoffman, A.: Examining response to a one-to-one computer initiative: student and teacher voices. Res. Middle Level Educ. Online **36**(6), 1–18 (2013)

Tearle, P.: The Implementation of ICT in UK Secondary Schools. BECTA and University of Exeter, Coventry (2004)

Wong, H.K.: New teacher induction: the foundation for comprehensive, coherent, and sustained professional development. In: Portner, H. (ed.) Teacher Mentoring and Induction: The State of the Art and Beyond. Corwin Press, Thousand Oaks (2005)

Transforming Teaching and Learning: Implications of a One-to-One Laptop Initiative for Professional Learning and Teacher Practices

Veronica Garcia Garza(✉)

Mobile Technology Learning Center,
University of San Diego, San Diego, CA, USA
vgarza@sandiego.edu

Abstract. Increased access to technology in school districts across the United States has sparked a growing demand for teachers and administrators to transform traditional teaching and learning models. These changes require a clear vision and plan to support educators through the transition. This paper presents findings from the second year evaluation of a one-to-one student laptop initiative in a large urban district in the United States that illustrate the impact of vision and planning on efforts to support changes in teacher practice, classroom culture, and student engagement. Additionally, this paper details how an outside evaluation has informed practice within the district and mobilized leaders to move towards a more personalized professional learning approach designed to leverage the power of technology. Strategies and recommendations for how to better support district and school leaders in using technology to enhance teaching and learning are provided.

Keywords: Instruction · Technology integration · Competency-based professional learning system

1 Introduction

Although studies show teachers believe in the many benefits of technology, such as being able to provide instruction in new ways and reinforce and expand concepts (PBS 2011), the literature also indicates high levels of technology integration (or use) is not being achieved in meaningful ways (Cuban and Kirkpatrick 2001; Gray et al. 2010). For example, in a 2009 survey by the National Center for Education Statistics of 3,159 teachers, few teachers reported their students engage in what is considered more creative uses of technology. These activities may include conducting experiments, blogging, or designing/creating their own content or products. Conversely, many more teachers have their students use technology to prepare written text or practice basic skills (Gray et al. 2010).

Conversations in the United States about transforming learning in technology-rich environments are not slowing down. Rather, the push to transform teaching and learning via the use of technology is being fueled at the national level. Initiatives such as

T.H. Brown and H.J. van der Merwe (Eds.): mLearn 2015, CCIS 560, pp. 31–45, 2015.
DOI: 10.1007/978-3-319-25684-9_3

President Obama's Future Ready Call to Action and P21's Framework for 21st Century Learning are encouraging educators, students, and communities to commit to preparing students to be critical thinkers, problem solvers, communicators, and innovators (P21 Partnership for 21st Century Learning; Office of Educational Technology U.S. Department of Education 2014). With new technologies and the push for digital learning environments, a widely adopted expectation is that teachers will need to change their practice to integrate technology in meaningful ways. This change in practice requires districts and school leaders to think differently about professional development systems and the supports provided to teachers.

The findings reported in this paper have implications for districts' planning efforts, particularly around professional learning systems that incorporate technology integration. It will share how the evaluation of one large urban school district's secondary technology initiative has helped the district move towards a more personalized professional learning approach designed to leverage the power of technology. In this paper, the following questions will be addressed: (1) What kinds of teaching practices are present in a secondary one to one technology initiative?; (2) How do these practices impact student engagement and classroom culture?; and (3) How do these practices inform a district's professional learning system? If educators are truly invested in supporting students to be ready for the 21st century society and want to teach innovatively, then teacher practices and a district's professional learning systems must be aligned and connected. Without alignment, these outcomes in these technology initiatives will likely not be achieved.

2 Literature Review

2.1 Instructional Practice

The education field has defined core practices and learning environments that are most effective for student achievement. Diverse learners must be able to access the curriculum in multiple ways, including personalized or learner-centered environments (Richardson 2012). Students must have access to flexible learning environments that promote curiosity, collaboration, and critical thinking via use of culturally relevant materials (Ladson-Billings 1995). Students need opportunities to make decisions, engage in metacognitive strategies, pursue individual goals, apply learning, and assess personal growth (Donovan and Bransford 2005). The classroom is a space that allows students to develop proficiency in creating and analyzing multimedia texts to skillfully communicate and collaborate with global audiences (P21 Partnership for 21st Century Learning).

One approach to creating classrooms that embody the values and ideals above is sociocultural learning theory, also known as a constructivist approach to learning. Constructivism is regarded as a positive teaching approach to student-centered instruction because of its focus on individuals constructing knowledge together (Rogoff 1990). Children, with the guidance of adults, co-construct meaning for themselves and with others (Rogoff 1990). This student-centered approach provides an opportunity for students and those around them (i.e., peers or teachers) to use their own ideas and draw conclusions using prior knowledge.

Student-Centered Instruction and Technology Integration. The relationship between teacher beliefs and technology integration has also surfaced as a critical factor in technology integration (Ertmer 2005; Ertmer and Ottenbreit-Leftwhich 2010; Inan and Lowther 2010; Ritzhaupt et al. 2012). Studies suggest it is important to examine the reasons why teachers feel challenged in their use and acceptance of technology. For example, Ertmer (2005) has discussed the issue of teacher beliefs and technology integration within the context of first and second order barriers. First order barriers are extrinsic and revolve around more technical issues teachers might encounter that challenge their use of technology such as equipment issues, insufficient training, and the lack of supports (Ertmer 2005). Second order barriers are more difficult to address and resolve because they focus on teachers' beliefs about teaching and learning. Ertmer (2005) advocates for the need to examine teachers' feelings and support teachers in developing goals for technology use in their instructional practices.

Additionally, there is a growing body of literature both in the United States and internationally indicating teachers who hold beliefs valuing student-centered practices or a constructivist approach to teaching use technology more so than their traditional counterparts (Overbay et al. 2010; Sandholtz and Reilly 2004; Tondeur et al. 2008; Windschitl and Sahl 2002). Although it is unclear if access to technology leads to constructivist teaching or if teachers with an already assumed learner-centered approach are more willing to use technology, there is evidence that technology use can potentially have more impact when aligned with a constructivist/student-centered approach to teaching. For example, Tondeur et al. (2008) studied elementary teachers in Belgium and found that teachers with stronger constructivist beliefs reported higher frequency of computer use. Teachers with traditional beliefs were more likely to use computers for drill and practice types of uses (Tondeur et al. 2008). Similarly, Overbay et al. (2010) studied a program designed to support K12 teachers to create 21st century learning environments and also found an important role for constructivist beliefs and teachers use of technology. Teachers' beliefs in student-centered approaches along with positive beliefs about role of instructional technology in their teaching practices were strongest predictors of technology use rather than other variables such as years teaching or gender (Overbay et al. 2010).

Based on the literature for effective instructional practice, teachers should build on students' prior knowledge, engage them in meaningful and relevant learning with others, allow for reflective and metacognitive actions, and hold students to high expectations. Student-centered or constructivist practices are one approach that, when done in authentic ways, can support these outcomes. The studies above provide evidence to suggest that student-centered classrooms have the potential to engage students and teachers in use of technology for more integrated practices.

2.2 Professional Learning Systems

Research-Based Characteristics of Professional Learning Systems. Professional learning (or professional development) systems in education play a critical role in supporting teachers with their practice and also help facilitate a culture of lifelong learning and professionalism. Research suggests there are approaches to professional learning systems that best support teachers in examining their beliefs, sharing knowledge, and integrating new learning into their practice. For example, professional learning systems can follow a systems-approach, which provides opportunities for individuals to connect across departments and organizational structures. These individuals and their organizations align to make the system functional at large (Senge et al. 2000 as cited in Levin and Schrum 2013; Thorton et al. 2004). Distributed leadership is another approach for professional learning systems to build on the strengths of individuals as the focus is on the individuals and how they function to build on people's strengths (Spillane 2005; Spillane et al. 2001).

Communities of Practice also characterize strong professional learning systems. In these communities, a support system is in place for the exchange knowledge and relationship-building among individuals within the context of the larger system(s) (Wenger 2000). Individuals "negotiate competence through an experience of direct participation" (Wenger 2000, p. 229). They engage one another, share and act upon resources of the community, and even hold one another accountable (Wenger 2000). A Professional Learning Community (PLC) is another type of community in which teachers are valued as experts who share their knowledge and expertise instead of an outside entity curating the knowledge (Vescio et al. 2008). When constructed and organized authentically, PLCs can foster a space for collaboration, enhanced teacher relationships, and critical thinking with the goals to improve teacher practice and student achievement (Vescio et al. 2008).

Lastly, consistent observations and coaching as part of professional learning systems are also research-based components that support teacher growth (Joyce and Showers 2002; Marzano et al. 2005; Ingersoll and Smith 2004). Similarly, integrating opportunities for coaching and mentoring into professional learning systems provides teachers with support networks and build collaborative practices while concurrently improving teacher practice and effectiveness (Ingersoll and Smith 2004).

Effective professional learning systems encompass many components, but collaboration and exchange of knowledge amongst educators are key (Ingersoll and Smith 2004; Joyce and Showers 2002; Marzano et al. 2005; Spillane et al. 2001; Vescio et al. 2008; Wenger 2000). Individuals in these community-oriented structures work together in ways that establish relationships, promote intellectual growth, exchange knowledge, and ultimately have the potential to impact student achievement outcomes.

Professional Learning Systems and Technology Integration. In studies addressing issues of technology integration and professional learning, the alignment of curriculum and instructional frameworks and professional learning systems is cited as critical to the success of the initiative and overall technology integration by teachers in their classrooms (Anthony 2012; Dexter 2005; Levin and Schrum, 2013; Sandholtz and Reilly 2004; White et al. 2002). In two studies examining schools and districts that implemented technology initiatives, for example, the researchers found professional development structures were differentiated, flexible, and allowed for teachers to learn from one another (Dexter 2005; Levin and Schrum 2013). Cross-functional departments worked together to ensure that the training for teachers focused on meaningful instructional practices rather than professional development practices that emphasized basic uses of devices. In another study, two middle school teachers (one science and one English & social studies) were followed during three years of a technology initiative (Anthony 2012). One teacher integrated technology seamlessly throughout that time, however, the second teacher's use was more inconsistent. This latter teacher's experiences were complicated by issues such as lack of curriculum alignment, too many initiatives to implement, and lack of structures in place for peer collaboration. Specifically, the teacher who struggled the most to integrate technology cited that professional development "did not emphasize ways in which technology supported, constructivist-oriented teaching might differ from teachers' existing practice" (Anthony 2012, p. 348). The district revised its program to address these challenges, which positively affected teachers and allowed for this teacher to gradually increase her use of technology. The study reaffirms the importance of aligning teachers' technology integration plans with the district's technology plan.

With the increasing presence of technology initiatives in education, it is essential that professional learning systems attend to the curriculum and instructional needs of its teachers. Despite what is known about professional learning systems and technology integration, one key gap remains: the literature does not suggest how professional learning systems can incorporate and align technology integration with the overall instructional goals of the district. This has been cited as a concern in other studies as well (Anthony 2012; Zhao and Frank 2003). This study aims to fill this gap by sharing findings about teacher practice from one large urban district's secondary technology initiative and share how its comprehensive professional learning system is addressing this need to align the technology initiative with the district's instructional goals.

3 Methodology

3.1 Context

This paper will draw on findings from Year 2 of a three-year study of a secondary one-to-one technology initiative in Elmore Unified School District (EUSD).[1] The study was conducted by researchers at the Mobile Technology Learning Center (MTLC). MTLC was contracted by EUSD to study their secondary technology initiative across the districts 42 comprehensive high schools for three years. MTLC is a university-based research and professional learning center at the University of San Diego. MTLC has conducted research in diverse school districts to understand how teachers are using technology, teachers' challenges and needs, and how leadership and support impacts the changing role of the teacher. MTLC's goal is to help schools and districts make evidence-based decisions that ignite innovation in education and improve student outcomes.

EUSD is a large urban school district in the southwestern United States serving just over 200,000 students in 283 schools. Approximately 80% of students are economically disadvantaged. The majority of students are Hispanic (62%) and African American (25%). EUSD is located in a state with a long history of participation in high-stakes reform (Darling-Hammond, 2008). Currently, this state evaluates its public

[1] All names have been changed to pseudonyms.

schools and school districts on a yearly basis. From third grade until graduation, students are tested annually on their knowledge of the core subjects. Students must pass five standardized end of course exams at the "Satisfactory Academic Performance" level to earn their high school diploma.

In fall 2013, EUSD announced the launch of a one-to-one technology program that would provide laptops for all the district's high school students. The purpose of the initiative is to digitize all high schools in the district and transform teacher pedagogy. In this initiative, the goal is for students to be prepared for 21st century learning skills. The initiative, combined with the entire goals and focus of the district, aims to support increases in student attendance, student engagement, and academic achievement, while decreasing disciplinary incidents and suspensions. A specific technology staff person in addition to a district-assigned support person supports each high school on campus. Over the course of three years, every EUSD high school student in the district will receive a laptop to use at school and home during the school year. Since the first two years of the initiative, approximately 40,000 laptops have been distributed to students and teachers for their immediate use in the classroom.

3.2 Participants

In Year 2 of the study, researchers worked with the district to identify a list of six high schools to participate in the study via teacher interviews. Schools were selected based on their similarity to the district as a whole. Three of the schools began the technology initiative in 2013–2014. Three schools began the technology initiative in 2014-2015. At each site, researchers met with the principal and in some cases, key administrators, to share an overview of the study, clarify expectations for participation, and answer questions.

3.3 Individual Teacher Participants

At the beginning of the initiative in 2014–2015, researchers worked with the three sites to solicit a small group of 9th and 10th grade classroom teachers to participate in individual interviews and classroom observations. Thirteen teachers who represented a range of classroom technology integration skills were ultimately selected at these three sites to participate in individual interviews and observations. See Table 1 for overview of teacher participants.

Table 1. Individual teacher participants

	Female	Male	Class observed
English	3	1	9th Grade *one class advanced
English	2	1	10th Grade *one class advanced
Algebra	3	0	9th
Geometry	1	2	10th *one class advanced

Teacher Focus Groups. Ninth and tenth grade English Language Arts (ELA) and math teachers were invited to participate in focus groups. During focus groups, teachers were asked about their pedagogical beliefs, beliefs around technology, current practices in the classroom, and professional development experiences. In Year 2, 69 teachers participated in focus groups. See Table 2 for breakdown of focus group teachers by content.

Table 2. Focus group teacher participants by content

Content area	# Teacher participants
Math	33
English	36
Overall Total	69

Classroom Observations. Classroom observations lasted between 30 and 45 min, and researchers typically stayed for the entire class period. Researchers used a revised version of the 2008 International Society for Technology in Education (ISTE) Classroom protocol. The ISTE protocol allowed researchers to capture instruction in these classrooms as well as student and teacher roles. These monthly classroom observations were carried out from November 2014 to April 2015. Researchers slightly modified the protocol by adding the following items to note in the classroom within the first five minutes of observation: "Tech Check In" (to observe who was facilitating technology if at all) Laptop Check In (how many laptops were on students' desks at time of arrival and if at all). Consent forms for interviews and observations were distributed to all teachers and students at the nine sites. See Table 3 for breakdown of observations by grade and content.

Table 3. Classroom observation outcomes (63)

	Observations prior to start of technology initiative	Observations during technology initiative	Total observations
9th ELA	8	12	20
10th ELA	6	10	16
9th Algebra	6	7	13
9th and 10th Geometry	5	9	14

3.4 Data Analysis

To ensure validity of findings, focus groups were coded and analyzed together to identify patterns and themes in participant responses. Codes that aligned to the overall research design, such as pedagogy, professional development, school site expectations, and challenges, for example, were used. Using content analysis to identify patterns and themes, three researchers analyzed the transcriptions from the focus group interviews (Hsieh and Shannon 2005). Through repeated readings, themes emerged and were organized into specific findings and agreed upon by the research team that are supported by multiple forms of evidence and consistent data.

Using similar process, researchers also reviewed classroom observation data to determine the focus of the lesson and code appropriately. Codes that aligned to the research design and observation protocol, such as student groupings and learning activities, for example, were used to identify patterns and themes from the observations. In most cases, observations were conducted with two people in the class to ensure the lesson was captured accurately. Researchers also debriefed classroom visits together and reflected on the process throughout the school year to ensure consistent observation note-taking. Again, through these repeated readings and analyses of classroom observation notes, themes emerged and were organized into specific findings and agreed upon by the research team.

4 Findings

Finding #1: The majority of instruction is teacher centered; students had little opportunity to engage in constructivist classroom experiences.

ELA Classroom Observations. In 31 of the 36 observations, the lessons were teacher directed and did not allow for students to collaborate in critical ways or in ways that suggested an exchange of knowledge. Students worked individually to complete classwork or engage with the teacher. In 11 observations, the lesson focused on individual persuasive writing. In eight observations, students read on their own and answered questions about content. In two observations, students specifically reviewed for a test by answering questions. In five observations, the lesson was specifically on students practicing for the stakes' high-stakes exam. In five observations, there were a variety of activities that occurred: students learned Greek terms, summarized and defined poetry terms, and studied the Shakespearean era. In five of the 36 observations students were given the opportunity to engage in conversation about class content or present to one another. However, this was not entirely without teacher presence or direction. For example, in one of these five observations, students presented their individual PowerPoint presentations about a book the student read. However, after students presented for about five minutes, there was no discussion or questions for the student from classmates. The teacher provided feedback individually to the student. In another example, the teacher instructed students to share their writing with the student next to him/her. Students then worked in small groups to discuss grammar edits to a sample sentence. Additionally, teacher centered instruction did not change even when students had laptops. Of the 36 observations, students used technology in 15 observations. For example, in 11 of the 15 observations, students accessed the district's learning management system (LMS) to submit assignments, read content online, or access study questions. In one observation, students were asked to individually download an article from the class website, read, and submit responses to questions about the article to the LMS.

In 32 ELA classroom observations, student groupings were categorized as "individual student work". In 4 of the ELA observations, student groupings were also recorded as "small groups". In these observations, however, the small groups were unstructured and students did not always work collaboratively in their groups. For example, in one observation, the teacher had students work in groups to come up with effective reading habits but not all students participated in the group discussion; rather, the same student completed the group tasks.

Math Classroom Observations. In 27 observations in both algebra and geometry courses, the classroom lesson focused on practicing or solving problems for a test. The majority of the time students used worksheets or notebook paper. In one class students had individual whiteboards to solve problems. While students were asked to provide answers to the problems, teachers provided explanations to problems and directed the problem solving process in all observations. In only one observation of a 9th grade Algebra class did a student have the opportunity to use the Smartboard to share his problem solving process with classmates. Students engaged in their classwork in these observations both individually and in small groups, however, the majority of time students worked individually. In four observations, the teachers used a timer to monitor students' time to finish the practice problems or quiz during allotted class time. In five observations, students took a quiz to test their knowledge. In six observations, students were specifically told that the lesson was to review for an upcoming test. In three observations, teachers explicitly stated that purpose of the work was to practice for the district's high-stakes assessment. Similar to the ELA classroom observations, teacher centered instruction in math did not change even when students had laptops. Laptops were used in 12 of the 36 math observations. In one of 12 observations, students used laptops to take a survey for the teacher. Twice laptops were used to play Kahoot (an online application that can be used to quiz/assess students). In nine of the 13 observations, the district's learning management system (LMS) was used for students to either submit a quiz or warm-up to the teacher (3), access class assignments (2), or watch teacher videos uploaded on the LMS (4).

In all 27 math classroom observations, student groupings were categorized as "individual student work". In 8 of the math observations, student groupings were also recorded as "small groups", however, the small groups were unstructured and students did not always work collaboratively in their groups. For example, in one observation, the teacher said to work in small groups to complete the worksheet, but the students worked individually. Additionally, the students' work in groups consisted of answering math questions, usually on a worksheet.

Finding #2: Professional development opportunities for teachers primarily reflected traditional methods.

Teachers in all six ELA focus groups and all six math focus groups reported that the majority of professional development experiences were not differentiated to their content area or grade level. Teachers described trainings as general and lacking specificity for how technology use would align with curriculum and even daily lessons in their content area. For example, one math teacher described attending a writing workshop that was geared more towards ELA teachers; this resulted in feeling that training was time wasted. In another example, a teacher who described herself as having strong technology skills described going to a training focused on lower-level or basic uses of technology. On the contrary, teachers reported that they learned most from peers on campus. Teachers in all six ELA focus groups and in five math focus groups expressed positive comments towards professional learning experiences that were provided by peers and other colleagues on their campus.

5 Discussion

Given the varied experiences of professional development, particularly, the lack of content and skill specific trainings, it is not surprising classroom practice was traditional in nature and overall limited in student engagement. Students were not provided opportunities to be critical thinkers, innovators, or risk-takers in their learning. The individual work culture in the classroom was counter to the kinds of research-based student-centered practices that can support 21st century skills. Students worked alone the majority of the time in their classes and when they did work in small groups or pairs, it was not to think critically about new information or content. Rather, the tasks were to find predetermined answers. There was an absence of critical dialogue and exchange of knowledge among students and teacher and students with one another. The majority of time, teachers provided all the information for class without requests for students to contribute their prior knowledge. The observations highlight a primarily individualistic culture for students in these early grades. In addition, students' use of technology was limited to basic uses such as downloading information, submitting assignments, or taking quizzes, rather than more complex uses of technology such as conducting research or collaborating with experts outside of the classroom walls. Teachers' professional learning experiences were overall inconsistent and did not meet their needs. In particular, teachers' comments suggest the district training did not support their content and skill levels. Teachers felt most supported when learning from their own peers because they shared the same content areas and could digest technology use in ways that were clear and beneficial.

Based on the findings, the district is revising its professional development system. In 2015-2016, the district is piloting a competency-based professional learning system that will not only support the kinds of teacher practice and student growth envisioned with the technology initiative, but that also embodies the pedagogical goals of the district's many other initiatives. With this type of competency based professional learning system, educators are able to identify for themselves the kinds of skills or competencies that are important to their professional growth and students' needs. This approach to professional development gives teaches a choice in what they attend or receive with professional development, which supports the kinds of content and skill specific professional learning opportunities EUSD teachers want. These efforts to revise the focus of the district's professional development system, however, may come with multiple potential challenges. First, a shift towards teacher choice and teacher skills and competencies in EUSD's professional development system that address a variety of students' needs does not necessarily align with the accountability focus on ensuring students pass standardized tests and schools meet district and state test score targets. The district has a long-standing history in the high-stakes reform movement. Thus, there may be conflict surrounding the kinds of teaching practices envisioned with technology initiatives and high stakes reform, and this conflict will need to be addressed if the technology initiative is to be successful. Secondly, while this study focused on ELA and math, other subjects, such as science or history, must also be provided opportunities to learn about and apply student-centered approaches with technology integration in their content areas. It will be important for EUSD's professional learning system to model these kinds of student-centered teaching practices across content areas, as well as incorporate them into the competencies and skills teachers have the choice to attain.

6 Conclusion

The findings of this study suggest the importance of quality professional learning opportunities for teachers that allow them to understand technology integration within the context of effective pedagogy. The integration of technology in classrooms across the United States has potential and promise, but there must be meaningful opportunities for teachers to learn from effective professional learning systems about what it means to transform learning in technology-rich environments. When this happens, teachers can organize their instructional practices in student-centered ways and their students will engage more fully in 21st century learning with their peers and teachers.

Appendix A

University of San Diego
Institutional Review Board
Classroom Observation Protocol

For the research study entitled:
Elmore Unified School District's One-to-One Technology Program

Setting

Content:	Course Name:	Grade Level:
School:	Date:	# of Students in Course:
Observer:	Start time:	End Time:

Purpose: The purpose of this observation is to capture the integration of technology in classrooms as part of EUSD's secondary technology initiative.

Technology Check In (Document at time of arrival)

At time of arrival, check the answer that best describes the classroom:

/ No technology
/ Teacher facilitating use of technology
/ Students working independently using technology
/ Students working with one another using technology
/ Students and teachers working together with technology

At time of arrival, approximately how many laptops are present on desks:

/ Less than half
/ About half
/ More than half

Room Description and student characteristics:

____
____
____

Objective of Lesson (if posted):

____

Topic:

____

Student groupings (check all that apply):

Individual student work   Small groups
Student pairs   Whole class
Other (explain):______________________

Teacher Roles (check all that apply):

Lecturing   Facilitating/Coaching
Interactive direction   Modeling
Discussion
Other (explain): ______________________

Learning Activities (check all that apply):

Creating presentations   Test-taking
Research   Drill and practice
Information analysis   Simulations
Writing   Hands-on skill training
Other (explain):______________________

How essential was technology to the teaching and learning activities:

____
____
____

Overall Classroom Experience: On a scale of 1 (classroom experience is low technology integration) to 4 (classroom experience is high technology integration): ______

Explain overall classroom experience below:

1. Enhancement:
2. Engage
3. Student Ownership:
4. Personalization:
5. Relevance

Appendix B

EUSD Secondary Technology Program

Teacher Focus Group Protocol

1. Can you all share about what a typical day is like in your ELA classes? What tends to happen in your classrooms?
2. How do students work together? What kinds of work do students produce in your classes?
3. Do you use technology in your classrooms? If you are using technology in your classroom, can each of you share how? If not, can you please explain why not?
4. The ways in which you are describing how you use technology, are these expectations set by your site about how you will use technology in the classroom? Or your own expectations? Can you explain?
5. Have you noticed the ways in which students are being impacted (or not) by technology? Has it changed students' behaviors in your classes? Has the use of technology influenced relationships in the classroom among students? Or the student-teacher relationship? How has this initiative influenced expectations in these particular classrooms?
6. What kind of professional development have you received to support your participation in the technology initiative for your classes? Can you share some examples of what you have experienced?
7. What kinds of professional development do you feel you need or will require as this initiative moves forward?
8. We want to know how the initiative may be influencing what happens at the school-wide level. What is a typical day at your school? How would you describe your school environment, in terms of how students interact with each other? How adults and students interact with each other? Has the initiative influenced these interactions and/or relationships at the school-wide level? Please explain.

Concerns/Recommendations

9. What concerns, questions, or recommendations do you have about the roll-out of the One-to-One Technology Program?
10. Is there anything else you would like to add that would help us understand the One-to-One Technology Program in the District?

References

Anthony, A.B.: Activity theory as a framework for investigating district-classroom system interactions and their influences on technology integration. J. Res. Technol. **44**(4), 335–356 (2012)

Dexter, S.: School technology leadership: artifacts in systems of practice. J. Sch. Leadersh. **21**, 166–189 (2011)

Cuban, L., Kirkpatrick, H., Peck, C.: High access and low use of technologies in high school classrooms: explaining an apparent paradox. Am. Educ. Res. J. **38**(4), 813–834 (2001)

Donovan, S.M., Bransford, J.D.: How Students Learn: Science in the Classroom. National Research Council, Washington (2005)

Ertmer, P.: Teacher pedagogical beliefs: the final frontier in our quest for technology integration? Educ. Technol. Res. Dev. **53**(4), 25–39 (2005)

Ertmer, P., Ottenbreit-Leftwhich, A.: Teacher technology change: how knowledge, confidence, beliefs, and culture intersect. J. Res. Technol. Educ. **42**(3), 255–284 (2010)

Gray, L., Thomas, N., Lewis, L.: Teachers' use of educational technology in U.S. public schools: 2009 (NCES 2010–040). National Center for Education Statistics, Institute of Education Sciences, U.S. Department of Education. Washington, DC (2010)

Hsieh, H., Shannon, S.E.: Three approaches to qualitative content analysis. Qual. Health Rese. **15**(9), 1277–1288 (2005)

Inan, F.A., Lowther, D.L.: Factors affecting technology integration in K12 classrooms: a path model. Educ. Tech Res. Dev. **58**, 137–154 (2010)

Ingersoll, R., Smith, T.M.: Do teacher induction and mentoring matter? NAASP Bull. **88**(638), 28–40 (2004)

Joyce, B., Showers, B.: Designing Training and Peer Coaching: Our Needs for Learning. ASCD, Alexandria (2002)

Ladson-Billings, G.: But that's just good teaching! the case for culturally relevant pedagogy. Theor. Pract. **34**(3), 159–165 (1995)

Levin, B.B., Schrum, L.: Using systems thinking to leverage technology for school improvement: lessons learned from award-winning secondary schools/districts. J. Res. Technol. Educ. **46**(1), 29–51 (2013)

Office of Educational Technology at U.S. Department of Education. Future Ready District Pledge (2014). http://tech.ed.gov/futureready/

Overbay, A., Patterson, A.S., Vasu, E.S., Grable, L.L.: Constructivism and technology use: findings from the IMPACTing leadership project. Educ. Media Int. **47**(2), 103–120 (2010)

Marzano, R.J., Waters, T., McNulty, B.A.: School Leadership that Works: From Research to Results. ASCD, Alexandria (2005)

Public Broadcasting Services and Grunwald Associates LLC, 2 February 2011. Deepening Connections: Teachers Increasingly Rely on Media and Technology. http://www-tc.pbs.org/about/media/about/cms_page_media/182/PBS-Grunwald-2011e.pdf

P21 Partnership for 21st Century Learning. Framework for 21st Century Learning. http://www.p21.org/about-us/p21-framework

Richardson, W.: Preparing students to learn without us. Educ. Leadersh. **69**(5), 22–26 (2012)

Ritzhaupt, A.D., Dawson, K., Cavanaugh, C.: An investigation of factors influencing student use of technology in K-12 classrooms using path analysis. J. Educ. Comput. Res. **46**(3), 229–254 (2012)

Rogoff, B.: Apprenticeship in Thinking: Cognitive Development in Social Context. Oxford University Press, New York (1990)

Sandholtz and Reilly: Teachers, not technicians: rethinking technical expectations for teachers. Teach. Coll. Rec. **106**(3), 487–512 (2004)

Spillane, J.P., Halverson, R., Diamond, J.B.: Investigating school leadership practice: a distributed perspective. Educ. Res. **30**(3), 23–28 (2001)

Thorton, B., Peltier, G., Perreault, G.: Systems thinking: a skill to improve student achievement. Clearing House **77**(5), 222–227 (2004)

Tondeur, J., Hermans, R., van Braak, J., Valcke, M.: Exploring the link between teachers' educational belief profiles and different types of computer use in the classroom. Comput. Hum. Behav. **24**, 2541–2553 (2008)

Vescio, V., Ross, D., Adams, A.: A review of research on the impact of professional learning communities on teaching practice and student learning. Teach. Teach. Educ. **24**, 80–91 (2008)

Wenger, E.: Communities of practice and social learning systems. Organ. **7**(2), 225–246 (2000)

White, N., Ringstaff, C, Kelley, L.: Getting the most from technology in schools. WestEd, pp. 1–12 (2002)

Windschitl, M., Sahl, K.: Tracing teachers' use of technology in a laptop computer school: the interplay of teacher beliefs, social dynamics, and institutional culture. Am. Educ. Res. J. **39**(1), 165–205 (2002)

Zhao, Y., Frank, K.A.: Factors affecting technology uses in schools: an ecological perspective. Am. Educ. Res. J. **40**(4), 807–840 (2003)

Rhizomatic Principles in mLearning: A Synthesis of Existing Qualitative Research

Lydia Mbati(✉)

Institute for Open and Distance Learning,
University of South Africa, Pretoria, South Africa
mbatilsa@unisa.ac.za

Abstract. Educational technological innovation to enhance the learning experience of students requires a sound understanding of intended learning outcomes. Similarly, an understanding of the pedagogical affordances of technology is required in order to make appropriate choices regarding which technologies are most suitable to achieve intended outcomes. While mLearning is perceived as the future of learning (Arrigo et al. 2013), an understanding of its application in facilitating the achievement of specific learning objectives is limited. This may lead to negative quality perceptions and subsequently have a negative impact on the adoption of potentially rich technological resources. The challenge for educators is to create learning environments based on sound didactical principles (Brown 2003). The purpose of this study is to highlight rhizomatic principles in mLearning practice. This may contribute to creating an awareness of rhizomatic principles in mLearning practice and this in turn may improve their practice.

Using a qualitative research synthesis approach, this study integrates the findings of published research with the aim of highlighting mLearning practices that stimulate rhizomatic learning in mLearning students.

Keywords: Qualitative research synthesis · Rhizomatic learnng · Mobile learning

1 Introduction

While mLearning has been in existence for a number of years, as a formalised form of learning, mLearning is relatively new. mLearning began to make its mark as a viable facilitator of individualised learning in the early 2000s (Brown 2014). Great strides have been made in the field with mLearning initiatives are seen in around the world (Ally and Tsinakos 2014, 3). Despite the mLearning initiatives taking place around the globe, adoption of mLearning is hindered by a number of factors including digital illiteracy (MacCallum et al. 2014) and limited understanding of its possibilities in facilitating the achievement of specific learning objectives. However, the incorporation of potentially learning-enrichment mobile technologies can be influenced by the teachers' belief system regarding teaching and learning strategies. The existing challenge is to create learning environments based on sound didactical principles (Brown 2003).

T.H. Brown and H.J. van der Merwe (Eds.): mLearn 2015, CCIS 560, pp. 46–57, 2015.
DOI: 10.1007/978-3-319-25684-9_4

'If universities are serious about enhancing learning through the use of innovative technologies, much needs to be done to demonstrate how this might take place'
(Kennedy et al. 2006 in Litchfield et al. 2007).

New pedagogies, supported by the affordances offered by mLearning, are emerging. Some of these pedagogies attempt to explain personalised negotiated meaning offered by mLearning. Rhizomatic learning, derived from the work of Deleuze and Guattari (1987), views ideas as multiple, interconnected and self-replicating and having no beginning and end. This belief system calls for educational models that allow for the fluidity of knowledge conception, in a world where cutting edge knowledge becomes obsolete due to the ephemeral nature of the Web (Cormier 2008).

The purpose of carrying out this research synthesis is to provide a heuristic approach to viewing learning. The intention is not to provide guidelines for employing rhizomatic principles in mLearning, but rather to make practitioners aware of rhiomatic learning processes. This in turn may positively influence their learning facilitation practices. This study explores the findings of qualitative research in the area of mLearning application in order to identify existing practices, aligned to rhizomatic principles.

2 Mobile Learning

mLearning provides opportunities for personalised and contextual learning through the affordances of mobile technologies. These affordances allow for contextual and situated learning, the merging of formal and informal learning, personal publishing and sharing. In addition, mobile devices that support software that allows for seamless and ubiquitous learning (Brown and Mbati 2015).

3 Theories in mLearning Practice

As mLearning has become more pervasive in mainstream learning settings, a number of theories for mlearning have been proposed.

One such theory is the dual coding theory which recognises two subsystems of learning, one processes non-verbal objects or events and the other processes verbal language and audio (Wang and Shen 2012, 562). Imagery is seen as an agent for the preservation of memory and linked to language as a form of expression. In applying this theory to mLearning, application of audio-visual affordances present in mobile devices are employed.

Activity theory has been used to design frameworks for mLearning in practice (Gifford and Enyedy, 1999 in Zurita and Nussbaum 2007). Activity theory attempts to explain social interaction within the complex interplay of contextual systems.

Networked learning theories are currently used to guide networked learning practice. Some prevalent theories in use include social constructivism, cultural historical activity theory, activity theory, constructivism, navigationism and connectivism.

Rhizomatic principles are based on unstructured networks forming organically. Rhizomes need not be thought of as chaotic but rather as a self-regulating structure responsive to learner's needs, as determined by mechanisms in place for determining such needs (Lian 2011, 11). Learning communities created through rhizomatically communicate with each other on shared learning interests, which in turn leads to an improvement in knowledge generation within the community.

The rhizomatic learning principles are:

1. Connection and heterogeneity. The principle of connection and heterogeneity implies any node of a rhizome may be and must be connected to any other node forming the network. The connecting nodes ought to be conspicuously diverse and heterogeneous.
2. Multiplicity. Multiplicity refers to the formation of new knowledge through the interconnectedness between knowledge. The multiple is then treated as a substantive and ceases to have any relation to the single subject (Deleuze and Guattari 1987, 8). Multiplicity is the connection of nodes that can be seen as a rhizomatic whole, where the single node is seen as valuable only as part of the whole.
3. Assigning rapture. Refers to the de-centralization of academic learning from the confines of the learning institution. As a rhizome can be broken and can start growing again on its old line or on a new line (Mackness and Bell 2015).
4. Cartography and decalcomania are the capacity of inclusion and diversity to spread. The metaphor of cartography, then, suggests that knowledge is never permanent, but always provisional, useful at best, and harmful when it becomes dogma (Hamon, 2012 in Cormier 2012). In explaining cartography, Hamon (2012 in Cormier 2012) describes it as mapping against a shifting, organic, adaptive reality. Decalcomania is the transfer of an original pattern to a new location. However, it is important to note that the pattern does not remain constant but is emergent and in constant transition throughout the transfer process.

It is important to note that these principles, while represented in this article as separate entities are interconnected and do not operate as separate parts but synchronously.

4 Methodology

The qualitative research synthesis approach used in carrying out this study

4.1 Paper Selection

Using the EBSCO HOST search engine and Academic Search Premier and ERIC databases, a search was conducted on 23rd of March 2015. The search terms were "mobile learning" and "application" and the search criteria was:

- Qualitative research articles
- References available
- Full papers
- Published between January 2010 and January 2015

The initial search yielded 74 results. On applying the selection criteria, a total of 51 quantitative studies and 19 conceptual articles were set aside. Consequently a sample of 4 sources was arrived at (Table 1 below).

Table 1. Results of primary source search

References of selected articles
Munoz-Cristobal et al. (2015). Coming down to earth: Helping teachers use 3D virtual worlds in across-spaces learning situations. Educational Technology & Society 18(1), 13–26
Price et al. (2014). Fostering geospatial thinking in science education through a customisable smartphone application. British Journal of Educational Technology 45(1),160–170.
Boticki et al. (2011). Supporting mobile collaborative activities through scaffolded flexible grouping. Educational Technology & Society 14(3), 190–202.
Demouy and Kukulska-Hulme (2010). On the spot: using mobile devices for listening and speaking practice on a French language programme. Open Learning 25(3), 217–232.

4.2 Appraising the Studies

Using an assessment scale adapted from Campbell et al. (2003) the 4 selected articles were appraised by 2 appraisers. This was an attempt to include articles which met the criteria for conducting the synthesis. The appraisal depicted on Table 2 below, reflects frequency counts for the four articles initially selected for the synthesis with indications of when the 2 appraisers agreed and partially agreed on the quality of the articles based on the criteria reflected under assessment questions.

During the appraisal exercise, one of the articles was deemed to be largely quantitative with some respondents invited to orally record the activities they participated in. Based on the oral record, and the potential contribution to the synthesis, this article was included in the synthesis.

4.3 The Synthesis

As a way of placing the synthesis in the context of the selected studies, an overview of the four studies is given. This is followed by the concepts and activities related to rhizomatic learning.

Munoz-Cristobal et al. (2015): The paper reports on the design of a prototype for the creation of across-spaces learning situations in a variety of technological ecosystems comprising multiple learning spaces. Thus, the system enables activities taking place in multiple physical, 3D virtual worlds at the synchronously and asynchronously. Additionally, learning designs can be shared and re-used in different technological ecosystems.

Price et al. (2014): The paper brings geospatial approaches to science teaching and learning, fosters the use of mobile technologies in pre-service teachers and customises mobile applications to foster creative teaching.

Table 2. Appraisals of articles (adapted form Campbell et al. 2003)

	Assessment questions	Agree	Partially agree	Disagree	Other
	Is this qualitative research				
1	Relevant to synthesis	3	1		
2	Aims	4			
3	Qualitative methods appropriate	3	2		
4a	Theoretical perspective identified	1	1	2	
4b	Which theoretical perspective	1	1	2	
5a	Sample where	3	1		
5b	Setting why	3	1		
5c	Who selected	3	1		
5d	Why sample selected	3	1		
5e	How sample selected	3	1		
5f	Sample size	3	1		
5g	Adequate	3	1		
	Sampling strategy appropriate?				
6a	Setting data collection	4			
6b	Setting chosen	4			
6c	Purpose explained	4			
6d	How data collected	4			
6e	Why data collected	4			
6f	How data recorded	4			
6g	Whether methods modified	4			
6h	Who collected data	4			
	Data collection addresses research issue?				
7a	How the analysis was done	3	1		
7b	Categories derived	2	2		
7c	Adequate description	3	1		
7d	Feedback	2	2		
7e	Different sources	4			
7f	Reliability	4			
	Data analysis rigourous?				
8a	Examine role	4			
8b	Relationship between researchers	4			
9a	Possible to summarise findings	4			
9b	Findings explicit	4			
	Key concepts				
10a	Sufficient data presented	4			
10b	Quotes identified	2	2		
10c	Data selection explained	4			
10d	Links between data and interpretations	2	2		

(*Continued*)

Table 2. (*Continued*)

	Assessment questions	Agree	Partially agree	Disagree	Other
10e	Negative cases	2	2		
10f	Discussion for and against	2	2		
	All data taken into account				
11a	Congruence	3	1		
11b	Transferable	3	1		
12a	How useful to synthesis	4			
12b	How important are findings to practice	4			
13a	Overall assessment	4			
13b	Include in synthesis	4			

Boticki et al. (2011): This paper reports on the design of in-class collaborative synchronous learning with flexible small groups, enabling students to practice communication, negotiation and coordination skills in the process of forming their own groups to solve a group goal.

Demouy and Kukulska-Hulme (2010): This reported study was aimed at looking at how mobile devices (iPods, MP3 players and mobile phones) could offer more opportunities for students to practise listening and speaking skills independently and thus enhance the learning experience.

5 Emergent Concepts Related to mLearning Practice for Rhizomatic Learning

During this part of the synthesis, emergent themes and concepts were aligned to the rhizomatic principles.

5.1 Connection and Heterogeneity

The principle of connection and heterogeneity implies any node of a rhizome may be and must be connected to any other node forming the network. The connecting nodes ought to be conspicuously diverse and heterogeneous.

Munoz-Cristobal et al. (2015, 21): The designed prototype allowed students to work across three spaces; the classroom, the streets and online as they explored digital literacy and the impact of advertising in primary schoolers.

The proposed system may also help improve the connection of activities across the different spaces

Price et al. (2014, 164–165): A mobile application was designed to create an in situ experience of geospatial concepts and representations in science. This was achieved through the use of cameras, video data logging, and QR codes to access lecturer selected web-based information…

PSTs (Pre-Service Teachers) selected a number of in-application features, illustrating adaptive use with various groups of students. Primary features chosen were the camera, QR codes, plant characteristics, video and ambient data section accessible on the "collect data" page

Cameras were used to take pictures

Ambient data logging on mobile devices

QR codes were used to give students access to information not readily available in situ

QR codes linked to different representations related to the same concept.

Boticki et al. (2011, 193): In trying to achieve a learning goal, *students worked in groups to identify and, through a series of mobile group invitations sent over their smart phones students, rearrange themselves into new groups.*

The study explores the space of collaborative activities in which students have to search and form their own groups in doing the activity.

Demouy and Kukulska-Hulme (2010, 226): "First of all I did this exercise after I had worked through the text. In this case, it's probably OK because it's quite a long text to memorise and to memorise is more difficult than actually talking about it. So in combination with the text which one had read before, it's a good exercise.."

5.2 Multiplicity

Multiplicity refers to the formation of new knowledge through the interconnectedness between knowledge. The multiple is then treated as a substantive and ceases to have any relation to the single subject (Deleuze and Guattari 1987, 8). Multiplicity is the connection of nodes that can be seen as a rhizomatic whole, where the single node is seen as valuable only as part of the whole.

Munoz-Cristobal et al. (2015, 21–22): Collaboratively, each group had to create a counter-ad based on one of the analysed advertisement. The counter ad is geo-positioned in the place where it is created. After the deployment, she reviewed the resulting learning environment in the wiki and in Google Earth.

Price et al. (2014, 162): Information was mapped onto broader science learning ideas, promoting a geo-spatial approach to thinking about science.

Demouy and Kukulska-Hulme (2010, 225): The participants in this study experienced realistic language listening skills and acquired good and quick response skills in a foreign language.

'Although daunting, I appreciate the chance to do authentic listening and speaking activities'.

'..although it wasn't easy, this activity provided real-life type of practice'

5.3 Assigning rapture

This refers to the de-centralization of academic learning from the confines of the learning institution. As a rhizome can be broken and can start growing again on its old line or on a new line (Mackness and Bell 2015).

Price et al. (2014, 162): Participants in the study into the design and use of a smartphone application for teaching science outside of the classroom experienced confidence in using the device and the application afforded them opportunities to use various pedagogical approaches.

Demouy and Kukulska-Hulme (2010, 222): Group 1 responses show that students engaged with the project activities in a variety of settings; 'Other' locations included at work, in the streets or public spaces, in hotel rooms, at the beach or at the supermarket.

5.4 Cartography and Decalcomania

The metaphor of cartography suggests that knowledge is never permanent, but always provisional, useful at best, and harmful when it becomes dogma (Hamon, 2012 in Cormier 2012). In explaining cartography, Hamon (2012 in Cormier 2012) describes it as mapping against a shifting, organic, adaptive reality. Decalcomania is the transfer of an original pattern to a new location. However, it is important to note that the pattern does not remain constant but is emergent and in constant transition throughout the transfer process.

Price et al. (2014, 162): The camera and abiotic data were designed to prompt tagging of data and uploading onto Google Maps. This enables information to be mapped onto broader science learning ideas, prompting a geo-spatial approach to thinking about science.

6 Line of Argument Synthesis

In the line of argument synthesis, an interpretation is constructed around rhizomatic learning principles in mLearning practice. Figure 1 is diagrammatic illustration of the findings from the line of argument synthesis.

Connection and Heterogeneity. The principle of connection and heterogeneity implies any point of a rhizome may be and must be connected to any other part of the network. This particular principle was prominent in all four studies. The synthesis revealed a number of perspectives through with this principle may be observed.

The first perspective is connections made across various diverse environments. The findings from Munoz-Cristobal et al. (2015) revealed connections made using mobile technologies across the conventional classroom, the street and the online environments. This was achieved through the design of a mobile device supported three dimensional virtual world which consisted of user interfaces of different learning environments.

A second perspective of connection and heterogeneity is the connections made between diverse mobile devices and applications. These connections were

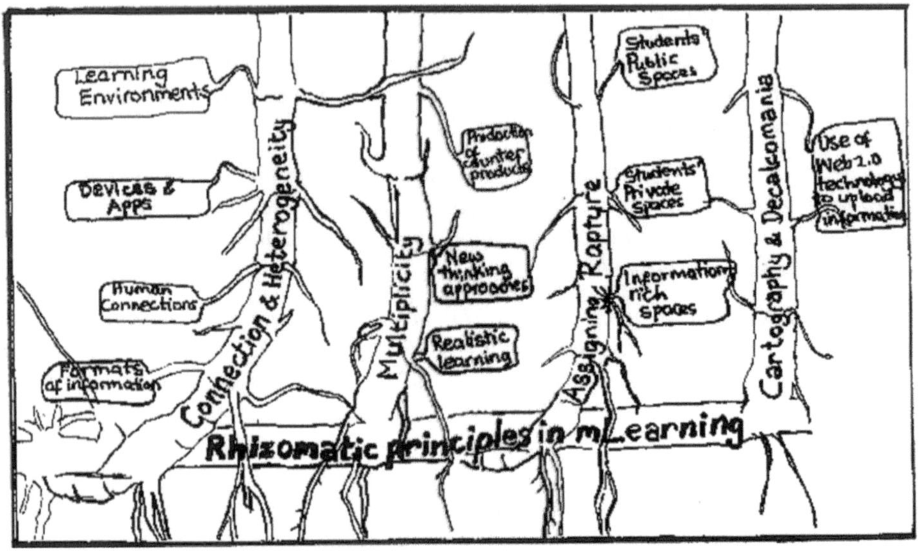

Fig. 1. Rhizomatic learning principles in mLearning practices

demonstrated in Price et al. (2014) where an *in situ* experience was created using diverse mobile technologies incorporated into an application. A camera was used by science education students to take pictures of various plants. QR codes provided information accessed and loaded by the teacher about the plant. Abiotic data (related to humidity and temperature of the plant environment) was used with the camera to prompt tagged information regarding the photographed plant on site.

A third perspective of connection and heterogeneity was demonstrated by Boticki et al. (2011) as human connections established through the use of mobile phones. These connections were made by students through negotiation and exchange in order to fulfil a given learning objective. Using mobile phones, students sent invitations to other groups of students who could help them meet the required learning objective.

The connection between various forms of information is demonstrated in the use of text and audio to achieve learning goals (Demouy and Kukulska-Hulme 2010).

Multiplicity. Multiplicity refers to the formation of new knowledge through the interconnectedness between knowledge. The multiple is then treated as a substantive and ceases to have any relation to the single subject (Deleuze and Guattari 1987, 8).

In Munoz-Cristobal et al. (2015), students taking part in a collaborative activity, analysed existing advertisements and each group had to create a counter-ad based on one of the analysed and assessed various advertisements. As part of the learning activity students were required to produce a counter advertisement which was geo-positioned in the place where it is created. After the deployment, she reviewed the resulting learning environment in the wiki and in Google Earth. In this way a new product is produced as a substantive, using mobile technology. This was achieved using a three dimensional virtual world.

In another example of multiplicity in rhizomatic learning, information was mapped onto broader science learning ideas, promoting a geo-spatial approach to thinking about science. This produced new information and a new approach to thinking about science (Price et al. 2014).

Demouy and Kukulska-Hulme (2010), report on a language skills study where the participants experienced realistic language listening skills through the use of mobile phones, iPods and MP3 players. As a result, they acquired good and quick response skills in a foreign language. The mobile devices provided real life learning opportunities for the participants as the devices allowed for the simulation of real conversations. One participant reported:

'Although daunting, I appreciate the chance to do authentic listening and speaking activities'.

'Although it wasn't easy, this activity provided real-life type of practice'.

Assigning Rapture. Refers to the de-centralization of academic learning from the confines of the learning institution

Munoz-Cristobal et al. (2015) reporting on a collaborative project on the impact of advertising report that each group that was formed to analyse and assess existing geo-positioned advertisements, were required to create a counter-ad based on one of the analysed advertisement. The counter ad was geo-positioned in the place where it is created. This activity took place outside and demonstrated rapture of learning from the physical confines of the learning institution.

Another example of assigning rapture is illustrated by Price et al. (2014). Participants in the study into the design and use of a smartphone application for teaching science outside of the classroom experienced confidence in using the device and the application afforded them opportunities to use various pedagogical approaches.

In a project on language skills enhancement rapture was demonstrated in the responses from the participants which indicated students engaged with the project activities in a variety of settings; 'Other' locations included at work, in the streets or public spaces, in hotel rooms, at the beach or at the supermarket (Demouy and Kukulska-Hulme 2010).

Cartography and Decalcomania are the capacity of inclusion and diversity to spread. Additionally, learning designs can be shared and re-used in different technological ecosystems.

This rhizomatic learning principle was evident in Price et al. (2014). The camera and abiotic data used in a geospatial science project were designed to prompt tagging of data and uploading onto Google Maps. This enabled information to be mapped onto broader science learning ideas, prompting a geo-spatial approach to thinking about science.

7 Conclusion

Rhizomatic principles applied in networked learning environments offer the potential to enrich students' learning experience. This research revealed rhizomatic principles in current mLearning practice. The purpose of the research was not to create a set of guidelines to be applied in mLearning, but rather to contribute in making mLearning practitioners aware of ways in which rhizomatic principles occur in mLearning practice. This awareness, it is hoped, can lead to application of the principles when they are deemed useful in achieving mLearning goals.

The findings from this research synthesis provide a groundwork for further research employing alternative methodologies and focusing on alternative ways in which rhizomatic principles may be used in mLearning practice thus building on these findings and advancing practice.

References

Ally, M., Tsinakos, A.: Introduction: enhancing access to education with mobile learning. In: Ally, M., Tsinakos, A. (eds.) Increasing Access Through Mobile Learning. Commonwealth of Learning, Vancouver (2014)

Arrigo, M., Kukulska-Hulme, A., Arnedillo-Sanchez, I., Kismihok, G.: Meta-analyses from a collaborative project in mobile lifelong learning. Br. Educ. Res. J. **39**(2), 222–247 (2013)

Boticki, I., Looi, C.-K., Wong, L.-H.: Supporting mobile collaborative activities through scaffolded flexible grouping. Educ. Technol. Soc. **14**(3), 190–202 (2011)

Brown, T.H., Mbati, L.: Mobile learning: moving past the myths and embracing the opportunities. Int. Rev. Res. Open Distrib. Learn. **16**(2), 115–135 (2015)

Brown, T.H.: Beyond the misperceptions - towards new trends in mobile learning. In: Invited Keynote Address Delivered at the Teaching Trends 2014 Conference, 15–16 October 2014, Carl von Ossietzky University of Oldenburg, Oldenburg (2014)

Brown, T.H.: The role of m-learning in the future of e-learning in Africa? Presentation at the 21st ICDE World Conference, June 2003, Hong Kong (2003). http://matheasy.webstarts.com/uploads/The_role_of_m-learning_in_the_future_of_e-learning_in_Africa.pdf

Campbell, R., Pound, P., Pope, C., Britten, N., Pill, R., Morgan, M., Donovan, J.: Evaluating meta-ethnography: a synthesis of qualitative research on lay experiences of diabetes and diabetes care. Soc. Sci. Med. **56**, 671–684 (2003)

Cormier, D.: Embracing uncertainty and the strange problem of habituation (2012). http://davecormier.com/edblog/2012/01/26/embracing-uncertainty-and-the-strange-problem-of-habituation/. Accessed 20 July 2015

Cormier, D.: rhizomatic education: community as curriculum (2008). http://davecormier.com/edblog/2008/06/03/rhizomatic-education-community-as-curriculum/. Accessed 26 March 2015

Deleuze, G., Guattari, F.: A Thousand Plateaus: Capitalism and Schizophrenia. Continuum Books, London (1987)

Demouy, V., Kukulska-Hulme, A.: On the spot: using mobile devices for listening and speaking practice on a French language programme. Open Learn. **25**(3), 217–232 (2010)

Lian, A.P.: Reflections on language-learning in the 21st century: a rhizome at work. RJAS **1**(1), 11 (2011)

Litchfield, A., Dyson, L.E., Lawrence, E., Zmijewska, A.: Directions for m-learning research to enhance active learning. Ascilite 2007, Singapore (2007)

MacCallum, K., Jeffrey, L.: Factors impacting teachers & apos; adoption of mobile learning. J. Inf. Technol. Educ. Res. **13**, 141–162 (2014)

Mackness, J., Bell, F.: Rhizo14: a rhizomatic learning cMOOC in sunlight and in shade Open. Praxis **7**(1), 25–38 (2015)

Munoz-Cristobal, J.A., Prieto, L.P., Asensio-Perez, J.I., Martinez-Mones, A., Jorrin-Abellan, I. M., Dimitriadis, Y.: Coming down to earth: helping teachers use 3D virtual worlds in across-spaces learning situations. Educ. Technol. Soc. **18**(1), 13–26 (2015)

Price, S., Davies, P., Farr, W., Jewitt, C., Roussos, G., Sin, G.: Fostering geospatial thinking in science education through a customisable smartphone application. Br. J. Educ. Technol. **45** (1), 160–170 (2014)

Wang, M., Shen, R.: Message design for mobile learning: learning theories, human cognition and design principles. Br. J. Educ. Technol. **43**(4), 561–575 (2012)

Zurita, G., Nussbaum, M.: A conceptual framework based on activity theory for mobile CSCL. Br. J. Educ. Technol. **38**(2), 211–235 (2007)

Mobile Learning in a Flipped Multimedia Higher Education Classroom

Chrisna Botha-Ravyse[1], Seugnet Blignaut[2(✉)], and Martin Booth[2]

[1] TELIT-SA, School of Economic Sciences,
North-West University, Vanderbijlpark, South Africa
Chrisna.Botha@nwu.ac.za
[2] TELIT-SA, School of Information Technology,
North-West University, Vanderbijlpark, South Africa
{Seugnet.Blignaut,Martin.Booth}@nwu.ac.za

Abstract. Flipping classrooms from traditional teaching approaches to technology-enhanced interactive classrooms requires that previously designed software be revisited for mobile use. This paper: (i) describes how an existing custom-made test-and-quiz multimedia application, originally created in Articulate Storyline™, was re-designed for Adobe Flash™ to encapsulate the original functionality for use on an array of mobile devices; and (ii) qualitatively evaluates students' perceptions of the value of the flipped-classroom approach. The self-evaluation mobile assessment was integrated as part of a flipped-classroom with seventy two (N = 72) Nutrition students. The module used technologies during a flipped-classroom approach to facilitation. The study captures students' perceptions of the usefulness of the approach of students' use of the mobile application from (i) students' course evaluations and (ii) students' evaluations in their nutrition competency portfolios. The analysis indicates that the students readily accepted the flipped classroom approach augmented with any-time-and-place classroom-based self-evaluation applications.

Keywords: Flipped classroom · Qualitative analysis · Self-evaluation mobile application · Re-designing of multimedia content

1 Introduction

The pedagogical approach of flipping classrooms draws on education concepts like active learning, student engagement, hybrid course design, and course podcasting (Educause 2012). A flipped classrooms approach aims at repurposing class time as active workshops where students corroborate course content, test their knowledge, apply their skills and knowledge to authentic cases, and interact within groups in hands-on activities.

Technology-enhanced learning (TEL) actively supports the swapping of homework for classwork in order to foster frequent and insightful interaction between lecturers, students and learning content. Such a flipped approach demands thoughtful selection and use of a palette of learning technologies. Flipped classes demand the use of new tools to support the out-of-class portion of the curriculum. The ongoing development of powerful mobile devices will put a wider range of rich, educational resources into the

T.H. Brown and H.J. van der Merwe (Eds.): mLearn 2015, CCIS 560, pp. 58–69, 2015.
DOI: 10.1007/978-3-319-25684-9_5

hands of students, at times and places most convenient to them (Educause 2012). During a flipped classroom approach, students are requested to view short video lectures at home before classes, while class time is subsequently devoted to exercises, projects, discussions and formative evaluation. Pre-recorded lectures and other course-related short videos could be podcast to students for access and interaction prior to formal classes. Students, in advance, receive pertinent pieces like journal articles to read, and perform relating Internet searches as part of their homework. Class time is thus freed up for the productive facilitation of content areas and engagement with hands-on activities (Ash 2012). In flipped classrooms, mobile devices compel students to embrace the responsibility for self-study of course content outside classes in order to, interact with problem solving tasks and other applied learning activities like role play inside flipped classes (Goodwin and Miller 2013). During classes, the involvement of lecturers changes to the roles of coaches and advisors while they individually and collaboratively encourage and enable students (Educause 2012).

For decades, the reductionist role of lecturers to teaching and learning in higher education was that of instructors imparting knowledge to students. Very little interaction took place between the concerned parties, and students became passive receivers of second-hand knowledge (Chuang 2015). Kuh and Hu (2001) state that the use of technology in teaching and learning does not only improve learning, but also improves interactive teaching. In order to change the passive and un-involved participation of students, in flipped classes short activities and multiple choice quizzes could assist in assessing and enhancing students' newly acquired knowledge and content skills (Chuang 2015). Mobile devices allow immediate interaction with the content which enhances both students' learning experiences and their actual learning (Caldwell 2007). An array of interactive mobile devices enable students to respond to multiple-choice questions to promote increased interactive learning and effective communication (Beekes 2006). Students from the Y-Generation also demand the use of technology in learning inside and outside classrooms (Prensky 2001).

Teaching with mobile technology opens education to the vast possibilities which technology-enhanced education affords. The literature frequents studies on the beneficial use of mobile devices for student learning outside classrooms (Naismith et al. 2004, Traxler 2010). Learning technologies provide students and lecturers alike the freedom to access digital resources and class activities at any time and any place (Kearney et al. 2012), for students to take ownership of their learning (Traxler 2010). On their own, mobile technologies cannot develop and support higher-order thinking skills (Chuang 2015, Dangel and Wang 2008). Lecturers have the new role to foster higher order thinking in their students through the development of bespoke applications for on-the-spot assessment to provide immediate feedback on pertinent curriculum issues. The use of such applications could also entice engaged classroom discussions and project-based activities where lecturers could devote class time for the application of concepts. In flipping their classrooms, lecturers also have more opportunities to detect misconceptions in students' thinking. Lecturers and students should reflect together on the way students learn, how students understand the content, and how to use and apply the learning content in real-life issues (Educause 2012).

Botha-Ravyse and Reitsma (2015) show how the use of multimedia tailored for specific courses could assist during the flipping of a classroom. They conclude that mobile technology enables the accessibility of learning content both inside and outside classrooms. This ground-breaking study indicates how, in a developing country where student Internet access in higher education is often inadequate, course information is not readily online, usability evaluations of courses are often not performed, funding for the development of apt mobile applications is infrequent, and devices for mobile learning reside in the pockets of students. These restraints impact not only students' readiness to participate in flipped classrooms, but also the institution's ability to support new developments in the use of TEL in higher education. It therefore becomes important that previously designed applications also be flipped, i.e. transformed for tailor-made use in flipped classrooms. Examples of such applications designed for use in computer laboratories may include tests and quizzes, tutorials, simulations, serious games, PowerPoint slides, lengthy videos, online tests, and other digital teaching learning content. For courses where the content remains relatively stable (e.g. content on nutrition), many of these technologies could be effectively used as part of students' self-study activities at home on their personal mobile devices. A severe downside of this approach is that these applications, most of the time, do not readily transport well from the computer laboratory network to the mobile devices in students' pockets.

2 The Intervention

2.1 Background

The test-and-quiz application under the microscope in this study was originally designed in Articulate Storyline™. Storyline™ is a software package that enables lecturers to easily create interactive learning content for both online and offline use of interactive slideshow presentations, as well as quizzes. Articulate Storyline™ projects are mainly exported to Shockwave Flash™ format (SWF). Adobe's Flash Player™ is required to view the content in the SWF format. Unfortunately, Adobe™ no longer provides support for Flash Player™ on mobile devices. This means that only computers or devices which use desktop operating systems (e.g. Windows 8™ and Mac OSX™) can display Flash™ content. Also, Flash Player 12™ is the last version that is supported on Linux™ and is no longer in regular use. Articulate Storyline™ provides its own mobile player to run Storyline 1™ content on iOS™ devices. Android™ devices are not officially supported. Articulate Storyline 2™, however, now provides support for devices running on Android 4.1™ or later.

At the time of the study, Articulate Storyline 2™ was not yet available. In order to provide a suitable equivalent experience to students, the authors turned to Adobe Flash™. Although Flash™ applications are no longer supported on mobile web browsers, they can run as standalone mobile applications on Android™ and iOS™ platforms. This is possible through the Adobe AIR™ framework. SWF files are created when Adobe Flash™ source files are compiled, and can therefore not be edited afterwards. This prevents developers from reversing engineer existing SWF files and porting them to mobile platforms through Adobe AIR™. Ultimately, a solution similar to Articulate Storyline™ quizzes needed to be developed from scratch in Adobe Flash Professional™.

Another reason for choosing the Adobe Flash™ rather than another platform to redesign, was mainly a financial one. Since this project was for a single lecturer enhancing a flipped classroom, the developer had to make use of programs that his particular University already had licenses for.

2.2 Redesigning the Test-and-Quiz Application

The existing in-house designed test-and-quiz multimedia application, created in Articulate Storyline™, needed to be redesigned as an Adobe Flash™ application to encapsulate the original functionality, but enable it for use on an array of smart mobile devices. The rationale for this re-design was that the original application was developed for computer laboratory use and could not readily be transported to mobile platforms without considerable manual work. Also, the lecturer aimed to implement the test-and-quiz application during classes where students would bring their own mobile devices.

There are a number of major differences between personal computers and mobile devices, which may affect the design and implementation of a mobile application concerning processing power, storage space, and screen size. Adobe AIR™ handles different screen resolutions by either adding borders or by stretching the display to fit the screen. However, scaling the display to smaller screens may disrupt user input.

Students are familiar with the format and style of Articulate Storyline™ quizzes, and the same look-and-feel was used for the Adobe Flash™ application. Fortunately, the existing resources that were used in the Articulate Storyline™ quizzes could be reused in Adobe Flash™. Different question types are available in Articulate Storyline™, such as multiple choice questions (single selection), multiple choice questions (multiple selection), ordering questions, matching columns questions, and hotspot questions. Figure 1 shows two question types used in the redesigned test-and-quiz application.

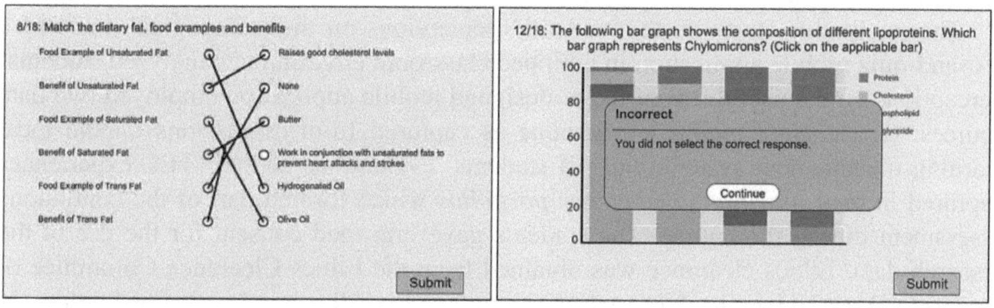

Fig. 1. Screenshots of the matching columns and hotspot question types

The sets of quizzes that had to be redesigned in Adobe Flash™ contained a few hundred questions. Manually recreating each question clearly would not be an efficient solution. Instead, a framework was developed that could create these types of questions automatically. This framework could then be populated with content. For example, a multiple choice question contains question text, a number of choices, the correct answer(s) and an optional picture. For each multiple choice question, the application reads the content and loads it into the framework. The framework would initially position the different parts of a question in fixed locations. This very quickly became problematic. Some questions contained more text, and some questions encompassed more choices or steps than others. This required that the application should attempt to use the available screen space efficiently. Some choices from questions are short enough to fit two columns of choices could fit on one screen.

Students could interact with the application via touch-and-drag gestures. Touch gestures were used to select specific choices. Dragging gestures were used to reorder steps in an ordering question, or to draw lines between two columns in a matching columns question. Adobe AIR™ deals with different screen resolutions by either adding borders or by stretching the display to fit the screen.

3 Research Methods

This paper addresses two relating issues: (i) How effective was the technical re-design of the test-and-quiz for use on an array of smart mobile devices? and (ii) Did the flipped classroom approach warrant the use of a self-assessment test-and-quiz application based on the students perceptions after using it?

3.1 Research Setting

The student group comprised seventy two (N = 72), mainly female (n = 65) Dietetics students in their second year of study and enrolled for a foundation Nutrition course at a residential university in South Africa. The module extensively used learning technologies like laptop computers, tablets and smart mobile phones during the facilitation of its flipped-classroom approach to course facilitation. This approach was unique at the time in the sense that it was not used in other Nutrition under-graduate courses.

The qualitative study on the students' perceptions on the pedagogical value of a test-and-quiz mobile application in a flipped classroom environment analyzed students' perceptions on the usefulness of the re-designed mobile application employed two data sources: (i) *student's course evaluations* as captured from discussions on the local learning management system; and (ii) students' evaluations of their TEL experiences captured in their *nutrition competency portfolios* which formed part of the continuous assessment during the course. The students gave informed consent for the use of the research data. Ethics clearance was obtained from the Ethics Clearance Committee of the North-West University for research on students' and lecturers' use of technology in classroom settings according to formative and summative methodologies. The relating ethics clearance number is NWU-00026-13-A4.

3.2 Data Analysis

3.2.1 Walkthrough Analysis of the Test-and-Quiz Mobile Application

The technical designer together with a team of mobile designers performed a walk-through evaluation on the test-and-quiz mobile application to ensure that the application functioned well and displayed satisfactory. They also tested the application on an array of smartphones and mobile devices that students carried in their pockets.

3.2.2 Thematic Content Analysis

This paper made use of the thematic content analysis inductive approach to coding (Boeije 2002) and analyzed the data with ATLAS.ti™ version 7, a computer-assisted qualitative data analysis software. Similar categories were collated under specific themes (Saldana 2009). The themes were developed on the basis of the coding process and were developed gradually and collaboratively. The final code system comprised the four themes: usability, immediate feedback, motivation, and added value (Table 1 and Fig. 2). Each of these themes encompassed eight categories and fourteen codes. The categories which emerged most frequently were *ease of use* and *anytime use*.

Table 1. Count of responses in each category.

			Total of students comments on topic
Immediate feedback			
Learning content	Examination preparation	Students' learning	
22 (35 %)	18 (25 %)	29 (40 %)	72
Usability			
Ease of use	Anytime use	Not used	
33 (56 %)	14 (24 %)	1 (0.02 %)	58
Motivation			
Enjoyment	Repeated use		
34 (51 %)	30 (44 %)		68
Added value			36
Total:			**234**

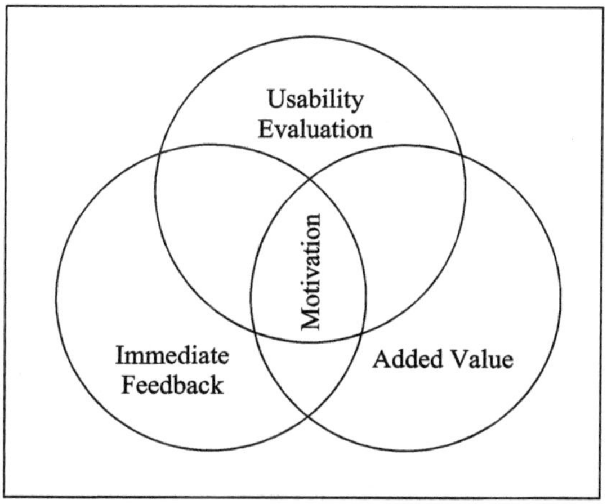

Fig. 2. Venn diagram indicating the three themes, sharing a central theme

4 Findings and Discussion

4.1 Findings from the Walkthrough Evaluation of the Redesign of the Application

On opening the test-and-quiz mobile application, students could choose a specific quiz from a list. Each quiz draws questions from a question pool. Some quizzes draw all the questions in the pool, while others only draw from a subset. The questions could be posed in random order. The application notifies students whether their response(s) were correct or not before moving on to the next question (Fig. 1). Once students have completed a quiz, they have the opportunity to review each question from the specific quiz. Thereafter, the students' answers are displayed together with the correct answers. Correct student responses are marked in green, while incorrect student responses are marked in red, allowing students to instantaneously view their misconceptions. Students can also see which correct choices (with multiple choice questions) they have missed.

4.2 Findings and Discussion of the Qualitative Analysis

The most prevalent theme, that emerged most, was *immediate feedback*. The comments relating to the categories of *summary of content* and *preparation for evaluations* were more frequent (60%), compared to the *learning* that took place (40%). This, however, suggests that the students appreciated the fact that the tests aided them to identify areas that they should spend more time on:

> *The tests on the phone after class helped me to determine how much I still need to learn and how much I know already.*
> *The self-test was handy seeing as we could do it on our phones and it didn't count any marks but it made you aware of what you know and what not.*
> *I used it for class preparation as a summary and to prepare for the exams.*

The aim of formative feedback is to increase student knowledge, skills, and understanding of some content area and address misconceptions in their knowledge base (Shute 2008). Hattie and Timperley (2007) report that feedback about how well a task is accomplished or performed, i.e. distinguishing correct from incorrect answers as in this case, is called *corrective feedback*. They emphasize the powerful value of timely feedback. Access to correct information is a foundation on which the processing and self-regulation are built. Hattie and Timperley (2007) are of the opinion that *knowledge feedback* Hattie and Timperley (2007) [17] is more powerful when it is about addressing misconceptions and not on students' insufficient information about the issue. When students have insufficient knowledge on a relating topic, further content facilitation is more powerful than feedback information. In the case of this study, the flipped classroom approach compelled the students to take responsibility for their learning, and knowledge feedback would therefore strengthen their efforts.

There are further advantages to knowledge feedback: (i) It can highlight a gap between a current level of performance and some desired level of performance or goal. Resolving this gap can motivate higher levels of effort (Song and Keller 2001), and (ii) It can also effectively reduce the cognitive load of a student, especially novice or struggling students (Paas et al. 2003). When feedback is given in small chunks, cognitive overload is diminished during learning with high performance demands.

The aim of this study was not to test usability of the mobile application, but to record students' perceptions on the usefulness of the test-and-quiz application in a flipped classroom setting. The analysis of students' utterances made it clear that the newly developed mobile application worked well and they perceived it as valuable. This indicates that they felt positive about the usability of the mobile application. None of the utterances directly pointed to the usefulness of the application, but the over-arching gist of their perceptions valued the smooth execution of the application and beneficial interaction with the learning content. Hartson et al. (2009) describe various methods to test usability. Based on the description of their methods, as well with how the codes emerged from our analysis, our study relates to the category of user evaluation. User evaluation refers to the specific critical incidents during a usability evaluation. Hartson et al. (2009) describe critical incidents as those which allow for the identification of events or phenomena that occur during task performance which could be indicators of usability issues or successes. The phenomenon in this case refers to the usefulness of the new mobile test-and-quiz application.

From the identification of three repeating ideas on the usability of our study, three categories emerged: *ease of use*, *anytime use*, and *no use*. The students regularly (80%) mentioned the first two categories in the discussion forum in the LMS and in their learning portfolios. Only one student mentioned that he/she did not use the mobile test-and-quizzes in class or elsewhere. Based on these repeating ideas, transformed as coding themes, we found that taking the trouble of redesigning the test-and-quizzes for mobile use was worth the effort, time and cost. The students perceived the mobile application to be easy to use and they were pleased with the fact that they could use it anytime and anyplace for course revision as a real benefit to them:

> *I liked the fact that I could use the material anywhere and also quickly check if I have a good grasp on the work, sitting in the SS* [Sic: Student Centre] *sipping a cool drink.*

During the usability testing of a mobile application it is important to consider three aspects for all types of software (Nayebi et al. 2012). The students made mention of all three aspects:

> *More efficient to use: takes less time to complete a particular task.*
> *Easier to learn: operations can be learned by observing the object.*
> *More user satisfaction: meets user expectations.*

Half of the students (50%) indicated that they engaged with the test-and-quiz application after classes and that they perceived that it added value to the flipped classroom approach:

> *I like the classes they are always fun and I learn something new every time. What I thought was valuable was the fact that the self-test on our phones would bring everything together and helped us to focus what has been done.*
> *It was very valuable to see that all the activities in the classroom led to my knowledge of the work by doing the phone tests.*

From the analysis, we identified *student motivation* as the intersectional aspect which linked to the three themes (Fig. 2). Although motivated students are easy to recognize, they are difficult to find (Skinner and Belmont 1993). Academic motivation is a complex phenomenon, partly because it stretches above and beyond the education domain to the broader social context in which the student is situated. Academic attitudes and behavior are strongly influenced by social concepts in the student's environment, whether these are lecturers, parents, or friends (Legault et al. 2006). Motivation as a theme developed through the recurring ideas that some sort of drive motivated the students to use the test-and-quiz mobile application. Some indicated that they enjoyed using it, and others that they used it, not just after the class, but also while they prepared for the examination. It was not clear whether these motivations were extrinsic or intrinsic in nature, but the students felt compelled to engage with the test-and-quiz mobile application:

> *It was fun doing tests on your phone it beats the boring old multiple tests on paper.*
> *I enjoyed using the mobile application and used it to prepare for class as well as for the exam.*

Three themes, usability, immediate feedback and added value emerged from the analyses which lead to student motivation (Fig. 2). Various studies have shown that once a student is motivated, learning increases (Deci and Ryan 2000, Legault et al. 2006, Serge et al. 2013). These studies also show that feedback is an important aspect as it increases learning behavior and motivation, depending on the learner's attention and ability to adapt learning behavior (Serge et al. 2013). In a digital environment the usability of the application could also contribute to the student's motivation to engage with it (Deci and Ryan 2000). We therefore theorize, based on students' perceptions and experiences that the added value of the test-and-quiz application motivated them to use the application and to learn.

5 Conclusions and Recommendations

The technical redesign and use of the test-and-quiz framework was beneficial:

- Questions could be created and presented consistently. The same elements from the different questions would always appear at the same location on the screen.
- Consecutive changes could be executed only once, e.g. if the space between two choices needed to be larger, the change only had to be made once.
- The file size of the individual quizzes could be kept low since the questions mainly consisted of text. However, the addition of supplementary images will have a more noticeable impact on the file size.
- An arbitrarily large number of questions can be included without any additional programming. This feature simplifies manual fixes and future updates.
- The framework can be reused to create quizzes for other subject areas.

Publishing an Android™ application through the Google Play Store™ requires a waiting period before the application can be accessed on devices. Although the waiting period is short—often within a few hours—it is a design aspect out of the control of the developer. The authors of the new test-and-quiz application opted to make the application available on the university's local learning management system (LMS). Students could log in to the LMS and download the application directly to their devices.

Unfortunately, subsequent updates had to be implemented manually. Every time a new quiz became available, the older version of the Android™ application is replaced with the new one. Students consequently have to download the newer version and reinstall the application. The size of the Android™ application is small (roughly 11 MB) and it could therefore easily be made available on the university's LMS for students to download and install multiple times without depleting their mobile data bundles. Future revisions of the application could include the functionality to download quiz content from a server, without having to reinstall the application on the student's device. This is an option envisioned for the future after the completion of the usability evaluation of the test-and-quiz application.

From the lecturer's point of view *usefulness* was the important factor which this paper also set out to test. The researched aimed to capture the added value a redesigning of a handy application could add to the flipped classrooms and the learning that this type of mobile application could illicit. From the findings it became evident that learning took place and students used the mobile application to gauge their progress, as well as to use it for preparation for examinations. The conclusion can therefore be made that the mobile application did prove to be useful for use in a flipped classroom, and it added value to the class seeing as students could monitor their own progress. As flipped classrooms rely heavily on self-directed learning where students take responsibility for their own learning, the lecturer felt compelled to include this tool as part of her teaching pallet in order to provide a scaffold to support students. The analysis indicated that this tool was handy for students' self-evaluation in class, as well as in conjunction with other activities.

However, from the eyes of students it seems as though the usability of the application was more important than its usefulness in a classroom setting. This might indicate that an application might be useful, but if the usability is not there, a student might not want to use it. This emphasizes the need for usability testing by the end user. The students were definitely more focused on the way in which this application worked or added to their learning strategy than whether or not it is useful in a class. Furthermore it was clear that the students were motivated using this application, not just inside the classroom but also outside of the classroom. The learning expectations of the Y-generation students during a flipped classroom approach, as well as their technology expectations during the use of technology enhanced learning, were met.

Based on the positive outcome of the students' acceptance and use of the self-assessment mobile application intertwined in a flipped classroom, the conclusion can be made that it was worth the effort. Its added value to the flipped classroom approach was that the students' knowledge base developed before classes and cemented during class. It also gave clear indications to the students on how well they understood the learning content. The application also enabled them to ask questions in time before the formal examination. The use of the application also provided the lecturer with feedback on the self-study and preparation of the students for the flipped classroom. This feedback also provided a tidy summary of students' competencies with the activities performed in the flipped class. The analysis indicated that the students readily accepted the flipped classroom approach which matched their expectation of the any-time-and-place classroom-based self-evaluation mobile application.

This paper contributes to knowledge on the useful redesign of existing multimedia applications for a new approach to teaching and learning. It indicated that spending cost, time and effort used during the redesigning of the mobile self-assessment test-and-quiz application was worthwhile and that its use was profitable in a flipped classroom approach. An additional benefit is that the once-off design of the framework could be used with a large number of test items, as well as for other subject areas. The clever design warrants its continued use in flipping Nutrition classrooms while adding value to students' learning experiences.

Acknowledgements. This work is based on research in part funded by (i) the National Research Foundation (NRF) of South Africa. Any opinion, findings and conclusions or recommendations expressed in this material are those of the authors and therefore the NRF does not accept any liability in regard thereto; (ii) the research participants that voluntarily gave their time to the research and shared their perceptions on the flipped classroom approach with the researchers; (iii) the North-West University for resources and support.

References

Ash, K.: Educatorts view "flipped model" with a more critical eye (2012). http://www.edweek.org/ew/articles/2012/08/29/02el-flipped.h32.html. Accessed 29 August 2015

Beekes, W.: The 'millionaire' method for encouraging participation. Act. Learn. High Educ. **7**(1), 25–36 (2006)

Boeije, H.: A purposeful approach to the constant comparative method in the analysis of qualitative interviews. Qual. Quant. **36**, 391–409 (2002)

Botha-Ravyse, C.R., Reitsma, G.: Engaged nutrition learning in a multi-media enhanced flipped classroom. Progressio **37**(1), 1–14 (2015)

Caldwell, J.E.: Clickers in the large classroom: current research and best-practice tips. CBE-Life Sci. Educ. **6**(1), 9–20 (2007)

Chuang, Y.-T.: SSCLS: a smartphone-supported collaborative learning system. Telematics Inform. **32**(3), 463–474 (2015)

Dangel, H.L., Wang, C.X.: Student response systems in higher education: moving beyond linear teaching and surface learning. J. Educ. Technol. Dev. Exch. **1**(1), 93–107 (2008)

Deci, E.L., Ryan, R.M.: The "what" and "why" of goal pursuits: human needs and the self-determination of behavior. Psychol. Inq. **11**(4), 227–268 (2000)

Educause. 7 Things you should know about Flipped Classrooms (2012). https://net.educause.edu/ir/library/pdf/eli7081.pdf. Accessed 20 July 2015

Goodwin, B., Miller, K.: Evidence on flipped classrooms is still coming in (2013). www.ascd.org. Accessed 25 March 2015

Hartson, H.R., Andre, T.S., Williges, R.C.: Criteria for evaluating usability evaluation methods. Int. J. Hum. Comput. Interact. **13**(4), 373–410 (2009)

Hattie, J., Timperley, H.: The power of feedback. Rev. Educ. Res. **77**(1), 81–112 (2007)

Kearney, M., Schuck, S., Burden, K., Aubusson, P.: Viewing mobile learning from a pedagogical prospective. Res. Learn. Technol. **20**, 1–17 (2012)

Kuh, G.D., Hu, S.: The relationships between computer and information technology use, student learning, and other college experiences. J. Coll. Stud. Dev. **35**(2), 217–232 (2001)

Legault, L., Green-Demers, I., Pelletier, L.: Why do high school students lack motivation in the classroom? Toward an understanding of academic amotivation and the role of social support. J. Educ. Psychol. **98**(3), 567–582 (2006)

Naismith, L., Lonsdale, P., Vavoula, G., Sharples, M.: Literature Review in Mobile Technologies and Learning. Future Lab Series, pp. 1–44. FutureLab, London (2004)
Nayebi, F., Desharnais, J.-M., Abran, A.: The state of the art of mobile application usability evaluation. Paper Presented to the Canadian Conference on Electrical and Computer Engineering (2012)
Paas, F., Renkl, A., Sweller, J.: Cognitive load theory and instructional design: recent developments. Educ. Psychol. **38**, 1–4 (2003)
Prensky, M.: The games generations: how learners have changed. In: From Digital Game-Based Learning, pp. 1–23. McGraw-Hill (2001)
Saldana, J.: The Coding Manual for Qualitative Researchers. SAGE, London (2009)
Serge, S.R., Priest, H.A., Durlach, P.J., Johnson, C.I.: The effects of static and adaptive performance feedback in game-based training. Comput. Hum. Behav. **29**(3), 1150–1158 (2013)
Shute, V.J.: Focus on formative feedback. Rev. Educ. Res. **78**(1), 153–189 (2008)
Skinner, E.A., Belmont, M.J.: Motivation in the classroom: reciprocal effects of teacher behavior and student engagement across the school year. J. Educ. Psychol. **85**(4), 571–581 (1993)
Song, S., Keller, J.: Effectiveness of motivationally adaptive computer assisted instruction on the dynamic aspects of motivation. Educ. Technol. Res. Dev. **49**(2), 5–22 (2001)
Traxler, J.: Students and mobile devices. Res. Learn. Technol. **18**(2), 149–160 (2010)

Infinite Possibilities for Using Eyetracking for Mobile Serious Games in Order to Improve User Learning Experiences

A. Seugnet Blignaut(✉)

TELIT-SA, School of Information Technology,
Faculty of Economic Sciences and Information Technology,
North-West University, Vaal Triangle Campus,
Potchefstroom, South Africa
Seugnet.Blignaut@nwu.ac.za

Abstract. Serious games have, to some degree, relocated from desktops to palmtops. Developers of serious games employ eyetracking as part of their evaluation of user learning experiences on an array of devices. Those who do not use eyetracking for usability evaluation agree that it seems a good idea. This paper provides an initial analysis of literature findings selected according to stringent search criteria to contribute towards a conceptual framework for the use of eyetracking for serious games to improve user learning experiences. Electronic articles were analyzed of which (i) the time span was 1999–2015; (ii) the document type was articles in journals; (iii) the keywords for searches were "eye tracking AND serious games" and some permutations thereof; and (iv) the articles spanned all disciplines. The qualitative analysis of the six identified articles rendered an unexpected large number of 34 findings suited to compilation of the conceptual framework. The findings grouped as six themes; three relating to user learning aspects during gameplay and three relating to eyetracking measures.

Keywords: Eyetracking · Serious games · Systematic literature review · Serious mobile games · Usability evaluation

1 Introduction

This paper integrates the findings of published empirical studies that employed eyetracking technology to explore the construct of users' learning experiences while they engaged with serious games over the past fifteen years (1999–2015). My interest in the topic was kindled when I read the work of Johansen et al. (2006) in which they argue that, in spite of the indisputable value of eyetracking, "usability evaluation is still not a well-integrated part of the development of computer games, and usability practitioners are still in want for better methods and procedures to help them work specifically with the improvement of usability of games." While Moreno-Ger et al. (2012) are of the opinion that only "moderate information" is available on the use of eyetracking and serious games, others (Johansen et al. 2006, Marsh 2007, Renshaw et al. 2009) reflect on the small number of scholarly publications which are available on

T.H. Brown and H.J. van der Merwe (Eds.): mLearn 2015, CCIS 560, pp. 70–83, 2015.
DOI: 10.1007/978-3-319-25684-9_6

the use of eyetracking for the usability evaluation during the development of serious games. With the introduction of mobile devices with touch screens, the question orbits out how eyetracking could contribute towards the playability of serious games, also on mobile devices.

2 Serious Games, Eyetracking and User Learning Experiences

Serious games have become important teaching and learning tools. The New Media Consortium (NMC) lists games and videos as the two primary ways students learn outside of their schooling and the NMC also predicts that the educational use of games and gamification will make significant impact within the near future (Johnson et al. 2015). However, the sobering voice of Giessen (2015) reminds us that "we are still far away from a general result on whether serious games are successful or not. However, success is not guaranteed, nor is failure necessary." Maybe the use of eyetracking, in a small way, could contribute towards the quality of a learning tool at the hype of technology use in learning. Blignaut et al. (2015b) propose a conceptual framework for user learning experiences through the lens of serious games, emotive learning and usability evaluation. The following paragraphs provide an explanation of the value of the construct of learning experiences of serious game players (Fig. 1).

2.1 Serious Games

Learning with serious games represents a dichotomy as a *game* represents enjoyment and excitement, while *serious* is often associated with the profound. As early as 1980, Malone 1980 in his model of intrinsically motivating instruction which for many years influenced game design, provides guidelines for the design of enjoyable (fun) learning with games and game-based learning (Djamasbia et al. 2010, Nacke et al. 2010). Malone includes guidelines for challenge, fantasy, and curiosity; the guidelines also stipulate direction for the evaluation of user experiences. Farber (2014) argues that "a coating of sweet does not make the learning suddenly fun." Jordan (1999) presents a hierarchical model of pleasure needs (for enjoyment or fun) which game developers could use during game design. He argues that the type of fun in games follows from usability evaluation (which depends on functionality). He lists four types of fun as: (i) physio-pleasure (evoked tactile and olfactory stimuli), (ii) socio-pleasure (evoked by relationships, society, personal status, or indicative of social identity), (iii) psycho-pleasure (cognitive and emotional reactions), and (iv) ideo-pleasure (aesthetics and ideological value). This model considers "fun" as the main component of the game play experience, as it was constructed from emotional and cognitive responses of game players (Nacke et al. 2010). Although the Faber taxonomy seems hierarchical of nature, the fun encountered in most serious games mainly derive from psycho-pleasures which elicit both cognitive and emotional reactions in game players.

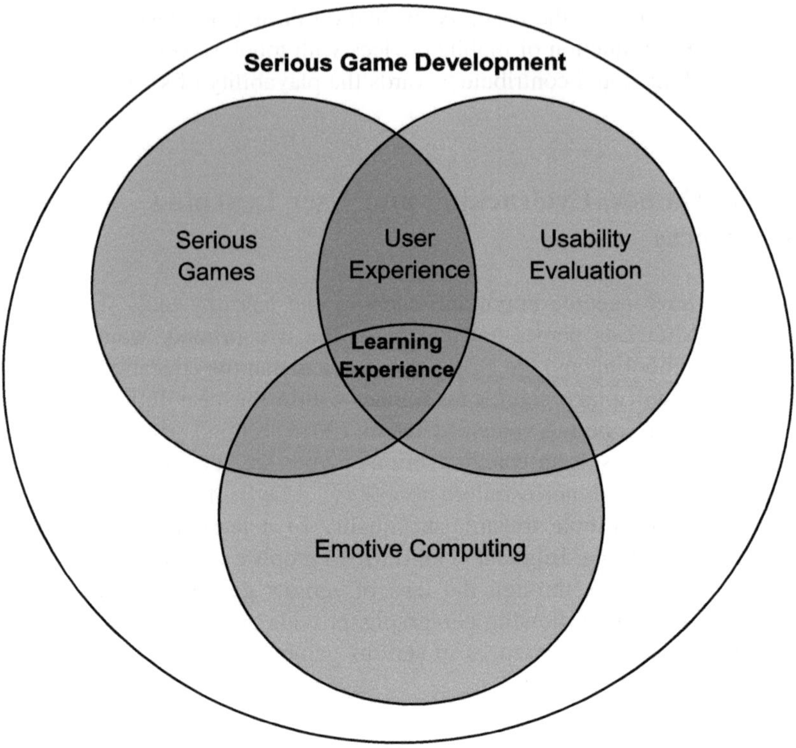

Fig. 1. Conceptual framework for user learning experiences through the lens of serious games, emotive learning and usability evaluation (Blignaut et al. 2015a).

2.2 Usability Evaluation

An ultimate challenge for serious game development is to generate enlightening formative and scientifically sound summative evaluation which on the one hand address gaming aspects, and on the other hand, foster meaningful learning (Kickmeier-Rust et al. 2011). The caveat for the testing of games is that classic usability testing does not suffice, since the standard metrics of effectiveness in task completion and efficiency in error rate are not directly applicable to all aspects of digital games. In the past the evaluation of digital games was mostly informal. However, the serious gaming developers are now adopting more formal techniques which originate from the human-computer interaction discipline. Evaluating user experiences to assess and improve serious games has become important. Although traditional usability evaluation metrics remain relevant, they have to be supplemented with physiological and metrical assessments in order to become relevant to serious games. Many principles used in the evaluation of the usability of general software may not be applicable to serious games (Wechsung and Naumann 2008). The criteria of usability evaluation are adapted to meet the needs of serious games according to gameplay experiences (Connolly et al. 2012). Hartson et al. (2001) classify usability evaluation methods (UEM) as four areas and they develop criteria for each: (i) expert evaluations, (ii) model evaluations, (iii) user evaluations and (iv) location evaluations. Location evaluations encompass three types of evaluations: controlled experiments, laboratory evaluations and remote evaluations. Eyetracking is classified as a laboratory evaluation where individual participants, whose profiles match those of the target users of the game, could evaluate typical tasks in a prototype game (Hartson et al. 2001). Eyetracking as a UEM could indicate game players' interpersonal attitudes and emotions. Its close relationship to the perceptions and visual attention mechanisms of people aligns with the internal state of the game player, seeks motives for their past behavior, and predicts their future actions. Most game developers demand some form of gaze control system during the development of games (Peters and Qureshi 2010). Although the individual aspects of fun and learning competencies must be outstanding, the game in its entirety should excel. Evaluating serious games must therefore consider both performance and recreational aspects (Kickmeier-Rust et al. 2011).

Observation of users' eye movements has a long tradition in UEM and its use has increased in recent years. In general, eyetracking is based on identifying fixations (processing of attended information with stationary eyes) and saccades (quick eye movements occurring between fixations without information processing) (Connolly et al. 2012). When a person interacts with a visual environment, he/she makes a sequence of fixations separated with saccades. Fixations and saccades are matched according to on-going mental processes during interaction with a visual object. However, it does not tell whether or not the person comprehends the information that he or she was looking at (Kiili et al. 2014). Eyetracking should always be augmented with complementary measures such as those used in usability evaluation (Kickmeier-Rust et al. 2011).

2.3 User Experience

Serious games should meet the demands from the consumer market and the expectations of Y-generation gamers who grew up with immersive fidelity, scalable and adaptive interaction, and engaging mechanics in multimedia applications. Serious games (educational digital games; games for learning) often fail in the consumer market, as game players, used to the dazzle of commercial games, desire interfaces that are both entertaining and captivating. Serious games consequently compete with triple A-class commercial games to provide a comparable product that also supports learning of fundamental nature. While some serious games present purposeful content, others deal with mind-numbing boring subject matter. Most successful serious games have a degree of enjoyment (fun) at their roots. Living with a life-threatening disease like HIV/AIDS (Amory 2007), fighting Malaria (Farber 2014), or saving forcibly displaced persons (Gonsalves et al. 2012) are examples of deadly serious learning content where fun dissipates to the background in favor of serious content.

Serious games promote engagement, which could be either behavioral, cognitive, or affective engagement (Sedano et al. 2013). Due to its duality of expectations, usability evaluation of serious games has to take into account the intended learning outcomes (Bellotti et al. 2013). Assessment of the performance of the students should provide an indication of achievement of learning outcomes in order to provide guidelines to game developers (Bellotti et al. 2013). Michael and Chen (2005b) describe three main types of assessments used during the evaluation of user learning experiences: (i) completion assessment, (ii) in-process assessment, and (iii) teacher assessment. Completion assessment could comprise both formative and summative measures. Formative assessments, like if the student successfully completed the game, the levels the students were able to complete, gaming scores achieved, currency collected, puzzles solved, and other game mechanics are indicators of both fun and learning engagement. In-process assessment indicates how, when, and why student made certain choices, and teacher assessment focuses on the instructor's evaluations of students' gameplay (Bellotti et al. 2013).

2.4 Emotive Computing

Affective computing relates to the role of affective experiences and the emotional expressions of people during their learning with computers and other digital devices. In some cases, applications are taught to mimic human emotions in order to establish computer-human interaction (Esterhuizen et al. 2012), while others interact with information of facial expression in order to adjust teaching strategies to provide personalized learning environments (Picard 2006). This study focuses on the emotional experiences of students while they cognitively engage with serious games. The data is gathered similar to the cues humans use to perceive emotions in others. Video cameras, body posture and gestures, capturing of speech, and physiological data that captures emotional like skin temperature or Electroencephalography (EEG) provide most of the cues (Salminen and Ravaja 2007).

Recognizing emotional experiences requires the extraction of meaningful patterns from gathered data from Electroencephalography (EEG) as an applied area of eyetracking (Blignaut et al. 2015b). Electrical activity in the brain generates at least four distinct rhythms. Measurement of the changes in the alpha and theta brain wave rhythms reflects what is happening in the participant's information processing situation, e.g. boredom, confusion, engagement and frustration. When a person is frustrated, his/her mind emits a particular pattern of brain waves which is picked up by the EEG. Software algorithms interpret these patterns as a graphical representation that indicates when a person was frustrated or excited (Blignaut et al. 2015b, Kruger et al. 2013).

Little information is available on the effect of serious games on learners' emotional states. Some studies have attempted to capture game experiences and demonstrate the psychological effects of gameplay with the use of real-time physiological measures in order to align game features with players' emotive experiences (Kivikangas et al. 2011).

2.5 Learning Experiences

"Learning experience refers to any interaction, course, program, or other experience in which learning takes place, whether it occurs in traditional academic settings (schools, classrooms) or nontraditional settings (outside-of-school locations, outdoor environments), or whether it includes traditional educational interactions (students learning from teachers and professors) or nontraditional interactions (students learning through games and interactive software applications)" (Glossary for Education Reform 2013). Some authors (Foko and Amory 2008, Gee 2005, Michael and Chen 2005a) promote the learning aspects of serious games, i.e. advanced goals or training of a certain knowledge domain. They are of the opinion that broadening of usability applications will assist in investigating users' learning experiences in terms of underlying pedagogical principles to improve serious games. Arnab et al. (2015) are of the opinion that the game industry and research practice alike disagree on concrete guidelines, taxonomical relationship or methodologies for assessment of gameplay learning experiences. Employing eyetracking measures during the developing of serious games may identify deficiencies as a means of early detection to improve the learning experiences of serious game players (Kivikangas et al. 2011).

3 Rationale for the Study

The above sections unpacked a conceptual framework for user learning experiences through the lenses of serious games, emotive learning and usability evaluation. However, a sound theoretical grounding for the use of eyetracking methods during usability evaluations of specifically serious games in laboratory settings should be established in order to ascertain the extent and the depth to which this method is grounded in theory as explicated from previous applicable quality research in order to compile a framework for the scholarly use of eyetracking during the development of serious games. This paper provides an initial analysis, and an integration of literature findings selected according to a stringent set of search criteria, to describe the building blocks of initial guidelines on the use of eyetracking for serious games.

4 Method

The literature pool for this review was retrieved from the electronic databases available to the Library Services of the North-West University. These comprised EbscoHost, Emerald, GoogleScholar, JSTOR, Science Direct, Scopus and Web of Science, and they were all searched individually. The criteria of the literature search were: (i) The time span was from 1999 to the present (2015). In spite of the extensive time span of the fifteen years for a fast developing field in computer science, the journal articles which matched the search terms only covered the years 2007 to 2014. (ii) The document type was limited to articles published in journals in order to capture peer reviewed work of comparable quality and e-book collection with evidence of peer review. (iii) Articles across all disciplines and fields were considered, but those relating to video and entertainment games were excluded as the basis of serious games fundamentally differs from video games. (iv) The keywords for searches used the Boolean operator 'AND' and comprised "eye tracking/eye movement AND serious games/digital learning games /computer-based games for learning." The researcher aimed to uncover the overlap of these two well-established concepts in research on user learning experience. The researcher acknowledges that the possibility exists that some data may have been lost, as authors sometimes do not indicate video games as intended for learning. The study therefore focuses on games aimed at learning and not games mainly intended for entertainment. I consequently systematically and manually screened the article titles, abstracts, keywords of the filtered articles according to the search criteria to ensure their inclusion in the analysis, and that they provided empirical evidence on usability evaluation of a serious game using eyetracking measures.

This systematic literature search resulted, surprisingly and disappointingly, in the low number of six journal articles which seemed much less than the even "moderate information" Moreno-Ger et al. (2012) cite on the use of eyetracking with serious games! These six papers comprised the dedicated dataset of this review and were consequently subjected to a qualitative analysis process.

The content analysis consisted of three stages: (i) The researcher meticulously affirmed that the selected papers adhered to the criteria of the systematic literature review. Papers not matching all the set criteria were not included in the qualitative analysis. (ii) The six selected papers were assigned to Atlas.ti™ version 7, a computer-assisted qualitative data analysis system. (iii) The content of each assigned paper was systematically coded according to the Boeije (2002) protocol of constant comparative analysis where all text was considered according to four pre-defined codes of (a) research question/objectives; (b) sampling conditions; (c) empirical design; and (d) findings which could contribute towards guidelines for a framework for the use of eyetracking for serious games (Table 1). (iv) I performed a secondary analysis on the findings captured according to the predefined codes according to an axial coding procedure. The aim was to link the findings as an initial (emerging) conceptual framework on the use of eyetracking during serious games to explore the concept of user learning experiences. Such findings could assist during the making of design decisions during the development of serious games as part of early detection of user learning experiences.

5 Findings

The findings of this initial literature review is presented according to the predefined codes, as explicated in the sections indicated in Table 1, namely research questions (objectives), sampling conditions, empirical designs, and findings relevant to the proposed framework that emanated from the literature review.

5.1 Research Questions or Objectives

The integrated dataset of six papers displayed diverse objectives for their respective investigations, indicating that saturation of researchable issues could not be established (Table 1). They are holistically clustered as the three categories of using eyetracking during (i) learning experiences (Alkan and Cagiltay 2007, Kickmeier-Rust et al. 2011, Kiili et al. 2014, Renshaw et al. 2009), (ii) technical explorations (Peters and Qureshi 2010), and (iii) theoretical models (Knoepfle et al. 2009).

Table 1. Analysis of the sources and their connection to eye tracking and serious learning

Authors	Research Question/Objectives	Sampling Conditions	Empirical Designs	Findings towards the Conceptual Framework
Alkan and Cagiltay (Alkan and Cagiltay 2007)	Investigate how novices learnt to play a computer game: a) Which strategies are used to learn a new computer game? b) How does attention of participants change during game playing at different levels and different parts of the computer game? c) What are the usability issues of the computer game played by participants?	• Selected 15 undergraduate university students • Data of 2 participants eliminated due to errors in data	• Eyetracking equipment recorded the eye movements of participants' gameplay of selected game • Demo-version of a not-widely known decision-making and problem-solving computer game • Game constructs applicable to educational settings • Mouse-played game • Eye movement data comprised fixations and saccades • Eyetracking followed by interviews	• Although participants searched the in-game information for hints for gameplay, none followed the hints. The use of documentation in a computer game does not contribute to the users understanding of the game • Provide sufficient control and freedom to players • Participants also search for information on gameplay through (i) trial and error and (ii) friends as sources of information • The differences between fixation times and patterns of gaze at different areas of interest showed that the types of cognitive processes of participants changed subconsciously • The highest values of fixation times were obtained in the contraptions area, where the participants think about the possibilities of the solution • The menu area have low values in terms of fixation times because there is nothing to do in the menu area
Renshaw and Denton (Renshaw et al. 2009)	a) Provided developers with detailed re-playable records of how a player interacts with a game b) Explored a variety of techniques (including eye tracking) to explore participants' insights of interaction c) Considered user satisfaction, engagement or immersion	• Study selected 5 male participants proficient at game playing, aged 20-29 • Participants were educated to degree level • All participants had previous game playing experience • No participants have played the selected game at the designated levels before	• Participant responses on how they felt while playing the game was recorded manually	• Participants have difficulties in articulating how they feel during gameplay • In spite of more negative emotive utterances than positive utterances on usability, on strengths of rating of the emotions, no significant differences can be detected • Participants' rating of their skills levels not accurate. Determining their skill based on the scores they achieved in a similar game more accurate • Participants experienced difficulties in articulating how they felt while playing • Complexity of games causes cognitive overload, diminishing verbal accounts, and indicates the importance of eyetracking methods
Knoepfle and Wang (Knoepfle et al. 2009)	a) How well five models predicted the actual choices of players b) How often players looked at information relevant to executing a particular learning rule	• Participants played 4 asymmetric non-zero-sum two-player 4x4 normal form games • Experiments were conducted in groups of 6; 2 participants were eye-tracked • 12 participants each played 4 games was played 10 times in a random-matching protocol with feedback (44 repeats recorded) • Order of games was fixed	• Gaze location and pupil dilation samples at 250Hz processed as fixations and saccades	• Learning is a sophisticated concept, and the appropriate comprehensive evaluation models should be developed • Research should aim towards specifying sophisticated learning rules that would relate to good approximation of true cognitive processes • Mouse-tracking designs have much less noise, but they relate to exogenous costs • Future studies could use a hybrid design combining mouse-tracking features with eyetracking recording
Peters and Qureshi (Peters and Qureshi 2010)	a) Are some blinking strategies, accompanying gaze shifts, perceived as more natural than others? b) Are different eye-head ratio configurations perceived as more natural than others? c) Are there differences in the perception of horizontal and vertical gaze shifts made by virtual characters?	• The study selected 6 participants (5 males and 1 female) of computer science background, aged between 20 and 28	• Participants were shown multiple animations of a male virtual character making a series of eye and head movements • Participants rated the naturalness of a virtual character's behavior on a scale of 1-10 at the end of trials • Participants provided textual description of their impression of the behavior of the virtual character	• Eyetracking has different purposes in each: • Long range gaze is an element in an ambient background where crowd members should be seen to look around, attend to each other, and the events in their environments • Medium range gaze may signal recognition and openness towards opening an interaction with the viewer, or cueing the viewer's attention towards other events of interest in the environment • Short range gaze behavior is important in face-to-face interactions to signal interest and conversation, and to direct attention towards objects related to the ongoing conversation • Conversational, emotional, or attentional factors are intended as a complementary evaluation • The gaze shift model should also be compatible with conversational control models
Kickmeier-Rust, Hillemann, and Albert (Kickmeier-Rust et al. 2011)	a) Determined if high and low performing students in terms of learning have distinct gaze patterns b) Evaluated the relationships and mechanisms in the context of using computer games for learning relating to three game situations (flying, instructive, and simulation)	• The study selected 9 Austrian learners: 4 girls and 5 boys ranging between 11-16 years	• Pre and post paper-pencil knowledge test with motivational, usability and attention-related scales • Gaze analysis of predefined AOI • Selected 1 scene for eyetracking from 3 games situations: flying, instructive, and simulation	• Learners benefit from playing computer games for learning purposes • Extreme groups like high and low performers exhibit different visual patterns • Distinct gender differences indicated in the interaction style with different game elements • From the use of gaze density maps, design recommendations can be made for improvements to games and prototypes • Eyetracking can successfully measure critical aspects with regard to the quality of serious games
Kiili,	a) Studied the meaning of feedback in educational	• Considered 4 educational games:	• Studied the playing behavior, adoption of games' user interfaces	• Different kinds of players perceive games differently in the way they grasp game elements

Authors	Research Question/Objectives	Sampling Conditions	Empirical Designs	Findings towards the Conceptual Framework
Ketamo, and Kickmeier-Rust (Kiili et al. 2014)	games b) Considered the usefulness of eyetracking in game based learning research and educational game design	• Mathematics game: 10-11 years old Finnish primary school pupils (N=14) randomly selected from a class of 27 pupils • Geography game: 10-11 years old Finnish primary school pupils (N=16) randomly selected from a class of 27 pupils • Mathematics elements study: 23 first class pupils divided into 2-4 pupils per groups • Feon's Quest game for teaching geography to 13-14 years: 9 Austrian children; 4 girls and 5 boys ranging between 11-16 years	and effectiveness of cognitive feedback in four different educational games • Measured time to first fixation, fixation counts • 3 experiments with a teachable agent; 4th studied the usefulness of eye tracking measures in game based learning research	• Distinct gender differences in the interaction style and perceptual paths • Some players miss relevant information during playing. Explains why some games fail to meet learning objectives • The sooner a player notices cognitive feedback and grasps it meaning, the better he/she can play the game • Extraneous elements should be eliminated in games in order to avoid incidental processing in crucial moments • Eye tracking can provide important information from the visual design of games, the usefulness of provided feedback as well as the whole game based learning process • Based on only fixation counts and fixation lengths one cannot determine whether the user has understood the game elements that he has fixated on or not • Complementary evaluation methods augment understanding of eyetracking data • Timing is important when interpreting eyetracking data of dynamic games. Fixation count or length does not tell whether the player has seen a game character in the certain time when the character has provided vital information for gameplay

5.2 Sampling Conditions

Eyetracking produces a huge amount of data (Knoepfle et al. 2009). Due to cost and time issues (Johansen et al. 2006), developers select as few participants as possible to address their respective development issue. Guidelines for exact numbers of participants are however not readily available. Renshaw et al. (2009) selected five participants; Peters and Qureshi (2010) employed six participants; Kickmeier-Rust et al. (2011) chose nine participants; Alkan and Cagiltay (2007) used thirteen participants; Kiili et al. (2014) selected four different games in which they respectively reported on nine, fourteen, sixteen, and 23 participants; and Knoepfle et al. (2009) indicated 44 gameplay repeats from twelve participants. From these observations, I conclude that the statistical model used for the analysis of the data provides the minimum required observations. Due to the huge amount of data that eyetracking measures produce, data saturation could be reached with a relatively small number of research participants, taking into account the time and cost involved with individual user learning experiences (Cutrell and Guan 2007).

5.3 Empirical Designs

The empirical designs of the six empirical studies were as diverse as the objectives of their research (Table 1). I therefore selected to report on how eyetracking protocols were augmented with complementary observation protocols—an issue deliberated across the literature (Moreno-Ger et al. 2012).

Two studies (Knoepfle et al. 2009, Peters and Qureshi 2010) of this dataset did not employ complementary observation protocols besides eyetracking measures. These studies did not relate to user learning experiences, but focused on technical aspects and models for the use of eyetracking. These augmented protocols are in line with the opinion of Marsh (2007), who argues that there is "a lack of serious analysis and design methods and approaches for serious games.

Alkan and Cagiltay (2007) followed their eyetracking experiments with interviews. They asked their research participants: (i) whether it is easy to learn the experimental game; (ii) to compare learning strategies of experimental game and games that they had played previously; (iii) how they classified the experimental game; and (iv) to compare the experimental game to games they had previously played. The augmented findings revealed information about how players explore a serious game that they do not know how to play in a naturalistic manner.

Renshaw et al. (2009) manually recorded participants' responses as a verbal pole (how they were feeling) while they played the experimental game. They also interviewed each participant about his/her experience of playing the second level of the experimental game. The researchers showed the participants the videos of their interaction with the game along with the overlay eyetracking data. The authors reported that most participants had difficulty in articulating how they felt during the gameplay. The analysis of these interviews indicated frustration as the predominantly stated emotion the participants uttered, as well as the prevalence of eleven additional emotions. The authors contributed the interview challenges to the cognitive overload caused by the complexity of the game rather than the participants' inability to express themselves under demanding circumstances. They concluded that this highlights the value of eyetracking that contributed little stress to the participants' gameplay.

Kickmeier-Rust et al. (2011) utilized paper-pencil knowledge tests comprising pre and post knowledge assessments with motivational, usability, and attention scales. They followed the eyetracking experimental phase with qualitative interviews with the research participants in order to identify design recommendations for further improvements of the game prototype.

Kiili et al. (2014) employed eyetracking to explore the game-based learning as well as users' perceptions of game interfaces of four educational games. During gameplay the researcher stopped the eyetracking recording at crucial places and posed questions to participants like: "Did you notice the gestures of your bird when it answered to questions?" and "Do you know what the bird's gestures mean?" The researchers also used retrospective interviews and gaze replays as complementary methods. They were of the opinion that such complementary methods were useful to provide deep and useful information about the participants' behavior and understanding that they believed eyetracking could not provide. The downside of retrospective interviews is that they are time consuming and participants do not remember small details during the interviews. Eyetracking provided thorough and objective information for the design of game interaction and layout which was useful to developers during the design and developing of storytelling, dialogue and game mechanics.

5.4 Proposed Conceptual Framework

Frameworks for the evaluation of video games and serious games are not new, and frequent the literature databases. De Freitas and Oliver (2006) propose an evaluation framework which focuses on (i) the application context of a serious game, (ii) learner characteristics, (iii) didactical/pedagogical aspects, and (iv) the extent and quality of the game story's world. Marsh (2007) proposes the Hierarchical Activity-Based Scenario

(HABS) which provides a flexible and dynamic conceptual framework that supports game research and development according to five steps. HABS (i) provides hierarchical structure which aids design and modelling of scenarios and narratives; (ii) allows evaluators and developers to dynamically model user-player behavior and interactions with/within the scenario during game play; (iii) offers concepts help to identify disruption to user's interaction from problematic design features; (iv) incorporates a method to structure and reason about the degree to which a game scenario or backstory has been successful through the fulfilment of tasks and objectives, as well as the degree to which experience from gameplay has been successful; (v) incorporates a way to reason about the situation in which an action becomes so stimulating that it drives itself and transforms into an activity.

In spite of the above-mentioned and other significant game development frameworks, no conceptual framework is yet available for the overlapping area of eyetracking evaluation of serious games in order to improve user learning experiences. During the first phase analysis of the six articles reporting on empirical studies which met the criteria of using eyetracking during the development of serious games (Table 1), the data analyzed according to the Boeije (2002) method of constant comparative qualitative data analysis rendered 34 noteworthy individual findings (Table 1). These findings were captured as a Word document and consequently assigned to the same integrated Atlas.ti™ dataset for subsequent axial coding and analysis. Six further themes emerged from this analysis; three relating to user learning aspects during gameplay and three relating to eyetracking measures. The gameplay-relating aspects were: (i) using of sophisticated learning models for gameplay; (ii) considering of individual learner (user) characteristics; and (iii) planning for applicable learner (user) control of the game. The eyetracking-related aspects were: (iv) selecting of fitting eyetracking protocols; (v) deliberating of game information; and (vi) tapping in on complementary user evaluation protocols.

6 Conclusions

Systematic literature reviews identify, appraise, select and synthesize all quality research evidence relevant to a specific question in order to provide a clear understanding of the scope of knowledge at a certain point of time. The aim is to reduce bias and provide a comprehensive body of knowledge on a particular subject, and/or evidence for a particular intervention (Adolphus 2015). The aspects this systematic literature review entailed were the use of eyetracking for serious games to improve user learning experiences. It selected only peer reviewed published articles of empirical design.

Many, if not most, serious game developers employ eyetracking evaluation as part of their evaluation of user learning experiences. Despite this, these evaluations often remain proprietary and details are not published (Peters and Qureshi 2010). Those who do not use eyetracking during usability evaluations agree that it seems a good idea (Hyönä 2010). It therefore remains disappointing to have identified only six published papers in the designated fifteen years on the empirical use of eyetracking during serious game development.

This qualitative analysis of the six identified articles rendered an unexpected large number of 34 findings suited to a framework for using eyetracking for serious games to improve user learning experiences. These findings readily grouped as six themes for the framework, resulting as the two main patterns of eyetracking and serious games (Mcmillan and Schumacher 2006). This is an initial and untested conceptual framework, not yet implemented or formally peer reviewed or confirmed according to another constellation of serious game aspects. Time will tell its usability, acceptance, and how others will augment this initial framework. Despite these limitations, much information on the conceptual aspects of using eyetracking for user learning experiences, also for mobile devices has emerged.

Acknowledgements. The author would like to acknowledge (i) that this work is based on the research in part funded by the National Research Foundation (NRF) of South Africa. Any opinion, findings and conclusions or recommendations expresses in this material are those of the authors and therefore the NRF does not accept any liability in regard thereto; and (ii) the North-West University for time and resources for research on usability issues of serious games.

References

Adolphus, M.: How to conduct a systematic or evidence-based literature review (2015). http://www.emeraldgrouppublishing.com/authors/guides/write/evidence_based.htm?part=1. March, 11 2015

Alkan, S., Cagiltay, K.: Studying computer game learning experience through eye tracking. Br. J. Educ. Technol. **38**(3), 538–542 (2007)

Amory, A.: Game object model version II: a theoretical framework for educational game development. Educ. Technol. Res. Dev. **55**, 51–77 (2007)

Arnab, S., Lim, T., Carvalho, M.B., Bellotti, F., Freitas, S.D., Louchart, S., Suttie, N., Berta, R., Gloria, A.D.: Mapping learning and game mechanics for serious games analysis. Br. J. Educ. Technol. **46**(2), 391–411 (2015)

Bellotti, F., Kapralos, B., Lee, K., Moreno-Ger, P., Berta, R.: Advances in human-computer interaction. Adv. Hum. Comput. Interact. **2013**, 11 (2013)

Blignaut, A.S., Matthew, G., Botha-Ravyse, C.R.: Examining chocolate-covered broccoli: eyetracking evaluation of the ExMan serious game. In: Paper Presented to the EdMedia 2015 - World Conference on Educational Media and Technology, Montréal, Québec, Canada (2015a)

Blignaut, A.S., Matthew, G., Botha-Ravyse, C.R.: Students' learning experiences of a serious food service management game under the lens of eyetracking and electroencephalography. J. Eye Mov. Res., 2015(under review) (2015b)

Boeije, H.: A purposeful approach to the constant comparative method in the analysis of qualitative interviews. Qual. Quant. **36**(4), 391–409 (2002)

Connolly, T.M., Boyle, E.A., MacArthur, E., Hainey, T., Boyle, J.M.: A systematic literature review of empirical evidence on computer games and serious games. Comput. Educ. **59** (2012), 661–686 (2012)

Cutrell, E., Guan, Z.: What are you looking for? an eye-tracking study of information usage in web search. In: Paper Presented to the CHI 2007: Gaze & Eye Tracking, San Juan, CA (2007)

De Freitas, S., Oliver, M.: How can exploratory learning with games and simulations within the curriculum be most effectively evaluated? Comput. Educ., **46** (Special Issue on Gaming), 249–264 (2006)

Djamasbia, S., Siegel, M., Tullis, T., Generation, Y.: Webdesign, and eyetracking. Int. J. Hum. Comput. Interact. **68**(2010), 307–323 (2010)
Esterhuizen, H.D., Blignaut, A.S., Els, C.J., Ellis, S.M.: Computer literacy learning emotions of ODL teacher-students. In: Amiel, T., Wilson, B., (eds.) World Conference on Educational Multimedia, Hypermedia and Telecommunications 2012 Denver, CO. pp. 586–595 (2012)
Farber, M.: Why serious games are not chocolate-covered broccoli (2014). http://www.edutopia.org/blog/serious-games-not-chocolate-broccoli-matthew-farber. February 27 2015
Foko, T., Amory, A.: Social constructivism in games based learning in the south african context. In: Weippl, E., Luca, J. (eds.) World Conference on Educational Multimedia, Hypermedia and Telecommunications (EDMEDIA) 2008, pp. 5757–5764. Vienna, Austria, AACE (2008)
Gee, J.P.: Why Are Video Games Good For Learning? (2005). http://www.academiccolab.org/resources/documents/MacArthur.pdf. July 25 2015
Giessen, H.W.: Serious games effects: an overview. Procedia–Soc. Behav. Sci. **174**(2015), 2240–2244 (2015)
Glossary for Education Reform (2013). Learning Experience. http://edglossary.org/learning-experience/. July 31 2015
Gonsalves, A., Ternier, S., Vries, F.D., Specht, M.: Serious games at the UNHCR with ARLearn, a toolkit for mobile and virtual reality applications. In: Specht, M., Sharples, M., Multisilta, J. (eds.) The 11th International Conference on Mobile and Contextual Learning 2012, Helsinki, Finland, October 16–18, 2012: CEUR. pp. 224–247 (2012)
Hartson, H.R., Andre, T.S., Williges, R.C.: Criteria for evaluating usability evaluation methods. Int. J. Hum. Comput. Interact. **13**(4), 373–410 (2001)
Hyönä, J.: The use of eye movements in the study of multimedia learning. Learn. Instr. **20**(2), 172–176 (2010)
Johansen, S.A., Nørgaard, M., Rau, J.: Can eye tracking boost usability evaluation of computer games? In: Paper Presented to the Proceedings of CHI, 2008–itu.dk (2006)
Johnson, L., Adams Becker, S., Estrada, V., Freeman, A.: NMC Horizon Report: 2015 Higher Education Edition (2015). http://www.nmc.org/publication/nmc-horizon-report-2015-higher-education-edition/. July 31 2015
Jordan, P.W.: Pleasure with products: Human factors for body, mind and soul. In: Green, W.S., Jordan, P.W. (eds.) Human Factors in Product Design: Current Practise and Future Trends UK: Taylor & Francis, pp. 206–217 (1999)
Kickmeier-Rust, M.D., Hillemann, E., Albert, D.: Tracking the UFO's paths: using eye-tracking for the evaluation of serious games. In: Shumaker, R. (ed.) Virtual and Mixed Reality, HCII 2011, Part I. LNCS, vol. 6773, pp. 315–324. Springer, Heidelberg (2011)
Kiili, K., Ketamo, H., Kickmeier-Rust, M.D.: Eye tracking in game-based learning research and game design. Int. J. Serious Games **1**(2), 51–65 (2014)
Kivikangas, J.M., Chanel, G., Cowley, B., Ekman, I., Salminen, M., Järvelä, S., Ravaja, N.: A review of the use of psychophysiological methods in game research. J. Gaming Virtual Worlds **3**(3), 181–199 (2011)
Knoepfle, D.T., Camerer, C.F., Wang, J.T.-Y.: Studying learning in games using eye tracking. J. Eur. Econ. Assoc. **7**(2–3), 388–398 (2009)
Kruger, J.-L., Hefer, E., Matthew, G.: Measuring the impact of subtitles on cognitive load: eye tracking and dynamic audiovisual texts. In: ETSA 2013, (ed.) Eye Tracking South Africa, Cape Town: ACM New York, NY, USA ©2013. pp. 62–66 (2013)
Malone, T.W.: What makes things fun to learn? Heuristics for designing instructional computer games. In: Paper Presented to the Cognitive and Instructional Sciences, Palo Alto, CA (1980)

Marsh, T.: Informing design and evaluation methodologies for serious games for learning (2007). https://www.researchgate.net/profile/Tim_Marsh2/publication/260749304_Informing_Design_and_Evaluation_Methodologies_for_Serious_Games_for_Learning/links/0a85e5321ceb8799b3000000.pdf. February 19 2015

McMillan, J.H., Schumacher, S.: Research in Education: Evidence-Based Inquiry, 6th edn. Pearson, Boston (2006)

Michael, D., Chen, S.: Proof of learning: assessment in serious games (2005a). http://www.gamasutra.com/view/feature/130843/proof_of_learning_assessment_in_.php. July 25 2015

Michael, D., Chen, S.: Proof of learning: assessment in serious games (2005b). http://www.gamasutra.com/view/feature/2433/proof_of_learning_assessment_in.php. May 10 2015

Moreno-Ger, P., Torrente, J., Hsieh, Y.G., Lester, W.T.: Usability testing for serious games: making informed design decisions with user data. Adv. Hum. Comput. Interact. **2012**, 13 (2012)

Nacke, L., Drachen, A., Göbel, S.: Methods for evaluating gameplay experience in a serious gaming context. J. Comput. Sci. Sport **2010**, 1–12 (2010)

Peters, C., Qureshi, A.: A head movement propensity model for animating gaze shifts and blinks of virtual characters. Comput. Graph. **34**(6), 677–687 (2010)

Picard, R.W.: Affective computing (2006). http://affect.media.mit.edu/pdfs/95.picard.pdf. July 31 2015

Renshaw, T., Stevens, R., Denton, P.D.: Towards understanding engagement in games: an eye-tracking study. Horizon **17**(4), 408–420 (2009)

Salminen, M., Ravaja, N.: Oscillatory brain responses evoked by video game events: The case of Super Monkey Ball 2. Cyberpsychology Behav. **10**(3), 330–338 (2007)

Sedano, C.I., Leendertz, V., Sutinen, E., Ellis, S.: Hypercontextualized learning games: fantasy, motivation, and engagement in reality. Simul. Gaming **44**(6), 1–25 (2013)

Wechsung, I., Naumann, A.B.: Evaluation methods for multimodal systems: a comparison of standardized usability questionnaires. In: André, E., Dybkjær, L., Minker, W., Neumann, H., Pieraccini, R., Weber, M. (eds.) PIT 2008. LNCS (LNAI), vol. 5078, pp. 276–284. Springer, Heidelberg (2008)

A Mobile Game World for Māori Language Learning

Tyne Crow[1] and David Parsons[2(✉)]

[1] Massey University, Auckland, New Zealand
tyne141@yahoo.com
[2] The Mind Lab by Unitec, Auckland, New Zealand
david@themindlab.com

Abstract. This paper describes the development and evaluation of a mobile assisted language learning tool that teaches some aspects of the Māori language within a virtual game world. The game uses a simulated world, which reflects aspects of Māori art and culture, to structure Māori language learning experiences. It was developed using the Corona SDK and can be deployed onto multiple platforms. Android tablet devices were used for our evaluations with learners. The approach to language learning theory embodied in the game is based on a well-established Māori language learning technique known as 'Te Ataarangi.' This is modelled on 'The Silent Way' method which uses Cuisenaire Rods. However, rather than rods, the game uses the relationships between virtual characters and artefacts in the game. A design science research methodology was used, with prototypes being developed and tested with teachers, students and academics as design partners. This involved testing early prototypes with educators, then subsequently whole classes of students. In between testing, the software was redeveloped based on the observations and feedback collected. Classroom observations during the iterative development cycle showed the tool was both engaging and effective for vocabulary learning. Knowledge was generated about how a wide range of game mechanics can be used in a game world to structure mobile, Māori language learning experiences. Quantitative evaluation showed that students were able to learn vocabulary over a short time using the tool.

Keywords: Māori language learning · The silent way · Gamification · Virtual game world

1 Introduction

This paper describes a mobile assisted language learning tool that teaches some aspects of the Māori language within a virtual game world. The Māori language, which is the indigenous language of New Zealand, has been going through a process of rejuvenation since the mid-1900s. A wide range of multimedia resources have been created to support the process of language rejuvenation, but computer games are under-represented in the wealth of Māori language resources, and globally there have been few language learning tools developed within purpose-built simulated game worlds. There is growing interest in the application of modern game mechanics

T.H. Brown and H.J. van der Merwe (Eds.): mLearn 2015, CCIS 560, pp. 84–98, 2015.
DOI: 10.1007/978-3-319-25684-9_7

(gamification) to mobile learning [1]. The work described in this paper applies dynamic features of modern games within a simulated game world to structure Māori language learning experiences.

1.1 Māori Language Learning and Mobile Devices

There is currently limited literature on Māori language learning on mobile devices. However, McKenzie [2] provides an extensive study of how mobile devices can play a part in revitalising the Māori language. A focus of this study was using the audio and video functions of mobile devices. The key findings of the study were that the portability and discretion of mobile devices allowed for learning in a wide variety of contexts. Timoko [3] investigated an indigenous model of effective mobile learning and the development of a mobile learning model adapted to meet the needs of teachers and students within a Māori environment, in order to improve outcomes for Māori learners.

These two studies represent the most relevant academic work to date on Māori language learning on mobile devices. There are, however, a number of mobile Māori language learning applications available. These include 'uTalk Māori' [4] a Māori vocabulary learner that utilises pictures and audio and has structured interactive 'flash-card' type activities for memorisation of vocabulary. It mainly focuses on single words rather than phrases. Kaitiaki [5] is not specifically a language learning app; rather, it is an ecology game app for school students that is bi-lingual. Kura [6] is a Māori language learning app that is 'gamified', and users compete against other learners for places on leaderboards. It is designed more for immersion education than second language learning and has a variety of activities that go beyond vocabulary learning. Puna [6] is an app developed by the same researchers that created Kura and it builds on the effective features of Kura. It has more options for customising content and structures learning across levels that are laid out on a minimap. It allows users to listen to audio in male and female voices and has structured handwriting activities. Te Pūmanawa [7] is a full online Māori language course that is available as an app for mobile devices and in browsers. It is designed to be a comprehensive beginner's course, including lessons, audio, learning management and the ability to record your own voice for practice. Hika [8] is an app that is based around sentence construction. It splits the sentences into parts that the user can substitute to create different meanings.

1.2 Target Users

The software tool was developed and tested mainly with a mixed class of primary school aged students and a limited number of high school aged students. While the benefit of engaging, game based learning is the ability to scaffold learning experiences for younger learners, it was designed to be engaging and relevant to older learners too. Beginning language learners have to learn the same basic vocabulary and sentences regardless of their age. One of the key areas of investigation was the potential of features of modern, mobile software to structure diverse levels of challenge to different learners so the software was not developed with an upper age limit in mind. In terms of language learning level it was structured for beginning learners in that it taught vocabulary and sentences from scratch and used game mechanics to scaffold the repetition and practise required to learn the language.

1.3 Gamification

Gamification is the use of game based mechanics in a non-game context. It is a relatively new term; Deterding et al. [9] date its first documented use to 2008 and widespread adoption in 2010. The term can often be misinterpreted as no more than placing educational content within a game or the basic implementation of stars and badges. Various authors have put forward multiple views of the components of gamification. Hamari, Koivisto and Sarsa [1] categorised the motivational affordances of gamification as points, leader boards, achievements/badges, levels, story/theme, clear goals, feedback, rewards, progress and challenge. Reeves and Read [10] described a range of successful elements of games, including self-representation with avatars, three-dimensional environments, narrative context, feedback, reputations, marketplaces, competition and time pressure. Robinson and Bellotti [11] categorised seven features of gamification; general framing, general rules and performance framing, social features, intrinsic incentives, extrinsic incentives, resources and constraints, and feedback and status information. Each of these seven categories has several different types of features.

Despite these various interpretations, there is some consensus in relation to the types of features that define gamification. Notably, more abstract concepts like progress and challenge have been listed alongside more observable features like badges and leaderboards. Most features of gamification predate the widespread use of the term; the term was created as a result of the increasing trend in applying these features to non-game contexts.

The game described in this paper has a number of features not previously explored in Māori language learning games. In particular it has a more developed gamification approach than previous examples, with a 2D virtual world within which learners explore interactive language learning activities and tools.

1.4 Mobile Aspects of the Software Tool

Beyond physically being developed and tested on Android devices there were several aspects of the project that related to mobile learning. The software tool created was designed to develop knowledge about specific mechanics and features from modern mobile games applied to language learning experiences. Features such as the interface, user controls, level structures, 3 star system and level progression were based on features in many modern, mobile games. More specifically they were based on more 'casual' games that are widely accessible and provide diverse levels of challenge for a wide range of users. Breaking the individual learning experiences into small tasks with frequent and diverse levels of feedback was a key feature; this is essential to new usage trends associated with mobile learning where learning can take place in a wider range of times and places. Breaking the learning into smaller chunks also had a significant positive impact on motivation and engagement as it increased the learners' sense of progress.

2 Theory and Method

When investigating Māori language learning methods, an effective approach was identified that had many conceptual and structural similarities to the potential concepts and structures of tasks afforded by a virtual game world. Te Ataarangi [12] is one of the well-established Māori language learning techniques in New Zealand, and is modelled on 'The Silent Way' method established by Caleb Gattegno [13]. As part of this technique learners listen to instructions relating to actions they carry out with coloured rods called Cuisenaire Rods and then give instructions to other learners.

2.1 Applying the Silent Way

The three major features of The Silent Way as summarized by Richards [14] are:

- Learning is facilitated if the learner discovers or creates
- Learning is facilitated by accompanying physical objects
- Learning is facilitated by problem solving involving the material to be learned

A key part of this is that learners relate the instructions they are giving and receiving to physical actions carried out on real objects by themselves and other learners. A specific example of this would be asking a learner to pick up four orange rods and place them on top of green rods. This concept of the learner creating understanding through their own actions rather than interpreting a teacher's explanations or reference material is valuable in the context of modern mobile learning tools.

2.2 The Relevance of the Tasks in the Silent Way

One key feature of The Silent Way as a language-teaching method is that it focuses more on the propositional meaning than the communicative value of sentences. Focus is given to learning the underlying structures of the language and the meaning attached to different words and sentence structures. An example of a common area focused on in Māori language learning and The Silent Way is locative prepositions, for example, 'The red rod is on top of the green rod'. These sentence structures are studied for the understanding the meaning of the sentences not their immediate communicative value. The specific nouns/objects used in the sentences relate to physical props the learner can interact with. Traditionally in The Silent Way, plastic rods of varying colours and sizes known as Cuisenaire Rods have been used; this is so learners can construct meaning by physically interacting with objects that relate to the meaning of sentences. Varying colours and sizes of rods create opportunities to use sentences that contain adjectives. Importantly the relative position of nouns, adjectives and locative prepositions varies between languages. Practising sentences relating to physical props the learner can physically interact with helps develop understanding of the underlying propositional meaning of the sentence. This understanding is transferable to sentences with communicative value in other contexts. On a more basic level vocabulary can be learnt by building associations between the physical objects and the word in the target language rather than relying on translating back to the first language.

2.3 Nature of Language Learning Tasks in the Simulated Game World

In the simulated game world the learner can physically interact with a range of game objects that can conceptually take the place of Cuisenaire Rods. A 2D platform game is well suited to building an understanding of locative words and sentences as it has a clear spatial component in which learners can physically move objects similar to the way props are used in The Silent Way. In the game, users create meaning from sentences with locative prepositions by moving rideable objects to positions relative to other objects in the sentence; the game then provides feedback but, if incorrect, gives the learner time to keep searching for the right answer, similar to a teacher in The Silent Way. Figure 1 shows a screen capture from the game, where the learner has to position a moa (a now-extinct bird from Māori history) on top of a coloured box, and compares this activity with the use of coloured rods in The Silent Way.

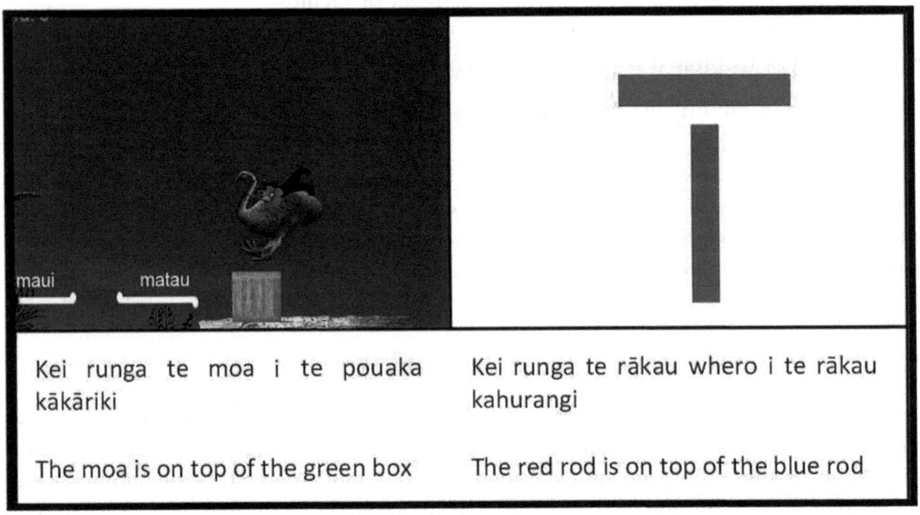

Fig. 1. Similarities between activities in the software tool (left) and the silent way (right)

The transferable knowledge about the relative position of different words in the sentence is the valuable part of what is being learned. In the sentence above the literal word by word translation would be more like ‘at top the moa of the box green’; notably the nouns and adjectives change position and the locative preposition is at the start of the sentence. Correctly using parts of speech like adjectives and locative prepositions is a common difficulty of language learners and many learners beginning to learn languages that swap the order of adjectives and nouns struggle to learn the new sentence structures. While the learner may practise with rods, moas and boxes the sentence structures are used in many contexts. Importantly when a learner uses a sentence structure to talk about something that is not applied to the Cuisenaire Rods or game world they will likely have some sort of conceptual visualisation or understanding of the concept they are communicating like they have when they are physically interacting with the task. On a more basic level the game world also allowed the key concept from The Silent Way of building associations between physical objects and the vocabulary in the target language without referring back to the English words. Because of the time limitations in the project more development was carried out on the more basic learning progressions relating to vocabulary learning that the more complex and lengthy progressions of learning experiences requires to scaffold the understanding of sentences containing locative prepositions. This is outlined in the results section.

The role of the game world in helping learners learn vocabulary and sentences is similar to that of the rods in The Silent Way; learners have an interactive, physical representation of the sentence and vocabulary they are learning in front of them. In the software tool the game mechanics and structure of the game help structure the learning tasks in a similar way to a human instructor.

2.4 Iterative Design and the Design Science Research Process

We utilised a Design Science Research Process [15] with prototypes being developed and tested with teachers, students and academics as design partners. Aspects of human centered design were used within iterative design cycles to ensure that design partners were involved in the whole design and research process. In practice this involved testing early prototypes with educators, then subsequently whole classes of students. In between testing, the software was redeveloped based on the observations and feedback collected. The game was designed over iterative cycles of development, testing and evaluation; each testing session provided the basis for the next iteration. Knowledge generation was increased through iterative improvement. Knowledge about the implementation of game mechanics in a virtual game world to structure language learning experiences was generated through iteratively implementing and evaluating specific features. Most of the data gathered was qualitative, with some quantitative assessment in the final iteration. This process of knowledge creation through artefact creation was beneficial in the context of this project where a novel combination of features was being investigated.

3 Game Development

From reviewing the wide range of development kits available, and the potential dynamic content each can create, it was concluded that the Corona SDK would be the best tool to develop the game. Corona is optimised for 2D applications and allows the easy addition of a physics engine. It also allows the creation of original functions and code to create new features in the software more easily than some more graphical tools that do not fully support scripting. The other major feature of Corona is that it allows for software to be programmed and deployed to Android, Windows Phone 8 and, in the future, Mac and Windows desktop. The game design uses a 2D side-on format, which allows the easy control of a player character and more action intensive game play. The representation of space in side-on games is also ideal for representing objects and concepts in language learning as the perspective allows for the representation of smaller objects, and positions above and below other objects, more easily than top down views.

3.1 Culturally and Nationally Relevant Game Content

When consulting teachers and other design partners, a common feature that was reported to be important was culturally significant content. These features were included in the software tool during development in the form of vegetation, structures, animals, design elements and characters. Another popular feature was the idea of relating different levels of the game to common Māori conceptualisations of the natural environment; specifically, earth, air, sea, forest and sky in relation to the deities/gods of these regions; this represents a common theme in visual art, performing arts and traditional stories. Another culturally significant feature is the abstract patterns and designs used as graphics in the game; the incorporation of designs into menus and buttons creates a uniquely New Zealand and Māori feel to the software.

Culturally relevant visual themes and content were consistently reported as important by teachers and other adults who were interviewed as part of the research process. Great care also has to be taken in choosing designs that are appropriate. While they are unlikely to be final designs developed into any widely distributed version of the software, the designs shown in Fig. 2 are original designs developed by people involved in the project. At no point were designs taken or copied. The grey design in the background was given by a wood carver who created it and chose it as an appropriate design to use in the software. The manaia figures were designed by the researcher and carved by students at the school where the research took place. The appropriateness and meaning behind designs is a very important consideration.

Fig. 2. Example of draft designs

3.2 The Virtual Game World

There were several reasons to use a virtual game world as the context for learning tasks in the software tool. The most fundamental one is motivation and engagement. Computer games and interactive media represent a medium that is underrepresented in many areas outside of entertainment. Specifically virtual game worlds represent a potential context for learning experiences in software tools but are very seldom used. Most studies relating to learning and virtual worlds use existing virtual game worlds rather than purpose built game worlds. The opportunities presented by existing or purpose built software applied to learning are very different. Creating purpose built virtual worlds allow a level of customisation to shape specific learning experiences through tailoring game mechanics to incentivise specific user behaviours that help achieve particular learning outcomes. Pre-existing virtual worlds on the other hand offer vast resources with more open learning experiences that are different in nature.

One of the main reasons that few educational software tools have tried utilising virtual game worlds is the resourcing and expertise required to create interactive virtual worlds. Games are financed largely from sales and as an entertainment medium they are generally bought and consumed more widely than educational software. Educational software is often created with limited resourcing that is not sufficient to develop many more advanced features of interactive media. This is changing as more powerful tools are developed for creating modern interactive media. Educational software is also becoming more widely purchased and monetised through app stores. It is likely that there will be more educational software developed that makes use of features of modern interactive media like virtual game worlds and a subsequent increase in interest.

3.3 Game Mechanics

In addition to the virtual game world and learning tasks, specific game mechanics were developed within the software tool. Techniques such as scores, coins, star systems, ranks and in-game currency with purchasable rewards were developed and tested.

An aim in the project was to iteratively develop game mechanics as an integral part of the structure of the learning experiences that were being developed in the learning tool rather than superficially adding scores or stars that played no functional role. The mechanics were used to incentivise certain behaviours that were designed to increase identified learning outcomes and additionally motivate and engage users. Vocabulary learning was the main skill being targeted. A desired behaviour was for learners to repeat levels where they made mistakes in order to practice the words more. Getting learners to repeat tasks multiple times is not always easy; however, incentivising rather than forcing repetition helped shape the learning. Importantly the right mechanics offer differentiated incentives for users based on previous interactions. The most fundamental mechanic is the three star system.

The three star system is a way of rating user performance for a specific task which usually relates to one game level; users can receive between 0-3 stars for each task. It has increased in popularity as a mechanic due to its prevalence in modern mobile games. Modern mobile games are also often referred to as casual games due to their wide appeal and usability, a feature that is also desirable in learning tools. Usability in modern mobile games is increased by creating more differentiation in challenges; there is a very low skill threshold for progression but a high skill threshold for perfection in contrast to other formats of games in which there is consistently a high skill threshold for passing every level. The applicable concept for structuring learning experiences is that of giving all users a consistent sense of progression while still incentivising perfection. In the 3 star system obtaining at least 1 star is a requirement to unlock the next level and is normally very easy.

In this project each level contained a specific amount of vocabulary to be learnt; users had to read instructions that required them to navigate to specific objects in levels. If learners had not learnt the words they would struggle to match them correctly but still be able to complete the level through trial and error. This is where the 3 star system is useful as a game mechanic; completing a level through trial and error still unlocked the next level but only one star was given if more than one mistake was made. Making only one mistake would gain the user a 2 star rating and no mistakes earnt a 3 star rating. Differentiation in feedback and next learning steps is an important feature of this mechanic. While it is not an overly complex way of tracking and displaying achievement it is very effective when compared to some other systems of feedback. We could compare it to standalone quizzes with percentage scores. A key feature of the star system is the overview screen that shows all of the levels. This allows users to view a summary of their performance on every level indicating the next level to progress to or previous levels that can be perfected.

Implementing this mechanic throughout iterative cycles in the research provided valuable findings. The effectiveness of the 3 star system was dependent on the specifics of how they were implemented. It was consistently found that spreading the learning in smaller chunks over more levels was more effective than learning the same content within fewer levels. Increasing the frequency of feedback and reward had a noticeable effect on motivation. Importantly, the nature of the levels as part of the structure of the program are an integral part of shaping the user experience and making other mechanics effective. This was directly observed across the iterative cycles of development, observation and evaluation. In early iterations, more words were included in each level and at sometimes repetition of words was required. When early levels were more lengthy engagement was noticeably lower than when early levels were shorter and gave users a sense of achievement very quickly. The levels can then be steadily increased in difficulty as the user progresses. One observation that seems quite logical and intuitive is that once users had achieved 3 stars in earlier levels they would then persevere on more difficult levels to achieve the higher star rating; if they were presented with harder levels early on they were much less likely to aim for perfection.

4 Results

Classroom observations during the iterative development cycle showed the tool was both engaging and effective for vocabulary learning. Knowledge was generated about how a wide range of game mechanics can be used in a game world to structure mobile, Māori language learning experiences. The quantitative evaluation showed that students were able to learn vocabulary over a short time using the tool.

The results of the study were based on qualitative observations and two sets of quantitative pretests and posttests. The qualitative data gathered in observations were part of the iterative design cycles; observations were followed by subsequent cycles of evaluation, design and testing. The pretests and posttests were part of the last two iterative design cycles. Quantitative data was not gathered earlier on as its purpose was not to provide actionable information to inform the next iterations. The qualitative observations were focused on testing how game mechanics and the game world affected students' learning experiences in order to make actionable observations about features of the game world and learning tool.

4.1 Qualitative Observations from Iterative Cycles

Figure 3 summarises some of the most important observations from user testing within the iterative design cycles. For the sake of brevity the 10 iterative cycles have been summarised into iterations 1–3 and 4–10. Iterations 1–3 have been grouped together as they tested a single game level with teachers and some limited testing with small groups of students. Iterations 4–10 tested multi-level progressions with a whole class and groups of four students at a time. Some features in the early iterations were immediately successful; the 2D game platform itself, the use of 'rideable' objects for locative prepositions and vocabulary matching activities, where users had to match a set number of words with a score counter. Other features were not so successful. The ability to carry and place objects turned out to be neither very usable nor very intuitive, and carrying and placing objects seemed contrived to the users. This feature was abandoned. Other features needed further work. For example the tasks related to making meaning from sentences with locative prepositions, and carrying out corresponding actions in the game world, were functional but required some optimisation to be understood better by all users.

In iterations 4–10, the successful features were a splash screen to collate all levels with a 3 star system and padlocks displaying the status of each level, and score and coin bonuses. Repeating words for random revision was perceived negatively by testers as it created some confusion as to what was required to pass the level, so this was abandoned. Features that required improvement included the number of new words in each level, enemies (actually mosquitoes - while users enjoyed some challenge within the game, many users were not gamers who enjoyed very difficult challenges) and introductory screens at each level; these had to be given some dynamic content to make them worth using.

Although this is a major simplification of the actual process, it gives an indication of the way that the interaction with users in the design science framework led to gradual evolution of the final game.

4.2 Summary of Iterative Design Cycles

The iterative design cycles were invaluable for creating and evaluating a range of features. The overall focus on knowledge creation rather than the completion of the final product within the limited timeframe allowed the repeated implementation of new features rather than volume of content; this created valuable findings relating to the use of and effectiveness of game mechanics and the virtual game world. The most important observations related to how tasks were structured within and across levels. The 3 star and padlock system created a great way to structure learning experiences by allowing all learners to progress but incentivising repetition for learners who had not perfected vocabulary lists. In different iterations vocabulary sets were varied and

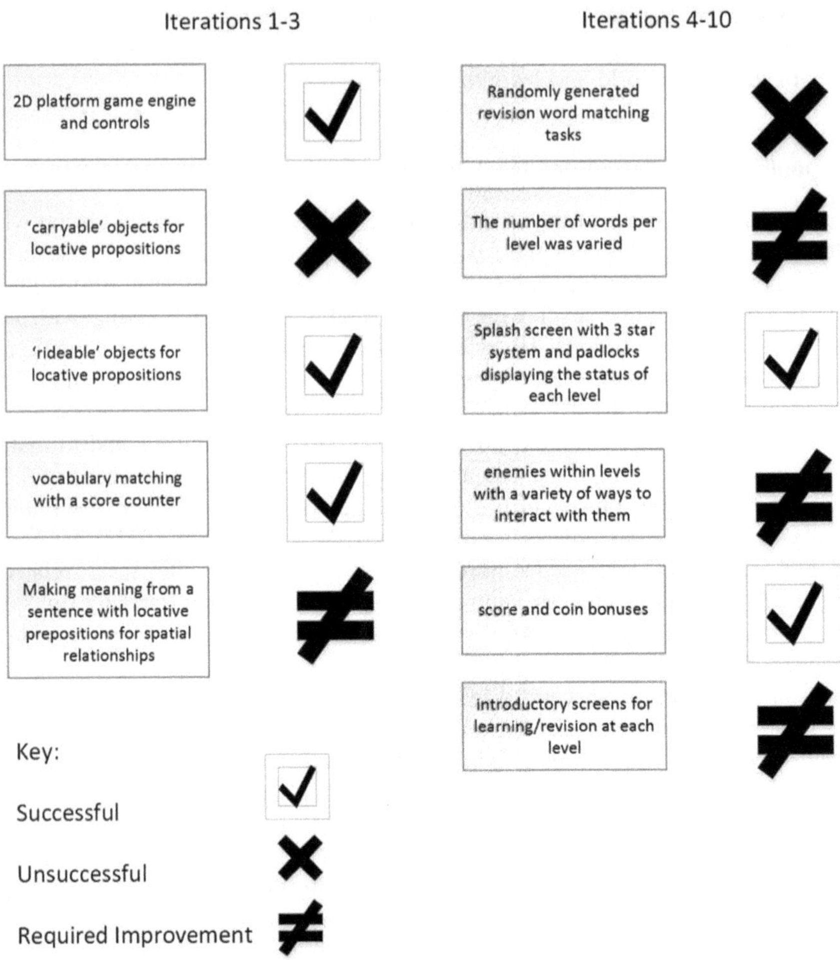

Fig. 3. Overview of the two main phases of iterative development

observations showed that users gained confidence quicker when initial levels contained smaller vocabulary sets with around 5 words; these could then be increased to around 8–10 words in later levels. Users were observed to more readily repeat levels that required more vocabulary learning if they had already achieved well in the preceding levels. Similar observations were made about other game mechanics like star ratings, enemies, bonuses and the user interface; only a sample have been listed in this publication.

A secondary observation relates to engagement and motivation. While it was always expected that different students would have different levels of interest in the software, it was observed that students universally seemed to be engaged by the software and throughout every one of the iterations did not put the test device down until they had completed every one of the levels; most users would repeat all levels until a 3 star rating was achieved. Users were never told they had to complete all levels or keep using the software.

4.3 Testing Locative Prepositions

While the observations from iterative design cycles indicate that modern game mechanics can help structure learning experiences, structuring learning progressions relating to more complex sentences containing locative prepositions was only preliminarily tested during iterations because of time constraints. Tasks involving locative prepositions were tested and definitely provided proof of concept. Users who had a basic understanding of sentence structures found the activities relating to complex sentences involving locative prepositions and adjectives engaging. The problem was that from observing the structure of learning progressions required to teach vocabulary and sentence structures from scratch, it was evident that the learning progressions required to properly scaffold complex sentences would be too lengthy to quickly iterate upon during the iterative design research process. For this reason quantitative testing was only carried out on vocabulary learning tasks and more focus was given to testing different aspects of other game mechanics.

4.4 Quantitative Testing

During the last two iterative cycles of classroom observations, quantitative pre-tests and post-tests were used to evaluate how much vocabulary was being learnt in the testing sessions. The quantitative evaluation of the software tool was based on a paper in which a dialogue based CALL tool was developed for Māori language learning [16]. There was no control group used in this study; partly for ethical reasons but also because it was not a comparative study. The main question to be answered from the quantitative evaluations was whether vocabulary could be learnt effectively with the software tool.

The tests consisted of connecting twelve words with their definition in the first pre-test and post-test in Iteration 9, then ten words in the second pre-test and post-test in Iteration 10. Individual results and averages were compared.

The tests were carried out on a group of students that had a wide range of abilities; they were not offered any extra instruction relating to the vocabulary or any special instruction on how to use the software, though they had used it before with different vocabulary lists. During both sets of testing the users played through 6 levels which required them to learn the required words in 2 smaller vocabulary groups and repeat them across revision levels. The change from 12 words in the first test down to 10 words in the second test was made in order to repeat the vocabulary more often over the same amount of levels. While this meant that the results of the 2 tests could not be compared, there was little value in comparing separate iterations of the software anyway as other features were changed between the iterations. The amount of words that learners already knew in the first test is far greater as more effort was put into finding completely unfamiliar vocabulary in the second test. In the first test, vocabulary that hadn't been used in previous iterations and user testing was used; however, many of the students had some existing knowledge of vocabulary. In the second pre-test and post-test completely unfamiliar vocabulary was used; the 2 correct words achieved by 4 students represent words that were possible to guess.

The results of the two different tests showed some variation. This was because they involved different vocabulary and were tested during different iterations. The first test used a word set that students already partially knew; this is not a problem in itself as sometimes learning tools are used to reinforce vocabulary that is already known. The results showed an average improvement of 6.875/12 to 10/12. The results of this test are shown in Fig. 4.

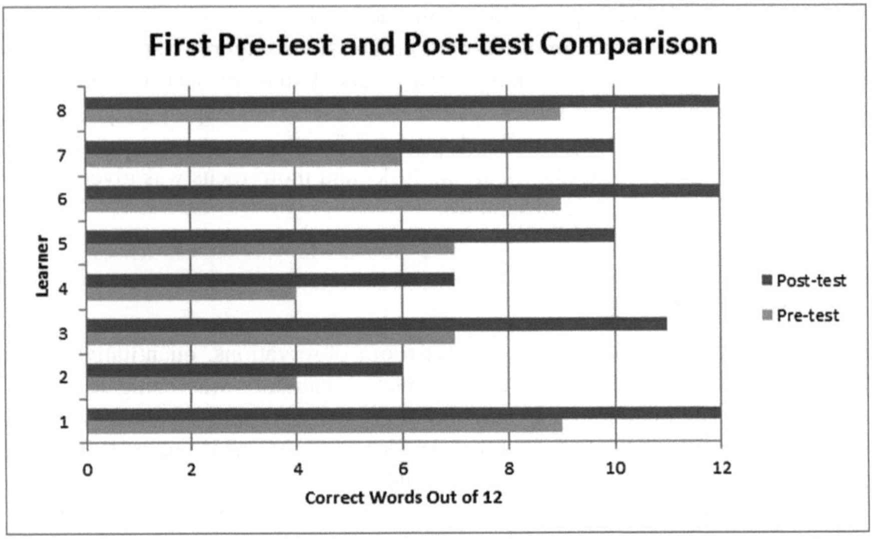

Fig. 4. Results of first quantitative pretest and posttest

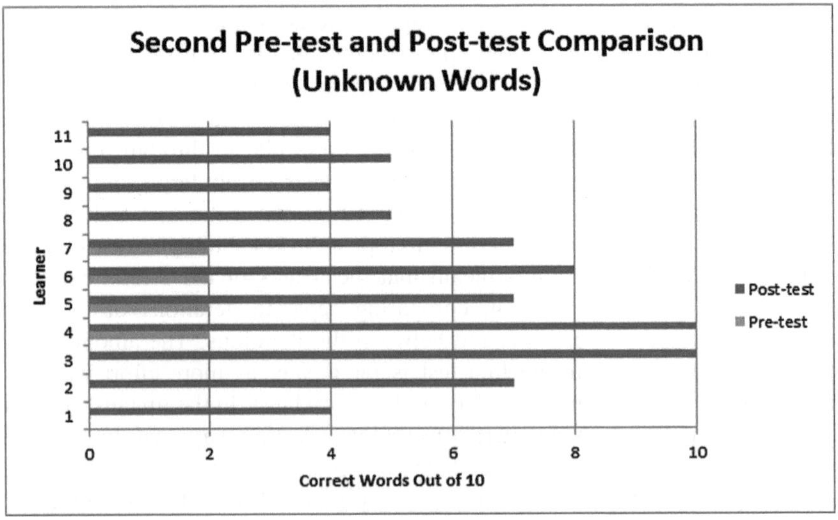

Fig. 5. Results of second quantitative pretest and posttest

The second quantitative test tested a vocabulary set that was unknown to the students; there were still two words that some students knew or managed to guess in the pre-test. This test showed an average improvement from 0.72/10 to 6.45/10, as shown in Fig. 5. T values and P values strongly indicated that there was a low chance the results were accidental. The results are good overall considering a lot of the users were younger students who did not have a lot of existing strategies for memorising vocabulary. It can be hard to recall more than 7 items from memory at once so the 12 word and 10 word vocabulary sets for a 10 min playing session were on the higher side. It is notable that all learners showed some improvement.

5 Conclusion

This study used the Design Science Research Process to create knowledge about game mechanics used in a virtual game world to structure Māori language learning experiences. Progressive iterations built upon each other and provided valuable observations and knowledge about how particular mechanics could be used in specific ways to enhance learning experiences. Importantly, the specific details about how mechanics were balanced was repeatedly evaluated and implemented. While the study did not provide a comprehensive quantitative comparison between the software and other learning methods it provided a large amount of comparisons of progressive implementations of game mechanics and the virtual world. Given the novel nature of the software tool these comparisons and observations throughout the iterations were of more utility in developing the tool than any comparison with other methods.

The virtual game world provided a highly engaging context for learning which students instantly wanted to explore. The ability of the game engine and game world to run its own logic and rules meant that there was no explanation needed for students to start interacting and learning; students could easily interpret feedback relating to where they were within the learning task and what they should do next. The virtual game world allows the instructional designer to structure learning experiences in a way that gives users a sense of freedom and exploration while maintaining a high level of control over the overall structure and progression of learning.

References

1. Hamari, J., Koivisto, J., Sarsa, H.: Does gamification work? – a literature review of empirical studies on gamification. In: 47th Hawaii International Conference on System Sciences (HICSS), pp. 3025–3034 (2014)
2. McKenzie, T.G.K.: The Challenges and Opportunities of Using Mobile Devices to Attain Māori Language Proficiency. Ph.D. thesis. Victoria University of Wellington, Wellington, New Zealand (2014)
3. Timoko, T.: Towards an indigenous model for effective mobile learning. In: Kalz, M., Bayyurt, Y., Specht, M. (eds.) mLearn 2014. CCIS, vol. 479, pp. 315–320. Springer, Heidelberg (2014)
4. EuroTalk. uTalk Māori (2015). https://itunes.apple.com/nz/app/utalk-classic-learn-Māori/

5. Game and Learn ltd. Kaitiaki (2012). https://itunes.apple.com/nz/app/kaitiaki/id529616251?mt=8
6. Te Kura Māori. Kura (2013). https://itunes.apple.com/nz/app/kura/id658132814?mt=8
7. Māori Multimedia. Te Pūmanawa - Learn Māori Language (2015). http://www.Māori.ac.nz/te-pumanawa-an-explanation/
8. Hika Group. Hika Lite / Hika Explorer (2015). http://www.hikagroup.com
9. Deterding, S., Sicart, M., Nacke, L., O'Hara, K., Dixon, D.: Gamification: Using game-design elements in non-gaming contexts. In: CHI 2011 Extended Abstracts on Human Factors in Computing Systems, pp. 2425–2428. ACM (2011)
10. Reeves, B., Read, J.L.: Total Engagement: How Games and Virtual Worlds Are Changing the Way People Work and Businesses Compete. Harvard Business Review Press, Boston (2009)
11. Robinson, D., Bellotti, V.: A preliminary taxonomy of gamification elements for varying anticipated commitment. In: Proceedings of ACM CHI 2013 Workshop on Designing Gamification: Creating Gameful and Playful Experiences (2013)
12. Te Ataarangi. Te Ataarangi Web Site (2011). http://www.teataarangi.org.nz/
13. Gattegno, C.: Teaching Foreign Languages in Schools: The Silent Way. Educational Solutions World, New York (1963)
14. Richards, J.: Approaches and Methods in Language Teaching: A Description and Analysis. Cambridge University Press, Cambridge (1986)
15. Vaishnavi, V.K., Kuechler, W.: Design Science Research Methods and Patterns: Innovating Information and Communication Technology. Auerbach Publications, Boston (2008)
16. Vlugter, P., Knott, A., McDonald, J., Hall, C.: Dialogue-based call: a case study on teaching pronouns. Comput. Assist. Lang. Learn. **22**(2), 115–131 (2009)

Going Mobile: Using SNSs to Promote STEMI on the Backseat of a Taxi Across Africa

Ronald Beyers and Seugnet Blignaut(✉)

TELIT-SA, Faculty of Economic Sciences and IT, School of IT, North-West University, Vanderbijlpark, South Africa
ron@yesa.org.za, seugnet.blignaut@nwu.ac.za

Abstract. This paper reports on the establishing of an educational service to promote Science, Technology, Engineering, Mathematics and Innovation (STEMI). The service uses MXit, a cost effective social media based on a Wireless Application Protocol (WAP) to reach low income users primarily across Africa, though not necessarily restricted to this continent. Users are encouraged to submit STEMI-related questions to the care of MXit, a web or Facebook interface. The findings indicate a growing and diverse user group of 15 to 25 years old. The initial phases of the project showed South Africa as the highest user base. Analysis of the feedback from the users was used to refine the service through action research. Students asked a variety of questions which were assigned to 22 different categories of which Biology, Physics, Chemistry and general knowledge featured as the most frequent questions. Career Guidance and Health related categories were also prominent. Statistics indicate regular use of the service over a 24 h period, with prominent peaks before and after school, intimating that users were accessing the service from the back seat of a taxi on route to and from school.

Keywords: Social network service (SNS) · STEMI · Mxit · Developing country

1 Introduction

Mobile technologies profoundly impact the way we learn and communicate in business, education, government, and society (Education Business 2014). It is a phenomenon that is acknowledged across the globe and continues to impact various facets of our lives. As witnessed by its popularity, mobile innovation inspires flexibility and accessibility to learning. It also has the capacity to bridge the digital divide while transforming the way we teach and learn (Guy 2010). This is a global phenomenon which is setting the pace primarily in first world countries, but with a growing trend in many third world countries, where the challenges to overcome the digital divide are even greater.

More than half of the people around the world have cell phones. Mobile phones have become the mode of communications technology of choice, particularly in developing countries. People are using social networking sites to stay in touch with family and friends and to share their views on an array of topics, including popular culture, religion and politics. People around the world are using their cell phones for a

T.H. Brown and H.J. van der Merwe (Eds.): mLearn 2015, CCIS 560, pp. 99–110, 2015.
DOI: 10.1007/978-3-319-25684-9_8

variety of purposes, especially for texting and taking pictures, while smaller numbers also use their phones to get political, consumer and health information. Mobile technology is also changing economic life in parts of Africa, where many are using cell phones to make or receive payments. About sixty percent of all South Africans regularly use mobile phones for a variety of needs (Pew Research Centre: Global Attitudes and Trends 2015).

Although half of the fifty million people in South Africa live below the poverty line, more than 75 % among those in low-income groups who are fifteen years or older, own a mobile phone. Mobile ownership at the base of pyramid (BoP)—households with an income of less than R432 per month (US$40 per month) per household member—is relatively high compared to other African countries (Infodev 2012). Of low-income groups who own mobile phones in South Africa, 98.5 % have a prepaid SIM card where the usage of data applications is low. The one exception here is the MXit social networking service (SNS) platform. Other applications, such as Mobile Money, do not seem to attract such a wide audience among poorer people.

There are some clear distinctions between urban and rural mobile phone owners in the low-income groups. In urban areas, users are knowledgeable about available applications and use social media and instant messaging to communicate with friends, watch videos and mix music. Urban users mostly browse the Internet on their mobile devices for job opportunities, information about schools and bursaries, and educational grants. Rural participants, however, are more sceptical about the value of mobile applications, sometimes even suspicious of them. Those mobile owners who do not use the Internet, are unaware of the availability of its useful applications. They mostly rely on traditional media such as newspaper, TV and radio for information, and on voice and SMS text services to communicate (Peyper 2013).

South Africa, with its high mobile phone penetration rate and persistent social inequalities, is the target of many "mobiles for development" (M4D) initiatives. There is often virtually no mention of negative externalities in the M4D literature. Most of my South African informants had a mobile phone, which ostensibly supports the observation of mobile phones' "ubiquity." The report highlights that many respondents' comments cast doubt about the "affordability" assessment, where more than three quarters of the interviewees characterized cell phone ownership as expensive, particularly owing to the costs of keeping sufficient airtime available on their mobile phones (Chenxing 2012, Pew Research Centre: Global Attitudes and Trends 2015).

2 The Young Engineers and Scientists of Africa

The Young Engineers and Scientists of Africa (YESA, http://wwww.yesa.org.za) was incubated within the Africa Advanced Institute for Information and Communication Technologies, commonly referred to as the Meraka Institute. Its inception was in response to the need to create a pipeline for Science, Technology, Engineering, Mathematics and Innovation (STEMI). A challenge that STEMI faces is the need to speedily renew human capital in the fields of science, engineering and technology. In South Africa, the Youth into Science Strategy (YiSS) seeks to contribute to a shortage of skills, addressing what the Government describes as the single greatest impediment in South Africa. The career sectors mostly affected by this shortage include professionals like engineers, scientists, surveyors, chartered accountants, actuaries, project managers, artisans, and information technology specialists. These shortcomings are addressed through interventions that aim to widen the pool of a demographically representative youth with talent and potential in science, technology, engineering and mathematics (Beyers 2010, Beyers et al. 2012). Within the context of YESA there are a number of different interventions:

- FabKids: promoting creativity and innovation in Fabrication Laboratories (FabLabs).
- FabTeachers: teaching a FabKids pedagogy.
- Digital Kids: teaching digital literacy through the development of multimedia.
- *My YESA Passport*: promoting STEMI to learners on the back seats of a taxi.
- Destination Zero Carbon: making use of Hydrogen Fuel Cell cars.
- Competition Pathways: create a better vision of the future for learners.
- Virtual Interactive Classrooms: digitally share teachers across communities.

This information is displayed as a skills grid to identify the strengths of the YESA interventions (Fig. 1).

The findings of the setup phase of YESA, together with a decade of research in the classroom, was delineated as a PhD thesis entitled "*Promoting Human Capital*

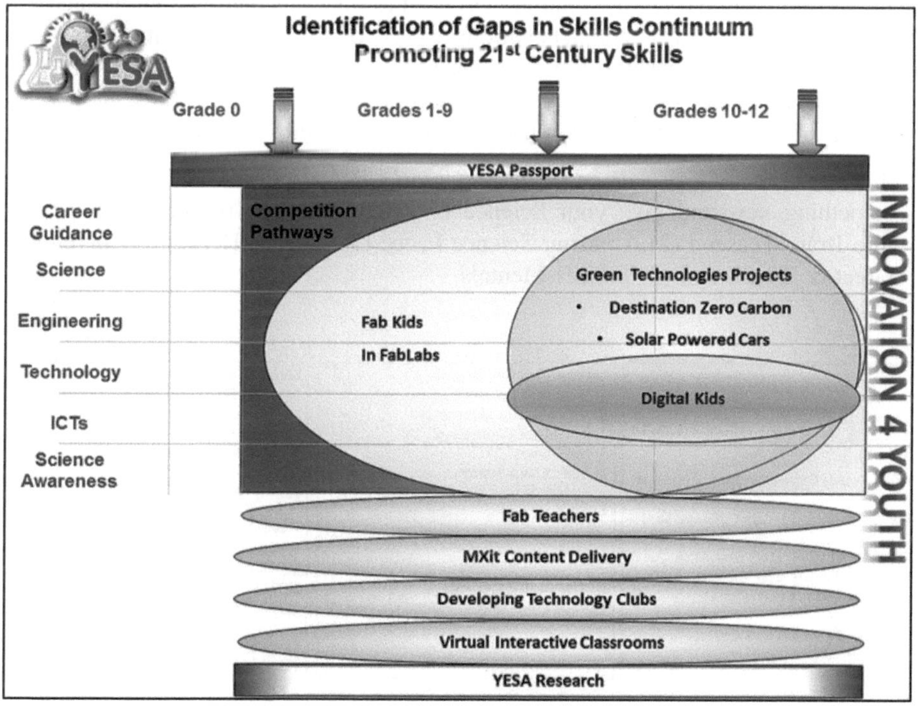

Fig. 1. The YESA skills grid to contextualise the YESA projects according to grades and areas of importance (Beyers et al. 2012)

Development through ICT Creativity and Innovation" (Beyers 2010). It laid the foundation for the formation of YESA as a non-profit organisation. All the YESA interventions serve to support various national policies and other programmes:

- Youth into Science Strategy (YiSS) (Mangena 2007);
- Innovation for Youth (Department of Science and Technology 2011);
- Department of Science and Technology's Ten Year Strategic Plan (Hanekom 2009);
- National System of Innovation (Engelbrecht 2008); and
- White Paper on e-Education (Department of Education 2004).

3 The Intervention

The original intention was to develop a portal to share STEMI-related information with the youth, not necessarily only restricted to school goers. Initial developments were around the use of the World Wide Web (WWW) as a medium of reaching the youth. A portal was established using Blue Ray software as the backend. The South African Finland Partnership (SAFIPA) provided funding for the endeavour during YESA's incubator phase. The initial response to the portal was low, which promoted the decision to port the system over to a MXit (getmxit.com) platform based on a Wireless Application Protocol (WAP) using Every1Mobile (http://www.every1mobile.com) as the developers. Limited private funding was used to fund this phase of the project. The series of screenshots (Fig. 2) depicts various aspects of the Evo portal (http://mxit-evo-pc.apponic.com/) with desktop access to the MXit portal version.

A number of other systems were put in place to ensure stickiness (product loyalty) within the system in order to retain users within the system:

- *A Daily Atom a day will keep the bad marks away!!* Come here every day for something new and give your Science knowledge a daily boost! (1) Word Picture Brain Teasers; (2) Amazing Science Facts; (3) Science Heroes; (4) Inventions Great & Small; and (5) Fun-da-Mentals.

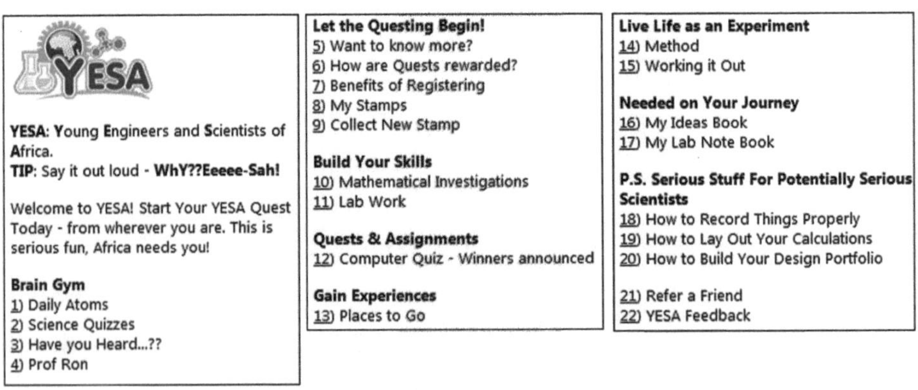

Fig. 2. Screenshots of the *My YESA Passport* portal on MXit

- *Science Quizzes*: Your mind is the most powerful tool you have for carving out a career in the sciences. Here are some quick quizzes to help keep it sharp. (1) Supertekkie Quiz!; (2) Science IQ; (3) Mythbuster; (4) Hazard Symbols, (5) Chemical Elements; (6) Chemical Formulae; (7) SI Units; (8) Young Animals; and (9) Mental Maths.
- *Ask Prof Ron:* Have all your burning Science, Technology, Engineering, Mathematics and Innovation questions answered (Fig. 2).
- *Your Ideas Book:* Wake up in the middle of the night with a spark of genius in your head? Get it down before you forget it. You probably have many ideas bubbling away inside, but are you really making the most of them. Your creative ideas are what make you special, different and valuable. Write down your "hunches", as they come to you, and then come back to them over time. Some will be worthless in the cold light of day. But a few will be worth cultivating.

4 Methods

As part of Sect. 23 of the portal, the users were asked to voluntarily respond to three questions posed on the *My YESA Passport* services: (i) What did you like about the *My YESA Passport*; (ii) What did you not like about the *My YESA Passport*?; and (iii) What changes would you like to see to the *My YESA Passport*? Users voluntarily answered the three-section questions, using only the keyboards on their mobile phones to formulate their responses which contributed to the brief nature of some responses. The responses from the users were logged and downloaded for analysis.

This paper reports on only one aspect of the *My YESA Passport* initiative, namely the qualitative feedback the users received from the *My YESA Passport*. In another part of the main project, Beyers and Blignaut (2015) reported on the quantitative analysis of other aspects captured from the *Ask Prof Ron* portal. The qualitative dataset comprised 395 text-based responses, downloaded from the *My YESA Passport* portal over a period of about seven months. Atlas.ti version 6 (Atlas.Ti. 2013)—a powerful workbench for the qualitative analysis of large bodies of textual, graphical, audio and video data—was used during the qualitative data analysis of the responses.

Three main themes emerged from the data as (i) what the users liked about the *My YESA Passport* portal; (ii) what the users did not like about the *My YESA Passport* portal; and (iii) what the users would like to see changed in the *My YESA Passport* portal. The integrated dataset was coded to match the gist of the responses emerged according to a constant comparative mode of analysis where every code is compared to each response (Boeije 2002). Codes with single responses were excluded for the purposes of this qualitative analysis resulted in a total of 92 codes pertinent to the learners' experiences with the *My YESA Passport* portal. The codes were subsequently imported into the Network Viewing tool of Atlas.ti™ and linked to the thirteen matching categories as indicated in Figs. 6, 7 and 8. The codes were then arranged in descending order for each category to indicate trends. The findings from the dataset are discussed according to the identified frequencies and trends.

5 Findings

The growing on-line community of disadvantaged users responded positively to the initial phase of the implementation of the project. The number of unique visits over the trial period of February 2012 to August 2012 was 118 961, with 395 users responding, indicating a 0.33 % response rate. The descriptive statistics (frequencies and percentages) relate to the number of visits, number of pages served, and average pages per visit for the trial period (Fig. 3). The *Ask Prof Ron* section of the portal closed at the end of August 2012 which demarcated the end of the trial. This may have had an influence on the decrease in the responses from the users by the end of the project.

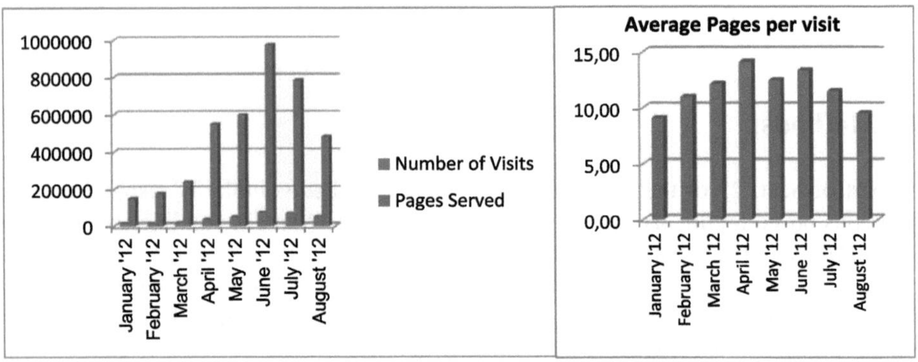

Fig. 3. Number of visits, number of pages served and the average pages per visits from February to August 2012

Figure 4 indicates the countries from which responses from users came. South Africa frequented the highest number of visits of eighty per cent, indicating the need for STEMI-related information in poor and developing areas.

During this analysis, the researcher (*Prof Ron*) addressed all the queries of the learners. With the growing number requests from learners, it was increasingly becoming almost impossible to keep this up. This issue could be alleviated in the future by the assistance of a pool of experts who would field the questions, or even expert participants from the user community. However, the current analysis of the *Ask Prof Ron* data indicates that the researcher (*Prof Ron*) answered questions mostly about Biology, Physics, general knowledge and Chemistry. The section on Career Guidance was also ranked high, proving it a key service amongst the concerned community of many users from disadvantaged communities (Fig. 5).

5.1 What Did You like About the *My YESA Passport*?

In response to the data relating to which aspects of the portal the users liked, a total of 32 codes emerged. They were grouped into four categories (Fig. 6): (i) The category *Personal* (21.5 %) highlighted issues such like learners' perceptions that they regarded

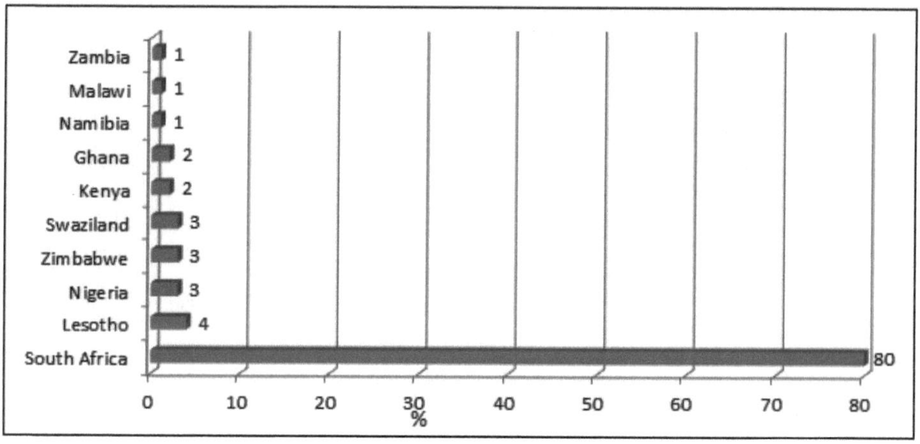

Fig. 4. Analysis of the countries reached January to May 2012 as percentages

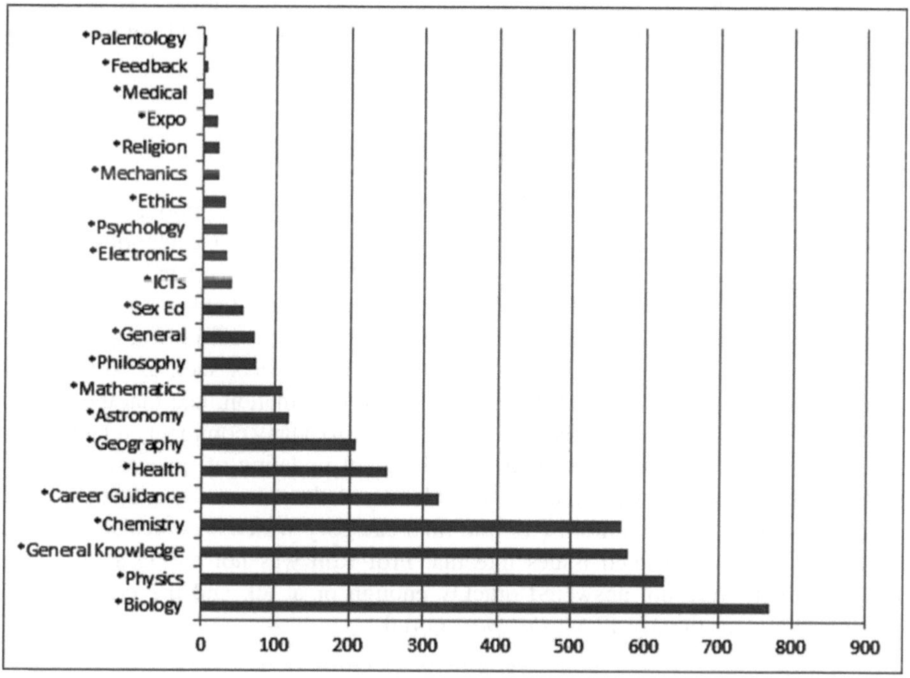

Fig. 5. Analysis of the *Ask Prof Ron* section of the *My YESA Passport*

the portal as motivational; it improved their knowledge, and it provided career orientation to them. (ii) In the category *Portal Specific* (37.2 %), users maintained that the portal was informative. They complemented YESA and they enjoyed everything it provided; (iii) The category *Portal General* (34.4 %) related to users' indications that

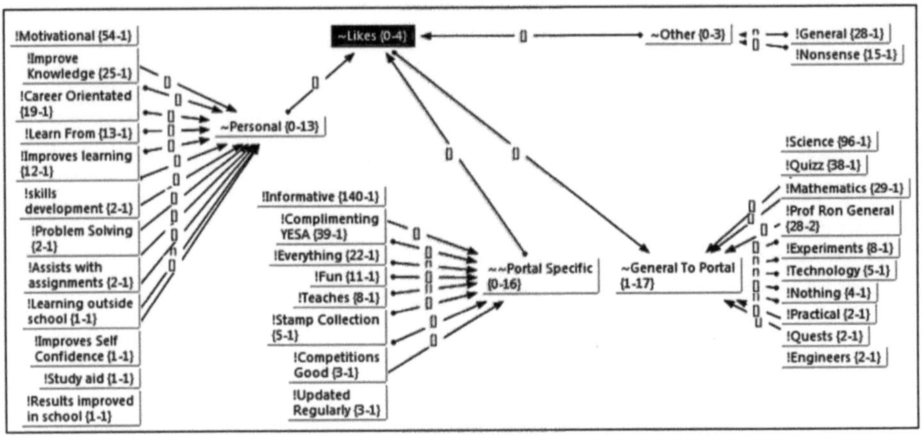

Fig. 6. Responses from the users to the question of which aspects of the portal they liked

they enjoyed Science, as well as the way quizzes and Mathematics were presented. (iv) The category *Other* (6.9 %) contained general comments which did not relate to the portal.

5.2 What Did You not like About the *My YESA Passport*

In response to the data on which aspects of the *My YESA Passport* portal the users did not like, a total of 27 codes emerged, which were linked to four categories (Fig. 7). Three of the categories comprised: (i) *General* (69.9 %) which related to user comments where they indicated that there was nothing that they disliked (49.6 %). The researcher classified some dislikes as irrelevant to the *My YESA Passport* portal (8.9 %). (ii) *Portal specific* dislikes (18.6 %) included aspects such as, some information was not clear to them, that they needed more information, and that the level of information was too difficult for them to understand. (iii) Many comments related to the quizzes specifically. The users wanted more frequent updating of quizzes. They also disliked that no rewards were made to completion of the quizzes, and that they perceived the competitions as unfair. (iv) The final category which specifically related to *Prof Ron* (11.5 %), clustered issues like that Prof Ron was not online all the time, questions which were not answered quickly enough or at all, and the prevalence of repeat questions on the *My YESA Passport* portal.

5.3 What Changes Would You like to See to the *My YESA Passport*?

In response to what the users would like to see changed, a total of 43 codes emerged which were linked to five categories (Fig. 8). Users' responses related to: (i) *More of improvements* (51.9 %) which suggested that they requested more career information (6.5 %), more quizzes, more mathematics information, and more competitions. (ii) The *general improvements* (5.3 %) indicated that the portal should be yet more informative,

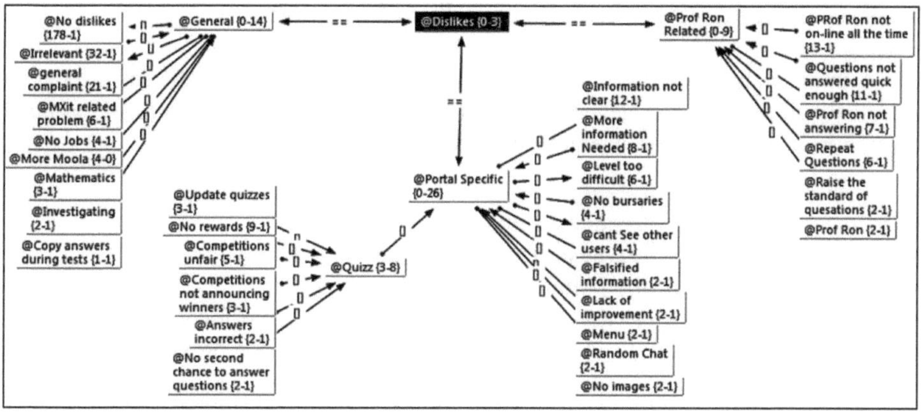

Fig. 7. Responses to the question of which aspects of the portal the users did not like

address advocacy, and provide more fun aspects. (iii) The suggested improvements of *Prof Ron* (6.5 %), highlighting issues of Pro Ron not answering all questions, that Prof Ron should come back, and that Prof Ron should answer all questions immediately (iv) Portal specific *improvements* (11.1 %) indicated that they wanted more rewards, more information updated more frequently. (v) *Other improvements* (25.2 %) included comments indicating that the users required no improvement of the *My YESA Passport* portal, as well as compliments to YESA in general.

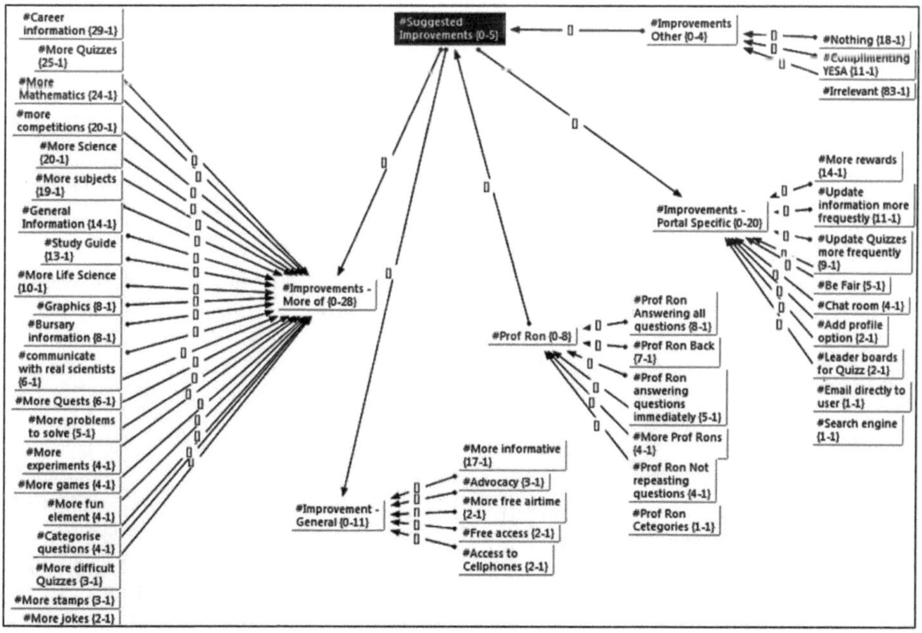

Fig. 8. Responses from the users to the question of which aspects of the portal they like to see improved

6 Recommendations and Future Developments

The overall analysis of the data captured from the user group indicates a positive acceptance of the portal in general. This has provided an important platform to launch into the next phases of the operation in order to:

- increase the number of users;
- increase the number of countries involved;
- provide a more informative service to the youth;
- refine key sections of the portal where possible;
- reintroduce the *Ask Prof Ron* section with a more restricted focus; and
- add more functionality to improve the quality of the service provided.

Though there were aspects of the portal that were not as well adopted as expected, indications point to the fact that once technical issues were resolved users made use of these services more frequently. The concept of users accumulating virtual stamps for various activities to post them in their Passports after the completion of certain experiments is one such example.

Data analysis from the *Ask Prof Ron* section highlights the possibilities of using the system to identify individuals with talent in STEMI. This includes the development of user profiles especially in the areas of scarce skills. Using this information it may be possible to identify these individuals and to encourage them to pursue careers in STEMI with the necessary support and encouragement.

Twenty years into democracy, South Africa remains a highly unequal society where too many people live in poverty and too few have work. The quality of school education for most black learners is poor. Apartheid spatial divide continues to dominate

Fig. 9. South African School-going youth on their way to and from school often make use of taxis as means of daily transport

the landscape. A large proportion of young black people feel that the odds are stacked against them. The legacy of apartheid continues to determine the life opportunities for the vast majority. These immense challenges can only be addressed through a steep change in the country's performance (National Planning Commission 2012). The My YESA Passport may be viewed as one building block in contributing to the educational journey of a growing number of youth who have been able to access the STEMI-related information from the backseat of a taxi—a regular mode of transport for many school-going youth in South Africa—at an affordable rate while using MXit as a means of communication and information seeking (Fig. 9).

Acknowledgements. This work is based on the research support in part by the National Research Foundation of South Africa. Any opinion, findings and conclusions or recommendations expresses in this material are those of the authors and therefore the NRF does not accept any liability in regard thereto.

The Meraka Institute of the CSIR for continued interest.

References

Atlas.ti: Atlas.ti: the Qualitative Data Analysis & Research Software (2013). www.atlasti.com/. Accessed 15 April 2015

Beyers, R.N.: Promoting Human Capital Development Through ICT Creativity and Innovation Unpublished Ph.D. thesis, North West University Potchefstroom (2010)

Beyers, R.N., Blignaut, A.S.: Using MXit to promote STEMI to students on the back seat of a taxi across Africa. In: EdMedia 2015 - World Conference on Educational Media and Technology, pp. 1459–1466, Montréal (2015)

Beyers, R.N., Blignaut, A.S., Herselman, M.: The young engineers and scientists of Africa: initiating the STEMI pipeline. Acta Acad. **2**, 105–126 (2012)

Boeije, H.: A Purposeful Approach to the Constant Comparative Method in the Analysis of Qualitative Interviews. Qual. Quant. **36**(4), 391–409 (2002)

Chenxing, H.: South african perspectives on mobile phones: challenging the optimistic narrative of mobiles for development. Int. J. Commun. **6**, 2057–2081 (2012)

Department of Education. White Paper on e-Education: Transforming learning and teaching through information and communication technologies (2004). http://www.gov.za/sites/www.gov.za/files/26734_1.pdf. Accessed 24 March 2014

Department of Science and Technology. Innovation towards a knowledge-based economy: Ten Year Innovation Plan (2011). http://www.esastap.org.za/download/sa_ten_year_innovation_plan.pdf. Accessed 1 August 2015

Education Business. Gove: Technology is changing the way we teach, learn and assess (2014). http://www.educationbusinessuk.net/index.php/features/5-/3371-gove-technology-is-changing-the-way-we-teach-learn-and-assess. Accessed 20 August 2015

Engelbrecht, L.: Govt pushes space science and tech (2008). http://www.itweb.co.za/index.php?option=com_content&view=article&id=3301&tmpl=component&print=1. Accessed 1 December 2011

Guy, R. (ed.): Mobile Learning: Pilot Projects and Initiatives. Informing Science Press, Santa Rosa (2010)

Hanekom, D (2009). Key Note Address by Deputy Minister Derek Hanekom, at the official launch of the French South African Technology Institute in Electronics Satellite Programme. http://www.gov.za/keynote-address-deputy-minister-derek-hanekom-official-launch-french-south-african-technology. Accessed 23 April 2015

infoDev. Mobile usage at the base of the pyramid in South Africa (2012). http://www.infodev.org/infodev-files/final_south_africa_bop_study_web.pdf. Accessed 15 October 2014

Mangena, M.: Address by Minister Mosibudi Mangena at the press launch of the South African Research Chairs Initiative (SARCHI) (2007). http://www.dst.gov.za/media-room/speeches/address-by-minister-mosibudi-mangena-at-the-press-launch-of-the-south-african-research-chairs-initiative-sarchi/?searchterm=PhD%20Innovation%20target. Accessed 12 April 2013

National Planning Commission. National Development Plan 2030: Our Future - Make it work (2012). http://www.gov.za/sites/www.gov.za/files/NDP-2030-Our-future-make-it-work_r.pdf. Accessed 1 August 2015

Pew Research Centre: Global Attitudes and Trends. Emerging Nations Embrace Internet, Mobile Technology: Cell Phones Nearly Ubiquitous in Many Countries (2015). http://www.pewglobal.org/2014/02/13/emerging-nations-embrace-internet-mobile-technology/. Accessed 20 August 2015

Peyper, L.: Mobile phone usage in SA (2013). http://finweek.com/2013/01/22/mobile-phone-usage-in-sa/. Accessed 12 April 2013

The Ship Has Left the Harbour, but the Captain is MIA: Mobile Adoption within Higher Education Institutes

Verona Leendertz(✉) and Marieta Jansen van Vuuren

TELIT-SA, North-West University, Vanderbijlpark, South Africa
{Verona.leendertz,marietajansenvanvuuren}@nwu.ac.za

Abstract. Mobile technology enables access to information through a variety of transmission media, like voice, text, video, and two-dimensional barcodes, anywhere, anytime. Therefore the current students expect mobile integration for teaching and learning to be the norm at Higher Education Institutes (HEIs). The purpose of this paper was to explore students' adoption of mobile devices for programme delivery versus the lecturers' acceptance or resistance to investigate the use of and potential for integrating mobile technologies for authentic teaching and learning in HEIs. The study used a multi-mode research design and methodology. Data collection strategies included: (i) a survey distributed in 2014 to 207 first and second year students from the Faculties of Humanities and Economic Sciences and Information Technology at the Vaal Triangle Campus (VTC) of the North-West University, and (ii) two individual interviews with lecturers from the two faculties. The quantitative and qualitative data were analysed with the use of the Technology Enhanced Learning (TEL) framework and the Technology Acceptance Model (TAM) to predict whether the students and lecturers adopt the use of SMARTguides on tablets/iPads for authentic teaching and learning at VTC. Results indicate that students adopt mobile technologies for programme delivery; however, even though lecturers should steer the integration of mobile technologies for authentic teaching and learning, lecturers are reluctant to use SMARTguides as a teaching and learning tool due to institutional constraints, and have mixed feelings on the use of and the potential for integrating mobile technologies for programme delivery.

Keywords: Mobile adoption · Technology enhanced learning framework · Technology acceptance model · Authentic teaching and learning · Multi-mode research design and methodology

1 Background

The changing demands of a higher education society, as well as the migration towards e- and online learning, have introduced a new paradigm to the educational scene, where the effective creation and application of knowledge are becoming increasingly important aspects. The mission of NWU is to develop, educate and empower, through innovative and high quality teaching-learning, well rounded graduates who are able to think laterally and critically in their service to the country and its people, the continent

T.H. Brown and H.J. van der Merwe (Eds.): mLearn 2015, CCIS 560, pp. 111–128, 2015.
DOI: 10.1007/978-3-319-25684-9_9

and the world (Department of Higher Education and Training 2013). The challenge is to develop a well thought out, focussed, e-learning strategy that could accommodate a blended teaching and learning approach within a multimodal delivery system. NWU strategic goals mirror this in mission element statements such as *the investigation and development of new and innovative approaches to teaching and learning technology*, as well as *to initiate pilot projects for the development of blended learning programmes*. Resulting from these strategic goals, a strong need was evident for practical guidelines and recommendations to facilitate the development and delivery of a pedagogically effective e-learning environment at the university. The creation of pedagogically effective e-learning material for online learning, or as supplement to face-to-face contact sessions in a blended learning environment, requires the application of sound instructional design principles, but also custom made application software to ensure the delivery of a high quality end product.

Adapting to this mode of content delivery poses challenges for the institution (Emerson and Mackay 2010) as numerous aspects should be taken into consideration before developing for blended or e-learning. Van Deventer and Blignaut (2013) developed a framework for Technology Enhanced Learning (TEL) in higher education. Figure 1 illustrates the TEL framework with the elements which play a role for the implementation of technology in higher education: (i) students; (ii) lecturers; (iii) Internet access; (iv) e-Communication; (v) comperacy; and (vi) course content.

As seen from Fig. 1, each one of the six aspects of TEL should be in place when developing in a blended or an e-learning environment. Students are central to the teaching and learning, therefore before planning a blended or e-learning environment, the following regarding the students should be taken into consideration: (i) background of the students, (ii) their versatile learning styles; (iii) access to technology and the

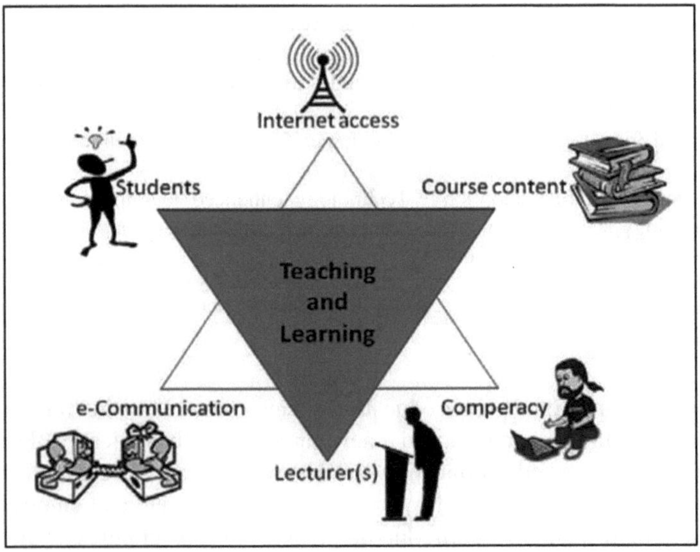

Fig. 1. Framework for technology enhanced learning (Van Deventer and Blignaut 2013)

Internet; and (iv) their comperacy (computer literacy). The lecturers should develop towards a different context from what they have been doing previously, therefore they should have sound technological, pedagogical and content knowledge (TPACK). TPACK which describes the relationship between technology, pedagogy and content. In order for technology to add value to teaching and learning, it cannot be regarded as context-free, but must be linked to pedagogy. Content knowledge (CK) refers to the quality and organisation of knowledge in the thought processes of lecturers. Lecturers who have the appropriate CK to be able to teach the subject fluently, have the pedagogical knowledge (PK) to select appropriate methods of teaching the particular course content to students. Pedagogical content knowledge (PCK), the interface between subject and pedagogical knowledge, is referred to as specialised content knowledge (Shulman 2004). Pedagogical content knowledge becomes evident when teachers have the ability to build on their students' prior knowledge and adapt their teaching strategies to best facilitate the new content to students (Mishra and Koehler 2006). Last, but not least, the NWU VTC should supply the students and lecturers with the infrastructure, finances, and support, to enable students to become critical, yet reflective thinkers, and lecturers to guide students through teaching and learning to become efficient and self-directed critical thinkers.

Therefore, NWU VTC Academic Development and Support (ADS) conducted a needs and context analysis to determine which options would best suit the university to develop a blended or e-learning model, and the concept of SMARTguides materialised. With the implementation of SMARTguides, VTC could adhere to the aspects of TEL.

SMARTguide is a *tool* (SMART) to support a blended learning approach, using a combination of contact and online learning, catering for versatile learning experiences, accommodating diverse learning styles, and creating a media rich learning experience for the students, simultaneously taken into consideration students' access to Internet and devices. The *S* indicates students to become self-directed; the *M* signifies the learning management as the capacity to achieve learning outcomes based on the notion of design with intent; the *A* indicates assessment of and for learning; the *R* defines a responsive environment, remediation, revision and reflection of learning, and the *T* allows for tracking of students' participations and learning. A SMARTguide additionally supplies students with a guide for their academic programme.

In 2013, as part of a five year implementation plan, fourteen lecturers at VTC, from the Faculties of Economic Sciences and IT as well as the Faculty of Humanities, with an interest for ICT integration in their teaching and learning, were identified to take part in the development of the SMARTguide pilot project. The academic and e-learning advisor designed and developed templates for the creation of the SMARTguides in Microsoft PowerPoint, which would then be incorporated, with links to videos, articles, learning management systems, and newspapers, into Articulate Storyline program software. This format was the first phase of the project, and fourteen modules were available and implemented in electronic form. The students involved in the project either received an android tablet, an iPad or brought their own devices to access the SMARTguides. With the proliferation of mobile initiatives (tablets/iPads) on VTC, before the project could move to the next phase, an evaluation of the pilot had to take place. For these initiatives to improve students' learning and lecturers' teaching, it has to be embraced by students and lecturers, therefore the opinions of those involved in the project had to share their experiences. With the increase of mobile computing initiatives across campuses; evaluation of such initiatives becomes the logical next step. Yet for such initiatives to improve students' learning and teaching effectiveness, such technology-based initiatives must be accepted by students and lecturers alike (El-Gayer and Moran 2007). The researchers used the TEL framework and the three factors of the Technology Acceptance Model (TAM) Abbad et al. (2009) in the e-learning domain to: (i) ascertain to which extent students adopted to the SMART-guides, and (ii) what were lecturers' experiences with the use of SMARTguides on mobile devices for programme delivery based on the TAM proposed by (Davis 1986).

2 Technology Adoption Model: Theoretical Background

Based on social psychology and sociology theories like the *Theory of Reasoned Action,* several models for acceptance and use of technology were developed. The TAM was developed by Davis (1986) which became prominent in research focussing on the acceptance and use of technology. The key purpose of TAM was to provide researchers and practitioners with a guide to trace the impact of external factors on internal beliefs on students' ability to use and accept technology. TAM states that the acceptance of a technology depends on two types of beliefs: the technology's perceived usefulness and its perceived ease of use (Davis et al. 1989). *Perceived usefulness* is rooted in the users' subjective belief that using a particular system will increase their performance when conducting a particular tasks within their existing context. *Perceived ease of use* refers to the users' belief that to use the system does not acquire any effort from their part.

Therefore, TAM was expanded further with three central factors which motivate users to embrace any form of multimedia or technology: (i) perceived ease of use; (ii) perceived usefulness; and (iii) attitude towards using the systems (Davis et al. 1989). Figure 2 illustrates the TAM used for this research.

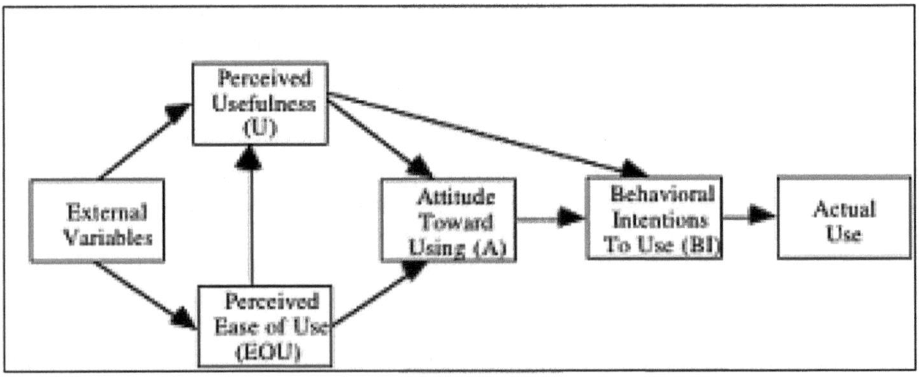

Fig. 2. Technology acceptance model (Davis et al. 1989)

2.1 Perceived Ease of Use

As seen from Fig. 2, TAM distinguishes between two mechanisms which influences the ease of use: self-efficacy and instrumentality. *Self-efficacy* refers to an individual's belief in his or her capacity to execute behaviours necessary to produce specific performance attainments (Barnhart and Barnhart 1990). Self-efficacy also exhibits confidence in the ability to exercise control over one's own motivation, behaviour, and social environment (Bandura 1977). Additionally self-efficacy triggers intrinsic motivation (Bandura 1977), which highlights the relationship between ease of use and attitude. The easier it is for the user to navigate and interact with the system the greater the self-efficacy and personal control regarding his/her ability to operate the system and complete the tasks. The aspect of *instrumentality* refers to improvements in the ease of use which add to increase performance, as the students are able to perform more tasks with the same amount of effort as before the implementation of the multimedia or technology.

2.2 Perceived Usefulness

Perceived usefulness is synonymous to external factors when it comes to technology acceptance. There are numerous things which influence or have an impact on perceived usefulness: (i) the training, support, academic consultations sessions and training material; (ii) the system features such as the mouse, icons, and a touchscreen, are also known to enhance the ease of use, but influence perceived usefulness; and (iii) the design characteristics (frames and screen). Even if there are two distinct systems, one with sound quality and the other with poor quality design characteristics, the latter would be perceived as more useful (Chuttur 2009).

2.3 Attitude Towards Technology

Through several previous studies conducting factor analyses, it became evident that perceived usefulness and perceived ease of use are two distinct dimensions, but are both important when it comes to the use and adoption of technology. TAM also articulates that a person's behavioural intention is viewed by a person's attitude towards using the system and the perceived usefulness of the system. *Attitude* is the tendency to respond positively or negatively to a particular technology, and perceived usefulness is the degree to which a person believes that using a particular system will enhance his or her job performance. Perceived usefulness has a stronger hold on attitude than ease of use. It was found that perceived usefulness and ease of use both have a positive effect on attitude (Davis et al. 1989).

Therefore, for students to accept technology, there should be a strong link between the aspects of ease of use, perceived usefulness, and attitude towards using the system (Fig. 2). In order for the researchers to ascertain whether the SMARTguides on mobile devices are adopted by students and lecturers at VTC, three aspects (ease of use, perceived usefulness, and attitude) independently and coherently should be considered central when conducting research.

3 Research Design and Methodology

In order to: (i) ascertain to which extend students adopted to the SMARTguides, and (ii) what are lecturers' experiences with the use of SMARTguides on mobile devices for programme delivery the research used a multi-mode research design and methodology. The quantitative data collection included an instrument developed, adapted and refined, based on previous studies (Abbad et al. 2009, Davis et al. 1989) and the TEL framework (Van Deventer and Blignaut 2013) which were distributed to the first and second year students who participated in the pilot project. The qualitative data collection included a focus group interview with the lecturers from the Faculties of Economic Sciences and IT and Humanities, and a written reflection regarding their experiences with the use of SMARTguides in their classrooms.

3.1 The Instrument

The survey included questions relating to: (i) demographic information, which included aspects like home language, gender, field of study, place of residence (on or off campus), type of mobile devices, and Internet access (TEL); (ii) perceived ease of use of the tablet and SMARTguide (TAM); (iii) perceived usefulness of the tablet and SMARTguide (TAM); (iv) user satisfaction (TAM and TEL); (v) design aspects (TAM and TEL); (vi) university infrastructure (TEL); and (vi) three open ended questions on what they liked, disliked and would change about the SMARTguide (TAM and TEL). The survey used a five point Likert Scale (1 = strongly disagree, 2 = agree, 3 = neutral, 4 = disagree, and 5 = strongly disagree) to measure their level of agreement and disagreement. Therefore the survey was designed including components of TEL as well as TAM.

3.2 Focus Group Interview and Reflection

As lecturers are role players in TEL, it was imperative to capture their experiences with the use of SMARTguides and tablets for teaching and learning at VTC. The researchers conducted an in-depth focus group interview with the targeted research participants. The researchers wanted to know about their concerns and perceptions regarding the use of SMARTguides and tablets used to deliver their first and second year modules at NWU VTC (Mcmillan and Schumacher 2001). The participants received the interview schedule in advance to enable them to prepare for the research conversation. The interview was conducted in Afrikaans (Home language of all the participants). The focus group schedule comprising semi-structured questions, was used as a guideline, but not asked in the specific order (Merriam 2009). The questions were compiled based on the TEL framework (Van Deventer and Blignaut 2013) and previous research which related to technology acceptance (Chuttur 2009). The interview was recorded and transcribed for analysis.

3.3 Research Participants

The survey was distributed to students involved in the SMARTguide tablet project of which 207 students from the fourteen modules completed the survey.

Two academic advisors, also coordinators of the pilot SMARTguide project, interviewed five lecturers from the two faculties to ascertain their experience with the implementation of SMARTguides and tablets/iPads for teaching and learning in their classrooms.

4 Data Analyses

The researchers conducted qualitative as well as quantitative data analyses.

4.1 Quantitative Data Analyses

The quantitative data were analysed by means of descriptive (frequencies and percentages) and inferential statistics (principal axis factor analysis).

In order to validate the survey, a principal axis factor analysis extracted individual items of the survey into factors according to the correlation between items. The factor analysis enabled the researcher to explore the data for patterns, verify, and decrease the number of variables within the survey (Cohen et al. 2011). Subsequent factors are, in turn, intended to account for the maximum amount of the remaining common variance until, hopefully, no significant common variance remains (Suhr 2006). With factor analysis the variables clustered the data into homogeneous groups, created new factors, and the researcher gained insight into the constructs underlying the data (Garrett-Mayer 2006). Barlett's test of sphericity tested whether the correlation matrix was an identity matrix, which would indicate that the variables are unrelated and unsuitable for structure detention. Significance values ≤0.05 indicated that the factor analysis could be useful. The Kaiser-Meyer-Olkim (KMO) tested whether the observed data and their correlations were large enough to form a concise factor structure. A measure of, or above, 0.9 indicated a good fit. Cronbach's Alpha was used to measure the reliability of the questionnaire as it is known as the most appropriate type of reliability for survey research (Mcmillan and Schumacher 2001). Values above 0.7, and in many cases a value of 0.5, would have sufficed (Nunnally and Berstein 1994) with an average inter-item correlation in the range of 0.15–0.50.

4.2 Qualitative Data Analysis

A constant comparative content analysis (Boeije 2002) was executed with Atlas.ti™, a qualitative analysis computer data analysis system (QACDAS). The qualitative data were analysed inductively with the aim of organising and exploring the data into categories and identifying patterns to gain insight on the phenomenon (Mcmillan and Schumacher 2001). During the inductive data analysis, the researchers systematically made sense of the data through selecting, categorising, comparing, synthesizing and interpreting the data. TEL (Fig. 1) and TAM (Fig. 2) was used as an analytical framework in the qualitative analysis of the focus group interview to grasp the lecturers' perceptions regarding SMARTguides and tablets/iPads in the classroom as a teaching and learning tool. Four reflections and one focus group were analysed with Atlas.ti™.

5 Findings

The findings of the quantitative data are displayed as descriptive statistics (demographic information), and pattern matrixes of the factor analyses. The qualitative analyses are integrated to substantiate or contradict the findings from the quantitative analyses.

5.1 Descriptive Statistics of the Survey

Table 1 illustrates the descriptive statistics of the demographic information which consist of frequencies and percentages are used to explicate the data from questions two to ten in the survey. Question (Q1) was optional for students to complete.

As seen in Table 1, the majority of the participants (83.1 %) speak African languages as NWU VTC has a larger group of African students. The two gender groups were well represented with 57 % male and 43 % female. Students from both faculties took part in the survey. The majority of the students reside off campus (81.2 %) which explain why so many of them (72.5 %) do not have Internet access. Most of the students who completed the survey (54.1 %) use a laptop and only 6.8 % have an iPad or iPad mini. What is important to take note of is that only 2.4 % of the participants thought that the Internet access on campus is adequate for teaching and learning (Table 1).

Table 1. Descriptive statistics of demographic information

Item			Frequencies	Percentages
2	Home language	Afrikaans	10	4.8
		English	25	12.1
		African languages	172	83.1
3	Gender	Male	118	57.0
		Female	89	43.0
4	Field of study	Behavioural Sciences	18	34.8
		Languages	2	4.3
		Basic Sciences	9	8.7
		Education Sciences	30	10.6
		Accounting Sciences	72	14.5
		Economic Sciences	22	26.1
		Information Technology	54	1.0

(Continued)

Table 1. (*Continued*)

Item			Frequencies	Percentages
5	Residence	On campus	168	81.2
		Off campus	39	18.8
6	Access to the Internet	Yes	150	27.5
		No	57	72.5
7	Types of Internet access	3G modem	24	29.0
		NWU WiFi	47	11.6
		Telkom	13	16.9
		On campus network	35	6.3
		Via mobile phone	28	13.5
		Other	60	22.7
8	Rationale for no Internet access	Accommodation does not provide	39	18.8
		Too expensive	5	2.4
		Do not need it	1	0.5
		Campus access is adequate	5	2.4
		Other	152	73.4
9	Devices	Android tablet	34	16.4
		Desktop	22	10.6
		iPad	28	13.5
		Laptop	112	54.1
		Windows tablet	2	1,0
10	iPads	iPad mini	14	6.8
		iPad	14	6.8

5.2 Findings from the Factor Analyses and Focus Group Interview

A principal axis factor analysis with Oblimin rotation was conducted on Questions 12–21 of the survey. The factor analysis validated the correlation coefficient between the factors. The shaded areas in the tables indicate the group items loading on each factor. All factor loadings ≤0.3 were deleted from the tables. The variables which had more than one factor loading were grouped according to the best interpretability. All the factors had a Cronbach Alpha of more than 0.5.

5.2.1 Perceived Ease of Use

Tables 2 and 3 illustrate the pattern matrixes of the factor analyses for Q12 and Q13, which addressed specific questions relating to perceived ease of use of the tablets and SMARTguides. Table 2 provides the pattern matrix of the factor analysis of the twelve items of Q12 of the survey.

The factor analysis clustered the items in Q12 into three homogeneous groups (Garrett-Mayer 2006). The factor analysis revealed three factors (Table 2) (Field 2009).

Table 2. Pattern matrix of Question 12

Perceived ease of use		Pattern matrix		
		Factor 1	Factor 2	Factor 3
7	I feel confident using my SMARTguide on my tablet/desktop	0.820		
8	I feel confident using my SMARTguide on my tablet/laptop	0.805		
5	Learning how to use my tablet was easy	0.593		
3	I feel confident to use my tablet for non-academic purposes	0.514		
12	I use my tablet for purposes other than my academic work	0.383		
10	Compared to laptop my tablet is more useful for academic purposes		0.837	
9	Compared to desktop my tablet is more useful for academic purposes		0.824	
2	I feel confident using my tablet for academic purposes		0.485	
6	I feel confident accessing my SMARTguide on my tablet		0.427	
1	I believe that working with tablets is complicated		0.353	
11	I use my tablet for academic purposes			0.746
4	I feel that I could use my tablet after the training at ADS			0.669
Percentage variance		22.218	15.163	12.728
Cumulative percentage		22.218	37.381	50.109
Cronbach Alpha		0.62	0.58	0.70
Kaiser-Meyer-Olkin measure of sampling adequacy				0.517
Percentage of total variance				159.873

Five variables clustered as Factor 1, five variables clustered as Factor 2, two variables clustered as Factor 3. The KMO measure of 0.517 indicated an adequate data for factor analysis (Cohen et al. 2011). The Barlett's test of sphericity showed a significance of $p < 0.000$ for this factor analysis (Cohen et al. 2011). The three extracted factors explained a total variance of 159 %. A thorough scrutiny revealed that Factor 1 corresponds with *self-efficacy with tablets*, Factor 2 relates to *instrumentality*, and Factor 3 corresponds with *use of tablets*. The self-efficacy relates to the students' ability to use the tablets with ease and confidence. The instrumentality relates to the extent which the students can use the tablets with ease. In general students were positive and confident to use their tablets, especially after a training session at ADS.

One of the lecturers highlighted the students' self-efficacy with tablets:

Once you get your students hooked or interested then they will continue to look for things in their own time (P1:22).

The lecturers also highlighted the following regarding instrumentality and the specific improvements which should be made to improve the ease of use:

Make the instructions clear and give as much guidance as possible (P1:21).

From the above it is clear that self-efficacy and instrumentality is of importance to ease of use of tablets.

Table 3 provides the pattern matrix of the factor analysis of Q13 of the survey.

The factor analysis clustered the items in Q12 into two homogeneous groups (Garrett-Mayer 2006). Two factors (Table 3) which were extracted according to the Kaiser's criteria (Field 2009). Three variables clustered as Factor 1, and three variables clustered as Factor 2. The KMO measure of 0.653 indicated an adequate data for factor analysis (Cohen et al. 2011). The Barlett's test of sphericity showed a significance of $p < 0.000$ for this factor analysis (Cohen et al. 2011). The extracted factors explained a total variance of 56 %. A thorough scrutiny revealed that Factor 1 corresponds with *SMARTguides and ease of use*, Factor 2 relates to use of *SMARTguides and the frustrations.*

Table 3. Pattern matrix of Question 13

Perceived ease of use		Pattern matrix	
		Factor 1	Factor 2
1	I feel the SMARTguide is easy to use	0.829	
3	Navigation in my SMARTguides was easy	0.826	
4	Downloading the off-line version of my SMARTguide was easy	0.715	
6	I feel frustrated whilst working with my SMARTguide		0.838
2	I access my SMARTguide on my cellphone		0.684
5	My lecturer(s) seem(s) confident using the SMARTguide in class		−0.345
Percentage variance		36.578	21.456
Cumulative percentage		36.578	58.034
Cronbach Alpha		0.79	0.62
Kaiser-Meyer-Olkin measure of sampling adequacy			0.653
Percentage of total variance			55.585

Students indicated that it was easy for them to use the SMARTguide. However, they became frustrated whilst working with the SMARTguides. The lecturers on the other hand also encountered many frustrations:

A student told him that the only time she used the guide a lot was close to the exams just for all the example questions that are in the guide (P1:16).
Student are lazy (P1:17).
Students that don't attend training that claim they cannot email, but there is nothing in the guide that students cannot access (P1:19).
Students use the tablets to play games and for social media (P2:2).

5.2.2 Perceived Usefulness

Tables 4 and 5 provide pattern matrixes of the factor analysis relating to perceived usefulness. The pattern matrix of the factor analysis of Q16 is illustrated in Table 4.

Table 4. Pattern matrix Question 16

Perceived usefulness		Pattern matrix	
		Factor 1	Factor 2
2	Using a tablet will improve my academic success	0.845	
1	I believe that a tablet is very useful for academic purposes at university	0.836	
3	Although I have a tablet, I prefer to use my SMARTguide on my laptop or desktop computer	−0.543	
4	Using my SMARTguide on my tablet allowed me to prepare for class more effectively		0.766
5	Using my SMARTguide on a tablet made it easier for me to access eFundi for activities		0.721
Percentage variance		36.440	23.711
Cumulative percentage		36.440	60.151
Cronbach Alpha		0.73	0.74
Kaiser-Meyer-Olkin measure of sampling adequacy		0.525	
Percentage of total variance		37.271	

The factor analysis clustered the items in Q16 into two homogeneous groups (Garrett-Mayer 2006). Two factors (Table 4) which were extracted according to Kaiser's criteria (Field 2009). Three variables clustered as Factor 1, and three variables clustered as Factor 2. The KMO measure of 0.525 indicated an adequate data for factor analysis (Cohen et al. 2011). The Barlett's test of sphericity showed a significance of $p < 0.000$ for this factor analysis (Cohen et al. 2011). The extracted factors explained a total variance of 37 %. A thorough scrutiny revealed that Factor 1 relates to *ease of use for academic purposes and success*, and Factor 2 relates to *ease of use for academic activities and preparation*. The students indicated that it is useful to be able to prepare for class and access their activities on eFundi and their SMARTguides via the tablets.

Even though students indicated that tablets are easy to use, lecturers experience difficulties when students often cannot access the SMARTguides:

Students do not have access to the activities linked to the SMARTguides if the WiFi is off (P1:3).
Many of the second year students to not have tablets to activate the SMARTguides (P4:2).
My students had to do an electronic evaluation, but were not able to (P1:4).

Table 5 provides the pattern matrix of the factor of Q17.

The factor analysis clustered the items in Q17 into three homogeneous groups (Garrett-Mayer 2006). The factor analysis extracted three factors (Table 5) according to Kaiser's criteria (Field 2009). Twelve variables clustered as Factor 1, four variables clustered as Factor 2, four variables clustered as Factor 3. The KMO measure of 0.830 indicated adequate data for factor analysis (Cohen et al. 2011). The Barlett's test of sphericity showed a significance of $p < 0.000$ for this factor analysis (Cohen et al. 2011). The three extracted factors explained a total variance of 958 %. A thorough scrutiny revealed that Factor 1 corresponds with *perceived usefulness of design characteristics*, Factor 2 relates to *perceived use of SMARTguides*, and Factor 3

Table 5. Pattern matrix of Question 17

Perceived usefulness		Pattern matrix		
		Factor 1	Factor 2	Factor 3
12	I find the SMARTguide to be mentally stimulating	0.822		
11	I will use the SMARTguide to do revision before tests and exams	0.777		
7	Using a SMARTguide will improve/enhance my academic success	0.758		
4	Using a SMARTguide makes my academic work more interesting	0.741		
5	Using a SMARTguide helped me to understand my work better	0.733		
6	The SMARTguide improved the quality of the study guide compared to the traditional paper guides	0.627		
10	I find the assessment activities in the SMARTguide useful	0.559		
8	Using the SMARTguide in class enhanced student participation	0.526		
15	I use my SMARTguide(s) more often than my printed study guides	0.525		
14	The use of video material in a SMARTguide will contribute to my learning	0.517		
19	The explanation of the action words in the SMARTguide is useful	0.420		
18	My lecturer(s) use the SMARTguide(s) effectively during class		−0.951	
17	My lecturer(s) use the SMARTguide(s) in class		−0.879	
2	I prefer using a SMARTguide to a printed study guide		−0.420	
1	I prefer the SMARTguide to power point slides		−0.401	
3	I can use my SMARTguide effectively on my cellphone			0.799
16	My lecturer(s) never use the SMARTguide			0.698
13	A SMARTguide should only include guidelines and minimum content			0.534
9	The offline version of my SMARTguide allows me freedom to use it when I am not at the university			0.362
Percentage variance		34.069	10.205	8.053
Cumulative percentage		34.069	44.274	52.326
Cronbach Alpha		0.59	0.66	0.60
Kaiser-Meyer-Olkin measure of sampling adequacy				0.830
Percentage of total variance				958.267

corresponds with *usability of SMARTguides*. The students did not encounter any problems with using the SMARTguides, and in general they were satisfied with the design characteristics of the SMARTguides. However, students indicated that lecturers do not use the SMARTguides as a teaching tool, and some students prefer the printed guides and presentations previously used. This was confirmed by one of the lecturers:

During the contact sessions I prefer to make use of my presentations, I refer to it, but students need to have Internet access and tablets to use it (P4:3).
A lot of the blogs and Web pages which are linked in the guides is not available anymore, then I as a lecturer are really embarrassed when that happens (P4:4).

5.2.3 User Satisfaction

Table 6 provides the pattern matrix of the factor analysis of Q18 which focussed on user satisfaction.

Table 6. Pattern matrix of Question 18

User satisfaction		Pattern matrix
		Factor 1
3	I prefer to use SMARTguides for all my modules	0.658
2	I think positively about using electronic study material (SMARTguide) on a tablet	0.641
5	I need an off-line version of my SMARTguide	0.443
1	Using a tablet at university is a status symbol	0.516
Percentage variance		27.476
Cumulative percentage		27.476
Kaiser-Meyer-Olkin measure of sampling adequacy		0.526
Percentage of total variance		6.580

The factor analysis clustered the items in Q18 into one homogeneous groups (Garrett-Mayer 2006). One factor (Table 6) was extracted according to Kaiser's criteria that all factors with eigenvalues larger than one be extracted (Field 2009). Five variables clustered as Factor 1. The KMO measure of 0.526 indicated an adequate data for factor analysis (Cohen et al. 2011). The Barlett's test of sphericity showed a significance of $p < 0.000$ for this factor analysis (Cohen et al. 2011). The extracted factors explained a total variance of 7 %. Factor 1 corresponds with *user satisfaction with SMARTguides and tablets*. In general the majority of the students were satisfied with the concept of study guides as multimedia on a tablet.

One of the lecturers highlighted the following:

We will only see the effects for using technology and SMARTguides in 2016 when the 1st years are through (P1:21).
The majority of the students are positive when they use the SMARTguides (P1:10).
Some students like to use the SMARTguides before, during and after class (P4:1).

5.2.4 Design Aspects

The pattern matrix of the factor analysis of Q23 relating to design aspects is illustrated in Table 7.

Table 7. Pattern matrix of Question 23

Design aspect		Pattern matrix
		Factor 1
10	I like the way more information is grouped on a page by using clickable buttons	0.795
11	I like to click on items/buttons in my SMARTguide to reveal more information	0.679
3	I like the design and layout of my SMARTguide(s)	0.656
9	I like the use of scrollbars in the SMARTguide(s)	0.647
12	The use of white icons to indicate that internet is required for an activity is useful	0.603
8	The visual elements (images, graphics, text, colours etc.) in the SMARTguide(s) contribute to my learning experience	0.464
10	I like the way more information is grouped on a page by using clickable buttons	0.795
Percentage variance		38.482
Cumulative percentage		38.482
Cronbach Alpha		0.66
Kaiser-Meyer-Olkin measure of sampling adequacy		0.834
Percentage of total variance		642.787

The factor analysis clustered the items in Q18 into one homogeneous groups (Garrett-Mayer 2006). One factor (Table 7) which was extracted with eigenvalues larger than one is extracted (Field 2009). Seven variables clustered as Factor 1. The KMO measure of 0.834 indicated an adequate data for factor analysis (Cohen et al. 2011). The Barlett's test of sphericity showed a significance of $p < 0.000$ for this factor analysis (Cohen et al. 2011). The extracted factors explained a total variance of 642 %. Factor 1 corresponds with *design elements of multimedia*. Students were satisfied with the outline, design, visual elements, and the colour coordinated icons. The lecturers did not comment on the design aspects as they designed the SMARTguides.

Table 8 illustrates the pattern matrix of the factor analysis of Q24.

The factor analysis clustered the items in Q24 into two homogeneous groups (Garrett-Mayer 2006). Two factors (Table 8) which were extracted with eigenvalues larger than one (Field 2009). Three variables clustered as Factor 1, and three variables clustered as Factor 2. The KMO measure of 0.530 indicated an adequate data for factor analysis (Cohen et al. 2011). The Barlett's test of sphericity showed a significance of $p < 0.000$ for this factor analysis (Cohen et al. 2011). The extracted factors explained a total variance of 44 %. A thorough scrutiny revealed that Factor 1 corresponds with *IT assistance*, Factor 2 relates to Internet access. The students who were part of the

Table 8. Pattern matrix of Question 24

University infrastructure		Pattern matrix	
		Factor 1	Factor 2
3	When I need help with my SMARTguide, I know where to go for assistance	0.821	
4	When I need help with my tablet, I know where to go for assistance	0.806	
1	The Wi-Fi on campus is good enough to connect to the internet anywhere on campus		0.846
2	The Wi-Fi on campus is good enough to connect to the Internet in all classes		0.764
Percentage variance		38.769	27.639
Cumulative percentage		38.769	66.407
Cronbach Alpha		0.81	0.81
Kaiser-Meyer-Olkin measure of sampling adequacy			0.530
Percentage of total variance			43.625

SMARTguide tablet were satisfied with the IT assistance which they received and had adequate WiFi access in their classes and on campus.

This is contradictory to what the lecturers revealed in their reflection and during the focus group interview particularly relating to Internet access:

Network frequently off, no WiFi in classrooms (P1:1-2).
To be honest, it is the instability of the Internet on this campus (P1:23).

Even though training, support and comperacy were not directly addressed in the survey or during the focus group interview and the reflections the lecturers highlighted the importance of comperacy:

We should attend training, because training help use (P1:18).
A suggestion is that lecturers get more training with technology (P1:19).
Students also struggled due to the fact that they had no training (P1:20).

6 Conclusions

As explicated by the TEL framework, in order for technology to be integrated seamlessly into the teaching and learning in HEIs, all aspects should be in place. From the findings it is evident that there are several of these aspects which should be amended before the next phase of blended or e-learning implementation at NWU VTC. In general students who adopted to the SMARTguides and tablets, were confident in their ability to use the SMARTguides and tablets, perceived the SMARTguides as useful, and had a positive attitude towards SMARTguides and tablets. However, to enhance the adoption of technologies in HEIs, Table 9 provides recommendations, using the TEL framework, which resulted from the qualitative and quantitative analyses.

Table 9. Improved technology enhanced learning at Vaal Triangle Campus

TEL framework	Recommendations for implementation of mobile technologies
Students	• Access to tablets, Internet and WiFi • Attend training to use SMARTguides and tablets
Lecturers	• Guide students to use the SMARTguides and integrate these into their teaching and learning • Have WiFi in their classroom • Monitor students' progress using the SMARTguides • Regularly check the content and the links • Develop their TPACK through professional development • Adopt the e-learning and blended learning strategy of the NWU
Course content	• Embed in the SMARTguides • Include clear instructions for the students
TEL framework	Recommendations for implementation of mobile technologies
Comperacy	• Provide students and lecturers with training to enhance their comperacy
e-Communication	• Provide students with alternative methods of communication • Introduce students to the communication tools available
Internet access	• NWU VTC should make sure that there are WiFi in all the classrooms and around campus

For seamless implementation and adoption of SMARTguides and tablets at NWU VTC, each of the role players (students, lecturers, ADS, and institutional management) should be proactive in addressing the recommendations to cultivate critical and reflective thinkers. Students should be able to have access to mobile devices, tablets, Internet, as well as sufficient training for seamless integration. Pertaining to the results from the above analyses, ADS and institutional management has started to put strategies in place for improving the student and Internet access, supplying basic computer literacy skills training, and enhancing the design elements of the SMARTguides. From the analyses ADS realized it is not possible for the ship to leave the harbour (SMARTguides and tablets to be implemented in the class), and the captain (lecturers) are missing in action and not navigating the ship to the reach the harbour. Therefore, ADS has started to motivate and support lecturers to explore with the use of various software on mobile devices (iPads, tablets, and smartphones), develop their TPACK, and expose them to the pedagogical benefits of ICT so that they come on board with mobile use for teaching and learning.

References

Abbad, M.M., Morris, D., De Nahlik, C.: Looking under the bonnet: factors affecting students adoption of e-learning systems in Jordan. Int. Rev. Res. Open Distance Learn. **10**(2), 1–25 (2009)

Bandura, A.: Self-efficacy: toward a unifying theory of behavioral change. Psychol. Rev. **84**(2), 191–215 (1977)

Barnhart, C., Barnhart, R.: The world book dictionary. In: Zenely, R.O. (ed.), pp. 1168–2430. Merchandice Mart Plaza, Chicago (1990)

Boeije, H.: A purposeful approach to the constant comparative method in the analysis of qualitative interviews. Quant. Qual. **36**, 391–409 (2002)

Chuttur, M.: Overview of the technology acceptance model: origins, developments and future directions. Sprouts Working Pap. Inf. Syst. **9**(37), 1–23 (2009)

Cohen, L., Manion, L., Morrison, K.: Research Methods in Education, 7th edn. Routledge, Abingdon, OX (2011)
Davis, F.D.: Perceived usefulness, perceived ease of use, and user acceptance of information technology. MIS Q. **13**(3), 319–340 (1986)
Davis, F.D., Bagozzi, R.P., Warshaw, P.R.: User aceeptance of computer technology: a comparison of two theoretical models. Manage. Sci. **35**(8), 982–1003 (1989)
Department of Higher Education and Training. White paper for post-school education and training: Building an expanded effective and integrated post-school system (2013). http://www.dhet.gov.za/LinkClick.aspx?fileticket=236NoC18lB4%3D&tabid=36. Accessed 23 January 2014
El-Gayer, O., Moran, M.: Examining students acceptance of tablet PC using TAM. Issues Inf. Syst. **VIII**(1), 167–172 (2007)
Emerson, L., MacKay, B.: A comparison between paper-based and online learning in higher education. Br. J. Educ. Technol. **42**(5), 727–735 (2010)
Field, A.: Discovering Statistics Using SPSS, 3rd edn. SAGE Publications, London (2009)
Garrett-Mayer, E.: Statistics in psychosocial research lecture 8 factor analysis I (2006). http://ocw.jhsph.edu/courses/statisticspsychosocialresearch/pdfs/lecture8.pdf. Accessed 14 June 2013
McMillan, J.H., Schumacher, S.: Research in Education: A Conceptual Introduction, 5th edn. Addison Wesley Longman, Virginia (2001)
Merriam, S.: Qualitative Research: A Guide to Design and Implementation, 2nd edn. Jossey-Bass, San Francisco (2009)
Mishra, P., Koehler, M.J.: Technological pedagogical content knowledge: a framework for teacher knowledge. Teach. Coll. Rec. **108**(6), 1017–1054 (2006)
Nunnally, J.C., Berstein, I.H.: Psychometric Theory, 3rd edn. McGraw-Hill, New York (1994)
Shulman, L.: The Wisdom of Practice: Essays on Teaching, Learning, and Learning to Teach. Jossey-Bass, San Francisco (2004)
Suhr, D.D.: Exploratory or confirmatory factor analysis? Paper Presented to the SUGI 31, San Francisco, Carlifornia (2006)
Van Deventer, M., Blignaut, S.: Taking the plunge from classroom teaching to technology enhanced learning at a residential university journal of information technology and application. Education **2**(3), 105–116 (2013)

Use of Web 2.0 and Mobile Technologies for Developing Argumentative Skills

Susan Gwee(✉) and Shalini Damodaran

English Language Institute of Singapore, Singapore, Singapore
gwee@mac.com

Abstract. Web 2.0 and mobile technologies have the potential to support learning outside formal learning spaces. In this paper, we examine the extent to which the use of Web 2.0 and mobile technologies has an impact on the argumentative skills of Grade 11 students in a Singapore high school. Using a quasi-experimental and mixed method research design, we looked at the quality of students' writing at the end of a six-week intervention that involved students using *Schoology* to read assigned materials, share new materials, post arguments, and respond to their classmates' arguments. We also examined both student and teacher interview transcripts to gain an understanding of how students and teachers viewed *Schoology* as an e-learning tool. Students in the experimental group showed higher levels of argumentation skills compared to students in the control group. Findings from student and teacher interviews concerning the use of Web 2.0 and mobile technologies to help them develop argumentative skills were mixed. The analysis of the interviews revealed that some students felt that it was distracting because they tended to veer into social media sites and preferred to use them in the classroom, while others felt that *Schoology* provided a great platform for them to develop argumentative skills as peer feedback gave them multiple perspectives. It developed a community of learners, and provided an interesting and interactive experience. The participation rate was higher on the online platform compared to classroom discussion. The teacher reported that students' essays became more coherent and their content more relevant.

Keywords: Mobile · Web 2.0 · Argumentation

1 Introduction

Web 2.0 and mobile technologies have the potential to support learning in formal and informal learning spaces. Cochrane (2014) reported that there had been considerable research on the use of mobile devices in the educational context. However, he noted that the research tended to focus on teacher-generated rather than student-generated content. With the affordances of mobile and Web 2.0 technologies, it has become easier for students to generate their own content. However, the informal learning space has to be designed in a way that encourages students to take a bigger role. Hew and Cheung (2013) after having reviewed evidence-based pedagogical approaches related to the use of Web 2.0 technologies in both K-12 and higher education settings, noted that future

T.H. Brown and H.J. van der Merwe (Eds.): mLearn 2015, CCIS 560, pp. 129–142, 2015.
DOI: 10.1007/978-3-319-25684-9_10

research needed to examine how Web 2.0 technologies could support students' use of mobile devices for learning purposes.

In this paper, the authors examined the extent to which the use of Web 2.0 and mobile technologies had an impact on the development of argumentative skills in Grade 11 students, and the perceptions that students and the teacher had of the intervention helping students develop argumentative skills.

1.1 Web 2.0 and Mobile Technologies

Web 2.0 tools make it easy for people to create and publish, communicate their work, and collaborate, to either a select group of people or to a much wider audience (Thomson 2008). Web 2.0 applications include Facebook, Schoology, and Google Drive. With Web 2.0 technologies, students and teachers can easily contribute to the online forum discussions without much technical expertise. They are no longer limited to mere reading of contributors, but they themselves become contributors. This study did not stipulate the type of application or website that the teacher could use as it is more concerned with its pedagogical, social and technical affordances. It is believed that these interactive, asynchronous technological spaces enable students to "explore, experiment, construct, converse and reflect on what they are doing so that they can learn from their experience" (Jonassen et al. 1999, p. 194). The teacher research participant was therefore given the free reign to select the Web 2.0 e-learning tool according to the learning outcomes she wished to achieve.

There are a few studies that have examined the use of Web 2.0 tools to improve language learning in K-12 (Wong and Hew 2010) and higher education settings (Arslan and Shain-Kizil 2010; Hsu and Wang 2011; Neumaan and Hood 2009; Pae 2007; Rick et al. 2002; Wichadee 2010). These studies have made use of the affordances of Web 2.0 tools and peer critique was an important feature in these interventions. For example, in Wong and Hew's (2010) study, fifth-grade students in Singapore commented on each other's drafts posted on their blogs during classtime. For the second draft, they commented on vocabulary and linking words. For the third, comments were made on sequencing, development, and relevance of their classmates' ideas. However, many of the studies did not report the use of Web 2.0 tools to improve language learning on mobile devices (Hsu and Wang 2010; Pae 2007; Rick et al. 2002; Wichadee 2010; Wong and Hew 2010). Smartphones and tablets were not as ubiquitous then and thus it was not as feasible to use them for language learning.

With mobile devices becoming more popular, especially with the young, the use of Web 2.0 technologies together with these devices has also increased. Smartphone ownership is now very common in Singapore. It was reported at the beginning of 2015 that 90 % of the respondents to a survey conducted in Singapore by Deloitte's Global Technology, Media and Telecommunications, owned a smartphone ("Smartphone Penetration" 2015). In 2013, 97 % of Singapore residents between the ages of 15 and 24 reported using smartphones (Infocomm Development Authority of Singapore 2013). Therefore, to bridge the gap between the students' everyday experiences and their school experiences, using Web 2.0 and mobile technologies to help them learn argumentative skills will ensure a form of learning that comes closer to their out-of-classroom experiences.

1.2 Argumentation Skills

Prior research shows that students are generally known to have problems with the construction of arguments (e.g., Means and Voss 1996). Argumentation skills that include critical thinking and critical reasoning skills are also considered to be vital to meet the demands of the 21st Century. Furthermore, given the comfort level of students with Web 2.0 tools, research findings would provide more insight into the affordances of such technology, and if they should be exploited to create learning opportunities for students to express their arguments cogently. Previous research suggests that students generally had difficulty with argumentative writing skills, and the use of technology in most instances may create positive learning experiences and outcomes in students constructing cogent arguments (Chandrasegaran and Kong 2006; Jonassen and Kim 2010; Kuhn 1991; Means and Voss 1996; Reznitskya et al. 2001).

Reznitskya et al. (2001), Kuhn (1991), and Means and Voss (1996) have emphasized the need to explore the effectiveness of Web 2.0 e-learning environments to promote argumentative writing skills as they claim that many teenage students do not understand argumentative discourse. These students have been found to experience difficulty writing persuasive essays, comprehending written arguments, differentiating between theory and evidence, and generating genuine evidence, alternative theories, counterarguments or rebuttals (Jonassen and Kim 2010). A local empirical study of Singaporean students confirms the claim of Reznitskya and his colleagues. It revealed that only 4.4 % of the 159 online postings displayed the ability to produce dialectical balanced arguments with teachers complaining that students do not know how to argue (Chandrasegaran and Kong 2006).

1.3 Theoretical Underpinnings

The model of Community of Inquiry was used as the theoretical framework of the present study (Garrison et al. 2000) where three elements constituting the educational experience which is embedded within a Community of Inquiry, namely, cognitive presence, social presence, and teaching presence, interact with each other to provide students a meaningful educational experience. The key participants of the Community of Inquiry, the teachers and the students, construct meaning through sustained communication with each other: teachers with students, and students with other fellow students. The cognitive presence plays an important role in critical thinking while the social presence that encompasses the affective aspects of the educational process, indirectly facilitates the process of critical thinking by the community of learners. The teaching presence in particular is important because the teacher has the dual function of designing the educational experience and of facilitating the discussion. For the first function, the teacher selects the e-learning tool that suits the profile, attitudes, and aptitudes of their students and creates an e-learning environment that is meaningfully designed to support the development of students' argumentative skills. He or she provides opportunities for online student discussions by posting appropriated triggers for such discussions. For the second function, the teacher facilitates the thinking processes of their students by monitoring and mediating online discussions, and by evaluating students' arguments and giving feedback. The teaching presence element therefore supports and enhances social and cognitive presence for the purpose of achieving student outcomes.

Garrison and Kanuka (2004) noted that in blended learning, the teaching presence is particularly important as the teacher will have to facilitate both synchronous verbal communication in a face-to-face setting as well as asynchronous written communication in the online setting to support critical discourse and higher order learning. Here, they explained that the teacher scaffolds student learning by moving them from a position of acquiring information to a higher level of accepting responsibility for constructing meaning and confirming understanding in a community of inquiry.

2 Methodology

2.1 Research Design

Creswell and Plano Clark (2011) defined a quasi-experimental research design as one in which "the researcher assigns intact groups the experimental and control treatments, administers a pre-test to both groups, conducts experimental treatment activities with the experimental group only, and then administers a post-test to assess the differences between the two groups." In this study, we used a quasi-experimental and mixed-methods design. Both groups of Grade 11 General Paper students (15 experimental students and 24 control group students) covered the same content as detailed in the scheme of work to ensure parity. They were taught using the same reading and writing materials by the same teacher though they were free to generate and share new material acquired by them. Both groups were taught how to plan their essay using the following questions:

(1) What is my purpose for including this argument?
(2) What are my viewpoints?
(3) How can I support my viewpoints?
(4) What evidence do I have?
(5) What are alternative viewpoints?
(6) How should I respond to them?

The authors collected pre- and post-intervention essays from both groups and conducted a post-intervention interview with the experimental group.

The online learning management tool used was *Schoology*. It allows users to create, manage, and share content and resources. It has a social media interface that enables users to collaborate with one another. The teacher in the present study used it to create a pedagogical experience to develop argumentation skills. She wanted to use the online platform so that students would be involved in crafting arguments regularly outside class time. That is, she wanted more informal learning to take place. For both experimental and control classes, she uploaded reading materials on the topics of *Youth and Family*, and *Education*. However, unlike those in the control class, students in the experimental class were required to hold discussions online once a week during class time as well as to post their comments and feedback outside class time. Some of these students downloaded the *Schoology* app so that they could post their arguments and feedback more easily on their mobile devices that they accessed throughout the day. The students in the experimental group were given specific guidelines on the rules of online engagement on *Schoology* such as relevant sentence starters, and teacher prompts on the form and purpose of an argument. Students were taught to comment on their peers' written work using the four-step approach:

(1) Clarify (Ask a question to seek clarification; e.g., When you wrote X, did you mean....?);
(2) Value (Write a statement that expresses what you value about the ideas presented; e.g., I really value the notion of Y that comes very clearly in the second paragraph.);
(3) Concerns (Express your concerns about the ideas presented; e.g., I am concerned about the flow of your arguments as it seems rather disjointed due to the lack of connectors in paras 3 to 5 especially.); and
(4) Suggest (Suggest how your classmate can improve his or her writing; e.g., Perhaps you could use phrases suggest as "in contrast" or "taking into consideration various perspectives" to improve the flow of your ideas.).

Below is an excerpt of the online discussion that students had on *Schoology* (see Fig. 1). Here, Simon began with a topic sentence followed by supporting details and an evaluation. Matthew responded to his argument. Then Tilly contributed a paragraph stating her stand, supporting details, and evaluation. This was followed by responses by Simon and Matthew on her paragraph.

The advantage of using *Schoology* is that quiet or shy students, or students who lack content knowledge in the topic being discussed, to construct arguments, are able to participate more easily in the online context, i.e., non face-to-face discussions.

After a six-week intervention, students in the control group who were deprived of the possible benefits of the intervention were compensated with the technological intervention in their lessons. The principal's approval and ethics clearance from student participants, and their parents if below the age of 21 were obtained before the start of the intervention.

2.2 Data Analysis

The authors rated the argumentation levels of pre- and post-intervention essays of both experimental and control groups using Erduran et al. (2004) analytical framework for assessing quality of argumentation, which is based on Toulmin's (1958) Argumentation Pattern. Level 1 argumentation, the most basic level of argumentation, consists of arguments that are a simple claim versus a counter-claim or a claim versus a claim. The first example in Fig. 2 shows an excerpt of a student's work that makes it an example of Level 1 argumentation. All examples are excerpts from uncorrected student work.

Simon	Was life for young people in Singapore better in the past than it is today?
	(Topic sentence) - Life for young people in Singapore was better in the past than it is today. (Supporting details) - There was much lesser competition in the past as compared to now. Young people had carefree lives and they could do whatever they wanted. Parents were more relaxed with their children's academic and professional achievements as the bench mark for success was much lower and people were generally less mercenary as they are today. In contrast, things are much more complicated and competitive now. Life isn't what it used to be. Pushed by the economic success of many people, parents now have very high expectations of their children, which inevitably create lots of stress to the children in both their studies and working life. (Evaluation)- As the world is changing and technology is advancing at such a fast pace, it would be normal for the demand of humans' ability to increase with time to improve the world, and make it a better place. As a result of this, life if getting harder and harder as time goes by, thus, life was better back in the past.
Matthew	The idea that youth led carefree lives and could do whatever they wanted isn't exactly correct. Contrary to what you may think, not all youths of the past lived easy lives. Parents were a lot more demanding in terms of them contributing to the family with them leaving school much earlier and working so much harder. But I do agree that there are values in the past worth holding on to in today's world. However, we shouldn't look back and wish we lived in the past. We should instead acknowledge the past, embrace the present, and look forward to the future, however stressful life might be.
Tilly	Was life for young people in Singapore better in the past than it is today? Topic sentence - Another aspect in favour of the lives of youths today is the plethora of opportunities that come across for them in terms of education and lifestyle. Supporting details - With rapid advancements in technology that had led the world to shrinking considerably, long gone are the days of a youth in pursue of passion and a good education bounded by geographical constraints. Industries are ever-changing and expanding, hence introducing even more job opportunities for youths today in search for a potential career. The world is an oyster for a student in search of higher education, for the array of accessible institutions all over the globe is greatly overwhelming. Evaluation - This shows that young people today definitely have a wider window to achieve their life goals as the world morphs into a single landscape of opportunity.
Matthew	I agree with the fact that technology has made life for young people better in the past, however i think it may be better to categorize the paragraph under "Technology", followed by using education and lifestyle as an example to backup and support why the improvement in technology affects youths' lives and has made it better. But I still would like to think that this is a well written argument. :)

Fig. 1. Excerpt of online discussion on *Schoology*

Simon	I agree with what you said about how the world is changing and expanding. Your sentence structure is unique and way better than mine, and good job on the use of good vocabularies.

Fig. 1. (*Continued*)

Level 2 argumentation has arguments consisting of a claim with either data, warrants, or backings but do not contain any rebuttals. Level 3 argumentation has arguments with a series of claims or counter-claims with either data, warrants, or backings with occasional weak rebuttal. Level 4 argumentation shows arguments with a claim with a clearly identifiable rebuttal (see Fig. 3 for an example of a Level 4 argumentation student essay). Such an argument in this level may have several claims and counter-claims. Level 5 argumentation, the highest possible level that students could achieve, displays an extended argument with more than one rebuttal. Figure 2 shows an example of a student who displayed Level 4 argumentation in his essay.

The authors also assessed the essays according to the content rubrics of the Cambridge A-level examinations for General Paper (Cambridge International Examinations 2012). The authors gave a mark range of 0 to 6 marks for essays showing inadequate content with little substance and very limited illustration. A mark range of 7 to 12 was awarded to essays exhibiting vague ideas, unsubstantiated statements, factual inaccuracy and insufficient focus on the topic. For essays where the more obvious points were mentioned but not adequately developed and where there was some digression and where there was a tendency for the student to generalize rather than discuss in detail, 13 to 15 marks were given to the essay. For the following three bands, a passing mark was given. Sixteen to 19 marks were given to essays that were competent with major points adequately developed, supported by a reasonable range of examples and that were reasonably structured. For essays that were totally relevant, well focused, with major points well developed and supported by a good range of examples and that are logical and effectively structured, with systematic discussion, 20 to 25 points were given. For top-notch essays that displayed a very good and comprehensive knowledge of the topic, 26 to 30 marks were given. These essays displayed comprehensive coverage with totally relevant material with thoughtful and enlightening illustration, using both local and international examples. The essays were also well structured showing sensitivity and maturity of the student who engaged in a coherent and engaging discussion of the topic.

The second author graded all of the essays while the first author graded 29 % of all the essays. Both had graduate degrees and had taught essay writing to high school students for more than ten years. The percentages of exact and adjacent agreement for argumentation and content scores were 100 % and 95 %, respectively.

To determine whether there were differences in content scores and argumentation levels, based on Toulmin's (1958) argumentation model, of students' pre- and post-interventions essays, a Welch test was performed. The authors conducted a content analysis of the student and teacher interviews and used the data to discuss the findings of this study.

Topic: The media is solely responsible for the breakdown of the family today. Do you agree?	
Family, a basic unit of society, nowaday (sic) is not stable but can be broken up every easily. Breakdown of family is becoming very prevalent since few decades ago worldwide. For instance, there is generally increasing trend in number of total divorces and annulments in Singapore since 1970. There are several reasons besides the media, for this phenomenon to occur. An economic factor such as poverty and a social factor such as gambling also contribute to the breakdown of the family today. Such factors act as a hindrance and an obstacle for relationship among family members to be strengthened. Hence, I do not agree with the statement as I believe that the media is not solely responsible for the breakdown of the family today, but partially responsible for it.	
The media is responsible for the breakdown of the family today. It can isolate the children in their rooms and lead them to be unwilling to communicate with their parents as they would rather choose to spend their time being engaged with social media and trends than with their parents, who are from different generation with their children. Moreover, with smartphones, youth can access to their social network accounts such as Twitter and Facebook and other social media platforms. With such an easy access to those accounts thanks to advancement in technology, it became ordinary for children to check their phones than to interact with their family members during the meal time. With the lack of communication, understanding and compromise, the family would be prone to face quarrels, conflicts and fights frequently due to misunderstanding, and disconnection, which would eventually result into family breakdown.	Claim without supporting evidence
In addition, poverty is another factor for the breakdown of the family today. Due to unemployment, there would be no breadwinner for a family who can support and provide their needs. With an unstable and uncertain income, family tend to be easily stressed, tense and very pressurized. Due to poverty, family members would have less opportunities to spend their time together and to communicate effectively. This would mean that it is easier for family to be angsty (sic) and disconnected. With poverty, it is impossible for parents to provide financial support to their children such as school fee, and tuition fee, and to provide themselves with basic necessities. This would cause a strain in family relationship that they would find 'giving up' is the better method for themselves as then they only need to take care of themselves only. Therefore, poverty is responsible for the breakdown of the family today.	Claim without supporting evidence

Fig. 2. Example of Level 1 argumentation

3 Findings

Students in the experimental group showed higher changes in argumentation skills compared to students in the control group (see Table 1). The mean argumentation scores for the pre-intervention essays were 1.9 and 1.2 for the experimental and control groups, respectively, and increased to 2.8 and 1.3 for the post-intervention essays. The change in argumentation scores was significantly higher for the experimental group ($M = 1.18$, 95 % CI [.52, 1.84]) than the control group ($M = .20$, 95 % CI [–.09, .49], $F(1,14.44) = 9.05$, $p = .009$).

In the same vein, the mean content score of the experimental group increased from 12.2 to 13.5 whereas the increase was less with the control group with the mean content score increasing from 11.2 to 11.6. The change in content score was also significantly higher for the experimental group ($M = 1.55$, 95 % CI [.73, 2.36]) compared to the control group ($M = .35$, 95 % CI [–.03, .73], $F(1, 15.06) = 8.56$, $p = .010$). The effect sizes for changes in content and argumentation scores were .27 and .29, respectively.

Analysis of student and teacher interviews concerning the use of Web 2.0 and mobile technologies to help them develop argumentative skills were mixed. Some students felt that it was distracting because they tended to veer into social media sites and preferred to use them in the classroom, while others felt that *Schoology* provided a great platform for them to develop argumentative skills as peer feedback gave them multiple perspectives.

> Like sometimes when you give biased views, they will pinpoint out. Sometimes when you talk about it, you don't really that is a bit biased or one-sided. Then they will tell me, show me the other side. Like they will argue about the other side as well. Then I will get to know, like both sides. Then I can see.

The online experience also developed a community of learners, and provided an interesting and interactive experience:

> It's sort of like, I would put it as Facebook but with educational purposes because what it does is that it creates a social group, a community for students to come and share their ideas and articles that are interesting. It makes it interesting to learn, rather than the old-fashioned way of studying notes and reading like newspapers and stuff. It's a bit more interesting because students can get together and discuss and it doesn't necessarily have to be in the classroom, because now they can do it on an online platform, at home, in front of a computer or on the cellphone. So it's a rather interesting and interactive learning experience and it helps, I suppose.

The teaching presence is important as the teacher has a key role in sustaining students' interest in online discussion as well as ensuring that the discussion is constructive and develops students; argumentative skills. One student commented:

> I think it does because what the teacher does is that she encourages us to argue with each other and pose constructive statements and arguments on it to develop our skills in GP (General Paper) like talk with each other, communicate properly and understand arguments and interesting articles. So I think it does help quite significantly in our ability to create constructive arguments and statements.

The teacher commented that students were more engaged on the online platform and that they responded to each other's arguments as well as providing different perspectives:

Topic: Politics has no place in the lives of the young. Do you agree with this statement?	
In the political chaos of post World War II, more and more civil wars are ignited as young people demand greater rights and freedoms, yet not all youths in the world are embroiled in political conflict, or even involved in politics at all. Thus there is the need to address the scope of the above statement (ie in which places do politics not have a place in the lives of the young, and in which areas do youths are politically active) and the reasons for which this is so, as well as whether politics should have a place in the lives of the young, and to what extent.	
The politics seem to play an almost non-existent role in the lives of the youth in countries with authoritarian states, such as Singapore and China. These states have effective single party systems, in which opposition parties have never overturned the domination of the ruling party.	Claim
One reason for this could be that people in these authoritarian states often fear that reprisal from the state. In the past, opposition to the government was easily met with cruel methods of torture to silence dissenters. The young students in Tiananmen Square of 1989 who refused to heed their elders' worries, had the Chinese government crack down on them with tanks and assault rifles. That historical moment will serve forever as a reminder that in a system where a single power can decide what is acceptable and what is punishable, the peace that we take for granted is sustained only by our compliance to the authorities. Of course, things are better now, with safer outlets of political expression, but the mothers and fathers those youths and other youths today were aware of these horrors, and thus have tried to instill in their children the lesson that politics is best left alone.	Claim Evidence Rebuttal
Another reason could be that politics also appears to be irrelevant to youths, as the political workings and formation of policies are often unexplained to youths, or at most, covered very briefly in school (Social Studies in Singapore and "thoughts and politics class" in China). Politics is often presented as a distant and far away activity, because the effects of policies we learn about in secondary school are only applicable to us when we are working adults and have to bear the costs of living, which would be much letter. Thus, there is an apparent failure to care about politics past and present.	Claim Evidence

Fig. 3. Example of Level 4 argumentation

Furthermore, although the public's opinion of government decisions and policies are taken up into account, they do not make any significant change in these policies, only slight adjustments, as evident in the controversy of casinos in the Integrated Resorts (IRs), when widespread criticism and petitions against the opening of casinos did not hinder the opening of the IRs. In all hopelessness, it can be said that the people of authoritarian states are dead to the possibility that political activism could bring about any real change, which might be the most pertinent reason as to why there is an inherent apathy to politics in these areas. Youths, most of whom are unable to vote, see even less reason to even keep themselves updated with political matters, and politics hold no meaning for them in their busy self contained lives.	Claim Evidence
However, this seeming apathy can co-exist with actual political engagement. Young people use the Internet for various purposes, one of which being political. A recent survey by NTU showed that during the 2011 General Election, people aged between 21 and 34 were more actively involved in online politics, such as writing about the elections on blogs (28% of youths, 10% of total population) and sharing online content (20% of youths, 10% of total population). Chinese youths spread viral images on Weibo, China's equivalent of Twitter, broadcast the injustices of the system, which quickly translates to offline protests and marches. And in other corners of the globe, youths are interacting with politics in new and forceful ways.	Rebuttal Evidence

Fig. 3. (*Continued*)

Table 1. Comparison of pre- and post-intervention mean content and argumentation scores between experimental and control groups

Variable	*Pre-intervention*	*Post-intervention*	*Maximum possible score*
Content score			
Experimental	12.2 (1.8)	13.5 (2.3)	30
Control	11.2 (1.3)	11.6 (1.2)	30
Argumentation score			
Experimental	1.9 (.8)	2.8 (1.2)	5
Control	1.2 (.4)	1.3 (.6)	5

Note. The standard deviation is reported within the brackets.

At the beginning they weren't very sure, the parameters, the guideline, so like you can imagine there needed to be certain rubrics even how to give feedback and then I had to post these things up and they tried, they became more structured rather than trying to be funny doing it like Facebook style. So once it was more structured, then they were forced to respond to each other's comments and not just to generate their own comments. It became quite good because they were more engaged and they were forced to weigh out the pros and cons of what they were talking about and to bring out other perspectives as well.

The teacher commented that students in the experimental group participated more on the online platform compared to when they were in the classroom:

> Mmm...only from an aspect whereby I saw that they were able to do more than what I had seen in class. It changed my interaction in the sense that I believed in them more and I saw that what I was getting in class is really not their full potential.

The teacher also reported the importance of the teacher's role in the implementation of an online discussion so that students could take part in discussions regularly, not just in the classroom but outside the classroom. She remarked that she had to show students how to give feedback before setting them the task of giving feedback:

> As I mentioned before, even before I came to be with this project, I was already using *Schoology* and I already saw it as something I wanted to use because in JC (junior college) sometimes you see them twice a week and what they need to do, somehow GP (General Paper) always gets sidelined you know, than Physics or Math. It gets very frustrating when they think you can't study GP and so I wanted it to be a platform to force them to be part of their everyday revision, every day. So I guess it was good experimental field to figure out what were the best ways to implement it and what are some things to be mindful of, for example giving feedback and how sometimes I can't just tell them, you go into *Schoology* and you just do. You have to show them and model a bit more before I set them certain tasks.

In addition, the teacher reported that the students' content had improved as well as their argumentation:

> I could see slight improvement in the writing of the essays. I didn't have strict tools to assess but I could see the writing becoming better. There was more content. There was slightly more structure, more reasoning in the essay and also the quality of the comments they were putting in and also the perspectives they were beginning to look at, rather than initially everything was very basic and rudimentary.

4 Discussion and Conclusion

This study provides support for the hypothesis that having students use Web 2.0 and mobile technologies to generate and critique arguments is positively related to the quality of their argumentative skills and of the content of their essays. The treatment has a statistically significant positive association with Grade 11 students' content essay scores and argumentative levels.

As reported in the student interviews, fellow students provided the cognitive support by offering multiple perspectives and by critiquing their peers' arguments. The teaching presence described in the Community of Inquiry model is particularly important in this study as the teacher had to design the online experience of her students, facilitate student discussion, give appropriate feedback and sustain students' interest in the discussion. Students also reported feeling a social presence as there was a community of learners who came together to share online their perspectives on different issues. The three elements of teaching, social, and cognitive presence contributed to students having a meaningful experience of learning how to express their opinions, giving evidence to support them and evaluating the evidence. All these resulted in students achieving better scores on content and argumentation.

There are several limitations to this investigation. One is related to one of the common issues with classroom-based research: the lack of random assignment to experimental or control groups, which could have led to non-equivalent groups. Another is the small sample size.

The implications for instructional practice that emerge from this investigation are the following. First, when teachers make use of Web 2.0 technologies on mobile devices to improve students' argumentation skills, they can capitalize on informal learning that comes closer to the daily digital experiences of their students. High school students should be actively involved in posting and critiquing arguments online on a regular basis outside the classroom. This will help bridge the gap between formal and informal learning opportunities. Second, to help students engage in written discourse practices found in argumentative essays, teachers can teach students the necessary linguistic structures that they need to express their arguments and to critique their peers' arguments on the online platform.

Acknowledgements. This research was made possible by a grant to the authors from the ELIS Research Fund administered by the English Language Institute of Singapore (Grant ERF-2014-02-SD).

References

Arslan, R.S., Sahin-Kizik, A.: How can the use of blog software facilitate the writing process of English language learners? Comput. Assist. Lang. Learn. **23**(3), 183–197 (2010)

Cambridge International Examinations Mark scheme for the October/November 2012 series (2012). http://www.cie.org.uk/images/155164-november-2012-mark-scheme-12.pdf

Chandrasegaran, A., Kong, C.K.M.: Stance-taking and stance-support in students' online forum discussion. Linguist. Educ. **17**(4), 374–390 (2006)

Cochrane, T.D.: Critical success factors for transforming pedagogy with mobile 2.0. Br. J. Educ. Technol. **45**(1), 65–82 (2014)

Cresswell, J.W., Plano Clark, V.L.: Designing and Conducting Mixed Methods Research, 2nd edn. Sage, Thousand Oaks (2011)

Erduran, S., Simon, J., Osborne, J.: Tapping into argumentation: developments in the application of Toulmin's argument pattern for studying science discourse. Sci. Educ. **88**(6), 915–933 (2004)

Garrison, D.R., Anderson, T., Archer, W.: Critical inquiry in a text-based environment: Computer conferencing in higher education. Internet High. Educ. **2**(2–3), 87–105 (2000)

Garrison, D.R., Kanuka, H.: Blended learning: uncovering its transformative potential in higher education. Internet High. Educ. **7**, 95–105 (2004)

Hew, F.H., Cheung, W.S.: Use of Web 2.0 technologies in K-12 and higher education: the search for evidence-based practice. Educ. Res. Rev. **9**, 47–64 (2013)

Hsu, H.-Y., Wang, S.: The impact of using blogs on college students' reading comprehension and learning motivation. Lit. Res. Inst. **50**, 68–88 (2010)

Infocomm Development Authority of Singapore. Annual survey on infocomm usage in households and by individuals for 2013. At Infocomm Development Authority of Singapore website (2013). http://www.ida.gov.sg/~/media/Files/Infocomm%20Landscape/Facts%20and%20Figures/SurveyReport/2013/2013HHmgt.pdf. Accessed 1 July 2015

Jonassen, D.H., Kim, B.: Arguing to learn and learning to argue: design justifications and guidelines. Educ. Technol. Res. Dev. **58**(4), 439–457 (2010)

Jonassen, D.H., Peck, L., Wilson, B.G.: Learning with Technology: A Constructivist Perspective. Merrill, Upper Saddle River (1999)

Kuhn, D.: The Skills of Argument. Cambridge University Press, Cambridge (1991)

Means, M.L., Voss, J.F.: Who reasons well? Two studies of informal reasoning among children of different grade, ability, and knowledge levels. Cognit. Instr. **14**, 139–178 (1996)

Neumann, D.L., Hood, M.: The effects of using a wiki on student engagement and learning of report writing skills in a university statistics course. Australas. J. Educ. Technol. **25**(3), 382–398 (2009)

Pae, J.-K.: Wiki-based English writing: Its effect on English writing proficiency and anxiety and Korean learners' perceptions. Multimed. Assist. Lang. Learn. **10**(1), 81–105 (2007)

Reznitskya, A., Anderson, R.C., McNurlin, B., Nguyen-Jahiel, K., Archodidou, A., Kim, S.Y.: Influence of oral discussion on written argumentation. Discourse Process. **32**(2–3), 155–175 (2001)

Rick, J,, Guzdial, M., Carroll, K., Holloway-Attaway, L., Walker, B.: Collaborative learning at low cost: coWeb use in english composition. In: Proceedings of Computer Support for Collaborative Learning Conference, pp. 435–442, Boulder (2002)

Smartphone penetration in Singapore the highest globally: Survey. At Today website, 11 February 2015. http://www.todayonline.com/singapore/smartphone-penetration-singapore-highest-globally-survey. Accessed 1 July 2015

Thomson, H.: Wikis, blogs and web 2.0 technology. At University of Melbourne website (2008). http://www.unimelb.edu.au/copyright/information/guides/wikisblogsweb2blue.pdf. Accessed 14 February 2014

Toulmin, S.: The Uses of Argument. Cambridge University Press, Cambridge (1958)

Wichadee, S.: Using wikis to develop summary writing abilities of students in an EFL class. J. Coll. Teach. Learn. **7**(12), 5–10 (2010)

Wong, R.M.F., Hew, K.F.: The impact of blogging and scaffolding on primary school pupils' narrative writing: a case study. Int. J. Web based Learn. Teach. Technol. **5**(2), 1–17 (2010)

Journey of Self-determination: Succeeding Through Mobile Phones

Gloria Thupayagale-Tshweneagae(✉) and Sambulelwe Sibanda

Department of Health Studies, University of South Africa,
P. O Box 392, Pretoria, South Africa
{tshweg, sibans1}@unisa.ac.za

Abstract. Mobile phone use by small businesses and informal traders in Africa has been celebrated as both transformational and revolutionary. However this revolution is slowly extending to other sectors most notably the open distance learning (ODL) which is not tailored for face to face communication. As such mobile phones generate new viable and innovative ways for postgraduate student supervision. However, the use of mobile phones is not without its challenges testing the supervisor and supervisee's knowledge, skill, attitude and in general the operative culture of supervision in higher education. The aim of this study was to unveil the challenges faced by postgraduate students and the novelty brought about by use of mobile phones in supervision. The study was conducted as a case study which profiled a doctoral student living in a remote area susceptible to frequent electricity cuts in Southern Africa. The Interaction Equivalency Theorem (IET) served as a base for the study. The device used by this student was just a basic mobile phone which facilitated just voice calls and short message (SMS) exchange only. Data was collected through the student's personal accounts and interviews with triangulation achieved through the reports of the supervisor. The findings of the study showed that student focus and self-determination in combination with mobile phone use can breed success to remote postgraduate supervision.

Keywords: Case study · Mobile phones · Mobile learning · Postgraduate students · Southern Africa · Supervision

1 Introduction

Mobile devices have evolved from basic cell phones with short message service (SMS) and voice calls to the sophisticated 'smart' devices with enhanced functionality that are currently being used. The 'smart' devices have evolved in line with wireless technology to make them more appealing to people as they are portable compared to fixed personal computers (El-Hussein and Cronje 2010). Whilst different mobile devices are currently used, the mobile phone remains the widely used and popular device. There are an estimated 1.5 billion mobile phones in the world and this is testimony to the evolution of the mobile phone from being an elitist device of the middle and upper class to being an important communication tool for people of all walks of life (Lącohée et al. 2003). Mobile phones have evolved from just being a communication tool to being a basic requirement to keep up with the demands of

T.H. Brown and H.J. van der Merwe (Eds.): mLearn 2015, CCIS 560, pp. 143–155, 2015.
DOI: 10.1007/978-3-319-25684-9_11

everyday for most people (Ng'ambi et al. 2012). The wide use of mobile phones and the advancements in functionality have made mobile phones practical not only as a communication tool but also relevant for on-demand information sharing, training and learning (Luisito 2008).

One mobile phone functionality, the short message service (SMS) which allows the exchange of texts is widely used and popular outside of academia and educators just have to import and adapt this tool to suit (Lominé and Buckhingham 2009). The popularity of SMS amongst students provides an innovative opportunity in teaching and learning (Ng'ambi et al. 2012). A survey of American universities found that text messaging (SMS) and emailing were the two commonly used functions on smart phones among college students and the psychology behind this was the perception that voice calls were intrusive and did not provide freedom in terms of response (Turkle 2011). The incorporation of mobile phones in education and learning led to the evolution of this new paradigm termed mobile learning (Muyinda et al. 2007).

Though different definitions exist for mobile learning (m-learning), the essence across the spectrum is undoubtedly the same and converges towards "the use of small and portable devices to facilitate mobile learning". Mobile learning is a vital element of distance education as it facilitates constant communication with the students. The contemporary uptake of M-learning extends back to the invention of the personal digital assistants (PDA) in the 1970s over 30 years ago. This technology and innovative way of learning and teaching is here to stay and enjoys great success stories of m-learning in higher education. The main focus of M-learning is to bridge the shortcomings of conventional E-learning and facilitate learners receiving and updating data without location specificity constraints (Nyiri 2002; Ismail et al. 2010). Many universities (e.g. University of Wolverhampton in UK) have previously published case studies on the successful use of bulk SMS to enhance student support, inclusion and retention (Riordan and Traxter 2005). Other UK teachers in higher education have successfully made use of SMS in various ways such as prompt for course requirements, polling classes, timetable reminders and examination date reminders among others (Ferry 2008). Mobile learning projects in South Africa have also been successfully used to improve the teaching system especially teaching biology subjects (UNESCO 2012). However, El-Hussein and Cronje (2010) assert that the mobility of learners is linked to the mobility of both the technology and learners. In a way the existence of a mobile device alone is not enough as such Attewell and Savill-Smith (2005) define m-learning as "learning using wireless devices that can be used whenever the learner's device can receive unbroken transmission signals". Therefore the successful implementation of m-learning in any institution is reliant on other external factors not just the availability of teaching material. The information sent to the student has to be received in its intended form and this process is dependent on internet connectivity, poor infrastructure and other factors such as electricity availability especially in developing regions. These represent political and socio-economic underpinnings to the success of m-learning in some regions. M-learning as an educational tool opens up the mind to the possibilities of radically new paradigms which enables people to abandon the constraints of habitual ways of thinking, learning and communicating (El-Hussein and Cronje 2010).

Background. M-learning is also on the rise in developing countries in some developing countries. The rapid growth of access to mobile phones in Africa and Middle East regions provides a conduit for improving teaching and learning which translates into national educational systems transformation (UNESCO 2012). The University of South Africa is a distance education institution and like all distance education institutes is mandated to help students by minimising isolation, minimising dropout rates and also improving the student experience (Louw 2005). On average it takes UNISA students 9 years to complete their degree programmes and only about 15 % persevere to the end (Louw 2005). The Department of Health at UNISA enrols students from across South Africa as well as many other countries on its undergraduate, postgraduate and research programmes. Most of these students are employed in their respective provinces (in South Africa) and countries; as such regular attendance of seminars and workshops on campus and at regional centres is logistically difficult. With these challenges, mobile learning more so communication with students using SMS and email becomes practical in effective support of the students. However, such support is dependent on the availability of fully functional mobile infrastructure in the respective countries. Many students from Zimbabwe are enrolled at UNISA, and the student featured in this case study is Zimbabwean. Zimbabwe is a developing country with a reported 97 % of people in both rural and urban areas owning a mobile phone (Nyarai et al. 2011). However, most rural centres in Zimbabwe do not have internet connectivity nor are they electrified. SMS has thus been widely explored as a communication tool for these students to also enable them to interact with other students. SMS technology is one of the most stable technologies which address the communication needs of students (So 2009). (Huang et al. 2009) state that mobile learning applications can facilitate students learning contents conveniently and also interacting with others collaboratively anytime anywhere. Despite mobile phones being widely available in Zimbabwe their effective use in distance education is hampered by regular electricity cuts, poor communications infrastructure and poor internet connectivity (Kabweza 2013). The phones that some people use might just have basic functionality (obsolete in other countries) without 'smart' features which are the standard in some m-learning platforms.Although not purposively arranged this paper gives a case study of a doctoral student from Zimbabwe who studied for her doctoral studies through distance learning relying only on short messaging service (SMS) and occasional voice calls from their supervisor on their basic mobile phone. This paper is perhaps an appraisal of the continued effectiveness of basic m-learning infrastructure in contemporary higher education settings which now largely rely on 'smart' mobile devices.

Conceptual Framework. The Interaction Equivalency Theorem (IET) by Anderson (2003a) served as a basis for this study. The Anderson Interaction Equivalency theory is an advancement of three part model of interaction postulated by Moore (1989) believed to be the first model to define the concept of interaction within distance education systematically. The Anderson Interaction Equivalency Theorem sought to clarify the different economies in distance education typified in independent-oriented and interactive-oriented learning strategies and activities. Anderson (2003a) stresses the importance of cost and sustainability as well as pedagogical value in the selection of appropriate mixes of interaction. The model typology is summarised in Fig. 1.

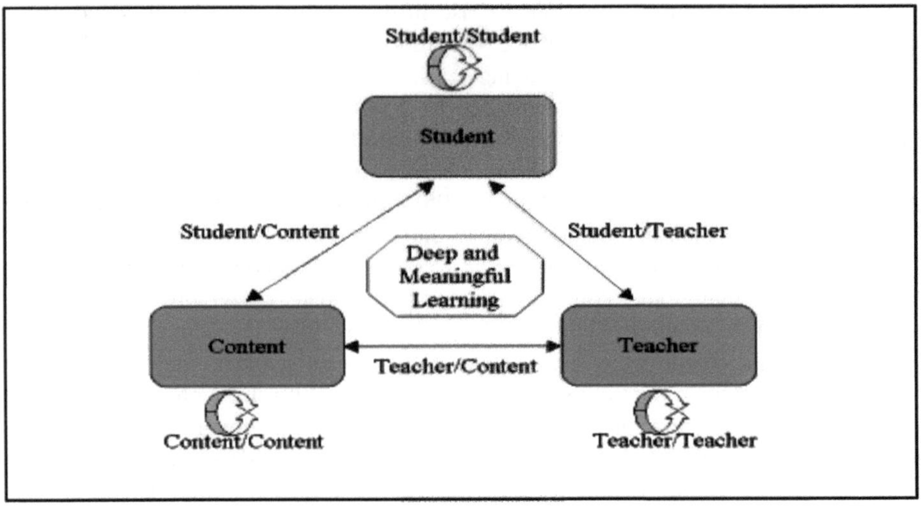

Fig. 1. The interaction typology (Garrison and Anderson, 2003)

The Anderson IET proposes that deep and meaningful formal learning is supported if one of the three forms of interaction (student-teacher; student-student; student-content) is at a high level. The model further postulates that the other two levels can be eliminated or offered at minimal level without compromising the educational experience. Anderson (2003a) further proposed that high levels of more than one of these interaction modes were likely to provide a more satisfying educational experience with less cost and time effectiveness compared to other less interactive sequences.

Aim of the Study. The aim of this study was to unveil the challenges faced by distance education postgraduate students and the novelty brought about by use of mobile phones in supervision in a developing country.

Participants. The doctoral supervisor, who is the first author of this article, was enthralled and amazed by how one individual could be so determined and overcome different impediments to complete her studies by use of a basic mobile phone. The supervisee was contacted and the intention to document their experience as a case presentation was explained. The supervisee gave express consent to taking part in the case study.

Ethical Considerations. Study approval was sought and granted by the Higher Degrees Committee of the Department of Health Studies, University of South Africa (UNISA). Written consent and permission was also sought from the supervisee and was granted. Participants were made aware of the intention to tape record the interviews. The right to withdraw their participation at any time was also made clear so was the right to request for the tape recorder to be switched off in case any information was deemed sensitive or uncomfortable. The two participants in this case study were free to give an uninterrupted account.

2 Methods

Case Study Design. Case studies are expected to unravel situations or a situation that gives them a particular relevance the qualitative case study approach to research facilitates exploration of a phenomenon within its context using a variety of data sources. A qualitative case study approach was used in this study to facilitate exploration of the journey of self-determination by the doctoral student. A descriptive approach to case study was selected as it allows for triangulation of many sources considered appropriate for in-depth-understanding of the phenomenon. According to Yin (2003), the descriptive case study is feasible as it allows both a confirmation and an extraction of new information concerning a specific topic of research. The decision to involve both the supervisor and the student allowed for the integration of experiences and perceptions and develop a wholesome picture of the subject of concern.

Data Collection. Data collection was achieved through telephonic interviews and summary accounts which were confirmed through the supervisors' departmental records. Face to face interview was conducted with the doctoral supervisor to augment the data. The student and supervisor were interviewed separately by the second author who explored similar themes from the perspective of each individual. Following the tenets of constant comparison each interview was analysed prior to any subsequent interviews. Emergent themes from summary accounts and the in-depth interviews were developed in subsequent interviews. The leading questions to both the supervisor and the supervisee were:

(i) Can you narrate to me what you remember about this doctorate journey from beginning to the end?
(ii) What were stand out challenges in this distance learning supervision journey?
(iii) How were these challenges overcome?
(iv) What lessons can be learnt from this case study?

The telephonic interviews with the supervisee and the face to face interviews with the supervisor were all audio-recorded with their permission. All interviews were conducted in English and the written reports were also in English.

Data Analysis. The audio recordings from the interviews were transcribed verbatim by the second author shortly after the interviews. Both authors were involved in the data verification process to ensure accuracy and also avoid researcher bias. Qualitative content analysis was used to analyse the transcribed data and both authors were involved in the process.

3 Findings

Demographics. Both the supervisor and supervisee were females aged above 50 years. The supervisee was single with children and the supervisor was married. The supervisee was employed in a remote and underdeveloped area of Zimbabwe a country in Southern Africa.

Supervisor and Supervisee Contexts. Further to the requests to give a summary account of the whole supervision journey without any promptings or guiding questions to avoid researcher bias, the supervisee and supervisor's accounts are summarised below.

Supervisor's Context

> *"In March 2011 I was assigned to supervise a doctoral student from a remote one area in Zimbabwe. At the beginning of supervision it became apparent to me the student was unable to access any of the emails that were being sent. It was at the point when I called the student that I discovered there was no internet where they were living and working. It became clear that her outdated mobile phone (Nokia 2110) was to be the only source of communication for the next three years. As a supervisor this meant that I had to adjust and adapt my supervision style to suit this student. Around the project proposal stage the student would send weekly SMS messages to me detailing the work they had done and this frequency was increased to maybe three times a week. When the student sent the short messages to me, I responded via SMS or if there urgent issue then I used voice to voice calls to give feedback. Written work posted from Zimbabwe took at least a week to reach the supervisor as the student relied on an infrequent and often unreliable postal service. It was on the odd occasion that the student would send written work by email as attachments. The frequency of such was very low as the student said they had to travel far to get to an internet café. At times even when they got to the internet café, they couldn't send the work due electricity outage which were frequent and could last for some weeks".*

Supervisee's Context

> *"I was at a point where I needed to better myself I registered and was offered a place at the distance learning university. I had this determination I could complete my studies within three years. However shortly after commencing my studies, I was transferred to a remote area which experienced frequent electricity blackouts. At this workstation, we had to rely on solar power which was not reliable at all. There was a point when I became so discouraged having to deal with all this and I remember at some point in time my son saying "mom you can still complete your studies but you need to focus, maybe have two cell phones". I managed to buy an additional second hand basic Nokia phones that just allowed for text messaging and voice to voice call as that was all I could afford. As a single mother of three children I was restricted financially and what I did was buy airtime for all my mobile phones at the end of the month for a total of US$30.00. The additional phone was exclusively allocated for my studies and the second was for my day to day work. When my supervisor sent me emails that went unanswered she then telephoned me. Initially when I explained my situation she was very pessimistic and thought it might be futile attempt to delay doing my work. With time she understood and began sending me text messages as well. When she called me, I would read sections of my work off to her and she would tell me where to correct and ask that I send the corrected work as soon as possible. If I was lucky and there was electricity I would do my work right away and then travel the following day to email the work at the business centre internet café. I would then wait a day or two for confirmation via text messaging that she had emailed back her feedback. This carried on for three years and there are times when I thought I would never complete my studies but thankfully I did."*

Close consideration and analysis of the supervisee and supervisor personal contexts and the follow up telephonic and face to face interviews revealed the following themes considered in the context of m-learning in open distance mobile learning; mobile device limitations, social and environmental factors and the convergent attributes and attitude of the learner and supervisor.

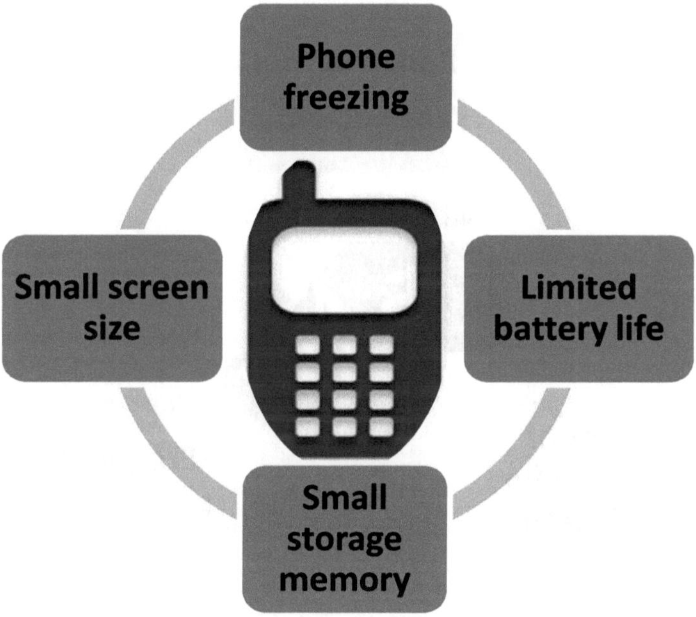

Fig. 2. Mobile device limitations

Mobile device limitations. A basic mobile phone (Nokia 3210) was being used by this student for communication. The functionality of this mobile phone was limited and as highlighted in the following extracts presented challenges to the learner. The numerous mobile phone challenges that are depicted in the extracts from the learner are summarised in Fig. 2.

> *"My phone had a small screen size so I had to send many segments of a single message which cost a lot. Even when I received SMS from the supervisor I had to read and delete them as the phone had limited storage"*

> *"At times I could not read messages as the phones froze and the small screen made it difficult to read accurately."*

> *"Because the electricity would go for many days, at times my phone had no battery so I could not receive any messages. Even if my supervisor tried to call they could not reach me, and this affected my progress. I wish I had a better phone"*

Socio-economic and environmental pressures Even when their phone was fully functional, there were additional pressures which were related to the remote location of this student as well as their socio-economic situation. These challenges meant that the student could not access mobile learning totally at times and also all. These economic challenges are presented in the following extracts and illustrated in Fig. 3.

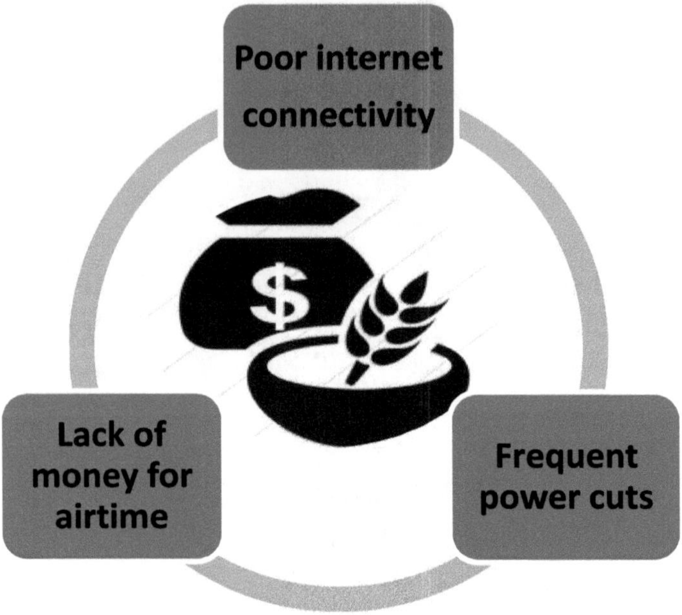

Fig. 3. Socioeconomic challenges to mobile communication

> *"Having no electricity for days and at times up to a week was difficult as during this period I could not use my phone. I could not go to the business centre as the shops there were also affected"*

> *"Sending multiple messages at a time was very expensive and with the little salary I am earning and taking care of my kids, it was difficult"*

> *"I also struggled to send the written work on time as I had to rely on the slow postal system. I could not afford to use DHL as it was expensive. This delayed my feedback and I was always working under pressure"*

Attributes of the Learner and Supervisor. Considering the personal contexts of the supervisor and the learner jointly showed that they both had to make deliberate and positive adjustments to make this relationship work. The students who was in a different setting to that of the supervisor had to make a deliberate effort to be positive and convince the supervisor to keep believing in them and assisting them.

> *"At some point I thought my supervisor was getting fed up with my excuses and explanations. I was afraid she might not want to continue with me"*

The supervisor made adjustments as well as they had to use unconventional means to stay connected with this student and also ensure that their situation did not disadvantage them at all in their studies. The two parties forged a good and rewarding working relationship as they appreciated the efforts of the other. The extracts below summarise this context.

"The supervision started off in difficulty but I began to enjoy it and appreciate the effort this student was making"– Supervisor

"Somehow my studies gave me more than I anticipated, they were socially appealing (my supervisor and I somehow became like friends, Saturday mornings I would expect a call from my supervisor"– Supervisee

"if my phone was engaged I will receive short message soon after and she would check on progress and convey instructions"- Supervisee

"The simplicity of sending SMS meant I did not have to learn new tricks and just allowed me to resort to something I used more often to reach out to my student"- Supervisor

4 Discussion

For m-learning to succeed and be effective there has to be mobility and the three components defined by Kynaslahti (2003) are convenience, expediency and immediacy. Consideration of the facts of this case study reveals that these components were seriously compromised and as such the success of mobile distance learning was seriously threatened. These learner mobility components were seriously affected by environmental as well as socio-economic factors. This position is endorsed by the proposed practical framework on three key areas that have to be factored in before SMS is used with learners (Lominé and Buckhingham 2009). As Fig. 4 shows, there has to be a consideration of the available technology as well as the cost complications to the learner and teacher as the sending and receiving messages bears a cost. In this case the student was in an underdeveloped area and they had financial limitations which hampered their flexible utilisation of mobile learning offered.

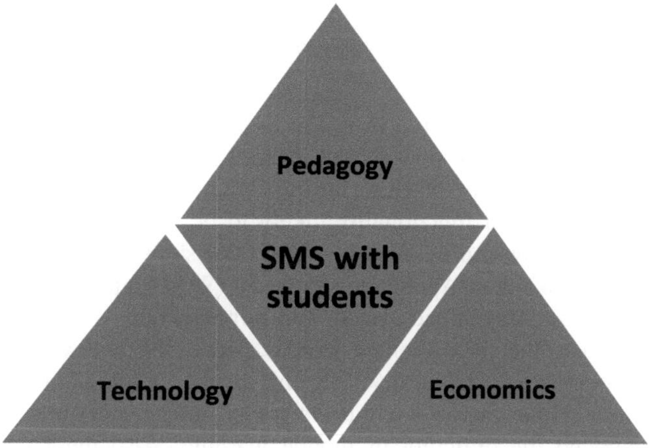

Fig. 4. P-E-T Framework for SMS use in m-learning (Lominé and Buckhingham 2009)

Ismail et al. (2010) state that M-learning allows students to learn free of location constraints but perhaps that disregards the fact that all the factors associated with M-learning have to line up and be functional. More so, this case study also highlights that the success of M-learning in higher education is not only dependent on the technological development of the mobile devices but in developing regions socio-economic and political factors are major determinants.

Whilst this case study perhaps exposed some of the frailties of m-learning in open distance education settings it nevertheless highlighted how the attitude and focus of the user can negate these shortcomings. This case study proves that the success and effectiveness of m-learning does not just depend on the availability of the device and the mobility of the learner but that there has to be a synergistic link in all components, mobile device, environmental factors and intended learning outcomes. An exploratory study of a mobile assessment system Wong et al. (2006) was presented schematically as shown in Fig. 5.

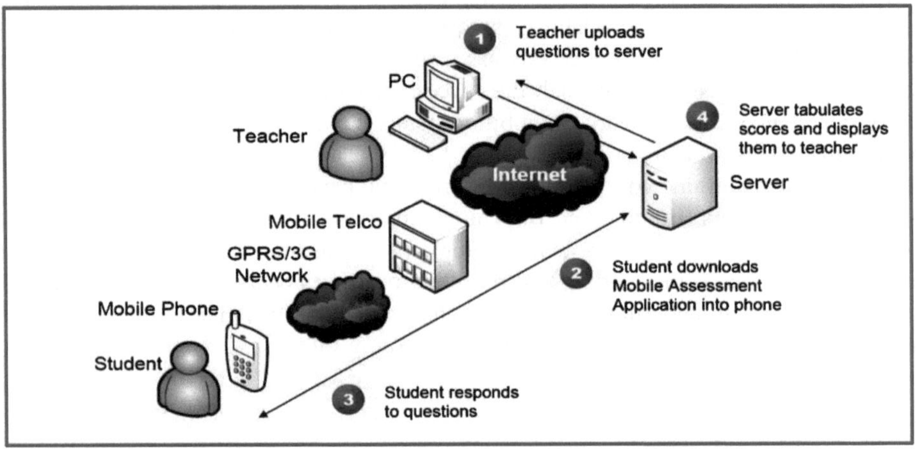

Fig. 5. Typical m-learning assessment pathways (Wong et al. 2006)

The illustration is perhaps borne from the fact that in Singapore where the study was based, 978 in 1000 people own mobile phones (Singapore Department of Statistics). This context assumes that developed infrastructure is in place and also the mobile devices used have enhanced functionality, likely to be 'smart devices'. A brief technical description of the system by Wong et al. (2006) shows that the technology they evaluated were SMS, wireless Application Protocol (WAP) and Java to Micro Edition (J2ME) typifying a well-developed system and infrastructure.

In the case study that is presented in this paper, the pathway can at best be described as antiquated as it relied on SMS only as the mobile phone in use was not internet compatible. Other factors such as electricity outage, storage size and constant freezing compounded the difficulty in mobile learning. Also there was reliance on internet cafes to send responses to the supervisor so the system was not entirely mobile and the student had no flexibility and that is driven by mobile learning.

In the case study there was over reliance on SMS as it was the only possibility with the handset that the learner had. The SMS were also used to alert the learner of emails that had been sent because the handset could not receive emails. The occasions voice calls that augmented the SMS cannot be considered entirely in the context of mobile learning they did not allow the learner to 'learn contents conveniently and interact collaboratively anytime and anywhere' according to (Huang et al. 2009) in his appraisal of mobile learning applications. As typified in this case study, the terms 'anytime and everywhere' are limited from being universally true due to connectivity as well as safety restrictions (Saccol et al. 2010).When m-learning shortcomings are discussed in the context of higher education settings, the focus tends to be on software development, speed of access and perhaps compatibility issues. However in some developing countries the problems are more or less centred on none existent or obsolete infrastructure as well as politically motivated factors such as underdevelopment of certain regions and the lack of basic resources.

Notwithstanding the combined challenges of the mobile phone functionality, socio-economic factors which hampered progress in this distance learning programme, there was overall success. The fact that this not so classic case of m-learning ended in success perhaps shows that other components are central to the success of m-learning more so in setting in developing countries. Different definitions mention learner freedom, mobility and convenience all which were constantly and frequently compromised in this case study. The attributes and attitude of the learner contributed immensely to their success despite relying on obsolete technology for their learning. The determination shown by the student of this case study is congruent with the assertion by Ryan and Deci (2000) that intrinsic motivation and thus higher quality learning, flourishes in contexts that satisfy human needs for competence, autonomy, and relatedness. The findings are resonant with the assertion by Anderson (2003a) that deep and meaningful learning can be supported without compromising the educational experience as long as at least one form of open distance learning interaction is maintained (Fig. 6).

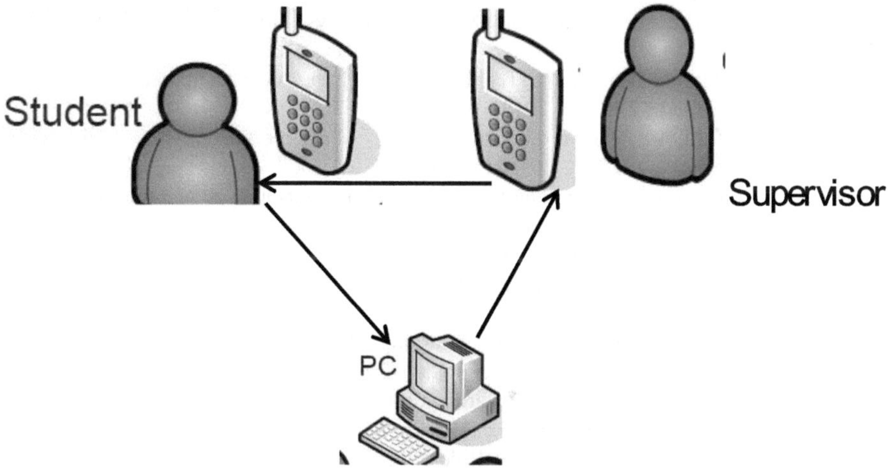

Fig. 6. Case study M-learning pathway schematic

5 Conclusion

It is unequivocal that the success of this open distance learning student was underpinned by their inherent determination and desire to achieve their objectives and succeed. The most basic of mobile devices can be successfully and effectively used to supervise open distance education learners provided necessary adjustments are made and the level of interaction between the student and the supervisor is maintained at the highest level possible. This case study further highlighted the need to develop a multi dimension approach to the improvement of m-learning by taking into cognisance the infrastructure capabilities in different regions of the world. Technological advancements in mobile device technology should be paralleled by infrastructure development in developing countries especially in the higher education setting for mobile learning to be practical.

References

Anderson, T.: Getting the right mix again: an updated and theoretical rationale for interaction. Int. Rev. Res. Open Distance Learn. **4**(2), 1–14 (2003)

Attewell, J., Savill-Smith, C.: Mobile Learning Anytime Everywhere. Learning and Skills Development Agency, London (2005)

Baxter, P., Jack, S.: Qualitative case study methodology: study design and implementation for novice researchers. Q. Report **13**(4), 544–559 (2008)

El-Hussein, M.O.M., Cronje, J.C.: Defining mobile learning in the higher education landscape. Educ. Technol. Soc. **13**(3), 12–21 (2010)

Ferry, B.: Using of mobile phones to augment teacher learning in environmental education. In: Proceedings of Ascilite on hello! Where are you in landscape educational technology? (2008)

Huang, Y.M., Jeng, Y.L., Huang, T.C.: An educational mobile blogging system for supporting collaborative learning. Educ. Technol. Soc. **12**(2), 163–175 (2009)

Ismail, I., Gunasegaran, T., Koh, P.P., Idrus, R.M.: Satisfaction of distance learners towards mobile learning in the Universiti Sains Malaysia. Malays. J. Educ. Technol. **10**(2), 47–54 (2010)

Kabweza, L.S.M.: Mobile Penetration. Techzim (2013). http://www.techzim.co.zw/tag/mobile-penetration/. Accessed 12 March 2013

Lacohée, H., Wakeford, N., Pearson, I.: A social history of the mobile telephone with a view of its future. BT Technol. J. **21**(3), 203–211 (2003)

Lominé L., Buckhingham C.: M-learning: texting (sms) as a teaching & learning tool in higher arts education. ELIA Teachers' Academy 2009, Sofia (2009)

Louw, W.: Taking the distance out of distance education through the means of m-learning. In: 4th World Conference on M-Learning - Cape Town, South Africa, 25–28 October 2005 (2005)

Luisito, C.H.: Enhancing Teaching and Learning through SMS mediated Lectures in Mathematics. New Era University, Quezon City (2008)

Muyinda, P.B., Mugisa, E., Lynch, K.: M-learning: the educational use of mobile communication devices. In: Migga, K.J., Muhirwe, J., Aisbett, J., Getao, K., Mbarika, V.W., Patel, D., Rodrigues, A.J. (eds.) Strengthening the Role of ICT in Development, pp. 290–301. Fountain Publishers, United Kingdom (2007)

Ng'ambi, D., Gachago, D., Ivala E., Bolzalek, V., Watters, K.: Emerging technologies in South African higher education institutions: towards a teaching and learning practice framework. In: 7th International Conference on e-Learning held at the Chinese University of Hong Kong, 21–22 June, 2012 (2012)

Nyiri, K. (2002) Towards a philosophy of m-learning. In: IEEE International Workshop on Wireless and Mobile Technologies in Education (WMTE 2002)

Ryan, R.M., Deci, E.L.: Self-determination theory and the facilitation of intrinsic motivation, social development, and well-being. Am. Psychol. **55**(1), 68–78 (2000)

Riordan, B., Traxter, J.: The use of targeted bulk SMS texting to enhance student support, inclusion and retention. In: IEEE International Workshop on Wireless and Mobile Technologies in Education, Tokushima, Japan (2005)

Saccol, A., Barbosa, J.L., Schlemmer, E., Rienhard, N.: Corporate m-learning: applications and challenges. In: Guy, R. (ed.) Mobile Learning: Pilot Projects and Initiatives. Information Science, California (2010)

Singapore Department of Statistics. http://www.singstat.gov.sg/publications/publications-and-papers/reference/yearbook-of-statistics-singapore

So, S.: The development of a SMS-based teaching and learning system. J. Educ. Technol. Dev. Exch. **2**(1), 113–124 (2009)

Tunjera, N., Mukabeta, T., Zivanai, J.: Increasing interaction by integrating short messaging services (Smss) into the Virtual Open and Distant Learning (VODL) teacher education programme: a case of Bindura University in Zimbabwe. Greener J. Educ. Res. **3**(4), 191–199 (2011)

Turkle, S.: Alone Together, pp. 187–209. Basic Books, Philadelphia (2011)

UNESCO (2012) Mobile learning for teachers in Africa and the Middle East: Exploring the potentials of mobile technologies to support teachers and improve practices (2012). http://unesdoc.unesco.org/images/0021/002163/216358e.pdf

Wong, C.C., Sellan, R., Lee, L.Y.: Assessment using Mobile Phones: An Exploratory study (2006). http://www.iaea.info/documents/paper_1162a2913.pdf

Yin, R.K.: Case Study Research: Design and Methods. Sage Publishing, Beverley Hills (2003)

Facilitating Knowledge Visualisation as Communication and Knowledge Transfer Mechanism in Postgraduate Learning

Judy van Biljon[1(✉)] and Karen Renaud[1,2]

[1] School of Computing, University of South Africa, Pretoria, South Africa
vbilija@unisa.ac.za
[2] School of Computing Science, University of Glasgow, Glasgow, Scotland, UK

Abstract. Advances in technology and subsequent access to inexpensive software have made visualisation, as a method of knowledge creation and transfer, more accessible. Visualisations have been used to support knowledge representation and transfer in teaching but the focus has primarily been on creating visualisations for learner consumption. The idea of students becoming active participants in producing visualisations, as part of knowledge creation and learning, has largely been overlooked.

The study reported here investigated the use of visualisation for summarising knowledge at postgraduate level. The student's need to *assimilate and organise* knowledge is an important part of their learning. We suggest that it would be useful for students to learn how to produce knowledge visualisations as part of this activity. The production is an act of knowledge creation, which can improve their comprehension of the research literature.

Producing visualisations is not necessarily straightforward and it is therefore advisable to scaffold the process. We propose a *faded-struts* learning process that gradually removes scaffolding as the learner masters the principles and becomes more adept. The contribution of this research is to present the idea of providing worked examples and faded examples to support postgraduate learning. This helps postgraduates to craft knowledge visualisations so that they can slowly become more proficient and independent. Due to the ubiquity of mobile devices we propose providing this support on these devices, incorporating their unique constraints and affordances in our learning process.

This is essentially a proof of concept paper, suggesting how the idea could be realised. Further work is necessary to test the idea with students and to extend the repertoire of mobile learning (m-learning) visualisation tasks.

Keywords: Knowledge visualisation · Knowledge transfer · Post graduate learning · Faded-Struts approach

1 Introduction

Critical factors for the successful adoption of m-learning include interactivity, coordination, negotiation and communication, organization of material and mobility. Mobility is central to the intersection of these factors, supporting dialectic relations and

T.H. Brown and H.J. van der Merwe (Eds.): mLearn 2015, CCIS 560, pp. 156–171, 2015.
DOI: 10.1007/978-3-319-25684-9_12

convergences between the contextual, semiotic, technological and pedagogical dimensions of m-learning (Petit and Santos 2014). This calls for a reflection on how teaching and learning content presentation can be optimized to exploit mobility in general, and the role of visualisation in particular, the focus of this paper.

Visualisations have a powerful capacity to improve inter-personal communication and interaction, but this can only be realized if the visualisation is appropriate and effective (Burkhard 2005). Our proposal is that postgraduates should include visualisations in their dissertations. There are two benefits of doing this. The first is that visualisations will improve the dissertation by transferring knowledge more effectively. The second is that the production of visualisation, in and of itself, can help students to conceptualise and comprehend the knowledge they are assimilating (Laseau 2000).

If visualisations are to mediate in the postgraduate context it is necessary to foster the nuanced understanding required to deploy visualisations appropriately and effectively. This is especially true in the mobile context where people need to steer clear of deployment and crafting risks (Bresciani and Eppler 2008). Providing support is particularly important in the m-learning environment with its unique constraints and affordances. Various authors have proposed information visualisation guidelines that could help but *knowledge* visualisation has received very little attention. The target group for this study is postgraduate students in an open distance-learning environment in South Africa.

Sharples et al. (2010) argue that the convergence of learning and mobile technologies allows people to learn in a life-long fashion, no longer constrained by classroom-based attendance. This applies particularly in this case since many of these students are employed full time and spend time traveling to work on public transport where the only computing devices available to support learning are mobile devices (smart phones and tablets). Being able to use mobile devices to facilitate the knowledge visualisation learning process can extend their learning time and opportunities.

Traxler (2009) reviews the state of play in m-learning, and reports on its use primarily in supporting children or undergraduate students. Wishart (2009) reports on the use of mobile technology to support teacher training. We argue that there is potential for postgraduates, too, to benefit from the availability and affordances of mobile devices in an m-learning context.

The nature of a postgraduate's "learning" is different from that of undergraduates in some very profound ways. According to James (1998), postgraduates have to demonstrate that they understand related research, can relate their own work to such research and can interact vigorously with the content. Crucially for the svisualisation context, they have to be able to show that they can organize principles and integrate ideas. This is usually achieved by writing about the work coherently, and presenting an argument that demonstrates understanding. There is another way to demonstrate this: by crafting a visualisation to demonstrate such understanding, engagement and ability to synthesize (Chen et al. 2009).

A side benefit might even be that an improved understanding emerges from this activity (Laseau, 2000). In Sect. 2 we establish the nature of data, information and knowledge, and visualisation thereof. We discuss learning styles and how learners can be supported in learning to visualise. Finally, we present the constraints of the mobile environment as a mechanism for supporting knowledge visualisation in m-learning. We then suggest the building blocks for knowledge visualisation m-learning. We propose a faded-struts learning process that moves from worked examples, to faded worked examples, to active production, supported by peers, in Sect. 3. Section 4 walks through an example of the proposed learning process. Section 5 concludes.

2 Background Literature

2.1 Knowledge, Information and Data Visualisation

When considering knowledge visualisation, we need to establish a shared understanding of the meaning of the terms data, *information* and *knowledge*. For the purpose of this paper data, information and knowledge are described as follows (Chen et al. 2009):

- *Data* - facts, concepts, or instructions suitable for interpretation or processing by humans or by software.
- *Information*– data with the associated meaning assigned by humans suitable for visualisation to encourage the revealing of patterns or insights into the data.
- *Knowledge*– information, together with understanding, awareness, or familiarity acquired through interpretation and application of information.

According to these definitions processed data becomes information and interpreted information becomes knowledge. Each level of processing adds bias due to the subjective selection of processing procedures. The only way to manage the accountability of the process is to state the assumptions and take cognisance of the constraints at each step of the process (Muller et al. 2012).

In the context of learning, visualisation is expected to lead to new insights. An individual's sense-making, the progression from data to gaining understanding and insight, is fundamental to knowledge acquisition and transfer. We therefore find it useful to revisit the differences between data, information and knowledge visualisations as illustrated by van Biljon and Renaud (2015) in Table 1.

Eppler and Burkhard (2007) structure the visualisation formats into seven main groups, namely: structured text/tables, mental (non-material) visualisation and visual storytelling, heuristic sketches, conceptual diagrams/concept maps, visual metaphors, knowledge maps, and graphic interactive environments. Taking cognisance of the variety of visualisation formats is important towards grasping the potential for knowledge creation, representation and transfer. The narrow perception, that visualisation encapsulates only the use of pictures and diagrams, is a limiting factor for its potential use and usefulness.

Table 1. Differences between data, knowledge and information visualisation (van Biljon and Renaud 2015)

Table 1: Differences between data, knowledge and information visualisation (van Biljon and Renaud, 2015)[38]			
	Data Visualisation	**Information Visualisation**	**Knowledge Visualisation**
Goal	Support Exploration of data using graphical metaphors	Support Exploration of Large Amounts of Data & Knowledge Creation	Ease Knowledge Transfer; Creation of New Knowledge
Benefit	Make data mining available to everyone, not just experts	Identification of patterns, exploration of large data sets	Augmenting knowledge transfer between individuals; communicating knowledge
Content	A large volume of data	Explicit data such as facts and	Experiences, insights, instructions,
	which needs to have meaning identified	numbers	assumptions
Answers Question	Where	What	Why, Who, How
Recipients	Data miners	Data Explorer, Pattern Spotter	Knowledge Workers
Influence	Data mining	Data analysis, Data exploration	Knowledge Transfer
Example	Pie chart representing of visualisation's distribution in a set of masters dissertations 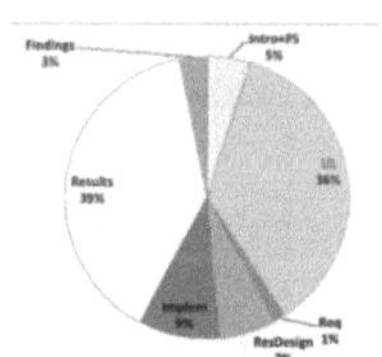	Depiction of an author's research areas to differentiate topics 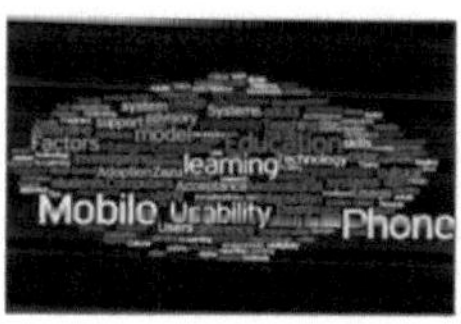	Representation of the relationship between data, information and knowledge. 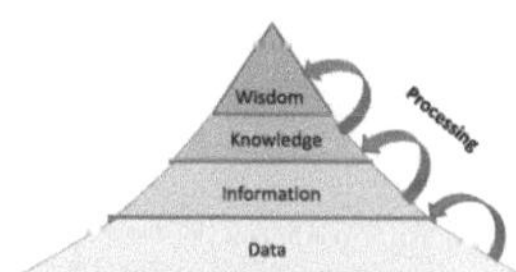

2.2 Learning Styles and Learning How to Visualize

Cognitive learning styles have been defined as "*the information processing habits of individual learners*" (Keefe, 1991). While individuals are different in their ways of seeking and processing information, cognitive styles serve as relatively stable indicators of how learners perceive and interpret information, and respond to learning environments (Wolfe & Johnson 1995). Learning styles have been categorised in terms of visual, kinaesthetic and aural modal preferences (Fleming 1995) and that may well impact the learning that will result from any activity. One study revealed that students' cognitive styles were not significantly correlated with their attitudes and preference for instructional delivery modes (Oh and Lim 2005). However, other factors, such as learners' attitudes, previous online learning experience and computer competency were indeed significantly correlated with students' learning outcomes and attitudes toward online instruction. A comprehensive discussion of learning styles is beyond the scope of this study. However, knowledge visualisation can be considered a complementary activity where some may benefit more than others but individual learning styles should not exclude any individual from benefitting.

Kirshner and Merriënboer (2008) describe learning in terms of the development of new schemata, a structured chunk of related knowledge (Robins et al. 2003) and the moving on to their establishment and maintenance. As these schemata become well established it becomes easy for the learner to match them to new situations. Before they are established the learner has to use valuable working memory to make sense of new situations and therefore becomes easily overwhelmed by too many new concepts (Cowan 2012). This suggests that the introduction of new material has to be managed very carefully not to overwhelm the learner. Visualisation, and the principles underlying visualisation, is no different; the limitations of mobile devices may even complicate the learning if not given due consideration. We therefore have to introduce new knowledge in such a way that learners can apply existing knowledge in a novel setting, acquiring new knowledge by building on existing knowledge (Al-Shuaily 2013). New material has to be introduced slowly and mindfully (Larkin 1989). Throwing a learner into the deep end by asking them to construct visualisations, without their having mentally constructed the required schemata, forces them into engaging in a trial and error process, and not really learning basic principles during the process. This is depicted in Fig. 1. We wish to provide enough scaffolding and support so that it is not necessary for the learner to go down the "trial and error" route in order to cope.

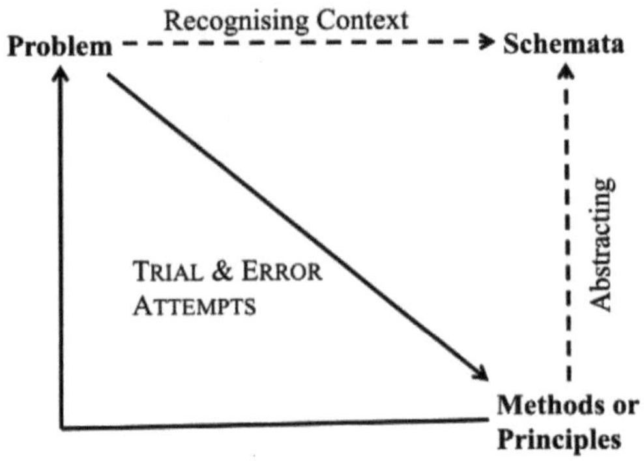

Fig. 1. Knowledge assimilation approach (Al-Shuaily 2013) (p.233)

How have people been supported in creating visualisations in the past? Mostly by the provision of guidelines. Kelleher and Wagener (2011) provided guidelines for effective data visualisation in scientific publications. Forsell and Johansson (2010) proposed a heuristic set for the evaluation of information visualisations. Engelbrecht, Botha and Alberts (2014) also provide information visualisation guidelines. Despite a number of publications offering guidelines, evaluation guidelines remain a key research challenge within the international Information Visualisation community (Forsell and Johansson 2010). Moreover, the deployment of knowledge visualisation in an m-learning context has not been researched in any depth. Our proposal is not merely a new approach but the first for supporting the production of knowledge visualisations on a mobile platform. In coming up with learning support in this context we first consider the unique constraints of the mobile environment.

2.3 Mobile Learning Constraints

Mobile devices, as a newly emergent and ubiquitous display context, have specific device and infrastructure constraints that have to be considered during the production of m-learning initiatives. Mobile devices, as a learning tool, have some significant differences from the usual classroom environment:

- Their **context of use** is variable. A classroom is a strictly controlled environment with the presence of a teacher or assistant taken for granted, and where other learners surround a learner. A mobile learner's context is unpredictable and unknowable. It could be noisy, quiet, solitary or busy. A learner could easily be interrupted while busy learning, by a call coming in. The device has to maintain state seamlessly; allowing re-establishment of context once the activity is resumed.
- **Connectivity**, with servers or other required support structures, cannot be guaranteed. Despite the incredibly speedy laying down of infrastructures by mobile service providers some users still experience periods of poor or no connectivity. This is still a fact of life for mobile users in developing countries. This intermittent connectivity means that the mobile learner cannot rely on being able to access servers so that the m-learning package has to be designed to continue to function when not connected.
- The **memory** on the device is constrained. Memory, data storage devices, has become cheaper and more plentiful year by year since Moore proposed his law (Schaller 1997) predicting this development. It does not apply to mobile devices yet, though. Memory is constrained, as is processing power, mainly because of limited battery power. Moreover, the write time is relatively expensive, in the context of a battery-powered device, so that this has to be constrained if the battery is not to be drained too fast.
- **Power** is the biggest challenge. The device has been designed to spend most of its time sleeping. Any sustained use drains the battery and might render the device useless for its core purpose, communicating with other people.
- The mobile phone has a **new development environment** that is limited in terms of debugging tools and available libraries. This makes it a challenging environment to develop for.
- The **screen is small**, as compared to a desktop device. The kinds of techniques used by user interface developers on a large screen are not suitable. For example, overlapping windows cannot be used, nor can multiple buttons. Menu hierarchies have to be limited, since they can easily get too big for the screen. This essentially means that decisions have to be made about what can be shown, and what needs to be left off the screen.

The power and scope of these devices is developing daily so many of these challenges may well diminish as time goes by. The constraints caused by the size of the screen, however, can be expected to endure since it is determined by the size of an average pocket. Any visualisation has to take this limited space into consideration.

3 Proposed Learning Support: The Faded-Struts Approach

The research question we consider is "*How can the production of knowledge visualisations be supported in an m-learning context?*" The first step is to model the visualisation production process, then to consider how best to support postgraduates learning on how to produce visualisations.

One task that is engaged in by all postgraduates is the synthesis and summarization of a body of knowledge in a particular area. They are all required to read a number of academic papers and to produce a coherent story that interleaves these while rigorously citing the sources. Many students will subsequently summarize these in tabular format. Tabularisation is a mechanism to support the selection, combination and integrations of information from different sources in order to provide a balanced representation of the core knowledge available to the person on the topic under summarisation. We therefore focus on this summarization process, in launching a discourse on the use of visualisation in m-learning.

To model the visualisation of knowledge in this context we adapt the knowledge management process suggested by Zeiller (2005). He suggests a set of building blocks making up the knowledge management process. We have revised his building blocks to support developing the *knowledge visualisation development process*, incorporating the insights we gained from the literature review (Fig. 2).

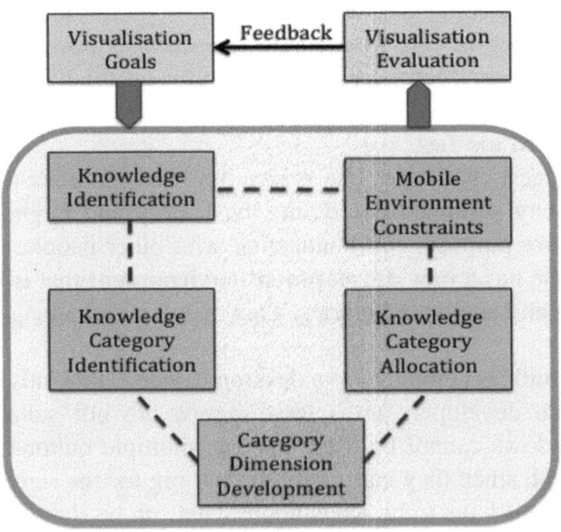

Fig. 2. Knowledge visualisation building blocks (adapted from Song (2014))

The stages involved in crafting the visualisation are:

1. **Knowledge Identification:** This is driven by the given task, the available knowledge resources and the width and depth of the expected outcome of the postgraduate student's task.
2. **Knowledge Category Identification:** This is the result of an abstraction the student carries out: it demonstrates an ability to rise above minutiae, to focus on getting core information and abstract principles from the individual research the student has read.
3. **Category Dimension Development:** This leads on from the previous activities. Having fixed on a set of description categories, the student now expands these categories into individual descriptors/dimensions.
4. **Knowledge Category Allocation:** The student now mines the literature to allocate individual research ideas, papers or items of work to the intersections between the descriptive categories.
5. **Mobile Device Constraints:** These will take the form of listen constraints and considerations, based on the discussion in Sect. 2.3.

The next step is to consider how learners can be supported through this process. We propose using a variation of the faded-examples learning process proposed by Song (2014). This adapted process ought to teach learners how to produce visualisations, in this case tables, depicting an overview of the literature they have researched. Song points out that apprenticeship is the gold standard of learning. The idea is that learners work through example after example, supervised by the ever-present master, until they assimilate enough experience to start working independently. The master removes the scaffolding of their assistance slowly as the learner demonstrates the ability to work independently (Lave and Wenger 1991).

This one-to-one apprenticeship is no longer feasible, but we can use the principles thereof to develop a slow and incremental learning process, similar to the approach proposed by Song (2014): examples, followed by faded examples (some support removed) and finally a peer-review process (Fig. 3). This fosters the slow and incremental development of the schemata, and ensures that the learner does not become overwhelmed during the learning process.

The faded-struts process starts with worked examples, a number of them, as suggested by Atkinson et al. (2000). The next step comprises faded examples, as suggested by Renkl and Atkinson (2003). Here some of the supports (struts) are removed, and the learner fills in the blanks, as it were. Song (2014) then suggests two more stages, guided discovery and minimal guidance. Instead, we propose that learners start interacting with each other, since the best way to learn is by teaching others. The skills being taught by Song's process are far simpler than knowledge visualisation and we do not believe that support can ever be withdrawn completely. Hence we propose moving from faded examples to peer review, providing minimal yet significant social support as learning continues and skills develop. The constant presence of the master is replaced by peer support as the learner starts to work independently.

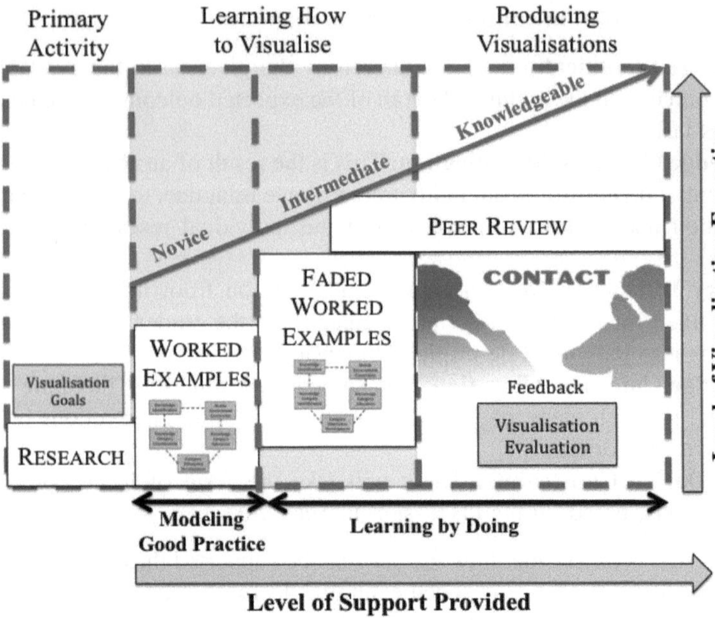

Fig. 3. Teaching postgraduates to visualise using a faded-struts approach adapted from (Song 2014)

Limitations. There are known risks to using knowledge visualisation (Bresciani and Eppler 2008). The risks could be both designer- and user-induced and relate to cognitive, emotional and social human aspects of the communication process. These can be exacerbated by the known m-learning constraints as noted in Sect. 2.3. By providing a stepped example-driven development process we attempt to minimise the risks and m-learning constraints.

4 Proof of Concept Example of the Faded-Struts Approach

One of the things all postgraduates are required to do is to gather information about a specific topic and then to provide a synthesis thereof (Golding et al. 2014; James 1998; Mullins and Kiley 2002). This is a time-consuming process and, despite the availability of similarity checking tools, plagiarism remains a concern. Provision of such a synthesis in a visual format, in this case in tabular format, is often particularly helpful. Yet we cannot expect students to know how to do this automatically. Hence, supporting the synthesis task on a mobile device, helping people to produce such a visualisation, would be valuable. We now step through this particular task in order to demonstrate the proposed knowledge-visualisation facilitated synthesis process.

Author(s)	Focus	Source
Brown & Mbati	Myths and opportunities	http://hdl.handle.net/10500/18589
Chipangura, van Biljon & Botha	Mobile-centric teaching and learning	http://researchspace.csir.co.za/dspace/bitstream/10204/7731/1/Botha2_2013.pdf
Koole	Pedagogical issues of information overload, knowledge navigation, and collaboration	https://www.jisc.ac.uk/full-guide/mobile-learning
Kukulska-Hulme	Learner attributes, skills and competences	http://www.ifets.info/journals/13_4/2.pdf
Sharples	Contexts, Curricula, Cultures, Ethics, Tools, Learning activity, Access to information and people.	https://www.google.co.za/webhp?sourceid=chrome-instant&ion=1&espv=2&ie=UTF-8#q=sharples%20small%20design%20big%20issues

Fig. 4. Identifying sources from the Literature

4.1 Worked Example

Consider that a postgraduate student has the task of reviewing the literature for m-learning constraints in order to produce a synthesis thereof. The building blocks in Fig. 2 would be traversed as follows:

1. ***Knowledge Identification:*** The student searches for relevant literature and reads it in order to understand the current state of play. He or she now identifies the set of papers and other sources that need to be included in the synthesis.
2. ***Knowledge Category Identification:*** The knowledge can be categorised in a number of different ways, but as to start off the student is expected to use at least the following categories as columns (1) author(s), (2) focus and (3) source. Figure 5 shows a selection from the data capturing on the topic of *mobile learning constraints*.

Focus	Author(s)	Source
Technological	Chipangura, van Biljon & Botha	http://researchspace.csir.co.za/dspace/bitstream/10204/7731/1/Botha2_2013.pdf
	Brown & Mbati	http://hdl.handle.net/10500/18589
Social	Sharples	https://www.google.co.za/webhp?sourceid=chrome-instant&ion=1&espv=2&ie=UTF-8#q=sharples%20small%20design%20big%20issues
	Petit & Santos	http://link.springer.com/chapter/10.1007%2F978-3-319-13416-1_1#page-1
Learner	Kukulska-Hulme	http://www.ifets.info/journals/13_4/2.pdf
	Koole	https://www.jisc.ac.uk/full-guide/mobile-learning

Fig. 5. Structured according to m-learning constraint categories

3. ***Category Dimension Development:*** The previous step is intended to develop a more nuanced understanding of the task. Students should now be made aware of the fact that the constraints highlight particular aspects of the literature that describe the area. This step now takes them further to show how the literature can be organised in different ways. The previous step was generic, and probably applicable to any

research area. This step now specialises the synthesis for the particular research domain.

During this phase a new table is created with the categories selected according to the specific domain area: m-learning constraints. In this case Koole's Frame model (2009) was selected, with the technological (device), the social and learner aspects as the three fundamental and overlapping sections. Columns are reorganised to ease the ordering of the dimensions (rows) as depicted in Fig. 5. The sources are the links to where the resource was found and the citation in the correct format is only extracted later.

4. ***Knowledge Category Allocation***: there is an intersection between each of the aspects of m-learning and the constraints. During this stage the learner allocates particular papers to each intersection. The papers are organised chronologically to depict developments over time. For example, connectivity was identified as a constraint in 2002 (Sharples et al. 2002) this is mentioned by Brown and Mbati (2015) as an issue in the developing country context and hence it is retained as a constraint (Fig. 6).

	M-Learning Constraints		
	Connectivity	**Device**	**Cost**
Technological	Sharples et al. (2002, 2007)	Chipangura *et al.* (2013)	Chipangura *et al.* (2012)
	Brown & Mbati (2015)	Traxler (2009)	Brown & Mbati (2015)

Fig. 6. Refined m-learning constraints

This example was launched using the basic and inexpensive Summary Pro App on an iPad. The App has two windows, a resource window and summary window. Appropriate information is selected in the resource window (displaying a Web page or other online source) and dragged to the summary window to build a editable collection of items as depicted in Fig. 7. The App allows the user to create an electronic file (containing all the information) which automatically includes the online references. This constitutes the "Knowledge Identification" building block in Fig. 2. The information in that file can then be used to create the tables (visualisations), continuing with the subsequent knowledge visualisation building blocks (Fig. 2).

5. ***Mobile Device Constraints:*** A mobile device was used to carry out the time-consuming task of collecting and tagging that information and saving the related source, with the focus where appropriate. In the Summary Pro App items can be saved as an electronic file which automatically includes the online references. Creating a table is fundamental to the principles of a mindful literature gathering strategy and expecting students to continually keep track of the sources emphasises ethical research. The App does not provide further support towards structuring the list of information sources into a table and it might be worth investigating the development of such an App in the future. Any other App could be used to create the table in Fig. 4 but, given mobile device constraints in switching between windows, this remains a clunky process.

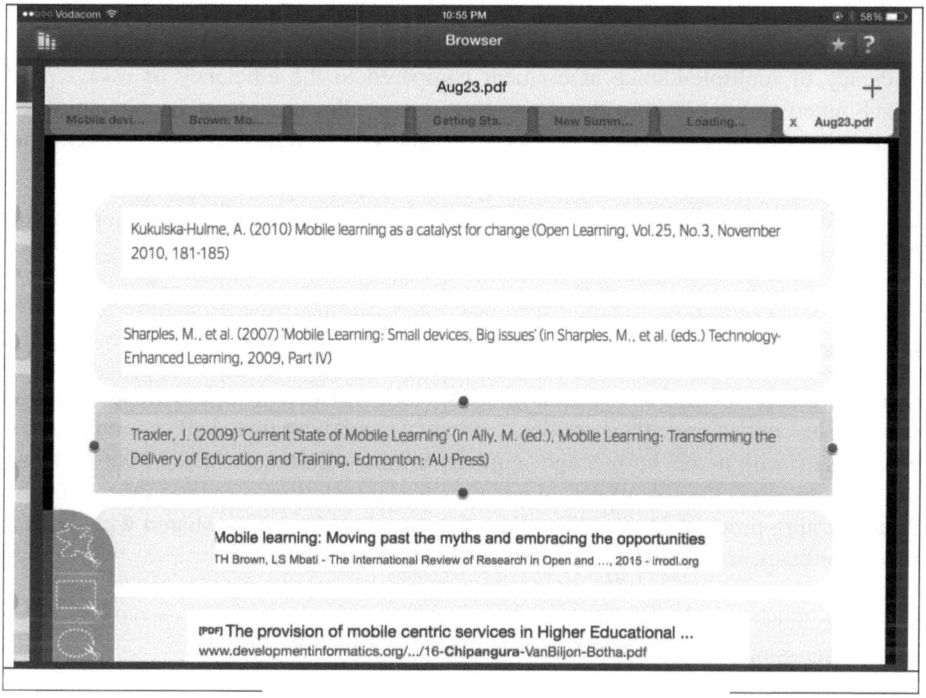

Fig. 7. Sources selected using the Mobile App

4.2 Faded Example

In the faded examples the students have to become more active in the learning process. The starting categories of author, focus and source would remain the same for the first table. Students would be given some dimensions of the second table and then be asked to add more themselves. An example follows.

Consider that a postgraduate student has been reviewing the literature on m-learning assessment. He/she now has to produce a summary of the literature. The building blocks would be traversed as follows:

1. ***Knowledge Identification***: The student undertakes a search for all relevant papers.
2. ***Knowledge Category Identification:*** The first three categories are always the author, article focus and source. So the student sorts all the relevant papers into these three categories.
3. ***Category Dimension Development:***

   - The dimensions could now be expanded into: *efficiency*, e.g. time, cost and effort, and *rigour*
   - More dimensions to be added by the student researcher.

4. ***Knowledge Category Allocation:*** There should be an intersection between each kind of assessment and the learner's category dimensions. For example, the efficiency of multiple-choice assessment compared to the efficiency of essays, both submitted online. During this stage the learner allocates research publications to each intersection. The summary serves to show how well the learner understands the relevant literature.

The idea is that a number of these faded examples will be worked through before the student is expected to do the visualisation independently.

4.3 Peer Review

M-learning is advocated as supporting the social construction of knowledge amongst learners by enhancing their critical, creative, collaborative and communicative engagement within the knowledge application sites (Cobcroft et al. 2006). Brown (2005) emphasises the role of communication and interaction as critical success factors in the learning process. During this phase the visualisation can be shared with peers to obtain feedback so as to improve the visualisation.

4.4 Discussion and Future Work

This paper proposes a process to support postgraduate students to develop visualisations, in order to ease knowledge communication. The literature survey was selected as an exemplar research task with structured text (tables) as visualisation choice. The mobile App used to support summarisation, namely Summary Pro (iOS), combines online searching functionality with the functionality to copy and paste information items and save that in an electronic format together with the relevant links. Further investigation and possibly bespoke development will be pursued in order to provide adequate, free Apps to support knowledge visualisation as a tool for postgraduate students.

This is but one possibility for using visualisation in research reporting. Research flow diagrams are another task where the faded-struts concept is relevant. The App we used for the tabular synthesis but a different kind of App would be needed for creating a research-flow diagram.

The fact that visualisation software packages are visualisation-specific complicates the use of visualisation. On the other hand, the proliferation of mobile Apps suggests that this is a minor issue and unlikely to prevent this kind of m-learning approach.

5 Conclusions

Data, information and knowledge visualisations have an under-utilized yet powerful ability to support communication and interaction in m-learning. Given the barriers and pitfalls to developing successful knowledge visualisations for mobile phones it is easy to understand why visualisations have, thus far, been the domain of the visualisation experts. However, the improved accessibility to visualisation software, the ubiquity of mobile devices and the clear pedagogical value support our argument that it is time to involve students on creating knowledge visualisations and that is the rationale for this study.

Advances in technology and access to software have made visualisation, as a method of knowledge creation and transfer, accessible to anyone with access to a standard computing device. The progress has been in developing visualising knowledge for consumption by the learner, i.e. for teaching. The novelty of this paper lies in the focus on learners creating knowledge visualisation rather than simply consuming them. The proposed process relies on a wider definition of visualisation which includes structured text as a form of visualisation. Besides the intrinsic value of engaging the students in creating the visualisation there are also the potential benefits of collaboration, knowledge transfer and sharing.

The contribution of this research is to present the idea of creating knowledge visualisation by students and provide worked examples and faded examples as proof of concept on how to implement the idea. Further work is necessary to test the idea with students and extend the repertoire of m-learning visualisation tasks.

References

Al-Shuaily, H.: SQL pattern design, development & evaluation of its efficacy Doctoral dissertation, University of Glasgow (2013)

Atkinson, R.K., Derry, S.J., Renkl, A., Wortham, D.: Learning from examples: instructional principles from the worked examples research. Rev. Educ. Res. **70**(2), 181–214 (2000)

Bresciani, S., Eppler, M.J.: A classification of disadvantages associated with graphic representations of information. ICA Working Paper 1/2008, The Risks of Visualisation, pp. 1–22 (2008)

Brown, T.H.: Towards a model for m-learning in Africa. Int. J. e-learn. **4**(3), 299–315 (2005)

Brown, T.H., Mbati, L.S.: Mobile-Learning: moving past the myths and embracing the opportunities. Int. Rev. Res. Open Distrib. Learn. **16**(2), 115–135 (2015)

Burkhard, R.A.: Towards a framework and a model for knowledge visualisation: synergies between information and knowledge visualisation. Knowl. Inf. Visualisation **3426**, 238–255 (2005)

Chen, M., Ebert, D., Hagen, H., Laramee, R.S., Liere, R.: Data, Information, and Knowledge in Visualisation. In: Visualisation viewpoints (Vol. January/February 2009), pp. 12–19. IEEE Computer Society (2009)

Chipangura, B., van Biljon, J.A., Botha, A.: Towards a mobile centric framework for inclusive sustainable interactions. Progressio **34**(3), 161–182 (2012)

Chipangura, B., van Biljon, J., Botha, A.: Evaluating mobile centric information access and interaction compatibility for learning websites. In: Pan African International Conference on Information Science, Computing and Telecommunication (2013), pp. 218–222, Zambia, 2013. http://www.meraka.org.za/icast2013/ICAST2013_proceedings.pdf

Cobcroft, R.l.S., Towers, S., Smith, J., Bruns, A.: Mobile learning in review: Opportunities and challenges for learners, teachers, and institutions. In: Proceedings of 2006 Conference on Online Learning and Teaching (OLT) (2006)

Cowan, N.: Working memory capacity. Psychology Press, Hove (2012)

Engelbrecht, L., Botha, A., Alberts, R.: Information visualisation view design: principles and guidelines. In: Proceedings of the International Conference on Computer Science, Computer Engineering, and Social Media, Thessaloniki, Greece (2014)

Eppler, M.J., Burkhard, R.A.: Visual representations in knowledge management: framework and cases. J. Knowl. Manage. **11**(4), 112–122 (2007)

Fleming, N.D.: I'm different; not dumb. Modes of presentation (VARK) in the tertiary classroom. Research and development in higher education. In: Proceedings of the 1995 Annual Conference of the Higher Education and Research Development Society of Australasia (HERDSA), vol. 18, pp. 308 – 313 (1995)

Forsell, C., Johansson, J.: An heuristic set for evaluation in information visualisation. In: International Conference on Advanced Visual Interfaces- AVI 2010, Rome, Italy 26-28 May 2010

Golding, C., Sharmini, S., Lazarovitch, A.: What examiners do: what thesis students should know. Assess. Eval. High. Educ. **39**(5), 563–576 (2014)

James, P.: Progressive development of deep learning skills through undergraduate and postgraduate dissertations. Educ. Stud. **24**(1), 95–105 (1998)

Keefe, J.W.: Learning Style: Cognitive and Thinking Skills. National Association of Secondary School Principals, Reston (1991)

Kelleher, C., Wagener, T.: Ten guidelines for effective data visualisation in scientific publications. Environ. Model Softw. **26**(6), 822–827 (2011)

Kirschner, P. A., Van Merriënboer, J.: Ten steps to complex learning a new approach to instruction and instructional design. In: Good, T.L. (Ed.), 21st Century Education: A Reference Handbook, Chapter 26, pp. 244–253. Sage, Thousand Oaks (2008)

Koole, M.L.: A model for framing mobile learning. In: Ally, M. (ed.) Mobile Learning: Transforming the Delivery of Education and Training. Athabasca University Press, Edmonton (2009)

Kukulska-Hulme, A.: Mobile learning as a catalyst for change. Open Learn. **25**(3), 181–185 (2010)

Larkin, J. H. (1989). What kind of knowledge transfers. Knowing, Learning, and Instruction: Essays in Honor of Robert Glaser. L B Resnikc (Ed.) (pp. 283–305). Chapter 9

Laseau, P.: Graphic thinking for architects and designers. John Wiley & Sons, New York (2000)

Lave, J., Wenger, E.: Situated Learning: Legitimate Peripheral Participation. Cambridge University Press, Cambridge (1991)

Muller, H., van Biljon, J.A., Renaud, K.V.: Information visualisation in research reporting: guidelines for representing quantitative data. In: Southern African Computer Lecturers' Association, Black Mountain Leisure & Conference Hotel, Thaba 'Nchu, outside of Bloemfontein, pp. 13–19 (2012)

Mullins, G., Kiley, M.: 'It's a Ph.D., not a Nobel Prize': how experienced examiners assess research theses. Stud. High. Educ. **27**(4), 369–386 (2002)

Oh, E., Lim, D.: Cross relationships between cognitive styles and learner variables. J. Interact. Online Learn. Summer **4**(1), 53–66 (2005). ISSN: 1541-4914

Petit, L., Santos, G.L.: Mobile Learning: An ergonomic alternative for learning awaited educational changes. In: Mobile as Mainstream-Towards Future Challenges Mobile Learning. 3rd World Conference on Mobile and Contextual Learning, m-Learn, November 3–5, Istanbul, Turkey (2014)

Renkl, A., Atkinson, R.K.: Structuring the transition from example study to problem solving in cognitive skill acquisition: a cognitive load perspective. Educ. Psychol. **38**(1), 15–22 (2003)

Robins, A., Rountree, J., Rountree, N.: Learning and teaching programming: a review and discussion. Comput. Sci. Educ. **13**(2), 137–172 (2003)

Schaller, R.R.: Moore's law: past, present and future. Spectr. IEEE **34**(6), 52–59 (1997)

Sharples, M., Taylor, J., Vavoula, G.: A theory of learning for the mobile age. In: Medienbildung in neuen Kulturräumen VS Verlag für Sozialwissenschaften. pp. 87–99 (2010)

Sharples, M., Corlett, D., Westmancott, O.: The design and implementation of a mobile learning resource. Pers. Ubiquit. Comput. **6**, 220–234 (2002)

Sharples, M., Arnedillo Sánchez, I., Milrad, M., Vavoula, G.: Mobile learning: small devices, big issues. In: Balacheff, N., Ludvigsen, S., de Jong, T., Lazonder, A., Barnes, S. (eds.) Technology Enhanced Learning: Principles and Products Kaleidoscope, pp. 233–249. Springer, Netherlands (2007)

Song, Y.: An authoring and presentation environment for interactive worked examples Ph.D. thesis, University of Glasgow (2014). http://theses.gla.ac.uk/view/creators/Song=3AYulun=3A=3A.html

Traxler, J.: Current State of Mobile Learning. In: Ally, M. (Ed.) Mobile Learning Transforming the Delivery of Education and Training. AU Press, Athabasca University (2009)

Van Biljon, J., Renaud, K.: Do visualisations ease dissertation assessment?. In: Proceedings of the 44th Annual Southern African Computer Lecturers Association 2015 (SACLA), Renewing ICT Teaching And Learning: Building on the Past to Create New Energies, pp 177–185 (2015)

Wishart, J.: Use of mobile technology for teacher training. In: Mobile learning: Transforming the delivery of Education and Training, Ally, M., (Ed.) pp. 265–278 (2009)

Wolfe, R.N., Johnson, S.D.: Personality as a predictor of college performance. Educ. Psychol. Meas. **55**, 177–185 (1995)

Zeiller, M.: A case study based approach to knowledge visualisation. In: Information Visualisation, 2005. pp. 377–382. IEEE (2005)

Developing a Sense of Identity as a Governor Within a Mobile Learning Community

Susan Gwee(✉) and Ek Ming Tan

English Language Institute of Singapore, Singapore, Singapore
gwee@mac.com

Abstract. Using a quasi-experimental design, this paper examines 36 Grade 9 students in a Singapore high school developed their sense of identity as a governor within a mobile learning community. In the traditional social studies classroom, students are taught how governors should govern their towns or countries in an ideal situation. *Statecraft X*, a mobile-phone game-based curriculum supporting the learning of principles of governance, however, allowed students to have a first-hand experience of being a governor within a mobile learning community, to assume the identity of a governor and to communicate with each other as governors. The server-based game design of *Statecraft X* ensures that there is a common experience within groups of players as well as between groups. It was hypothesized that civic learning mediated through a mobile game would help students develop a stronger sense of identity as a governor than those who learnt in traditional social studies classrooms. The final student assignment of this study was the presentation of a speech, which enacted students' understanding of principles of governance, based on their game experience, and in-class and outside-classroom activities. Data sources included surveys and written speeches. Analysis of the surveys showed how students developed their identity as governors and adopted civic values. The analysis of the written speeches indicated that students had enacted their sense of identity as governors as shown by their scores in relevance of proposed policies, perspective, and personal voice.

Keywords: Mobile · Game · Identity · Civic learning · Civic values

1 Introduction

With the proliferation of mobile devices among adults and teenagers, mobile learning is a field which is advancing at a rapid pace. Mobile learning allows learners to gain access to the learning environment outside the classroom. The convergence between mobile devices and games is of interest in the educational context. Educators can harness the potential of using a game installed in a mobile device to support student learning. The social studies mobile game-based curriculum proposed in this study is different from traditional curricula in that civic learning is mediated by a mobile game that requires learning across different spaces. Players are not required to be logged in at the same time and they can weave in and out of game play into the activities of their daily lives as their play is asynchronous. At the same time, students can also use the

T.H. Brown and H.J. van der Merwe (Eds.): mLearn 2015, CCIS 560, pp. 172–183, 2015.
DOI: 10.1007/978-3-319-25684-9_13

in-game chatline and the mobile phone to have synchronous communication with their team members. In this learning paradigm, learning takes place in school as well as out of school, across a multitude of spaces thanks to the portability of the mobile device used. Thus, there are possibilities for both asynchronous and synchronous communication and collaboration.

This research study deals with the concepts of games and learning and also relates them to the role of mobile technologies in the processes of game-based learning. In this study, the mobile nature of the *Statecraft X* game, a multiplayer strategy game installed in iPhones, where students take on the role of governors, allows students to play the game continually both in school as well as in out-of-school settings. This immersive virtual game experience that students experience is similar to that of leaders running a real government as described in the principles of governance found in the social studies textbook for Grade 9 students in Singapore. It is hypothesized that since the affordances of mobile technologies allow students to take actions in the game and to communicate to one another throughout the day, across different spaces, students participating in the mobile game-based curriculum are more likely to develop a stronger sense of identity as a governor compared to those taught in traditional social studies classrooms.

In traditional social studies classrooms, students are taught how governors should govern their towns or countries in an ideal situation. There is no opportunity for students to experience being a governor and develop a sense of identity as a governor. *Statecraft X*, a mobile phone game-based curriculum supporting the learning of principles of governance, allows students a first-hand experience of being a governor within a mobile learning community (Chayko 2007, 2009), to assume the identity of a governor, and to communicate with one another as governors. Students have constant access to the game and to one another through in-game chatlines, forums, and blogs. The server-based game design of *Statecraft X* also ensures that there is a common experience within groups of players as well as between groups, so that they can consult other student governors. This mirrors the real world where civic leaders or ministers and prime ministers also consult one another regarding issues of governance within the same cabinet in their own country.

1.1 Serious Games and Identity

Gee (2005) noted that "video games are all about identity. The player 'plays' some character; the player takes on, carries out and identifies with some special identity in a virtual world" (p. 19). Gee (2005) concluded that video games are good for learning because "they can create an embodied empathy for a complex system" and that "they are action-and-goal preparations for, and simulations of, embodied experience." Indeed, Hofer and Swan (2014) concurred that researchers have explored using role playing games and simulations to build historical empathy and skills.

There is a growing interest in the use of serious games in education. Game-based learning is an emerging paradigm for learning that can help students inhabit and act in virtual worlds so that they can develop situated understandings, shared values, ways of thinking, and powerful identities in a particular community of practice (Shaffer *et al.* 2005). Shaffer *et al.* (2005) noted that "video games are important because they let people participate in new worlds. They let players think, talk and act in new ways. Indeed players come to inhabit roles that are otherwise inaccessible to them" (p. 105). Although social studies teachers can use other ways of immersing students in civic learning, serious games allow students to learn by doing and hypothesizing what will happen if certain actions are carried out, rather than passively reading social studies content.

1.2 The Role of Mobile Technologies

Research on the use of mobile technologies for learning in the K-12 classrooms has shown that students find it more meaningful to learn with mobile devices and are also more engaged (Schmitz *et al.* 2014; Su and Cheng 2013; Wijers *et al.* 2010). Mobile devices are increasingly used to support learning in and outside the K-12 classroom (Davidsson 2014; Huizenga *et al.* 2009; Looi and Wong 2014; So *et al.* 2009; Wijers *et al.* 2010). Mobile games have also been used to support student learning (Facer *et al.* 2004; Huizenga *et al.* 2009; Squire and Jan 2007; Wijers et al. 2010). Situated learning is the focus of many studies on the use of mobile games among K-12 students (Facer *et al.* 2004; Huizenga *et al.* 2009; Squire and Jan 2007). As pointed out by Petit and Santos (2014), there have been many definitions of mobile learning. For example, Martin and Ertzberger (2013) noted that mlearning comprised three important aspects: accessibility, authenticity, and experience. Martin and Ertzberger (2013) defined it as "…learning that occurs when learners have access to information anytime and anywhere via mobile technologies to perform authentic activities in the context of their learning. Here and now mobile learning gives students the opportunity to be in the context of their learning and have access to information that is related to what they are seeing and experiencing at the moment" (p. 77).

In the current study, the mobile technologies of the serious game *Statecraft X* in this mobile game-based curriculum offer the mobile learning affordances identified by Martin and Ertzberger (2013): accessibility, authenticity, and experience. In terms of accessibility, the gameplay by the participants of the current study was not subject to the constraints of classroom environments. The mobile game was installed in a smartphone, which students could bring with them wherever they went and which they could use whenever they wanted to outside the classroom. Students did not need to rush through or complete the game within a prescribed lesson time. Students were also not limited to information resources in class but could access the Internet or contact fellow classmates for information while playing the game. Besides accessibility, the mobile game also offered students an authentic experience of being governors. Real governors respond to issues and emergencies that arise throughout the day, and they need to respond to these issues by interacting with others using information and communication technologies. Similarly, while playing the mobile game, students could communicate with one another via chatlines, forums, or by calling and texting one another. In other words, the *Statecraft X* mobile game-based curriculum simulated for students the actual experiences that real governors go through in their daily lives.

The purpose of this paper is to examine how Grade 9 social studies students in a Singapore high school developed their sense of identity within this mobile learning environment.

The research questions are:

1. What impact does the design of *Statecraft X* curriculum have on students' construction of identity as a governor?
   a. To what extent do students identity themselves as governors?
   b. To what extent do students show emotional responses for citizens under their charge?
2. How do students enact their identity as governors?
3. What civic values do students hold?

1.3 Theoretical Underpinnings

The authors draw on Collen's (2003) framework on human inquiry, which views human learning as a process of inquiry. Collen (2003) defined it as the practices of persons who go about doing their daily work and private lives. These practices concretize abstract concepts which constitute knowledge that they hold. Collen (2003) defined human inquiry as the processes of discovery, investigation, observation, and questioning.

The authors also draw on Dewey's (1916) philosophy that the habits and virtues required for democracy should be developed by participating in democratic communities that are characterized by dialogue and active participation reflecting social concerns. In the *Statecraft X* curriculum (see Table 1), students formed a community that engaged in governor practices and civic learning while playing the *Statecraft X* mobile game. In the classroom, they role-played as governors in the fictional world of Bellalonia. Consequently, students were able to act as governors in their daily lives during the duration of the intervention. They could also read and write blogs about their experiences as governors and discuss their experiences in small and large groups in forums, in-game chats, and in classroom discussions. Adopting the role of a governor in both game and fictional worlds gave students the perspective of a governor, in addition to their perspective as a citizen in the real world and the textbook perspective. Acting as governors in the game and fictional worlds enabled students to experiment with different civic values and engage in civic learning.

2 Methodology

2.1 Research Design

This study used a quasi-experimental research design. The data sources used in this paper include two surveys and the written speeches. To address the first research question, survey questions were administered to the experimental group (see Table 2). To address the second research question, both experimental and comparison groups were required to write a speech to the prompt:

Table 1. Proposed learning objectives of *Statecraft X*

Knowledge and understanding	To understand why the principles of governance are necessary for policy formulation and implementation;
	To understand how to use available resources to meet the social and economic needs of citizens;
	To understand the importance of social cohesion in a country;
	To learn from experiences in the game and fictional world and have multiple perspectives and ways of solving new problems.
Skills and processes	To engage in critical inquiry by testing hypotheses in the game world and reflecting on the outcomes;
	To evaluate information from the game, fictional and real worlds, and draw conclusions with strong arguments and evidence;
	To propose multiple perspectives and novel ways to solving problems in new scenarios.
Values and attitudes	To value social cohesion;
	To use non-violent approaches to solve conflicts;
	To understand that decisions made by the government have implications for citizens.

Table 2. Alignment of research questions, data sources, dependent measures, and analysis strategies

Research question	Data source	Dependent measure	Analysis strategy	Group
What impact does the design of *Statecraft X* curriculum have on students' construction of identity as a governor?	Survey 1	Identity	Descriptive Statistics	Experimental (n = 36)
How do students enact their identity as governors?	Written Speech	Relevance, Perspective, and Voice scores	Welch Anova	Experimental (n = 34) Comparison (n = 38)
What civic values do students hold?	Survey 2	Social cohesion, power, diplomacy, and agency scores	Welch Anova	Experimental (n = 34) Comparison (n = 39)

"Imagine that you are running for an election to be a member of parliament and that you have to formulate policies to convince the citizens of your country that you are the best candidate. Justify your proposed policies by using examples from what you have learnt, what you have read, and your personal experiences."

To answer the third research question, survey questions examining the constructs of social cohesion, agency, and power were administered to both experimental and comparison groups to determine whether there were differences in values held by students regarding governance at the end of the intervention. Eighteen survey items formed four constructs:

(a) valuing social cohesion which is the valuing of harmonious relations between people from different ethnic or racial backgrounds, and the respect and appreciation for cultures, customs, and traditions of various ethnic communities;
(b) valuing diplomacy over unthinking use of force to resolve conflicts between countries;
(c) recognizing that government power is inextricably bound to responsibility for the common good; and
(d) possessing agency, as a citizen, to influence the present and the future through participation in society.

2.2 Scoring of Student Written Speeches

The authors assessed (a) relevance, (b) perspective, and (c) personal voice. Relevance refers to how relevant the policies proposed by students are to the social and economic needs of the different segments of the country's population and whether they have given examples from both traditional and non-traditional sources to support their proposed policies. Perspective refers to whether students could give multiple perspectives to the proposed policies and integrate them or whether they could only give the textbook perspective. Personal voice refers to the voice used by students and whether it matched the situation, how authentic the voice was, whether opinions were well-defined and detailed, whether they communicated strong feelings and honest statements, and whether they showed that they cared about the topic.

The authors assessed each written speech separately and awarded a mark for each criterion. They both held graduate degrees, had at least eight years of teaching experience in Singapore schools, and were part of the *Statecraft X* research team. The first author also had three years of experience in an improving teachers' assessment literacy research project where she trained teachers to assess student work based on a scoring guide and exemplars of student work during assessment workshops. She also acted as an adjucator during score resolution sessions if two teams of teachers gave different scores to the same student work. After having assessed all written speeches separately, they came together to moderate the marks for each criterion in each written speech. When there was a discrepancy between the mark given by the two authors, they compared the features of the written speech with the benchmark performance given in the scoring guide and discussed why the student should be awarded a certain score. They considered any evidence that challenged the original scores and achieved a consensus score. They then assigned this consensus score for each criterion.

The results of Johnson *et al.* (2005) study suggest that when scores differ between two raters, discussion as a core resolution method is the best method compared to the averaging of two scores. Johnson *et al.* (2005) reported that for the use of an analytic rubric for grading essays, the scores arrived at after discussion between two raters were closer to expert-criterion scores than averaged scores between the two raters. To calculate exact and adjacent agreement between the first and second authors, the first author transformed the students' scores to the level scores as indicated in the analytic rubric, i.e., scores of 1–5, 6–10, 11–15, and 16–20 were transformed to level scores 1, 2, 3, and 4, respectively.

2.3 Participants

Thirty-six Grade 9 students (14 boys and 22 girls) participated in this intervention study. Two students in the experimental group were absent in the collection of post-intervention survey and writing task data. Two social studies teachers participated in the study. Thirty-nine students Grade 9 (28 boys and 11 girls) formed the comparison group. One student in the comparison group completed the survey but did not write the written speech. All students were in the Express academic track in the school. On average, they were 14 to 15 years of age.

2.4 Mobile Game

The back-story of the mobile game *Statecraft X* is that King Tropez of Velar died without leaving an heir. Thus, players have to lead political factions to look over their own towns and try to take over the capital city. One of the game objectives is that players belonging to each faction have to win the trust of the people residing in their towns as well as neutral town and towns belonging to other factions, developing the towns. The second objective is that players from different factions have to work together to ensure that the kingdom of Velar can resist the attacks neighboring kingdoms. The game ends when the players have successfully defeated the invaders. The winning faction is the faction that has the highest composite score of average happiness of citizens, economic score (profit), and population levels in the towns under their charge. During the intervention period of the current study, the server triggered events

Fig. 1. Players checking the effectiveness of their player actions

involving the game such as famine, bandit attacks, influx of refugees, and health epidemics. Students had to take player actions to mitigate the effects of these events. See Fig. 1 for a screenshot of the mobile game.

In every time interval, students were awarded action points that they could use for various player actions. Actions that they could take to develop a town included building a farm or factory, setting the tax rate for the factory, and setting water price. Military or defensive actions included moving a soldier on the world map, and hiring a soldier while diplomatic actions included requesting friendly relations with a neutral town or requesting peace treaty with another faction.

2.5 Procedure

Prior to the intervention, consent was sought from the teachers and the parents of the students to participate in the research study. The teachers then participated in a two-day professional development workshop designed to prepare them for the enactment of the *Statecraft X* curriculum. They were trained to play the mobile game and were shown the *Statecraft X* curriculum prepared by the authors. They gave feedback on the lesson plans designed, and worked with the authors to finalize the in-class and outside classroom activities of the learning program.

Outside classroom activities included mobile game play, blog, forum, and in-game chatlines. A web-portal was set up to provide a space for students to be informed of events happening both in the game world of Velar and the fictional world of Bellalonia and to write blogs and contribute to forums. Additional materials from the real world were provided to help students consider experiences from real world countries. In-class activities included classroom discussion, individual seatwork, and presentation of individual speeches. The intervention class was divided into two groups for game play as well as for discussions. All lessons were video recorded.

The control group did not receive any special treatment. The students in the control group participated in classroom activities such as lectures on government formation, and seatwork on principles of governance and solutions to low birth rate. Students also engaged in using inquiry-based learning approaches to evaluate posters, articles, and statistical data on traffic flow or in classroom discussion on World Corruption Perception Index, population growth, and low birth rate.

3 Findings and Discussion

As shown in Table 3, students displayed high scores of assuming the identity of a governor. Survey items 1 to 5 indicated that students identified themselves as governors. In survey items 6 to 9, students showed that they experienced feelings of happiness and sadness as a result of the actions that they had taken as governors in the mobile game. They felt happy when the citizens in their town were happy, trusted each other, and when they felt that they took good care of their citizens. In other words, they showed high levels of emotional responses to citizens under their charge in the mobile game. In sum, the *Statecraft X* learning program had an impact on their construction of identity as a governor.

Table 3. Mean scores of display of students' identity as governors

Items	*M*	*SD*
1. I feel less like a student in the *Statecraft X* curriculum.	4.75	.87
2. Being a governor in the *Statecraft X* curriculum helps me understand how to be a better governor.	5.06	.41
3. I feel like a governor when I play *Statecraft X*.	5.06	.71
4. I feel that the *Statecraft X* classroom is different from other places in the school.	5.08	.69
5. I thought about *Statecraft X* all the time while I participated in the study.	4.28	1.25
6. I feel happy when the citizens in my town(s) are happy.	5.47	.56
7. I feel sad when the citizens in my town(s) leave my town(s).	5.42	.73
8. I feel happy when I take good care of my citizens.	5.56	.56
9. I feel happy when the citizens in my town(s) trust each other.	5.56	.50

Note. The maximum possible score is 6.

There were significant differences between the experimental and comparison groups for two dependent constructs in the survey: social cohesion and agency (see Tables 4 and 5), and for three dependent measures in quality of student work in terms of relevance, perspective, and voice (see Table 6). The exact and adjacent agreement rates between the authors were 85 %, 97 %, and 94 % for relevance, perspective and voice, respectively whereas the exact agreement rates were 47 %, 65 %, and 41 %, for relevance, perspective, and voice, respectively.

Table 4. Comparison of constructs social cohesion, agency, diplomacy, and power between experimental and comparison groups

Construct	*df1*	*df2*	*F*	*p*	η^2
Social cohesion	1	58.59	19.53	<0.001	0.21
Agency	1	66.48	5.44	0.02	0.07
Diplomacy	1	69.94	0.20	0.66	0.002
Power	1	69.84	0.00	0.99	0.000

Note. *df* = degree of freedom; η^2 = eta squared or effect size.

The effect sizes of relevance, perspective, and voice were very large at 0.604, 0.654, and 0.453, respectively. Students in the experimental group felt a much higher sense of social cohesion and agency than students in the comparison group. The social cohesion (SC) survey items in Table 5 showed that trust, multiculturalism, and working well and happily with people from different races, were important to students.

As Dewey (1916) had recognized, active participation reflecting social concern and dialogue in a community helped develop in students the habits and virtues such as valuing social cohesion and diplomacy, required for citizens. Students were able to engage in critical inquiry, as suggested by Collen (2003), by testing their hypotheses in

Table 5. Comparison of results of specific survey questions on social cohesion (SC), agency (A), diplomacy (D), and power (P) between experimental and comparison groups

Items	*df1*	*df2*	*F*	*p*	η^2
I feel that trust between races is important (SC).	1	58.83	21.81	<0.001	0.221
I think that it is important for people of different races to live together happily (SC).	1	59.81	11.87	0.001	0.134
I want to work well with people from different races (SC).	1	65.71	11.51	0.001	0.133
I find it easy to work with people from different races (SC).	1	67.65	11.00	0.001	0.129
A multicultural society is preferable to one with a single dominant culture (SC).	1	69.29	5.35	0.024	0.068
The government will listen to citizens who keep complaining (A).	1	71.00	5.70	0.020	0.073
Building a strong defense force will help prevent other countries from invading Singapore (D).	1	49.92	6.68	0.013	0.078
The government's decision is always best for its citizens' welfare (P).	1	68.72	4.12	0.05	0.053

Note. *df* = degree of freedom; η^2 = eta squared or effect size.

Table 6. Summary of the welch ANOVA analysis of quality of written speeches between experimental and comparison groups

Variable	*df1*	*df2*	*F*	*p*	η^2
Relevance	1	69.78	109.00	< 0.001*	0.604
Perspective	1	64.51	138.46	< 0.001*	0.654
Voice	1	62.18	61.01	< 0.001*	0.453

Note. *df* = degree of freedom; η^2 = eta squared or effect size.

the game world and by reflecting on the outcomes. The findings of the current study seem to suggest that a social studies mobile game-based curriculum can help students achieve higher levels of civic skills compared to a traditional social studies curriculum. The advantage of the mobile game is that it is more easily incorporated in the school's social studies curriculum as it does not need to fit in with the prescribed school timetable. For all these reasons, this social studies mobile game-based curriculum should be incorporated into social studies practitioner's toolkit as it allows students to:

- learn by actively playing the game;
- assume the identity of a governor;
- engage in critical inquiry;
- develop multiple perspectives to different scenarios;
- solve problems in novel and different ways; and
- develop civic skills.

4 Conclusion

Students who participated in this mobile game-based curriculum displayed high scores of assuming the identity of a governor. The affordances of a mobile game allowed students to engage actively in the business of governing throughout the day. The curriculum design has also included components of forums and blogs where students could reflect and dialogue with one another. Consistent with Dewey's (1916) philosophy and Collen's (2003) framework, the active experimentation, dialogue, and inquiry reflecting civic concerns, which occurred during the mobile game-based curriculum, resulted in students adopting civic values of social cohesion and agency, where students showed that they valued social cohesion and believed that they possessed the agency to influence the present and the future. The affordances of the mobile technologies offered students the opportunities to engage actively in civic learning that led to civic learning outcomes.

Future research can look at whether these civic learning outcomes are sustained by investigating whether students participate more actively in civic activities after having experienced a social studies mobile game-based curriculum. It is of utmost importance that students take the initiative and responsibility of improving community conditions and of addressing social problems in their own community setting.

Acknowledgements. The National Research Foundation, Singapore, provided funding for the research reported in this paper through grant number NRF2007–IDM005–MOE–007CYS. We thank the Principal Investigator of the research project, Prof. Yam San Chee for having given us the opportunity to be part of the research team, and the Learning Sciences Lab, National Institute of Singapore, Nanyang Technological University for the rich research-oriented environment that it provided for us. We also acknowledge and thank other team members who contributed to this work: Mingfong Jan, Ahmed Hazyl Hilmy, Liu Qiang, Eric Salim Lim, Daniel Gan, Rave Tan, and Aldinny Abdul Gapar.

References

Chayko, M.: The portable community: envisioning and examining mobile social connectedness. Int. J. Web Based Communities **3**(4), 373–385 (2007)

Chayko, M.: Portable Communities: The Social Dynamics of Online and Mobile Connectedness. SUNY Press, Albany (2009)

Davidsson, M.: In the eye of the beholder: promoting learner-centric design to develop mobile games for learning. In: Kalz, M., Bayyurt, Y., Specht, M. (eds.) mLearn 2014. CCIS, vol. 479, pp. 238–249. Springer, Heidelberg (2014)

Dewey, J.: Democracy and Education: An Introduction to the Philosophy of Education. Macmillan, New York (1916)

Collen, A.: Systemic Change Through Praxis and Inquiry. Transaction Publishers, New Brunswick (2003)

Facer, K., Joiner, R., Stanton, D., Reid, J., Hull, R., Kirk, D.: Savannah: mobile gaming and learning. J. Comput. Assist. Learn. **20**(6), 399–409 (2004)

Gee, J.P.: Why video games are good for learning (2005). http://www.academiccolab.org/resources/documents/MacArthur.pdf. Accessed 14 April 2015

Hofer, M.J., Swan, K.: Technology and disciplined inquiry in the social studies. Contemp. Issues Technol. Teacher Educ. **14**(3), 25–30 (2014)

Huizenga, J., Admiraal, W., Akkerman, S., ten Dam, G.: Mobile game-based learning in secondary education: engagement, motivation and learning in a mobile game city game. J. Comput. Assist. Learn. **25**(4), 332–344 (2009)

Johnson, R.L., Penny, J., Gordon, B., Shumate, S.R., Fisher, S.P.: Resolving score differences in the rating of writing samples: does discussion improve the accuracy of scores? Lang. Assess. Q. **2**(2), 117–146 (2005)

Looi, C.-K., Wong, L.-H.: Implementing mobile learning curricula in schools: a programme of research from innovation to scaling. Educ. Technol. Soc. **17**(2), 72–84 (2014)

Martin, F., Ertzberger, J.: Here and now mobile learning: an experimental study on the use of mobile technology. Comput. Educ. **68**, 76–85 (2013)

Petit, T., Santos, G.L., Klemke, R., Specht, M.: Mobile learning: An ergonomic alternative for long-awaited educational changes? In: Kalz, M., Bayyurt, Y., Specht, M. (eds.) mLearn 2014. CCIS, vol. 479, pp. 1–14. Springer, Heidelberg (2014)

Schmitz, B., Kalz, M., Klemke, R., Specht, M.: In the eye of the beholder: promoting learner-centric design to develop mobile games for learning. In: Kalz, M., Bayyurt, Y., Specht, M. (eds.) mLearn 2014. CCIS, vol. 479, pp. 92–106. Springer, Heidelberg (2014)

Shaffer, D.W., Halverson, R., Squire, K.R., Gee, J.P.: Video games and the future of learning (2005). http://eric.ed.gov/?id=ED497016

So, H.-J., Seow, P., Looi, C.K.: Location matters: leveraging knowledge building with mobile devices and Web 2.0 technology. Interact. Learn. Environ. **14**(4), 367–382 (2009)

Squire, K.D., Jan, M.: Mad city mystery: developing scientific argumentation skills with a place-based augmented reality games on handheld computers. J. Sci. Educ. Technol. **16**(1), 5–29 (2007)

Su, C.-H., Cheng, C.-H.: A mobile game-based insect learning system for improving the learning achievements. Procedia Soc. Behav. Sci. **103**, 42–50 (2013)

Wijers, M., Jonker, V., Drijvers, P.: MobileMath: exploring mathematics outside the classroom. ZDM Math. Educ. **42**(7), 789–799 (2010)

Small Talk Versus Smart Talk: Providing Accounting Content and Emotional Support in a Distance Education Course

Annelien A. van Rooyen[1(✉)] and Jacobus S. Wessels[2]

[1] Department of Financial Accounting, College of Accounting Sciences, University of South Africa, Pretoria, South Africa
vrooyaa@unisa.ac.za

[2] Department of Public Administration and Management, College of Economic and Management Sciences, University of South Africa, Pretoria, South Africa
wessejs@unisa.ac.za

Abstract. Integrating mobile phones into higher education, and more specifically in the distance education context, is no longer regarded a strange phenomenon. Mobile devices are widely used by distance education institutions to make learning available and accessible to increasingly more students. Although mobile learning provides more mobility and convenience to these students than online learning, students may still experience the distance gap if communication and guidance are not incorporated into the presentation of a course. Börje Holmberg refers to this guidance of the student by the facilitator as 'didactic conversation'. His theory postulates conversation as essential in a distance education course to explain content, and to correct and redirect the student. By creating a sense of emotional involvement, students will feel more connected to the course than before, which will inevitably increase study pleasure and motivate students to learn.

This paper reports on a case study of a selected group of students' perceptions and experiences of the use of mobile phones in an accounting module at the University of South Africa to bring about more didactic conversation. Making use of short message service (SMS) and instant messaging software on mobile phones, regular communication between the facilitator and the students was increased. The qualitative data provided insight into how participating students perceived the use of these tools to assist them in their studies. Based on the evidence provided, it was evident that mobile phone intervention increased communication and exchanging of views. Creating a feeling of empathy and belonging, students enjoyed their studies and felt motivated to persist throughout the semester.

Keywords: Accounting · Didactic conversation · Emotional support · Mobile phones

1 Introduction and Background

Research conducted by the South African Institute of Chartered Accountants (SAICA) reveals a current shortage of approximately 17 000 accountants and more specifically 5 000 chartered accountants (CAs) in South Africa (Marshall 2014;

T.H. Brown and H.J. van der Merwe (Eds.): mLearn 2015, CCIS 560, pp. 184–197, 2015.
DOI: 10.1007/978-3-319-25684-9_14

PricewaterhouseCoopers 2012; SAICA 2012). Institutions of higher education play a pivotal role in reducing the shortage of this scarce skill that appears twelfth on the official list of top 100 scarce skills (Republic of South Africa 2014:17). Attempts are made to reduce this shortage by way of undergraduate and postgraduate qualifications offered by 14 SAICA-accredited residential universities in South Africa as well as the University of South Africa (Unisa), the largest open distance learning (ODL) university in the country (SAICA 2014; Van der Post 2010). The bulk of accounting students (60 %) in South Africa complete their undergraduate qualification on a full-time basis at residential universities (Olivier and Bulman 2009).

Students who want to pursue their CA career on a part-time basis (as most BCompt students at Unisa do), are required by SAICA to enter into a five-year training contract with a registered training office and obtain their undergraduate degree within five years (SAICA 2012). Research conducted by SAICA reveals that the throughput rates of both undergraduate and post-graduate accounting students studying at the various distance learning institutions in South Africa is considerably lower compared to that of students studying at residential universities (Olivier and Bulman 2009). While Unisa has a major market share in accounting education in South Africa (around 40 %) (College of Accounting Sciences 2014), its throughput rates (of about 20 %) compared to national figures are considerably lower than those of residential universities (see Table 1).

Table 1. Accounting students' enrolment: comparison between South Africa and Unisa

Year	National			Unisa			Total market	Percentage graduates produced for the sector
	Head-counts	Graduates	Through-put rate	Head-counts	Graduates	Through-put rate		
2005	88 062	12 267	14 %	34 516	2 099	6 %	39 %	17 %
2006	94 530	14 019	15 %	39 070	1 773	5 %	41 %	13 %
2007	95 125	14 465	15 %	41 618	2 087	5 %	44 %	14 %
2008	95 410	14 341	15 %	44 375	2 185	5 %	47 %	15 %
2009	97 613	14 591	15 %	44 284	2 060	5 %	45 %	14 %
2010	93 753	14 196	15 %	42 841	3 153	7 %	46 %	22 %
2011	95 925	14 408	15 %	45 422	3 043	7 %	47 %	21 %
2012	81 306	14 635	18 %	33 446	2 895	9 %	41 %	20 %

(College of Accounting Sciences 2014:online)

Being employed full-time as trainee accountants while studying part-time at Unisa unavoidably places many challenges on the successful completion of these tough qualifications (Olivier and Bulman 2009), resulting in low retention and throughput rates of these students. Furthermore, distance education (DE) students are required to have sufficient discipline to work through course material and assignments on their own and at their own pace. They have no or limited contact time with facilitators as well as other students and may struggle to stay focused and motivated in their studies (Holmberg 2005; Olivier and Bulman 2009; Simonson, Smaldino, Albright and Zvacek 2012).

Considering the high dropout and low throughput rates of accounting students at Unisa, the researchers have embarked on a research project to explore the possibilities of enhancing student support to accounting students enrolled at Unisa to increase their throughput rate, as this will inevitably help to alleviate the shortage of accountants and CAs in South Africa. The purpose of this paper is thus to report on a case study to understand the possible effect of mobile technology in improving the retention and throughput of a selected group of accounting students at Unisa by applying Holmberg's (1982) theory of didactical conversation. This paper commences by contextualising the case study within the current scholarly discourse, followed by a brief exposition of the research design and a description of the mobile intervention as case. The paper concludes with a summary of the main findings as well as a conclusive reflection on the study.

2 Literature Review

Research by a variety of scholars in the DE and ODL fields (refer Bates 2005; Birch and Volkov 2007; Garrison and Vaughan 2008) has established that students' success depends not only on the quality of the learning package, but also on the quality and scope of support given to these students. Studies have shown that motivation is important in DE courses (Rice 2006; Simonson *et al.* 2012; Simpson 2002; 2004) and, although literature confirms that motivation is an important factor in dropout rates of students in DE and ODL institutions (Berge 2001; Perraton 2000; Simonson *et al.* 2012), retention rates have always been lower in DE when compared to traditional face-to-face education (Simpson 2004). Some have criticised DE for its lack of personal contact (Frank, Reich and Humphreys 2003) and noted the sense of isolation students feel in DE courses (Abrami, Bernard, Bures, Borokhovski and Tamim 2011; Abrami and Bures 1996).

Research has shown that high dropout rates can be improved through blended instruction (Rowley et al. 2002), motivational messages (Visser et al. 2002) as well as other means of student support to improve performance and retention. Thayer, Newman and McClain (1994:910) explain that emotion is related to motivation as people tend to do things they hope will lead to happiness and satisfaction, or as Bradley (2000:602) describes it, "both emotion and motivation are fundamentally related to action". Sincero (2012:online) defines emotion as "the conscious and subjective experience that is characterised by mental states, biological reactions and psychological expressions". In addition, Sincero (2012:online) postulates three links between emotion and motivation, namely–

- both activate or energise behaviour;
- emotions often go together with motives; and
- basic emotions have motivational properties.

The theories of Maslow (1970) have shown to be still relevant to understand the role of motivation in the learning process, namely being a psychological process where behaviour is directed towards a goal based on an individual's needs. Bandura (1989:729) is of the opinion that self-efficacy is related to motivation in that if students believe they have the capability to perform a task and that performance would then lead to a positive result, they would be motivated to perform. Additionally, Hurd (2000:61) claims that for DE students, the demanding nature of self-instruction together with the shift in the locus of control from facilitator to student implies that only those students who maintain their level of motivation are likely to succeed. Motivation is hence a major factor in a student's study efficiency, and its effect on students' success has been explored by various authors (Koen 2007; Pizzolato 2004; Robotham and Julian 2006; Yorke 2004).

Literature has also shown that various factors can influence the motivation of students. In this regard, Keller (1999:7) argues that, although motivation is personal, student motivation can also be affected by external factors. Hurd (2000:61) identifies difficulty in assessing personal progress and perceived inadequacy of feedback as examples of such factors related to the distance learning environment. In order to be successful, students need to be persistent. In research conducted by Morgan and Tam (1999:99), four categories of persistence barriers that may have an effect on a student's motivation were identified, namely:

- *situational barriers*, which arise from a student's particular life circumstances (such as a changed employment situation, changed marital status or having a baby);
- *institutional barriers* are difficulties students experience with the institution (such as admission requirements, course pacing and limited support services);
- *dispositional barriers* are personal problems that affect students' persistence behaviour (such as a student's attitude, confidence, learning style and motivation); and
- *epistemological barriers* are impediments that are caused by disciplinary content knowledge or the relative perceived difficulty of that content.

Considering that students are not passive receivers of education, but active participants who are positioned in specific socio-economic, capital, habitus, attribution, locus of control and self-efficacy circumstances which have an effect on their motivation (Prinsloo and Subotzky 2009; Subotzky and Prinsloo 2011), involving students emotionally in their studies is especially relevant in a DE module. Motivation is essential for learning and performance, especially in a technology-mediated environment where students must take an active role in their learning (Lee 2000) and motivation is optimised when students are exposed to a large number of motivating experiences on a regular basis (Debnath 2005; D'Souza and Maheshwari 2010; Palmer 2007). Communicating effectively and with ease with students via electronic means, independent of time and place, is perceived by many to be a real advantage (Ebersole and Vorndam 2003:15; McCorkle et al. 2001:16).

Considering literature relating to students' emotional involvement and motivation, the present study set out to understand students' perceptions on and experiences of the use of mobile phones to involve them emotionally in their second-year Accounting module (FAC2602). The study made use of mobile phones to provide the students with motivational messages and by doing so to increase the didactic conversation necessary for emotional support. The didactic conversation theory, which was introduced by Börje Holmberg (1982), highlights the importance of dialogue between facilitator and student. Holmberg's theory (1982) implies the creation of a feeling of connectedness promoting study pleasure and motivation, particularly if two-way communication exists. Holmberg (1989:162) has this to say:

> Central to the learning and teaching in distance education are personal relations, study pleasure, and empathy between students and those representing the supporting organisation.

Holmberg's theory implies that by increasing the use of technologies in a DE student's study package, student support is improved as the didactic conversation is increased between facilitators and students (Kelsey and D'Souza 2004; Simonson *et al.* 2012). This was especially relevant to this research project which made use of mobile phones to support students. If the mobile phone could provide a motivating stimulus or incentive to generate a need or desire that causes a student to act (Williams and Williams, 2011:1), the participating FAC2602 students would hopefully react on the stimulus.

Mobile technologies enable people to communicate regardless of their location (Zawacki-Richter et al. 2007). As mobile phone networks extend to rural areas (especially in South Africa) (Barker et al. 2005; Brown 2004; Sharples et al. 2005), they allow people in rural communities not only to make phone calls but also to enjoy the benefits of mobile services, such as text and multimedia messaging. Not only does mobile support have the potential to improve students' throughput rates and enhance the quality of the learning experience, but research also confirms that students find mobile learning fun (Pieri and Diamantini 2009). Besides, students in mobile learning project trials have indicated that they not only enjoy the content, but they also love the collaboration (Colley and Stead 2004).

The research project reported on in this paper was part of a case study examining the effect of technologies on the retention and success rate of accounting students at Unisa. This paper reports on students' perceptions on the possibilities of using SMSes (short message service) and MXit (instant messaging software application developed in South Africa that runs on mobile phones) to assist with the transfer of accounting concepts and providing emotional support. By applying the framework of Holmberg (1982), this paper makes a contribution to the deepening understanding of the retention and throughput rates of accounting students in an ODL environment. The study has shown that retention and throughput rates can be improved through the lessening of the transactional distance between facilitator and student and by improving the quality and extent of the two-way didactic conversation in the learning process.

3 Research Design and Execution

The study participants were the 2 732 students registered during the second semester of 2012 for the second-year Financial Accounting module FAC2602. These students formed part of the mobile phone intervention project. Before the study commenced, these students received printed study material only. This project consisted of an introduction to the use mobile phone technology– such as SMSes and MXit– by the facilitator of the FAC2602 accounting module to communicate with students. These students were invited to make use of these applications to ask the facilitator questions and to communicate with other students. The interventions have been introduced and observed, and are discussed in the following subsection.

3.1 SMS Intervention

The first mobile phone intervention commenced by using SMSes to communicate with the FAC2602 students on a weekly basis. The SMS-to-student intervention was aimed at giving advice and making suggestions to students by providing information related to their studies. The FAC2602 module is a semester module, and a semester generally runs over 15 weeks (from close of registration to the start of the examination period). The SMSes were compiled by taking the total pages of the FAC2602 study guide (thus indirectly the course content) and dividing the total number of pages by 15. However, the difficulty level of the topics, the number of pages per topic and the assignment due dates were also considered when these SMSes were compiled, which resulted in a total of 12 SMSes per semester. Every SMS had a limitation on the number of characters; 160 characters or fewer. The SMSes were sent to students (always including the FAC2602 code) on a Monday morning to inform the students which section of the study material they had to cover during the particular week. Another objective was to incorporate a more personal conversation style between the lecturer and the students and to involve the students emotionally (to encourage and motivate them). Some of the SMSes sent to the FAC2602 students during the second semester of 2012 are included in Table 2. All SMSes are repeated here verbatim.

Table 2. SMSes sent to FAC2602 students during second semester of 2012

Wording of SMS
Welcome to FAC2602! Lecturers will SMS every week with workload for that week. Start 20/7.No text book for this module
FAC2602. Let's do pages 1-36 of guide this week. Do all exercises-do not just read thru text.1st compulsory assignment due 10/8
FAC2602.Do revision. WORK thru Q1-Q14 in tut 102.Do not look at answer b4 Q completed. Mark. Must complete within time
Good luck with FAC2602 exam Tuesday. Do all questions! Show all calculations. U've come a long way-u can do it!!

3.2 MXIT Intervention

The second mobile intervention used during the research project was MXit, which is an inexpensive instant messaging software application developed in South Africa, and which runs on mobile phones. Founded in 2003 by Namibian-born software developer Herman Heunis, MXit has since attracted more than 15 million users in the developing world (Heunis 2009). Although MXit users in South Africa have decreased from 10 million in 2012 to 5 million in 2014 (Groupe Speciale Mobile Association [GSMA] 2014:16), MXit allows users to send and receive one-on-one text messages to and from other users. Currently, MXit is a free mobile social application (MXit Lifestyle 2014). As the MXit function on mobile phones allows for instant messaging or communication between people, the FAC2602 facilitator was hoping that the MXit intervention would help to increase the didactic conversation.

At the start of the present research, an SMS was sent to all registered FAC2602 students. The SMS included the MXit number, and invited the students to connect with the lecturer via MXit. The relevant weekly MXit times were included in the SMS and were mostly at night (between 19:00 and 23:00) as many of Unisa students work during the day and study at night. On average less than 10 % of the FAC2602 students per semester registered for MXit. Although the number of students who actually participated in the MXit intervention seem low, texting and communicating with on average 10 % of these students at a time was quite daunting as the two-way conversations are instantly and every participant expected the lecturer to answer as quickly as possible. For this reason, the lecturer decided to increase her available time for questions on MXit, to allow students to ask questions over a longer period of time (including during the day) and that resulted in fewer students being active on MXit at a given time.

MXit language is different from the traditional English language, and the participating FAC2602 students also made use of this language, which is similar to SMS language. The students often made use of emoticons or textual portrayals of their moods or facial expressions. In addition, MXit users mostly do not use their family name; they prefer to register with an alias. Table 3 gives a few examples of abbreviations and emoticons used in MXit messages as well as one lecturer–student conversation (verbatim).

The instant two-way communication MXit provides assisted the lecturer to provide students with the emotional support they so often need before sitting for an examination. Two lecturer–student conversations a day before an FAC2602 examination appear in Table 4 (verbatim).

3.3 Assessing These Interventions

In order to understand the possible effect of these interventions on the didactical conversations (Holmberg 1982) and subsequently on the retention and throughput rates of these students, the FAC2602 students were asked to share their perceptions and experiences on the use of mobile phones through a self-administrated questionnaire with 11 open-ended questions. This questionnaire was piloted in November 2012. Feedback was received from five students. On 22 November 2012, the questionnaire was made available on *my*Unisa (an on-line student academic portal) to all registered FAC2602 students. A total of 70 questionnaires were returned. Thus, by adding the five pilot studies, a total of 75 questionnaires were collected. Although a small percentage of students completed the questionnaire, rich data was received and the researchers were of the opinion that saturation had been reached. The qualitative data was analysed using Atlas.ti and various themes and codes were identified for interpretation. The interpretation of the themes and codes specifically related to the theory of didactic conversation is discussed in the next section.

Table 3. MXit language and MXit lecturer–student conversation during semester

MXit abbreviation	English word or phrase
Hw r u, hru Gtg, g2g brb b4 cos, coz, bcoz gr8	How are you Got to go Be right back Before Because Great
zaksi (20:16)	Hell0..
zaksi (20:19)	In study guide..study unit 4..ques 1..page 53..why is pr0fit f0r the year in d inc0me statement and pr0fit f0r the year in the analysis tw0 different am0unts?
zaksi (20:20)	S0rry..page 51 and 52
Lecturer (20:21)	Which amounts? R538 000? And?
zaksi (20:20)	340 000 and 168 000..pr0fit after tax
Lecturer (20:23)	The R168 000 is the profit of the sub. Refer calc page 53. The R340 000 is the profit of the group (parent and sub 168 000).
zaksi (20:24)	0h yes! Thank y0u ☺
Lecturer (20:25)	Pleasure

Table 4. MXit lecturer–student conversations one day before an examination

bianca (15:28)	thanks btw I wish every module had this help
bianca (15:29)	Enjoy ur day guna go thru more questions and if I got a prob il come online
bianca (15:29)	☺
Zaakir (14:41)	Thanx.. So nervous 4 tomoro
Lecturer (14:42)	Not to worry. U have worked during the semester and Im sure u r ready 4 the exam. Will do well!! Good luck!
Zaakir (14:43)	Thx mam ☺

4 Findings

The didactic conversation theory of Holmberg (1982) emphasises the imperative of a two-way conversation between the facilitator and the student. It furthermore postulates that when the conversation encompasses emotional aspects, this will enhance student retention and throughput. Codes used to describe the participating FAC2602 students' perceptions and experiences on the use of mobile phones to involve them emotionally are identified in Table 5. These codes have been classified as either negative or positive.

Table 5. Codes used to describe emotional involvement

Theme identified	Related codes
Involve emotionally	Negative – alone, depression, hopeless, introvert, lonely, stress, surprise
	Positive – belonging, boost, connected, contact, cool, encourage, enjoy, entertain, feeling, freedom, friend, happy, interesting, involve, looking forward, motivate, reassurance, recognition, relationship, surprise, team, wow

The negative codes relate to the participants' uneasy experience of a learning environment lacking didactic conversation, and are associated with failure, stress, depression and fighting a lonely battle. The positive codes relate to participants' encouraging experience of support, success, good morale and self-esteem, and confidence.

Regarding the language used in the SMSes and MXit conversations, participants were pleased. One participant explained the conversation "was easy going and I didn't feel the need to get my back up with someone telling me what to do" (P27)[1]. The regular interaction also motivated the students and changed their "negative attitude towards our studies" (P33), while one participant explained the emotional involvement by saying, "it feels like the lecturers actually cares about the students & you're just not another number that's on the registration file" (P63). Another participant described the involvement as "a sense of belonging, as you know there are many others also studying to pass this subject" (PS3)[2].

Concerning the use of the various mobile phone interventions, one participant indicated, "the sms's kept me motivated and felt more like a varsity with class schedules than studying on my own" (P63) and another participant was of the opinion that "all modules should be embracing the use of podcasts and sms's as for me it was having a friend on a journey where u really need a friend" (P21). One participant described his/her experience with the mobile technology intervention as:

[1] P27 refers to feedback received from participant number 27.

[2] PS3 refers to feedback received from participant number three who was part of the pilot study.

> We need to feel like full time student by always receiving information from your lectures relating to that module. It makes one feel important that at least the lectures care about us making it to pass (P28).

The interventions assessed in this study undoubtedly comprised an emotional aspect as experienced by the participating FAC2602 students. Participants felt connected to the module and the lecturer, which was experienced as a decrease in the transactional distance. The analysis of the qualitative data provided adequate evidence that the application of mobile technologies in the teaching of the FAC2602 module at Unisa indeed contributed to the didactical conversation between students and the lecturer involved in the particular module.

5 Conclusion

The research reported on by this paper responded to the low retention and throughput rates of accounting students at Unisa. The researchers have consequently started to explore the possibilities of enhancing student support to increase their throughput rate. The subsequent case study to understand the possible effect of mobile technology in ultimately improving the retention and throughput rates of the selected group of accounting students was directed by Holmberg's (1982) theory of didactical conversation.

The research has shown that the use of mobile technologies for academic support kept the students on track, while it also motivated and encouraged them to persevere with their studies. As most of the participating students were working full-time and had limited time available for studies, these interventions have shown to be successful in enhancing didactic conversation as they provided quick and timeous connections between the student and the facilitator. Learning problems and queries were resolved almost instantly through these interventions as the participating students reported feeling like full-time students attending a face-to-face session. The contribution of this research is not the use of mobile phone interventions such as SMSes and MXit in supporting DE students, but the application of Holmberg's (1982) theory of didactic conversation in understanding student retention and throughput in a DE environment. This mobile intervention case study has shown that successful didactic conversation depends on the immediateness of the two-way communication technique used. Considering that Holmberg's (1982) theory of didactic conversation postulates a correlation between improved didactic conversation and student retention and throughput, this research has shown that a nearly insignificant intervention, such as the use of SMS communication between students and lecturers, may contribute to improved throughput and retention rates.

References

Abrami, P.C., Bernard, R.M., Bures, E.M., Borokhovski, E., Tamim, R.M.: Interaction in distance education and online learning: using evidence and theory to improve practice. J. Comput. High. Educ. **23**(2), 82–103 (2011)

Abrami, P.C., Bures, E.M.: Computer-supported collaborative learning and distance education. Am. J. Distance Educ. **10**(2), 37–42 (1996)

Bandura, A.: Regulation of cognitive processes through perceived self-efficacy. Dev. Psychol. **25** (5), 729–735 (1989)

Barker, A., Krull, G., Mallinson, B.: A proposed theoretical model for m-learning adoption in developing countries. In: Conference Proceedings: Mobile Technology: the Future of Learning in your Hands, Fourth World Conference on mLearning, October 25–28, Cape Town (2005)

Bates, A.W.: Technology, e-learning and distance education, 2nd edn. Routledge, New York (2005)

Berge, Z.L.: Sustaining distance training: integrating learning technologies into the fabric of the enterprise. Jossey-Bass, San Francisco (2001)

Birch, D., Volkov, M.: Assessment of online reflections: engaging English Second Language (ESL) students. Australas. J. Educ. Technol. **23**(3), 291–306 (2007)

Bradley, M.M.: Emotion and motivation. In: Cacioppo, J.T., Tassinary, L.G., Berntson, G.G. (eds.) Handbook of psychophysiology, pp. 602–641. Cambridge University Press, New York (2000)

Brown, T.: Exploring future learning paradigms: will m-learning survive. Conference proceedings: Conference keynote address, Mobile learning anytime everywhere, July 5–6, Rome (2004)

CAS (College of Accounting Sciences) (2014). About the College of Accounting Sciences. http://www.unisa.ac.za/Default.asp?Cmd=ViewContent&ContentID=96659. 15 October 2014

Colley, J., Stead, G.: Mobile learning = collaboration. Conference proceedings: Mobile learning anytime everywhere, July 5–6, Rome (2004)

Debnath, S.C.: College student motivation: An interdisciplinary approach to an integrated learning systems model. J. Behav. Appl. Manage. **6**(3), 168–189 (2005)

D'Souza, K.A., Maheshwari, S.K.: Factors influencing student performance in the introductory management science course. Acad. Educ. Leadersh. J. **14**(3), 99–120 (2010)

Ebersole, S., Vorndam, M.: Adoption of computer-based instructional methodologies: A case study. Int. J. E-Learn. **2**(2), 15–20 (2003)

Frank, M., Reich, N., Humphreys, K.: Respecting the human needs of students in the development of e-learning. Comput. Educ. **40**(1), 57–70 (2003)

Garrison, D.R., Vaughan, N.D.: Blended learning in higher education: framework, principles, and guidelines. Wiley, San Francisco (2008)

GSMA (Groupe Speciale Mobile Association) (2014). The mobile economy: sub-Saharan Africa 2014. http://www.gsmamobileeconomyafrica.com/GSMA_ME_SubSaharanAfrica_Web_Singles.pdf. 10 May 2015

Heunis, H.: Mobile communications and communities in South Africa: MXit's Herman Heunis (2009). http://mobilebeyond.net/mobile-communications-and-communities-in-south-africa-mxits-herman-heunis/. 12 September 2013

Holmberg, B.: Weiterführendes Hochschulfernstudium (1982). http://deposit.fernuni-hagen.de/1784/. 13 August 2010

Holmberg, B.: Theory and practice of distance education. Routledge, New York (1989)

Holmberg, B.: The evolution, principles and practices of distance education. Oldenburg: Bibliotheks- und Informationssystem der Carl von Ossietzky Universität (2005)

Hurd, S.: Distance language learners and learner support: beliefs, difficulties and use of strategies. Links and Letters 7: Autonomy in L2 Learning, 61–80 (2000)

Keller, J.M.: Motivation in cyber learning environments. Int. J. Educ. Technol. **1**(1), 7–30 (1999)

Kelsey, K.D., D'Souza, A.: Student motivation for learning at a distance: does interaction matter? (2004). http://www.westga.edu/~distance/ojdla/summer72/kelsey72.pdf. 27 March 2013

Koen, C.: Postgraduate student retention and success: a South African case study (2007). http://www.hsrcpress.ac.za/product.php?productid=2205&freedownload=1. 28 April 2013

Lee, C.Y.: Student motivation in the online learning environment. J. Educ. Media Libr. Sci. **37**(4), 367–375 (2000)

Marshall, N.: Special report– employees (2014). http://www.accountancysa.org.za/special-report-employees/. 10 April 2015

Maslow, A.H.: Motivation and personality, 2nd edn. Harper and Row, New York (1970)

McCorkle, D.E., Alexander, J.F., Reardon, J.: Integrating business technology and marketing education: enhancing the diffusion process through technology champions. J. Mark. Educ. **23**(1), 16–24 (2001)

Morgan, C.K., Tam, M.: Unravelling the complexities of distance education student attrition. Distance Educ. **20**(1), 96–108 (1999)

MXit Lifestyle (2014). MXit. http://mxit.android.informer.com/. 8 April 2015

Olivier, M., Bulman, F.: News – Distance learning education (2009). http://www.accountancysa.org.za/resources/ShowItemArticle.asp?ArticleId=1783&Issue=1086. 1 June 2012

Palmer, D.: What is the best way to motivate students in Science? Teaching Science. J. Aust. Sci. Teachers Assoc. **53**(1), 38–42 (2007)

Perraton, H.D.: Open and distance learning in the developing world. Routledge, New York (2000)

Pieri, M., Diamantini, D.: From e-learning to mobile learning: new opportunities. In: Ally, M. (ed.) Mobile learning: Transforming the delivery of education and training, pp. 247–264. AU Press, Edmonton (2009)

Pizzolato, J.E.: Coping with conflict: self-authorship, coping, and adaptation to college in first-year, high-risk students. J. Coll. Student Dev. **45**(4), 425–442 (2004)

PricewaterhouseCoopers (2012). Mathematical talent in short supply. http://www.bbqonline.co.za/articles/empowerment/skills-development/479-mathematical-talent-in-short-supply. 6 June 2012

Prinsloo, P., Subotzky, G.I.: Modelling throughput at Unisa: the key to the successful implementation of ODL. Unpublished Report. Pretoria: Unisa (2009)

Rice, K.L.: A comprehensive look at distance education in the K-12 context. J. Res. Technol. Educ. **38**(4), 425–448 (2006)

Robotham, D., Julian, C.: Stress and the higher education student: a critical review of literature. J. Further High. Educ. **30**(2), 107–117 (2006)

Rowley, K., Bunker, E., Cole, D.: Designing the right blend: combining online and onsite training for optimal results. Perform. Improv. **41**(4), 26–36 (2002)

RSA (Republic of South Africa) (2014). Call for comments on the National Scarce Skills List: the top 100 occupations in demand. Notice 380 of 2014. Government Gazette, No. 37678. Government Printer

SAICA (South African Institute of Chartered Accountants) (2012). Becoming a CA. https://www.saica.co.za/Training/BecomingaCA/tabid/157/language/en-ZA/Default.aspx. 19 February 2013

SAICA (South African Institute of Chartered Accountants) (2014). List of SAICA accredited programmes – 2014. https://www.saica.co.za/Portals/0/LearnersStudents/documents/List%20of%20accredited%20programmes.pdf. 16 October 2014

Sharples, M., Taylor, J., Vavoula, G.: Towards a theory of mobile learning (2005). http://www.mlearn.org.za/CD/papers/Sharples-%20Theory%20of%20Mobile.pdf. 10 March 2012

Simonson, M., Smaldino, S., Albright, M., Zvacek, S.: Teaching and learning at a distance: foundations of distance education, 5th edn. Pearson Education, Boston (2012)

Simpson, O.: Supporting students in online, open and distance learning. Kogan Page, London (2002)

Simpson, O.: The impact on retention of interventions to support distance learning students. Open Learn. **19**(1), 79–95 (2004)

Sincero, S.M.: Motivation and emotion (2012). https://explorable.com/motivation-and-emotion. 4 November 2014

Subotzky, G., Prinsloo, P.: Turning the tide: a socio-critical model and framework for improving student success in open distance learning at the University of South Africa. Distance Educ. **32**(2), 177–193 (2011)

Thayer, R.E., Newman, J.R., McClain, T.M.: Self-regulation of mood: strategies for changing a bad mood, raising energy, and reducing tension. J. Pers. Soc. Psychol. **67**(5), 910–925 (1994)

Van der Post, W.: CA training in South Africa (2010). http://www.greyconsulting.co.za/mediareleases/CA%20TRAINING%20IN%20SOUTH%20AFRICA.htm. 22 May 2012

Visser, L., Plomp, T., Amirault, R., Kuiper, W.: Motivating students at a distance: the case of an international audience. Educ. Technol. Res. Dev. **50**(2), 94–110 (2002)

Williams, K.C., Williams, C.C.: Five key ingredients for improving student motivation. Res. High. Educ. **12**(3), 1–23 (2011)

Yorke, M.: Retention, persistence and success in on-campus higher education, and their enhancement in open and distance learning. Open Learn. J. Open, Distance e-Learn. **19**(1), 19–32 (2004)

Zawacki-Richter, O., Brown, T., Delport, R.: Mobile learning – a new paradigm shift in distance education? (2007). http://auspace.athabascau.ca:8080/dspace/bitstream/2149/1258/1/Zawacki-Richter_Brown_Delport%20mlearn06.pdf. 10 April 2015

Designs for Heritage Language Learning: A Photography Project in the UK Supplementary Education

Koula Charitonos[1(✉)] and Marina Charalampidi[2]

[1] The Institute of Educational Technology, Open University, Milton Keynes, UK
koula.charitonos@open.ac.uk
[2] University of Warwick, Coventry, UK
m.charalampidi@warwick.ac.uk

Abstract. Supplementary Schools in the UK offer educational opportunities for children and young people outside mainstream school provision. The paper reports an enquiry undertaken by practitioners in Greek Supplementary Schools in the UK to explore how features of mobile technologies may be leveraged to foster heritage language learning. It draws on the view that mobile learning can be a way for learners to explore the language informally and direct their own development (Kukulska-Hulme 2015) and may also shape the learners' 'habits of mind' (Wong 2012, p.22) in learning—and consequently their language competencies.

The project #ItsAllGreekToUS set to investigate how to create learning designs to incorporate effective use of mobile technologies within language learning and teaching. It draws on action research orientation and uses the idea of 'Bring Your Own Device' (BYOD) (JISC, 2013) in educational settings. The study involved several sessions around the concept of 'loanwords' and representations of this vocabulary in artefacts created with the use of mobile phones and a popular photography application (e.g. Pinterest).

The participants were fourteen students (12-13s) attending a pre-GCSE class in a Greek School in London and nine students (12-14s) attending a GCSE class in a Greek School in Leicester.

Evidence from user-generated content, the pupils' views around the project and the practitioners' observations are considered. The paper will discuss how students' practices associated with mobile technologies are integrated into teachers' practice. Particular attention will be drawn to designing language learning by blending traditional language classroom practices along incorporating the practices of sharing and curating content, as well as allowing 'visibility' through artefacts created by the learners.

Keywords: Mobile learning · Photography · Supplementary education · Heritage language learning

1 Introduction

The popularity of mobile devices equipped with various cameras and apps makes possible for people to take photos and share their experiences on various media 'anytime, anywhere'. Indeed, mobile photography has advanced rapidly over the last

T.H. Brown and H.J. van der Merwe (Eds.): mLearn 2015, CCIS 560, pp. 198–216, 2015.
DOI: 10.1007/978-3-319-25684-9_15

few years and is increasingly gaining traction among young people (OfCom 2014), who seem to adopt the 'image-as-conversation' (Williams 2014). Whereas such practices are well 'embedded' in young people's lives, it is also recognised that these relationships are formed primarily 'in the domain of popular culture' (Buckingham 2007) and not in schools. Therefore, examining how learning occurs within the context of young people's activities with mobile technologies and on social network sites—how knowledge is produced and represented through interaction—might contribute to gaining an understanding of their experiences, cultures and communication practices, which can then be built within formal learning programmes. This paper focuses on the practice of taking/crafting and sharing photos to put forward the argument that this could be used as a resource within formal learning settings and a way to break down the classic distinction between formal and informal learning.

In this paper we present an intervention study '#ItsAllGreekToUs' with a focus on heritage language learning to examine the integration of mobile photography in the classroom and beyond. This study emphasises creative learner content outputs and draws attention to a learning design that blends the physical and the digital contexts and directs the learners to use the mobile technology to interact with their physical environment. It also highlights a design that incorporates an arts dimension—the art of photography—into the learning and teaching of community languages. This intervention locates itself within a body of research seeking to identify more clearly a pedagogical approach to the use of technology in a learning setting which is sensitive to the context, the situation of the learners and which also has the potential to contribute significantly in creating opportunities for the teacher to engage with his/her pedagogic practice.

The study is informed by sociocultural perspectives of learning with a focus on mediating artefacts in the development of understanding in situated learning activities. Using largely qualitative research methods, data was collected from two Greek Supplementary Schools in London and in Leicester. Through an 'action research' orientation of this study important insights were gained into identifying the impact on learners, the pedagogy and the use of technology and these are also commented upon in the paper.

2 Literature Review

2.1 Community/Heritage Language Classroom

In the United Kingdom (UK) community languages are typically taught in supplementary/complementary schools. These schools offer educational support (language, core curriculum, faith and culture) and other out-of-school activities to children attending mainstream schools (Evans and Gillan-Thomas 2015). They operate in community centres, youth clubs, religious institutions and mainstream schools. There are an estimated 3000–5000 such schools in England (NRCSE 2015) and while many are run by small local groups, others are part of larger organisations that provide a range of services. An example for the latter are the Greek Supplementary Schools, that provided the context of the study presented in the paper. They run under the auspices of three institutions: the Cyprus High Commission in the UK (as a branch of the Ministry of Education and Culture in Cyprus), the Embassy of Greece in the UK, and the Greek Orthodox Archdiocese of Thyateira and Great Britain.

In this paper we are using a broad definition of 'community languages' as "languages in use in a society, other than the dominant, official or national language" (McPake et al. 2007, p.7). We are also employing the term 'heritage language', to point to the language used in home or familiar contexts, and at the same time to emphasise its broader cultural associations and significance (for a discussion around definitions see King and Ennser-Kananen 2013). In other words, we differentiate heritage language learners from first or second language learners whilst recognising that this creates an issue in the context of teaching and learning a heritage language because it cannot be assumed that the heritage language is in fact the students' native language; many students may only have a passive knowledge of the language or not speak it at all, as it was the case with many of the participants of the study in this paper. This is the reason why Anderson (2009) expresses a concern within the area of community language teaching which is the question of pedagogy and how best to address the needs of a highly diverse group of learners for whom neither a 'foreign language' approach nor a 'mother tongue' approach is appropriate.

Another issue well recognised within this context is that English tends to become the dominant language for students from ethnic or other minority backgrounds, with the shift towards English increasing across the generations. Therefore, it is not necessary for these students to learn their community language in order to communicate. Yet, there are good reasons for learning the language, including the benefits of having a second language for further language learning. Having said this, the United Kingdom suffers from a general lack of emphasis on development of multilingual skills within the general population and within the education system (Speak to the Future 2015) and as a result, a decline in the take-up of languages has been observed (Handley 2011). Apart from motivational issues to study the community languages, other factors influencing the operation of the supplementary schools include constraints on resources, e.g. qualified teachers, infrastructure.

2.2 Mobile Learning in the Language Classroom

Mobile learning has been one of the most significant areas of research across education over the last fifteen years with many studies focusing on second/foreign language acquisition. According to UNESCO (2013) the unique benefits of mobile learning include the ability to bridge formal and informal learning. For language learners, for example, this might be translated to access to supplementary materials beyond the classroom or to capture and document difficult terms and phrases which can be brought back into the classroom (UNESCO 2013). Mobile-Assisted Language Learning (MALL) has emerged as an area of Computer-Assisted Language Learning (CALL) and maintains important promise "for significant change in teaching and learning practices" (Kukulska-Hulme 2009, p. 1) since it allows the learners to locate resources and information in context 'anytime, anywhere' and ultimately to "re-interpret their everyday life contexts as potential resources for learning" (Pachler 2009, p. 5). It is precisely the situated nature of learning allowed by mobile technologies that distinguishes current MALL research from previous studies in early 2000s, which were either content or design-oriented studies (Kukulska-Hulme and Shield 2008). In addition to the connectivity, portability and flexibility afforded by mobile technologies, such technologies are also a means of communication and social interaction in the target language.

Many studies in CALL or MALL focus on vocabulary learning, since it is one of the most important aspects of language learning. Burston's (2013) comprehensive bibliography of MALL studies shows that there have been more than 150 reports of studies related to vocabulary acquisition—almost a fourth of all the published work relating to MALL over the period 1994–2012. Many studies in this context often employ mobile devices and develop systems to 'push' content to learners (e.g. Kennedy and Levy 2008), often adapted to the needs of the learners, i.e. interests, proficiency level (e.g. Li et al. 2010).

A study particularly relevant to the work presented in this paper is the project 'Move, Idioms!' (Wong et al. 2012) carried out with primary school children learning Chinese as a second language. This project emphasised contextualised learner content creation and meaning making with their daily encounters. As with Wong et al.'s (2012) work—albeit in a different cultural and educational context—the aim of our study was to foster our students' skills in identifying and appropriating in situ resources to mediate their learning activities in any learning space, rather than always being directed by the resources that the teacher provides. Also, unlike most of the published MALL studies (approximately 85 %) which have been conducted within higher education (Burston 2013), our study took place within K12 settings and aimed to address questions about how technologies mediate representations of learning and the production of meanings by young people.

It is noted that in an extensive review of CALL in English as a second language in the primary and secondary education, the evidence that technology has a direct benefit on linguistic outcomes is 'slight' and 'inconclusive' (Macaro et al. 2012). Macaro et al. (2012) find it difficult to recommend that technology in general or specific software should be used to improve vocabulary development. Their review, however suggests that technology may have an indirect positive impact on learner attitudes, behaviours and collaborative work. Importantly, the pedagogical approach underpinning most of MALL implementations has been criticised as adopting "a behaviorist, teacher-centered, transmission model of instruction" (Burston 2014). It is also our view that any successful implementation of MALL depends less on the technological advancements and more on the pedagogy. It is therefore important to examine the affordances of mobile technologies in ways that support constructivist, collaborative, task-based learning across formal and informal settings.

A key point that needs careful consideration in introducing technology in formal learning settings is the tension that might occur between students' informal uses of such tools (e.g. peer communication) and the rather more formal aims and activities of teachers, e.g. assessment (Crook 2012). The nature of Web 2.0 might be seen as having "a disruptive influence… and present[ing] specific challenges to existing notions of academic authorship and authority" (Selwyn et al. 2012, p. 25), which may not be desirable in the current school culture with rigid practices and behaviours in place.

Despite these issues, researchers refer to 'missed opportunities' (Kukulska-Hulme 2015) regarding achieving mutual benefit between formal and informal learning. Formal education is seen as 'detached' from rapid socio-technological change, whereas informal learning is 'sidelined' or 'ignored' when it could be used as a resource or a way to discover more about evolving personal and social motivations for learning (Kukulska-Hulme 2015). This paper describes a study that sought to allow connections between formal language instruction and informal practices associated with Web 2.0 tools. It also sought to allow connections between the heritage language and the English Language and to highlight creative approaches to heritage language learning.

3 Research Questions

The key questions we sought to address in this study were:

RQ1: What contribution can creative work with mobile technologies make to the learning and teaching of heritage languages in supplementary school contexts?
RQ2: How do students experience the innovative pedagogic practices?
RQ3: What are the implications for pedagogy, i.e. opportunities opened up, conditions for learner's participation?
RQ4: What are the enablers or barriers of how students' practices associated with mobile technologies are integrated into teachers' practice?

4 Mediation by Artefacts

Within the sociocultural perspective of learning, knowledge is seen as being mediated through the use of 'tools' or 'artefacts'. A broad definition of artefacts is the one that includes physical and symbolic artefacts (e.g. signs, language, text, objects, instruments and machines). Tools are essentially a part of the 'cultural tool kit' (Wertsch 1991) available in a particular sociocultural setting. It is through engagement in socioculturally situated goal-oriented activities that tools are given meaning and both activities and artefacts are transformed (Wells 1999). In this paper, the photographs (online and physical) are products of specific social contexts and are viewed as a mediating artefacts for the participants across time and space. Essentially, photographs are viewed as material representations of meanings (Kress 2010) made by the students within and outside the classroom and are accessible to us through the specific medium (i.e. Pinterest). The focus of this paper is to examine the role of the photographs as part of the resources available for meaning making within the context of heritage language learning.

5 Context of the Study

5.1 Aims and Objectives

The research design involved a classroom intervention that had a broad focus on the concept of 'loanwords', defined as "a word that at some point in the history of a language entered its lexicon as a result of borrowing (or transfer, or copying)" (Haspelmath 2009, p. 35). The stated aim of the project was to develop students' vocabulary knowledge, as well as to raise awareness among the students about the concept of borrowing words from one language to another. The learning objectives included the students to identify and collaboratively form a list of loanwords; to create visual representations of the loanwords through the medium of photography that would be uploaded online; to curate content and communicate their knowledge and understanding to an audience; and to evaluate and reflect on the artefacts they produced.

5.2 Participants

The study took place in two Greek Supplementary Schools, one in North London (School A) and the second in Leicester (School B). The participants were a pre-GCSE class (12–13 years old, N = 14) and a GCSE class (12–14 years old, N = 9) respectively. School A operates twice in a week for five hours in total, while School B once in a week for a total of 4.5 h. The study was implemented in two phases: in School A from February to July 2014 and in School B from March to June 2015. All the participants had personally owned mobile devices or access to tablets owned by their parents and an initial assessment determined that their perceived familiarity with their use was ranked from very good to excellent.

5.3 Tools

5.3.1 Pinterest

Pinterest (www.pinterest.com) is a popular social networking site that lets people discover, collect, and share pictures. It saw significant growth between 2012 and 2014 and according to Pew Internet Research it is now the third largest social network site in the US (Duggan et al. 2015). The users of Pinterest can 'pin' pictures with links to items they find on the web or upload themselves and organise them into boards representing themes (e.g. recipes), tag/title and share them with their social network on the site.

Pinterest was targeted for the present study precisely because of its focus on pictures. Also, the way the pictures are displayed resembles a school display board. Images or pictorial information where shared on the site through a secret board #ItsAllGreekToUs that was created by the teachers (see Fig. 1). However due to the age of the participants (12–14 years old), the use of the site as a social network site (i.e. create a profile, establish a relationship with other users) was not utilised to its full potential. To explain, Pinterest 'Terms of Use' refer to thirteen years old as the minimum age for a user. As a result, the teacher in School A was the administrator of the board and the one uploading the pictures to the site. In School B the students had access to the board and could upload the pictures themselves through a common username/password. Due to the two different time phases, students from School B could view the pictures taken by the participants of School A.

Fig. 1. Pinterest board

5.3.2 Mobile Technologies - 'Bring Your Own Device'

Most schools have policies in place that ban the use of mobile phones in the school, as was the case with both the supplementary schools in the study. Having said this, the 'Bring your own device' (BYOD) (JISC 2013) policy is gaining traction among educational organisations, encouraging or requiring students to provide their own device for learning purposes. Proponents of BYOD suggest that it helps promote better outcomes via a more personalised learning and an enhanced engagement between home, school and other spaces, hence an increasing number of studies examine how BYOD works in a learning environment (e.g. see Song 2014).

The decision to introduce the BYOD policy in the study was made partly due to lack of access to technological infrastructure in the school and partly due to practical reasons. We determined that the external environment (i.e. students' access to mobile phones/tablets that were Internet-ready and with a camera) was mature enough to proceed with this option.

5.4 Description of the Study

In the study we facilitated the participants to examine Greek 'loanwords' in English and vice versa. We also considered other borrowing phenomena that are more or less closely related to loanwords, such as words that had phonological or morphological adaptation (e.g. use of prefixes such as 'mono-', 'tri-', 'tele-'). A number of activities with specific goals that span over several sessions took place in the classroom (see an outline in Table 1). The plan varied from one school to another due to time restrictions (i.e. participants from School B had to sit the GCSE in Modern Greek exams).

The students were instructed to use their smartphones to take photos in their daily lives or in the school that could represent words identified in the classroom. Each student was asked to select a few loanwords that s/he could capture with their mobile phones. In School A, often the parents (and less the students) were emailing the

Fig. 2. 'Campaign word posters'

Table 1. Outline of #ItsAllGreekToUs activities per school

Description	School A	School B
1. In groups of three or four, students brainstormed words that are borrowed or are similar in both languages. An initial list was created, which was then put in alphabetical order. The list was updated throughout the project work with words identified during classroom instruction (e.g. in texts) or through discussions with parents/grandparents and the teacher.	x	x
2. Students grouped the words identified in categories (e.g. medicine, mathematics, sports).	x	x
3. Each group was assigned specific letters (e.g. A-D) and students in groups selected words and gave definitions/brief descriptions of these words in Greek.	x	
4. Students explored the school and a few took photos based on their encounters in this space and associations they could make with loanwords.	x	x
5. Students selected loanwords that they would like to photograph.	x	x
6. Students practiced grammar activities with loanwords, e.g. nouns, endings, plural formation	x	x
7. Students in groups created a 'probe' and an invitation for the photography exhibition. The probe was left in the school space prior the exhibition for others to find it. The invitation was sent to parents and school staff.	x	
8. Each student created one or two 'campaign word posters' associated with a loanword. They were then photographed by fellow students (see Fig. 2).	x	

(*Continued*)

Table 1. (*Continued*)

Description	School A	School B
9. Students curated content and set up a photography exhibition. Students and members of the community voted for the best photograph (see Fig. 3)	x	x
10. During the exhibition, the audience added new words to a display that included all the words identified by the participants.	x	
11. Students with their teacher created a short film about their project utilising the school spaces and their photographs. The film was screened for the parents and fellows students to see during the assembly.	x	
12. Students created a power point with all the pictures and their labels. The power point was projected for the parents to see during the photography exhibition.		x
13. Photographs on Pinterest were screened on the Interactive Whiteboard in the class on a weekly basis.	x	
14. Printouts of the photographs were displayed in the school and the class throughout the duration of the project.		x

pictures to the teacher and the teacher was then uploading them on Pinterest. In School B, the students could upload the pictures themselves, although most of them opted for sending them to their teacher.

An outcome of the project work was the organisation of a photography exhibition in the schools to display the students' photographs (see Fig. 3). The exhibition took place as part of the end-of-year activities for parents and members of the community. During this event the audience was asked to vote for the best photograph, i.e. the one that represented the word more succinctly/creatively.

Fig. 3. Photography exhibition

6 Methods and Data Collected

6.1 Action Research

The project was largely driven by the authors' desire to examine how to create learning designs to incorporate effective use of mobile technologies within language learning and teaching. We follow an action research orientation because the study presented in this paper is firmly located in the realm of us, as practitioners who look to "improve the rationality and justice of their own practices, their understanding of these practices, and the situations in which the practices are carried out" (Carr and Kemmis 1986, p. 162). Our intention is to link practice and ideas with an aim of investigating an inquiry in which questions examined are brought to bear on significant practical issues regarding teaching and learning with mobile technologies. The study is an example of engagement with a small group of learners in an attempt to work toward practical outcomes, and also about creating new forms of understanding. Our approach, drawing on Lewin's definition of action research as "proceed[ing] in a spiral of steps, each of which is composed of a circle of planning, action and fact finding about the results of the action" (1946/1948, p. 206), involved more or less systematic cycles of action and reflection. In action phases practices were tested and evidence was gathered. This paper can be seen as an outcome of the reflection stage, where we attempt to make sense of the evidence, discuss and plan further actions. In doing this we acknowledge, as other have, that this inquiry "had different purposes, is based in different relationships, has different ways of conceiving knowledge and its relation to practice" (Reason and Bradbury 2008, p. 8) compared to conventional academic research.

6.2 Data

In order to build up a picture of the processes and perspectives as they have manifested themselves through the project, various types of data were collected:

- Pre-test Questionnaires (School A) (N = 14)
- Field-notes by the two teachers
- Reflection forms (School A) (N = 9)
- Focus group interview with participants (N = 6) (School B)
- Teaching plans and resources (School A and School B)
- Students' Artefacts (photographs, film)

In this paper we present content generated by the participants (photographs) and we focus on the analysis of the interview data and the self-reflection forms to examine how students perceived and experienced the innovative pedagogic practices and whether this work opened up any opportunities for the students.

7 Findings

7.1 Reflection Forms

Following the completion of the project work students were asked to fill in a reflection form, which included four direct questions and one open-ended question, as following:

Q1. What did we do well?
Q2. How I felt we achieved?
Q3. What could we have done differently/better?
Q4. What was the value of doing this project in the Greek School?
Q5. I think my overall benefit from this project was…

Nine forms in total were collected from the participants in School A (five students were absent).

For each of the questions a content analysis was performed. Codes were assigned to describe the thematic content of the comments. Responses per theme were quantified to make their relationship to the wider population apparent. Table 2 shows the themes and a few exemplar responses that demonstrate the analysis.

Table 2. Analysis of the reflection forms (N = 9)

Questions	Themes	Exemplar Quotes by participants
Q1. Project work perceived as successful or well implemented	• team work (n=6) • artefacts created (n=4) • specific tasks (n=4) • performance/presentation (n=3)	• All the photographs were colourful and creative (Student #6) • I think that it was a very good idea for people to vote for pictures and to add new words (Student #5) • I think our presentation was brilliant (Student #7)
Q2. Feelings	• accomplishment (n=5) • satisfaction (due to audience's reactions/feedback) (n=3) • purposeful (n=4) • enjoyment (n=3)	• I felt that we did very well as we got very positive feedback and everybody seemed to enjoy it (Student #8) • We achieved by working as a team and having fun while doing it (Student #6)
Q3. Project work perceived as requiring improvement	• inclusion of contextual information (n=4) • reach out more people for bigger impact (n=2)	• We could have had a bit of information with each picture to make it easier to understand. (Student #8) • We could have involved more people to make it well known (Student #4)
Q4. Perceived value	• learn vocabulary (n=5) • develop an awareness about 'loanwords' (n=4) • raise awareness in their audience (n=4) • reinforce the value of heritage language (n=3)	• This project helped us and our audience understand how much of the english language is influenced by greek. Also it was very fun making it and we learnt a lot of new vocabulary as well (Student #5) • To show how important and special Greek Language is (Student #3)
Q5. Perceived benefit	• learn vocabulary (n=8) • develop an awareness about 'loanwords' (n=4) • advance skills (e.g. team work, ICT) (n=5) • bond with peers (n=2) • enjoyment (n=2)	• I think we made people more aware…(Student #7) • learning how to work as a team properly…(Student #5) • …getting to know my classmates better through a group activity (Student #8)

Two important themes emerge from this analysis: the first, importantly, is a perceived development of vocabulary knowledge, alongside an enhanced awareness of the concept of 'loanwords'. The second, is an acknowledgment of an audience, since many of the students' responses considered the impact and the value their work had, not only for themselves but for other people as well.

7.2 Students' Photographs

Students created 83 photographs in total (N = 83), (n = 51 from School A, n = 32 from School B). All the participants, except four, contributed photos. For the analysis of the photographs we drew on the analysis suggested by Wong et al. (2010) in the 'Move, Idioms!' project. The researchers analysed the photographs with respect to two dimensions: (1) types of physical setting and (2) types of meaning making. Of the two dimensions only the first is relevant to our analysis since it refers to the sources of the physical setting captured by each photo. Following this, the researchers classified the photos into categories: (1) natural setting, (2) physical object manipulation, (3) human enacted scenario and (4) previously published materials, e.g. TV illustrations, screenshots. Table 3 features examples of different types of photos.

The analysis shows that the photographs predominately depicted objects (n = 37). Few (n = 10) were based on a 'human-enacted scenario'. Notably, the top photos—as ranked in the exhibitions—are included in the latter category. The students were not given specific instructions about how to approach the task of taking pictures. Therefore, the photographs are viewed as evidence of students' creativity by crafting contexts that associate with specific loanwords. The variety of artefacts reflected students' engagement with, and attention to their surroundings. This is also verified by the interview data that is discussed in the following section.

7.3 Focus Group Interview Data

The focus group interview took place with six participants (School B). The interview was structured around three main themes: (1) views about the Greek Supplementary School (2) views about the use of mobile phones, including questions about the practice of taking photographs and (3) the project experience. Due to the fact that the interview took place prior to the completion of the project work no data related to the photography exhibition was collected. The duration of the interview was approximately an hour. All the data was transcribed and thematic analysis was performed. A few themes that emerged from this analysis are discussed below.

Vocabulary Learning. All the interviewees held strong views about the project contributing to the development of their vocabulary knowledge (Q. What was the value of doing this project in our school?). Participation in the project was seen as helping towards preparation for their exams, and as such, taking pictures was treated as a weekly homework. They referred to the value of this learning method and evaluated it as fun, enjoyable and effective. Importantly, four of the interviewees referred to the notion that taking pictures assisted them in remembering the words. This is evident in the following quotes:

Table 3. Analysis of the students' photographs (N = 83)

'Types of physical setting'			
Natural setting	**Physical object manipulation**	**Human-enacted scenario**	**Previously published materials**
n = 17	**n = 37**	**n = 10**	**n = 19**
		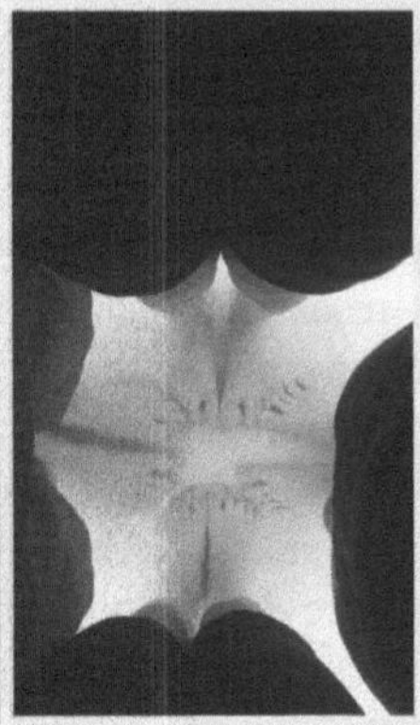	
Geography (Γεωγραφία)	Pyramid (Πυραμίδα)	Octopus (Οχταπόδι)	Frappe (Φραπέ)

Museum (Μουσείο)	Photosynthesis (Φωτοσύνθεση)	Phobia (Φοβία)	Bible (Βίβλος)

> I didn't know there were so many words that sound and mean the same. I didn't know the meaning of some words but now I do and this also helped me with the exams, like the word "seminar" or the word "Europe" which I used to forget sometimes. After taking the pictures, I can now remember the meaning and it stuck in my mind (Girl A).
>
> We learned words we didn't know before and even if we knew them before we just wouldn't think to use them but now they come to mind straight away cause we've taken a picture of them. But even if we knew them before we probably wouldn't think of them while doing an essay but now we think of them. If you take a picture of them it stays in your head (Girl B).

Selection of Words to Photograph. The interviewees elaborated on how they approached the task of selecting words that would be captured in a photograph (Q.

How did you go about deciding which word to photograph?). Half the interviewees referred to being attentive to the surrounding environment and taking pictures of objects available to them. One was particularly driven by his interests (i.e. music) and another one by identifying words viable to capture. Two interviewees tried to make associations with loanwords after having a picture of a random object taken. This, as well as the involvement of the student's social environment, are illustrated by the following quote:

> Basically, me and my brother were trying to make one of them [a pyramid], and I thought I should take a picture cause it took me ages so once I did I took a picture of it and then I realised it was like a pyramid so then I remembered it was on the list… (Girl B).

Constraints. Time and workload emerged as the main factor influencing students' participation in the project. The following quote provides evidence for this:

> We had to spend more time to revise rather than taking pictures. Even though it helped before, as we got closer to the exams we needed to do some proper revising and to practise essays, past papers (Girl A)

Moreover, the interviewees referred to a need for guidance and being reminded, e.g. one student said "Once you forget to do it once, you just forget to do it all the time!" (Boy A)

Value of Heritage Language. Almost all the interviewees referred to the idea of the project creating or reinforcing positive attitudes towards their heritage language. One interviewee referred to "feel[ing] proud for being Greek" (Girl C).

8 Discussion

In this section we discuss the evidence presented earlier and we provide some insights from our engagement with this study to address the four research questions and discuss implications for using mobile technologies in the language classroom.

- *RQ1: What contribution can creative work with mobile technologies make to the learning and teaching of heritage languages in supplementary school contexts?*

  The study overall has highlighted how the practice of photography encouraged learner creativity and provided a means of developing language skills as well as cultural understanding. The integration of mobile photography in the classroom, as presented in this paper, shows that learning can occur in ways which incorporate experiential, affective and cognitive dimensions. For example, the analysis of the reflection forms and the interview data points to a perceived development of the vocabulary. Additionally, it reveals the creation or reinforcement of a feeling of valuing the heritage language. Importantly, a sense of achievement and pride felt by the participants is noted. As discussed in earlier section of this paper, our students often lack motive or question the value of the heritage language, hence this "renewed sense of pride in their bilingual and bicultural identities" (Anderson and Chung 2012, p. 278) might provide an incentive for studying the language.

- *RQ2: How do students experience the innovative pedagogic practices?*

  The evidence collected from the reflection forms point to the participants largely valuing the opportunities given to work with fellow students and to draw upon each others strengths. Each one's contributions was becoming a part of a bigger whole, while curating content and setting up the exhibition created a sense of solidarity and a feeling of accomplishment among them. Students appeared to be seeing their classmates in a new light, since the project work brought a realisation of others' skills and competences beyond language skills. It is noted that the students' involvement flourished in the weeks preceding the exhibition whereas their appreciation of what they achieved was consolidated upon experiencing the final event. Importantly, the use of the mobile technologies seemed to make the participants 'oriented to an audience' (Charitonos 2015) and as a result they viewed the project work as helping them towards presenting, performing or making an impact to this audience.

  Observation data revealed that a few students were less engaged in the project work and it could be argued that the total amount of photographs is not particularly high. This might be because many of the mobile devices that learners have access to provide services that were not designed for learning, hence learners find them difficult to use for the activities that teachers expect them to undertake. Related to this is Stockwell's (2010) review of studies suggesting that while learners have a positive view of mobile learning, and feel that there are the potential benefits, not all students are willing to engage in it. It might also be the case that the students were not sufficiently motivated to contribute photos, perhaps due to the fact that the project was seen as another school activity.

- *RQ3: What are the implications for pedagogy, i.e. opportunities opened up, conditions for learner's participation?*

  Drawing on our involvement in this project, our current thinking supports the view that the integration of mobile technologies in the language classroom is most effective when based on a learning design which involves:

  (1) aligning the work with the curriculum; (2) blending physical with digital artefacts and allowing their visibility within the classroom/school space; (3) working towards a 'tangible' creative output, e.g. the photographs and the exhibition (and the film in School A); (4) drawing on practices that are well established among young people (e.g. taking pictures) and (5) engaging an 'audience' (e.g. parents, school community to vote for the best photograph). Related to the design of the activities are the issues of structure and guidance a teacher should provide to his/her students. Throughout the project we felt that in designing the activities (see Table 1) we adopted a rather rigid 'schooling' perspective (e.g. assign homework, grammar activities). This was partly due to our aim of maintaining a focus on the learning objectives of a curriculum and partly due to a concern of a change in the dynamics of the classroom when mobile technologies are brought into this context. Throughout the project work we were questioning whether this approach was

'appropriate'. We now believe that it is necessary to maintain such a perspective for the following reasons: (1) students (and parents) view this work as associated with regular classroom activities; (2) alignment with the curriculum and school events (e.g. end-of-year show) releases anxiety from the teacher that this work takes time away from 'real work'; and (3) levels of structure with direct guidance provide a frame within which students can work creatively. In other words, it is important to work within boundaries, but at the same time to allow certain levels of choice (e.g. select words, content).

- *RQ4: What are the enablers or barriers of how students' practices associated with mobile technologies are integrated into teachers' practice?*

  It is our view that the practice of photography offered the children a 'known territory' for engagement with issues of language. Though this arts-related task, learners were encouraged to be creative, whilst their creativity could be made visible by everyone. Moreover, the specific medium allowed the artefacts to be shared in both digital and physical form and this, arguably, affords different uses in the classroom. Further to this, we view the notion of 'trust' as key in any work with mobile technologies in the classroom. Our experience showed that when we showed trust to our students and "once they sense they're trusted, kids [a]r[o]se to the occasion" (MacGibbon 2012). On the other hand, the issue of students' familiarity with technologies might be a barrier. Evidence from this work points to lack of skills among young people. For example, three students did not know how to email their photos from their smartphones and many could not adjust settings for higher quality of pictures. It is a fact that when designing studies with young people and technologies it is often assumed that they have advanced ICT skills. This might be true for some students, but not for all. In line with this, it is noted that the BYOD model was employed assuming that this would cause the minimal disruption to learning because the student will know how to use the device. In actuality, this apparent convenience opened the door to a more complex set of challenges, e.g. there were different devices/apps/software for which we were required to provide support. While no one questions the central role a teacher has in orchestrating the activities with technology (Dillenbourg and Jermann 2010), at times this was felt like an 'additional burden' (Sharples 2015).

9 Conclusions

This paper offers an account of a study which approached vocabulary learning based on student-generated resources rather than resources that the teacher supplied to the students. It provided some insights into ways in which activities with mobile technologies could be integrated into heritage language learning through an example of engagement with a small group of students. Its importance lies in that through such micro-practices the practitioners increase their ability to reflect upon, make sense and improve their practices in a meaningful way.

The paper considered new opportunities to develop language skills by acknowledging that learners' expectations are changing and would welcome the chance to use their mobile device in ways that could help them enhance their learning. The analysis showed that students had a positive experience, while the benefits from this intervention are viewed mainly in terms of vocabulary learning and an enhanced awareness of the concept of 'loanwords'. Moreover, the analysis highlighted that the use of technology should be aligned with the adoption of appropriate pedagogies and points to some considerations regarding the learning design, such as blending physical and digital artefacts, working towards 'tangible' creative outputs and engaging an 'audience', while maintaining a focus on the curriculum.

Still, there is clearly a need for further work on the way this can be achieved most effectively at different levels. The insights gained here allow us to engage with yet another 'cycle of action and reflection' to link practice with ideas and inform learning designs with the use of mobile technologies.

References

Anderson, J.: 'Relevance of CLIL in Developing Pedagogies for Minority Language Teaching'. In: Marsh et al. (eds) CLIL Practice: Perspectives from the field (2009). http://www.icpj.eu/?id=contents. Accessed 20 July 2015

Anderson, J., Chung, Y.-C.: Community languages, the arts and transformative pedagogy: developing active citizenship for the 21st century. Citizenship Teach. Learn. **7**(3), 259–271 (2012)

Browne, C., Culligan, B.: Combining technology and IRT testing to build student knowledge of high frequency vocabulary. JALT CALL J. **4**(2), 3–16 (2008)

Buckingham, D.: Beyond Technology: Children's Learning in the Age of Digital Culture. Polity Press, Cambridge (2007)

Burston, J.: Mobile-assisted language learning: a selected annotated bibliography of implementation studies 1994–2012. Lang. Learn. Technol. **17**(3), 157–225 (2013)

Burston, J.: MALL: the pedagogical challenges. Comput. Assist. Lang. Learn. **27**(4), 344–357 (2014)

Carr, W., Kemmis, S.: Becoming Critical: Education Knowledge and Action Research. Falmer, Lewes (1986)

Charitonos, K.: An investigation into the use of a microblogging technology in school trips to museums. Ph.D. thesis. The Open University (2015)

Crook, C.: The "digital native" in context: tensions associated with importing Web 2.0 practices into the school setting. Oxford Rev. Educ. **38**(1), 63–80 (2012)

Dillenbourg, P., Jermann, P.: Technology for Classroom Orchestration. In: Khine, S.M., Saleh, M.I. (eds.) New Science of Learning. Cognition, Computers and Collaboration in Education, pp. 525–552. Springer, New York (2010)

Duggan, M., Ellison, N., Cliff, L., Lenhart, A., Madden. M.: Social Media Update 2014. Pew Research Centre 9 January. http://www.pewinternet.org/2015/01/09/social-media-update-2014/. Accessed 20 July 2015

Evans, D., Gillan-Thomas, K.: Supplementary Education. Descriptive analysis of supplementary school pupils' characteristics and attainment in seven local authorities in England, 2007/08—2011/12 Paul Hamlyn Foundation (2015). http://www.phf.org.uk/publications/supplementary-schools-research-report/. Accessed 10 July 2015

Handley, S.: Promoting community language learning in the United Kingdom. Lang. Learn. J. **39**(2), 149–162 (2011)

Haspelmath, M.: Lexical borrowing: concepts and issues. In: Haspelmath, M., Tadmor, U. (eds.) Loanwords in the World's Languages: A Comparative Handbook. De Gruyter Mouton, Berlin (2009)

JISC BYOD Legal Toolkit (2013). http://www.jisclegal.ac.uk/ManageContent/ViewDetail/ID/3070/BYOD-Toolkit-1-May-2013.aspx. Accessed 5 April 2015

Kennedy, C., Levy, M.: Litaliano al telefonino: using SMS to support beginners" language learning. ReCALL **20**(3), 315–330 (2008)

King, K.A., Ennser-Kananen, J.: 'Heritage languages and language policy'. Chapelle C.A. (ed.) The Encyclopaedia of Applied Linguistics, Blackwell Publishing Ltd. (2013)

Kress, G.: Multimodality: A Social Semiotic Approach to Contemporary Communication. Routledge, London (2010)

Kukulska-Hulme, A.: Will mobile learning change language learning? ReCALL **21**(2), 157–165 (2009)

Kukulska-Hulme, A., Shield, L.: An overview of mobile assisted language learning: From content delivery to supported collaboration and interaction. ReCALL **20**(3), 271–289 (2008)

Kukulska-Hulme, A.: Language as a bridge connecting formal and informal language learning through mobile devices. In: Wong, L.-H., Milrad, M., Specht, M. (eds.) Seamless Learning in the Age of Mobile Connectivity, pp. 281–294. Springer, Singapore (2015)

Lewin, K.: Action research and minority problems. In: Lewin, G.W. (ed.) Resolving Social Conflicts, pp. 201–216. Harper and Row, New York (1946/1948)

Li, M., Ogata, H., Hou, B., Hashimoto, S., Liu, Y., Uosaki, N., Yano, Y.: Development of adaptive Kanji learning system for mobile phone. Int. J. Distance Educ. Technol. (IJDET) **8**(4), 29–41 (2010)

Macaro, E., Handley, Z., Walter, C.: A systematic review of CALL in English as a second language: Focus on primary and secondary education. Lang. Teach. **45**(1), 1–43 (2012)

MacGibbon, A.: 'BYOT signals a move to students using their own technology, writes Ainslie MacGibbon', The Sydney Morning Herald, 28 May 2012. http://www.smh.com.au/technology/technology-news/smarter-use-of-home-devices-20120527-1zcry.html#ixzz3hSadjxdX. Accessed 28 July 2015

McPake, J., Tinsley, T., Broeder, P., Mijares, L., Latomaa, S., Martynuik, W.: 'Valuing All Languages in Europe' Graz: European Centre for Modern Language (2007). www.ecml.at/mtp2/publications/Valeur-report-E.pdf. Accessed 10 July 2015

NRCSE (2015). Supplementary Education http://www.supplementaryeducation.org.uk/supplementary-education-the-nrc/. Accessed 10 July 2015

OfCom 'Children and Parents: Media Use and Attitudes Report' (2014). http://stakeholders.ofcom.org.uk/binaries/research/media-literacy/media-use-attitudes-14/Childrens_2014_Report.pdf. Accessed 10 July 2015

Pachler, N.: Research methods in mobile and informal learning: some issues. In: Vavoula, G., Pachler, N., Kukulska-Hulme, A. (eds.) Researching Mobile Learning Frameworks: Tools and Research Designs. Peter Lang, Bern (2009)

Selwyn, N., Crook, C., Noss, R., Laurillard, D.: 'Education 2.0? Towards an educational web 2.0' in TLRP-TEL (2012). Education 2.0? Designing the web for teaching and learning http://www.tlrp.org/pub/documents/TELcomm.pdf. Accessed 2 April 2015

Sharples, M.: Seamless learning despite context. In: Wong, L.-H., Specht, M., Milrad, M. (eds.) Seamless Learning in the Age of Mobile Connectivity, pp. 41–55. Springer, Singapore (2015)

Song, Y.: "Bring Your Own Device (BYOD)" for seamless science inquiry in a primary school. Comput. Educ. **74**, 50–60 (2014)

Speak to the Future. 'RT news report on poor UK language skills' 14 April 2015. http://www.speaktothefuture.org/rt-news-report-on-poor-uk-language-skills/. Accessed 25 May 2015

Stockwell, G.: Using mobile phones for vocabulary activities: examining the effect of the platform. Lang. Learn. Technol. **14**(2), 95–110 (2010)

UNESCO. Policy Guidelines for mobile learning (2013). http://unesdoc.unesco.org/images/0021/002196/219641e.pdf. Accessed 25 July 2015

Wertsch, J.V.: Voices of the Mind: A Sociocultural Approach to Mediated Action. Harvard University Press, Cambridge (1991)

Williams, Z.: 'Now I get the naked selfie – at its core it is citizen porn' Guardian 5 September 2014.http://www.theguardian.com/theguardian/2014/sep/05/saturday-sketch-naked-selfie-citizen-porn. Accessed 30 July 2015

Wong, L.-H., Chin, C-K., Tan, C-L., Liu, M., Gong, C.: Students' meaning making in a mobile assisted chinese idiom learning environment. In: ICLS 2010 Proceedings, vol. 1, pp. 349–356 (2010)

Wong, L.-H., Chen, W., Jan, M.: How artefacts mediate small-group co-creation activities in a mobile-assisted seamless language learning environment? J. Comput. Assist. Learn. **28**(5), 411–424 (2012)

Wong, L.-H.: A learner-centric view of mobile seamless learning. Br. J. Educ. Technol. **43**(1), E19–E23 (2012)

Introducing an iPad Innovation into Accounting Tutorials

Laurel Evelyn Dyson(✉), Jessica K. Frawley, Jonathan Tyler, and James Wakefield

University of Technology, Sydney, Australia
{Laurel.E.Dyson, Jessica.Frawley, Jon.Tyler, James.Wakefield}@uts.edu.au

Abstract. This study reports on the second phase of a trial to change tutorials in an Introductory Accounting subject into more interactive, student-centred learning experiences using an iPad combined with sharing and annotation technology. The technology allows student homework to be photographed, shown to the class instantaneously through a data projector and annotated live by the tutor using the iPad, with student input. The innovation addresses calls from the Accounting Profession for educational approaches which use technology in imaginative ways to engage students and shift from the didactic paradigm that has dominated so much of accounting education in the past. The approach has the advantage that only one iPad is required per class and is used in conjunction with free software: it is thus cost effective and scalable to the large numbers of students enrolled in the subject. The trial reported in this paper involved two classes conducted with the iPads and two traditional classes without. Evaluation comprised observations of the four classes and a survey of the students regarding their experiences in the tutorials. The results revealed that the use of the technology did not of itself transform the classes into interactive, student-centred events: the teaching style of the tutor to a large extent determined how the iPads were used and how much interaction occurred. However, students in classes with the iPads were mostly enthusiastic about their use, even if the results of the survey generally failed to show statistically significant differences between the classes with iPads and those without.

Keywords: Tablet PC · Student–centred learning · Student engagement · First-year experience · Accounting education

1 Introduction

Since April 2010, when Apple first launched the iPad, there has been a phenomenal growth in ownership. A study by the Pew Research Center showed that 42 % of adults in the USA owned an iPad or other tablet PC in 2014, with the figure growing every year. In Australia, with its high adoption rates of mobile technology, the Mobile Industry Group found 56 % of surveyed adults aged 18 to 75 owned a tablet PC in 2013, up from 38 % in 2012, and 16 % in 2011 (MacKay 2013). Ownership amongst students is also high: a 2014 study of undergraduates and postgraduates across a range of disciplines at the authors' university showed 62 % of students surveyed owned a tablet.

T.H. Brown and H.J. van der Merwe (Eds.): mLearn 2015, CCIS 560, pp. 217–228, 2015.
DOI: 10.1007/978-3-319-25684-9_16

It is not surprising, then, to find educators interested in using the device to enhance their students' learning. Despite its origins as a device for consuming media (Fisher, Lucas and Galstyan 2013), the tablet PC lends itself to a variety of learning activities. These include its affordance for note-taking and annotation, multimedia viewing, interactivity and sharing, collaboration and communication, and both consumption and creation of content (Churchill, Fox and King 2012). It supports mobile learning because it is lighter and therefore more portable than a laptop, and also superior in face-to-face sharing: Fisher et al. (2013) found that mathematics students were able to share their solutions to problems in class much more easily when using an iPad compared with a laptop, since the laptop screen acted as a barrier, restricting the ability of other students to view their peers' work. Furthermore, studies have shown that tablets can increase students engagement and be highly motivating (Amelink, Scales and Tront 2012), and promote an active, student-centred pedagogy (Hargis et al. 2014). Wakefield and Smith (2012) presented a case study in which students located, critically evaluated and shared information in and out of the classroom instead of being given course materials and listening to lectures; this shifted the course to a student-centred, collaborative model in which the teacher guided and advised.

However, Daccord and Reich (2015, 22) note how resistant to change educational practices are and that, unless tablet PCs are "paired with investments in teacher capacity", transformation is unlikely. In an early study by van Oosteveen, Muirhead and Goodman (2011) the deployment of tablets was not transformative and students used them largely as a note-taking tool. Fisher et al. (2013) emphasize that much remains to be learnt about the deployment of the technology, particularly for supporting student interaction in face-to-face learning situations.

In this paper we present our findings of a trial in which we used iPads to improve student interactivity and to create a more student-centred learning experience in the tutorials of a large Introductory Accounting subject. Despite calls by the Accounting professional over many years for more innovative uses of technology to engage students, there is still a largely didactic approach at both the lecture and tutorial level (Stevenson, Ferguson and Power 2014). A major report of accounting education in Australia recently showed that accounting was lagging behind other disciplines in the use of new technologies: despite student expectations of technology use in their studies, accounting lecturers lacked engagement with technology, were resistant to change and suffered from workload and time constraints (Watty, McKay and Ngo 2014).

The paper will begin with a description of how iPads were introduced into the tutorials and the problem that they were intended to overcome. We report on the results of an earlier small trial in which one tutor used an iPad for one semester and how this provided proof of concept for the innovation to be continued. We then describe our evaluation methods and the findings in a larger trial involving four tutorials, in which iPads were deployed in half the classes while the other half followed the more traditional format. Some of the findings were surprising, in that we expected higher levels of interactivity in both tutorials in which the iPads had been deployed, but this was not automatically the case, despite generally high levels of student satisfaction when iPads were used in the class. Our discussion explores the issues raised and suggests further work.

The study contributes to our understandings of using iPads in moving towards more student-centered learning approaches in face-to-face education contexts. It is innovative in accounting education since we believe it is the first report in the literature of using iPads in this way. Furthermore, it has implications in other disciplines, particularly where there is a core body of knowledge that must be mastered by students.

2 The Implementation of iPads in Tutorials and Initial Findings

The first-year undergraduate subject in which iPads were trialled in 2014-15 is typical of introductory accounting in being a core subject for all Business students and having very large student numbers: approximately 1,500 in first semester and another 700 in the semester following the mid-year intake. There are a number of reasons why students study introductory accounting, including the plan to undertake an accounting major, acquire a basic knowledge of accounting in order to enhance business decision-making, or purely to satisfy a requirement of their course. Based on these different reasons, there is a great diversity in the motivation and dedication of students to their studies.

Apart from attending lectures, students are also provided with tutorials, for which they are expected to prepare by undertaking homework exercises, mostly consisting of accounting problems. Tutors work extensively through the exercises, in some cases, writing the solutions on the whiteboard while talking through them and allowing students the opportunity to ask questions. Students then form the expectation that tutors will continue with the process and tutorials become centred on the tutor and his or her solutions and explanations, with students adopting a passive role.

To motivate students to participate and engage in tutorials to a greater extent, we introduced iPad-enabled sharing and annotation technologies. Because of the large student enrolment it was imperative that the adoption of any new technology be cost effective. Hence, unlike other studies reported in the literature, where each student is equipped with a device (e.g., Fisher et al. 2013, Wakefield and Smith 2012), our implementation requires only one device per tutor. The iPad allows photos of handwritten student homework to be taken, transmitted wirelessly to a desktop or laptop computer connected to the classroom projector, which shows the images to all students in the class instantaneously on the large screen. The tutor annotates the homework on the iPad, if possible with student input, and these annotations are again projected live to the class (Fig. 1). Thus, instead of tutors giving the answer, images of individual student exercises become the centre of discussion.

In adopting this technology and shifting the focus of student attention away from the tutor's solutions to students' own work, we sought to answer a question posed by Prosser and Trigwell (1999, 99): "Approaches to learning are relational, hence changes to the learning context may be sufficient to change students' approaches to learning. What factors in the learning context might be related to students' adopted approaches?" The provision of tutors' solutions was reasonably assumed to be the factor related to student passivity and lack of participation. Hence, changing the learning context to focus on students' solutions was hypothesized to be a way of increasing engagement, peer learning and encouraging students to participate more.

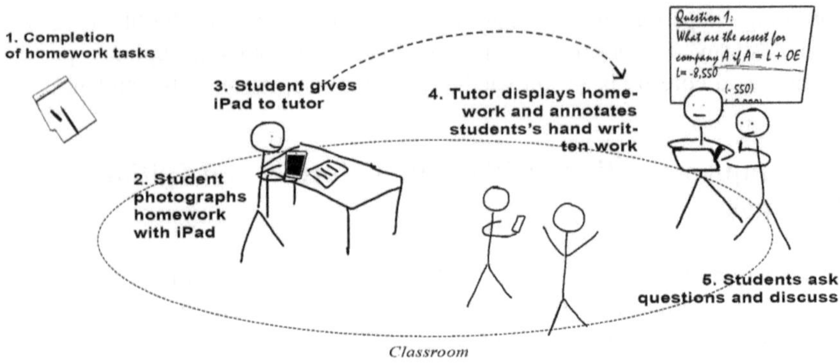

Fig. 1. Image sharing and annotation process in class

A small trial with one tutor in 2014 demonstrated that the technology was easy to use in class. The trial was evaluated by two focus groups: one of students attending a tutorial in which the iPad technology had been used and the other from a tutorial conducted in the traditional manner (Dyson, Frawley, Tyler and Wakefield 2014). Students who had experienced the iPad innovation were extremely enthusiastic about its use in the class, whether they were one of those who volunteered their homework for display or never did so. They appreciated being able to get instant feedback and seeing where their work stood with respect to other students. The lack of anonymity in providing answers did not seem to worry them. Furthermore, they appreciated being able to cover a large number of the homework exercises quickly. The inability to cover all the required content in class was a major concern for the students from the traditional tutorial who had participated in the second focus group. These students confirmed much of the lecturer's views how the tutorials are normally conducted, namely the adoption of a very teacher-centred approach, with little interaction between students. They voiced their preference for a more engaging method of teaching in which they could interact with each other, get to know each other, and also do more of the work in the class (Dyson et al. 2014).

The findings of this exploratory study gave us encouragement to continue with this innovation on a larger scale in 2015 with a more thorough evaluation undertaken.

3 Experimental Design and Research Methods

Three tutors were selected to trial the iPad annotation technology in 2015 in their tutorials, which last 1½ hours. They were more senior staff who had extensive experience of running tutorial classes and were thus considered in the best possible position to identify the added value of the new approach over prior semesters and suggest potential improvements. To maximize the benefits, since we felt its use would change classroom dynamics, tutors started using the innovation from week one following a briefing session. They were asked to use the technology as a supplement to existing practices. For instance, some exercises still need to be worked through on the whiteboard, given their greater complexity and the challenge posed to students. Tutors were asked, therefore, to consider the setup of the tutorial room: projecting the live annotation to a screen beside the whiteboard was considered the best way to leverage both the new and old resources available. They were also asked to clearly emphasize the shared nature of the technology through allowing student volunteers to take photos of their own homework, rather than the tutor standing over them and forcing them to share their homework. We felt that such a forced approach would lead to student resistance to the new technology, rather than improve engagement. In actual practice, only two tutors decided to adopt the iPads, the original academic who had trialled the technology initially and was so enthusiastic about it that he decided to use it in all his tutorials, and a tutor who tried it in one of his classes, while using the traditional teaching method in his other class.

Reflective of the comparative, experimental nature of this study, the image-sharing and annotation approach was evaluated across four tutorials, two of which employed the iPads (experimental condition) and two without (control group) (Table 1).

Two methods were employed to evaluate the trial: firstly, observations of the four tutorials for one week by two of the research team who are unconnected with teaching the subject, and secondly a survey of all the students in the four tutorials. Thus two different perspectives were obtained: the researchers' and the students'. Details are as follows.

Table 1. Experimental design

	iPad sharing and annotation technologies	Traditional teaching method (non-iPad)
Tutor A	Tutorial 1	
Tutor B	Tutorial 2	Tutorial 3
Tutor C		Tutorial 4

3.1 In-Class Observations

The researchers observed the four tutorials over the course of a single week during the latter half of the semester. Observations were recorded using the time, type of interaction, and any comments or issues that were observed. Researchers were seated at the back of the classroom and all recordings were done by hand, without the potentially intimidating presence of any recording equipment that might have affected student and tutor behavior. Though this approach is less likely to affect student behavior it does have limitations, for example, the difficulty of separating multiple responses to one question, or noting private interactions between friends or small groups. The researchers recorded the general atmosphere of the class; however, notes on interactions are limited to what was observable within open class discussion. From these notes, the interactions were then summarized (see Findings).

3.2 Student Surveys

Surveys were administered in hard-copy format to students in the four tutorials at the end of semester. Hard copy ensured that all students present completed the surveys. Questions were devised based firstly on the student feedback received during the two focus groups of the initial trial, and secondly from the in-class observations. All students used 5-point Likert scales to rate 14 common questions, with an additional 9 questions specifically for those students who had attended the tutorials in which the iPad had been used. The questions were designed to elicit information about how teacher- or student-centric the pedagogy was (teacher talk versus student talk); the level and nature of interaction (students asking or answering questions, listening to the tutor, peer learning); receiving feedback (from tutor or from peers); and learning the process of accounting versus learning accounting content. The questions and the results are presented in Tables 2 and 3. For the sake of convenience of comparison, the results from the two experimental tutorials were grouped, and the results from both control classes were grouped.

There was also an open-ended question, either "Briefly describe your experience of having the iPads used in the tutorials", or "Briefly describe your experience of the tutorials in this subject" for the non-iPad students. Sample answers from the student responses are reported in the Findings section.

4 Findings

4.1 In-Class Observations

Core findings from the tutorial observations were:

- *Levels of student participation did not depend solely on iPad use*

Tutorial 1 had the greatest number of positive, on-task student interactions (57 observed). These interactions included student-teacher (e.g., asking and answering questions, asking the tutor to go over work again, volunteering or explaining their homework answer, and discussing with the tutor) as well as student-student interactions (e.g., discussing the work with another student). Tutorial 4 had a much lower number of on-task interactions (14). Like Tutor C, Tutor B had few students asking or answering questions, or discussing the work with the whole class (Tutorial 2: 14 interactions; Tutorial 3: 12 interactions). However, he enhanced classroom interactivity in both his iPad and non-iPad tutorials by using a traditional method, that of small-group work.

- *Individual tutors structure their classes differently*

Observations of the three tutors highlighted the different ways that tutors structured their tutorials – whether these classes were *with* or *without* the iPad innovation. Tutor A, who *only* taught with the iPad, used it within a wider student-centric approach to teaching that began by asking students which problems they wanted to work on and handing the iPad over to a volunteer to take the photo. There was no "off-task" work observed. Tutor B used small-group discussion time (45 min per tutorial) to let students work through the homework together. This approach encouraged interactivity in otherwise not highly interactive classes, but in the non-iPad class resulted in lots of students being distracted or off task (16 off-task behaviours observed, plus 25 students who left early). However, in Tutor B's iPad tutorial the class was very focused on the work they were doing (only 3 off-task interactions), even though they had little choice in what work they covered, with the tutor selecting which exercises to work through and photographing student work during the small group activities. Tutor C, who only taught without iPads, structured the class around homework exercises and had a largely didactic tutorial with little student participation. However, her students seemed reasonably well focused and engaged with the work (10 off-task behaviours observed). What this emphasizes is that whilst all tutorials taught the same content, tutors had their own existing teaching approaches, which pre-dated the implementation of the iPad innovation. How well this innovation worked in Tutorials 1 and 2 depended, not solely on the technology, but its place within the tutors' teaching habits and the way they structured their class.

- *Integration of the technology into teaching*

In Tutorial 1 the iPad was integrated seamlessly with other approaches to teaching. Tutor A was quick in navigating between photos of student work and annotating it in a way that was easily visible to the class. The iPad was used to support wider interactivity through questions, answers, discussion. In contrast, in Tutorial 2 the iPad was used in a way that was supplementary, as opposed to integrated, within the tutor's pre-existing teaching. For Tutor B the iPad was an alternative way of doing some of the class activities. However, in comparing Tutor B's iPad class with his non-iPad class, there was little change to the fundamental structure or way in which the class was taught. Thus the iPad was more a laminate, than an integrated part, of the class structure and conduct.

- *Tutor's manner of annotation*

There were several differences in the way Tutors A and B annotated the images of student work. Tutor A's annotations were large, written in a bright colour (e.g. red or green) and included marks that functioned as "gestures" to emphasize what the tutor was saying. For example, Tutor A might say "this bit here, this is really important" and circle the part of the equation that was related to what he was saying. In contrast, Tutor B did not use gestural marking and highlighting to the same degree that Tutor A did. Tutor B's writing was neater, smaller and sometimes less visible due to using a black "pen" which blended in with the black-and-white written student work.

- *Minor technical problems*

Only one technical malfunction was observed in Tutorial 1. This was caused by the iPad losing connection to the WiFi. Though this was an interruption, Tutor A handled it calmly and did not disrupt the flow or focus of the class.

4.2 Student Surveys

Table 2 shows the analysis of the answers to questions presented to all students in the four tutorials. Answers usually ranged from Strongly Disagree (1) to Strongly Agree (5), except for Questions A and B, where answers regarding frequency could be Never (1), Once (2), Occasionally (3), Mostly (4) or Every Class (5). The mean ratings for Tutorial 1 and 2 (iPad) and Tutorials 3 and 4 (non-iPad) are compared using an independent samples 2-tailed *t* test. It can be seen that, for only 4 questions out of the 14 was the mean rating significantly different between the iPad and non-iPad groups. Furthermore, for only 3 questions did the iPad group rate the questions higher: Q 4 "I have gotten to know many other students during class activities"; Q 5 "I learn a lot from other students' questions and comments in tutorials"; and Q 7 "During the class I learn a lot from comparing my homework with that of other students". For Q B, students in the non-iPad group actually rated their frequency of sharing homework with the class as significantly higher than the iPad group, contrary to expectations.

Table 3 shows the results for the questions asked solely of students in Tutorials 1 and 2, where iPads were in use. The mean ratings show that students were generally satisfied with the use of the deployment of the iPad sharing and annotation approach. For three questions, mean rankings were in excess of 4 on the scale of 1 to 5: students thought it was nice to see others' work because it made them feel they were not the only one who got it wrong or didn't understand (mean = 4.27); they didn't mind if the same students always had their work shown on the iPad (mean = 4.04); and they thought that the iPads were really helpful in a subject like accounting, where there was a right and wrong answer and a process to go through (mean = 4.13).

Student comments to the open-ended question were generally positive for both iPad and non-iPad tutorials. With regard to the iPad tutorials typical positive responses included: (Tutorial 1) "The use of iPad allowed me to learn from the mistakes of other students"; "I liked the use of the ipad because I could easily see the process other students used who got the answer correct and I could compare them to mine."; "Fantastic, especially for accounting H/W because there are lots of hard steps to go through in order to get the answer and the tutor goes through slowly & is able to write on the work through the ipad but not actually manipulate the work"; "Ipads were used well, quick and effective way of sharing homework"; (Tutorial 2) "It made the class a bit more engaging and interesting. It was an effective way to display the answer and to work through it as a class."; "My experience of having the iPad in my tutorial was pleasant, interactive, productive and engaging method and it certainly helped me throughout my learning process." Negative or mixed comments were fewer but included: (Tutorial 1) "It was quite time consuming have to take photos and switch between programs. Would of preferred for tutor to just write out and explain answers on whiteboard."; "The Ipad is a good way to see other peoples work, but sometimes I like to wate [to see] how its done.. then change/mark my work. with the ipad they move on quickly and the slide is gone."; (Tutorial 2) "The ipad's did not take clear photos and the program was slow and hard for the tutor to use. I found it more complicated trying to read others work on a blurry photo. good concept though."

The open-ended responses from students in the traditional non-iPad tutorials were also largely positive. Many students appreciated the tutors' explanations of content

Table 2. Survey questions common to iPad and non-iPad tutorials (n = 96)

Question	Mean likert scale rating		*t* (*df: 94*)	*p*	Significance Level
	iPad Tutorials	Non-iPad Tutorials			
1. Most of the talking in the tutorial is done by the tutor.	3.46	3.63	−0.904	0.368	–
2. In class I prefer to listen and think about what the tutor is saying, rather than ask questions.	3.56	3.59	−0.110	0.912	–
3. I feel comfortable asking and answering the tutor's questions in the class.	3.89	3.90	−0.063	0.950	–
4. I have gotten to know many other students during class activities.	3.47	2.95	2.152	0.036	$p < 0.05$
5. I learn a lot from other students' questions and comments in tutorials.	4.13	3.44	4.168	0.000	$p < 0.001$
6. I don't mind if the same people always ask or answer the tutor's questions.	4.11	3.83	1.804	0.075	–
7. During the class I learn a lot from comparing my homework with that of other students.	4.24	3.61	3.579	0.001	$p < 0.005$
8. It is really helpful to get the tutor's feedback on homework during class.	4.40	4.27	0.778	0.438	–
9. The tutor goes through the work step by step and breaks each problem down so that it is easy to understand.	4.49	4.54	0.304	0.762	–
10. The tutor's final answer is more important than seeing the steps you use to get there.	1.95	2.00	−0.305	0.761	–
11. We get through a lot of content during the tutorial.	4.15	4.00	0.959	0.340	–
12. I feel fully focused on the accounting exercises throughout the whole tutorial.	3.71	3.88	−0.951	0.344	–
A. How often did you ask or answer the tutor's questions in class?	2.82	2.66	0.768	0.444	–
B. How often was your homework shared with the rest of the class using the iPad?/How often did you share your homework with the class?	1.98	2.78	−2.986	0.004	$p < 0.005$

and/or process: (Tutorial 4) "Informative, helps to learn the content and generally does what it needs to do, I think it's good."; "Clear explanations/Step by step analysis/Good learning environment/Helpful with any queries and concerns." Only one student voiced a concern over the traditional, didactic method of teaching in Tutorial 4: "It was ok.

Table 3. Survey questions regarding the use of the iPad (n = 55)

Question	Mean	Median	Std. Dev.
13. Using the iPad is a quick way of getting feedback from the tutor.	3.89	4.00	0.92
14. I felt more students participate when the iPad is part of the class.	3.76	4.00	0.84
15. Using the iPad makes the tutorial more engaging by getting everyone working together.	3.86	4.00	0.93
16. Using the iPad is time consuming and a waste of time.	2.09	2.00	1.06
17. Knowing your homework might be shown on screen makes you actually do it.	3.27	3.00	0.99
18. If you volunteer your homework, there's no judgment if you get the answer wrong.	3.93	4.00	0.92
19. It is nice to see other students' work because it makes you feel you're not the only one who got it wrong or didn't understand.	4.27	4.00	0.56
20. I don't mind if the same students always have their work shown in class using the iPad.	4.04	4.00	0.64
21. For a subject like Accounting, where there is a right and a wrong answer, and a process to go through, the use of the iPads is really helpful.	4.13	4.00	0.75

I would have preferred it if the teacher was more innovative in the way she teaches and try to engage us in another way rather than just saying 'you have to listen because you need it!'" By contrast, several students in Tutorial 3 voiced their appreciation of the discussion and interactivity of the small-group discussion sessions: "Going through the homework with my peers first was helpful in both understanding the requirements as well as learning about them when explaining my answers to my peers and when they explain theirs to me."

5 Discussion

The findings demonstrated that it was more difficult than we had expected to change students' approaches to learning and make the tutorials more participative and learner-centred. Though Tutor A, who had previous experience with the iPad sharing and annotation technology in our initial trial, had fully integrated it into his teaching and was achieving the highest levels of student participation and interactivity, Tutor B retained an accepted method of fostering student participation, namely small-group work. For him, the iPad approach was a supplement to his established teaching practices. Moreover, this tutor was not as expert at annotating the students' homework on the iPad, and there were a couple of complaints in the student surveys about his photos being blurry and hard to read.

While this highlights the need for better training (Daccord and Reich 2015), it is also essential to respect the agency of tutors and the different ways in which they structure their classes. Thus, any staff development needs to accept that the iPad innovation will not be implemented into a homogenous learning and teaching environment. Tutors will have different epistemologies or "private theories" of teaching and learning, which will either impede or enhance their adoption of an innovation, and these will need to be taken into account if the affordances of iPad technologies for greater interactivity are to be realized (Churchill et al. 2012).

Furthermore, though the surveys revealed that students in Tutorials 1 and 2 were largely enthusiastic about the iPads in the classroom, the lack of significantly different responses to most common questions answered by these students and those in the traditional, non-iPad tutorials shows a level of acceptance of – and, indeed, occasionally, a preference for – traditional teaching approaches. A case in point was the student who would have liked the tutor "to just write out and explain answers on whiteboard", presumably in a similar way to that adopted by Tutor C. As Prosser and Trigwell (1999, 107) note, changing the learning context may be insufficient to improve learning approaches, given "students' perceptions of that context and of their learning situation". However, the positive comments regarding the interactivity of Tutor B's small-group discussions, practised in Tutorials 2 and 3 (with and without the iPad technology), show that students do react well to more participatory classroom techniques, if they are offered them.

6 Conclusion

Following our initial trial of the iPad to make student worked examples the focus of discussion in tutorials, we had believed that there would be a clearer demarcation between the new technology-supported approach and the traditional method of conducting tutorials, in which the tutor works through exercises on the whiteboard and the students occupy the more passive role of listening and correcting their homework, with the occasional question. Though the much higher level of interactivity in the first tutorial in which the iPad was employed in this larger trial demonstrates the shift that is possible towards student-centred learning, there are obviously issues with both the embedded teaching practices of tutors as well as student expectations of how they should be taught.

The two very different ways in which the iPads were deployed highlights the need to better understand the tutor's experience and its impact on learning. How the use of iPads in this new teaching approach shapes tutors' attitudes to teaching and learning is an important area for future research. In addition, the difference in pedagogies between the tutors who used iPads in tutorials 1 and 2, and between the tutors who did not use iPads in tutorials 3 and 4, probably obscured some of the findings, particularly in relation to the student surveys. For example, the students in Tutorials 2 and 3 all experienced a level of interactivity and participation through traditional small group discussions set up by Tutor B. Establishing a clearer understanding of this trial will form the basis of the next phase of our research: in particular, we intend to conduct a more sophisticated statistical analysis of the data we collected and compare survey responses for each tutorial with learning outcomes achieved by the students in their final exam.

References

Amelink, C.T., Scales, G., Tront, J.G.: Student use of the tablet PC: impact on student learning behaviors. Adv. Eng. Educ. Winter **3**, 1–17 (2012)

Churchill, D., Fox, B., King, M.: Study of affordances of iPads and teachers' private theories. Int. J. Inf. Educ. Technol. **2**(3), 251–254 (2012)

Daccord, T., Reich, J.: How to transform teaching with tablets. Educational Leadership, May 18–23 (2015)

Dyson, L.E., Frawley, J.K., Tyler, J., Wakefield, J.: Facilitating enhanced learning in tutorials through tablet computing enabled sharing and annotation technologies. Trans. Mob. Learn. **3**, 22–26 (2014)

Fisher, B., Lucas, T., Galstyan, A.: The Role of iPads in constructing collaborative learning spaces. Tech. Know Learn. **18**, 165–178 (2013)

Hargis, J., Cavanaugh, C., Kamali, T., Soto, M.: A federal higher education iPad mobile learning initiative: triangulation of data to determine early effectiveness. Innov. High. Educ. **39**, 45–57 (2014)

Mackay, M.M.: Australian Mobile Phone Lifestyle Index. Mobile Industry Group, AIMIA (2013)

Pew Research Center. E-reading rises as device ownership jumps (2014). http://www.pewinternet.org/files/2014/01/PIP_E-reading_011614.pdf

Prosser, M., Trigwell, K.: Understanding Learning and Teaching: The Experience of Higher Education. The Society for Research into Higher Education and Open University Press, Buckingham (1999)

Stevenson, L., Ferguson, J., Power, D.: The use of teaching resources in accounting education. The Routledge Companion to Accounting Education (2014)

van Oostveen, R., Muirhead, W., Goodman, W.M.: Tablet PCs and reconceptualizing learning with technology: a case study in higher education. Int. Technol. Smart Educ. **8**(2), 78–93 (2011)

Wakefield, J., Smith, D.: From Socrates to satellites: iPad learning in an undergraduate course. Creative Educ. **3**(5), 643–648 (2012)

Watty, K., McKay, J., Ngo, L.: CPA Australia Global Research Perspectives Program. Deakin University and CPA Australia, Melbourne (2014)

Assimilate or Accommodate? The Need to Rethink Current Use of the Term 'Mobile Learning'

Jocelyn Wishart(✉)

University of Bristol, Bristol, UK
j.m.wishart@bristol.ac.uk

Abstract. For a decade now, as mobile devices are found in an ever wider range of learning situations and contexts, mobile learning researchers have sought to define (Sharples, Taylor and Vavoula, 2007; Wexler et al. 2008) and redefine (Crompton, 2013) mobile learning in a way that is meaningful within this increasing range. However, the need to assimilate this ever increasing range of situations and contexts has become a progressively more complex challenge which is well illustrated by Park's (2011) paper that aims to categorise educational applications of mobile technologies into four types. Like many others Park includes the classroom as a pedagogical context for mobile learning. However, Sharples et al. (2007)'s original definition emphasised the assumption that, for learning to be mobile, learners are continually on the move which is clearly not the case for students using mobile devices in class to, say, record audio or video or as a classroom voting system. Yet we continue to try to assimilate these instances into our understanding of mobile learning. Is it not now time to accommodate this complexity and create a new concept reserving the original term 'mobile learning' for mobile technology supported learning opportunities that involve the learners physically moving between contexts? This paper will therefore engage its audience in a debate about whether it is time to rethink definitions of mobile learning to exclude static, classroom based learning opportunities using tablets such as iPads or students' own mobile devices. Such learning opportunities would need renaming, maybe 'handheld learning' or 'hand-e-learning'? Though that begs the question, is this not just another form of e-learning making a separate name unnecessary? Other suggestions will be invited on the day so as to involve both experienced and new researchers in this debate.

1 What Do We Understand by Mobile Learning?

The concept of mobile learning came into being along with the twenty-first century and was largely driven by the new learning opportunities offered by personal, portable technology that could connect to the Internet via mobile phone networks or wireless networking. Pioneers from both higher education and business introduced us to the term mobile learning in the year 2000. In the UK Mike Sharples published a framework for the design of personal mobile technologies for lifelong learning (Sharples, 2000) in a well-established academic journal. In the US, in an online magazine targeted at the 'New Economy', Clark Quinn announced a working definition of mLearning (short for mobile eLearning) - using a Palm OS personal digital assistant as a learning device (Quinn, 2000). So, for Quinn, mobile learning was eLearning delivered via mobile computational

T.H. Brown and H.J. van der Merwe (Eds.): mLearn 2015, CCIS 560, pp. 229–238, 2015.
DOI: 10.1007/978-3-319-25684-9_17

devices which, at the time, were Palms, Windows CE machines and some digital mobile phones. However, Sharples' work focussed more on the role of the learner than the technology and, with colleagues, he developed the definition of mobile learning to be used by Mobilearn, the first international research project to explore mobile learning. This was:

> *Any sort of learning that happens when the learner is not at a fixed, predetermined location, or learning that happens when the learner takes advantage of the learning opportunities offered by mobile technologies.* (O'Malley et al. 2003 p.7).

This was insightful as the technology changes rapidly however, the contrast in approaches has been an issue for researchers seeking clarity over the concept of mobile learning ever since. Another early authority Agnes Kukulska-Hulme recognised the challenge as she wrote in her introduction to the first Handbook of Mobile Learning edited with John Traxler:

> *Readers will probably position themselves differently in their own definitions of mobile learning, as indeed do the various contributors to this book: there are many ways to conceptualize, theorize about and experiment with mobile learning.* (Kukulska-Hulme and Traxler, 2005 p. 5).

Yet, by and large, the community of researchers and innovators in mobile learning have not been content with this eclectic approach and continued to define and redefine mobile learning. Changes to these definitions have been regularly prompted by the ever increasing range and contexts where mobile devices can be used. Brown (2005) describes this growth as the background to his placing of mLearning firmly as a subset of eLearning but one that provides "more mobility, flexibility and convenience" p. 10.

One of the most widely cited definitions gains credence from the authors' association of it with their aim to develop a widely applicable theory of mobile learning relevant to the broad range of learning opportunities available in the twenty-first century. Sharples, Taylor and Vavoula (2007) point out that the first step in developing a theory of mobile learning, surely, is to distinguish what is special about mobile learning compared to other types of learning activity. The obvious answer is that it starts from the assumption that learners are continually on the move. Their definition of mobile learning as:

> *the processes of coming to know through conversations across multiple contexts amongst people and personal interactive technologies* (Sharples, Taylor and Vavoula 2007 p. 4),

therefore reflects the dynamic, changing nature of mobile learning contexts and the authors' conception of learning as an interaction within a system.

Other definitions, not unsurprisingly, also reflect their authors' predominant conceptions such as this one emphasising productivity by Wexler et al. (2008) that was aimed at eLearning professionals in the US and presented in a report for the eLearning Guild exploring what mLearning is, why it matters and how to incorporate it into a learning strategy. Thus the eLearning Guild defines Mobile Learning (m-Learning) as follows:

> *Any activity that allows individuals to be more productive when consuming, interacting with, or creating information, mediated through a compact digital portable device that the individual carries on a regular basis, has reliable connectivity, and fits in a pocket or purse.* (Wexler et al. 2008, p. 7).

Another US based professional association, Educause, that was formed to serve the interest of higher education information technology community also starts their definition of M-Learning with a technological focus however it then moves on to restate the importance of mobility emphasising learning opportunities outside the traditional classroom.

> *Using portable computing devices (such as laptops, tablet PCs, PDAs, and smart phones) with wireless networks enables mobility and mobile learning, allowing teaching and learning to extend to spaces beyond the traditional classroom. Within the classroom, mobile learning gives instructors and learners increased flexibility and new opportunities for interaction. Mobile technologies support learning experiences that are collaborative, accessible, and integrated with the world beyond the classroom.* (Educause, 2015).

This definition also includes mobile technology enabled collaborative learning experiences, a notion also introduced by Sharples, Taylor and Vavoula (2007) as new pattern of mobile learning. However, for Educause the focus on mobility of mobile learning as "an essential defining attribute - is beyond dispute" as Oller (2012, p.1) pointed out in a research bulletin on the future of mobile learning created specifically for Educause.

However, this view is not endorsed by all within the mobile learning community. John Traxler, in reflection on both the content of this debate and its length, notes "After extended discussions within the mobile learning research community about the definition, it is probably just 'learning with mobile devices'" (Traxler, 2011, p. 4). Though he then immediately lists four key ways in which mobile learning opportunities can enhance, extend and enrich the both the concept and the activity of learning itself. He labels the first as contingent mobile learning and teaching, where learners can use personal, mobile devices to react and respond to their environment and their changing experiences both inside and outside the classroom. The second is situated learning, where learning takes place in surroundings that make learning meaningful. Traxler (ibid) exemplifies this with the examples of learning religious studies whilst visiting temples, mosques, churches and synagogues or learning about fish biodiversity whilst at sea. His third category of mobile learning opportunities are those that enable authentic learning, where learning tasks are meaningfully related to immediate learning goals, for example an app supporting nurse trainees doing drug calculations on hospital wards. The fourth is context aware learning, where learning is informed by information on the history and surroundings of the learner, for example in art galleries, botanical gardens and museums that is delivered via their device.

Other areas noted by Traxler (2011) where mobile learning is enriching the learner experience include location-specific student support systems such as the open source Mobile Oxford and My Mobile Bristol applications. These systems enable students at Oxford and Bristol universities in the UK to find any information they need, such as, for example, which bus to take them to the library holding the book they want at a particular moment in time, even allowing for multiple buses and multiple copies of the book being lent and returned at different libraries. Also he notes that assessments and tests are now increasingly exploiting mobile technologies, for example with physiotherapy students capturing visual proof of treatments in situ and trainee motor vehicle mechanics capturing evidence of their competence at engine maintenance procedures. In addition, ePortfolio systems such as Pebble Pad designed for students are migrating onto mobile phones allowing reflection on learning to be captured straightaway.

This wealth of learning opportunities afforded via mobile devices goes some way to demonstrate why the community has found it so hard to settle on a single, agreed definition of mobile learning. One of the latest, UNESCO tries to cover these multiple aspects.

> *Mobile learning involves the use of mobile technology, either alone or in combination with other information and communication technology (ICT), to enable learning anytime and anywhere. Learning can unfold in a variety of ways: people can use mobile devices to access educational resources, connect with others, or create content, both inside and outside classrooms. Mobile learning also encompasses efforts to support broad educational goals such as the effective administration of school systems and improved communication between schools and families.* UNESCO (2015).

Others have even announced that mobile learning is undefinable. Winters (2006) reflecting on the Big Issues in Mobile Learning workshop held by the pan-European Kaleidoscope Network of Excellence in 2006 reports "there was general agreement that a precise definition of mobile learning is unattainable" (Winters, 2006, p. 6). The expert group discussions moved on instead to propose four key characteristics of mobile learning. These included:

- That it enables knowledge building by learners in different contexts;
- That it enables learners to construct understandings;
- Mobile technology often changes the pattern of learning/work activity and
- The context of mobile learning is about more than time and space.

This stands in stark contrast to a recent, much more succinct definition, put forward by Helen Crompton in her historical overview of mobile learning in the, almost encyclopaedic, Handbook of Mobile Learning published by Routledge. She defines mobile learning as "learning across multiple contexts, through social and content interactions, using personal electronic devices" (Crompton, 2013, p.4).

Others take a different approach, aiming to frame (Koole, 2009) or categorise mobile learning (Park, 2011) thus avoiding the need to first wrestle with a definition. Koole (ibid)'s model, developed as a basis for assessing the effectiveness of mobile devices for distance learning, makes it clear that she defines mobile learning in terms of three distinct aspects: the device (technology and usability), the learner (their knowledge, experience and attitude), and the social (socio-cultural context). These aspects overlap and considering what happens at the intersections of these aspects will usefully inform the design of different mobile learning opportunities. For Koole, therefore, mobile learning is a combination of the interactions between learners, their devices, and other people. However, this conceptual model does not acknowledge the potential mobility of the learner whose technology enables them to use information and data from one context in another.

Park's (2011) aim is similar to Koole's (2009) in that the purpose of her categorisation of the educational applications of mobile technologies is to support instructional designers of open and distance learning in learning about the concepts of mobile learning and how mobile technologies can be incorporated into their teaching and learning more effectively. This categorization is based on a modified approach to transactional distance theory that includes opportunities for social mediation as a separate dimension to the transactional distance between learner and the source of that which is to be learned. Transactional distance itself is a concept based on the pedagogical, psychological and geographical space between instructor and learner introduced to distance learning by Moore (1997). It centres on the interactions between the learners, the learning resources, their tutor or instructor and their environment. The transactional distance itself is controlled and managed by three interrelated factors: (1) the taught programme's structure; (2) the dialogue that the tutor and learners exchange; and (3) the extent of the learners' autonomy. To this Park (ibid) added a third factor, social mediation, acknowledging the potential for collaboration via mobile technologies. Whether learners are working individually or collectively in a group was termed individualised m-learning or socialised m-learning respectively. This results in four categories: high transactional distance socialized m-learning in classroom based, group activities, (2) high transactional distance, individualized m-learning where there is instructional support or tightly structured content and resources such as in nurse education or mobile assisted language learning (MALL), (3) low transactional distance socialized m-learning which as loosely managed, unstructured group work is rarer and (4) low transactional distance individualized m-learning such as outside classroom, individual informal learning opportunities such as those involved in Citizen Science projects. Yet, as Park (ibid) herself acknowledges, though it is obscured by the emphasis on creating the four category model, transactional distance is, in fact, a continuum rather than discrete categories.

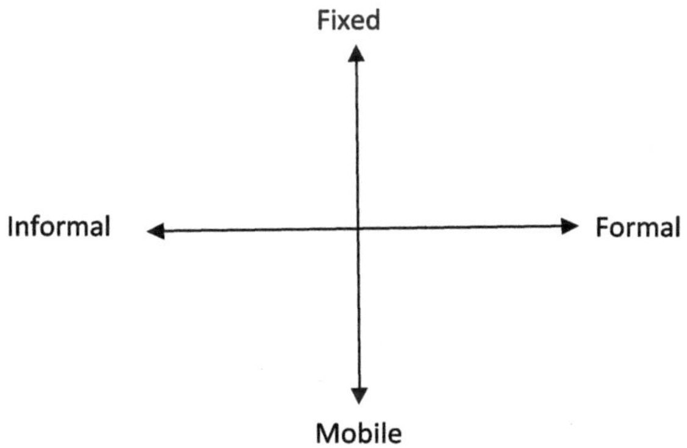

Fig. 1. Two possible dimensions of mobile learning

The approach of expanding the concept of mobile learning into a continuum was also taken up by Sharples (2013) in an overview of mobile learning research and practice written for the distance education community in China. He moves away from seeking to define what has, despite the efforts described above, become a nebulous concept that is difficult to seize and presents mobile learning on a continuum. This continuum or dimension, as Sharples (ibid) labels it, extends from enhancing classroom learning via devices such as handheld response systems and tablets to learning as part of everyday life through informal communication and knowledge sharing by mobile phone. Thus it extends from curriculum led learning opportunities in a fixed setting to informal, highly mobile learning opportunities. However, on closer inspection it actually comprises two dimensions, from the formal (curriculum based) to the informal (interest or hobby led) and from fixed (in a classroom) to mobile (in the field, crossing contexts) that can be represented orthogonally as shown in Fig. 1 below.

If we add in the individualised-socialised dimension as proposed by Park (2011) we have a neat three-dimensional model that encompasses a myriad of opportunities to engage in learning via personal, mobile technologies as shown in Fig. 2 below.

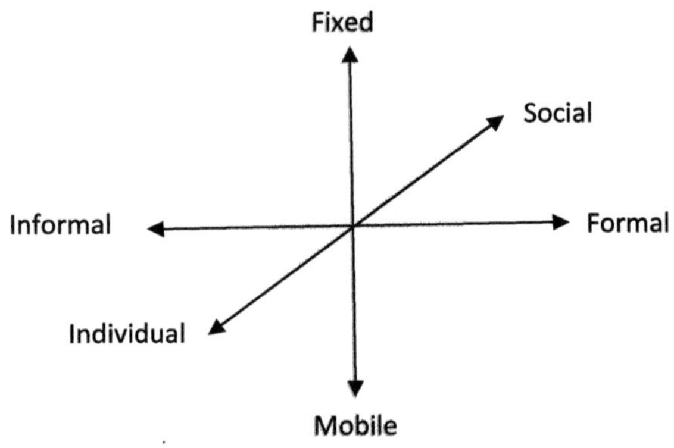

Fig. 2. Three possible dimensions of mobile learning

However, whilst this structure fits a range of learning opportunities that have been characterised as mobile learning such as Zurita and Nussbaum's (2004) mobile computer supported collaborative learning (MCSCL) activities in Chilean primary schools [Fixed, Social, Formal]; Priestnall et al's (2010) work on augmenting reality via mobile phones for earth science teaching [Mobile, Individual, Formal]; and the nature spotting app iSpot developed by the Institute of Educational Technology at the Open University, UK [Mobile, Individual, Informal], it is both hard to envisage and complex to work through all eight possible combinations. This is reminiscent of the way the definitions reported above increased in length and complexity as researchers struggled to capture the increasing range of mobile learning opportunities new and emerging technologies offer. On further reflection, how, for instance, should we include the rich visual learning opportunities now offered through augmented reality in the same model as a text-based quizzing app? With a fourth dimension?

2 The Dilemma: To Continue to Assimilate or to Accommodate?

Thus all of the framings, dimensions and categories discussed above have in common, along with the opportunities listed by Traxler (2011) and the more complex of the definitions presented earlier, the sense that their authors are trying to 'fit a quart into a pint pot'. The following concept map (Fig. 3) produced by Mirandanet, the global knowledge sharing online community for professionals engaged with digital technologies, members at a mobile learning conference in 2009 makes a valiant, if likely to be futile, effort to bring order to the resulting messiness.

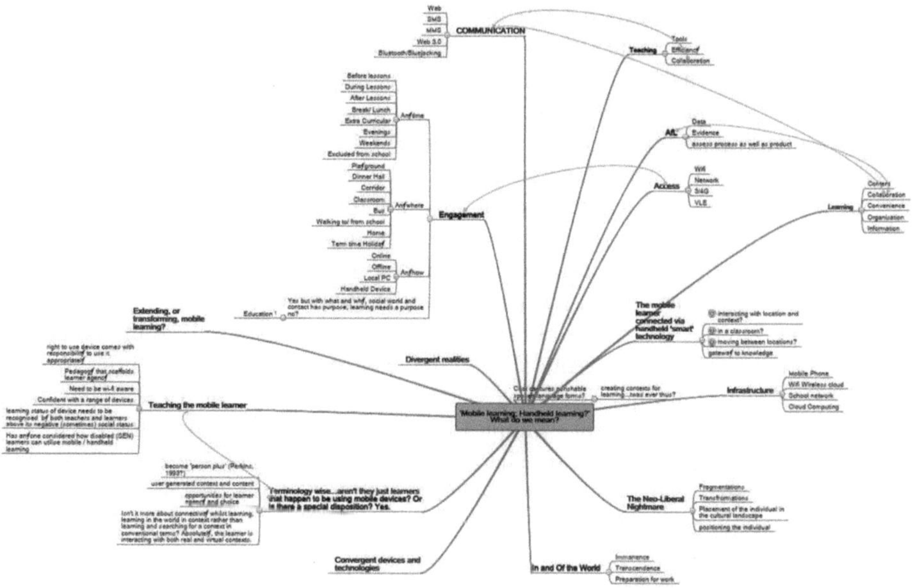

Fig. 3. Mobile learning: handheld learning? what do we mean?

A more successful approach was taken by Börner et al. (2010) who used both concept mapping and cluster analysis techniques to analyse mobile learning experts' perceptions of the most important educational problems that can be addressed by mobile learning. The identified problems were found to all relate to three main domain concepts "access to learning", "contextual learning", and "orchestrating learning across contexts" and thus confirming the essential nature of mobile learning relates to mobility of the learner supporting learning in and across a range of contexts rather than the device.

However, if we take a step out and reconsider these efforts to continually assimilate new learning opportunities via mobile technologies into our conceptual framing for mobile learning we can see that, whilst generating discussion and debate, it is not helping foreground mobile learning as a mainstream pedagogy. Rather, as pointed out by one of the reviewer of this paper, it has become a cyclical debate with similar arguments made nearly a decade ago. In 2007 John Traxler wrote "advocates of mobile learning attempt to define and conceptualise it in terms of devices and technologies; other advocates define and conceptualise it in terms of the mobility of learners and the mobility of learning" (Traxler, 2007).

Is it therefore not time, taking our lead from Jean Piaget's (1952) ground-breaking work on the origins of human intelligence, for us amend our concept of mobile learning the better to accommodate the range of learning opportunities available today? This process of accommodation features in Piaget's (ibid) descriptions of conceptual development which takes place firstly through the process of assimilation of new information into a growing schema (a framing for that concept) and then followed by its break up or 'accommodation' into several schemas when the range of assimilated information becomes too unwieldy to manage.

Thinking therefore, through the definitions presented above about the possible presence of sub-schemas, we note a prevailing distinction between those definitions that tend to lead with a focus on the technology being a mobile device and those which emphasise the mobility of the learner using such a device. When reviewing this latter point, the "essential defining attribute" of mobile learning (Oller, 2012), a question arises as to how this is managed when many researchers today, for example Park (2011), include the classroom as a pedagogical context for mobile learning. Here, learners such as school students using mobile devices in class for recording audio or video to support learning, or university students providing feedback via a classroom response app on their phones in a lecture, are clearly not continually on the move. There are indeed other context relevant learning opportunities for mostly classroom based learners such as learning in the field (Priestnall et al. 2010) or on visits outside the classroom (Chen et al. 2004; Vavoula et al. 2009). Or even, as highlighted by Yatigammana Ekanayake and Wishart (2011), for bringing personally relevant examples from the outside world into the classroom. However, fixed location teacher set classroom based tasks involving educational apps on phones or iPads, whilst involving handheld, mobile technologies do not match this mobility focused concept of learning.

3 Conclusion: Keep Mobile Learning to the Truly Mobile

Whilst it could be argued that the move from the virtual to the real when going online in the school classroom traverses learning contexts thus realising Crompton's (2013) recent definition of mobile learning as "learning across multiple contexts, through social and content interactions, using personal electronic devices" (p.4), classroom based learning is, in no way, truly mobile. Much of what we call classroom based mobile learning is Quinn's (2000) m-learning, simply 'using the current model of Smartphone as a learning device' and, largely follows what Cochrane (2014) describes as merely repositioning traditional teaching and learning resources and activities to online sources. It is now time to disassociate this perspective from that of location led, context relevant, situated and authentic mobile learning opportunities. This would create two conceptual framings with mobile learning being one and fixed location m-learning being the other. Thus examples of classroom based learning via mobile devices such as teacher set tasks involving educational apps on iPads now common to schools in many countries would need renaming. To call it m-learning would be confusing as 'm-'stands for mobile. One suggestion could be 'hand-e-learning' or maybe just 'handheld learning' and a more drastic approach would be to advocate tool agnosticism making it simply e-learning though that would preclude examples such as Cochranes's (ibid) creative pedagogy of using mobile social media in class. Other suggestions will be invited at the presentation of this paper at MLearn 2015 so as to involve both experienced and new researchers in this debate.

References

Dirk Börner, D., Christian Glahn, C., Slavi Stoyanov, S., Marco Kalz, M., Marcus Specht, M.: Expert concept mapping study on mobile learning. Campus-Wide Inf. Syst. **27**(4), 240–253 (2010)

Brown, T.H.: Towards a model for m-learning in Africa. Int. J. E-Learn. **4**(3), 299–315 (2005)

Chen, Y.S., Kao, T.C., Yu, G.J., Sheu, J.P.: A mobile butterfly-watching learning system for supporting independent learning. In: Proceedings of the 2nd IEEE International Workshop on Wireless and Mobile Technologies in Education, pp. 11–18. IEEE (2004)

Cochrane, T., Antonczak, L., Keegan, H., Narayan, V.: Riding the wave of BYOD: developing a framework for creative pedagogies. Res. Learn. Technol. **22**, 1–14 (2014)

Crompton, H.: A historical overview of mobile learning: toward learner-centered education. In: Berge, Z.L., Muilenburg, L.Y. (eds.) Handbook of Mobile Learning, pp. 3–14. Routledge, Florence (2013)

Educause. Current Topics: M-learning and mobility (2015). http://www.educause.edu/eli/programs/learning-technologies. Accessed 10 July 2015

Koole, M.L.: A model for framing mobile learning. In: Ally, M. (ed.) Mobile Learning: Transforming the Delivery of Education and Training, pp. 25–47. Athabasca University Press, Athabasca (2009)

Kukulska-Hulme, A., Traxler, J.: Mobile Learning-A Handbook for Educators and Trainers. Routledge, London (2005)

Moore, M.G.: Theory of transactional distance. In: Keegan, D. (ed.) Theoretical Principles of Distance Education, pp. 22–38. Routledge Studies in Distance Education, NY (1997)

Oller, R.: The Future of Mobile Learning (Research Bulletin). Louisville, CO: Educause Center for Analysis and Research (2012). https://net.educause.edu/ir/library/pdf/ERB1204.pdf. Accessed 24 July 2015

O'Malley, C., Vavoula, G., Glew, J.P., Taylor, J., Sharples, M., Lefrere, P.: Guidelines for Learning/Teaching/Tutoring in a Mobile Environment. MOBIlearn project report, D4.1 (2003). http://kn.open.ac.uk/public/getfile.cfm?documentfileid=7488. Accessed 21 July 2015

Park, Y.: A pedagogical framework for mobile learning: Categorizing educational applications of mobile technologies into four types. Int. Rev. Res. Open Distrib. Learn. **12**(2), 78–102 (2011)

Piaget, J.: The Origins of Intelligence in Children, vol. 8, issue 5, p. 18. International Universities Press, New York (1952)

Priestnall, G., Brown, E., Sharples, M., Polmear, G.: Augmenting the field experience: a student-led comparison of techniques and technologies. In: Brown, E. (ed.) Education in the Wild: Contextual and Location-Based Mobile Learning in Action. A Report from the Stellar Alpine Rendez-Vous Workshop Series, pp. 43–46. Learning Sciences Research Institute, Nottingham (2010)

Quinn, C.: mLearning: Mobile, wireless, in-your-pocket learning. LiNE Zine (2000). http://www.linezine.com/2.1/features/cqmmwiyp.htm. Accessed 21 July 2015

Sharples, M.: The design of personal mobile technologies for lifelong learning. Comput. Educ. **34**(3–4), 177–193 (2000)

Sharples, M.: Mobile learning: research, practice and challenges. Distance Education in China **3**(5), 5–11 (2013)

Sharples, M., Taylor, J., Vavoula, G.: A Theory of Learning for the Mobile Age. In: Andrews, R., Haythornthwaite, C. (eds.) The Sage Handbook of Elearning Research, pp. 221–247. Sage Publications, London (2007)

Vavoula, G., Sharples, M., Rudman, P., Meek, J.: MyArtspace: design and evaluation of support for learning with multimedia phones between classrooms and museums. Comput. Educ. **53**(2), 286–299 (2009)

Traxler, J.: Defining, Discussing and Evaluating Mobile Learning: The moving finger writes and having writ… Int. Rev. Res. Open Distrib. Learn. **8**(2) (2007). http://www.irrodl.org/index.php/irrodl/article/view/346/875. Accessed 21 July 2015

Traxler, J. (2011) Introduction in John Traxler and Jocelyn Wishart (Eds.) Making mobile learning work: case studies of practice. Bristol: ESCalate. http://escalate.ac.uk/8250. Accessed 21 July 2015

UNESCO: ICT in Education » Mobile Learning. UNESCO, Paris (2015). http://www.unesco.org/new/en/unesco/themes/icts/m4ed/. Accessed 24 July 2015

Wexler, S., Brown, J., Metcalf, D., Rogers, D., Wagner, E.: Mobile learning: What is it, why it matters, and how to incorporate it into your learning strategy (2008). http://www.elearningguild.com/research/archives/index.cfm?id=132&action=viewonly. Accessed 10 July 2015

Winters, N.: What is mobile learning? In: Sharples, M. (ed.) Big Issues in Mobile Learning:Report of a Workshop by the Kaleidoscope Network of Excellence Mobile Learning Initiative. University of Nottingham, Nottingham (2006)

Yatigammana Ekanayake, T.M.S.S.K., Wishart, J.: Investigating the possibility of using mobile phones for science teaching and learning: is it a viable option for Sri Lanka? Int. J. Cross-Discip. Subj. Educ. **2**(2), 372–380 (2011)

Zurita, G., Nussbaum, M.: A constructivist mobile learning environment supported by a wireless handheld network. J. Comput. Assist. Learn. **20**(4), 235–243 (2004)

Teachers Matter: Challenges of Using a Location-Based Mobile Learning Platform

Christian Sailer(✉), Joram Schito, Peter Kiefer, and Martin Raubal

Institute of Cartography and Geoinformation,
Chair of Geoinformation Engineering, ETH Zurich,
Stefano-Franscini-Platz 5, 8093 Zurich, Switzerland
{csailer,jschito,pekiefer,mraubal}@ethz.ch

Abstract. This paper presents the design of a learning management system for location-based mobile learning and reports on first experiences of ongoing user studies with a location-based mobile learning platform. This platform allows teachers to create location-based mobile learning units as editors that can be consumed by students using mobile devices with self-localization capabilities, such as the Global Positioning System or network positioning. We show hands-on challenges of location-based mobile learning and emphasize the role of teachers as learning unit designers. We determine five aspects relevant for the challenges of location-based mobile learning: environment, technology, teaching, learner, and teacher's spatial cognitive competences. For every aspect, predictable and non-predictable challenges may exist. We describe these five aspects and focus on the challenges encountered to enhance professionalism in the didactic use of location-based mobile learning based on related work, diaries, and interviews of initial studies with our learning platform. In this respect, our experiences with the ongoing project support the importance of teachers for the success of location-based mobile learning concepts.

Keywords: Location-based mobile learning · Location-awareness · Mobile learning management system · Context-awareness · Teaching

1 Towards Location-Based Mobile Learning

Mobile technologies are changing the way we interact with the world. The ubiquitous availability of information, combined with the contextual awareness these devices provide, enables us to learn and receive support whenever we need it and wherever we are. The potential in multi-functional and individualized learning through mobile learning applications show the limitations of traditional educational tools in classrooms, which were typically confined with regard to content, given location, and given functionality.

In our research, we focus on a particular type of mobile learning whose learning activities are performed at those places the teaching content is spatially related to (*location-based mobile learning, LBML*). In LBML, the learner interacts with the environment during contextualized learning activities by means of location-aware technologies (Patten et al. 2006).

From several previous studies with LBML applications, it is well-known that teaching place-related content at the respective location with mobile technologies can

T.H. Brown and H.J. van der Merwe (Eds.): mLearn 2015, CCIS 560, pp. 239–255, 2015.
DOI: 10.1007/978-3-319-25684-9_18

improve the learning effect by complementing conventional didactical methods. Mobile Virtual Campus, for instance, is a collaborative mobile learning system powered by the location-based dynamic grouping algorithm (Tan et al. 2010). This algorithm groups the learners primarily based on their location closeness but takes learners' learning profiles, learning styles, and learning interests as further grouping criteria. Environmental Detectives is a handheld augmented reality simulation game designed by Klopfer and Squire (2008). It supports learning in advanced introductory (late high school and early college) environmental science. Their goal was to understand the potential of augmented reality simulation games while also proposing the idea of a general software development platform including authoring tools for creating other handheld applications. CAERUS is a complete context-aware educational resource system for outdoor tourist sites and educational centers by Naismith et al. (2005). Their system is a working implementation of a complete context-aware educational tool for outdoor use with the goal of engaging visitors with their physical surroundings. Location-based multimedia content and activities are presented to visitors through Pocket PC handheld computers with GPS capability. Beside the handheld delivery application, CAREUS consists of a desktop administration application and provides a visual interface to add new maps, define regions of interest, and add theme-based multimedia tours. Rogers et al. (2004) presented Ambient Wood, a framework for the different forms of digital augmentation and the different processes by which they can be accessed. Using the framework, they designed an outdoor learning experience, aimed at encouraging students to carry out contextualized scientific enquiry and to reflect on their interactions. Pairs of pupils explored a woodland and were presented with different forms of digital augmentation at certain locations. This study showed that such kind of exploration promotes interpretation and reflection at a number of levels of abstraction for pupils.

In summary, teaching place-related content at the respective location with mobile technologies opens up a number of promising opportunities. However, implementing LBML in a real teaching setting comes with a number of challenges, thus impeding a broad adoption of LBML in school and university teaching. Moreover, there is a lack of platforms that support teachers in overcoming these challenges.

The success of LBML strongly depends on the context and situation during learning, which leads to a number of challenges in designing LBML management systems. Several approaches and models for supporting and evaluating learning with mobile technology have been proposed in related work. For instance, Sharples et al. (2010) observed a dialectical relationship between learning and technology and showed their convergence. Muyinda et al. (2011) developed a competence set of dimensions and sub dimensions for instantiating or evaluating mobile learning objects which are based on Khan (2001). They defined learning objects as a digital educational resource which is granulated into units that are reusable, adaptive, and can be re-purposed to different learning styles, knowledge levels and conditions. Tan et al. (2013) recommended their 5R adaptation framework concept to enhance learning in location-based learning environments by taking into consideration the factors of learner, location, time, and mobile devices.

While these examples demonstrate the breadth of mobile learning pointing in particular to the importance of the learner, we recognize missing literature on the evaluation and challenges of LBML management systems on the one hand, and literature focusing on the editor (teacher) on the other hand. We argue that—by focusing on the learner—the importance of teachers' abilities in the field of LBML is often underestimated. Technological, didactical, and spatial cognitive competences of teachers are diverse and have a major impact on the result of the design in the field of LBML. Further the teachers' understanding of the physical environment and the individual learners depends also of that design. In conclusion, teachers matter in view of successful implementations of LBML.

The rest of this paper is structured as follows: we describe the design of a LBML management system (OMLETH) in Sect. 2 and systematically report on challenges that occur in teaching with LBML in Sect. 3. Our list of challenges may serve as a guideline for teachers planning to use LBML in their courses, as well as for system developers responsible for LBML platforms. Future research on LBML may also be motivated by these challenges.

2 OMLETH: A Location-Based Mobile Learning Management System

OMLETH[1] is a prototype implementation of a LBML management system (Sailer et al. 2015a). It allows teachers to create LBML units as editors that can be consumed by students using mobile devices with self-localization capabilities, such as the Global Positioning System (GPS) or network positioning (IP address, WiFi, GSM/CDMA cell IDs).

Figure 1 provides a schematic overview of our prototypical platform. Editors (teachers) use the system through a map-based web application which can be accessed with conventional desktop browsers. The system enables the teacher to create and publish *learning modules*, where each module consists of one or (usually) several learning units – a concept known from common learning management systems. The teacher draws the spatial footprint of each learning unit, i.e., the zone in which it will be triggered on the students' phone, in an interface based on scalable web maps (Fig. 2a). Learning units are categorized by the type of learning activity they involve, similar to those found in common learning management systems. Examples of such activities include: consuming context information by text or photo, solving tasks by text input, multiple choice, voice or video recording, distance estimation tasks, or activities that involve the interaction with, learning from, and comparison of current and historical maps. These activities can be combined flexibly depending on the curriculum, learning goals, as well as didactical approaches. Teachers can save the module for self-testing and later publish it, thus making the module accessible in the students' mobile app.

Learners (students) access the learning module on their mobile devices by a mobile web application (right in Figures 1 and 2b). By pressing the "Locate me" button, students can trigger the localization and visualize their location on the map. Spatial

[1] Location-Based Mobile Learning at ETH Zurich (German: *Ortsbezogenes Mobiles Lernen an der ETH Zürich*, OMLETH).

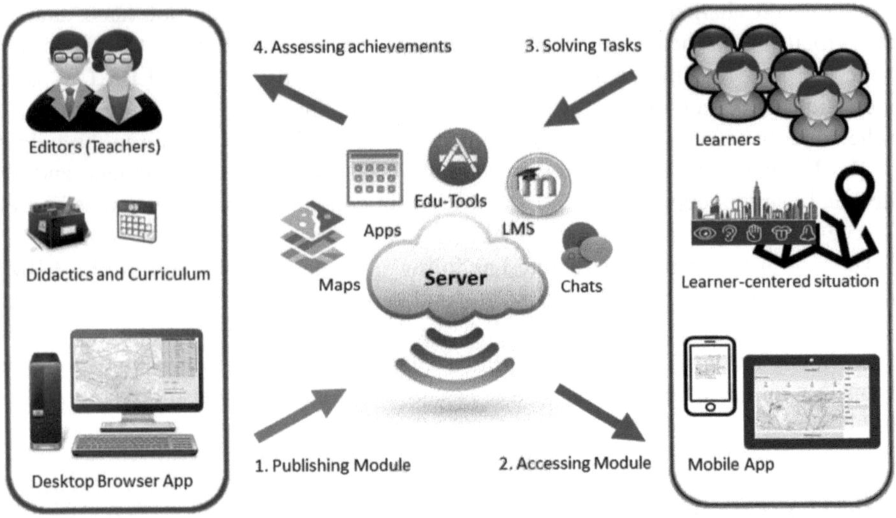

Fig. 1. Overview of OMLETH, a location-based mobile learning management system

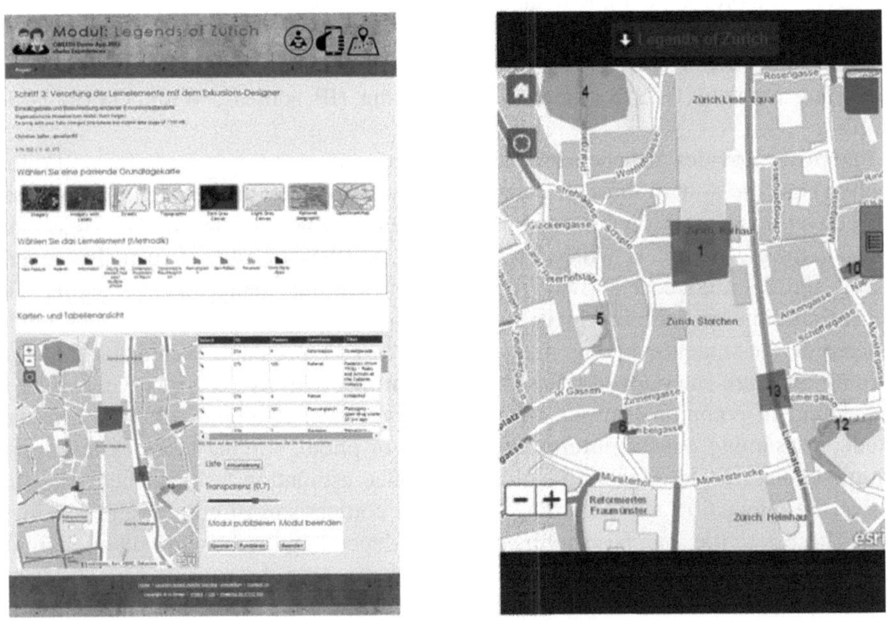

Fig. 2. (a) Editor App of OMLETH. (b) Learner App of OMLETH

footprints of learning units are visualized as polygons on the map, where the color-coding is based on the type of learning activity. As soon as the current location of the mobile device is inside the footprint (area) of a learning unit, the associated content is retrieved from the server and appears on the screen. The learner is asked to solve the unit, where the required activity depends on the type of learning unit (as explained above).

The teacher can follow and supervise the students' activities in two ways: during the execution of OMLETH learning modules, as well as after students have finished. The trackable students' data include the solutions to learning activities, students' feedback, as well as spatio-temporal trajectories. The latter can be visualized and aggregated in a second map-based interface and may be particularly useful for evaluating the design of the learning module. For instance, learners' speed and trajectories can be analyzed, and transportation mode as well as wayfinding problems can be detected through visual analysis of individual and aggregated student trajectories (Sailer et al. 2015b). Afterwards, the teacher can adapt the methodology of the learning module and dose or enhance the educational content.

In addition, a chat functionality enables teacher and students to communicate while the student is using the mobile app. Teachers can send instructions, hints or abruptly important notifications, whereas students can ask for help, immediate feedback or interesting findings.

3 Challenges of Location-Based Mobile Learning and Teaching

Our classification of challenges is inspired by the context model of Brimicombe and Li (2009): we determine five aspects relevant for the challenges of LBML: environment, technology, teaching, learner, and teacher's spatial cognitive competences. For every aspect, predictable and non-predictable challenges may exist (see Table 1). We describe in the following the five aspects and focus on the challenges encountered to enhance professionalism in the didactic use of LBML based on related work, diaries, and interviews of initial studies with OMLETH.

3.1 Physical Environment

In the following, we emphasize the environmental factors where mostly physical factors, such as weather, light, sound, and accessibility affect the planning of LBML activities.

3.1.1 Weather Conditions, Comfort

The planning of an outdoor LBML unit requires a diverse preparation and a confident handling of environmental factors, such as the season, and the actual weather conditions at a given time and location in order to recommend a suitable equipment (e.g., clothing, water-proof phone case) for the learning session.

Our experiences with OMLETH have shown that the weather is highly important: learners evaluate the conditions as good in dry weather, and rather bad in rainy weather. If the weather is bad, the motivation for solving the LBML unit conscientiously is low and thus the achievements are scarce. First experiences have shown that

Table 1. Challenges in LBML, structured by their predictability and the context aspect they relate to.

	Challenges where teachers are out of influence	Predictable challenges
Environment	- Weather conditions - Comfort - Safety risk - Accessibility of locations - Traffic	- Seasonal conditions of the climate - Safety risk - Environmental Noise, Light and Odor
Technology	- Hardware (Screen size, Battery, Accuracy of Positioning Sensors, Screen Reflection, Temperature and Humidity Extrema) -Software (Correctness, Usability / Learnability, Integrity, Reliability, Efficiency, Security, Safety)	- Hardware (Network) - Software (Security)
Teaching	- Curriculum - Learning success - Interaction between learners	- Group size and members - Learning goals and their integration into the curriculum - Time
Spatial cognitive competences	- Spatial knowledge - Spatial concepts	
Learner	- Character - Motivation	- Aims - Individual communication - Empathy - Age

learners do not like to rest too long at one learning unit when temperatures are below approx. 10°C whereas temperatures over approx. 25°C get learners tired and impatient. LBML becomes even more uncomfortable if extreme weather events like thunderstorms, vertical solar radiation, or heavy winds occur. Fortunately, predictions' reliability increased during the last years.

In summary, weather forecasts and uncertainties must be taken into consideration when planning an LBML unit. One option for dealing with weather uncertainties consists in preparing a second learning unit as a fallback solution in which learners, for instance, cover a shorter route or are less exposed to the weather.

3.1.2 Physical Accessibility

In OMLETH LBML units, learners usually have to visit learning units successively in a pre-defined order. The allocation of these learning units is based on the teacher's opinion of an ideal path. Although the teacher explores this path at least once while planning the LBML unit, circumstances are – especially in urban areas – changing on a daily basis, and direct access to an object might not be possible any longer. Construction sites, traffic jams, or barriers could intersect the learners' walk and force them to do a detour. OMLETH studies have shown that traffic can distract learners and render accessing a certain location effectively impossible: the learning module then fails because information about further procedure is lacking.

In conclusion, the physical accessibility of the learning units becomes more relevant for LBML than for general mobile learning, since the learning content is bound to specific locations.

3.1.3 Environmental Noise, Light and Odor

Environmental factors are manifold and have different effects on the perception by human senses. In the field of LBML, learners cannot turn off their ears, thus sound perception is always on and must be filtered based on the importance of the content (Schwartz 2003). Findings, how far sounds have a benefiting or obstructive influence on learning, are controversial. Personally preferred music tends to have a neutral effect on learning whereas environment noise is mainly perceived as neutral to obstructive (Reinhardt and Rötter 2013). Therefore, teachers can foster effective learning by the avoidance of areas with obstructive environmental noise.

Environmental ambient light changes during the day. Therefore, features in the environment appear differently depending on the time of day, and readability of mobile displays will also vary.

Our experiences from pilot studies with OMLETH indicate that the influence of some odorants on human behavior is highly affective. Teachers can integrate specific location-based odors in a LBML unit. Unique odors support the learners' long-term memorizing. However, extremely unpleasant odors can distract learners.

In summary, sound, light and odor are often underestimated factors in LBML designs. Teachers need to reflect about these factors during the planning of the LBML units.

3.2 Technology

Mobile technology plays a central role in LBLM. The fast growing mobile development and the change of hardware (mobile devices) and software solutions (platform and apps) poses ongoing challenges for LBML designers. Smartphones are convergent devices which empower users with internet access, music, audio and video playback and recording, navigation and communication capabilities (Sharples 2013, Brown et al. 2010, Vavoula and Sharples 2009).

When learners use their own mobile devices many technological factors are out of the teacher's control. This technology section is divided into two parts – hardware and software – each subsuming relevant issues and related work for technology usage where teachers have some influence in providing learning activities and where teachers are out of control.

3.2.1 Hardware

Although the development of hardware technology is a fast growing industry, mobile device users are still struggling with several issues. In the following we summarize challenges we were facing in studies with OMLETH.

Screen Size

LBML is based on handheld technology for the delivery of learning objects. Churchill and Hedberg (2008) found the key limitations of this kind of technology are the small screens. Meanwhile, a variety of screen sizes for mobile devices is available on the market, labelled as Smartphones, Phablets or Tablets. Studies with OMLETH and others (e.g., Bartoschek et al. (2013) have shown that devices with larger screens are preferred for map reading and navigation. However, not every learner may have access to a tablet, therefore screen size remains a challenge.

Battery

Larger screens, fast processors, frequent use of the positioning sensor and internet connectivity, and generally growing functionality come with the requirement for higher battery capacity to support operation throughout the learning session. Display use, processing power, feature-sets and sensors are bottlenecked by battery life, where the typical battery capacity of smartphones today is barely above 1500 mAh. Ferreira et al. (2011) presented solutions to allow users for longer smartphones battery life.

Finally, teachers must be aware of learners' hardware equipment even though excursions longer than two hours may anyway be questionable in terms of learners' motivation (see Sect. 3.4).

Accuracy of Positioning Sensors

Our experiences with OMLETH have demonstrated that positioning technology on older smartphones is rather unreliable or sometimes failing. Contrary, devices from the latest generation show better results (accuracy below 10 meters). However, accuracy is also influenced by the area in which learning takes place; for instance, GPS is known to have low accuracy in urban canyons (Montillet et al. 2007). Consequently, teachers need to consider both, the available hardware and the accuracy of positioning at the locations of the learning units.

Screen Reflection

In LBML we have to deal with a wide range of ambient lighting conditions (see Sect. 3.1.3). Besides simply increasing screen brightness, a typical solution consists in using anti-reflection coatings and treatments. Ma et al. (2012) have shown that the usage of such anti-reflection coatings, together with color and intensity scale management profiles based on the ambient light sensor, can significantly improve the situation. However, since it is the learner's choice to add such components or not, the screen reflection remains a challenge for teachers in the field of LBML.

Temperature and Humidity Extrema

Temperature does not only affect the learner, but also the resilience of the mobile device. Apple[2], for instance, recommends an operating temperature between 0 and

[2] Keeping iPhone, iPad, and iPod touch within acceptable operating temperatures (https://support.apple.com/en-us/HT201678, Call date: 24.07.2015).

35 degrees Celsius for iPhones, and a humidity of 5 to 95 percent non-condensing. They recommend cold-resistant, brave users texting gloves and winter-proofing gadgets. Manufacturers argue that any temperature condition that would be unsuitable for humans is also unsuitable for smartphones, and teachers should keep this in mind when deciding on starting an LBML activity.

Network (Bandwidth Capacity/Mobile Data)

LBML affords using multimedia teaching materials, thus avoiding traditional classroom methods, such as reading long texts. Streaming multimedia requires a sufficient bandwidth from the mobile network. In the case of OMLETH, the LBML platform uses a number of different multimedia online services, including photos, video watching and map exploration. The large internet downloads necessary for streaming such multimedia content across various locations has to be taken into account when designing a learning unit, especially if a learning activity is located in an area with limited bandwidth.

3.2.2 Software

Educational software has special requirements which are in the following presented based on Sharples' theory of learning for the mobile age in relation to teachers (Sharples et al. 2010). Factors influencing software quality are discussed in the second part.

Software Requirements

The goal of using learning software consists in supporting teachers to teach more effectively. The offer of educational software and apps, however, is tremendous, and choosing the right software for a particular teaching situation is challenging.

In the field of mobile learning, Hwang and Chang (2011) have emphasized the need for well-designed learning support to improve the students' learning achievements. Sharples et al. (2010) suggest learner centered, knowledge centered, assessment and community centered approaches for effective learning. The successful development of mobile learning depends on human factors in the use of mobile and wireless technologies.

Sharples (2013) stated that the majority of mobile learning activities continues to take place on devices not designed with educational ends in mind, and that usability issues are often reported. In conclusion, a teacher centered approach is often missing. For this reason, learning units in OMLETH can be designed in other e-learning systems teachers are already experienced with, and at the same time support the teacher's freedom and creativity w.r.t. didactic choices.

The knowledge centered approach as well as the assessment centered approach are based on teacher's personal choice and experience and are linked again to a teacher's choice of e-learning system. Recent developments show also growing gamification elements in learning software applications (Kapp 2012).

With regard to the community centered approach for outdoor education, educational software in the field of LBML should support learning in pairs or groups (see Sect. 3.3). Christie (2007) discovered that middle school teachers as well as students are highly motivated to use GPS and Geocaching. The Geocaching software creates technology-rich, constructivist learning environments and supports learning in communities.

Factors for Software Quality

The challenges teachers face in their daily work with educational software may be caused by several factors. McCall et al. (1977) presented a software quality schema to assess software in a structured way: they proposed a categorization of factors that affect software quality. These software quality factors focus on three important aspects of a software product such as operational, transitional and revisional characteristics.

Teachers' main challenges are found in the daily operation and are reflected in the following seven categories: (Table 2)

3.3 Teaching

Teaching is a complex activity that requires reflection on various levels and a thorough planning. Good and effective teaching is explained by various authors (Dubs 1995, Borich 2013, Hattie Hattie 2013) and always includes the reflection of a thorough planning process. The planning starts with a curriculum framework, from which first unit plans and then lesson plans are derived. In particular, lesson planning considers goals and objectives in the cognitive (Bloom 1956), affective (Krathwohl et al. 1964), and psychomotor (Harrow 1972) domains as well as learner's individual prerequisites and incorporates diverse teaching methods. In addition, teachers can also decide to plan a LBML unit based on a specific learning paradigm and thus use tasks and questions specified for that approach (Schito et al. 2015). In this regard, LBML is one method among many to contribute with its ability to implement different teaching strategies to diverse teaching and to lifelong learning.

3.3.1 Integrate LBML in the Curriculum

First, we focus on the question, when teachers best make use of LBML. Because LBML units require surpassing preparation time, they must be applied selectively and with care. Ideally, LBML is integrated within a topic that has a high teacher task orientation, and for which it is useful to reuse the results achieved during the LBML unit for further lessons. In this way, learner's achievements are appreciated insofar as their work becomes an essential part of the whole group's learning process. Another characteristic of LBML is its linkage to a specific place. In contrast to classroom learning, teachers choose tasks linked to a phenomenon that only occurs at a specific place. Thus, LBML crucially depends on the reliability that a phenomenon occurs satisfactorily noticeably at a specific place and time. The main teaching

Table 2. Matrix of daily software operations concerning seven categorizes

Operational Factors	Description	LBML challenges
Correctness	The software should meet all the specifications stated by the customer.	Errors in LBML software have, due to the lack of direct contact between teacher and learner, bigger impacts than in classroom learning.
Usability/Learnability	The amount of effort or time required to learn how to use the software should be small. This makes the software user-friendly even for IT-illiterate people.	E-learning tools often provide overwhelming functionalities and are not directly adapted to the user's mental model. These challenges teachers and results in terms of LBML design in different solutions.
Integrity	A quality software should not have side effects, i.e., it should not affect the functionality of other applications.	Using sensors like the positioning in OMLETH depends sometimes on third party running software and may lead to problems for some mobile web browsers.
Reliability	The software product should not have any bugs; most importantly it should not crash during execution.	Since teachers and learners in LBML are typically spatially separated, a real-time support by the teacher in case of problems with the application is not possible.
Efficiency	The software should make effective use of the available resources, efficient use of storage and processing power, obeying the desired timing requirements.	In the case of LBML, the required time for planning is a multiple of the effort for preparing e-learning or classroom lessons.
Security	The software should not have negative effects on data or hardware. Proper measures should be taken to keep data secure from external threats.	Security is a big issue in the field of LBML. Crowded systems like OMLETH and its third party apps need security regulations, in terms of privacy and geo privacy.
Safety	The software should not be hazardous to the personal context.	LBML risks higher safety issues than classroom learning (e.g., software-based positioning errors)

challenges are first to link location-based phenomena with learning, and second to integrate LBML units thematically and seamlessly into the curriculum by simultaneously considering the main goals and objectives.

3.3.2 Topics Appropriate to LBML

Teachers may question which contents and topics could best be taught with LBML. According to the statement above, LBML is not limited to geography classes. Instead, LBML is a means to an end that can be conveyed for every subject whose content is linked to a specific location. This opens opportunities for interdisciplinary learning: imagine for example an economy lesson in which learners must analyze the net production of agricultural products, map the occurrence of these products on a digital map, and suggest solutions to improve production and to foster ecosystem services. Thus, the topic should not act as a bottleneck for refusing the use of LBML. Instead, teachers are motivated to search for ideas, how a topic could be related to a specific place. Rather than aiming at completeness about a topic, regional features can be investigated exemplarily in case studies.

3.3.3 Special Characteristics of Teaching with LBML

In this section, we describe in which way teaching of LBML units differs from regular classes with regard to didactic approaches and learning. LBML is very suitable to promote constructivism and cooperation. Constructivism is fostered by an intensive confrontation with the subject matter with the aim to construct somebody's knowledge through experience. Therefore, time on task plays an important role: it should be chosen sufficiently high for learners to solve the task while operating with a device and analyzing the environment (Borich 2013). These interactions could not yield a learning effect if the time given was insufficient. However, learning progress can only occur if every learner actively participates in the learning unit. Therefore, splitting tasks into subtasks by assigning each learner a role and thus making him or her a specialist intensifies the learner's confrontation with the subject matter and increases the consciousness about a useful contribution to the final product and to the collective learning process (Borich 2013). Moreover, task splitting causes division of labor and makes learners become task specialists. In general, cooperation allows to place one's own contribution within the context of the work of others. This structure fosters the sharing of ideas and enhances the learning process based on the peer effect (Hoxby 2000).

3.3.4 LBML Unit Management

In contrast to classroom teaching, LBML does not provide an implicit classroom management. With LBML, teachers partially lose control of the learners because they are supposed to solve tasks away from school or at least outside the classroom. Even though teachers revert to technical monitoring solutions and provide communication opportunities they cannot guarantee that learners invest the maximum of time available to solve a task correctly. Instead, teachers can contribute to a pleasant atmosphere within the groups by choosing the group sizes and their members properly. Furthermore, teachers can steer by the tasks specified and the material provided the social climate between the groups, which can either be competitive or cooperative (Borich 2013). In this regard, interaction between learners can be prolonged more and intensified to increase the awareness for each other's learning. Thus, because interaction between the teacher and the learners is reduced, feedback, reinforcement, and support come mainly from peers. In this regard, teachers can only act as supporters who help the learners to reflect their own performance (Borich 2013).

3.3.5 Time

Depending on the time at which the learning takes place, the environmental effects can highly vary. Therefore it is important to determine an optimal time slot in which learners can proceed with the LBML unit and perceive the environmental effects as expected. Time is also a crucial factor since the time available for learning is often limited. Tasks should be solved within a given time frame to keep the focus straight on learning (Borich 2013). Second, especially during LBML units learners must move from one station to another which needs time again. For both, teachers must plan enough time to guarantee sufficient time on task used for learning. The teacher must also consider that the physical activity involved in LBML may lead to learners getting tired if the learning module takes too long.

3.3.6 Considering Safety Issues

Participants' well-being has the highest priority while conducting an LBML unit. In this regard, the avoidance of accidents or risky situations and the evaluation of natural hazards helps not only to increase the learning success, but also to prevent legal consequences in case teachers are responsible for the learners' health. For instance, teachers should be cautious, they must be prepared for unexpected situations, and they must recognize dangers in areas with challenging paths, steep abysses, slippery floors, potentially occurring natural hazards, obscured lighting conditions, or heavy traffic. Also, teachers must be informed if a learner needs medication, has a disease or is allergic to certain substances. Legal issues must be clarified in advance to avoid lawsuits. Keeping in mind safety issues might increase the learner's awareness of being cautious during the LBML unit. In addition, a safe environment supports carefree learning. Thus, teachers must propose solutions to any circumstances, best by following an emergency plan, in order to make learners feel safe. To prevent a learning gap, an elaborated lesson plan must contain content-related options, e.g., for tired or powerless learners.

3.3.7 Intensities of Assistance

The planning of an LBML unit opens various possibilities for the intensity of teacher's assistance. The assistance intensity depends on the formulation of the task and thus on the goals. First, a teacher can provide no assistance by refusing to set a time frame. In this regard, learners must decide by themselves how to organize their work, however, they practice self-responsibility. Second, a teacher can provide assistance selectively: at the beginning (briefing), at the beginning and at the end (debriefing) or at the beginning, at the end and in the middle (intermediate briefing). Ideally, teachers never refuse to assist the class during the beginning to explain the organization, the procedure or the goals of the LBML unit and during the end to summarize the observed phenomena. Third, teachers can provide full assistance which is not compatible with the constructivist paradigm and thus inappropriate for the use of LBML.

3.4 Learner

In this section, we focus on the learner as the protagonist to whom a teacher must draw his or her full attention. The learner is at the center of interest because teachers' actions aim at learners experiencing a noticeable learning progress. If such a learning progress did not occur, the teacher might have failed to focus on the learner's characteristics. Just like learners are unique, their learning approach and their motivation to learn also are individual. In this regard, the specific challenge lies in adapting the teaching approach according to the learner's characteristics to enhance the quality of teaching. As Borich (2013) wrote, teachers thus need empathy to foster learners of diverse characteristics.

Because motivation is a key factor of learning success, teachers should respond to the learner's character, background knowledge, social heritage, and age to motivate them to improve their skills. As premise, learners must be respected; otherwise they do not feel to be taken seriously and thus doubt the purpose of learning. Without the learner's participation or interest, teaching becomes senseless. Furthermore, power imbalance or age differences between teachers and learners inhibit open communication and enhance learners' distrust of teachers. Instead, learning from peers rates high because especially adolescents do not want to rank behind their peers (Hoxby 2000). If somebody has understood a subject matter, peers are also motivated to reconstitute the thoughts in order to prove mastery. In contrast, for the learner that has understood the matter, explaining the fact to peers deepens his or her understanding and enhances his or her social skills. Thus, teachers can benefit from these facts by planning tasks in a way that group members must cooperate and share knowledge to solve a task completely.

Beside the learner's characteristics, the reflective integration of knowledge, and the cooperative work in groups, Sharples et al. (2005) propose assessments to crucially contribute to learning success. Assessments offer diagnosis and formative guidance so that learners recognize a purpose behind learning. Such purpose can comprise mastery or competitive goals (Ames and Archer 1987). Furthermore, assessments allow students to calibrate their knowledge to a grade scale (Nicholls 1984). As teachers respond to learner's individual characteristics and encourage them individually to invest time for their learning process, chances are also high that learners will be motivated to do so.

3.5 Environmental Spatial Ability

While the concept of mobile learning mainly propagates to use mobile devices in general for teaching units, the concept of location based learning relates to a notion of teaching which aims at working on a topic at a concrete spatial location. Because in LBML knowledge is built in situ, it is embedded into a concrete context and in a real situation respectively (Brown et al. 2010).

Spatial ability is the capacity to understand and remember the spatial relations among objects, whose choice of an appropriate location to conduct a LBML unit, is crucial (Montello and Raubal 2013). OMLETH requires different spatial concepts for the LBML design. Furthermore, the map-based design of the LBML units needs also spatial knowledge of the real world.

3.5.1 Spatial Knowledge

Spatial knowledge is commonly defined as the ability of modeling the spatial environment in an intrinsic mental model. Planning learning units in OMLETH and simultaneously differ between different spatial objects, needs an excellent mental model known as mental maps. A teacher's mental map is based trough in situ or map-based exploring and experience. OMLETH shows that in situ exploration as well as map study such as the understanding of the topography are essential to design a well-constructed learning module.

3.5.2 Spatial Concepts

Spatial concepts consist of the orientation skills, spatial contexts, spatial proportions like angle or distance estimation. Experiences with OMLETH have shown that distance estimation is difficult and that teachers often underestimate the time needed to move from one station to the next (see 3.1.4). Thus, teachers should be motivated to allocate the stations close to each other to maximize the time on task and at best to keep the learner's motivation high.

Teachers' spatial knowledge and skills not only facilitate the design of LBML activities, but are highly relevant to plan them in a meaningful and beneficial way. Hegarty et al. (2002) developed a standardized self-report scale of environmental spatial ability, called the Santa Barbara Sense of Direction Scale (SBSOD). OMLETH could demand minimal environmental spatial abilities from teachers where this self-report could be used for evaluation purposes.

4 Conclusion

LBML is ideal to complement a given topic in the circumstances that a specific content can only be learned at a determined location. However, the planning of reflective LBML units is highly complex because the volatile challenges environment, technology, teaching, learners, and environmental spatial abilities must be considered. In this planning process, teachers play a key role because they can contribute to a successful LBML unit by their knowledge, skills, and by their decisions made to equally integrate the five volatile challenges and to optimally assist learners. In this respect, our experiences with the ongoing OMLETH project support the importance of teachers.

However, evidence from research in LBML with OMLETH should be treated with caution because LBML is a relatively new and rapidly growing research field and most studies concerning the effectiveness of LBML are less than ten years old. Moreover, research with OMLETH has not investigated privacy issues concerning the conduction, purpose and analysis of monitoring learner's behavior yet.

On the basis of the rapid development of mobile technology, growing user experience, and enhanced didactic research of LBML, the software development of OMLETH will continuously be adapted and extended. According to Sharples (2013) and Tan et al. (2013), we propose on the one hand to use diaries to record teacher's and learner's experience, whereas on the other hand, we propose data mining and data analysis to track learners' behaviors and to build learner profiles for enhancing personalized learning. In order to improve the technical understanding and handling, learners should be motivated to learn with their own device. These records help to evaluate the design, structure, and popularity of LBML and return essential insights to solve challenges in future work.

References

Ames, C., Archer, J.: Mothers' beliefs about the role of ability and effort in school learning. J. Educ. Psychol. **79**, 409 (1987)

Bartoschek, T., Schwering, A., Li, R., Münzer, S.: Ori-Gami–An app fostering spatial competency development and spatial learning of children. In: Proceedings of the 15th AGILE International Conference on Geographic Information Science. Springer-Verlag, Leuven (2013)

Bloom, B.S.: Taxonomy of Educational Objectives: The Classification of Education Goals. Cognitive Domain. Handbook 1. Longman, New York (1956)

Borich, G.D.: Effective Teaching Methods: Research-Based Practice. Pearson Higher Ed., New York (2013)

Brimicombe, A., Li, C.: Location-Based Services and Geo-Information Engineering. Wiley, New York (2009)

Brown, E., Sharples, M., Clough, G., Tangney, B., Wishart, J., Wijers, M., Jonker, V., Cook, J., Glahn, C., Börner, D.: Education in the wild: contextual and location-based mobile learning in action, Learning Sciences Research Institute, University of Nottingham (2010)

Christie, A.: Using GPS and geocaching engages, empowers, and enlightens middle school teachers and students. Meridian: Middle Sch. Comput. Technol. J. **10** (2007)

Churchill, D., Hedberg, J.: Learning object design considerations for small-screen handheld devices. Comput. Educ. **50**, 881–893 (2008)

Dubs, R.: Lehrerverhalten–Ein Beitrag zur Interaktion von Lehrenden und Lernenden im Unterricht [Schriftenreihe für Wirtschaftspädagogik, Band 23]. Auflage, Zürich (1995)

Ferreira, D., Dey, A.K., Kostakos, V.: Understanding human-smartphone concerns: a study of battery life. In: Lyons, K., Hightower, J., Huang, E.M. (eds.) Pervasive 2011. LNCS, vol. 6696, pp. 19–33. Springer, Heidelberg (2011)

Harrow, A.J.: A Taxonomy of The Psychomotor Domain: A Guide for Developing Behavioral Objectives. Addison-Wesley Longman Ltd., New York (1972)

Hattie, J.: Visible Learning: A Synthesis of Over 800 Meta-Analyses Relating to Achievement. Routledge, London (2013)

Hegarty, M., Richardson, A.E., Montello, D.R., Lovelace, K., Subbiah, I.: Development of a self-report measure of environmental spatial ability. Intelligence **30**, 425–447 (2002)

Hoxby, C.: Peer effects in the classroom: learning from gender and race variation. National Bureau of Economic Research (2000)

Hwang, G.-J., Chang, H.-F.: A formative assessment-based mobile learning approach to improving the learning attitudes and achievements of students. Comput. Educ. **56**, 1023–1031 (2011)

Kapp, K.M.: The Gamification of Learning and Instruction: Game-Based Methods and Strategies for Training and Education. Wiley, New York (2012)

Khan, B.H.: A framework for web-based learning. Web-based training, pp. 75–98 (2001)

Klopfer, E., Squire, K.: Environmental Detectives—the development of an augmented reality platform for environmental simulations. Educ. Tech. Res. Dev. **56**, 203–228 (2008)

Krathwohl, D.R., Bloom, B.S., Masia, B.B.: Taxonomy of Educational Objectives, Handbook II: Affective Domain. David McKay Co., New York (1964). Krathwohl's Taxonomy of Affective Domain

Ma, T.-Y., Lin, C.-Y., Hsu, S.-W., Hu, C.-W., Hou, T.-W.: Automatic brightness control of the handheld device display with low illumination. In: 2012 IEEE International Conference on Computer Science and Automation Engineering (CSAE), pp. 382–385. IEEE (2012)

Mccall, J.A., Richards, P.K., Walters, G.F.: Factors in software quality. volume i. concepts and definitions of software quality. DTIC Document (1977)

Montello, D.R., Raubal, M.: Functions and applications of spatial cognition. In: Waller, D., Nadel, L. (eds.) Handbook of Spatial Cognition. American Psychological Association, Washington (2013)
Montillet, J.-P., Meng, X., Taha, A., Roberts, G., Hancock, C., Ogundipe, O.: Achieving centimetre-level positioning accuracy in urban canyons with locata technology. Positioning, 1 (2007)
Muyinda, P.B., Lubega, J.T., Lynch, K., van der Weide, T.: A framework for instantiating pedagogic mlearning objects applications. In: Cerone, A., Pihlajasaari, P. (eds.) ICTAC 2011. LNCS, vol. 6916, pp. 194–217. Springer, Heidelberg (2011)
Naismith, L., Sharples, M., Ting, J.: Evaluation of CAERUS: a context aware mobile guide. In: Proceedings of mLearn 2005-Mobile technology: The Future of Learning in Your Hands, Cape Town, South Africa (2005)
Nicholls, J.G.: Achievement motivation: conceptions of ability, subjective experience, task choice, and performance. Psychol. Rev. **91**, 328 (1984)
Patten, B., Sánchez, I.A., Tangney, B.: Designing collaborative, constructionist and contextual applications for handheld devices. Comput. Educ. **46**, 294–308 (2006)
Reinhardt, J., Rötter, G.: Musikpsychologischer Zugang zur Jugend-Musik-Sozialisation. In: Heyer, R., Wachs, S., Palentien, C. (eds.) Handbuch Jugend-Musik-Sozialisation. Springer, Wiesbaden (2013)
Rogers, Y., Price, S., Fitzpatrick, G., Fleck, R., Harris, E., Smith, H., Randell, C., Muller, H., O'Malley, C., Stanton, D.: Ambient wood: designing new forms of digital augmentation for learning outdoors. In: Proceedings of the 2004 Conference on Interaction Design and Children: Building A Community. ACM, pp. 3–10 (2004)
Sailer, C., Kiefer, P., Raubal, M.: An integrated learning management system for location-based mobile learning. In: 11th International Conference on Mobile Learning 2015 (ML 2015), Madeira, Portugal (2015a)
Sailer, C., Kiefer, P., Schito, J., Raubal, M.: An evaluation method for location-based mobile learning based on spatio-temporal analysis of learner trajectories. In: MobileHCI 2015, Mobiscool - 1st Workshop on Mobile, Social and Culturally Oriented Learning, Copenhagen, Denmar, Copenhagen, Denmark (2015b)
Schito, J., Sailer, C., Kiefer, P.: Bridging the gap between location-based games and teaching. In: AGILE 2015 Workshop on Geogames and Geoplay, Lisbon, Portugal (2015)
Schwartz, H.: The indefensible ear: a history. In: Bull, M., Back, L. (eds.) The Auditory Culture Reader, pp. 487–501. Berg, Oxford (2003)
Sharples, M.: Mobile learning: research, practice and challenges. Distance Educ. China **3**, 5–11 (2013)
Sharples, M., Taylor, J., Vavoula, G.: Towards a theory of mobile learning. Proc. mLearn **1**(1), 1–9 (2005)
Sharples, M., Taylor, J., Vavoula, G.: A theory of learning for the mobile age. In: Bachmair, B. (ed.) Medienbildung in neuen Kulturräumen. Springer, Wiesbaden (2010)
Tan, Q., Jeng, Y.-L., Huang, Y.-M.: A collaborative mobile virtual campus system based on location-based dynamic grouping. In: 2010 IEEE 10th International Conference on Advanced Learning Technologies (ICALT). IEEE, pp. 16–18 (2010)
Tan, Q., Liu, T.-C., Burkle, M.: Location-based environments for formal and informal learning: context-aware mobile learning. In: Sampson, D.G., Isaias, P., Ifenthaler, D., Spector, J.M. (eds.) Ubiquitous and Mobile Learning in the Digital Age. Springer, New York (2013)
Vavoula, G.N., Sharples, M.: Meeting the challenges in evaluating mobile learning: a 3-level evaluation framework (2009)

Influencing Everyday Teacher Practices by Applying Mobile Digital Storytelling as a Seamless Learning Approach

Susanna Nordmark(✉) and Marcelo Milrad

Center for Learning and Knowledge Technologies (CeLeKT), Department of Media Technology, Linnaeus University, Växjö, Sweden
{susanna.nordmark,marcelo.milrad}@lnu.se

Abstract. The present study describes our on-going efforts aiming at refining and validating a Mobile Seamless Learning (MSL) approach supported by mobile Digital Storytelling (mDS). Considering learning factors of locality, formality and time, as well as elements of designs for learning and technical development, we have chosen six dimensions of the MSL framework (Wong and Looi 2011) to support our work. Guided by the principles of co-design (Spikol et al. 2009) and design-based research (Design-Based Research Collective, 2003; Ejersbo et al. 2008), we collaborated with 4 teachers and 54 pupils, devoting an extensive amount of time to design, develop and enact the phases of our proposed mDS workflow supported by mobile and web technologies.

Beyond the mobile application developed for mDS, we have developed and integrated web solutions that support the overall learning experience, and tools that allow teachers to orchestrate the activities. The mDS web serve as a platform for continued work over time, such as reflecting, remixing, and reusing the digital content generated during the activities. The web platform provides means for teachers to search, watch, group, and assess the pupils' mDS outcomes, and therefore serves as the interconnecting glue between all the learning activities involved in the mDS workflow. This study reports on the activities conducted in four classrooms in the spring of 2015, working with the five phases of the mDS approach. The outcomes of our efforts reinforced the importance of an active involvement by teachers to adopt and incorporate innovative technology enhanced learning (TEL) activities and solutions into their everyday educational practices, but most importantly on the need for schools to acquire self-governance on how to make use of their learning technologies.

Keywords: Mobile digital storytelling · Teacher practices · Sustainability · Seamless learning

1 Research Problem and Aim of Study

To implement sustainable TEL efforts in everyday teacher practices is part of an animated debate and much-discussed topic in Sweden, as well as worldwide (see e.g. the 2015 NMC Horizon report for Higher Education, and the 2015 NMC Technology Outlook for Scandinavian schools). Over the years, a rich variety of attempts have been

T.H. Brown and H.J. van der Merwe (Eds.): mLearn 2015, CCIS 560, pp. 256–272, 2015.
DOI: 10.1007/978-3-319-25684-9_19

put to the test, but many have failed and still do. To make teachers sustainably embrace TEL innovations into their practice, i.e. to continue using them also after the research effort has ended, have in many cases proven to be a considerably more diversified and difficult problem than expected. Our research interests lie in providing a workflow with a set of supporting technologies independent of subject disciplines, context and pupil age. The workflow aim at affording teachers and pupils means for innovative and engaging learning activities, as well as acting as a straightforward, introductory step for teachers to "dare" incorporate further technology supported activities into their every practices. Over the last four years of research we have refined the workflow of mobile storytelling (see Fig. 1 in Sect. 3 below). Hence, the specific questions we are trying to answer by conducting this study are formulated as follows:

1. What factors could make an innovative TEL effort sustainable and worthwhile to pursue for teachers; and
2. In what ways could mobile digital storytelling support TEL implementation and sustainability in teachers' daily practices?

The mDS workflow depicted in Fig. 1 is a proposed methodology accompanied by supporting mobile and web technologies for collaborative as well as individual learning activities (Nordmark and Milrad 2014, 2015). The mDS workflow has been iteratively co-designed by researchers together with our study participants. It provides an introductory and easily comprehensible approach that could pave the way for a sustainable set of consecutive TEL efforts, thus creating a continuous and sustainable flow of TEL methods into teachers' everyday practices. In order to support these efforts, we have redesigned our previous mDS iOS application from scratch, allowing it to interact and be seamlessly integrated with its complementary supportive technologies. Thus, the features of the mDS web serve as the interconnecting glue for the five phases of the mDS workflow, which over time could support the development of a sustainable TEL methodology.

The remainder of the paper is organized as follows: Section two outlines the theoretical background and related research efforts, and section three summarizes the mDS workflow and its accompanying supporting technologies. Section four illustrates how the present study was designed and enacted, while sections five and six contain a discussion of the outcomes and a brief outline of future prospects and developments.

2 Theoretical Foundations and Related Work

In this section, we present some of the major theoretical influences for our work and similar research efforts that inspired our work. We begin with the concept of multimodality as means for meaning making and learning, continuing with the importance of efforts of designs for learning inspired by multimodality, moving over to the impact of digital storytelling as means for teaching and learning as well as for pupil engagement, motivation and involvement. We end with what a mobile seamless learning (MSL) approach to digital storytelling could offer learners. Altogether, these theoretical underpinnings have inspired and guided us to design straightforward and versatile mobile and web tools with an accompanying pedagogical method which supports both formal and informal learning regardless of context, age, pre-understanding and technology confidence, and that encourages reflection and critical thinking.

Nowadays, when the use of mobile technologies and social media are more or less universal, and sharing of on-the-fly information is vital, speech and written text no longer suffice as the only modes for communicating and meaning making. This paradigm shift is related to the ease with which people use and produce so called "multimodal texts", a term that refers to text as incorporating different modes, including written words, film, audio, gestures, mimics, poses and images (Kress 2010). The term "multimodal" here refers to the research on media and meaning making across different modes (e.g. Jewitt 2006; Kress and van Leeuwen 2001; Kress 2010; Selander and Kress 2010). Selander and Kress (2010) share many years of successful collaboration related to multimodal designs for learning. Their work add a specific focus on integrating and implementing multimodal design for teaching and learning, a need expressed to the authors by many teachers and pedagogues, illuminating the reader on what the multimodal approach implies for communication and meaning making in contemporary education.

Digital storytelling (DS) offers excellent opportunities for anyone to creatively craft powerful stories, reports and messages – for personal use as well as for various learning situations (see e.g. Lambert 2007, 2013; Ohler 2007; Lundby 2008). But, since mobile technologies already are an integral and well-established component in young people's daily lives, bringing storytelling to a mobile platform offers unique affordances for meaning making, learning and self-expression (Nordmark and Milrad 2012a, Nordmark and Milrad 2012b, Nordmark and Milrad 2014, Nordmark and Milrad 2015). The concept of mobile digital storytelling (mDS) and its application to learning contexts is a relatively new field of research. Adding the mobile dimension allows users to participate, create and share their own "digital voice" by using a familiar tool that they consider to be their personal property, and perhaps also their foremost means for communication, a device they always carry with them wherever they go (e.g. Ito 2009; Pachler et al. 2010). Furthermore, making digital storytelling mobile also provides unique opportunities for promoting mobile seamless learning, which suggests that learners learn constantly and ubiquitously, i.e. regardless of where, when and how, by switching between these scenarios using mobile devices such as smartphones and tablets etc. (Milrad et al. 2013).

Wong and Looi (2011) have suggested ten different dimensions characterizing activities for MSL, of which we have focused on the following six: MSL1 *formal and informal learning*, MSL3 *learning across time*, MSL4 *learning across location*, MSL7 *multiple device type, multiple learning tasks*, MSL8 *switching between multiple learning tasks* & MSL9 *knowledge synthesis*. We believe these six to be the most applicable in connection to our specific effort on mobile digital storytelling, both by considering the factors of locality, formality and time, as well as the design of the activity and assignments, and the access to mobile technologies. Our ultimate goal is to develop a versatile approach with an accompanying methodology and technological support for ubiquitous access to creating, sharing, reflecting and learning regardless of context, by transferring the generally more stationary workmode of digital storytelling to a mobile platform. To do so, we started researching other similar efforts, where StoryKit and StoryBank were among the two first we encountered.

StoryKit, developed by Druin et al. (2009) is an iOS mobile digital storytelling application focused on informal and inter-generational storytelling by letting its users create "books" on the mobile device by arranging text, photos, drawings, and sounds. Bidwell et al. (2010) developed StoryBank to support non-textual information sharing expressing a mixture of development and community information in developing countries. Although these efforts explored how digital storytelling could be deployed on mobile units to support e.g. aspects of formal and informal learning, we noted that none of these efforts provided an accompanying methodology, and did not investigate how to support and provide a means for TEL innovation and sustainability.

Hence, the overall purpose for developing an mDS application of our own was to provide users with mDS functionalities that were not supported by available applications or fully covered in related research efforts, but also to offer a complete workflow and toolkit supporting the entire experience of mDS for education. Where our previous work has provided us with various outcomes and suggestions regarding technical requirements, methodological issues and design considerations that have constituted ratification for a continued work effort (Nordmark and Milrad 2012a, 2012b, 2014, 2015), our main aims for the present study were to test the extensively re-designed iOS application, and the prototype version of the mDS web services in an authentic school environment. We also wanted to further inspire teachers to actively try the mDS workflow and to implement ideas and procedures from their experiences into their everyday educational practices. The aim to involve teachers to take an active part in the overall study workflow and activities instead of us as researchers coming in and "taking over" their territory was essential for us to accomplish in order to address earlier encounters of teacher ownership and empowerment.

Overall, our study efforts were aligned with the ideas reported e.g. by Goodyear (2011) claiming two major changes in contemporary educational research: our altered understanding of when and where learning actually takes place, and our heightened perception of the importance of learning design.

The following section illustrates the complete mDS workflow, its methodology, and the supporting technologies.

3 The mDS Workflow

The mDS workflow is an approach to which relevant mobile and web technologies have been integrated, and applicable MSL characteristics addressed (see e.g. Nordmark and Milrad 2014). To fulfill the learning requirements co-designed with teachers, museum personnel and pupils, we have developed our own iOS application for mDS, and a supporting web platform which handles storage of the full stories and their individual components, such as images, audio, and meta-information of different kinds for reuse, remix and reflection efforts. We chose iOS because we at the launch of the development process already had an iOS infrastructure available, but also because there then were a few other iOS storytelling applications obtainable for comparison. The recently added mDS web platform and its associated services add possibilities for further collaborative working modes, as well as reusability of existing mDS stories and

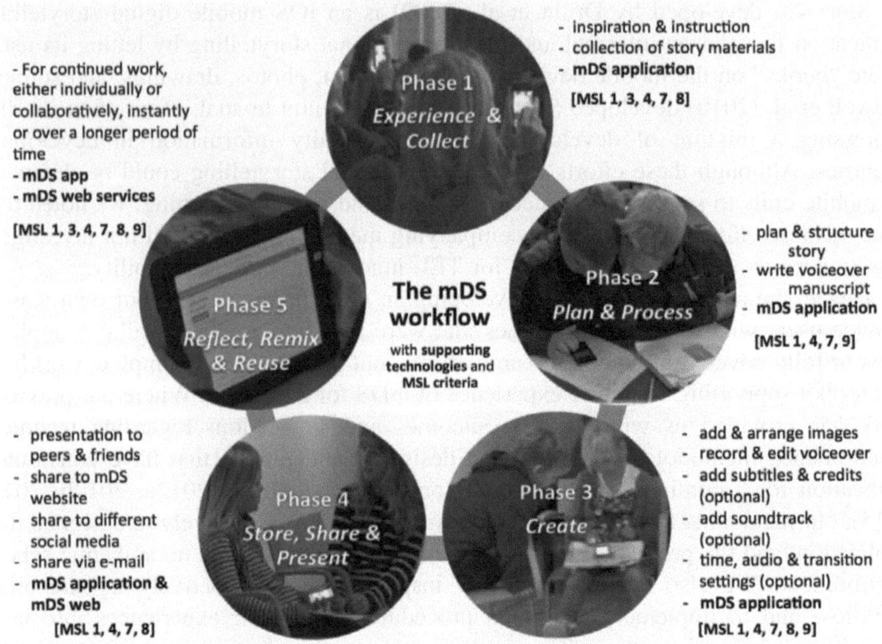

Fig. 1. The mDS workflow with current mDS technologies and MSL dimensions.

story elements, which provides potential for remixing stories into enhanced versions, or for creating altogether new stories, reusing already existing story components.

3.1 The mDS Workflow Approach

The mDS workflow as seen in Fig. 1 above, consists of five interrelated creative processes that progressively build on each other, starting with Phase 1, *Experience & Collect*, where the storytellers get their first acquaintance with the assignments ahead, and are instructed on how to proceed through the full cycle. Phase 2, *Plan & Process*, encourages the storytellers to reflect on the experiences so far, and to relate them and the materials gathered to their story theme. For the processing part, where the pupils storyboard and script their story, the pupils are to carefully consider and discuss what to use and why, and how they intend to combine the chosen images with their script to tell the story as planned. Phase 3, *Create*, invites the storytellers to the mDS application for assembling and completing their story. Following the planned storyboard they insert and arrange the selected images and record and edit the voiceover. They also have access to optional features such as subtitles, soundtrack, and title and credits screens, and a preview the finished story. All steps throughout the creation process are auto-saved as separate components to facilitate editing, sharing and remixing. Phase 4 *Store, Share & Present*, renders and stores the finished story (both the full story version and each story component) to the mDS web service. The user can also share the full story to e.g. YouTube, Vimeo, and Facebook or send it by e-mail. The final phase 5, *Reflect, Remix & Reuse*, offers possibilities for story reflection sessions, as well as for story remix and reuse with the mDS web services.

3.2 The mDS Technologies

Two main software solutions have been designed and developed to scaffold the five phases of the mDS workflow. The main focus has obviously been on the initial iOS application called *mDS*, which is devised specifically for mobile digital storytelling efforts in educational settings. Each individual story component is identified and stored in JSON format on the mobile client, and are then uploaded to the mDS web, which is a web-repository for storage, reuse, reflection and presentation. Using JSON for storing the content allows easy integration with the complementary technologies and other software applications that rely on web technologies and standards for data exchange. Figure 2 illustrates some examples of the user interface (UI) of the mDS application.

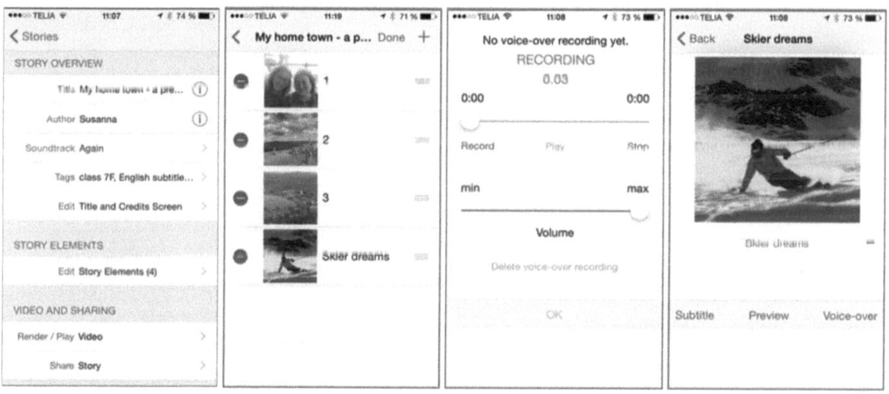

Fig. 2. Examples of the UI for the mDS mobile application

The recently developed mDS web platform adds several possibilities for further collaborative working modes, features for comments and reflection, and teacher orchestration of the activities. All mDS stories and their story elements stored by the web service provide potential for continued work, e.g. by remixing stories into enriched versions, or by creating altogether new stories by reusing existing story components. The service also contains a UI for reflections and commenting (see example in Fig. 3 below) to be used during phase 5 of the workflow, and will ultimately also contain teacher admin tools for grouping, grading, and reporting, to mention some.

The story data is transferred from the iOS application to the web platform and thereafter stored as individual and unique story elements. Figure 4 below outlines the architecture of the mDS web platform and the different components and its features and functionalities.

Fig. 3. The mDS web service UI for reflection sessions

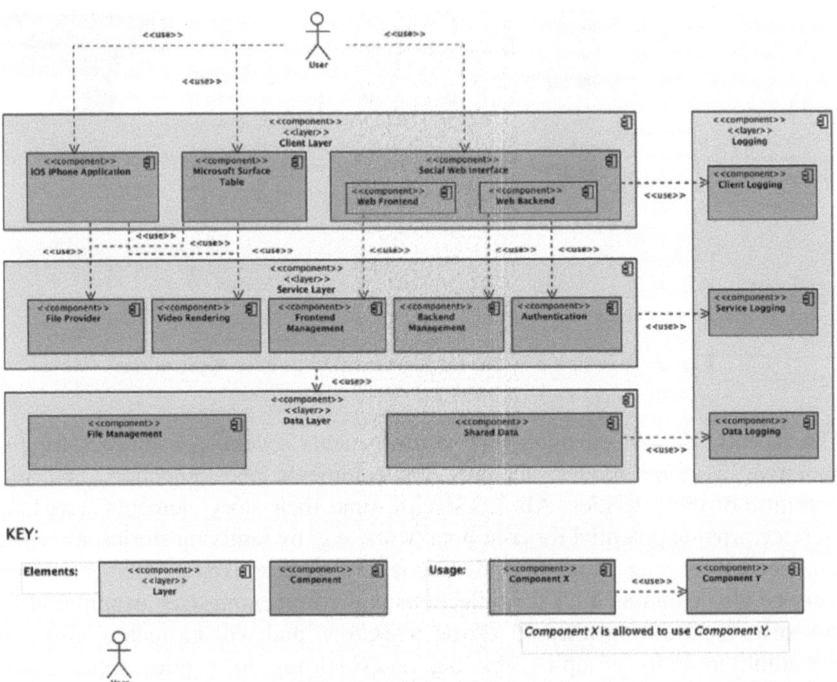

Fig. 4. The mDS web architecture (Eiter, 2015)

Finally, to scaffold the overall storytelling process for both teachers and pupils we also supply a set of optional – however not digital – tools, such as storyboard templates, time management agendas, and step-by-step mDS guides.

4 Research Intervention - Study Design and Results

Our first pilot study on mobile digital storytelling was carried out with the Pilbäck School of Växjö, Sweden, in 2011 (Nordmark and Milrad, 2012a). This initial study served as means for conceptualizing the by now fully established mDS workflow as seen in Fig. 1 above, and as a first step of trying out the overall ideas and plans for our upcoming work. The partaking of the Pilbäck School for the present study was initiated as we wished to come back to the school where we once began our mDS work, and hopefully also get a recurring participation of some of the teachers. As described more detailed in 4.2, a total of 4 teachers and 54 pupils participated in the study, where the actual pupil activities were carried out throughout a week's classroom work, and teacher the preparation and follow-up time added to that covered 12 two-hour-long sessions spread over a total of 6 weeks before and after the pupil activities.

As is the case with all our previous efforts, this study is guided by educational design research (Design-Based Research Collective, 2003; Ejersbo et al. 2008), where the general aim is to find out how, when, and why educational innovations work in real educational settings by making all involved partake as essential individual partners without whom the end result would not be sufficient. In this study, the design process mainly focused on testing and evaluating the two supporting technologies, and to provide the mDS workflow with some finishing touches in order to influence the overall intention of achieving practice sustainability. The mDS workflow has been iteratively designed, tested, assessed and redesigned throughout our previous mDS studies since 2011, and this time the focus on redesigning it was related to sustainability aspects.

Since one of the teachers participating in the first 2011 study was also involved this time, a welcome and thought-provoking longitudinal dimension to the overall teacher experiences was added, alongside further insights on the adaptation of TEL in everyday teacher practices. Since our first pilot trial in 2011, we have carried out a series of mDS studies and other mDS related efforts, both nationally and internationally. The majority of the participating school pupils have been in ages from 6 to 14, and the adult users have represented a range of different professions, for example teachers, teacher trainees, museum curators, museum pedagogues, project managers, school leaders, system and web developers, TEL designers and librarians (Nordmark and Milrad 2012a, 2012b, 2014, 2015).

The Pilbäck School study presented in this paper was divided into three subdivisions. Each will be described in detail in the forthcoming subsections: *Teachers' contribution and planning*, *study settings and requirements*, and *teacher follow-up sessions*.

4.1 Teachers' Contribution and Planning

After having completed a series of initial sessions with the teachers and headmaster where general information, presentations, overall aim, scope, and required experimental settings of the forthcoming study was presented, a more detailed planning and hands-on phase was initialized. As reported in our earlier studies (Nordmark and Milrad 2012a, 2012b, 2014, 2015), teacher ownership of any TEL activity seems to be crucial, why we spent extensive preparation time on making the contributing teachers feel comfortable both with the supporting technologies and the mDS workflow, as well as stressing the importance of connecting the activity to the syllabi and subject matter which in this case were those of Swedish, Civics, and Arts. All preparations were aimed at making the study fit smoothly to the already planned schedule, and to blend in the mDS activities as seamlessly as possible. A visual overview of the teachers' study commitment can be seen in detail in Table 1 below.

Table 1. The teacher activities

Teachers' activities			
1 Initial sessions	1.1 mDS Introduction and study presentation		
	1.2 Overall info and discussions on logistics etc.		
	1.3 Experimental settings		
	1.4 mDS methodology (repetition from introduction session) + tech walkthrough session		
2 Detailed planning	2.1 In this study, the mDS phase 1 "experience & collect" will be carried out as a classroom experience within the frame of their ordinary subject studies in Swedish, Arts and Civics.		
	2.2 Swedish grade 4 teachers are "interdisciplinary" by default...	2.2.1 As Swedish teachers, Teacher 1 & colleagues cover the "factual basis" for the storytelling sessions, which will be the first step of a series of lectures covering either the whole semester, or for the whole of year 4, if needed.	
		2.2.2 As Swedish teachers, Teacher 1 & colleagues support the overall story composition and voice-over scripting, and help out with subtitles if someone wants to use those	
		2.2.3 As Arts teachers, Teacher 1 & colleagues help with image collection and teach how to tell a story supported by images + how to storyboard	
		2.2.4 As Civics teachers, Teacher 1 & colleagues teach about copyright (for gathering images from the Internet) and for publishing (using Creative Commons)	
	2.3 Teachers' expected outcomes	2.3.1 To provide pupils with their first introduction to storytelling in general: Overall theme is "How to convey a message?" in which they will learn especially about interpretation, settings, and dialogue	
		2.3.2 Planned continuation of storytelling lectures for the whole of 4th grade (using mDS)	
	2.4 Follow-up sessions (see also 4.4 below)	2.4.1 Interviews / discussons with teachers about:	2.4.1.1 methodology
			2.4.1.2 technology
			2.4.1.3 pupil workprocess and outcomes
			2.4.1.4 views on teaching with support of mDS tech and the mDS workflow, compared to teaching "ordinary" storytelling sessions (i.e. without the mDS package)
			2.4.1.5 future use - suggestions, wishes, etc
			2.4.1.6 over time - if they continue to use mDS throughout year 4 - I would like to come back and do a "longitudinal follow-up" on the outcomes
	2.5 Pre- and Post-trial sessions on evaluation and assessment on multimodal texts	2.5.1 "Digital storytelling as an educational tool" & "Assessing digital stories". Chapters 3 & 4 in "Digital Storytelling in the Classroom" by Jason Ohler (2008)	
		2.5.2 "Assessment of students' texts from a multimodal perspective". Chapter 4 in "See the text - Multimodal Compositions in Subject Didactics" by Kristina Danielsson & Staffan Selander (2014). In Swedish.	
		2.5.3 "A sociocultural perspective on opportunity to learn" & "Language & Literacy [...]". Chapters 2 & 3 in "Collected Essays on Learning and Assessment in a Digital World" by James Paul Gee (2014)	
		2.5.4 "Suggestions on models for assessment and analysis of digital stories" by Maria Stam & Magnus Engvall (2009). In Swedish.	

The involved teachers were also encouraged to take charge of preparing the pupils' for the upcoming mDS activities, see Table 2 below. The pupils' overall course task was to start learning "how to tell a story/how to convey a message", a learning activity usually within the boundaries of the subjects of Swedish and Civics. In this case

Table 2. The pupils' activities

Pupils' activities			
1 Initial session	1.1 mDS method / what to do and when / mDS workflow walkthrough / equipment check / etc.		
2 Story creation	2.1 work in pairs; create 2 stories	2.1.1	Following the mDS workflow, make first story in relation to the teachings in course.
		2.1.2	Following a script make a second story about work process, involving a mDS workflow reflection, comments on methodological challenges, and on using the supporting technologies, both iOS app and web service.
3 Story presentation	3.1 classroom presentation using the mDS web as supporting technology. Show story 1 from mDS web, reflective discussion with teachers after trial, using "Two stars and a wish-method". Teacher and/or pupils note the reflective discussion in the mDS web interface.		

however it also involved the Arts subject because of the inherent multimodal approach that mobile storytelling embraces.

This time our research focus was not set primarily on the pupils' outcomes, since we have studied that extensively in earlier efforts. Instead, we focused on the testing of the completion of the full mDS workflow and its supporting technologies, the teacher embracement of the mDS concept, the impact on and incorporation of that concept in their everyday practices, and the adaptation of the activities to the syllabi and curriculum – all as an attempt to make the effort as sustainable as possible. However, for clarity of the pupil's part we include Table 2 below to give a brief outline of the study settings that were planned for the pupils.

4.2 Study Settings and Requirements

The study participants included 54 fourth graders (11–12 year olds) and their 4 teachers. The teachers involved all belonged to one of the school's four teaching divisions (the B-unit), and the effective study time took place in their 4 classrooms for the duration of one school week. We installed the mDS mobile application on all of the divisions' 30 iOS units, and we also set up a dedicated mDS web service for the forthcoming reflection sessions addressed in mDS phase 5. However, after other teachers at the school learned what was going on in the participating unit, several of them signed up as subsequent participants on a voluntary basis, i.e. they would shadow and test the method and technologies with the support and introduction from their colleagues primarily involved in the study, and who thus would function as "mDS pilots" for the rest of the school. This rewarding "long-tail-effect" consequently ended up in us installing the mDS iOS application on all of the school's iOS units ($\approx$ 100 new iPads), and also in setting up an entire mDS web server solitary dedicated to the continued mDS work at the Pilbäck school.

A total of 1 researcher and 3 observers participated in the school activities. Two of the observers are also actively involved in the design process as developers of the mDS iOS application and the mDS web platform. Data was collected by video recordings of the activities, mainly focusing on pupil accomplishment of the mDS workflow, their overall involvement in the reflective discussions and follow-up class discussions, and on teacher interactions with the supporting technologies and the workflow completion. Also, teachers were interviewed after testing each technology as suggested by the mDS workflow, and thoroughly briefed in the follow-up discussions on outcomes, experiences, assessment and future suggestions.

For the study realization we needed the school's iPad units to connect to the mDS web platform, something that proved to be the most cumbersome of all things to prepare and establish. It turned out that neither teachers nor the school could authorize what websites their technologies could connect to, meaning that the municipality restrictions obstructed pedagogical innovation, something we all agreed on to be a severe limitation for learning. This will be further discussed in Sect. 5.

4.3 Teacher Follow-up Sessions

mDS phases 1 and 2 were independently accomplished by the teachers following the mDS methodology within the ongoing coursework. Phases 3, 4 and 5 were introduced to the pupils by the researchers, and planned and realized collaboratively with the teachers, with us functioning only as supporting personnel when needed. This means that the participating teachers predominantly realized the activities 2.2 and 2.3 in Table 1 above, and all sessions in Table 2, which is a significant difference and a great improvement compared to the teacher outcomes of our earlier studies.

In the follow-up study sessions the participating teachers were asked to share and compare their expectations and experiences (±) – pre- & post study – based on three viewpoints:

1. *Methodological* (mDS workflow, pupil achievement, assessment and practice sustainability).

   We asked the teachers to compare how they usually teach these particular curriculum sequences when not using the mDS workflow, and how they had experienced those same sessions with mDS implemented. All participating teachers concurred that the mDS experience had given them a complete and easy-managed set of working-modes and tools to utilize, thereby providing something that had made all their pupils feel motivated, involved and engaged. Teachers also stated that during the "non-mDS" sessions where writing had been the only mode the pupils could use, and the method of progressing through the assignment had been very differently planned, many had lost interest and focus at an early stage, why a large number actually had not passed the assignment given. With the mDS workflow methodology, the levels of pupil motivation, focus, engagement and fulfillment had been greatly improved in comparison to the learning sessions without mDS. Teachers also agreed that the workflow methodology and accompanying technologies had been very easy to understand, follow and use for both learners and teachers, something they all had appreciated and unanimously felt were the strongest factors to continue using mDS, but also to scale up by implementing it in more subjects.

   As we have seen in earlier studies, assessing a multimodal text instead of a traditional written one often proves to be a serious challenge for many participants. To address this we provided discussions on a set of articles and book chapters covering assessment issues, and which the teachers took part of before running the study. In the last follow-up session before the school summer holidays we unfortunately ran out of time to fully discuss these readings as closely as planned, but all teachers established that they had read, understood, and found the texts very useful for their continued work. Neither of them had specific questions on the matter, nor did they express concerns on any level; a welcome result and improvement.

On the minus side of the study events were severe network issues that – despite careful preparations by the school – had to be re-negotiated in medias res with the municipality IT group. However, since these issues had nothing to do with the implementation of the mDS workflow as such, but instead with the overall IT policy of the municipality, all participating teachers as well as the headmaster resolutely agreed that the policy problem in fact had been opportunely highlighted by the mDS activities, and thereby had pinpointed an acute issue all school leaders and pedagogues in the municipality needed to jointly address to the municipality officials and representatives.

2. *Technical* (mDS application and web platform).

   From the study start and following mDS introduction we were adamant on focusing the teachers' attention on the simplicity of the tools, and how it's design and development has come to be, i.e. in close cooperation with other teachers, pupils and museum pedagogues; i.e. they were not a product of a closed and separate research group. Also, it is essential to point out that no components of the mDS workflow and technologies have been developed to impress and astonish on a technical level, but rather to give the user an impression of simplicity, straight forwardness, reliability and usability; factors that are crucial for teachers, and especially so in the initial stages of implementation. Our teachers were given a thorough introduction and extensive possibilities to test and evaluate the tools and workflow on their own in good time before the study, and we painstakingly considered their questions and ideas in a finishing tech walkthrough just before starting up the study. After the study ended, even the most "tech reluctant" of the 4 teachers said she now felt confident and relaxed about using the mDS workflow and technologies on her own. She and another teacher started to plan an immediate spin-off session already during the ongoing study, see further discussion in Sect. 5.

3. *Suggestions* (requirements, future use etc.).

   The participating teachers unanimously agreed that mDS is something they plan to continue using and also introduce in other subjects, e.g. English, Science and Mathematics. The built-in versatility of the mDS innovation is supporting the much-needed prospect of scalability and sustainability for educational innovations (Looi and Teh, 2015, p. 1 ff).

   The overall impressions of the mDS workflow established as mentioned that it worked very well, but teachers also agreed that the younger the pupils, the more formalized and well-planned their tasks has to be in order to get the desired outcomes. This is also something we have found when working with the youngest of the elementary school children (see Nordmark and Milrad, 2015).

   For future use the teachers established to encourage the children not to make extensive use the optional soundtrack feature (background music), since all of this particular school's iPads were equipped with a heavy cover that obstructed the internal microphone to clearly record the voiceover audio. Unfortunately, the covers could not be removed due to insurance policies. Careful use of the soundtrack option is also something we encourage generally, since voiceover sound quality is of essence in order to perceive the narration properly. However, including a soundtrack option has been one of the design requirements from earlier iterations, and is considered to add to the telling of the story when used with dueconsideration. The soundtrack setting will henceforth be set to "low" as default in the next application update. Finally, for uploading the full stories to the mDS web platform, the teachers provided valuable of ideas and suggestions on how to tag the stories in order to create smooth grouping, and classification e.g. to tag each story with the unique class code.

5 Discussion

Here, we intend to consider some of the most noteworthy outcomes from our study, starting on a broader scale with the overall viewpoints of the school staff and closing in on some of the effects of the mDS workflow and technologies on the everyday teacher practices. The research questions we aimed to answer were:

1. What factors could make an innovative TEL effort sustainable and worthwhile to pursue for teachers?
2. In what ways could mobile digital storytelling support TEL implementation and sustainability in teachers' daily practices?

As reported in Sect. 4.2 above, an unfortunate scenario in many Swedish schools is that municipality IT policies tend to hinder pedagogical development instead of underpinning and scaffolding innovative TEL efforts. Headmaster Edward Jensinger (in Grönberg 2015) discusses the sometimes-hopeless role of the school leader, and his/her two-faced responsibility and commission to support and develop TEL practices in school; two-faced here meaning that school leaders are under orders to take charge and act, but at the same time they aren't allowed to actually do anything. Instead of being given means for pedagogical freedom, school leaders and teachers run into case after case where their central IT department is acting as a downright operational hindrance rather than providing the support they reasonably should give. Jensinger attests that when the limitations of the school's pedagogical and financial freedom become so severe that neither headmaster nor teachers can really manage their own work, the overall directive of the school leader to transform their school into a so-called "IT-school" is really a dead heat already from the beginning. There simply is no flexibility in the system. Jensinger's conclusion is that technicians must never be allowed to interfere in policy-making or decisions concerning pedagogical matters. However, he also points out that school leaders in general must take a more active part in learning what the IT departments' suggested steps and measures actually implies for the schools' daily work, so that school leaders can act in time to put a stop to defective suggestions.

We as researchers have unfortunately observed cases like this at close hand over an extensive period of time, and as discussed above we also encountered it also during this study. In fact, we cannot really detect any significant change from when first starting working with novel TEL solutions including mobile technologies for more than a decade ago. In a recent article Khaddage et al. (2015) discuss the pedagogical, technological, policy and research challenges and concepts underlying mobile learning, and proposes a mobile learning framework with dynamic criteria. Based on their discussion and our own experiences, we consider the policy challenge to be the foremost concern in need of immediate attention, and also one of the factors that all too effectively hinders TEL innovation and sustainability in teacher practices. What schools and teachers need are solutions that matches the complex IT and TEL landscape of today, and that has flexibility to be easily adapted to and redesigned for the landscape of tomorrow. This is also supported by Looi and Teh (2015, p. 13–14), where they establish that it is the coordinated work of teachers and administrators that in concord can create sustainable innovation and transform education.

To get an interesting comparison and to provide a tangible eye-opener for the participating teachers, we asked them before running the study to describe how they normally would go about teaching the same sessions without using the mDS technology and methodology. These descriptions turned out to be very helpful when we during the follow-up sessions asked the teachers to compare the two as discussed in Sect. 4.3 above. All teachers reported that the levels of pupil motivation, interest, focus and accomplishment had skyrocketed, and even though some of the teachers had been reluctant towards TEL efforts before taking part in this study, all of them now felt confident and relaxed using the mDS tools and method on their own in various learning situations. Two of them, as reported above, became so committed that they even presented an immediate mDS spin-off that they wanted to initiate in the subjects of English and Mathematics, a very welcome result and something we were invited to follow-up later this fall, and as mentioned above we also got an early interest from several teachers not participating in the study; teachers who had heard what was going on and who expressed an interest in becoming introduced to the concept by their colleagues at a later stage. The word of mouth-factor and the following immediate spread of interest for mDS after the participating teachers introduced to colleagues was of great importance and also highly effective. How these efforts turned out will also be something we will come back to during the fall.

Conclusively, the teacher who was also involved in our mDS pilot study in 2011 was given a special interview session to share her TEL practices from then to now. What news, what differences, and what changes had she experienced? Her report turned out similar to several of those we've encountered in earlier studies – lack of time and money to find, buy, evaluate and implement relevant technologies, absence of appropriate methods accompanying the proposed technologies, shortage of support and help, and insecurity and non-existent confidence with technology which was often caused by earlier TEL experiences where the technology had failed and/or been far too complex to grasp, together with no time allowance for teachers to explore and learn for themselves – all of that constitute tangible impediments to pedagogic development. Since 2011, the only provided technology for teaching and learning at the school were interactive whiteboards. They were now only used without employing the interactivity, due to technical issues. However, the recent investment in 20–30 iPads per teaching unit she regarded as a very welcome addition, especially in the light of the recent mDS events. The simplicity and reliability of the mDS experience made her share a renewed technology confidence with us, and a hope to initiate a more TEL infused teaching practice. She also recognized a general use for tablets in all kinds of learning situations, and consequently an immediate need for investing in more iPads units in order to provide one unit for each pupil, instead of having to share them was the case when the study took place.

To summarize this section in relation to the two research questions, TEL innovation and sustainability are dependent on factors like accessibility, simplicity, stability and, scalability, which stood out as essential for making the teachers feel comfortable with the implemented approach, but also feeling confident enough to continue working with and developing new TEL features in their practices. As for the second question, outcomes such as heightened pupil motivation, increased engagement, happiness and task achievements acted as very strong arguments for a continued use of mDS in particular, but also as incitements to dare try new and other solutions. Both questions are intrinsically related to each other, so the outcomes of this study could in fact cover both questions. Lastly, the present constraints in teacher and school-leader authorization to administrate and unreservedly use their learning technologies, are pressing matters that needs to be solved urgently in order for this or any other TEL efforts not to be in vain.

6 Future Prospects

This study has been the latest in our work on completing a comprehensive mDS workflow as described above. It has also served to test the most recent version of the mDS mobile application, and the mDS web platform. As far as the methodological requirements and settings for the enactment of the mDS workflow in school settings, we now feel that we have reached a result that can be implemented irrespective of school subject, learning settings, pupil age and previous knowledge.. Left to accomplish regarding the supporting technologies are firstly some minor fine tunings of the mDS application, such as some redesign of the UI, to change the soundtrack options, and to implement a few more transition and sharing options before we launch it to the AppStore.

As for the mDS web platform, we need to adjust the UI according to the suggestions teachers and pupils reported during the follow-up sessions. These suggestions mainly concerned the placement of links and buttons, color choices, and how to organize the story tags in a more graphic and useful style, e.g. an active tag cloud, which we will address shortly.

Following these redesigns, and some other additions we already have planned for the mDS web, we need to discuss with our local interest groups on the future ownership and management of the whole mDS system in order to provide continuous and adequate service and support for schools and users. Finally, we intend to continue our collaboration with the Pilbäck School during the fall of 2015 and hopefully even longer, so that we can return and observe their continued mDS efforts with pilot teachers, their colleagues, and the various and continued mDS activities.

References

Bidwell, N.J., Reitmeier, T., Marsden, G., Hanson, S.: Designing with mobile digital storytelling in rural Africa. In: Proceedings of CHI 2010, pp. 1593 – 1602 (2010)

Design-Based Research Collective. Design-based research: An emerging paradigm for educational inquiry. Educational Researcher, 32, 5–8 (2003)

Druin, A., Bederson, B.B., Quinn, A.: Designing intergenerational mobile storytelling. In: Proceedings of the 8th International Conference on Interaction Design and Children, pp. 325–328. ACM, New York (2009)

Eiter, J.: Design and Development of a Web-Based Interface for a Mobile Digital Storytelling System. Bachelors' thesis from Technischen Hochschule Nürnberg Georg Simon Ohm (2015)

Ejersbo, L., Engelhardt, R., Frølunde, L., Hanghøj, T., Magnussen, R., Misfeldt, M.: Balancing product design and theoretical insights. In: Kelly, A.E., Lesh, R.A., Baek, J.Y. (eds.) The Handbook of Design Research Methods in Education: Innovations in Science, Technology, Engineering and Mathematics Learning and Teaching. Routledge New York(2008)

Goodyear, P.: Emerging methodological challenges. In: Markauskaite, L., Freebody, P., Irwin, J. (eds.) Methodological Choice and Design, Part 4, Vol. 9, pp. 253–266. Springer, The Netherlands (2011)

Ito, M.: Hanging Out, Messing Around, and Geeking Out: Kids Living and Learning with New Media. The MIT Press, Cambridge (2009)

Jensinger, E.: The Principal's role in a 1:1 school. In: Grönberg (ed.) Changing School with Technology: Beyond "One to One Computing" (2014). Örebro University Press. (In Swedish) (2014)

Jewitt, C.: Technology, Literacy and Learning: A Multimodal Approach. Routledge, London (2006)

Khaddage, F., Christensen, R., Lai, W., Knezek, G., Norris, C., Soloway, E.: A model driven framework to address challenges in a mobile learning environment. Education and Information Technologies, pp. 1360–2357. Springer, US (2015)

Kress, G.: Multimodality: A Social Semiotic Approach to Contemporary Communication. Routledge, London (2010)

Kress, G., van Leeuwen, T.: Multimodal Discourse: The Modes and Media of Contemporary Communication. Hodder Arnold Publication, London (2001)

Lambert, J.: The Digital Storytelling Cookbook: Center for Digital Storytelling. Digital Diner Press, Berkeley (2007)

Lambert, J.: Digital Storytelling: Capturing Lives, Creating Community. Routledge, New York (2013)

Looi, C.K., Teh, L.W.: Scaling Educational Innovations. Springer, Singapore (2015)

Lundby, K. (ed.): Digital Storytelling, Mediatized Stories: Self-Representations in New media. Peter Lang, New York (2008)

Milrad, M., Wong, L.H., Sharples, M., Hwang, G.-J., Looi, C.-K., Ogata, H.: Seamless learning: an international perspective on next generation technology enhanced learning. In: Berge, Z.L., Muilenburg, L.Y. (eds.) Handbook of Mobile Learning. Routledge, New York (2013)

NMC Horizon report: Higher Ed. edition. http://www.nmc.org/publication/nmc-horizon-report-2015-higher-education-edition/. Accessed 17 April 2015

NMC Technology Outlook: Scandinavian Schools. http://www.nmc.org/publication/2015-nmc-technology-outlook-scandinavian-schools/. Accessed 17 April 2015

Nordmark, S., Milrad, M.: Mobile digital storytelling for promoting creative collaborative learning. In: Proceedings of the Seventh IEEE International Conference on Wireless, Mobile, and Ubiquitous Technology in Education, WMUTE 2012, Takamatsu, Japan, 27–30 March 2012 (2012a)

Nordmark, S., Milrad, M.: Using mobile digital storytelling to support learning about cultural heritage. In: Biswas, G., Wong, L H., Hirashim; T., Chen, W. (ed.) Proceedings of the 20th International Conference on Computers in Education, ICCE 2012, pp. 408–412, 26–30 November 2012, Singapore. Asia-Pacific Society for Computers in Education (APSCE), Singapore (2012b)

Nordmark, S., Milrad, M.: Promoting sustainable innovation in technology enhanced learning: a teacher & pupil study using mobile digital storytelling (mDS). In: Proceedings of the 14th IEEE International Conference on Advanced Learning Technologies, ICALT 2014, Athens, Greece (2014)

Nordmark, S., Milrad, M.: Tell your story about history – a mobile seamless learning approach to support mobile digital storytelling (mDS).In: Wong, L.-H., Milrad, M., Specht, M. (eds.) Seamless Learning in the Age of Mobile Connectivity. Springer, Singapore (2015)

Ohler, J.: Digital Storytelling in the Classroom: New Media Pathways to Literacy, Learning, and Creativity. Sage, London (2007)

Pachler, N., Bachmair, B., Cook, J.: Mobile Learning: Structures, Agency, Practices. Springer, New York (2010)

Selander, S., Kress, G.: Designs for learning – a multimodal perspective. In: Swedish, Norstedts, Stockholm (2010)

Spikol, D., Milrad, M., Maldonado, H., Pea, R.: Integrating co-design practices into the development of mobile science collaboratories. In: Proceedings of the 9th IEEE International Conference on Advanced Learning Technologies, pp. 393–397 (2009)

Wong, L.H., Looi, C.K.: What seams do we remove in mobile assisted seamless learning? a critical review of the literature. Comput. Educ. **57**(4), 2364–2381 (2011)

Towards Design Patterns for Augmented Reality Serious Games

Alessandra Antonaci[1](✉), Roland Klemke[2], and Marcus Specht[2]

[1] Institute of Educational Technology (ITD) of the Italian National Research Council (CNR), Via de Marini, 6, 16149 Genoa, GE, Italy
Antonaci@itd.cnr.it

[2] Welten Institute – Research Centre for Learning, Teaching and Technology, Open University of the Netherlands, P.O. Box 2960, 6401 DL Heerlen, The Netherlands
{Roland.Klemke,Marcus.Specht}@ou.nl

Abstract. For professional workers today, keeping up with knowledge and the continuous technology progress is challenging. Increased innovation speed and dynamic work situations shorten preparation times for new tasks significantly. Traditional professional training approaches preparing employees for new tasks are becoming inappropriate. Thus new educational means are needed. These would help employees get acquainted with new situations faster and more efficiently.

According to learning theories such as action learning and situated learning, which embed the learning process in the application context and challenge the learner to be actively involved help to improve the learning process. These theories are the basis for mobile learning and serious games. From research in Serious Games we know that games have the potential to actively involve learners and to immerse them in a learning situation and increase their engagement.

With Augmented Reality (AR) and wearable devices a new generation of tools and applications becomes available, which inherently are mobile, contextualized and personalized. First successful application scenarios show the potential of these new technologies for education and training.

While the application of game-design patterns to learning processes help to systematically design learning games supporting specific learning outcomes, an empirically tested, systematic approach towards the design of AR-based learning solutions is still missing.

Based on the state of the art in AR research and in applying design patterns for serious games, we consequently propose a research methodology to apply game design patterns to augmented reality-based learning games for the training of professionals in dynamic situations.

Keywords: Augmented reality · Mobile serious games · Game-design patterns

1 Introduction

We live in a complex society where technology and knowledge are changing at a very fast rate (Aleandri and Refrigeri 2013). In today's 'high performance organizations',

T.H. Brown and H.J. van der Merwe (Eds.): mLearn 2015, CCIS 560, pp. 273–282, 2015.
DOI: 10.1007/978-3-319-25684-9_20

workers must be prepared for continuous growth and development on-the-job (ERIC Digest).

"In such fast-moving working contexts, skills and competences rapidly become outdated and need to be continuously implemented and empowered as a strategic factor for global competitiveness. Traditional models of learning both inside and outside of the workplace have become unable to explain the complexity of such a process" (Manuti *et al.* 2015).

In this context, learning plays an important role "in individual career development and organizational success". To better underline how important learning is in the workplace, Sambrook (2005) described the concept of *workplace learning*. His work is very connected with Eruat (2000) and gives an important contribution to the clarification of its meaning by distinguishing between different types of context where the learning process takes place:

- Learning *at* work: associated with planned training and education courses;
- Learning *in* work: correlated with the more informal processes implied in these activities, such as discussing, observing, asking questions, solving problems;
- Learning *outside* work: connected with the idea that some forms of learning could also occur outside the boundaries of the work setting.

Besides, these distinctions foster an easier parallelism with the formal, informal and non-formal learning definition retrieved from the educational/instructional field. This is why "in all or nearly all situations where learning takes place, elements of both formal and informal learning are present" (Manuti *et al.* 2015).

This concept is in line with the following learning theories: action learning theory, based on the idea that learning requires action in a *context* (formal or informal) and reciprocally action requires learning (Lewis and Williams 1994). Furthermore the situated learning theory is based on the premise that knowledge is not independent, but fundamentally situated; a product of the activity, *context* (either formal or informal), and culture within which it is developed (Brown 1988). Last but not least, according to the mobile learning theory, learning cannot be separated from everyday activities: it is integrated with non-learning tasks such as shopping or entertainment; it is organized into projects that are interleaved with everyday activities. Therefore "learning needs emerge when a person strives to overcome a problem or breakdown in everyday activity" (Sharples *et al.* 2005).

These theories are also the fundament for game-based learning (Wu et al. 2012), where systematic approaches towards the design of applications have already been explored with respect to delivering /providing the needed skills (Johnson et al. 2011), the motivational potential (Carstens and Beck 2010; Douch and Savill-Smith 2010) as well as their ability to address various target groups in the most effective way (Unterfauner *et al.* 2010; Liao *et al.* 2011).

In the remainder of this paper we discuss Game Design Patterns (GDP) for serious games, the characteristics of Augmented Reality (AR) and propose a new research idea focused on transferring the pattern-based approach onto designing AR Serious Games.

2 Serious Games and Game-Design Patterns

The Mobile Learning NETwork's (MoLeNET) review on learning game technologies suggests that mobile learning games provide potential for learning and teaching in terms of "assessment", "learner performance and skills development" or "social and emotional well-being" (Douch *et al.* 2010).

Still, the use of (mobile) serious games, as compared to the continuous boost in the games' market (GlobalCollect 2013; PWC 2010; National Gaming Survey 2009) is limited (Arnab *et al.* 2012). Reasons for this are partly due to:

- The high technical demands required to design games or simulations (Goosen *et al.* 2001); game development is complex and thus hard to realise within the educational budgets (Westera *et al.* 2008).
- The difficulty to organise/customise Serious Games in a way that they fit into the educational process (Klopfer *et al.* 2009). Games are often designed for a specific purpose (and not customisable) or they require specialised customisation skills (which can hardly be done by a teacher/educator, who is usually not a game designer or developer).

In the Serious Games research field, an approach to help simplifying the design process for Serious Games is through applying a pattern-based approach as known from the branch of the entertainment games (Björk and Holopainen 2004) and combining it with educational objectives (Kelle et al. 2011). While this approach has also successfully been applied to mobile learning games (Schmitz 2014), little is known on how to systematically apply game-design patterns to augmented reality.

We agree with Schmitz (2014), claiming that "Generally, mapping learning outcomes, patterns and context information may lead to a better understanding of AR and pervasive games for learning and feasible results, which are suitable as a base for design guidelines that define (a) patterns, which support the achievement of a desired learning outcome and (b) ways of applying them".

In the recent literature, we found some work by Wetzel (2013), "*Design Patterns supporting the Development of Mobile Mixed Reality Games*", who used the pattern-based approach to design a game in AR/mixed reality, but without providing any evaluation or evidence that indicates the connection between the game patterns used and their learning efficacy.

Considering the potential of AR for learning, which will be highlighted in the next paragraph, we consequently propose a research methodology that applies GDP to augmented reality-based learning games for the training of professionals in dynamic situations.

With our idea we propose to move two steps further from Wetzel's (2013) work by performing: (1) an evaluation of the patterns which are suitable for an AR Serious Games and (2) to study those patterns and understand the types of learning they are able to improve or stimulate in the users.

At this point clarification about the terms used is needed. What do we mean with game-pattern, what is it? Is it a game mechanic, an algorithm, or a concept more connected with pedagogy?

Computer game designers frequently use the term "game mechanic" both in the context of board games and that of technical programming (Lundgren and Björk 2003; Ott *et al.* 2014).

Lundgren and Björk (2003) outline game mechanics as "any part of the rule system of a game that covers one, and only one, possible kind of interaction that takes place during the game, be it general or specific (…) mechanics are regarded as a way to summarize game rules". Cook's (2006) claims: "game mechanics are rule based system/simulations that facilitate and encourage a user to explore and learn the properties of their possibility space through the use of feedback mechanisms". "A typical mechanic is "roll and move" that simply states that the dice are rolled and that something else is moved depending on the outcome of the dice roll. The mechanic does not state how and why something should be moved; this is determined in the rules for the particular game" (Lundgren and Björk 2003).

According to Björk and Holopainen (2004), however, we can look at patterns as a mean to support creative designing. Patterns are semiformal interdependent descriptions of commonly recurring parts of the design of a game that concern gameplay (McGee 2007). Through them it is possible to describe how the components and the individual aspects of the game interact to create a gameplay experience.

The origin of the concept of "design patterns" hails from the field of architecture and in particular was coined by Christopher Alexander (McGee 2007). The Design Pattern is a method of codifying design knowledge in separate but interrelated parts and has been used to describe game elements related to interaction. "The pattern approach has increasingly been applied to other areas such as the domain of educational science by way of pedagogical patterns (Kohls and Wedekind 2011), for example, or to the design of digital games" (Schmitz 2014).

The GDP approach, indeed, has been successfully used in Serious Games (Kelle, *et al.* 2011) and Mobile Games (Schmitz 2014) and in the literature examples of "Design Patterns supporting the Development of Mobile Mixed Reality Games" (Wetzel 2013) are already available.

Furthermore already in research the effects of AR solutions have been analysed, as will be shown in the next paragraph.

The purpose of this article is to highlight that AR Serious Games can be effective tools for training but need to be understood also how an AR game should be designed to be effective for learning.

3 Augmented Reality

In accordance with Bower *et al.* (2014) we believe that AR is "poised to profoundly transform education as we know it". Considering the widespread availability of the Internet, and the level of diffusion of mobile, smart and wearable devices, it is evident that technology is already part of our daily life. It is expected, that approaches towards AR will become a major trend in education and training once wearable glasses/devices and other display technologies become widely accessible to end-users (Freina and Ott 2015).

AR can be considered as "a system that enhances a person's primary senses (vision, aural and tactile) with virtual or naturally invisible information made visible by digital means" (Specht *et al.* 2011).

Thanks to a wide range of mobile devices, "AR is set to become a ubiquitous commodity for leisure and mobile learning. With this ubiquitous availability, mobile AR allows us to devise and design innovative learning scenarios in real world settings. This carries much promise for enhanced learning experiences in situated learning" (Specht *et al.* 2011).

The basic equipment/hardware needed for an AR system includes:

- Video camera to capture live images;
- Ample storage space for virtual objects;
- Powerful processor to either compose virtual and real objects or display a 3D-simulated environment in real time;
- An interface that allows the user to interact with both real and virtual objects (Bower *et al.* 2014) and
- Sensor infrastructure capable of identifying position, direction, movement (such as geo-localization system and head - or other part of the body - tracking movement sensor).

Due to its potential and the availability of the equipment needed for an AR system, it has been used in different contexts, such as medicine, military, entertainment, training, tourism, social networking, industrial applications, cultural heritage etc. Mobile AR has been used in different projects, a wide taxonomy of which is available in FitzGerald *et al.* (2013) work. Furthermore, the authors stress the educational potential of AR; they mention a series of studies that empirically indicate the efficiency of AR in

- Promoting engagement and motivation (Klopfer and Osterweil 2009; Luckin and Fraser 2011);
- Improving memorability, engagement (Luckin and Fraser 2011) and motivation (Di Serio *et al.* 2012);
- Improving spatial skills (Martin-Gutierrez *et al.* 2011; Schmalstieg and Wagner 2007);
- Supporting collaborative problem solving, (Cook 2010).

The use of AR in education has been profusely explored during the last decades, showing significant evidence of its benefits for learning (Muñoz-cristóbal *et al.* 2014). It is now necessary to explain how and why this medium differs from others in the training context and what the advantages and disadvantages are for the learner, taking into consideration Radu's (2014) literature review: the author compared 26 academic papers and underlined the positive impact that AR experiences have had on learners, as compared to non-AR initiatives:

- *Increased Content Understanding*: The studies examined by the author "generally indicate that students learn better when using AR than when using either printed media or using desktop software";
- *Long Term Memory Retention*: Research indicates that "content learned through AR experiences is memorized better than through non-AR experience";

- *Improved Physical Task Performance*: "Through an AR experience, maintenance tasks are performed with higher accuracy, and students are able to better transfer their learning to operate physical machinery";
- *Improved Collaboration*: in the Morrison *et al.* (2009) study it is shown that the group who used AR to create a shared space, contrary to "the more individual experience of a student using a GPS mapping application";
- *Increased Student Motivation*: "user motivation remains significantly higher for AR systems (vs. the non-AR alternative) even when the AR experience is deemed more difficult to use than the non-AR alternative".

The added value that AR has compared with other delivery techniques/tools comprise:

- Multi-modal visualization of difficult theoretical concepts;
- Practical exploration of the theory through tangible examples;
- Natural interaction with multimedia representations of teaching material;
- Effective collaboration and discussion amongst the participants (Liarokapis and Anderson 2010).

Starting from what has been highlighted until now, it is necessary to mention some disadvantages experienced by learners compared to non-AR systems, found in the literature and strictly connected with formal education, but relevant for our research idea:

1. *Attention Tunneling*; in the studies reported by Radu (2014) it is shown that learners needed more attention than usual not only to live the experience but also to understand how to use the AR tool with the consequence of "ignoring important parts of the experience or feeling unable to properly perform team tasks";
2. *Usability Difficulties;* "In several studies, users rate AR systems as more difficult to use than the physical or desktop-based alternatives";
3. *Learner Differences*: people with high-achieving or cognitive disabilities have some problems; for example "low-ability readers did not learn from parts of the AR experience which presented textual content. This is not surprising, but it does reinforce the issue that educational tools must be well tailored to the capabilities of their audience".

Usability problems are also highlighted in Klemke *et al.* (2014), which also recognizes the potential of AR wearable devices in overtaking the attention tunneling problem by making the interaction and the user experience as much as natural, immersive and intuitive possible, avoiding also the need from the user to switch his/her attention between the task deployed in the augmented context and the device in his/her hand.

Bacca *et al.* (2014) performed a detailed systematic review of the state of the art in AR, analysing the field of education, the target group, the type of AR, the reported purposes, advantages, limitations, affordances and effectiveness of AR in educational settings. While a number of successful AR-cases can be found according to this review, only limited research has been devoted to analysing the combination of AR and Serious Games with respect to realizing professional training for adults (Furió *et al.* 2013). Especially, while systematic approaches towards the design of AR games are emerging (Wetzel 2013), their underpinning with empirical research is still missing.

4 Conclusion: Applying Game-Design Patterns to Augmented Reality

While TEL-based educational approaches in general and game-based learning specifically proved to be helpful for learning, we found that research is needed studying the potential of AR based mobile learning games for professional educational scenarios. Especially, empirical evidence about how to design learning games using AR is missing.

Consequently, we propose to adopt the GDP approach as methodology, in order to investigate game design patterns suitable for AR games and determine whether they are effective for learning.

Therefore, empirical work is needed to understand which patterns are suitable for which type of learning (considering design, usability and learning outcome). A starting point for this work is the literature and previous research (Kelle 2012; Schmitz, 2014); that demonstrated the empirical evidence of the efficacy of the GDP approach in Serious Games and Mobile Games. We now propose to move forward by transferring this functional methodology to a different field: AR, and by analysing, studying and in case designing suitable new patterns for AR games.

Below some design patterns already identified by the authors of this paper, which take advantage of AR potential, are listed:

- Localization: adding information related to the user's position and orientation;
- Video recording and view sharing: sharing the user's view with another user or an expert;
- Synchronous communication: using communication features while performing a task;
- Contextualization: enriching the current view by providing contextual information (e.g. distance to specific points);
- Object recognition: enhancing or enriching an object in the field of vision of the user;

We expect, that the utilization of these patterns in AR-based games can be beneficial to task performance and learning effects. However, little is known so far, when and how these patterns should be used in order to foster positive effects. Consequently, a mapping to educational objectives will further help to describe design processes towards the systematic application of GDP for AR games.

Acknowledgements. The present paper has been realized in the framework of the Short Term Mobility Programme financed by Italian National Research Council (CNR) at the WELTEN Institute of the Open University in the Netherlands, in April/May 2015.

References

Aleandri, G., Refrigeri, L.: Lifelong learning, training and education in globalized economic systems: analysis and perspectives. In: Third World Conference on Learning, Teaching and Educational Leadership – WCLTA 2012, Brussels. Published by Elsevier Ltd. Procedia - Social and Behavioral Sciences, vol. 93, pp. 1242 – 1248 (2013)

Arnab, S., Berta, R., Earp, J., de Freitas, S., Popescu, M., Romero, M., Stanescu, I., Usart, M.: Framing the adoption of serious games in formal education. Electron. J. e-Learn. **10**(2), 159–171 (2012). http://www.ejel.com

Bacca, J., Fabregat, R., Baldiris, S., Graf, S., Kinshuk: Augmented reality trends in education: A systematic review of research and applications. Educ. Technol. Soc. 17, 133–149 (2014)

Björk, S., Holopainen, J.: Patterns In Game Design. Charles River Media, Hingham (2004)

Brown, J.S., et al.: Situated cognition and the culture of learning. Technical report, Palo Alto Research Center, Palo Alto, CA (1988)

Bower, M., Howe, C., McCredie, N., Robinson, A., Grover, D.: Augmented Reality in education – cases, places and potentials. Educ. Media Int. **51**(1), 1–15 (2014)

Carstens, A., Beck, J.: Get ready for the gamer generation. TechTrends **49**(3), 22–25 (2010)

Cook, D.: What are game mechanics? (2006). http://www.lostgarden.com/2006/10/what-are-game-mechanics.html, 29 July 2015

Cook, J.: Mobile phones as mediating tools within augmented contexts for development. Int. J. Mob. Blended Learn. **2**(3), 1–12 (2010)

Di Serio, Á., Ibáñez, M.B., Kloos, C.D.: Impact of an augmented reality system on students' motivation for a visual art course. Comput. Educ., 1–11 (2012)

Douch, R., Attewell, J., Dawson, D.: Games technologies for learning. More than just toys (2010). http://goo.gl/mazqJ, 29 July 2015

Douch, R., Savill-Smith, C.: The mobile learning network: the impact of mobile game-based learning. In: IADIS International Conference on Mobile Learning 2010, Porto, pp. 189–197 (2010)

ERIC Digest. New Ways of Learning in the Workplace. ERIC Digest, No. 161, 1–8. https://archive.org/details/ERIC_ED385778, 29 July 2015

Eruat, M.: Non Formal learning and tacit knowledge in professional work. Br. J. Educ. Psychol. **70**(1), 113–136 (2000)

FitzGerald, E., Adams, A., Ferguson, R., Gaved, M., Mor, Y., Thomas, R., Keynes, M.: Augmented reality and mobile learning: the state of the art. In: 11th World Conference on Mobile and Contextual Learning (mLearn 2012), pp. 62–69, Helsinki, Finland, 16–18 October (2013)

Freina, L., Ott, M.: A literature review on immersive virtual reality in education: state of the art and perspectives. In: eLearning and Software for Education - eLSE, Bucharest, Romania, April 23–24 (2015)

Furió, D., González-Gancedo, S., Juan, M.-C., Seguí, I., Rando, N.: Evaluation of learning outcomes using an educational iPhone game vs. traditional game. Comput. Educ. **64**, 1–23 (2013)

GlobalCollect: The Global Mmo Games Market: Payments, Intelligence and Trends. GlobalCollect Video Gaming Payments: knowledge series, Edition 2, July 2013. http://info.globalcollect.com/gaming-report-lading-page/

Goosen, K.R., Jensen, R., Wells, R.: Purpose and learning benefits of simulations: a design and development perspective. Simul. Gaming **32**(1), 21–39 (2001)

Johnson, L., Levine, A., Smith, R., Stone, S.: The 2011 Horizon Report. The New Media Consortium, Austin, Texas (2011)

Kelle, S., Klemke, R., Gruber, M., Specht, M.: Standardization of game based learning design. In: Murgante, B., Gervasi, O., Iglesias, A., Taniar, D., Apduhan, B.O. (eds.) ICCSA 2011, Part IV. LNCS, vol. 6785, pp. 518–532. Springer, Heidelberg (2011)

Kelle, S.: Game Design Patterns for Learning. Doctoral dissertation, Open Universiteit in the Netherlands, Heerlen, The Netherlands. SIKS Dissertation Series No. 2012-41. Publisher: Shaker Verlag, Aachen, 9 November 2012

Klemke, R., Ternier, S., Kalz, M., Schmitz, B., Specht, M.: Immersive multi-user decision training games with AR learn. In: Rensing, C., de Freitas, S., Ley, T., Muñoz-Merino, P.J. (eds.) EC-TEL 2014. LNCS, vol. 8719, pp. 207–220. Springer, Heidelberg (2014)

Kohls, C., Wedekind, J.: Investigations of E-Learning Patterns: Context Factors Problems and Solutions. IGI Global, Hershley, PA (2011)

Klopfer, E., Osterweil, S., Salen, K.: Moving Learning Games Forward, Obstacles Opportunities & Openness. Cambridge, MA: MIT/The Education Arcade (2009). http://education.mit.edu/papers/MovingLearningGamesForward_EdArcade.pdf

Lewis, L.H., Williams, C.J.: Experiential learning: past and present. New Dir. Adult Continuing Educ. **62**, 5–16 (1994)

Liao, C.C.Y., Chen, Z.-H., Cheng, H.N.H., Chen, F.-C., Chan, T.-W.: My-mini-pet: a handheld pet-nurturing game to engage students in arithmetic practices. J. Comput. Assist. Learn. **27**(1), 76–89 (2011)

Liarokapis, F., Anderson, E.F.: Using augmented reality as a medium to assist teaching in higher education. In: Eurographics 2010, pp. 9–16 (2010)

Luckin, R., Fraser, D.S.: Limitless or pointless? an evaluation of augmented reality technology in the school and home. Int. J. Technol. Enhanced. Learn. **3**(5), 510–524 (2011)

Lundgren, S., Bjork, S.: Game mechanics: Describing computer-augmented games in terms of interaction. In: First International Conference on Technologies for Interactive Digital Storytelling and Entertainment- TIDSE, Darmstadt, Germany, 24– 26 March 2003

Manuti, A., Pastore, S., Scardigno, A.F., Giancaspro, M.L., Morciano, D.: Formal and informal learning in the workplace: a research review. Int. J. Training Dev. **19**(1), 1–17 (2015)

Martin, S., Diaz, G., Sancristobal, E., Gil, R., Castro, M., Peire, J.: New technology trends in education: seven years of forecasts and convergence. Comput. Educ. **57**(3), 1893–1906 (2011). Elsevier Ltd

McGee, K.: Patterns and computer game design innovation. In: 4th Australasian Conference on Interactive Entertainment, at Storey Hall University, 3–5 December 2007

Morrison, A., Oulasvirta, A., Peltonen, P., Lemmela, S., Jacucci, G., Reitmayr, G., Nasanen, J., Juustila, A.: Like bees around the hive: a comparative study of a mobile augmented reality map. In: Conference on Human Factors in Computing Systems-SIGCHI, pp. 1889–1898. ACM (2009)

Muñoz-cristóbal, J.A., Martínez-monés, A., Asensio-pérez, J.I., Villagrá-sobrino, S.L., Hoyos-torío, J.E.: City ads: embedding virtual worlds and augmented reality in everyday educational practice. J. Univ. Comput. Sci. **20**(12), 1670–1689 (2014)

National Gaming Survey. Detailed data of gaming in the Netherlands. Newzo, TNS-NIPO (2009). www.nationaalgamingonderzoek.nl

Ott, M., Antonaci, A., Dagnino, F.M., Bellotti, F., Berta, R., De Gloria, A., Lavagnino, E., Mayer, I.F., Romero, M., Usart, M.: A gamified collaborative course in entrepreneurship: focus on objectives and tools. Comput. Hum. Behav. **51**, 1276–1283 (2014)

PWC. Global Entertainment and Media Outlook: 2010–2014 (2010). http://www.pwc.com/

Radu, I.: Augmented reality in education: a meta-review and cross-media analysis. Pers. Ubiquit. Comput. **18**(6), 1533–1543 (2014)

Sambrook, S.: Factors influencing the context and process of work-related learning: synthesizing findings from two research projects. Hum. Resour. Dev. Int. **8**, 101–119 (2005)

Schmalstieg, D., Wagner, D.: Experiences with handheld augmented reality. In: 6th IEEE and ACM International Symposium on Mixed and Augmented Reality, ISMAR 2007, pp. 3–18, Nara, Japan, 13–16 November 2007. IEEE (2007)

Schmitz, B.: Mobile games for learning: a pattern-based approach. Doctoral dissertation, Open Universiteit in the Netherlands, Heerlen, The Netherlands. SIKS Dissertation Series No. 2014–45, 12 December 2014

Sharples, M., Taylor, J., Vavoula, G.: Towards a Theory of Mobile Learning. In: 4th World Conference on mLearning, vol. 1, pp. 1–9, Cape Town, South Africa, 25– 28 October 2005

Specht, M., Ternier, S., Greller, W.: Dimensions of mobile augmented reality for learning: a first inventory. J. Res. Cent. Educ. Technol. **7**(1), 117–127 (2011)

Unterfauner, E., Marschalek, I., Fabian, C.M.: Mobile learning with marginal-ized young people. In: IADIS International Conference on Mobile Learning 2010, Porto, pp. 28–36 (2010)

Westera, W., Nadolski, R., Hummel, H., Wopereis, I.: Serious games for higher education: a framework for reducing design complexity. J. Comput. Assist. Learn. **24**(5), 420–432 (2008)

Wetzel, R.: A case for design patterns supporting the development of mobile mixed reality games. In: Foundations of Digital Games (2013). http://www.fdg2013.org/program/workshops/papers/DPG2013/b6-wetzel.pdf

Wu, W.H., Hsiao, H.C., Wu, P.L., Lin, C.H., Huang, S.H.: Investigating the learning theory foundations of game based learning: a meta analysis. J. Comput. Assist. Learn. **28**(3), 265–279 (2012)

The Adoption of Mobile Technologies in a Higher Education Institution: A Mixed Methods Study

Apostolos Giannakopoulos(✉) and Sunet Eybers

School of Computing, University of South Africa, Pretoria, South Africa
gianna@unisa.ac.za, sunet.eybers@yahoo.com

Abstract. This paper is about the implementation of mobile technologies to improve teaching and learning. By mobile technologies is meant any wireless and transferable device which includes laptops, smartphones, tablets, smart devices and PDAs. Research on the use of mobile technology for educational purposes is relatively new. As a result various findings might not be either generalizable or valid as review of literature showed that some findings are contradictory. However, these contradictions in literature areacceptable for any new idea that deals with human phenomena like education. Since mobile technologies are part of the broader ICT their appropriate usage could contribute to the teaching and learning situation be it distance or face to face education (secondary or tertiary).

A study was conducted at the International University of Management in Namibia to discover the impact of mobile technologies in the teaching and learning in the field of Business Information Systems, using one undergraduate and one postgraduate group. Structured interviews were conducted and a questionnaire was completedby both groups. 2 Tests were written by anexperimental and a control group. The results, although not generalizable, were very encouraging as it indicated that there was a significant difference in performance in the tests between the two groups.

Keywords: mLearning · Mobile technologies · Blended learning · Universities

1 Introduction

Low graduation rates in higher education institutions (HEIs) around the world have been observed for decades and The International University of Management in Namibia is no exception. HEIs strive to achieve high pass rates all the time as their subsidy is related to the graduation and throughput rates in all courses. HEIs are supposed to be the first to embrace new technological and scientific trends and incorporate them in their teaching andlearning situation.The advent of the Internet justified further the use of technology in education to decrease costs as well as enhance the teaching and learning situation. The introduction of Mobile Technologies (MT) into the realm of education opened the doors to new possibilities as well challenges as their real value to education has yet to be established.

The fact that the use of mobile technologies in education is a relatively new tool and research is in its infancy stage did not stop researchers to embark on a mission to

T.H. Brown and H.J. van der Merwe (Eds.): mLearn 2015, CCIS 560, pp. 283–299, 2015.
DOI: 10.1007/978-3-319-25684-9_21

test either a number of previous findings or become creative and innovative and introduce wherever possible new ideas. It can be argued that educators have either to adapt new technologies in their teaching or develop apps in existing technologies to augment their teaching.In both instances can only be to the benefit of the teacher and the learner provided that the technologies are used effectively, wisely and appropriately and not use them because everyone else is using it. The study investigated the problem of whether use of mobile technologies in a tertiary institution affects academic performance. The way the study is organized is: firstly the context and rationale is discussed. Here the context is very important since it deals with a developing country, Namibia, and thus successful applications of mobile technologies in a developed country will not necessarily produce the same results if applied in a developing country as the circumstances differ.The context is followed by the literature review where research done on the use of mobile technologies will be critically discussed.

Then, the research design, data collection, data analysis and discussions of findings take place. Finally, conclusions will be drawn and recommendations will be made.

2 Context and Rationale

It is common knowledge among the educators around the world that themassification of education, low graduation rates and decrease in government subsidies to HEIs is becoming an increased problematic situation. The last decade or so the use of mobile technologies for communication purposes as well for socialising has gained ground as such technologies are more and more affordable as their prices decrease (Sharples et al. 2007). In a tag cloud presented by Brown et al. (2010) the power of certain mobile devices are displayed (see Fig. 1).

Fig. 1. Mobile learning tag cloud

The study took place at the International University of Management of Namibia focusing on the teaching of Business Information Systems. The research question to be answered is: What impact if any has the adoption of mobile technology in the teaching and learning of Business Information Systems at the International University of Namibia?

3 Literature Review

Tyler (2002) gives a simplistic as well as a comprehensive definition of a mobile device:

- is any gizmo that uses batteries, fits in your pocket and stores information for later, convenient retrieval. More accurately;
- such as a PDA (personal digital assistant) or smart phone, that can store, access, create, allow to modify, organize, or otherwise manipulate data.

Mobile devices within an educational environment have advantages as well as disadvantages. Among the advantages are: enhancing a student's sense of individuality and community as well as his or her motivation to learn through participation in collaborative learning; they stimulate student's sense of ownership as (s)he participates actively in a variety of social, collaborative and cooperative activities (Tomasovic 2014; Tyler 2002); relatively of low cost (Pillay and Ramdeyal 2012); more readily available than laptops. Among the disadvantages could be: the relatively small screen and limited memory capacity and relatively low speed (Schreurs 2008), hinder real human interaction and can be disruptive (e.g. being destructed when we drive) (Tomasovic 2014) and most of them are dependent on a network's position of their transmitters (within the range or beyond the range) reception (Schreurs 2008).

The relative affordance of mobile devices has made mobile technologies very attractive of their usage for educational purposes as they are more cost efficient in developing countries (Pillay and Ramdayel 2012, p. 6) and close the digital gap (Van Weert 2005). Jimmy (2012) maintains that mobile devices are on the verge of replacing personal computers such as laptops and laptops. The author further states that 68 % of the teens use instant text messaging, 55 % use Wikipedia, 73 % use social working siteswhile Lenhart (2014) found that in 2014 97,5 % of students send messages to their friends.

Van Weert (2005) views mobile technology as an important avenue by which we can reduce the digital gap in a society where access to knowledge and information is increasingly important. The mobile cellular devices have the capacity to link to the Internet and deliver content and instruction that can enable students tolearn at any time and anywhere in a format that is culturally prestigious among people in the same age group (El-Hussein and Cronje 2010, p. 17).

In his article, "Mobile learning around the world", Avgoustos (2013), p. 33 identified the following major barriers to implementing mobile technology in education, namely, socio-economic and technology limitations, lack of human resources (skilled personnel) and hardware limitations. For socio-economic reasons, Avgoustos (2013) sites high start-up costs of mobile initiatives-the communication cost and the cost of mobile devices which are limiting the adoption of mobile learning. Equity issues among students' ability to access modern mobile phones such as smart phones due to low income or due to social-demographic origins, may also be an issue during. Such dilemmas arise not only in the poor areas of central Africa or of Afghanistan, Bhutan and Nepal but are also present in more wealthy regions such as New Zealand and the USA.

For lack of skilled personnel, Avgoustos (2013) states that as mobile learning is in its infancy, specific educational plans or guidance both for teachers and students on how to use their personal devices for educational purposes are rare. Insufficient teacher training and support, or even of high-quality educational content as reported in Canada, the USA, Russia and Asia, in addition to difficulties incorporating existing learning content to mobile initiatives, reinforces teachers' resistance to adopting mobile devices in schools.

With respect to hardware limitations Avgoustos (2013) includes battery life, user interface usability, device memory, hardware and/or ergonomic limitations—such as screen size, small keyboards for typing and security issues, are also listed among the most commonly reported barriers to mobile learning. Though such barriers are the least important as technology rapidly excels and new gadgets and more handy and advanced mobile devices emerge every year proving that mobile devices and smartphones are spreading faster than any technology in human history (Degusta 2012).

There are various ways in which mobile devices can be used by students in their studies. Davies et al. (2012) when they analysed the results from the focus group analysis about different uses of mobile technologies in education, identified the following ways:

1. Timely access to learning key facts in context
2. Consolidation of knowledge through repetition
3. A supplement rather than are placement
4. Making use of wasted time

Integration of mobile technology in teaching and learning needs not completely change the traditional ways of lecturing. Instead, it may incorporate some of the features that are in existence already.

Integration of mobile technology in teaching and learning need not completely change the traditional ways of lecturing. Instead, it may incorporate some of the features that are in existence already. According to Huang et al. (2008), p. 3, the environments in which the study of mobile learning have been conducted have some similar features with the previous studies. These features include:

1. Enhancing availability and accessibility of information networks;
2. Engaging students in learning-related activities in diverse physical locations; etcetera.

To enable the effective use of mobile technology in education, some key factors and requirements, from the literature review above, have to be considered during implementation. These according to Sharples et al. (2007) include:

- Ubiquitous access - This involves complete access to course materials at any time and from any location.
- Students must also be able to create and use various multimedia components such as digital sound, digital photos, and digital video as part of their curriculum.
- Mobile learning should also be personalised allowing the students to play videos, read e-books, listen to audio, and interact with social networking sites in a meaningful educational manner.

4 Research Design

The study was a case study at the International University of Management (IUM) of Namibia, and a mixed methods approach (quantitative and qualitative) was used (Johnson and Onwuegbuzie 2004). This approach is viewed in the light of, that there can be no pure qualitative or quantitative research but predominantly of the one than the other. Two subjects were chosen, the Business Information systems (BIS), a 2nd year of study subject and Digital Communication Technology (DCT) a 4th year of study subject. Both subjects were taught by the same lecturer. The study complied with all academic and research ethics as stipulated by IUM.

The quantitative study comprised of a questionnaire and a quasi-experiment which comprised of an experimental and control group. It was established beforehand that only students who possessed a smart device with the minimum requirement, being the ability to connect to the Internet would participate in the experimental group. The control group would use no devices. Two (formal) tests were given to both groups in order to establish if the use of mobile technology made any difference to academic achievement. Academic achievement was the dependent variable.

As use of mobile devices is relatively new, in order to minimise problems that could occur with the completion of the questionnaires, a pilot study was undertaken initially and the questionnaire was refined. Also the rules of engagement using mobile phones were also determined.

The qualitative study comprised of structured interviews and observations and one to one structured interviews. Various samples were used depending on the nature of data collection techniques. The samples were purposive/convenient samples. The design of the questionnaire was one of predetermined categories. However in order to enrich the questionnaire three open ended questions were asked. The reason was that on the one hand respondents could offer their personal views of how they feel about current mobile technologies in general, and on the other hand students can state how mobile technologies can be used in the day-to-day classroom for their studies more effectively. The third question was mostly informative which dealt with biographical data as well as technical information about the mobile technologies they use for educational purposes.

5 Data Collection

5.1 The Samples

The respondents were level 4 (Honours) and level 2 (undergraduate) students who were undertaking the BIS and Digital Communication Technology Honours degrees. All the respondents were coded from S1 to S50 for anonymity reasons. The values of N differed when different datatools were used. This was because some of the respondents were not available to participate at all times or did not satisfy certain criteria.

Questionnaires	N=48
Interviews	N=43
Experiment	N=50
Observations	N=50

5.2 The Questionnaire

The sample comprised of 48 students (25 DCT and 23 BIS) of which 25 were males and 23 females. The predetermined categories shown in Table 1 comprised of various themes and the total of answers for each are shown. The questionnaire comprised of 23 questions covering the categories shown in Table 1 using a 5 point Likert scale. The design of the questionnaire was based on research done on persistence, motivation, satisfaction and student engagement. Research (Chena et al. 2010; Coates 2005; Strydom et al. 2009) has found that among the many factors that affect student academic success is student engagement whereby if a student is actively and voluntarily involved in his/her studies and does all the necessary tasks (s)he is satisfied and integrates in the university environment will becomes motivated and persists till graduation. The context of the study had to be taken into consideration.

5.3 The Interviews

The structured interviews were aimed at establishing how students feel about their studies (progress made, lecturers), ownership of and competency with mobile devices as well as confirming the results of the questionnaires of the various categories so that the validity of the results could increase. The sample consisted of 43 students (23

Table 1. Results of the questionnaire

Categories (N = 48)	Strongly disagree	Disagree	Undecided	Agree	Strongly Agree
Mobile tech	1	1	2	30	14
Mobile devices	1	2	1	23	21
Networks	1	1	4	37	5
Lecture delivery	2	2	11	26	7
Educational reasons	1	1	1	19	26
Using mobile devices					
• Social	1	1	1	18	27
• Educational	1	3	2	17	25
• Communication	1	1	1	18	27
Internet access	1	3	2	17	25
Mobile ownership	11	16	2	12	7
Mobile fluency	1	2	1	5	39
Mobile disturbance	1	19	3	5	3
Online access	18	7	4	20	16
Online Library	1	2	1	25	19
Campus Library	1	3	2	27	14
Paperless Tech	2	20	2	10	5
Time creation	11	4	5	22	16
Motivation	1	7	9	20	11
Understanding	3	5	13	20	7

females and 20 males) of BIS. There were 9 questions. 38 of the students owned at least one mobile device (a smartphone or a laptop). At the end of the answers the numbers in brackets are frequencies. e.g. "I find the studies to be hard" (20). This means 20 respondents found their studies to be hard.

Q1. How are you finding your studies?

This theme dealt with the perceptions that students had about their studies. What was interesting is that about 50 % (20) found their studies to be 'good to excellent' while about 40 % (17) found their studies to be 'hard' as some respondents put it:

"the studies are hard"

"studies are difficult"

"studies very good"

"studies are interesting"

Q2. Do you feel you are making progress with your studies?

This question too produced mixed results. Results indicated that 71 % (31) students found the studies interesting and are making good progress (31, 71 %) while 23 % (10) found itboring and difficult as they lack of sufficient practice.

"Studies are boring and difficult"

"Studies are good and understandable"

Q3. Briefly tell us how lectures are delivered in lecture halls; both theory and practical classes?

Many students complained that there is not enough time to do practical classes mostly due to the fact that the university has a limited number of computer labs as well as not enough supervisors for the labs. This was also established in the pilot study and it became an extra reason to introduce mobile technologies. With respect to lectures in general, 50 % (22) of the students found the lectures to be "good" or "very well" or "theory is great." With respect to insufficient practicals many 60 % (26) voiced their dissatisfaction.

"There are not enough practical classes. Too much theory".

"Practical classes should be more effective".

"Not enough time allocated for practical classes".

Q4. What do you understand about mobile devices?

The answers to this question varied from "a phone" to "movable devices" to "it allows roaming". Probably students that gave answers like these concentrated only on the mobility aspect. But others concentrated on what the devices can do. Some of the other answers were:

"Mobile devices area technology that is portable, convenient, efficient" (19, 44 %)

"Mobile devices are used for research, communication and entertainment" (18, 42 %).

Q5. If you have a mobile device what do you use it for?

The majority of the respondents (38, 79 %) own at least one mobile device (smartphone), 4 (10 %) did not say whether they own one or not while the rest owned more than one (e.g. smartphone and laptop/tablet). Twenty-six (60 %) of the respondents used the devices for social reasons.

"I use it to chat with friends and family"

"I connect with people from all over the world via Facebook"

Some others use it for academic reasons (18, 42 %) when they state that they use it for "research"or "in their studies" or "do my projects" or "share ideas about various subjects".

Q6. How comfortable are you when using mobile devices (laptops, Tablets, Smartdevices)

The majority of the respondents (38, 88 %) stated that they felt very comfortable and competent when using such devices:

"I am very comfortable because it reduces paperwork and you can put it in your pocket"

"I love technology so I explore my mobile devices everyday"

"I am dangerous on this as if I was born with one, I own 4 smartphones including blackberry bold 9900."

Three of the respondents felt that they were between 60 % and 70 % confident while two respondents stated that they do not feel comfortable as they had bad experiences.

Q7. IUM has a wireless network accessible to all students. What do you use this network for?

A great majority (36, 86 %) of the respondents used it for academic purposes.

"I use it to download books and articles when doing assignments"

"I use it for research"

"I access the internet"

One respondent stated he is using it for entertainment while the rest indicated that the network is too slow and thus it frustrates them and they use their phones.

Q8. Do you think the use of mobile devices in classrooms and outside, can improve your understanding of the course?

37 (86 %) of the respondents think that mobile technology, if used in classrooms, can improve understanding

"..can improve because I can research information"

"yes, but we need more practical classes"

"of course, dealing with them will improve our skills"

The rest of the respondents did not think that mobile technology can have any effect in the teaching and learning.

Q9. How do you think these devices can be used to benefit your studies?
Here the answers varied somewhat between using the devices for research and study purposes (20, 47 %), to downloading of material (11, 26 %) and for storing information (9, 21 %).

"for knowledge acquisition"

"viewing what is happening around the world"

"doing assignments and researching"

"they should be used for researching rather than wasting time face booking"

5.4 The Experiment

The basic aim of the experiment was to investigate whether using mobile devices in a classroom situation had any effect on academic performance. In order to establish the effect preparation preceded the experiment in order to eliminate as many variables (extraneous, intermediate, latent, and intervening) as possible so that the only possible difference between two groups could be the one using mobile devices and the other not using them. Once the two samples (N = 25 each) (the experimental, Group 1, and the control group, Group 2) were established, it was ensured that all those using mobile devices were sufficiently competent in the use of the devices. These devices could be smartphones with the minimum requirements. In order to have the groups as similar as possible with the only disadvantage being the mobile device, open book tests were given, where Group 2 students could bring with any book and notes they wanted to do research.

Group 1 students could make use of data banks available on the IUM portal for their research. They didn't need to physically bring text books from the library since they had access to the IUM network. The students could also access online data banks through the IUM network. IUM network gives students access to certain educational websites where students can get helpful information on their studies. Group 1 students finished their exercises in a shorter time than Group 2 who had to manually search for information in the text books.

Group 1 students could also perform simple tests of their programs since the exercises they were doing had some programming questions. Group 2 students could not because they did not have access to any computers or mobile devices, so they could not test their programmes either.

Because of the availability of mobile devices, Group 1 students could also type their work and present it for marking in a more presentable way. Group 2 had to write their work on paper and hand it in to the lecturer for marking (Tables 2 and 3).

The following results were obtained:

Table 2. Group1 statistics

Descriptive statistics					
Group 1 - with devices	N	Minimum (%)	Maximum (%)	Mean (%)	Std. deviation
mark1	25	58	98	74.48	11.083
mark2	25	54	100	76.08	12.376
Av	25	61	93	75.32	10.007
Valid N (listwise)	25				

Table 3. Group2 statistics

Descriptive statistics					
Group 2 - without devices	N	Minimum	Maximum	Mean	Std. deviation
mark1	25	14	66	32.32	14.138
mark2	25	0	68	41.56	20.378
Av	25	11	63	36.92	14.280
Valid N (listwise)	25				

After the end of test 2 a discussion took place with the students that used mobile devices. A few shortfalls were identified which are in line with the findings of (Avgoustos 2013; Degusta 2012; El-Hussein and Cronje 2010; Schreurs 2008) such as difficulties with typing on a small keyboard and small screen.

Finally the last data collected was from observations on students using their mobile devices.

5.5 Observations

This data was collected while the students were doing the tests as well as after classes during discussions. Some students would use the computer labs, if space was available, others would resort to their mobile devices. Both groups encountered the same problem which was a very slow IUM network as during the day students try to make use of it.

Some of the students, though a handful, had 3G devices from a telecommunications company that they used to gain Internet access. Not everyone who was connected to the network and Internet was conducting academic research. Some students were seen socialising online on web pages such as Facebook whilst others were inquisitive, trying to find important information online. It was observed that students looked relaxed and comfortable using their devices. They seemed to know how to operate their mobile gadgets without any difficulties.

During the experiment, Group 1, which was using mobile technology, showed more interest in their work than Group 2. During the experiment, the students wrote two exercises. Group 1 attempted all the questions in the exercise whilst some of Group 2 students attempted part of the questions.

5.6 Validity and Reliability of Results

According to Saunders et al. (2012) and Creswell (2009), validity refers to the extent to which data collection method or methods accurately measure what they were intended to measure. Saunders et al. (2012), p. 680 states that: "Reliability refers to the extent to which data collection technique(s) will yield consistent findings." In this study the different data collection techniques used the same variables to add to the validity of the study.

To ensure reliability of the interview guide, two experts were identified and asked to rate its reliability. The degree of agreement of the two experts determined the reliability of the interview guide. Phelan and Wren (2006) described reliability as the degree to which an assessment tool produces stable and consistent results. The inter-rate reliability was used to rate uniformity of the interview guide.

For the quantitative part Cronbach's Alpha was calculated. After running reliability tests with SPSS, Cronbach's Alpha showed that the questionnaires used in this study were 74.4 %relevant to the study ($\alpha = 0{,}744$) while for the experiment 69.4 % ($\alpha = 0{,}694$).

6 Analysis of Quantitative Results

Statistical analysis using SPSS was used to process the questionnaire and the experiment data. The data that was collected using questionnaires was analysed using one-way Anova and frequencies. One-way Anova, considers from the analysis, only variables with a coefficient of significance 0.05 or less. The rest were eliminated.

Table 4 indicated that one-way Anova gave a coefficient of significance of .026 that is **F (3.44 = 3.390, p-value .026 < .05)** for variable mobile technology and this means that 97.4 %of the students understand the concept of mobile technology and how it enables us to access data and information from wherever we are. The variable mobile devices has a coefficient of significance of .028 that is **F (3.43 = 3.330, p-value .028 < .05)** meaning that 92.2 % of the students know and understand mobile devices and the analysis proved that the students understand that mobile devices work best with networks since the network variable had a significance of .000 which can be represented statistically as **F (3.43 = 12.424, p-value .000 < .05)** which is equivalent to100 %.

The variable lecture delivery has a statistical coefficient of significant differences of.023, statistically expressed as **F(3.44 = 3.507, p-value .023 < .05)** and mobile ownership. 004, F **(3.44 = 5.142, p-value .004 < .05).** Variables educational purposes, using mobile devices and theoretical lectures have a coefficient of significance of .001 **F (3.43 = 6.579, p-value .001 < .05)**,.013 **F (13.44 = 3.996, p-value .013 < .05)** and .037 **F (3.44 = 3.076, p-value .037 < .05)** respectively. The results aboves how that there are significant differences that can be brought about in education by implementing mobile technology.

Table 4. Statistical results of questionnaires

		Sum of squares	df	Mean square	F	Sig.
Mobile technology	Between Groups	4.115	3	1.372	3.390	.026
	Within Groups	17.802	44	.405		
	Total	21.917	47			
Mobile devices	Between Groups	6.675	3	2.225	3.330	.028
	Within Groups	28.729	43	.668		
	Total	35.404	46			
Networks	Between Groups	9.504	3	3.168	12.424	.000
	Within Groups	10.964	43	.255		
	Total	20.468	46			
Lecturedelivery	Between Groups	7.702	3	2.567	3.507	.023
	Within Groups	32.214	44	.732		
	Total	39.917	47			
Mobile ownership	Between Groups	14.098	3	4.699	5.142	.004
	Within Groups	40.214	44	.914		
	Total	54.313	47			
Educational purposes	Between Groups	23.052	3	7.684	6.579	.001
	Within Groups	50.225	43	1.168		
	Total	73.277	46			
Using mobile devices	Between Groups	11.023	3	3.674	3.996	.013
	Within Groups	40.456	44	.919		
	Total	51.479	47			
Theoretical lectures	Between Groups	6.844	3	2.281	3.076	.037
	Within Groups	32.635	44	.742		
	Total	39.479				

With respect to the experiment, from Table 5, the one-way Anova analysis gave the statistical coefficient of significance differences of .000 that is **F (1.48 = 121.242, p-value .000 < .05)** meaning that there are significant differences in students' performances when mobile technology is used.

Table 5. Statistical results of the experiment

ONE-ANOVA					
Av					
	Sum of squares	Df	Mean square	F	Sig.
Between groups	18432.000	1	18432.000	121.242	.000
Within groups	7297.280	48	152.027		
Total	25729.280	49			

7 Findings and Discussion of Results

This study that was conducted in Namibia, a developing African country, produced some very interesting results as the attempt was made to use mobile technology in the teaching and learning situation in a higher learning institution. Being a relatively new technology it has its advantages as well as disadvantages. The flaming question that any educator should ask before using any form of technology in the teaching and learning situation is: Will such technology add value into my teaching and the students' learning? It can be argued that any new technology is met with either 'eagerness' to use such technology, or apathy perhaps due to insufficient knowledge about such technology or overestimating/under-estimating such technology. Jimmy (2012), p. 191 warns against using technology for the sake of it rather than using it wisely and effectively. Therefore, it is absolutely necessary that the educator and the student are knowledgeable and feel comfortable with the use of such technology and they know what it can or what it cannot do, that is, knowing its limitations. This criterion was met by the majority of respondents (88 % and 81 % of the questionnaire and interviews samples respectively) in the study.

The literature review (Davies et al. 2008; Huang et al. 2008) showed that there are advantages as well as disadvantages associated with the use of mobile technologies. This study used the two important features of mobile technologies identified by Huang et al. (2008) availability and accessibility, engagement of students and Davies et al. (2008) using them for consolidation of knowledge, supplementing teaching and learning, accessing information on time and making use of wasted time.

By having quick access to information, in the palm of one's hand, makes education student-centred as it enables students to customise and adapt access to information in order to meet their own educational goals and needs (El-Hussein and Cronje 2010; Sharples et al. 2007; Van Weert 2005). Student engagement has been identified as one of the most important factors for academic success (Chena et al. 2010; Coates 2005; Strydom et al. 2009) as it was stated earlier. In this study the results from the questionnaire and interviews indicate that if students are given the freedom to use their mobile devices for their education they become more engaged with their studies especially if they feel competent enough to make full use of their devices. The more they use their mobile devices successfully, the more they benefit and thus become more motivated. Especially if the course is designed for collaborative learning (Tomasovic 2014; Tyler 2002) students could get involved with group projects and without realising it they are involved in Communities of Practice, since they share knowledge for a common goal (Lave and Wanger 1991). This is a very important attribute of mobile devices as Huang et al. (2008), p. 3 had identified.

The fact that most students from the convenience sample owned a mobile device, like a smartphone, is an indicator that in a developing country such device is cost effective and affordable which concurs with Pillay and Ramdeyal (2012), p. 6 who state that, "Mobile technology, in developing countries, is seen to be more cost efficient than other technologies which are necessary for eLearning. "These authors and Steinbacher (2011) add that since students do carry these devices then they can be utilised by the university at no extra cost to deliver education. The findings showed that the use of mobile technology does not benefit students alone. It also benefits the teachers/lecturers and thus the institution. These findings are in line with Davies et al. (2012), p. 1 findings who mention that the use of mobile devices in medical practice and education benefits both teachers and students.In actual fact according to El-Hussein and Cronje's (2010) when students come to a higher learning institution with their mobile devices they expect to be encouraged to use them for their education

The majority of the students' (88 % of the questionnaire and 86 % of the interviews) opinions supported the use of mobile technology in education. They believe, if properly used in classrooms and outside, mobile technology can improve their understanding. This is in line with El-Hussein and Cronje's (2010), p. 17 findings when they state that "The mobile cellular devices have the capacity to link to the Internet and deliver content and instruction that can enable learners to learn at anytime and anywhere in a format that is culturally prestigious among people in the same age group." Students believe that with mobile technology, they can better tackle their research work and find more study materials from various online libraries.

A very important aspect that was also highlighted by the respondents suggested that mobile devices should be used for practical classes and this would help eliminate the shortage of sufficient computer labs at all times. This could become a bit problematic and unethical if 100 % of the students do not possess mobile devices and with sufficient memory (Avgoustos 2013) as programs used for programming require huge amounts of memory and space. However (2008) found using PDAs in a study to deliver historic information about a given region and in laboratories for medical simulations memory and space is sufficient. Davies et al. (2012), p. 1 concur when they state that: "Their [mobile devices] used in medical practice and education is in line with the General Medical Council's (GMC) requirements and is generally thought to be of great benefit to both teachers and students."

When asked about their mobile device preferences, most of the students preferred smartphones and tablets. Reasons such as the portability, usability and cost of these devices were cited by the students. This is in line with the findings of Norris et al. (2011) when they state that, over 90 % of the students responded that they would prefer a mobile device small enough for them to carry with them at all times such as a smartphone

After a comparison of results from the experiment and the results obtained by IUM students in the last three years, it was realized that the students who used mobile technology during the experiment obtained better marks. One of the reasons to such good performance is that mobile technology provided various study materials for the students. One can then say that, if implemented in education, mobile technology can provide more study resources to students. The pass rates for the last three years were obtained from the students' records for the subject BIS. In the class of year 2012, 35 (57 %) students passed and 26 (43 %) students failed. In the class of year 2013, 56 (55 %) students passed and 46 (45 %) students failed. In the class of year 2014, 118 (70 %) students passed and 50 (30 %) students failed. The averages for the years 2012, 2013 and 2014 were 38, 39 and 44 percent respectively.

The fact that, the pass rate during the year that mobile devices were used was higher than the previous two years, cannot be concluded categorically that, the use of devices was the sole reason for such improvement. There could be other intervening variables such as change in syllabus and change of the lecturer and perhaps other variables (for example the 2014 cohort was not as homogeneous as the other cohorts). Of course also the limitation of the study that it is a case study, a small sample and the researcher also teaches those classes.

Finally what can be stated about this study as a whole is that in a developing country using mobile devices is cost effective, and such technology is accepted by students and they see value in using them for their studies. Since there could be a few students who cannot afford such devices (in the study was only 2 % that did not possess such devices) the university should supply students with such devices which should be seen as an investment and not as a cost since: (a) The devices can be used by the next cohort; (b) If they do have a positive effect on pass rates then the university will receive more subsidy; (c) If the country has stable and reliable cellular service provider then the students will be paying for such services outside the university.

The way forward is that Action Research will be used in 2015, mobile devices will be used as a predominantly collaborative tools as and problem based education (PBE) will be used while andthe formation of Communities of Practice (CoPs) among the students will be introduced. The value of CoPs has been acknowledged as one of the most important ways for knowledge sharing and innovation where it is the sharing of tacit knowledge that creates a competitive advantage in companies and in education the credo 'knowledge sharing is power' is very applicable (Amin and Roberts 2008; Borzillo et al. 2012; Nonaka and Takeuchi 1995; Retna and Tee 2011)

8 Conclusion

The use of mobile devices in education is gaining momentum in the last decade or so as it is evident in the increase of research on that field. For a developing country it is even more necessary to use these devices in education from cost effectiveness perspective but also for improving knowledge acquisition, knowledge sharing, accessing of information, and improving student engagement as it is more student centred education. Of course it is absolutely necessary that the teachers and the students are competent enough to use such technology. The mode of delivery has to be modified to accommodate such usage. The incorporation of the technology has to be an integral part of the lesson planning and to integrate the social, the educational, and the communication aspects of the mobile technology into one so that students will use it voluntarily because the see value in it. The study showed that adoping mobile technologies in a blended education classroom affects positively academic performance and could minimise the costs of deploying other forms of technologies such as computers. If the CoPs are also incorporated to increase knowledge sharing, then mobile technologies could only contribute to the betterment of education where the institution, the teacher and the student will be winners.

References

Amin, A., Roberts, J.: Knowing in action: beyond communities of practice. Res. Policy **37**(2), 353–369 (2008)

Avgoustos, T.: State of mobile learning around the world. Global mobile leraning and trends. 4–44. China Central Radio and TV University Press (2013)

Borzillo, S., Schmitt, A., Antino, M.: Communities of practice: keeping the company agile. J. Bus. Strat. **33**(6), 22–30 (2012)

Brown, J., Branon, R., Haag, J., Raasch, C.: Mobile Learning Technology: Strategy and Implementation workshop. mLearnCon, San Diego (2010)

Chena, P.D., Lambertd, A.D., Guidryb, K.R.: Engaging online learners: the impact of web-based technologies on college student engagement. Comput. Educ. **54**(4), 1222–1232 (2010)

Coates, H.: The value of student engagement for higher education quality assurance. Qual. High. Educ. **11**(1), 25–36 (2005)

Creswell, J.W.: Research Design: Qualitative, Quantitative and Mixed Methods Approaches, 3rd edn. Sage, Los Angeles (2009)

El-Hussein, M.O.M., Cronje, J.C.: Defining mobile learning in the higher education landscape. Educ. Technol. Soc. **13**(3), 12–21 (2010)

Davies, B.S., Rafique, J., Vincent, T.R., Fairclough, J., Packer, M.H., Vincent, R., Haq, I.: Mobile medical education (MoMEd) - how mobile information resources contribute to learning for undergraduate clinical students - a mixed methods study. BMC Med. Educ. **12**(1), 1–11 (2012). http://www.pubmedcentral.nih.gov/articlerender.fcgi?artid=3317860andtool=pmcentrezandrendertype=abstract. Accessed 23 June 2013

DeGusta, M.: Are smart phones spreading faster than any technology in human history?. In: Massachusetts Institute of Technology Review (2012)

Huang, Y.M., Huang, T.C., Hsieh, M.Y.: Using annotation services in a ubiquitous Jigsaw cooperativelearning environment. Educ. Technol. Soc. **11**(2), 3–15 (2008)

Jimmy, B.: Mobile technology in the classroom. In: Cases on Inquiry Through Instructional Technology in Math and Science, pp.1–676. Hershey, PA:IGIGlobal. (2012). doi:10.4018/978-1-4666-0068-3

Johnson, R.B., Onwuegbuzie, A.J.: Mixed methods research: a research paradigm whose time has come. Educ. Res. **33**(7), 14–26 (2004)

Lave, J., Wenger, E.: Situated Learning: Legitimate Peripheral Participation. Cambridge University Press, Cambridge (1991)

Lenhart, A.: Teens, social media and technology overview (2015). http://www.pewinternet.org/2015/04/09/teens-social-media-technology-2015/. Accessed 8 April 2015

Nonaka Iand Takeuchi, H.: The knowledge-Creating Company. Oxford University Press, New York (1995)

Norris, C., Hossain, A., Soloway, E.: Using smartphones as essential tools for learning. Educ. Technol. **51**(3), 18–25 (2011)

Phelan, C., Wren, J.: Exploring reliability in academic assessment. UNI Office of Academic Assessment (2005)

Pillay, F.R., Ramdeyal, P.K.: Student access to and use of ICTs and the implications for academic staff: views from a developing university of technology in SouthAfrica. In: 14th Annual Conference on World Wide Web Applications, Durban (2012)

Retna, K.S., Tee, N.P.: Communities of practice: dynamics and success factors. Leadersh. Organ. Dev. J. **32**(1), 41–59 (2011)

Saunders, M., Lewis, P., Thornhill, A.: Research Methods for Business Students, 5th edn. Financial Times/Prentice Hall, London (2012)

Schreurs, J.: Mobilee-learning course scenario model on PDA. Int. J. Mob. Learn. Organ **2**(4), 358 (2008). http://www.inderscience.com/link.php?id=20688. Accessed 15 April 2015

Sharples, M., Milrad, M., Arnedillo, S.I., Vavoula, G.: Mobile learning: small devices, big issues. In: Balacheff, N., Ludvigsen, T., de Jong, T., Lazonder, A., Barnes, S. (eds.) Technology Enhanced Learning: Principles and Products. Springer, Berlin (2007)

Steinbacher, M.: On campus going mobile Universities moving to keep up with technology. Bloomington Ill, United States (2011)

Strydom, J.E, Mentz, M., Kuh, G.D.: Enhancing success in higher education by measuring student engagement in South Africa (2009). http://sasse.ufs.ac.za/dl/userfiles/documents/SASSEinpresspaper_1.pdf. Accessed 15 October 2014

Tomasovic, N.: Advatanages and disadvatages of mobile phones: the smart phone generation (2014). https://blog.udemy.com/advantages-and-disadvantages-of-mobile-phones/. Accessed 10 April 2015

Tyler, T.: Mobile tech - defining mobile technology for legal professionals (2002). http://www.llrx.com/columns/mobiletech.htm. Accessed 20 November 2014

Van Weert, T.: Life long learning in knowledge society: implications for education. Educ. Knowl. Soc. **161**, 15–25 (2005)

The Utilisation of Mobile Technologies in Higher Education: Lifebuoy or Constriction?

Sunet Eybers and Apostolos Giannakopoulos(✉)

School of Computing, University of South Africa, Pretoria, South Africa
sunet.eybers@Yahoo.com, gianna@unisa.ac.za

Abstract. The utilization of mobile technologies for the purpose of mLearning has immense potential in education whether face to face, blended or distance. With the current high ownership rate of these devices around the world it is quite surprising that mobile devices are not utilized extensively.

This study is part of a larger study that investigated the utilization of mobile devices in a blended environment from the students' perspective. It uses the behavioral dimension as described in the 'Uses and Gratification Theory' (Balakrishnan and Raj 2012) to investigate behavioral issues in the adoption of mLearning approaches at the International University of Management in Namibia, a developing country. The main target population was students enrolled in Business Information Systems. The rich data collected contain a multi-dimensional aspect and in this paper the reasons that students use mobile devices and the reward they receive upon usage is analysed. It was hoped that by identifying such reasons for use of the devices and barriers that might exist in not using them can be used as a starting point to increase the use of mLearning using mobile devices within this environment. The main objective is to ensure that mLearning becomes a lifebuoy and not a constriction.

Keywords: Mlearning · Mobile devices · Adoption · Gratification Theory (UGT)

1 Introduction

Namibia, a developing African country, was a South African controlled country known as South West Africa till its independence in 1990. There is no reliable data as to the number of people who own mobile devices as a result it is assumed that similar trends are followed as those in South Africa. However a recent study by Research ICT Africa (RAI, 2012), indicated that although the usage of mobile device using Internet in the African continent is lower than the European, USA and Asia counterparts is on the increase. The study found that in South Africa, Nigeria, Kenya, Tanzania and Rwanda 70 % of the mobile users access Internet through their mobile devices. For South Africa, the latest research and statistics has shown that more than 75 % of South Africans with the age of 15 years and older, owns a mobile phone (Peyper 2013). The e-business handbook (2006) in 2006 found that about 35 million South African owned a mobile phone, compared to about 15 millions in 2003. That is a staggering 115 %

T.H. Brown and H.J. van der Merwe (Eds.): mLearn 2015, CCIS 560, pp. 300–314, 2015.
DOI: 10.1007/978-3-319-25684-9_22

increase which includes any variation of mobile phone (smart phone or no smart phone), without even considering other mobile devices.

It is reported in Europe that about 57 % (Spain has the highest 66 %) possess tablets or smartphones (Mobile Life Report, 2013). What makes this statistics remarkable is the fact that the main user group fall within the low-income groups. The implication is that the South African youth, irrespective of the income level, are connected. In other words, they have the ability to either connect on social level (chat mechanism, sharing photo's), for information purposes (to stay informed through browsing the Internet) or as communication mechanism (making calls). If the statistics by Jimmy (2012) (though not for South Africa) are added they support the idea that many young people use their cell phones. Jimmy (2012) found that 68 % of the teens use instant text messaging, 55 % use Wikipedia, 73 % use social working sites while Lenhart (2014) found that in 2014 97,5 % of students send messages to their friends. Furthermore, the ownership of mobile phones is influenced by the need for safety and privacy issues. Unfortunately research is vague when it comes to the utilization of these devices for educational purposes.

However, before mobile devices are used for educational purposes, it is necessary to establish why people buy such devices and how do such devices contribute to the gratification of a need, which could be similar to Maslow's (1970) basic need manifesting itself in a different form. This study is part of a larger study that investigated the utilization of mobile devices in a blended environment from the students' perspective. It uses the behavioral dimension as described in the 'Uses and Gratification Theory' (Balakrishnan and Raj 2012) to investigate behavioral issues in the adoption of mLearning approaches at the International University of Management in Namibia.

2 Context and Rationale

In a developing country such as Namibia, where access to education (in particular tertiary education) is often limited, the utilization of mobile technologies for learning purposes might be the lifebuoy to a better future for the youth and even those who want to further their studies. In fact, a developing country should be more eager to embrace new technologies, though the cost could be a factor, in order to overcome certain challenges in education. For example, not enough computers, computers not being available 24\7 and so on. One could lose out on great education opportunities at their doorstep. However, it should be interesting to investigate to what extent students at the International University of Management (IUM) in Namibia are currently utilizing mobile technologies for learning purposes and then experiment with incorporating such technologies in their day to day classes.

Will the utilization of mobile technologies be to the advantage or disadvantage of students? Will student participation rates increase as a result of such deployments? The assumption is that if it is possible to either allow or incorporate mobile devices in the teaching and learning situation it can increase student engagement, a factor that has been recognized by many authors (Chena, Lambertd and Guidryb 2010; Coates 2005; Strydom, Mentz and Kuh 2010) as a contributor to academic success. However, since we deal with education, the usage of such mobile devices must be used as a form of pedagogic interventions considering the social, psychological and cognitive aspects of the students. Since this is a case study in a developing African country it will be futile to make use of existing data and research done elsewhere especially in Europe or USA or even Asia and use mobile devices in a tertiary institution. An exploratory study is warranted. Therefore the purpose of this study becomes one of exploratory nature and subsequent limited implementation in the classroom.

3 Literature Review

Mobile devices have become part of our daily lives (Peyper 2013; Walsh and White 2006) and irrespective what one uses them for, (s)he uses them voluntarily and efficiently as far as they are concerned. Trying to use them for educational purposes and become part of the daily curriculum which adds a new dimension whose value has still to be determined beyond any reasonable doubt. Before such use in education can take place it is necessary to answer the simple question: Why people use such devices? To answer this question the multi-dimensionality of the mobile devices will dictate the answer, or part of the answer. For example if one is in an isolated place where there are no land lines such device might be useful, assuming there is reception in that area. Here the one dimension, communication (utility), is the dominant reason. A business man who has shares and can buy and sell shares will benefit by having access to stock exchange 24\7 as shares tend to fluctuate in a volatile market like presently. Here another dimension, 'anywhere anytime' access of information (utility), is the dominant reason.

In the past the individual was perceived as a helpless victim of mass communication by large companies (mass society theory), or a person with intelligence and self-esteem which drive an individual to media choice (individual differences) (West and Turner 2007). However, recent research has shown that the individual when (s)he uses media there is intent and reason why they use it and not because they have been brainwashed to use them. This new perspective gives rise to the Uses and Gratification Theory (UGT) (Balakrishnan and Ray 2012; West and Turner, 2007). This study is informed by UGT since the aim is to determine, why students use mobile devices and how do they benefit from such a use. A similar study that used the UGT was that of Chigona, Kamkwenda and Manjoo (2008) in South Africa and another on Malaysian youth by Balakrishnan and Ray (2012) form the foundation of this study. The former concentrated though on the mobile Internet usage only and the effects such a usage had on students. The latter concentrated "on the mobile use pattern, purchasing factors, motivations to use and behavioural issues related to mobile phone usage among urbanized youth between the ages of 17 and 27 years old" (Balakrishnan and Ray 2012). If used in education, the fact that the teacher intervenes and can dictate the rules of engagement and how mobile devices should be used for their education could create conflict as there could be a discrepancy between what the owner of the device thinks is useful for so (s)he can benefit and what the teacher thinks.

'Uses and Gratification Theory' (UGT) UGT "focuses on why consumers turn to technology to satisfy their social and psychological needs" (North, Johnston and Ophoff 2014:116). On a basic level the theory identifies a need (or a cause) seeking to obtain some sort of gratification. To obtain this gratification or satisfaction, a particular means or item is used to move towards the required satisfaction. External influences include the context in which the item is used (including environment and time for example) as well as attributes of the item used (interactivity, level of involvement required, etc) (Chigona et al. 2008). In general the main objective of the UGT focuses on understanding the motive and consequences of a particular technology (Leung and Wei 2000). For Leung and Wei (2000) UGT implies that consumers are actively (not passively as though brainwashed) involved in their decision to use and how to use technology to fulfill a need which is preceded by a motive to buy a technological item such as cell phone. In the instance of mLearning, if one can understand the behavioural aspects of why students are actively adopting an mLearning approach, one can identify the barriers to the utilization of mobile devices. Although this theory was introduced to investigate the social and psychological needs in the context of mass media the relevance to emerging technologies seemed applicable (Chigona et al. 2008).

As far as Leung (2007) is concerned application of UGT led to the general conclusion that "the gratifications sought motivate the use of a particular medium in an audience." Balakrishnan and Ray (2012) site a number of studies which examined the utilitarian dimension of UGT to examine consumer's motives for using Internet (Stafford, et al. 2004), social networking sites (Urista, et al. 2009) and mobile phones (Leung and Wei 2000; Leung 2007). A great number of factors have been identified by a number of researchers. What is of interest here is media had identified youth (perhaps ages between 15 and 25 years old) to be more prone to usage gratifications of mobile phones and it is confirmed by Auter (2007) and Sanders (2008) who found that most of the research on mobile phone is on youth and especially college students.

A great number of factors that lead to mobile device purchase and usage have been identified by a number of authors. For example, sociability, instrumentality, reassurance, entertainment, acquisition as well as time management (Leung, 2007) and Grellhesl and Punyanunt-Carter (2012) add status seeking and relaxation; Social inclusion and connectedness (Srivastava 2005); Reinforcing relationships between friends and family (Geser 2005); Improvement in status (Green 2002). These are just a few of a great number of other factors. However it must be borne in mind that there could be negative if not detrimental consequences on the users and the environment. Disruption of classes (Selwyn 2003) or disturbing the peace in a public place like a bus or a train (Ling 1997), use of mobile phone while driving (Pennay 2006), causing emotional distress, damaged relationships and falling literacy (James and Drennan 2005) while Walsh and White 2006 introduced the behavioural salience where user tend to check their phones continuously even if they are not on silence mode.

It is assumed that this exploratory study will create a foundation for future use of mobile technologies in education in order to alleviate the shortage of computers and supervisors of computer labs in IUM. It is believed that usage of mobile technology could satisfy social, psychological as well as cognitive aspects of a student if properly and effectively used. This implies that a good foundation has to be led and sufficient training of the teachers will have to take place before such incorporation into the teaching learning situation takes place.

4 Research Methodology

The study was part of a larger case study at the International University of Management (IUM) of Namibia. In order to determine the perceptions of the students as to why they use mobile devices and how it benefits them and feel satisfied (gratified), a questionnaire with pre-determined themes was designed and interviews were conducted on the same themes. Use of mixed methods approach (quantitative and qualitative) (Johnsonn and Onwuegbuzie Johnson and Onwuegbuzie 2004) was appropriate. The researchers view this approach in the light of that there can be no pure qualitative or quantitative, but predominantly of the one than the other. Two subjects were chosen, the Business Information systems (BIS), a 2nd year of study subject and Digital Communication Technology (DCT) a 4th year of study subject. Both subjects were taught by the same lecturer. The study complied with all academic and research ethics as stipulated by IUM. It was hoped that once the results were analysed they could be used to develop a mobile technology based education.

The samples were purposive/convenient samples. The design of the questionnaire was one of predetermined categories which were derived from previous research. However in order to enrich the questionnaire three open ended questions were asked. The reason was that on the one hand respondents could offer their personal views of how they feel about current mobile technologies in general, and on the other hand how they are used in the day today student life.

4.1 Data Collection

The respondents were level 4 and level 2 students who were undertaking the BIS and Digital Communication Technology honours degrees. All the respondents were coded from S1 to S50 for anonymity reasons. The values of N differed when different data tools were used. This was because some of the respondents were not available to participate at all times.

Questionnaires N = 48

Interviews N = 43

4.1.1 The Questionnaire

The sample comprised of 48 students (25 DCT and 23 BIS) of which 25 were males and 23 females. In Table 1 the first column contains the various categories and the 5 point Likert scale is used. The design of the questionnaire was based on research done on uses of mobile devices, competency in the usage of such devices, reasons for the usage, benefits derived from such usage.

What is of importance looking at Table 1 is that the majority of respondents as a rule agree or strongly agree with all the items except in the ownership but the question was phrased in a negative sense. For example: You do not need a mobile device for day to day functioning in life. With respect to 'time creation' about 25 % of the respondents did not think that a usin a mobile device could save one time to be used elsewhere more productively. Another important aspect that an informative question was whether they own a smartphone or a Tablet and 45 of the respondents owned at least a smartphone

Table 1. Results of the questionnaire

Categories (N=48)	Strongly disagree	Disagree	Undecided	Agree	Strongly Agree
Understanding of mobile technology	1	1	2	30	14
Examples of mobile devices	1	2	1	23	21
Mobile devices access to Inter/intra/extra-nets	1	1	1	19	26
Using mobile devices for:					
· Social	1	1	1	18	27
· Educational	1	3	2	17	25
· Communication	1	1	1	18	27
Mobile ownership	11	16	2	12	7
Mobile fluency/ competency	1	2	1	5	39
Time creation	11	4	5	22	16
Motivation	1	7	9	20	11
Understanding	3	5	13	20	7

while 9 possessed more than one mobile device (predominantly a Tablet) and only one respondent possessed an ordinary cell phone with the minimum functions (making a call, receiving a call, SMS).

4.1.2 The Interviews

The structured interviews were aimed at correlating the results from the questionnaires in order to ensure a better validity as the results would be used in the future to re-design the courses by incorporating mobile devices. The sample consisted of 43 students (23 females and 20 males) of BIS. There were 8 questions. 38 of the students owned at least one mobile device (a smartphone or a laptop). At the end of the answers the numbers in brackets are frequencies. e.g. "If I forget my cell at home I cannot function" (20). This means 20 respondents gave the same answer.

Q1. What do you understand about mobile devices?

The answers to this question varied from "a phone" to "movable devices" to "it allows roaming". Probably students that gave answers like these concentrated only on the mobility aspect. But others concentrated on what the devices can do. Some of the other answers were:

"Mobile devices is technology that is portable, convenient, efficient" (19, 44 %)
"Mobile devices are used for research, communication and entertainment" (18, 42 %).

Q2. If you have a mobile device what do you use it for?
The majority of the respondents (33, 77 %) own at least one mobile device (smartphone), 4 (9 %) did not say whether they own one or not while the rest owned more than one (e.g. smartphone and laptop/tablet). 26 (60 %) of the respondents used the devices for social reasons.

"I use it to chat with friends and family"
"I connect with people from all over the world via Facebook"

Some others use it for academic reasons (18, 42 %) when they state that they use it for "research", "in their studies", "do my projects", "share ideas about various subjects".

Q3. How comfortable are you when using mobile devices (laptops, Tablets, Smartdevices)
The majority of the respondents (38, 88 %) stated that they felt very comfortable and competent when using such devices:

"I am very comfortable because it reduces paperwork and you can put it in your pocket"
"I love technology so I explore my mobile devices everyday"
"I am dangerous on this as if I was born with one, I own 4 smartphones including blackberry bold 9900".

3 Of the respondents felt that they were between 60 % and 70 % confident while 2 stated that they do not feel comfortable as they had bad experiences.

Q4. Do you think the use of mobile devices in classrooms and outside, can improve your understanding of the course?
37 (86 %) of the respondents think that mobile technology, if used in classrooms, can improve understanding

"..can improve because I can research information"
"yes, but we need more practical classes"
"of course, dealing with them will improve our skills"
"more than you think" but "with class rules"

The rest of the respondents did not think that mobile technology can have any effect in the teaching and learning.

Q5. How do you think these devices can be used to benefit your studies?
Here the answers varied somewhat between using the devices for research and study purposes (20, 47 %), to downloading of material (11, 26 %) and for storing information (9, 21 %).

"for knowledge acquisition"
"viewing what is happening around the world"
"doing assignments and researching"
"they should be used for researching rather than wasting time face booking"
"they should be used for researching rather than wasting time face booking"

The three open ended questions were:

Q1. Why did you purchase a cell phone?
The content analysis of the responses revealed that the main reasons were firstly for communication (40, 93 %) (utilitarian reasons, socialisation, immediate access, safety).

"I can talk to my friends and family at any time and keep up with current issues"
"It is an extension of me. If I do not have it with me I feel I fall behind with news and events."
"I need the phone especially in case of emergency and I feel safe with one."
"Where I stay there are no land lines so I had to purchase a phone to connect with people."

The next reason was content accessibility. Here a great number of users felt that since the IUM does not have sufficient computers and they could not afford one or a laptop or a Tablet, since they were technology competent (40, 93 %) they sought a smartphone as a means to satisfy the need for quick access to information.

"With my smartphone I can download articles, get access to Internet and IUM's student portal."
"I can do research and even test my programmes"
"Sometimes my friend can record important parts of a lecture as I have to work some days."

The final predominant reason was entertainment. But the frequency used for this reason was low. On the average 23 (53 %) of the respondents would listen to music when they were bored., 'fill time'.

"When I wait for the bus, I kill time by listening to the music."
"Sometimes I put the ear phones even in a lecture, if it is boring, and listen to music"

There were other responses too but the frequency was so low that such responses were not significant for the study.

Q2. What made you choose what type of phone you will buy?
A great majority (41, 91 %) stated that the cost dictated what they can buy and not what they would like to buy. It was established from the biographical data that 68 % (29) of the respondents belonged in the average to low income group.

"My parents are poor and I could only afford a simple cell phone, but I would like to have bought a smartphone."

"I am working part time and I had to buy a smartphone so it could also help me with my studies."

"Although my parents could not afford for me to buy a smartphone they made a plan as they understood that it will assist me with my studies."

"I had to buy a smartphone as it is the end thing nowadays."

"I got a smartphone for my 21st birthday as a gift."

Q3. What problems do you think the use of cell phones can create?

There was a great variety of responses to this question. The predominant answer had to do with using the phone while driving (26, 60 %), while others had to do with phones ringing in the class (15, 35 %), or ringing in a public place such as a bus or a train. A small percentage (8,19 %) mentioned the negative effect it had in their relationship with a girl or a boy where the partner will check their messages.

"It is very irritating when the phone rings in the classroom."

"Sometimes my brother has the phone on in the night while I am sleeping and it wakes me up."

"I travel by train for almost an hour and I study in the train. Suddenly you hear a number of phones ringing."

5 Validity and Reliability of Results

According to Saunders, Lewis and Thornhill (2012) and Creswell (2009), validity refers to the extent to which data collection method or methods accurately measure what they were intended to measure. Saunders et al. (2012:680) states that: "Reliability refers to the extent to which data collection technique(s) will yield consistent findings." In this study the different data collection techniques used on the same variables add to the validity of the study.

Reliability of the interview guide could be attained by using two experts and asking them to rate its reliability. The degree of agreement between the two experts determined the reliability of the interview guide. Phelan and Wren (2006) described reliability as the degree to which an assessment tool produces stable and consistent results. The inter-rater reliability was used to rate uniformity of the interview guide.

For the quantitative part Cronbach's Alpha was calculated. After running reliability tests with SPSS, Cronbach's Alpha showed that the questionnaires used in this study were 74.4 % relevant to the study ($\alpha = 0{,}744$).

6 Analysis of Quantitative Results

The questionnaire's results were processed using the software SPSS. The categories were grouped into uses, benefits, understanding, and motivation.

Table 2. Statistical results of questionnaires

		Sum of Squares	df	Mean Square	F	Sig.
Understanding of mobile technology	Between Groups	4.115	3	1.372	3.390	.026
	Within Groups	17.802	44	.405		
	Total	21.917	47			
Examples of mobile devices	Between Groups	6.675	3	2.225	3.330	.028
	Within Groups	28.729	43	.668		
	Total	35.404	46			
Mobile ownership	Between Groups	14.098	3	4.699	5.142	.004
	Within Groups	40.214	44	.914		
	Total	54.313	47			
Mobile devices access to Inter/intra/extra-nets	Between Groups	23.052	3	7.684	6.579	.001
	Within Groups	50.225	43	1.168		
	Total	73.277	46			
Using mobile devices	Between Groups	11.023	3	3.674	3.996	.013
	Within Groups	40.456	44	.919		
	Total	51.479	47			
Mobile device competency	Between Groups	9.504	3	3.168	12.424	.000
	Within Groups	10.964	43	.255		
	Total	20.468	46			
Understanding	Between Groups	7.702	3	2.567	3.507	.023
	Within Groups	32.214	44	.732		
	Total	39.917	47			
Motivation	Between Groups	6.844	3	2.281	3.076	.037
	Within Groups	32.635	44	.742		
	Total	39.479				

The data that was collected using questionnaires was analysed using one-way anova and frequencies. One-way Anova, considers from the analysis, only variables with a coefficient of significance 0.05 or less. The rest were eliminated.

Looking at Table 2 we can see using one-way Anova gave us a coefficient of significance of.026 that is **F (3.44=3.390, p-value .026 <.05)** for variable mobile technology and this means that 97.4 % of the students understand the concept of mobile technology and how it enables us to access data and information from wherever we are. The variable mobile devices has a coefficient of significance of .028 that is **F (3.43=3.330, p-value .028 <.05)** meaning that 92.2 % of the students know and understand mobile devices and the analysis proved that the students understand that mobile devices work best with networks.

For mobile ownership the coefficient of significance was 0.004, F **(3.44=5.142, p-value .004 <.05).** Variables educational purposes, using mobile devices and theoretical lectures have a coefficient of significance of .001 **F (3.43=6.579, p-value .001 <.05),** .013 **F (13.44=3.996, p-value .013 <.05)** and .037 **F (3.44=3.076, p-value .037 <.05)** respectively. The results above show that there are significant differences that can be brought about in education by implementing mobile technology.

7 Findings and Conclusions

This study focused on the use of mobile devices and the motives behind purchasing such devices by students in the BIS and DCT subjects. It comprised of 48 students for the questionnaire and 43 students in the structured interviews with average age of 23 years.

Since Namibia is a developing country it was assumed that the patterns followed could be similar to those of other developing countries. The results derived were very close to other similar studies which were informed by UGT (Balakrishnan and Ray 2012; Chigona et al. 2008; Leung and Wei, 2000). The advantages and disadvantages were highlighted by the students' responses to the questions posed to them. There was a relative consensus among the respondents that cost played a central role in the purchasing of a mobile device. However, intent in view of satisfying a certain need occupied the central point as the decision to purchase such device was an informed and pragmatic decision. Possessing such a device then became more of a lifebuoy rather than a restrictor.

From the questionnaire (25 females and 23 males) gender did not play a role when it came to different usages of the mobile device since as a rule there was no distinct difference in the replies. With respect to use of mobile technology the fact that 97.4 % of the respondents understand the uses of such technology implies that when they purchased their devices they knew exactly what to use them for. Utility dominated the motive which subsequently leads to satisfying a certain need be it of social, cognitive or psychological nature. These findings concur with the findings by (Leung 2007; Leung and Wei 2000; North et al. 2014).

Furthermore since 92.2 % of the respondents know and understand mobile devices and especially that such devices give them access to networks added value to the motive of having to possess such device. Familiarity with a mobile device is a contributory factor if the full potential of the device is to be achieved. It happens that at times devices are purchased as a symbol of status (Leung and Wei 2000; Walsh and White 2006) with little knowledge of what the device can do. That is why it is necessary if such devices are going to be used for educational purposes the teacher must ensure that all users of such devices are sufficiently competent with the use of the device and not assume they are.

For mobile ownership almost 100 % (99.6 %) of the respondents possess one or another type of a mobile while some possessed more than one. This concurs with previous findings in other developing countries like Malaysia (Balakrishnan and Raj 2012) and South Africa (Chigona et al. 2008). Awareness of the usage of such devices for educational purposes was also almost 100 % (99.9 %) which is relatively higher than those reported around the world (Jimmy 2012; Lenhart 2012; Walsh and White 2006). This is quite encouraging and the teachers should take an advantage of that as they can use mobile devices to supplement lectures.

Using mobile devices as a means of intrinsic motivation and understanding better the content, the levels of significance were below 90 % (81 % and 76 % respectively) which were below the acceptable level of >95 %. However they cannot be totally excluded. On the contrary more comprehensive tests should be conducted on these two constructs as they can play a very important role if mobile devices are incorporated in the day to day lectures.

The interviews also produced valuable data as they correlated highly with the questionnaire findings. For a developing country, its youth does not appear to be very different to either developed or developing countries as ownership of a mobile device which should be considered as a luxury (Leung and Wei 2000) on the contrary it appears to be a basic necessity. Perhaps due to the fact that the youth is aware that we are living in a knowledge society and if they do not move with the rest of the world they will fall behind. Their desire to possess a smartphone is almost of the same intensity as other youth around the world as it is indicated by research (Balakrishnan and Raj 2012; Leung and Wei 2000; North et al. 2014).

Most of the respondents agreed that mobile devices are useful for socialising, keeping up to date with events in the family and friend's circles as well as being informed about world important events. The safety factor (Aoki and Downes 2003; James and Drennan 2005; Selwyn 2003), the use of the mobile device as necessary due to lack of land lines, entertainment (Katz, Blumler and Gurevitch 2011; Leung and Wei 2000), filling time and avoiding isolation (Rubin, Perse and Barbato 1988), and networking (Leung and Wei 2000) were also factors that satisfied certain needs. The fact that almost all respondents agreed that the possession of a mobile device was due the existing needs which needed to be gratified is in line with the UGT (West and Turner 2007; Katz et al. 2011; Balakrishnan and Raj 2012).

Therefore based on the findings, it can be stated (bearing in mind a number of limitations) that students at IUM in the subjects of BIS and DCT exhibit approximately the same desires, needs and how to satisfy such needs mobile devices dependent.

8 Limitations of the Study

Like all case studies' findings cannot be generalized but used as indicators for further research as this study was also an exploratory study and not a confirmatory one. The small sample and being not a random but a convenience sample adds to the limitation. Lack of sufficient data about number of mobile devices owned in Namibia and data from cell phone providers provides an extra limitation as comparisons cannot be made with other countries. However such limitations should not discourage further research at IUM on the contrary increase the need for such research as it can contribute to overcoming technological problems such as insufficient computers and insufficient time necessary to do research due to lack of personnel.

9 Conclusion

The use of questionnaires and interviews to establish reasons for possessing mobile devices, knowledge about such devices, and behavioural issues produced some very encouraging results. Since most of the findings are in line with many other findings around the world then through Action Research it could become possible to prepare the ground for a full inclusion of mobile devices in the teaching and learning situation. It can be accepted that having an informed user of such devices it can become an extra motivating factor for such incorporation in education. Especially in Namibia, a developing country, such incorporation could minimize the costs of IUM whereby if the majority of the students possess such devices then it will be cost effective to supply such devices to those that do not possess one. Such devices could be used by the next cohort.

References

Aoki, K., Downes, E.J.: An analysis of young people's use of and attitudes toward cell phones. Telematics Inform. **20**(4), 349–364 (2003)

Auter, P.J.: Portable social groups: Willingness to communicate, interpersonal communication gratifications, and cell phone use among young adults. Int. J. Mob. Commun. **5**(2), 139–155 (2007)

Balakrishnan, V., Raj, R.G.: Exploring the relationship between urbanized Malaysian youth and their mobile phones: A quantitative approach. Telematics Inf. **29**(3), 263–272 (2012)

Chena, P.D., Lambertd, A.D., Guidryb, K.R.: Engaging online learners: the impact of web-based technologies on college student engagement. Comput. Educ. **54**(4), 1222–1232 (2010)

Chigona, W., Kamkwenda, G., Manjoo, S.: Uses and gratifications of mobile Internet among South African students. S. Afr. J. Inf. Manage. **10**(3), 57–73 (2008)

Coates, H.: The value of student engagement for higher education quality assurance. Qual. High. Educ. **11**(1), 25 (2005)

Creswell, J.W.: Research design: qualitative, quantitative and mixed methods approaches, 3rd edn. Sage, Los Angeles (2009) e-Business Handbook. The E-business Handbook: the review of innovation at work in South African Business. Cape Town, South Africa, Trialogue (2006)

Geser, H.: Towards a sociological theory of the mobile phone. In: Zerdick, A., Picot, A., Scrape, K., Bugleman, J.C., Silverstone, R., Feldman, V., Wernick, C., Wolff, C. (eds.) E-Merging Media: Communication and the Media Economy of the Future, pp. 235–260. Springer Verlag, Berlag (2005)

Green, N.: Who's watching whom? Monitoring and accountability in mobile relations. In: Brown, B., Green, N., Harper, R. (eds.) Wireless Worlds: Social and Interactional Aspects of the Mobile Age. Springer, Heidelberg (2002)

Grellhesl, M., Punyanunt-Carter, N.M.: Using the uses and gratifications theory to understand gratifications sought through text messaging practices of male and female undergraduate students. Comput. Hum. Behav. **28**(6), 2175–2181 (2012)

James, D., Drennan, J.: Exploring addictive consumption of mobile phone technology. In: Australian and New Zealand Marketing Academy Conference (2005)

Jimmy, B.: Mobile technology in the classroom. Cases on inquiry through instructional Technology in Math and Science. IGI Global, Hershey (2012)

Johnson, R.B., Onwuegbuzie, A.J.: Mixed methods research: A research paradigm whose time has come. Educ. Researcher **33**(7), 14–26 (2004)

Katz, E., Blumler, J.G., Gurevitch, M.: Uses and Gratifications Research. The Public Opinion Quarterly 4th ser, 37 (1973–1974), 509–23 (2011)

Lenhart, A.: Teens, social media and technology overview. (2015) http://www.pewinternet.org/2015/04/09/teens-social-media-technology-2015/. 8 April 2015

Leung, L.: Unwillingness-to-communicate and college students' motives in SMS mobile messaging. Telematics Inf. **24**(2), 115–129 (2007)

Leung, L., Wei, R.: More than just talk on the move: uses and gratifications of the cellular phone. J. Mass Coummun. Q. **77**(2), 308–320 (2000)

Ling, R.: One can talk about common manners! The use of mobile telephones in inappropriate situations. In: Haddon, L. (ed.), Themes in Mobile Telephony Final Report of The COST 248 Home and Work Group (1997)

Manslow, A.H.: Manslow's Hierarchy Needs (1970). www.simplypsychology.org/Manslow.html. 20 March 2015

Mobile Life Report. Informe mobile life. Madrid, Spain: Ministry of Industry (2013)

Nonaka, I., Takeuchi, H.: The knowledge-creating company. Oxford University Press, New York (1995)

North, D., Johnston, K., Ophoff, J.: The use of mobile phones by South African university students. Issues Inf. Sci. Inform. Technol. **11**, 115–138 (2014)

Pennay, D.: Community Attitudes to Road Safety: Community Attitudes Survey Wave 18. Australian Transport Safety Bureau, Canberra (2006)

Peyper, L.: Mobile phone usage in SA (2013). http://finweek.com/2013/01/22/mobile-phone-usage-in-sa/. 10 April 2015

Phelan, C., Wren, J.: Exploring reliability in academic assessment. UNI Office of Academic Assessment (2005)

Research ICT Africa (RAI). Internet Going Mobile: Internet access and usage in 11 African countries (2012). http://www.researchictafrica.net/publications/Country_Specific_Policy_Briefs/Internet_going_mobile_-_Internet_access_and_usage_in_11_African_countries.pdf. 20 August 2015

Rubin, R.B., Perse, E.M., Barbato, C.A.: Conceptualization and measurement of interpersonal communication motives. Hum. Commun. Res. **14**, 602–628 (1988)

Saunders, M., Lewis, P., Thornhill, A.: Research methods for business students, 5th edn. Financial Times/Prentice Hall, London (2012)

Sanders, W.: Mobile Phone Usage Among Young, Urban Chinese, Conference Papers – National Communication Association. Communication and Mass Media Complete 1–27 (2008)

Selwyn, N.: Schooling the mobile generation: the future for schools in the mobile-networked society. Br. J. Educ. **24**(2), 131–144 (2003)

Srivastava, L.: Mobile phones and evolution of social behaviour Behavioral Information Technology **24**, 111–129 (2005)

Stafford, T.F., Stafford, M.R., Schkade, L.: Determining uses and gratifications for the internet. Decis. Sci. **35**(2), 259–288 (2004)

Strydom, J.E., Mentz, M., Kuh, G.D.: Enhancing Success in Higher Education by Measuring Student Engagement in South Africa (2010). http://sasse.ufs.ac.za/dl/userfiles/documents/SASSEinpresspaper_1.pdf. 15 October 2014

Urista, M.A., Qingwen, D., Kenneth, D.D.: Explaining why young adults use myspace and facebook through uses and gratifications theory. Hum. Commun. **12**(2), 215–229 (2009)

Walsh, S., White, K.: Ring, why did I make that call? Mobile phone beliefs and behaviour among Australian university students. Youth Stud. Aust. **25**(3), 49–57 (2006)

West, R.L., Turner, L.H.: Uses and Gratifications Theory. Introducing Communication Theory: Analysis and Application. McGraw-Hill, Boston (2010)

A Multiple Case Study Approach Exploring Innovation, Pedagogical Transformation and Inclusion for Mobile Learning

Kathryn Mac Callum(✉), Stephanie Day, David Skelton, Istvan Lengyl, and Michael Verhaart

Eastern Institute of Technology, Napier, New Zealand
{kmaccallum, sday, dskelton, ilengyl, mverhaart}@eit.ac.nz

Abstract. Mobile learning has enabled students to be active participants in their own learning. Students now have the ability to better develop and control their learning inside and outside the teaching context. Effective mobile learning practices require educators to develop an environment that fosters and supports their student's learning. Educators are however, still struggling with how to effectively support a learner-centred mobile learning environment.

In 2014, six New Zealand (NZ) tertiary institutions became involved in a nationwide project that aimed to explore how mobile technology could be effectively incorporated into tertiary education to provide increased inclusivity and to support innovative and transformative classroom practices. To guide the project, a framework was adopted to help support the teachers to better integrate mobile devices to facilitate learner-generated contexts. The framework adopted blends several interrelated learning frameworks interpreted within the pedagogy-andragogy-heutagogy (PAH) continuum.

This paper reports on four cases studies exploring how mobile technology was incorporated at one of the institutes involved in the wider project. These case studies explore how four lecturers have employed mobile devices to enhance students' learning opportunities within four different computing courses. Each case study focuses on how mobile technology has been integrated and includes a discussion on the benefits and issues of the technologies encountered within each case.

Keywords: Mobile learning · Mobile innovation · Pedagogical transformation · Inclusion · Case study

1 Introduction

Mobile learning provides opportunities to facilitate the learning interaction; between student and teacher, student and resources, and student and student, regardless of time restrictions or geographic proximity. As this relatively new learning environment emerges, it appears to foreshadow a paradigm shift in education which will require teachers to rethink how they design their teaching (Shee and Wang 2008). Mobile technology potentially offers a way to extend existing learning practices and expand on

T.H. Brown and H.J. van der Merwe (Eds.): mLearn 2015, CCIS 560, pp. 315–329, 2015.
DOI: 10.1007/978-3-319-25684-9_23

the advantages exploited by e-learning. However, despite the wide appeal and uptake of mobile learning, it has not necessarily guaranteed provision of enhanced learning opportunities (Cochrane 2012). It is important that effective pedagogical approaches be adopted to ensure effective mobile learning (Spencer et al. 2013).

To understand how mobile technology can be incorporated into the teaching and learning environment, case studies can be used to showcase effective practice. This paper reports on four cases studies exploring how mobile technology has been incorporated within a computing programme at a tertiary institution in New Zealand. These case studies discuss how four lecturers have used their own mobile devices and encouraged the use of students' mobile devices to enhance learning opportunities.

2 Background

At the beginning of 2014, six tertiary institutions became involved in a NZ nationwide project. This project, 'Learners and mobile devices (#NPF14LMD): A framework for enhanced learning and institutional change', aimed to deliver a "range of practical strategies for students, teachers and leaders to utilise the affordances of mobile devices for pedagogical transformation and empowering learners" (Ako Aotearoa 2014). The key project questions are derived from Traxler (2010), *Will learners' mobile devices deliver innovation, inclusion, and transformation—the main potential benefits for learners? If so, how? What is the 'framework for enhanced learning and institutional change' that will deliver these benefits?* As part of this research, lecturers from the participating institutes integrated and explored how mobile technology could be exploited to better support their teaching and learning within a variety of learning contexts. The project's aim was to help build a platform for future uptake of mobile technology within each institution and throughout the wider educational context.

3 The Study

One of the institutions involved in this nationwide research project is the Eastern Institute of Technology (EIT). EIT is a small regional tertiary educational institute providing a range of programs, from foundation studies through to applied professional study at Masters Level. To meet the needs of the East Coast and Hawke's Bay regions of New Zealand, EIT has two major campuses, one located in Taradale, Napier and the other situated in Gisborne. Several smaller campuses are located in suburban areas and smaller towns throughout the region.

Four lecturers from EIT's School of Computing were involved in the national research project. The project was shaped around developing a community of practice (COP) where lecturers could get together to discuss and support each other in exploring and integrating mobile technology in their teaching. As a result of the COP discussions, each lecturer took a unique approach to designing, developing and integrating mobile learning practices within the courses they taught. The following case studies discuss the different approaches, outcomes and issues each lecturer faced as they tackled the different needs and outcomes specific to their leaner context.

The outcome of this paper is to showcase how mobile technology can be incorporated into tertiary education and to provide strategies and advice to other educators and educationalists interested in adopting mobile learning.

4 Research Framework

A version of the Cochrane et al. (2014) framework was adopted to guide the project (Table 1). This framework was developed to support teachers better integrate mobile devices to facilitate learner-generated contexts: "The key aspect of Learner Generated Contexts is that they are generated through the enterprise of those who would previously have been consumers in a context created for them" (Luckin et al. 2010, p. 3). The framework blends several interrelated learning frameworks interpreted within the pedagogy-andragogy-heutagogy (PAH) continuum. The PAH continuum outlines the progression from pedagogy to andragogy to heutagogy (Luckin et al. 2010). The premise of the PAH continuum is that it can be scaffolded to support learning that is student-determined. Heutagogy foundations are rooted in andragogy and apply a holistic approach to developing learner capabilities so learning can be self-determined (Blaschke 2012). A heutagogical approach requires learners to approach their own learning in a mature and autonomous way (Canning 2010).

5 Data Collection and Analysis

Case studies explore and explain a current event or events, and include direct observations and participant feedback as sources of evidence within the research (Yin 2003). As part of this research, each case study relied on Lecturer explanation and observation of events and feedback from participating students. Overall student feedback was captured by way of opened ended survey questions delivered using an online survey tool at the end of the course. In class discussions and reflections captured from students' blogging exercises were also recorded and used as evidence. The feedback was then open coded and aligned to the three themed research areas of innovation, transformation and inclusion.

6 Case Study 1: IT Management

IT Management is a third year Bachelor of Computing Systems (BCS) paper comprising of 41 students. This paper provides a broad overview of all aspects of Information Technology (IT) and its management. Students are being offered the opportunity to participate in class activities using their mobile devices. As classes are not held in a computing lab, students are using their devices to facilitate research, work on collaborative activities and discussions, and to deliver assessment presentations. This case study will report on the preliminary findings of the effectiveness of using mobile devices as a research and presentation tool.

Historically, this particular class has been timetabled in a conventional computer room, however due to increased numbers and the need to run a simultaneous video

Table 1. A framework for using mobile social media to enable creative pedagogies

	Pedagogy	Andragogy	Heutagogy
Activity types	Content delivery	Teacher as guide	Teacher as co-learner
	Digital assessment	Digital identity	Digital presence
	Teacher-delivered content	Student-generated content	Student-generated contexts
	Teacher-defined projects	Student-negotiated teams	Student-negotiated projects
Focus	Teacher-directed	Self-directed	Self-determined
Locus of control	Teacher	Student	Student
Cognition	Cognitive	Meta-cognitive	Epistemic
Course timeframe and goal	Initial establishment of a course project and induction into a wider learning community	Early to mid-course: Student appropriation of mobile social media and initial active participation	Mid to end of course: Establishment of major projects where students actively participate within an authentic community of practice
Creativity (Sternberg, Kaufman & Pretz, 2007)	Reproduction	Incrementation	Reinitiation
Knowledge production	Subject understanding: lecturers introduce and model the use of a range of mobile social media tools appropriate to the learning context	Process negotiation: students negotiate a choice of mobile social media tools to establish an eportfolio based upon user-generated content	Context shaping: students create project teams that investigate and critique user-generated content within the context of their discipline. These are then shared, curated and peer-reviewed in an authentic COP
Supporting mobile social media affordances	Enabling induction into a supportive learning community	Enabling user-generated content and active participation within an authentic project COP	Enabling collaboration across user-generated contexts, and active participation within a wider professional COP
Ontological shift	Reconceptualising mobile social media: from a social to an educational domain	Reconceptualising the role of the teacher	Reconceptualising the role of the learner

(Source: Cochrane et al. 2014)

session to another campus (Gisborne) the three hour class now takes place in a standard classroom - although it does include multiple projectors and video capability. This placed more emphasis and need for students to bring their mobile devices and laptops to class for any Internet-based research or use of applications. If the class had been run in a computer room, then it is likely that less use of mobile devices would have ensued.

6.1 Innovation

One of the practical hands-on uses of mobile technologies in this class was the use of EZCast, a system allowing students to broadcast via Wi-Fi from their mobile device through a data projector. EZCast was selected to support sharing of screens since IT policy within the institute did not support many of the other solutions, such as Reflector and Apple TV. The EZCast solution was also selected as it supported a range of platforms and devices (Windows, Android and Apple computers, tablets and phones).

Student presentations were integrated into their first assignment with the option of mobile projection or traditional PC Powerpoint projection. The classroom lent itself to dual projection with one projector setup with EZCast, with the other projector at right angles projecting Powerpoint slides. Students alternated their presentations, with one student presenting with the aid of their mobile device (Windows, Android smartphone or tablet, iPhone or iPad), then the next student presenting with the aid of the class PC and projector. This alternation gave students and the lecturer some insights into the contrasting effectiveness of each technique.

The use of mobile devices for student presentations was of particular interest to this group of students (41) as they were IT degree students with a strong interest in harnessing technology for organisational aims. The technical setup of software, projector dongle, experimentation with the phone or tablet beforehand and the contrast between Apple and Android systems also enabled some practical technology learning for these IT students.

One of the challenges has been the lack of standardisation of devices in any one class, and the variability of students bringing their own various high-end devices to class. An initial survey was taken of this class seeking information on mobiles devices owned by students, and those they were prepared to bring to class. In future, some access to a class set of tablets with standardised operating systems and applications may enhance the integration into class exercises and activities.

6.2 Student Inclusion

The challenge of using mobile technology in this example included ensuring that organisational and technical policies were not a barrier and ensuring full testing was prepared before classes. The sessions involving mobile projection were supported by a learning advisor from EIT, to help overcome any technical issues. The effect on the learning environment was that students became more focussed and aware of their presentation. Some students mentioned they did feel more in control of their presentation as they were using their own personal device, although some also mentioned they were more nervous with less familiar technology setup. A small number of students experienced difficulty with their Android devices as these required an app to be installed.

6.3 Pedagogical Integration

This adoption of mobile devices is integrated into a current blended learning environment. Most tertiary institutions will already be using a blended layer of learning and teaching channels including face to face classes, a learning management system (e.g. Moodle, Blackboard), online activities, online content, communication technology, and so, as this example demonstrates, mobile learning and the use of mobile devices fits into this overall matrix as one more channel of communication and interaction. A previous matrix for blended learning environments has been proposed compiling all of the elements of blended/online/technology channels (Skelton 2009) and it may be helpful to teaching practitioners to consider further integration and use of mobile technology within such a framework rather than another isolated teaching technology. In fact, mobile learning can more easily enhance face-to-face teaching environments due to its portability and flexibility as well as enhance the online learning environments.

7 Case Study 2: User Interface Design

User Interface Design is a second year Bachelor of Computing Systems paper that covers the design principles and techniques of graphical interface design. The course adopts a user experience (UX) approach to design evaluation. Students evaluate and develop a range of interfaces to for usable design.

In 2015, student numbers increased significantly, from around twelve students to 29 students, and this highlighted a need to approach course assessment in a more effective and efficient manner. To support the new approach, the course was redesigned and adopted an agile software development methodology where teamwork formed the core learning approach. The students worked with an industry client to redevelop a website and develop a mobile application. The assessment was arranged into four self-managed teams comprising of 6–7 members. Each team investigated and developed a different part of the same system. Mobile technology was introduced to support team collaboration, lecture capture, feedback and learner supporter interaction.

7.1 Innovation

The course tutorials were redesigned around teamwork and focused on the project. Tutorials are no longer held inside a computer lab - since they did not support team communication, as communication was limited due to the arrangement of the lab room. Tutorials are now conducted in open plan room with a strong BYOD philosophy. The desks were configured into groups and students were encouraged to bring their own devices to work on in the class.

Inside the class tutorials, students in their teams work around common tasks but with different focuses due to them working on separate parts of the redevelopment. In the class, students could work either around a single group computer or their own computers. Students were also able to share work outside the teams to the wider class via screen sharing (EZCast). The screen sharing enabled the students to project their computer, tablet or mobile device (when taking photos of written work) screens and to share these screens with the rest of the class on the main projector. This enabled students to share work and discuss their team's work to get a feedback and support from the whole class. The teacher no longer controlled the sharing of work; rather the shared screens were controlled by the students to support class wide communication and feedback.

As with the previous case study, there were a few issues with the using the EZCast solution. The main issue was the reliability of the system. The EZCast software would often fail and students had trouble connecting. A significant amount of time was lost trying to fix these technical issues. A dongle also need to be manually plugged into projector and configured before the class. This process was cumbersome and also time consuming. Due to the technical infrastructure of the institute, alternative methods had been tried and tested with the EZCast solution being the most effective. To overcome some of these technical issues it has now been proposed that in the future each projector has its own dongle. This solution will therefore removing the issue of plugging in and removing the device every class and hopefully removing some of technical issues.

Lectures were still held for the course. The lecturers would cover much of the theory and important concepts that students needed to undertake their project. The lecturer would screen share the presentation from her tablet and video record the presentation. This recording would be shared with students after the class via the course Learning Management System (LMS). This approach was undertaken for three reasons: (1) so that the teacher was mobile inside the class and not stuck at the front of the class, (2) the presentation could be shared with students, where they could take control of the presentation and provide their own perception and content. This was particularly important when students were asked to provide examples or share opinions when discussing effective interface design. (3) Lectures were now permanently recorded. Students could watch the videos after class and rewind and re-watch parts that they may have missed or not understood.

7.2 Student Inclusion

For the assignment each team was able to choose and work on different parts of the system, based on core functionality supported by the system. Despite each team working on different parts of the system each would be facing many of the same or similar issues and constraints. So sharing outside the teams was as important as supporting communication within the teams. Therefore a number of Google Plus Communities were set up for students to share and discuss course content and assessment work inside and outside groups. Google Plus was adopted to support this communication. This was also selected, as they were easily accessible from all devices including mobile devices. The first community that was set up was an open access class community. This was set up to enable all students in the class to share and discuss common issues and class content. Separate private communities were set up, one per team, where they could discuss, share and work on their assessment.

Overall these communities were very successful with students' actively engaging and sharing work. However it was perceived that the team communities were more active and better used that the class community. Largely the class a community was run by the lecturer and most students were reluctant to add content or comment on the various posts compared to the team communities. This might be due to how the communities were perceived by the students. Student took ownership of the team communities and due to the size they had a higher level of comfort and trust within this group. The fact that these groups were also closed also contributed to the feeling of trust. The students however did not necessarily feel comfortable within the larger group. They still felt that this community was the domain of the teacher and therefore felt less comfortable to add content. In the next iteration of this course, it has been decided that more work be placed on the class communities to make it feel more like a community, where students feel comfortable and safe to place their own posts and share ideas and thoughts.

In addition to the Google Plus communities, team collaboration was supported via either shared OneNote or Google Drives. These were used to share work and support collaboration on their assignments. These resources were also shared with lecturer to support instant access by the lecturer and opportunity to provide instant feedback. Since OneNote and Google Drives are accessible via mobile devices, not only could students collaborate via their mobile devices, the lecturer was also able to get updates and view student work and provide feedback via her mobile device.

7.3 Pedagogical Transformation

The course was redeveloped to adopt a heutagogical approach that facilitated socio-cultural learning of the students. Mobile technology was used to drive and support this approach. Socio-cultural learning takes place in this course through social interactions, engagement and the changes made to the assessment. Sociocultural learning theories take a learner-centered approach (Crompton 2013). By adopting an Agile Software Development approach students were able to choose tasks that they wish to complete. A list of tasks that were to be completed to achieve the project was written as a team. However students within the group were able to select which tasks they wish to undertake on behalf of the team. This approach recognised students' prior knowledge and abilities and students where students could focus on what they preferred or felt best suited their existing abilities.

In the collaborative learning environment, students interact with learning tools and other members' in-group activities; they express and conceptualize their viewpoints and also listened to others in order to solve problems, to complete their tasks, or to generate new ideas. Relationships within the teams were encouraged and supported. In particular, students were encouraged to first to get to know their teams before work on the project started. This was supported inside and outside the class. For example, students were encouraged to sit together in the both the lecturers and the tutorials. Students were also asked to introduce themselves in the Google Groups (in whichever format they wished). This re-enforcement of teams feeling of belonging within and outside the classroom and helped to promote and bring teams together and reinforced the communities.

8 Case Study 3: Digital Learning Technologies

Digital Learning Technologies (DLT) is a third year Bachelor of Computing Systems paper that allows students to investigate technological developments, technology integration and pedagogical practices that influence education and training. A range of technologies and tools are used demonstrate good pedagogy and students are required to design a learning object that meets a defined learning outcome. This course presents an ideal environment to investigate mobile pedagogies and students are encouraged to use mobile technologies in a variety of contexts. This case study reports on the use of mobile technologies to enable remote student participation both in and out of the classroom.

Thirty five students were enrolled in the DLT class. These students were able to attend the class either face to face or remotely using Adobe Connect, a web conferencing system. This flexibility in attendance methods is available for every class, but as part of this case study, the dual method of attendance was extended from the classroom and into field based learning. While in the field, mobile devices running the Adobe Connect software allowed remote students to be included in the shared experience.

During this course, students are required to explore instructional design models and the relationship between pedagogy and technology. As part of this exploration and to experience the integration of technology as a classroom management option, students participated in a field trip and visited EIT's School of Music. The School of Music uses a classroom management system (CMS) that allows the class lecturer to take control of the students' computer to both monitor and limit student-computing behaviour. During the field trip, the students experienced the CMS features and engaged in discussion regarding the system and the related areas of privacy and ethics. Students were also encouraged to use mobile devices to capture multimedia evidence of their visit, and to use this as part of an assessed reflective activity in a shared class blog.

The student blog entries, a short electronic survey and a class discussion were used to capture student experiences with the mobile technologies used to enable the GxLearning environment and engage in the field trip.

8.1 Innovation

Field trips are recognised as a valuable short-term experiential learning activity (Scarce 1997) that increases student knowledge and motivation (Behrendt and Franklin 2014). The value of experiential learning lies in a participatory learner experience, reflecting on the experience and being able to apply the new learning in different ways (Kolb 1984).

Computer technologies have enabled virtual field trips by bringing real world experience into the classroom, but the use of mobile technologies to include students both in face-to-face mode and remotely, takes advantage of the pervasiveness of mobile to enable flexibility in these learning experiences. The use of technologies in this way has been coined "GxLearning" by Verhaart and Hagen-Hall (2012), who describe it as "a geographically distributed class, consisting of students in a face-to-face mode plus students in a remote location" (p. 111). The mobile supported GxLearning environment enabled remote students to virtually participate in the field trip. Students feedback showed they appreciated the flexibility offered by the GxLearning environment, *"When my children was sick I attended class via Adobe Connect, works great"*, and *"I could attend class from anywhere and anytime from any device."*

As part of the DLT field trip, learners were required to use the knowledge gained from this experience to blog about their experience, complete a SWOT analysis of the CMS and to reflect on the value of using mobile technologies to enable remote student participation. Students had previously blogged in their own blogs, but as part of this learning experience, the class were given access to a shared blog, and were to use this for reflection. The remote students were also able to complete the reflective blogging assessment and offer unique perspective of using these technologies in this manner.

8.2 Student Inclusion

Using the GxLearning paradigm students that were unable to attend the field trip either face-to-face or within the mobile enabled Adobe Connect classroom. During the field trip, mobile devices connected to the Adobe Connect classroom were used in a variety of ways. An iPad captured a video stream of the experience. This provided a portability not possible with a fixed computing device; allowing video streaming from multiple angles and perspectives. A laptop was used by the class lecturer to facilitate the discussion stream with the remote students. This allowed the remote students to ask questions and both the remote and face-to-face students could use the technology for peer-to-peer communication. As the GxLearning environment is web based, remote students could attend the class using any computing technology including smartphones, tablets, laptops or desktop computers with Internet access. The disadvantages centered on the quality of the audio provided to the remote students, *"sometimes the audio is not very clear"* and *"The sound quality is really poor. Especially for non-native speakers it is even harder to understand the lecturer when recorded in a poor sound quality"*. Students also noted engagement issues, *"The inherent remoteness of presence and sound making for a lesser quality learning experience"*. Although poor sound quality generally caused the most dissatisfaction amongst the students, the ability to be flexible, engage with a diverse student cohort and using the technology in a practical way was high on the list of enjoyment factors.

8.3 Pedagogical Transformation

GxLearning and the ability to include remote students into a class experience has become critical as life demands on students often prevent them from attending class, flexibility in delivery is expected and institutes widen their offerings into distant and blended learning modes. Such a shift requires a transformation from traditional class learning and teaching and requires student-centric focus inclusive of both cohorts of students. Activities in the DLT class use a variety of web based technologies alongside the GxLearning environment that allow both cohorts of students equal access and an equitable learning experience. These activities include collaborative editing in Google Docs, microblogging, blogging and contribution to a shared class blog. Student feedback showed that they had a good understanding of both the technological and pedagogical requirements of learning and teaching in this multi-modal environment. A student noted that "*the learning design and preparation needs to cover the increased demands of teaching across two channels at the same time*" and "*The teacher must be skilled (and preferably at expert level) across all domains: pedagogy, instructional design, the subject material to be presented, the technology used for delivery and managing two audiences before, during and after delivery*". Students were understanding of the set-up requirements when using complex technologies "*The more complex and more useful technologies go often hand in hand with higher requirements in terms of hardware and technical understanding*".

Careful planning was critical to success when using this teaching environment as was students' readiness and ability to engage with multiple technologies. Strong Wi-Fi or mobile data was needed to support the technologies used and good quality microphones and cameras needed to ensure the best experience for the remote students. Despite these issues, student responses to the activity were positive and the combination of mobile and web conferencing technologies enabled learning beyond the classroom and into the field.

9 Case Study 4: Help Desk

Help Desk is a second year BCS course and has been designed to provide the 33 enrolled students with the skills to analyse problems, identify solutions and prioritise those solutions with an IT focused lens. This course also aims to improve students' ability to communicate and listen to others in a professional manner. As part of meeting these learning outcomes, the assessment focuses on students work with a client to create a user guide (manual). The user guide is developed specifically for a client and provides them support with a particular system of their choice. This process of working with a client required students to attentively listen to requirements, communicate and accurately meet the desired outcome. This case study reports on the redevelopment, implementation and results of redesigning this course to include mobile technology to create student-generated resource in the form of e-book creation as an assessed activity.

9.1 Innovation

In the past, students were to develop the user guides as paper based reports comprising of just text and images. However to take advantage of the affordance of mobile technology, this assessment was redesigned where students were now required to create an interactive e-book for their client. The assessment still required students to work with a client however rather than creating a written report they now created an interactive e-book that meets the client's needs. Students are required to make the e-book accessible across multiple platforms and are encouraged to use mobile devices to both develop multimedia content and to test for cross platform usability.

The ebooks were created using iBook Author, a software package available on Apple computers and iPads. These ebooks must incorporate a range of multimedia elements such as images, videos, interactive quizzes, and other components as necessary to provide a client approved professional product. The students were encouraged to use mobile devices to capture and create content as required.

Based on this redevelopment student's feedback was extremely positive. Students felt that the user interface and tool-set provided by both the Mac OS and the iBook Author program was user friendly and intuitive. Since the software adopted was only available on the Apple platform this was however a major limiting factor, as not all students owned these devices. An additional 12 Apple iMacs are available at the EIT library, however the small number of iMacs available still limited the development of iBooks and simultaneous access to the resource. To overcome this issue alternative software was sought to develop these ebooks (such as Inkling), however these alternatives were found to be not as easy to use as the iBook Author software. This was a major limiting factor to the success of this project and of yet still not resolved. It is hoped that as ebooks software becomes more sophisticated that is issue will be resolved in the near future.

9.2 Pedagogical Transformation

Transforming a traditional approach where students need to create a tradition paper based user manual into an interactive e-book allowed students to express themselves more creatively. This transformation also enabled the inclusion of multimedia content and interactive quizzes in multiple formats allowing opportunity for the reader to reflect what they have learnt. Students engaged more in their assignment, as they explored their creative abilities and took pride in their accomplishments. Students acquired new knowledge of an Operating System (Mac OSX) and became very proficient in use of iBook Author. E-books allowed knowledge to be shared and fed forward. As many international organisations use e-books as a cost effective way to deliver training solutions to clients, the skills learned in this course will be of future value to students in the workplace.

Beyond the assignment these ebooks were also resources for other students within and outside the course.

The ebooks will be accessible through the library and end product will be available for use by all EIT students and will be used in the software packages course as a textbook. The ebooks will also become published works on the iBookstore and will be available for future download.

Overall, students created some wonderful polished interactive e-books that fulfilled their client's expectations. This form of assessment has been validated in this context and there is now opportunity to investigate plausibility of implemented this approach in other areas.

10 Conclusion

Overall each case study identified different ways that mobile technology was integrated into the classroom as part of EIT's contribution to the nationwide project. Each of the four lecturers involved in the project integrated and used mobile technology in different ways that better supported their learners in the context of their own course assessment requirements and learner outcomes. The following table (Table 2) summarises each activity that was adopted and how the learning approach was adapted, and could be further adapted to support a self-determined (Heutagogical) learning.

Table 2. Activities employed in the case study and how the teaching was redeveloped.

Activity	Past	Redeveloped	Redeveloped with possible adaptation
Presenting (Screensharing)	Content delivered by lecture presentations with class discussion Content delivered by lecture presentations with class discussion	Student presentations from computer in front of class Recording of lecture for students to view after class	Screen sharing from students own personal device and controlled by students to share work and collaborate Students recorder/created their own videos on class topics and shared with class
Online groups (Google plus)	Teacher led and controlled	Student leading and adding own content (Google Plus for course)	Student controlling own team and community building (Google Plus for team)
Team collaboration (Google drive and onenote)	Lecture controlled tasks typically individual	Group assessment with shared tasks but lecturer directed	Students able to use shared resources and choose their own tasks based on their own abilities. The lecturer providing support when requested by students.
Web conferencing (Adobe connect)	Teacher captures lectures and class discussion for remote viewing	Remote students actively participate in experiential learning using technology to enable virtual presence	Students control the virtual environment, with peer-to-peer support and discussion, shared video and resources
Blog	Teacher blogs interesting things to share with the class.	Students create individual blogs for assessment. Students comment on/engage with other student blogs	Students author a class blog where collaboration and shared reflection strengthen analysis and understanding.
Ebooks	Student written assignment	Student created ebooks for assessments	Student created resources to be shared with other students within and between classes

Integrating mobile technology into tertiary learning has provided the opportunity for learning to become learner-focused and determined. However the effective integration of this technology is not necessarily straightforward. In each case study there were various issues that were identified with some still not as yet resolved. These issues generally related to access, technical issues and limitations and institutional IT policy. However these four case studies illustrate different ways that mobile technology has begun to be implemented within one tertiary institution to provide inclusivity and support innovative and transformative classroom practices. These case studies provide an important starting point on describing how mobile technology can be adopted and the issues that can arise when using mobile technology. They provide an insight how learning could be extended and be supported in a connected world where ubiquitous ownership of a wireless mobile device has become the norm and where educators are grappling with how to effectively implement these devices into the educational environment.

References

Ako, A.: Learners and mobile devices (#NPF14LMD): a framework for enhanced learning and institutional change (2014). https://akoaotearoa.ac.nz/learner-mobile-devices

Behrendt, M., Franklin, T.: A review of research on school field trips and their value in education. Int. J. Environ. Sci. Edu. **9**, 235–245 (2014)

Blaschke, L.M.: Heutagogy and lifelong learning: a review of heutagogical practice and self-determined learning. Int. Rev. Res. Open Distrib. Learn. **13**(1), 56–71 (2012)

Canning, N., Callan, S.: Heutagogy: spirals of reflection to empower learners in higher education. Reflective Pract. **11**(1), 71–82 (2010)

Crompton, H.: A historical overview of mobile learning: toward learner-centered education. In: Handbook of mobile learning, pp. 3–14 (2013)

Cochrane, T.: Secrets of mlearning failures: confronting reality. Res. Learn. Technol. **20**, 123–134 (2012)

Cochrane, T., Antonczak, L., Keegan, H., Narayan, V.: Riding the wave of BYOD: developing a framework for creative pedagogies. Res. Learn. Technol. **22**, 1–14 (2014)

Kolb, D.A.: Experiential learning: experience as the source of learning and development (1984). http://academic.regis.edu/ed205/kolb.pdf

Luckin, R., Clark, W., Garnett, F., Whitworth, A., Akass, J., Cook, J., Robertson, J.: Learner-generated contexts: a framework to support the effective use of technology for learning. In: Lee, M., McLoughlin, C., (eds.) Web 2.0-Based E-Learning: Applying Social Informatics for Tertiary Teaching, pp. 70–84. Hershey, PA: IGI Global (2010)

Scarce, R.: Field trips as short-term experiential education. Teach. Sociol. **25**(3), 219 (1997). http://search.proquest.com/docview/223512647?accountid=39646

Shee, D., Wang, Y.: Multi-criteria evaluation of the web-based e-learning system: a methodology based on learner satisfaction and its applications. Computers & Education **50**(3), 894–905 (2008). http://www.sciencedirect.com/science/article/pii/S0360131506001424

Skelton, D. (2009). Blended is still best: Review of literature and commentary on optimal learning environments. AMCIS 2009 Proceedings. Retrieved from http://aisel.aisnet.org/amcis2009/615

Spencer, K.M., Coutts, T., Fagan, T., King, A.: Connections, diversity, coherence: three vignettes exploring learning with ipads in primary schools. Comput. NZ Sch.: Learn., Teach., Technol. **25**(1–3), 38–55 (2013)

Sternberg, R.J., Kaufman, J.C., Pretz, J.E.: The Creativity Conundrum: A Propulsion Model of Kinds of Creative Contributions. Psychology Press, Philadelphia (2002)

Traxler, J.: Will student devices deliver innovation, inclusion, and transformation? J. Res. Cent. Edu. Technol. **6**(1), 3–15 (2010). http://www.rcetj.org/index.php/rcetj/article/view/56/177

Verhaart, M., Hagen-Hall, K.: GxLearning, teaching to geographically extended classes. In: Lopez, M., Verhaart, M., (eds.) Proceedings of the 3rd Annual Conference of the Computing and Information Technology Research and Education of New Zealand Conference (Incorporating the 25th National Advisory Committee on Computing Qualifications Conference), Christchurch, New Zealand, 7–10 October, pp. 75–81 (2012)

Yin, R.K.: Case Study Research: Design and Methods, 3rd edn. Sage, Thousand Oaks (2003)

Heutagogial Approaches in the Understanding and Modelling the Adoption of Mobile Learning

Kathryn Mac Callum[1(✉)], Lynn Jeffery[2], and Kinshuk[3]

[1] School of Computing, Eastern Institute of Technology, Private Bag 1201 Hawke's Bay Mail Centre, Napier 4142, New Zealand
KMacCallum@eit.ac.nz

[2] School of Management, Massey University, Private Bag 11 222, Palmerston North 4442, New Zealand
L.M.Jeffrey@massey.ac.nz

[3] Faculty of Science and Technology, Athabasca University, 1 University Drive, Athabasca, AB T9S 3A3, Canada
Kinshuk@ieee.org

Abstract. The purpose of this paper is to investigate how the factors that influence a learner's ability to be self-directed (Andragogy) and self-determined (Heutagogy) may influence the understanding and modelling of mobile learning adoption. Heutagogy is seen as a progression along a continuum of pedagogical approaches from pedagogy to andragogy to heutagogy, where learners need to progress from each with the aim of becoming highly autonomous and mature learners. Due to the nature of mobile technology, learning can be orientated towards the learner to support their needs. Learners are now better equipped to manage and control their own learning as learning can take place anywhere and anytime. However not all students possess the required traits, such as self-management, self-control and desire for learning, that signal that are ready for learning that is no longer teacher-lead and directed.

The study examines the results of a survey (n = 446 students) assessing how the traits that indicate a readiness for learning that is self-directed and self-determined, can impact on students' perceptions and adoption of mobile learning. This model was tested using structural equation modelling. The findings showed that there was a strong association with the factors of self-management, self-control and desire for learning on the positive perception of mobile learning and adoption. The study reinforces the need for scaffolding and developing learners so that they are comfortable to succeed in an environment that is self- directed and determined.

Keywords: Andragogy · Heutagogy · Mobile learning adoption · Technology adoption model

1 Introduction

Mobile learning provides learners with new ways and opportunities to direct and manage their own learning paths, whenever and wherever they wish. These opportunities have however signalled a need for new approaches to be developed to better

T.H. Brown and H.J. van der Merwe (Eds.): mLearn 2015, CCIS 560, pp. 330–342, 2015.
DOI: 10.1007/978-3-319-25684-9_24

support learners. Heutagogy is one such approach that has received considerable recent interest (Blaschke 2012). Heutagogy foundations are embedded in andragogy and apply a holistic approach to developing learner capabilities so learning can be self-determined (Blaschke 2012). The heutagogical approach is a progression from pedagogy to andragogy to heutagogy (Luckin et al. 2010). A heutagogical approach requires learners to manage their own learning in a mature and autonomous way (Canning 2010). Mature learners are characterised as those that require less teacher control and course structure. These learners enjoy and want to be more self-directed in their learning. Less mature learners however require more guidance from the teacher and need learning to be scaffolded to encourage students to be more self-directed (Canning and Callan 2010; Kenyon & Hase, 2010).

Due to the ubiquitous nature of mobile learning, learners are able to learn the "right thing at the right time at the right place", but at the cost of less direct support and input from teachers (Sha et al. 2012, p 2). Typically, mobile learning devices are owned by the student (BYOD) and include a range of different types of device. Teachers have no direct overview of the amount or quality of the student's engagement with learning on these devices, so are unable to monitor student progress. Unless directly contacted by students, they cannot offer support, advice or interventions: students must take the responsibility to ask for help. Further, the types of activity provided on mobile devices are likely to be single-focus, app-like exercises that may vary in usefulness, importance and coverage of the topic. Students select which of these they believe to be most helpful, so the learning experience may vary greatly between students. By contrast, an online environment can be designed to guide students to important resources and activities in an appropriate order. These differences suggest that students' self-determination will play a more significant role in the adoption of mobile learning than has been found for e-learning generally (Sha et al. 2012).

For students to survive in an environment that is learner-driven and focussed, students need to be supported and scaffold so that they are confortable in manainge and controling their own learning. Learners need to be self-directed before they can self-determine their own learning (Blaschke 2012). Therefore the learner's readiness for self-direction is an important consideration when implementing mobile learning into a course.

The purpose of this paper is to investigate how the factors that influence a learner's ability to be self-directed (Andragogy) and self-determined (Heutagogy) may influence the understanding and modelling of adoption of mobile learning. Specifically the study examines the following research question, what impact does the students' desire for learning, the need for self-management and for self-control (over learning) have on the perceptions and adoption of mobile learning. The study examines the results of a survey (n = 446 students) assessing students' readiness for self-directed learning and their perceptions to the ease of use and usefulness of mobile learning. A modified version of the Technology Adoption Model was used to model the influence of self directedness on adoption. This model was tested using structural equation modelling.

2 Heutagogy as an Extension of Andragogy

Despite the opinion that mobile learning can support and facilitate learning that can be self-determined by a learner, learners first need to be able to manage and direct their own learning. Learners need to be scaffold and supported to successful and cope in learning that is continuing to be less teacher lead.

Andragogy, unlike pedagogy, has its foundation in adult learning. Merriam (2001, p 5), defines adult learners as those "who (1) has an independent self-concept and who can direct his or her own learning, (2) has accumulated a reservoir of life experiences that is a rich resource for learning, (3) has learning needs closely related to changing social roles, (4) is problem-centered and interested in immediate application of knowledge, and (5) is motivated to learn by internal rather than external factors." Andragogy is considered synonymous with self-directed learning whereby learning is a process which learners take responsibility under the guidance of an instructor to diagnose and manage his or her own learning.

Heutagogy however, is seen as an extension of the pedagogical and andragogical concepts focusing on a form of self-determined learning. Self-determined learning is a where learners take initiative for their own learning with the aim to increase their own learning capabilities (Blaschke 2012). Heutagogy is considered to extend these traditional concepts, such as self-directed learning, but also reflects additional concepts such

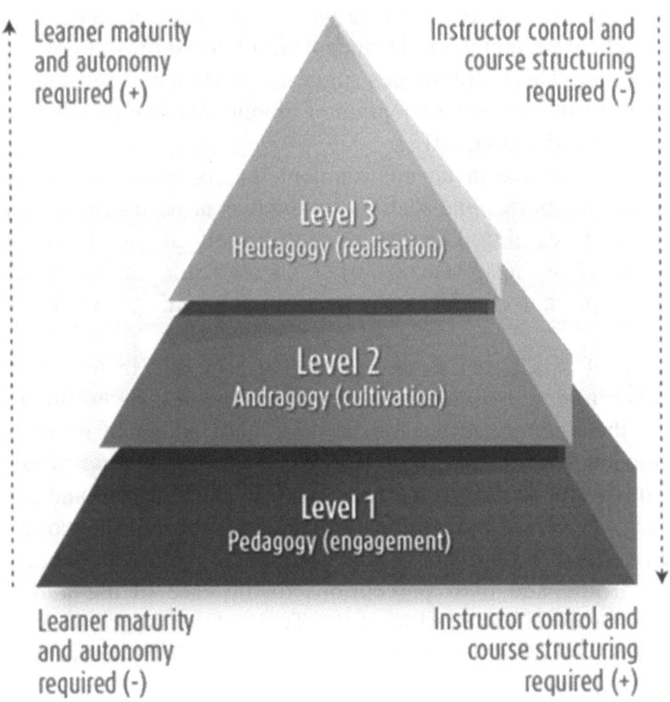

Fig. 1. Progression from pedagogy to andragogy then to heutagogy (Source Canning 2010, p. 63).

as collaborative learning. Hase and Kenyon (2007) identify heutagogy as focusing on student -centred learning. The student is seen as the major agent in his or her own learning. The teacher's role is no longer to control the learning experience but rather to transfer of knowledge and skills to the student. Heutagogy places a strong emphasis on learning that is more holistic and focuses on building the learner's independent capability (Hase and Kenyon 2001). With its basis in andragogy, heutagogy further extends the andragogical approach and can be understood as a continuum of andragogy (see Fig. 1).

3 Readiness for Self-directed and Determined Learning

The strong emphasis on student-centred learning has placed the emphasis on the learner. Learners need to be able to manage and control their own learning. Therefore students need to be self-directed and take responsibility for their own learning. These learners are able to plan, carry out and evaluate their own learning (Deepwella and Malikb 2008). Tertiary students are expected to have some level of self-directness to be successful in their studies. According to Higgs (1993) a "highly competent self-directed learner is a learner who is capable of exhibiting the following characteristics:

- a readiness for autonomous learning,
- [holding] the attitudes of responsibility and self-reliance,
- purposive independent and interdependent action in relation to the learning task,...
- effective use of learning and cognitive strategies (including metacognition and critical reflection), and,
- [having a] state of mind which involves self-awareness and self-evaluation" (p. 6).

Learners also require certain skills be self-directed, these include "the ability of the individual to organise their learning, being able to accurately self-assess in order to determine their learning needs, identify learning goals, select from a range of resources and methods and to evaluate the learning that has occurred" (Penman 2014, p 53). And finally, readiness to be a self-directed learner is determined by the attitudes, abilities and personality characteristics of the learner (Fisher et al. 2001).

The traits the indicate that a student is ready for learning the is learner directed has been of considerable debate with many different instruments being developed to measure a range of different traits (see Penman 2014 for a discussion of some of these traits and measures). However, Fisher et al. (2001), developed and tested three core characteristics, namely a students' need for self-management, self-control and desire for learning, that indicate that learners that are ready for self-directed learning. These characteristics have been found to be specific indicators of learners that will thrive in tertiary learning since they are typically more learner-centred whereby students are expected to learn more autonomously (Fisher et al. 2001; Fisher and King 2010).

There has been no specific instrument developed to measure readiness for self-determined learning. However since self-determined learning is considered to be the next level on the continuance of learning pedagogy it can be argued that many of the characteristics measured by Fisher et al. 2001 are important, if not more important, for self-determined learning. Therefore these same measures can be considered to also indicate that students are somewhat ready for self-determined learning.

4 Methodology

The aim of this study was to model how the ease of use and usefulness of mobile technology mediates the relationship between the factors that determine student's readiness for self-directed and determined leaning with the intention of students to use mobile learning in the future. A questionnaire was used to measure the major variables in this study. The questionnaire was given to a small pre-sample group who provided feedback on the clarity and easy of understanding of individual items.

A multi-stage stratified cluster sampling method was adopted to survey the students at three Universities/Polytechnics within New Zealand. Undergraduate students undertaking twenty-three business courses were randomly selected and asked to complete the survey. Of the approximate 1213 students invited to take part (based on numbers enrolled in each course), 446 completed the questionnaire giving a response rate of 37 %. From the original 446 completed surveys, a final sample of 413 was achieved after data screening. This included 227 females (55 %). The mean students age were between the age of 20-29 years ($\bar{x} = 2.21$; $s = .991$) and the majority of participants classified themselves as European or part European (68.3 %).

5 Theoretical and Research Model

5.1 TAM

To explain an individual's acceptances of technology a number of models have developed (see Venkatesh et al. 2003, for a detailed discussion). One of the most cited model is the Technology Adoption Model (TAM), which proposes that an individual's attitudes are the drivers for the adoption of the technology (Straub 2009). Perceived ease of use and the usefulness of the innovation have been shown to directly influence a users' intention to adopt a particular technology (Saadé & Kira, 2007). Davis (1989) defined perceived ease of use as the level of difficulty or effort needed to use the technology. Perceived usefulness is the level of belief an individual has about whether the technology will provide an advantage and lead to better outcomes than not using it (Venkatesh and Davis 1996). The model has also been tested to show a relationship between perceived usefulness and ease of use, with ease of use influencing perceived usefulness. The work with the model concludes that an innovation should be easy to use and learn, and not so complex that it negates it usefulness (Hackbarth et al. 2003). Studies suggest that the TAM model can be used to explain approximately 50 % of the variance in acceptance levels (Davis et al. 1992).

Two constructs of the TAM were used to determine intention to adopt (Venkatesh et al. 2003) and the items slightly modified to fit the mobile learning context of this study. Perceived usefulness and ease of use were assessed using 7 items of a 7-point likert-type scale where 1 represented "Strongly disagree" and 7" Strongly agree".

The two factors were analysed using exploratory factor analysis (EFA) to confirm the structure of the data and enable the selection of the strongest indicators of each construct (Pallant 2007). The composite reliability (internal consistency reliability) approach was estimated using Cronbach's alpha. Composite reliabilities of perceived usefulness resulted in score of. 93 and perceived ease of use had a score of .71, satisfying the threshold of 0.7 (Nunnally and Bernstein 1994).

Based on the TAM model three hypotheses were tested:

- H1: Students who perceive mobile learning as easy to use will have a more positive perception of mobile learning usefulness.
- H2: Students who perceive mobile learning as useful will be more likely to indicate that they intend to adopt mobile technology.
- H3: Students who perceive mobile learning as easy to use will be more likely indicate that they intend to adopt mobile technology.

5.2 Self-directed Readiness

Self-directedness was measured using Fisher et al. (2001) self-directed learning readiness scale (SDLRSNE). This scale was developed to assess nursing students' readiness for self-directedness. Despite this measure being developed for nursing students the items used are generic and applicable to any discipline. The purpose of the SDLRSNE was to develop an alternative to the popular Guglielmino's SDLRS to overcome criticism of reliability and validity (Fisher et al. 2001). The scale was based on key attitudes, abilities and personality characteristics of a self-directed learner. In particular they identify three core characteristics:

1. Self-management: Self-directed learners are able to identify what they need during the learning process, to set learning goals, to control their energy and time during learning, and to arrange work feedbacks.
2. Desire to learn: Such individuals have a strong motivation for acquiring knowledge.
3. Self-control: Self-directed learners are completely independent people who can analyze, plan, implement, and assess their leering activities independently.

Even though the SDLRSNE measure is still fairly new a number of studies have reported good reliability and validity (Newman 2004; Bridges et al. 2007; Smedley 2007; Torabi et al. 2013).

From the original SDLRSNE scale, 15 statements of the original 40 were selected to be included based on the pilot testing of the student survey. These items were measured using the same 7-point scale described earlier (Cronbach's alpha .83 or higher). The survey included a section in which respondents were invited to add comments they wished to make regarding the survey or the use of mobile technology in education.

Therefore this study will test the following two hypotheses:

- H4: Students with higher levels of desire for learning, self-control and self-management will more likely to see mobile learning as being useful.
- H5: Students with higher levels of desire for learning, self-control and self-management will be more likely to adopt mobile learning.

6 Results

Structural equation modelling was used to analyse the influence that self-directedness had on perceived ease of use, perceived usefulness and behaviour intention. Figure 2 shows all the significant standardised path coefficients for the student model. As recommended by Hooper et al. (2008), the goodness of fit statistics for the student model shows in general good fit (Table 1).

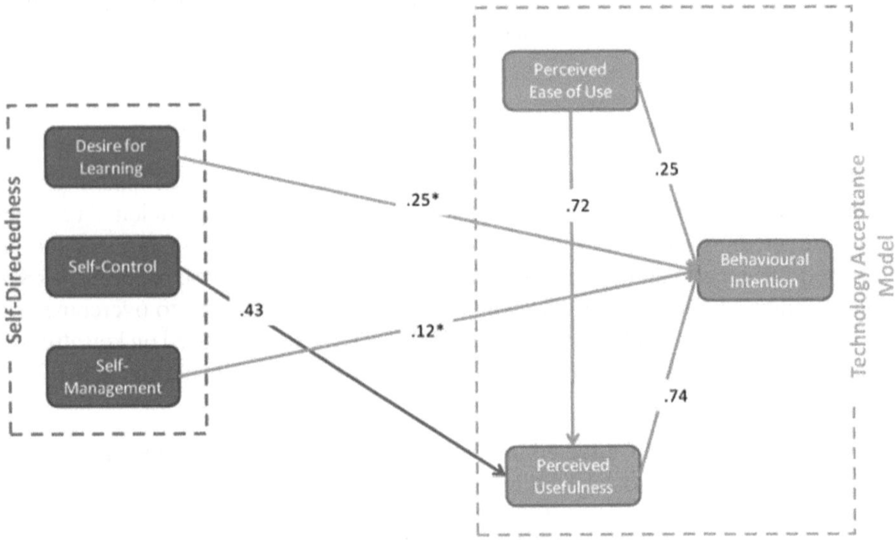

Fig. 2. Results of SEM for students Note: All paths that were significant at P < .000 unless indicated with a * where p > *.01*

Table 1. Model fit indices

	χ^2	χ^2/df	SRMR	NFI	CFI	PCFI	RMSEA
Recommended value		<3	<.08	>.90	>.90	>.50	<.10
Student Model	450.157	2.52	.07	.90	.94	.80	.06

This paper set out to examine the influence of self-directedness on the adoption of mobile learning. The results show that desire for learning (H5a), self-management (H5c), perceived ease of use (H2) and usefulness (H3) directly impacted the intention to adopt. Self-control (H4b) and perceived ease of use (H1) influenced the perceived usefulness of mobile learning.

7 Discussion

Students' self-directedness plays a major role in the adoption of mobile learning. Two of the dimensions of self-directedness, students' desire for learning and the ability for self-management, had a direct impact on student adoption. However, the need for control over their learning was not directly related to an intention to adopt, but was related to the perceived usefulness of mobile learning.

Student comments demonstrated their self-directedness in the adoption of mobile learning. A number of them were using mobile technology for learning without direction from educators, and many of these were keen to extend their usage further. For example one student stated that he could not wait to access learning on his iPad and iPhone, but also wished he could have a custom built application that would allow him to use his Learning Management System (LMS) more effectively. Another student wrote about how she had already tried to get connected to her LMS and how her learning would benefit if she was given access:

> *[Mobile learning is an] excellent idea. Coincidentally I sent an e-mail a few days [ago] asking about how [I] could I have access to Stream with my PDA/phone, as I tried and it doesn't work. Unfortunately, I didn't receive an adequate answer, I believe I was misunderstood. I work full time in rural areas, and to be able to access Stream on my phone would be wonderful and very convenient. I do carry with me (PDA SD card) the readings and study guide etc., but that is just not enough [S56].*

A small number of studies have examined the link between the self-management dimension of self directedness and mobile learning adoption. Wang et al. (2009) established that an individual who is highly autonomous would be more likely to use mobile learning than an individual who was less autonomous. However, later studies by Lowenthal (2010) and Donaldson (2011) found no relationship between self-management and behavioural intention to adopt mobile learning. Lowenthal's work, although based on Wang et al. (2009), used a relatively small sample (n = 113) compared to Wang et al. (2009) study (n = 330) and conducted the study in a different country (US rather than Taiwan). Lowenthal (2010) provided no explanation for his findings. Donaldson (2011) argued that operationalising self-directedness as the single dimension of self-management was the cause of the no finding in Lowenthal (2010) study.

There have been no empirical studies assessing the direct effects of self-control on the adoption of mobile learning. Self-control relates to the need of the student to have control over their learning. Students that have a need for self-control, but feel that they have no control over the learning process are more likely to disengage (Regan 2005). These learners are more likely to feel in control when they can be involved in determining their learning goals and activities (Ponton and Carr 2000). Several studies have asserted that mobile learning enables students to take greater control over their own learning. For example Ryu et al. (2010) explained that mobile learning supports learner collaboration and through this, students are able to expand and develop their own learning. They claimed that mobile learning can encouraged playful, exploratory behaviours that enable learners to experience a feeling of control over the whole learning activity with the result was that they were motivated to work on tasks for longer and be less distracted. Further to this, Zeng and Luyegu (2011) argued that user mobility made students more likely seek out (pulled) their own learning rather than learning necessarily being pushed onto the learner. They concluded that the ability of the learners to control their own learning processes and outcomes were important factors in their use of mobile technology. However, neither of these, nor other studies have tested these claims. This study provides early empirical evidence of the relationship between self-control and the perceived usefulness of mobile learning and suggests that higher self-control will positively influence the perception of usefulness of mobile learning. Students who feel that they want to control their own learning will see mobile learning as a good opportunity to do this; the mobility enables students to dictate when and where the learning takes place and what learning will be covered.

As explored by Hedman and Gimpel (2010), an individual's desire to learn and explore new things will often drive adoption of new technology. Mobile devices in particular offer a novelty value that stimulates an interest and curiosity to learn about the new technology. In this study, desire for learning had a strong influence on mobile learning adoption. Students with a strong desire for learning saw mobile learning as useful and indicated a strong intention to adopt mobile learning. Desire for learning as characterised by Fisher et al. (2001; Fisher and King 2010) has not be investigated before in terms of adoption of mobile learning. These findings provide strong evidence that students desire to learn will drive adoption of mobile learning.

8 Implications, Conclusions and Future Research

This study has reinforced the hypothesis that learners that wish to mange and control their learning are more likely to positively perceive mobile learning. With mobile technology learners can choose when, where and how often what they wish to learn. Mobile learning provides the expectations that learners will take more initiative in their own learning. Innovations that are enhanced by mobile learning, such as flipped learning and social media have highlighted the value of self-directed learning in education and highlighted the need for traditional classroom teaching needs to change and evolve. Mobile learning provides educators with a way to differentiate learning, change the role of learners and teacher in the classroom, alter the time/place of learning, and revolutionise traditional learning (Fischer and Scharff 2010).

The recommendation for both educators and researchers is to develop mobile learning activities that give students progressively more opportunities to manage their own learning. This should include tools which they can elect to use when and where they want. Tools that specifically help them to self-manage or control their own learning, when integrated into learning activities on mobile, will foster self directedness. Students that are highly motivated to learn will always seek new ways to learn. However students need to be made aware of how mobile learning can better support their learning if they are to be encouraged to adopt. Mobile learning can offer greater autonomy for the student, but it can also help to build such autonomy (Liu and Li 2009; Stone 2004). To use mobile technology students have to make a series of decisions about why, what and when to access learning content – decisions normally made by educators. Students may not even be aware of the process but by engaging in this activity they are self-managing. The more they use their mobile, the greater the responsibility they are taking for their learning. Several studies have looked at mobile technology activities that support self-directed learning (for example, Ebner et al. 2010, Lan and Sie 2010, Lawlor and Donnelly 2010; Lazzari 2009).

Overall, the study found evidence that desire for learning, self-control and self-management were associated with higher perceptions of the usefulness of mobile learning and their intention to adopt. This study brings clarity to the conflicting findings from studies on self-directedness. The overarching goal of this study was to contribute to the limited understanding of mobile learning adoption in tertiary education and create a clearer picture of factors that influence student adoption. The findings from this study suggest the importance of scaffolding student learning with mobile devices rather than expecting students to be sufficiently self-directed.

The intention to adopt mobile learning is determined by a complex set of interrelated motivational, perceptual and belief factors. This study aimed to establish some of the groundwork for further understanding the influences on the adoption of mobile learning. Support was found for some of the previous small-scale work done on mobile learning and new findings were also made. However, this was a cross-sectional study and longitudinal research is needed to establish the causality of relationships identified more firmly. In addition, the study itself was based on the Technology Adoption Model (TAM). The technology adoption model starts by from the position that people are already using the particular technology and then predicts future use. This study did not assume that participants had any experience of mobile learning but relied on users' experience with mobile technology generally. Participants were expected to project their understanding of mobile technology to the use of that technology for learning. This approach of developing a mobile learning adoption model based on limited experience is not new and a number of studies have used this same approach (Akour, 2009; Theng, 2009). In addition, future usage was calculated from a stated intention to adopt. Extensive empirical research has confirmed the causal link between intention to adopt and actual future adoption therefore giving some credence to using behavioural intention as an indicator of actual future adoption (Dillon 2001; Venkatesh 2000).

In summary, while this study is not without limitations, the methods adopted resulted in significant findings in an area that is new and emerging with little empirical research. Overall, even considering the limitation, these findings add significant value to our understanding of mobile learning adoption. Future research will focus on how this insight into the factors that will influence adoption of mobile learning will impact on how mobile learning is structured and scaffold so that learners are comfortable to succeed in an environment may be more self- directed and determined. In addition, future research will focus on how educators can be supported to implement this type of instruction.

References

Akour, H.: Determinants of mobile learning acceptance: an empirical investigation in higher education Doctoral dissertation. Retrieved from ProQuest Dissertations & Theses database (2009). (UMI No. AAT 3408682)

Blaschke, L.M.: Heutagogy and lifelong learning: a review of heutagogical practice and self-determined learning. Int. Rev. Res. Open Distrib. Learn. **13**(1), 56–71 (2012)

Bridges, P., Bierema, L., Valentine, T.: The propensity to adopt evidence-based practice among physical therapists. BMC Health Serv. Res. **7**(1), 103 (2007). doi:10.1186/1472-6963-7-103

Canning, N., Callan, S.: Heutagogy: Spirals of reflection to empower learners in higher education. Reflect. Pract. **11**(1), 71–82 (2010)

Davis, F.D.: Perceived usefulness, perceived ease of use, and user acceptance of information technology. MIS Q. **13**(3), 319–339 (1989)

Davis, F.D., Bagozzi, R.P., Warshaw, P.R.: Extrinsic and intrinsic motivation to use computers in the workplace. J. Appl. Soc. Psychol. **22**(14), 1111–1132 (1992). doi:10.1111/j.1559-1816.1992.tb00945.x

Deepwella, F., Malikb, S.: On campus, but out of class: an investigation into students' experiences of learning technologies in their self-directed study. ALTJ, Res. Learn. Technol. **16**(1), 5–14 (2008). http://repository.alt.ac.uk/749/

Dillon, A.: User acceptance of information technology. In: Karwowski, W. (ed.) Encyclopedia of Human Factors and Ergonomics. Taylor and Francis, London (2001)

Donaldson, R.L.: Student acceptance of mobile learning. Unpublished doctoral dissertation. Florida State University, USA (2011). http://www.rdonaldson.com/wpcontent/uploads/2011/05/Donaldson_R_Dissertation_2011.pdf

Ebner, M., Lienhardt, C., Rohs, M., Meyer, I.: Microblogs in higher education: a chance to facilitate informal and process-oriented learning? Comput. Educ. **55**(1), 92–100 (2010). doi:10.1016/j.compedu.2009.12.006

Fisher, M.J., King, J.: The self-directed learning readiness scale for nursing education revisited: A confirmatory factor analysis. Nurs. Educ. Today **30**(1), 44–48 (2010). doi:10.1016/j.nedt.2009.05.020

Fisher, M., King, J., Tague, G.: Development of a self-directed learning readiness scale for nursing education. Nurs. Educ. Today **21**(7), 516–525 (2001). doi:10.1054/nedt.2001.0589

Fischer, G., Scharff, E.: Learning technologies in support of self-directed learning. J. Interact. Media Educ. vol. 1998(2), Article 4 (2010)

Hackbarth, G., Grover, V., Yi, M.Y.: Computer playfulness and anxiety: positive and negative mediators of the system experience effect on perceived ease of use. Inf. Manage. **40**(3), 221–232 (2003). doi:10.1016/S0378-7206(02)00006-X

Hedman, J., Gimpel, G.: The adoption of hyped technologies: a qualitative study. Inf. Technol. Manage. **11**(4), 161–175 (2010). doi:10.1007/s10799-010-0075-0

Hooper, D., Couglan, J., Mullen, M.R.: Structural equation modelling: guidelines for determining model fit. Electron. J. Bus. Res. Methods **6**(1), 53–60 (2008). http://arrow.dit.ie/libart/4

Kenyon, C., Hase, S.: Moving from andragogy to heutagogy in vocational education (2001). http://www.avetra.org.au/abstracts_and_papers_2001/Hase-Kenyon_full.pdf

Lan, Y.-F., Sie, Y.-S.: Using RSS to support mobile learning based on media richness theory. Comput. Educ. **55**(2), 723–732 (2010). doi:10.1016/j.compedu.2010.03.005

Lawlor, B., Donnelly, R.: Using podcasts to support communication skills development: a case study for content format preferences among postgraduate research students. Comput. Educ. **54**(4), 962–971 (2010). doi:10.1016/j.compedu.2009.09.031

Lazzari, M.: Creative use of podcasting in higher education and its effect on competitive agency. Comput. Educ. **52**(1), 27–34 (2009). doi:10.1016/j.compedu.2008.06.002

Liu, Y., Li, H.: What drives m-learning success? drawing insights from selfdirected learning theory. In: Pacific Asia Conference on Information Systems (PACIS 2009), India July 2009

Lowenthal, J.N.: Using mobile learning: determinates impacting behavioural intention. Am. J. Distance Educ. **24**(4), 195–206 (2010). doi:10.1080/08923647.2010.519947

Luckin, R., Clark, W., Garnett, F., Whitworth, A., Akass, J., Cook, J., Robertson, J.: Learner-Generated Contexts: A Framework to Support the Effective Use of Technology for Learning. In: Lee, M., McLoughlin, C. (eds.) Web 2.0-Based E-Learning: Applying Social Informatics for Tertiary Teaching, pp. 70–84. IGI Global, Hershey (2010)

Merriam, S.B.: Andragogy and self-directed learning: Pillars of adult learning theory. New Dir. Adult Contin. Educ. **2001**(89), 3–14 (2001)

Newman, M.: Problem based learning: An exploration of the method and evaluation of its effectiveness in a continuing nursing education programme Project on the Effectiveness of Problem Based Learning (PEPBL) Research Report. Middlesex University, Middlesex, UK (2004)

Nunnally, J.C., Bernstein, I.H.: Psychometric Theory, 3rd edn. McGraw-Hill, New York (1994)

Pallant, J.: SPSS survival manual: a step by step guide to data analysis using SPSS for Windows, 3rd edn. Allen & Unwin, Crows Nest, Australia (2007)

Penman, M.: Do we have what it takes? An investigation into New Zealand occupational therapists' readiness to be self-directed learners Doctoral dissertation, University of Otago (2014)

Ponton, M.K., Carr, P.B.: Understanding and promoting autonomy in selfdirected learning. Current Research Social Psychology **5**(19), 271–284 (2000). http://www.uiowa.edu/~grpproc/crisp/crisp.5.19.htm

Regan, J.-A.: Facilitating students towards self-directed learning. In: Hartley, P., Woods, A., Pill, M. (eds.) Enhancing teaching in higher education: new approaches for improving student learning, pp. 93–108. Routledge, Abingdon (2005)

Ryu, H., Cui, J., Parsons, D.: Raising the bar of challenge with collaboration: social flow in mobile learning. In: 9th World Conference on Mobile and Contextual Learning (m-Learn 2010), Valetta, Malta, October 2010

Saadé, R., Kira, D.: Mediating the impact of technology usage on perceived ease of use by anxiety. Comput. Educ. **49**(4), 1189–1204 (2007)

Sha, L., Looi, C.-K., Chen, W., Zhang, B.H.: Understanding mobile learning from the perspective of self-regulated learning. J. Comput. Assist. Learn. **28**(4), 366–378 (2012). doi:10.1111/j.1365-2729.2011.00461.x

Smedley, A.: The self-directed learning readiness of first year bachelor of nursing students. J. Res. Nurs. **12**, 373–385 (2007). doi:10.1177/1744987107077532

Stone, A. (Ed.): Designing scalable, effective mobile learning for multiple technologies: Learning and Skills Development Agency (2004)

Straub, E.T.: Understanding technology adoption: theory and future directions for informal learning. Rev. Educ. Res. **79**(2), 625–649 (2009). doi:10.3102/0034654308325896

Theng, Y.-L.: Mobile learning for tertiary students: an exploratory study of acceptance of use. In: World Conference on Educational Multimedia, Hypermedia and Telecommunications 2009, Honolulu, HI, USA, June 2009. http://www.editlib.org/p/31606

Torabi, N., Abdollahi, B., Aslani, G., Bahrami, A.: A validation of a self-directed learning readiness scale among preliminary schoolteachers in Esfahan. Procedia-Soc. Behav. Sci. **83**, 995–999 (2013)

Venkatesh, V.: Determinants of perceived ease of use: Integrating control, intrinsic motivation, and emotion into the technology acceptance model. Inf. Syst. Res. **11**, 342–365 (2000). doi:10.1287/isre.11.4.342.11872

Venkatesh, V., Davis, F.D.: A model of the antecedents of perceived ease of use: development and test. Decis. Sci. **27**(3), 451–481 (1996). doi:10.1111/j.1540-5915.1996.tb00860.x

Venkatesh, V., Morris, M.G., Davis, G.B., Davis, F.D.: User acceptance of information technology: Toward a unified view. MIS Q. **27**(3), 425–478 (2003). doi:10.2190/EC.40.1.d

Zeng, R., Luyegu, E.: Mobile learning in higher education. In: Olofsson, A.D., Lindberg, J.O. (Eds.) Informed Design of Educational Technologies in Higher Education: Enhanced Learning and Teaching, pp. 292–306. IGI Global (2011)

Wang, Y.S., Wu, M.C., Wang, H.Y.: Investigating the determinants and age and gender differences in the acceptance of mobile learning. Br. J. Educ. Technol. **40**(1), 92–118 (2009)

Learning with Wearable Technologies: A Case of Google Glass

Daniyar Sapargaliyev(✉)

Almaty Management University, Almaty, Kazakhstan
dsapargalieff@gmai.com

Abstract. The purpose of this study is to determine how wearable are used in education. Different types of wearable technologies, such as smart watches, fitness trackers, smart glasses, HoloLens or even smart clothing are gradually changing the structure of global consumer market. These changes inevitably lead to transformation of educational spaces. This paper presents a review of scientific literature for the last three years (2013-2015) in the field of using Google Glass as a teaching and learning tool. We have analysed over thirty papers in reviewed journals, proceedings of conferences and scholarly web sources. In recent years, there has been an increasing amount of literature on the use wearable technologies in education. Wearable devices are used by explorers, librarians and educators at workplaces, university libraries, laboratories and classrooms. Learning with wearables is one of the most widespread trends in medical or especially surgical education. Wearable computers are actively used by library staff and assist to library patrons at universities. Some of the pilot projects in learning with wearables help students to study anatomy, physics and other discipline through application prototypes. Overall, some sources indicate that learning with wearable technologies has big perspectives while other ones show several examples of low efficiency in using wearable technologies in education.

Keywords: Wearable devices · Hands-free learning · Mobile learning · Google glass

1 Introduction

First wearable computers appeared in the early 1960s (Thorp 1998). In the end of 1990s, Steve Mann created the 'EyeTap Digital Eye Glass' that was the one of the first attempts to make a head-mounted display computer (Mann 2012). In 2013, Google started to sell a prototype of 'Google Glass', a new type of wearable technology with an optical head-mounted display. The Glass displays information in a smartphone-like hands-free format (Google 2015). In the next 5 years, the importance of wearable technology will significantly grow up and wearable computers will be used by the college-aged students (Johnson et al. 2015). In recent years, researchers have shown an increased interest in the use of different types of wearable computers, such as watches, brain-computer interfaces, body sensors and even digital tattoos in everyday life (Pedersen, 2013).

There is a growing body of literature that recognises the importance of using wearables in libraries, universities and other public spaces. One of the most popular

T.H. Brown and H.J. van der Merwe (Eds.): mLearn 2015, CCIS 560, pp. 343–350, 2015.
DOI: 10.1007/978-3-319-25684-9_25

wearable devices is Google Glass and several educators studied the best practices of using Google Glass in the classrooms and learning environment (Boykin 2014; Woodside 2015). This wearable computer allows involving students to team-based research projects (Paterson and Glass 2015) and could be used as real-time assistive teaching tool (Kirkham and Greenhalgh 2015). Nevertheless there are some studies of negative impacts of wearables (Norman 2013; Pedersen 2013).

However, much of the research up to now has been descriptive in the use of wearables in educational purposes. One of the main ideas in these studies is how to provide seamless transition from the use of hand-held devices to hands free wearables in the classroom and outdoor (Clark 2013).

The purpose of this paper is to review recent studies into the theoretical and practical use of wearable technologies in libraries, medical faculties and universities.

2 Method and Limitations

The method consisted of searching the relevant terms 'wearable technology (or technologies)' and 'Google Glass' in education, learning and teaching. We have used the numerous databases of peer-reviewed literature: such as ISI Web of Science, Scopus, IEEE Xplore, SpringerLink and EdITLib. The aim of our study was to find and analyse related academic literature in the field of the use wearable technologies in education. The main focus of the search was devoted to the use Google Glass as a teaching and learning tool. We considered the conference papers, reviews, reports, web-documents, magazines and journal articles written in English language in the period from January 2013 to July 2015. In most cases, the findings and materials were based on description of pilots and experiences in United States' universities. Due to practical constraints, this paper cannot provide a comprehensive review of the use of wearable computers in education.

3 Google Glass in Library Spaces

We start our study from the description and analysis the pilot projects in public and universities libraries. These organisations were one of the first participants of the Google Glass Explorer Programme (Google 2015) and they received technical possibilities to test a new type of wearable devices at learning spaces.

Today libraries remain the important educational sites with providing physical and digital access to information. But the fast development of information technologies reshapes these public buildings into virtual spaces. The use of wearable devices can crucially help library staff to attract new generation of readers. Emerging technologies allow presenting librarian interaction in different formats. For example, the workers of Arapahoe public library (Colorado, USA) used Google Glass as a new tool to access educational information. Locals and their kids started to visit the library for testing wearable devices and suggested the ways how to use these tools in the library spaces (Asgarian 2014).

The different situation is in university libraries. Evidently, there are many students and professors that visit university libraries every day and spend many hours for searching information at these spaces. Many university libraries invest in new technologies and try to improve digital access to learning materials (Table 1).

Table 1. Glassware apps for libraries.

Glassware	Aim	Library	Author
MyGlass app	Records debates from the first-person perspective to examine speech techniques	Claremont University Library	(Thomas 2014)
Scan and Deliver app	Allows library staff to fulfill patron scanning requests directly from the library stacks	Yale University Library	(Patrick 2014)
ShelvAR app	Identifies shelf reading and inventory management	Miami University Library	(Hawkins 2014)

For example, Miami University Library started to use Google Glass for shelf reading and inventory management. The special Glassware application "ShelvAR" frees the readers from the necessity of holding the mobile phone up to the books. Meanwhile the librarians complained of a difficult work on closed networks with this wearable device and also there was a lot of not secure data passing through Glass (Hawkins 2014).

Access services staff of the Yale University library developed special Google Glass application called "first-person scanner" which allows librarians to fulfill patron scanning requests directly from the library stacks (Patrick 2014).

The students of the Claremont University tried to create several Glassware apps for enhancing learning and providing different ways of accessing information. New applications allow examining speech techniques and tracking eye patterns in public speaking from the first-person perspective (Thomas 2014).

Together these examples provide important insights into using Google Glass and other wearables in the nearest future. How many university's libraries across the globe will demonstrate the possibilities of emerging technology for readers and visitors. Probably, the results of pilot projects are still not enough scalable for further implementations.

4 Wearables in Teaching and Learning

The first serious discussions and analyses in the use of wearable technologies in teaching and learning emerged during the last three years (2013-2015). Some studies have examined the relationship between mobile learning and the use of emerging technologies (including big data and wearables) in higher education. For example, Bower and Sturman (2015) investigated educational affordances of wearable technologies in teaching and presented wearables as a new generation of mobile learning tools. In another study, Llorente and Morant (2014) reported that modern wearable computers allow students and professors to communicate with big data resources in higher education environments.

There have been a number of pilot studies involving wearables for efficiency and effectiveness of using Google Glass in learning environment (Coffman and Klinger 2015). For example, Knight *et al.* (2015) reported that the use of Google Glass as a teaching tool can replace existing equipment and help to broadcast learning information onto mobile devices of the students. Also the Glass allows teacher to share information in various modes of interaction including flipped classroom (Parslow, 2014). Salamin (2014) describes the method of the use Google Glass to enrich printed books and strengthen students' motivation for learning by intertwining wearables and traditional textbooks.

Burke (2014) argues that one of the important features of Google Glass is to present text based translations in real time. This wearable computer can be helpful in mobile-assisted (or wearable-assisted) language learning and students would have the benefits of real time decoding in different languages.

All of the studies reviewed here support the idea that Google Glass can be successfully used in several educational directions – mobile learning, flipped classroom, mobile-assisted language learning and even the use of big data. But we want to consider practical examples of the use Glassware apps in possible learning situations. There are three Glassware prototype applications presented on Table 2, which allow using its in different educational goals.

Table 2. Glassware applications for teaching and learning.

Glassware	Aim	Authors
gPhysics App	'To perform an educational physical experiment in the area of acoustics'.	Weppner *et al.* (2014)
Glass Personal Inquiry Manager (GPIM App)	'To support the learning- and inquiry-process just in time and in an unobtrusive way'.	Suarez *et al.* (2014)
Glassist App	'To allow teachers to create individual portfolios for students, manage their information and share it with peers'.	Silva *et al.* (2014)

In their application prototype 'gPhysics App', Weppner *et al.* (2014) presented the tool for finding relationship between the frequency of the sound generated by hitting a water glass and the amount of water. The other researchers, Suarez *et al.* (2014) introduced the design and functionalities of a prototype for Inquiry-based learning (IBL) providing a more seamless learning experience. And the last example, Silva *et al.* (2014) demonstrated 'Glassist App' for helping teachers' management tasks. This tool can recognise students face and display relevant information about them.

Contrary to expectations, this study did not find a significant difference between the Glassware applications, because firstly all presented apps are still on testing stage and secondly these prototypes were realised in the local spaces without wide introduction.

5 Google Glass in Medical Education

In recent years, there has been an increasing amount of literature on using wearable technologies in medical education. The generalisability of much published research on this issue is problematic. The most of the studies were conducted only in one country with limited amounts of participants. The medical faculties and schools of the United States' universities started to use wearables in early 2013 and almost all these pilot projects were involved in Google Glass Explorer Programme. Meanwhile, there were some enthusiastic expectations of the revolutionary changing in medical education, but later the limitations of spreading the device required a pragmatic assessment in its use. Nevertheless the first use of Google Glass and other wearable devices in medical education slightly changed the vision of healthcare and shortened distance between the patient and caregiver (Nosta 2013). Today, there are three main directions in medical education that can be identified for successfully use Google Glass as a teaching and learning tool. We tried to describe how to use wearable devices for studying different disciplines such as surgery, cardiology and anatomy.

5.1 Surgical Education

There is a small volume of published studies describing the role of wearable devices in surgical education. But the study by Bola and Brighton (2015) offers probably the most comprehensive analysis of using Google Glass as a surgical training tool. The authors defined the three main ways of using the Glass for surgical practice:

1. Tool for self assessment.
2. Evidence for annual review of competence progress.
3. Consultant support (video conferencing to other consultants at different sites in cases of unusual anatomy or difficult cases).

Moreover, the Glass can help medical students to efficiently learn in difficult practical situations. For example, when emergency cases where a senior is not available, this wearable device provides communication between the junior and senior surgeon in real- time.

In the same vein, Ponce *et al.* (2014) in their study mention the usefulness of combining real-time augmented reality and wearable computing devices in the field of surgery. The authors described one of the first surgical cases adopting the combination of real-time augmented reality and the Google Glass. The surgical procedure was integrated with the virtual interactive presence and augmented reality system through Google Glass. This combination allowed the local surgeon to interact with the remote surgeon within the local surgical field.

5.2 Cardiology Teaching

One of the first studies in the use of wearable technology to improve cardiology learning was carried out by Vallurupalli *et al.* (2013). The authors explored different educational levels in cardiovascular practice for medical trainees. In this investigation, live streaming video demonstrated several practical actions in cardiology via Google Glass. Medical students received and saved learning information on their mobile devices.

The practice of remote and real-time mentorship relationships between students and experienced experts was described in a pilot study by Russell *et al.* (2014). The authors attempted to use Google Glass for telementoring of cardiac ultrasonography. In this study, medical students were able to obtain adequate imaging through Google Glass to determine a healthy patient's ejection fraction. These students received real-time telementored consultations through Google Glass via Google Hangout from a remotely located expert.

5.3 Studying Anatomy

A small but growing body of literature attempts to describe the use of the wearables in learning of anatomy. These studies discuss the recent experiences in using Google Glass for teaching of anatomy in medical schools. For example, Benninger (2015) demonstrated the method that melds traditional medical palpation with Google Glass in teaching of human anatomy. The Glass has provided access to a live ultrasound image for viewing anatomical plane while examining the patient. Ciomek et al. (2015) performed a similar study of using the Glass for clinical and educational value within anatomic pathology. The analysis of surgical specimens in pathology requires high quality photographic and video records. Video and photo fixation of the intact and fresh specimens at the time of initial dissection helps students to avoid potential errors in diagnosis and reporting.

The other successful example of using wearable devices for video recording was presented by Tully *et al.* (2015). In this study, medical students have used the Google Glass to record their first-person perspective for the further analysis and evaluation of their interpersonal communication skills and nonverbal behaviors with the patients.

The studies presented thus far provide evidence that the Glass is considered by the researchers as a tool for transmitting of live video for different practical situations and medical procedures. But sometimes Google Glass helps to improve communication between students and experienced practitioner and allows working in groups. Current stage in development of wearable technologies does not detect any evidence for widely usage the Glass and other devices in global aspect, but we expect that in the next five years the situation will change radically.

6 Conclusion

The main goal of the current study was to determine how wearable technologies are used in education. One of the more significant findings to emerge from this study is that wearables have a big potential for development and attractive opportunities for student and educators. We think that there will be very promising pilot projects on using wearable technologies in libraries. These spaces have much informal approach to learning with less technical (closed network, software incompatibility) and ethics (cyber security, privacy and face recognition) restrictions. Sometimes the use of Google Glass for teaching are considered by the researchers only in the classrooms, but the main potential of the wearables can be effectively used in outdoor spaces. Google Glass is one of the best tools for streaming live video, but with very short battery life. These problems will be solved in the next years and teacher should be ready to easy use wearables in their everyday practice.

We hope that the results of this study complement those of earlier studies. The most of them were based on suggestions and recommendations without significant practical findings. Robust and ubiquitous spread of mobile technologies and fast growth of wearables will lead to transition from handheld to hands-free approaches in learning and teaching in the nearest future. Further research could also be conducted to determine the effectiveness of the use wearable computers in outdoor and workplace learning. A future study needs to examine more closely the links between mature mobile learning projects and new pilots in learning with wearables.

References

Asgarian, R.: Arapahoe library invests in Google Glass. Libr. J. **139**(1), 16–18 (2014)

Benninger, B.: Google Glass, ultrasound and palpation: the anatomy teacher of the future? Clin. Anat. **28**(2), 152–155 (2015)

Bola, S., Brighton, G.: Can Google Glass be a surgical training tool? Br. J. Surg. **102**(5), 1–18 (2015)

Boykin, E.: Google Glass in the Class: Wearable Technology of the Educational Future (2014). https://dukedigitalinitiative.duke.edu/google-glass-in-the-class-wearable-technology-of-the-educational-future/. Accessed 25 July 2014

Bower, M., Sturman, D.: What are the educational affordances of wearable technologies?. Comput. Edu. **88**, 343–353 (2015)

Burke, M.: 5 ways Google Glass can be used in education (2014). http://www.emergingedtech.com/2013/04/5-ways-google-glass-can-be-used-in-education/. Accessed 25 July 2014

Ciomek, N., Zhu, H., Cordon-Cardo, C.: Diagnostic and educational uses of google glass in anatomic pathology. Lab. Invest. **95**(1), 395A–395A (2015)

Clark, D.: Google Glass: 7 amazing uses in learning (2013). http://donaldclarkplanb.blogspot.com/search?q=Google+Glass. Accessed 11 December 2013

Coffman, T., Klinger, M.: Google glass: using wearable technologies to enhance teaching and learning. In: Slykhuis, D., Marks, G., (eds.) Proceedings of Society for Information Technology & Teacher Education International Conference 2015, pp. 1777–1780. (2015)

Google: Google Glass explorer edition (2015). http://www.google.com/glass/start/. Accessed 11 July 2015

Hawkins, D.: Library services and Google Glass (2014). http://www.libconf.com/2014/04/09/library-services-google-glass/. Accessed 25 July 2014

Johnson, L., Adams Becker, S., Estrada, V., Freeman, A.: NMC Horizon Report: 2015 Higher Education Edition. Austin, Texas: The New Media Consortium (2015). http://cdn.nmc.org/media/2015-nmc-horizon-report-HE-EN.pdf. Accessed 19 July 2015

Kirkham, R., Greenhalgh, C.: Social access vs. privacy in wearable computing: a case study of autism. IEEE Pervasive Comput. **14**(1), 26–33 (2015)

Knight, H., Gajendragadkar, P., Bokhari, A.: Wearable technology: using Google Glass as a teaching tool. BMJ case reports (2015)

Llorente, R., Morant, M.: Wearable computers and big data: Interaction paradigms for knowledge building in higher education. In: Peris-Ortiz, M., Garrigós-Simón, F., Pechuán, I.G. (eds.) New Directions in Research, Practice and PolicyInnovation and Teaching Technologies, pp. 127–137. Springer, Switzerland (2014)

Mann, S.: Through the glass Lightly. IEEE Technol. Soc. Mag. **31**(3), 10–14 (2012)

Norman, D.: The paradox of wearable technologies. Technol. Rev. **116**(5), 101–103 (2013)

Nosta, J.: How Google Glass Is changing medical education (2013). http://www.forbes.com/sites/johnnosta/2013/06/27/google-glass-teach-me-medicine-how-glass-is-helping-change-medical-education/. Accessed 29 June 2013

Parslow, G.: Commentary: Google glass: a head-up display to facilitate teaching and learning. Biochem. Mol. Biol. Edu. **42**(1), 91–92 (2014)

Paterson, M., Glass, M.R.: The world through glass: developing novel methods with wearable computing for urban videographic research. J. Geogr. High. Edu. **39**(2), 275–287 (2015)

Patrick, A.: Google Glass available for faculty and student groups during spring Semester (2014). http://www.library.yale.edu/librarynews/2014/01/google_glass_available_for_fac.html. Accessed 25 July 2014

Pedersen, I.: Ready to wear (or not): examining the rhetorical impact of proposed wearable devices. In: Proceedings International Symposium on Technology and Society, pp. 201–202 (2013)

Ponce, B.A., Menendez, M.E., Oladeji, L.O., Fryberger, C.T., Dantuluri, P.K.: Emerging technology in surgical education: combining real-time augmented reality and wearable computing devices. Orthop. **37**(11), 751–757 (2014)

Russell, P., Mallin, M., Youngquist, S., et al.: First "Glass" education: telementored cardiac ultrasonography using Google Glass - a pilot study. Acad. Emerg. Med. **21**(11), 1297–1299 (2014)

Salamin, A.D.: Using Google Glass to enrich printed textbooks in a blended learning environment to meet digital natives' expectations. In: Bastiaens, T., (ed.) Proceedings of E-Learn: World Conference on E-Learning in Corporate, Government, Healthcare, and Higher Education 2014, pp. 1741–1748 (2014)

Silva, M., Freitas, D., Neto, E., Lins, C., Teichrieb, V., Teixeira, J.M.: Glassist: using augmented reality on Google Glass as an aid to classroom management. In: Proceedings - 2014 16th Symposium on Virtual and Augmented Reality, pp. 37–44 (2014)

Suarez, A., Ternier, S., Kalz, M., Specht, M.: GPIM: Google glassware for inquiry-based learning. In: Rensing, C., de Freitas, S., Ley, T., Muñoz-Merino, P.J. (eds.) EC-TEL 2014. LNCS, vol. 8719, pp. 530–533. Springer, Heidelberg (2014)

Thomas, J.: Library to lend Google Glass. the student life (2014). http://tsl.pomona.edu/articles/2014/2/14/news/4709-library-to-lend-google-glass. Accessed 13 July 2014

Thorp, E.O.: The invention of the first wearable computer. In: Proceedings of the 2nd IEEE International Symposium on Wearable Computers, pp. 4–8 (1998)

Tully, J., Dameff, C., Kaib, S., et al.: Recording medical students' encounters with standardized patients using Google Glass: providing end-of-life clinical education. Acad. Med. **90**(3), 314–316 (2015)

Vallurupalli, S., Paydak, H., Agarwal, S.K., Agrawal, M., Assad-Kottner, C.: Wearable technology to improve education and patient outcomes in a cardiology fellowship program - a feasibility study. Health Technol. **3**(4), 267–270 (2013)

Weppner, J., Hirth, M., Lukowicz, P., Kuhn, J.: Physics education with Google Glass gphysics experiment app. In: ACM International Joint Conference on Pervasive and Ubiquitous Computing, pp. 279–282 (2014)

Woodside, J.M.: Wearable technology acceptance model: Google Glass. In: Slykhuis, D., Marks, G., (eds.) Proceedings of Society for Information Technology & Teacher Education International Conference 2015, pp. 1800–1802 (2015)

Difficulties Experienced by Students Using Mobile Devices to Access E-Learning

A Case Study of Undergraduate IT Students in South Africa

Daniel Adeboye and Corné Johandia van Staden(✉)

Faculty of Information Technology, Midrand Graduate Institute,
Halfway House, Midrand 1685, South Africa
danno4krist@gmail.com, cornev@mgi.ac.za

Abstract. This paper reports on a study carried out to identify the challenges experienced by students in their voyage from e-learning to m-Learning. The study focused on identifying which devices (i.e. mobile technology or laptops) students are using to access the e-Learning environment. The type of device used to access the e-Learning environment is imperative as research has indicated that both the users and designers experience challenges in the transition. The move from accessing e-Learning using a laptop to accessing e-Learning from a mobile device such as a tablet, poses a number of challenges for both students and designers of the e-Learning environment. The study was guided by the following research question: What are the difficulties students face when learning takes place using a mobile device?

The research design used an interpretative philosophy, with a deductive approach and case study strategy. A non-probability sampling method was used to select the participants. A total of one hundred and eighteen undergraduate students from the Faculty of Information Technology at the Private Higher Education Institution participated in the study. A semi-structured questionnaire was used as a tool to obtain both quantitative and qualitative data and was analysed. The study results identified difficulties involving technical problems, distractions by applications on the mobile devices and issues of health such as eye constraint.

Suggestions made to solve or reduce these problems are the provision of suitable internet connection to students, provision of alternative forms of academic materials and a general online help-desk forum. Proper implementation of these recommendations will enhance learner satisfaction of students who want to engage and embrace m-Learning.

Keywords: Difficulties and solutions · M-Learning · Mobile technology · South africa

1 Introduction

Learning can generally be classified as either traditional classroom face-to-face learning or virtual or electronic-based learning (Chang and Chang 2012). Virtual learning is also called

T.H. Brown and H.J. van der Merwe (Eds.): mLearn 2015, CCIS 560, pp. 351–365, 2015.
DOI: 10.1007/978-3-319-25684-9_26

e/m-Learning. For the purpose of this study, the authors refer to m-Learning as educational learning which takes place via electronic media, typically on smart mobile devices which include smartphones and tablets. The growth in electronic-based learning can be traced directly to the increased access to information and communications technology (ICT) and the decreased cost of the e-Learning process itself (Naidu 2006). One key property of engaging ICT in learning is the flexibility of access to information and resources. ICT allows learners to have access to a variety of resources and the ability to use these resources anywhere, anytime and at the pace of the learner (Naidu 2006). Teaching with ICT as an enabling technology is an approach to maximize the development of human resources (van Biljon and Dembskey 2011), which is underdeveloped in South Africa according to Jonston, Tufvesson and Johnston (2010). Donner (2004) identified two factors which complicate teaching via ICT: access to information technology is constrained by cost and infrastructure in developing countries, which in turn has a detrimental effect on the education sector (Barker, Krull et al. 2006). To complicate matters further, students in Private Higher Education Institutions are often resource-constrained in terms of finances and academic preparedness when entering higher education in a South African context (Gregson and Jordan). Resource constraints may result in transport-to-campus problems which lead to students not attending classes and students are also faced with the high cost of text books (van Biljon and Dembskey 2011). The adoption of information technology tools in the e-learning environment is also influenced by factors such as infrastructure, perceived usefulness, perceived ease of use and social context (van Biljon and Renaud 2009). Mobile and wireless technology adoption in South Africa is challenging the adoption of information technology tools problems and low adoption rate (Botha and Ford 2008). Van Biljon and Renaud (2009) carried out research on how mobile phones could be used as a saviour technology to address the development of human resources in South Africa. Personalised learning, using mobile technology and tools and the movement from generic e-learning to individual based m-learning, has also become a major topic for discussion among Information Technology professionals.

Despite the flexibility of learning, cost effectiveness and social access that m-Learning affords a typical student in an academic environment (Bates 2005), students have not been able to harness these opportunities to enhance their learning process. This sentiment was supported by Petrides (2002) in his research when he observed that students experience difficulty with their academic learning, once they are not required to sit within the four walls of a conventional classroom and have to do the learning electronically. The researchers assumed that the voyage from e-learn to m-learn would be easy for IT students.

The aim of this research therefore is to explore the difficulties students generally face when using mobile devices as the primary tool for learning in Private Higher Education Institutions (PHEI).

The research is guided by the following questions:

- *What are the difficulties students face when learning material has to be accessed via a mobile device?*
- *How can the identified difficulties be overcome?*

The paper is organised as follows: Sect. 2 provides a discussion on the tools, challenges and the roles and responsibilities of the role players in a virtual learning environment. This is followed by an explanation of the research design in Sect. 3. The results from the survey are presented in Sect. 4. The findings regarding the challenges experienced by students in their voyage from e-learning to m-Learning are presented in Sect. 5.

2 Literature Review

Literature has indicated that there is a close relationship between e-Learning and m-Learning and that the latter cannot be understood without an explanation of the former. The structure of the literature study represents two tiers of the study, namely e-learning and m-learning. In Sect. 2.1 e-learning is discussed, while Sect. 2.2 focuses on literature on m-learning. Section 2.3 then elaborates on the difficulties students face when learning via mobile devices while Sect. 2.4 will look at proffered solutions to challenges student face from literature.

2.1 E-Learning

E-learning may be described as a way to present material to students through the use of technology (van Biljon and Dembskey 2011) and which includes use of the internet to find information as well as using learning management software to manage courses. Horton (2012) in his book offered a simple definition that e-Learning is the use of electronic technologies to create learning experiences. E-learning can comprise of any form of telecommunications and learning that is computer-based (Bates 2005). Cox (2012) referred to e-Learning as technology-enhanced learning and information technology (IT) in teaching and learning. Esgi (2013) while comparing different e-Learning types offered a broader definition of e-learning as "the practice of educational activities via computer or communication activities". Nicolau and Popescu (2013) seem to consider both definitions by defining e-learning as any kind of learning using the computer, the internet and modern technology. It is observed that in all the definitions, e-Learning comprises of making use of computer, communication technologies and the internet for educational purposes. The tools examined in the paper are the Moodle e-learning platform of the PHEI in South Africa and the ebooks the students access through their mobile devices (Samsung Galaxy Note 8). The e-Learning environment does not replace lectures but can be used to provide additional support to those students who need help, for example, when unable to be on campus because of transport problems - as mentioned by van Biljon and Dembskey (2011). The e-learning platform is also used by lecturers to communicate and exchange information with students or conduct quizzes in class. Students can then also use the e-Learning platform to submit assignments. The e-Learning platform allows lecturers to create, teach and manage courses online. The students are able to access the e-Learn platform from different devices be they PCs, laptops or mobile devices such as the tablets issued to students with their textbooks (Samsung Galaxy Note 8).

Some researchers refer to m-Learning as an extension or subset of e-Learning (Crescente and Lee 2012), but Parsons (2014) pointed out in his study that this view does not take into account any of the additional affordances of the mobile device.

2.2 M-Learning

The definition of mobile learning is constantly evolving as technology evolves. Sharples (2006) identified a broad category of current perspectives on mobile learning:

- Technocentric– where mobile learning is viewed as learning using a mobile device.
- The relationship to e-learning– mobile learning is an extension of e-learning. It is a stream of thought that tends to put mobile learning somewhere on e-learning's spectrum of portability (Taxler 2005).
- Augmented formal education – in mobile learning literature, formal education is often seen as face-to-face teaching, although distance education has been in existence for more than 100 years.

Geddes (2004:1) defined m-learning as "the acquisition of any knowledge and skills through the use of mobile technology, anywhere and anytime." The use of mobile learning assists in the reduction of traditional training infrastructure and it facilitates the learning process (Grohmann et al. 2005). Another advantage of mobile learning is that it contributes to improving the accessibility, inter-operability and reusability of educational resources, as well as the flexibility to learn at any convenient time and place (Murphy 2006). Korucu and Alkan (2011) view mobile learning as a type of learning that provides access to e-Learning content independently of specific location, utilisation of services and communication with others. Mobile learning can thus be defined as the type of learning that takes place when the student is not in a specific location but on the move. Learning takes place when the student takes advantage of the learning opportunity.

m-Learning is also about the mobile devices used in the learning experience. According to Brown and Mbati (2015), mobile technology should be regarded as "the enabler and not as the driver of our teaching and learning activities". Brown and Mbati (2015) conclude that the primary purpose of the integration of technology into the teaching and learning environment is to enhance the learning experience. Mobile phones are but one of the mobile devices that can be used for m-learning. Corbeil and Valdes-Corbeil (2007) also include laptops in their definition of mobile devices, while other researchers feel that laptops restrict the 'mobility' of a learner (Taxler 2007). The researchers agree with Brown and Mbati (2015) and Taxler (2007) that a mobile device should be one which is handheld. Mutlu et al. (2005) state that laptops, tablet computers, pocket PCs with phones, pocket PCs, portable media players, MP3 players and smart phones are examples of mobile informatics devices. Hashemi et al. (2011) agreed with Mutlu et al. (2005) and added other examples such as ultramobile PCs, mini notebooks or netbooks, handheld GPS or voting devices and specialised portable technologies used in science labs. Tablet PCs are the newest mobile technologies available. While these are lighter than laptops they are more expensive and are heavier than smart phones but in terms of screen sizes and usage facilities, appear to be more convenient than laptops (Korucu and Alkan 2011). In this study the students accessed the e-learning environment using their tablet PC as a mobile device. All the first year students were given a Samsung Galaxy Note 8 tablet with registration. The textbooks for modules were also loaded on the tablet in epub or ePdf format. Instead of students learning from hard copy textbooks they accessed information from a soft copy textbook on the tablet. 2014 was the first year that the institution made use of electronic textbooks as prescribed learning material. The tablet cost was included in the registration fees.

2.3 Student Difficulties with M-Learning

Sun et al. (2008) in their research discussed some of the critical factors which influence learner satisfaction among m-learning students. They discovered that although most colleges now offer compulsory computer and/or technology courses for high school students, anxiety regarding the use thereof may still exist for certain technology users. To increase user satisfaction, basic computer education and relevant technology training must be given to students. Sun et al. (2008) further observed that the teacher attitude towards the course and the technical expertise of the lecturer will impact the students' attitudes and affect their eventual performances.

Fichten et al. (2009) study focused on students with disabilities. In their study they identified that these students had technical difficulties ranging from the inability to being able to hear audio in online material to being unable to see visual presentations uploaded onto learning sites. Other students mentioned difficulties such as connecting to websites; video clips taking a long time to download; web pages that would not load and problems opening and downloading uploaded files (Fichten et al. 2009). Cheon et al. (2012) assert that students are not likely to use mobile devices for learning because of the limitations of m-learning. These include technical limitations of mobile devices (Haag 2011; Lowenthal 2010) e.g. small screens with low resolution display; memory that is insufficient; slow network connectivity and speed as well as a lack of standardisation and comparability (Cheon et al. 2012). Corbeil and Valdes-Corbeil (2007) identified pedagogical limitations: the use of mobile devices in class may hinder learner concentration and interrupt class progress.

Despite the potential that an m-learning environment has to offer, there are a number of challenges in the adoption thereof. In studies conducted by Attewell (2005) and Attewell and Savill-Smith (2003) students did not demonstrate any preference for future use of m-Learning at the end of their projects. Corbeil and Valdes-Corbeil (2007) further indicated that despite advanced mobile technologies, many students and education programmes are still not ready to adopt an m-Learning strategy. The adoption of ICT tools in e-Learning is influenced by various factors including infrastructure, perceived usefulness, perceived ease of use and social context (van Biljon and Renaud 2009), which makes it difficult to understand which individual factor played a role in the adoption of e-Learning and m-Learning tools.

Brown and Mbati (2015) identified the following challenges that may impede the adoption of an m-Learning strategy:

- Resource-rich m-Learning of rural learners – growth in wireless infrastructure in developing countries does provide mobile connectivity but the bandwidth is still low. A further challenge is the fact that poorer communities cannot afford the more expensive devices.

- Connectivity costs and data costs – due to financial constraints the majority of developing countries do not qualify for, or cannot afford, fixed monthly contracts for voice and data services. The rates of service providers in Africa for data are too expensive for pre-paid clients to afford. This then is counterproductive to m-learning which is driven by access to affordable and reliable connectivity.
- Smart devices ownership– in rural contexts, learners will share smartphones or tablets. While m-learning is reliant upon the ubiquity of the mobile device, the learner ought to have the mobile device with him in order for formal/informal learning to occur within various contexts at various times.
- Digital literacy – the literacy of both learners and educators remains a challenge.
- Content-driven paradigm – an approach to education characterised by curriculation and educational activities which focus on subject content.

Although m-Learning is a model which is designed to meet educational needs and which offers students learning and access opportunities at any given time, there are still challenges which students and educators face in the adoption of m-learning in Higher Education Institutions (HEI).

2.4 Proffered Solutions to M-Learning Difficulties

Literature has indicated some solutions to the difficulties students encounter with m-learning and how these can be overcome. It is thus important to note the impact of the internet on the educational process and how this affects the skills and the roles of students and educators (Crisan and Enachne 2015). Sun et al. (2008) recommended that lecturers themselves must show a great level of enthusiasm towards the course in order to properly motivate students. They further advised that a lecturer must seek to improve his/her technical skills regarding the use of mobile devices and properly engage them for teaching and learning purposes. It was also stated that a proper and well-designed e-learning system that takes mobile devices and interfaces into consideration will result in a high level of performance by students. As stated by a participant, "*the easier a system is to use, the less effort required to carry out a given task.*"

Fichten et al. (2009) recommended that if students received alternate forms of materials, this would solve problems such as videos not playing or PDFs not opening online. Providing technical staff to assist students with technical problems like logins, webpages not loading etc. will also ease the online experience.

3 Research Methodology

Considering the literature review on e-Learning, m-Learning and the challenges students face with m-Learning, the authors identified the following as the main area to be researched: Challenges that students might face in their voyage between e-Learning and m-Learning environments using different mobile devices.

With Sects. 1 and 2 as background, the following questions emerge:

- *What are the difficulties students face when learning material has to be accessed via a mobile device?*
- *How can the identified difficulties be overcome?*

In this section, the researchers will discuss the research aim, research respondents, data collection and data analysis respectively.

3.1 Research Aim

The research is guided by the following objectives:

- To explore the difficulties students face when learning has to be done via a mobile device.
- To explore ways in which the difficulties may be overcome.

3.2 Research Participants

This study used a non-random sampling technique to collect data (Creswell 2012). The participants for this research were undergraduate students from the Faculty of Information Technology at a PHEI in South Africa. The students voluntarily signed up to be research participants. The students use the institution's e-Learning platform, to access their registered module material using laptops or their Samsung Galaxy tablet PC. A limitation to the study is the number of students who participated. The researcher specifically targeted the first year IT students, because the first year textbooks were in an electronic format as opposed to those of the second and third years which were hardcopy textbooks. A total of one hundred and eighteen (118) students responded to the questionnaire out of the hundred and thirty five (135) in total. As shown in Table 1, twenty-six (26) respondents, which accounted for 22 % of the total, were females while ninety-two (92), accounting for 78 %, were males.

Table 1. Gender distribution of participants in the survey

Gender	Frequency	Percentage
Male	92	78 %
Female	26	22 %
Total	118	100 %

3.3 Data Collection

The research used a survey to gather data. The researcher used a customised questionnaire after investigating the use of existing standard surveys. As Frechtling (2002) indicated, cost and time constraints can affect the choice of data collection method while the validity and reliability of the data collection depends on the design and structure of the questionnaire. For validity purposes the questionnaire was given to research experts to evaluate and review questions. Adjustments and revisions were made based on the recommendations prior to full implementation. The questionnaire was designed to examine user's behaviour on the internet and preference of reading and learning in an attempt to find out the difficulties these students face while using their tablet PCs to access their books or module(s) on the e-Learn platform. The survey instrument contained both open-ended and closed questions to gather information from the students in terms of their general demographic information, computer proficiency level and access to mobile devices. The survey allowed the researchers to gather some quantitative data. It was important to capture information regarding the number of students who own and use mobile devices to access the internet. The students had been working with the tablet PC for at least six months before the data was gathered. However, to capture participants' perceptions and feelings towards the use of tablet PC for e-learning, open-ended questions were included. The collected data was then captured in a database which could be used to derive conclusions. The next section will describe how the analysis was carried out.

3.4 Data Analysis

As previously explained, both quantitative and qualitative data were gathered from the questionnaires. It was therefore necessary to do both a quantitative and qualitative analysis. Complete anonymity has been ensured, so that the respondents cannot be identified in the reports. The results cannot be generalised because it will be drawn on the experience of a small purposefully chosen group of people.

Quantitative data collected was analysed and visual summaries were drawn. Qualitative results obtained were grouped into categories and themes and these responses and results were presented to show relationships. The next section describes the results and findings of the analysis performed. Qualitative data was analysed through the following process: summarising, categorising and structuring of data as recommended by Saunders et al. (2009). Overall categories and themes were identified from the responses and results presented to show relationships. Microsoft Excel was used for data analysis and different visual summaries were drawn.

4 Research Findings

This section discusses the results obtained from the analysed data and the critical findings.

4.1 Results

The results indicated the following:

- More than 80 % of the respondents consider themselves proficient with the use of computers.
  - Very proficient – 47 (40 %)
  - More than average – 56 (47 %)

- Less than average – 13 (11 %)
- Not proficient – 2 (2 %)

- Students frequently browse academic sites and study downloaded academic materials from their mobile devices. The interesting discovery by the researchers here was the fact that students do in fact go to online academic sites to study and also to download materials for offline study. The chart below further explains the results on the frequency of students' interaction with these two activities on any mobile device in three months as shown in Fig. 1.

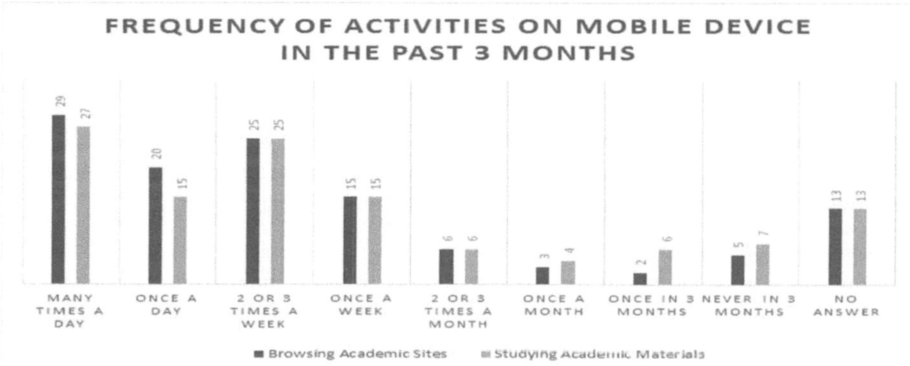

Fig. 1. Frequency of activities of students on mobile device in the past three months

- Figure 2 shows visually the number of participants that have participated in various forms of e/m-learning, like massive open online courses (MOOC), reading of e-books, participating in online academic sites and learning via video lectures and tutorials. It can be observed that MOOCs are the least participated-in form of e-learning while video lectures and tutorials are the most participated-in form of e-learning by the participants.

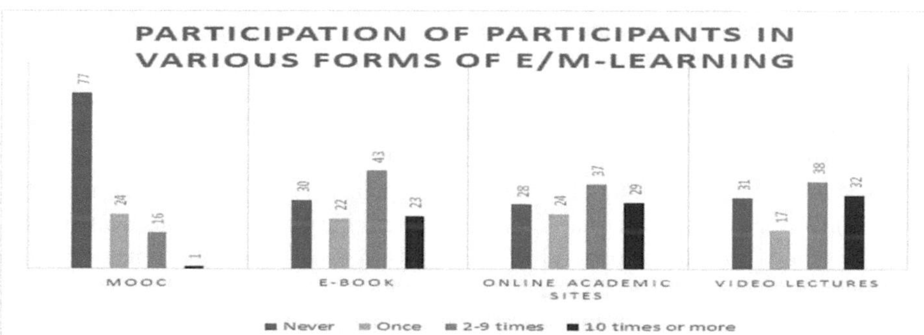

Fig. 2. Participation of participants in various forms of learning

- Preferences of students with the use of electronic tools
  - 91 (77 %) prefer to read printed materials while 27 (23 %) prefer to read materials via a mobile device.
  - 107 (91 %) prefer to learn in a face-to-face classroom environment while 11 (9 %) prefer to learn via electronic means.
  - 50 (42 %) prefer to submit an assignment by hand to the lecturer, 31 (26 %) prefer to submit it as an e-mail attachment while 37 (31 %) prefer to submit an assignment via the school e-portal.

The next section will discuss these results and show general themes from the qualitative aspect of this study.

4.2 Discussion

Three distinct themes emerged from the results: preference of students, difficulties of students and possible solutions to the difficulties. The next section will discuss each of these themes in more detail in order to answer the main research question.

- *Preference of Students*
  From the results shown above, the researchers found it interesting that despite the perceived eagerness of students to visit online academic sites and download academic materials, students still prefer printed coursework and learning without those devices. Students' prefer the non-electronic presentation of material than electronic with regard to reading and learning. This showed the students were experiencing some difficulties as demonstrated in detail below.
- *Difficulties of Students*
  From the results of the open-ended aspect of the questionnaire, findings were used to establish patterns using correlations and identification of relationships. Participants described various difficulties they encounter when having to interact academically in a mobile environment.
  - Technical problems

  One of the most prevalent difficulties mentioned by participants in the research related to technical issues. This finding was not surprising to the researchers as difficulties related to technical issues are common in any electronic environment, whether e-learning or m-learning (Haag 2011; Lowenthal 2010). In this research, sixty-four (64) participants (which accounts for 54 % of the total population) assert this difficulty. Electronic mobile devices such as smartphones, tablets, kindles and even laptops all make use of batteries; students complained that these devices usually run out of power and could thus affect reading or assimilation - a point also identified by Hashemi et al. (2011). As one participant stated, "…these electronic based materials switch off at random times [due to low battery] and this tends to make you lazy at times." Another participant mentioned that: "Since all my textbooks are electronic, I have to go about with my charger because of the battery of my tablet." The lack of battery power is an issue which has been mentioned before in literature and it is still a problem that could affect students' learning experience.

  There were several problems relating to a lack of, or poor, internet connection available for use. In the mobile learning environment, access to the internet is critical and

"...a lack of stable and fast internet can suck" as one participant stated. This in turn affects access to webpages, course materials and videos that require internet connection. A participant also commented that "...these things take so long to load, and I get tired waiting most of the time." Another participant said the slow internet made it difficult for her to access her textbooks and submit assignments at the right time.

– Not easy to use

About 31 % of the participants in this research (36 participants) complained about the difficulty they found in using the devices and learning systems to maximize their learning experience. Van Biljon and Renaud (2009) also identified students' perception of ease of use as a challenge. As one participant expressed, "I don't know how to use the tablet, I have to always look for someone who knows how to use it before I can learn with it." This appears to be a major challenge because for non-IT students, learning to use the tablet would require mastering an additional skill. However, in this survey the participants were in fact IT students and thus the comment came as a surprise to the researchers, contradicting the hypothesis that the voyage from e-learn to m-learn would be easy for IT students.

Many participants have been used to physical interaction with the contents of their textbooks and notebooks e.g. flipping pages, making custom notes in handwriting, underlining or highlighting texts and they found this very difficult to do on electronic devices. One student stated, "I like to jot down notes in the textbook while the lecturer is speaking and these electronic devices just make it difficult."

– Distractions from the device and the internet

Results in this research showed that twenty-two (22) participants, accounting for about 19 % of the population, reported that they were distracted while learning electronically. Petrides (2002) found that students experience difficulty in learning if they are not required to sit within the four walls of a conventional classroom but rather have to do the learning electronically. Participants complained that other fun apps like social networking and gaming apps available on the devices usually serve as a distraction for them while studying.

One student said, *"I usually find myself browsing other sites like YouTube when I am on the internet and that distracts me a lot."* This can potentially pose a challenge as getting lost in an app or in a website means the student has to postpone reading until another time.

– Health concerns for the eyes

The research revealed that twenty-seven (27) participants in this research, accounting for 23 % of the population, had difficulties using electronic devices due to the strain on their eyes. This correlates to a study conducted by Fichten et al. (2009) who focused on students with disabilities. This study also raised concerns regarding the inability to hear audio online material and the inability to see visual presentations uploaded to learning sites. A student said, *"After I read for a while, my eyes begin to ache and I have headaches too."*

The next section suggests some solutions as to how these difficulties can be overcome from the participants' view.

- *Possible solutions to these difficulties*

The questionnaire gave students an opportunity to proffer possible solutions to the difficulties they were experiencing. The following were possible suggestions to handle these difficulties:

- A properly established, strong and fast internet connection which is also more cost effective should be made available for students' use. Elements also identified by Brown and Mbati (2015) as challenges that may impede the adoption of m-learning. Where an effective internet connection is already available, an increase in its bandwidth should be considered. This encourages students to use the internet more often for their learning.
- Academic materials like module outlines, textbooks and assignment sheets should be made available both in electronic format and also in hardcopy format. Students would, however, have a choice of which format to use.
- Regular technical training should be organised to teach students how to maximize the m-learning system of the institution to their advantage. Many participants in this survey suggested a regular training session for students who have difficulties with using the electronic devices. Participants feel that if they were taught how to use these, it would be a worthwhile tool to improving their learning.

5 Contribution

In this section, the researchers will answer the second question: how can the identified difficulties be overcome? The contribution of this study is the improvement of mobile learning in institutions of higher education by providing considerations for the design of m-learning platforms.

1. *Ease of use and access by students*
   Academic e-learning platforms should be easily accessible with mobile devices. These systems should be designed in such a way that all users can quickly and easily access whatever information is needed, when it is needed. The integration of technology into teaching and learning should be to enhance the students' learning experience and should thus be easy to use and accessible. The systems should be designed intuitively, so students can, with little effort, learn to use them on their own. m-Learning customised mobile applications could be designed to further ease access and increase interactivity with relation to both content and also other users, whether students or lecturers.
2. *Ease of access to help*
   Students may still from time to time encounter problems while engaging these electronic platforms for their work. A good m-learning environment must have a help component as an integral part of the environment. Users of the system should be assured of prompt help when they need it. A technical help team must be appointed with the responsibility of ensuring that users have access to the necessary help to make their experience easier.
3. *Accompany non-electronic element*
   One of the suggestions made by several participants in this survey was to introduce a combination of both electronic and non-electronic elements to the learning

experience. Face-to-face components and alternative hardcopy academic materials give a balance to the much needed electronic part of any learning experience. Incorporating these non-electronic components together with the electronic, makes the experience richer and effective.

6 Conclusions

In conclusion, the researchers in this study examined the difficulties students experience when learning has to be done electronically (especially via tablet PCs) and is not the traditional face-to-face or classroom learning. These challenges include technical problems; non-intuitive and non-user-friendly tools and systems; distractions caused by the device; connectivity and eye strain. Some suggestions put forward which may smooth the voyage of adopting m-learning and reduce these problems include the availability of suitable internet connection to students; provision of alternative forms of academic materials; organisation of regular technical training for students and introduction and maximizing of computer software and mobile apps. All these will enhance learner satisfaction of students engaged in e-learning, especially via a mobile device.

This study provided insight into how m-learning management systems can be designed for an effective learning environment. Such systems must be designed in a way that the students find them easy to learn and use. A help component must be integrated into the process so that students can find help quickly when needed. Social networks and gaming apps can be incorporated into the learning experience to increase engagement from students. If these are taken into consideration, the students can maximize this growing technology and eliminate, or at least reduce, the effects of these difficulties, and then have an e-learning academic environment that works and benefits all.

References

Attewell, J.: Mobile Technologies and Learning. A Technology Update and M-Learning Project Summary. Learning and Skills Development Agency, London (2005)

Attewell, J., Savill-Smith, C.: Mobile learning and social inclusion: focusing on learners. In: Proceedings of MLEARN 2003 Conference-Learning with Mobile Devices, London, UK (2003)

Barker, A., Krull, G. et al.: A proposed theoretical model for M-Learning adopting in developing countries (2006)

Bates, A.W.: Technology, E-Learning and Distance Education, 2nd edn. Taylor & Francis e-library, New York (2005)

Botha, A., Ford, M.: Digital like skills for the young and mobile digital citizens. In: Proceedings of the MLearn: The bridge from Text To Context. Shropshire, United Kingdom (2008)

Brown, T.H., Mbati, L.S.: Mobile learning: moving past the myths and embracing the opportunities. Int. Rev. Res. Open Distrib. Learn. **16**(2), 115–135 (2015)

Chang, I., Chang, W.: Effects of e-Learning on learning performance: a case study on students in tourism department in Taiwan. Pak. J. Stat. **28**(5), 633–644 (2012)

Cheon, J., Lee, S., Crooks, S.M., Song, J.: An investigation of mobile learning readiness in higher education based on theory of planned behavior. Comput. Educ. **59**(2012), 1054–1064 (2012)

Corbeil, J.R., Valdes-Corbeil, M.E.: Are you ready for mobile learning? Educause Q. **30**(2), 51–58 (2007)

Crescente, M., Lee, D.: Critical issues of m-learning: design models, adoption processes and future trends. J. Chin. Inst. Indus. Eng. **28**(2), 111–123 (2012)

Creswell, J.W.: Educational Research: Planning, Conducting, and Evaluating Quantitative and Qualitative Research, 4th edn. Pearson Education, Upper Saddle River (2012)

Crisan, A., Enache, R.: The role of Internet in education – change and transformation. E-Learn. Softw. Educ. **3**, 199–204 (2015)

Cox, M.J.: Formal to informal learning with IT: research challenges and issues for e-Learning. J. Comput. Assist. Learn. **29**(1), 85–105 (2012)

Donner, J.: Micro entrepreneurs and mobiles: an exploration of the uses of mobile phones by small business owners in Rwanda. Inf. Technol. Int. Develop. **2**(1), 1–21 (2004)

Esgi, N.: Comparison of effects of e-Learning types designed according to the expository teaching method on student opinions. Int. J. Acad. Res. **5**(5), 443–450 (2013)

Fichten, C.S., Ferraro, V., Asuncion, J.V., Chwojka, C., Barile, M., Nguyen, M.N., Klomp, R., Wolforth, J.: Disabilities and e-Learning problems and solutions: an exploratory study. Educ. Technol. Soc. **12**(4), 241–256 (2009)

Frechtling, J.: User friendly handbook for project evaluation. Westat: S.N. (2002)

Geddes, S.J.: Mobile learning in the 21st century: benefit for learners. Knowl. Tree e-J. **528**(10), 65–95 (2004). 6th edn. http://knowledgetree.flexiblelearning.net.au/edition06/download/Geddes.pdf

Grohmann, G., Hofer, A., Martin, G.: ARIS MOBILE: helping to define the future of mobile learning. In: Proceedings of the International Conference on Mobile Business 2005. Sydney (2005)

Haag, J.: From e-Learning to m-Learning: the effectiveness of mobile course delivery. In: Interservice/Industry Training Simulation, and Education Conference (I/TSEC), Orlando, Florida. USA (2011)

Hashemi, M., Azizinezhad, M., Najafi, V., Nesari, A.J.: What is mobile learning? Challenges and capabilities. Proceida -Soc. Behav. Sci. **30**(2011), 2477–2481 (2011)

Horton, W.: E-Learning by Design, 2nd edn. S.l. Pfeiffer, San Francisco (2012)

Johnston, K.A, Tufvesson, I. et al.: Maximising Human Resources in South Africa. In: International Development Informatics Association Conference (IDIA 2010), Cape Town, Monash University (2010)

Korucu, A.T., Alkan, A.: Differences between m-Learning (mobile learning) and e-Learning, basic terminology and usage of m-Learning in education. Procedia Soc. Behav. Sci. **15**(2011), 1925–1930 (2011). http://www.sciencedirect.com

Lowenthal, J.: Using mobile learning: determinates impacting behavioral intention. Am. J. Distance Educ. **55**(3), 1211–1219 (2010)

Murphy, A.: Mobile learning in a global context: a training analysis. In: Proceedings of the International Conference on Networking. International Conference on Systems and International Conferences on Mobile Communications and Learning Technologies, Morne, Mauritius (2006)

Mutlu, E.M., Yenigun, U.H., Uslu, N.: On education, mobile learning: open e-learning services evaluation of the possibilities of utilization of mobile computing devices (2005)

Naidu, S.: E-Learning: a guidebook of principles, procedures and practices, 2nd edn. Common wealth Educ. Media, Asia (2006)

Nicolau, G.N., Popescu, M.: E-Learning innovations in higher education. Rom. Rev. Soc. Sci. **1**(4), 34–47 (2013)

Parsons, D.: The future of mobile learning and implications for education and training. In: Ally, M., Tsinakos, A. (eds.) Perspectives on Open and Distance Learning: Increasing access through m-Learning. Common wealth of Learning and Athabasca University, Vancouver (2014)

Petrides, L.A.: Web-based technologies for distributed (or distance) learning: creating learning-centered educational experiences in the higher education classroom. Int. J. Instruct. Media **29**(1), 69–77 (2002)

Sharpels, M.: Big issues in mobile learning. England, University of Nottingham, Nottingham (2006)

Sun, P., Tsai, R., Finger, G., Chen, Y., Yeh, D.: What drives a successful e-Learning? an empirical investigation of the critical factors influencing learner satisfaction. Comput. Educ. **50**(4), 1183–1202 (2008)

Saunders, M., Lewis, P., Thornhill, A.: Research Methods for Business students. Pearson, Edenburg, Essex, England (2009). http://www.pearsoned.co.uk/HigherEducation/titlesby/Saundersetal/. ISBN 978-0-273-71686-0

Taxler, J.: Mobile learning it is here but what is it? Interactions **9**(1), 1–12 (2005)

Taxler, J.: Defining, discussing and evaluating m-Learning: The moving finger writes and having writ… International Review of Research in Open Distance Learning, vol. 8(2) (2007). http://www.irrodl.org/index.php/irrodl/article/view/346/882

Van Biljon, J., Dembskey, E.: Learning tools in resource constrained environment: learning from e-learning in the time of m-learning. In: IDIA 2011 Conference, Lima Peru (2011)

Van Biljon, J., Renaud, K.: Distance Education as enabler in crossing the digital divide: Will the Phoenix Fly? In: IDIA2009 Development Informatics Conference, 28–30 October 2009. Bergendal, Kruger National Park, South Africa, Monash South Africa (2009)

Sense-it: A Smartphone Toolkit for Citizen Inquiry Learning

Mike Sharples[1(✉)], Maria Aristeidou[1], Eloy Villasclaras-Fernández[2], Christothea Herodotou[1], and Eileen Scanlon[1]

[1] Institute of Educational Technology, The Open University, Milton Keynes, UK
mike.sharples@open.ac.uk
[2] City University, London, UK

Abstract. We describe a toolkit for Android smartphones and tablets that enables a user to access all the sensors available on the device. Data from individual sensors can be viewed as dynamic graphs. Output from one or more sensors can be recorded to a spreadsheet, with the sampling rate set by the learner. As a tool for inquiry learning, the sensors can be linked to 'missions' on the nQuire-it website, allowing learners to sample and share data for collaborative crowd-sourced investigations.

Four nQuire-it missions have employed the sensor toolkit for investigating environmental noise, sunlight levels, air pressure and rainfall, and the speed of lifts (elevators). These four investigations represent a variety of methods to initiate, orchestrate and conclude inquiry science learning. Two of the missions are in the context of a study to develop a community of inquiry around weather and meteorology. The others are intended to engage members of the public in practical science activities. Analysis of the missions and the associated online discussions reveals that the Sense-it toolkit can be adopted for practical and engaging science investigations, though the issue of calibrating sensors on personal devices needs to be addressed.

Keywords: Inquiry science learning · Smartphone sensors · Crowd-sourced learning

1 Introduction

Citizen science activities engage members of the public in carrying out scientific investigations on behalf of, or in partnership with, professional scientists (see e.g. Silvertown 2009). Some citizen science projects, such as the US Annual Christmas Bird Count (Cohn 2008), or Galaxy Zoo (to classify astronomy observations; Lintott et al. 2008), enable thousands of people to interact with scientists in activities that require mass engagement to collect or classify data. But these projects do not offer opportunities for citizens to initiate their own investigations and undertake the entire process of planning an investigation, selecting the equipment, recruiting participants, collecting data, and analysing and presenting results. While there are claimed benefits to volunteers through enjoyment, finding a social community and participating in real science (Raddick 2009) there is a lack of evidence relating to the learning benefits of

T.H. Brown and H.J. van der Merwe (Eds.): mLearn 2015, CCIS 560, pp. 366–377, 2015.
DOI: 10.1007/978-3-319-25684-9_27

engaging in citizen science projects. A study by Brossard and colleagues (Brossard et al. 2005) of participants in a citizen science project on ornithology found the participants had gained knowledge of bird biology, but there was no statistically significant change in participants' attitudes towards science nor in their understanding of the scientific process.

In a previous project, to address these issues of how to engage young people in personally-meaningful inquiry-based learning, we designed an online environment named nQuire that guided children through an entire cycle of inquiry, connecting learning within and outside the classroom. The typical approach was for the teacher to propose or negotiate a 'big question' in class, such as 'is my diet healthy?' or 'are birds scared away from cities by noise?'. Then the children used mobile devices (for nQuire these were netbook computers, but nowadays they would be tablets) to collect evidence. For example, to explore whether birds are scared by noise, the children worked in groups to measure the ambient noise in different parts of the playground, then they placed bird feeders in quiet and noisy areas. They took photos of birds feeding and measured the amount of food eaten after two days. The unexpected result was that in the study, more food was eaten from noisy areas than quiet ones. Their photos of the habitats showed that a greedy pigeon, unaffected by noise, ate food in the noisy area. A repeat controlled experiment in a garden with two trees, one with a noisy radio attached, showed the result that small birds ate more from the quiet environment (Anastopoulou et al. 2012).

The birds and noise study was proposed by the children, aged 12–13, in collaboration with their teacher and a wildlife expert, and involved them in a complete investigation in an authentic setting, with unexpected but explainable results. The nQuire project showed that children were able to operate the equipment and we observed the groups engaging in scientific methods including framing appropriate questions, planning investigations, selecting measures, and collecting and comparing data. A controlled test of the children's scientific inquiry skills, using a measure devised for the project, showed a significant improvement in the accuracy of their understanding inquiry science decisions from pre- to post-test for the children using the nQuire system (Sharples et al. 2014). A measure of their attitudes towards science showed that 'enjoyment of science lessons' was maintained for the nQuire group from start to end of the project, but declined for a non-intervention control group.

Despite these modest successes, the nQuire project would be difficult to scale into widespread adoption without substantial investment in equipment, lesson planning and teacher development. It required the running of a series of well-planned classroom lessons and outdoor or home activities, and placed high demands on the teacher to integrate the data collected by the students into a coherent final lesson where they shared and presented results and drew conclusions.

2 Citizen Inquiry

For these reasons, in our more recent work we have explored the concept of 'citizen inquiry', as the fusing of citizen science and inquiry-based learning. In citizen inquiry, members of the public (of all ages) explore aspects of practical science through shared investigations on a web-based platform. It combines methods of crowd-sourced project initiation (similar to Kickstarter[1], but with scientific curiosity rather than financial incentives), social networking, and reputation management to enable science inquiry projects to be initiated and managed by citizens with differing levels of knowledge and expertise.

Typically, an individual or group will initiate a new investigation (or 'mission') around a question or topic of interest or concern. They will encourage others of all abilities, including trained scientists, to join and contribute to the mission. All the data collected as part of the mission is made visible and available for download and sharing. As the mission progresses, the participants discuss the topic online, through comments and replies linked to the mission and each item of data, and attempt to reach a consensus about the findings. Social network features allow users to 'like' data items and be notified of comments and likes from other users. Themes (such as 'investigate the weather') can combine a set of missions with differing aims, methods and contributors.

The benefits of the citizen inquiry approach over personal inquiry learning, are that it does not rely on a teacher to initiate a project (though a teacher may propose a citizen inquiry theme or a mission as part of a school project), it draws on the power of the crowd to provide data and comments, and it can be applied across a broad range of topics in the physical, environmental and social sciences.

3 Sense-it: Mobile Technology for Citizen Inquiry

Central to citizen inquiry is the use of mobile devices for collecting and sharing data. Given the broad range of possible themes and missions, in designing mobile technology it was important to offer a generic toolkit, rather than a set of specialist domain-specific tools.

A modern mobile phone comes equipped with a wide range of sensors including:

- Motion sensors, to measure acceleration and rotation;
- Environmental sensors, for ambient air temperature, noise, illumination, air pressure, magnetic field and humidity;
- Position sensors, including GPS location and orientation.

All these sensors can be accessed by software developers[2] but there has been no previous application that gives a user the opportunity to access and view data from any sensor on a mobile device, nor to process and connect multiple sources of data to learner-led science investigations. This is the basis of the Sense-it application (app).

Development of the Sense-it app was carried out as part of the nQuire: Young Citizen Inquiry project, funded by Nominet Trust. The project involved collaboration with Sheffield University Technical College (UTC), a technology college specialising in project-based work in collaboration with industry. The teacher from this college

---

[1] www.kickstarter.com.

[2] http://developer.android.com/guide/topics/sensors/sensors_overview.html.

proposed that a set of sensor tools on mobile devices would engage the students in practical science investigations. A design workshop with students aged 14-15 developed the initial interaction design and example investigations. Development of Sense-it then continued at The Open University (OU), with trials among OU staff members and with Sheffield UTC.

Sense-it is an Android app that can be downloaded from Google Play[3]. It gives the user access to all the sensors on an Android smartphone or tablet. A data stream from one or more sensors can be viewed on the mobile device as a dynamic graph. The user can also record data by setting the rate of sampling, then starting and stopping the data stream. The captured data is stored in.csv format for downloading to a spreadsheet. The third method of interaction is to connect Sense-it with a web-based platform named nQuire-it[4], to upload data to its citizen inquiry missions.

The main screen of Sense-it shows three tabs: Explore, Record and Share (see Fig. 1).

3.1 Explore

Selecting the Explore tab displays all the sensors that can be accessed on the user's mobile device, which depending on the device could be 15 or more (Fig. 1). Clicking on the icon for a sensor shows a dynamic graph of the sensor output. For example, clicking the Orientation icon shows three moving graphs with the orientation of the device in three axes (tilt, pitch and rotation).

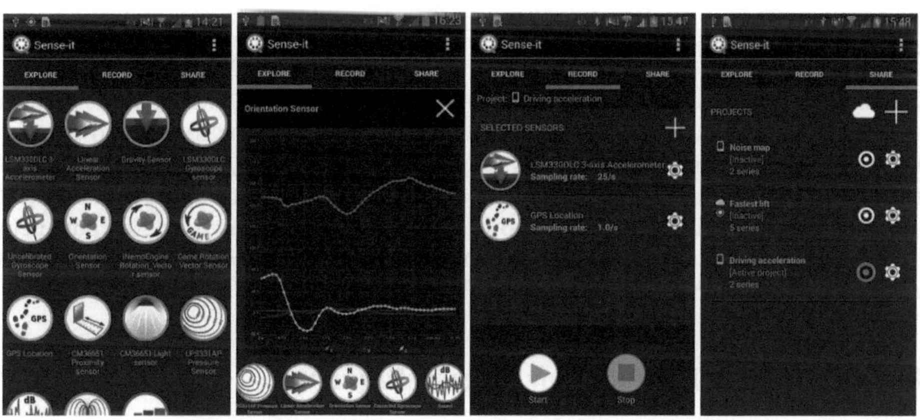

Fig. 1. The Explore, Record and Share tabs of Sense-it

---

3 https://play.google.com/store/apps/details?id=org.greengin.sciencetoolkit&hl=en_GB.

4 www.nquire-it.org.

3.2 Record

Selecting the Record tab allows the user to choose one or more sensors, set the sampling rate, and then start and stop the data sampling. The recorded data can be viewed as a static graph for each sensor, or the stream of data exported in.csv format to a spreadsheet for analysis. Figure 2 shows the data, imported into Excel, produced from the Orientation sensor, sampling 10 times per second, when an Android device is rotated, then tilted and pitched.

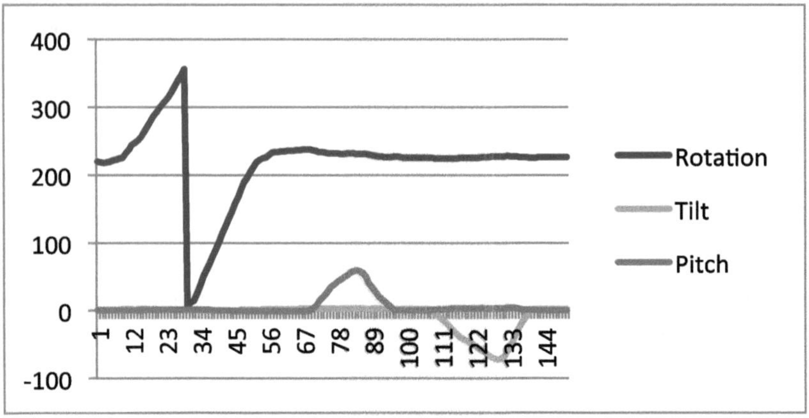

Fig. 2. Data exported from Sense-it into Excel

3.3 Share

The Share tab allows a user to set up projects that collect and view a series of data samples under one name (e.g. 'My orientation samples'). The user can also connect directly with the nQuire-it platform, by clicking the 'cloud' icon, to join on or more of its missions. On joining a mission, the title of that mission is added to the list of project and the sensors selected and configured to collect data for the mission. Any data item can then be uploaded and displayed on nQuire-it, to be shared with other people who have joined that mission.

4 nQuire-It: A Platform for Citizen Inquiry

The nQuire-it platform (www.nquire-it.org.uk) (Fig. 3) was also developed during the nQuire: Young Citizen Inquiry project (see Herodotou et al. 2014). It provides a site for a variety of citizen inquiry missions, ranging from 'objects and their stories' to creative ways to measure the height of a building or tree. The nQuire-it site has a responsive interface so that it can be accessed on internet-connected smartphones and tablets as well as laptop or desktop devices.

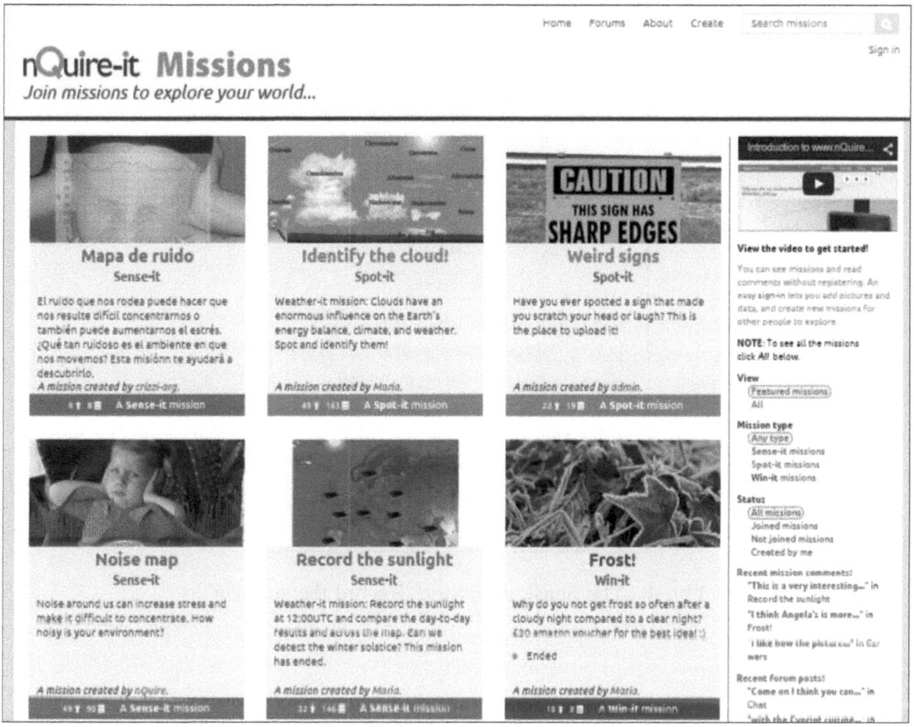

Fig. 3. The nQuire-it platform available at www.nquire-it.org.uk

For this paper, we focus only on one category of nQuire-it mission – that connects with the Sense-it mobile app. A Sense-it mission provides a means to initiate sensor-based citizen inquiries, collect and share data, and report results.

To date, four Sense-it missions have been created on the nQuire-it platform, as follows:

4.1 Record the Sunlight

This mission (Fig. 4) was created and facilitated by Maria Aristeidou, a PhD student at the Open University, and co-author of this paper. The aim is for people to use the light sensor to measure the ambient light level at midday, and compare it across different locations, and over time.

4.2 Air Pressure and Rainfall

The aim of this mission is to investigate the question 'Does it rain when the pressure is low?'. Users measure barometric pressure, using the pressure sensor on some newer mobile devices and record whether or not it is raining. This mission was initiated by a member of the nQuire-it community.

Fig. 4. The Sense-it mission 'Record the sunlight'

4.3 Noise Map

This mission is to record the ambient noise at different locations, e.g. to find the quietest or noisiest working environment, or the noise in a particular setting such as on a London Underground train. It was created by Mike Sharples, a co-author of the paper. (A Spanish version of Noise Map has also been initiated by a user of nQuire-it based in Buenos Aires).

4.4 Fastest Lift

The idea for this mission came from the workshop with Sheffield UTC and was proposed by a college student. The aim is to find the fastest lift (elevator) by going to the ground floor of a building, holding the device firmly against the lift wall in a vertical position, starting the recording, travelling to the second floor and stopping the recording. The uploaded accelerometer data is automatically processed to find the maximum velocity (Fig. 5).

5 Creating Sense-it Missions

The nQuire-it platform provides an environment to create new Sense-it missions. Clicking on the Create tab on the platform (shown on the top right of Fig. 3), opens an authoring tool. Here, a user can initiate a new mission, give it a title, add instructions to other users on how to engage with the mission and collect data, and configure the sensors for the mobile device. Then, whenever that mission is synchronised with the

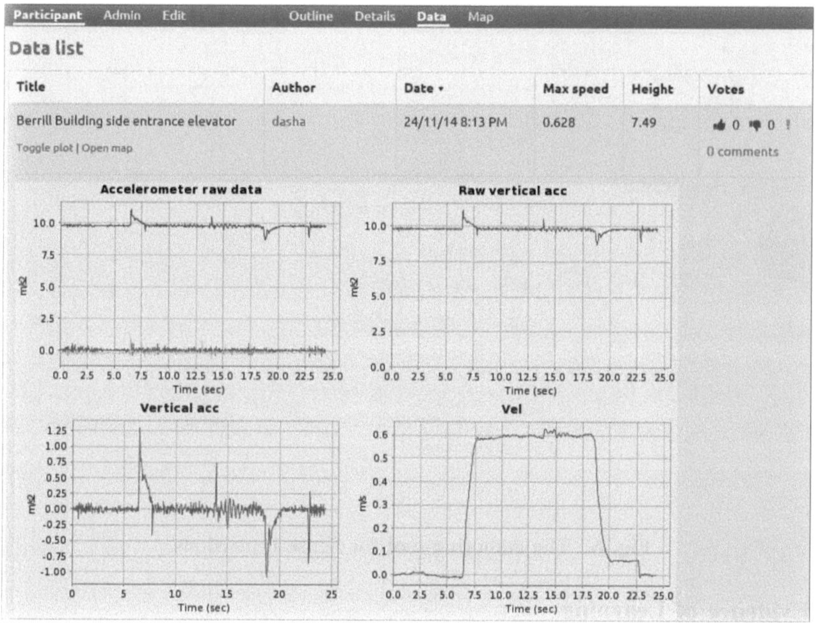

Fig. 5. Plot of one data recording on nQuire-it for the 'fastest lift' mission

Sense-it app on a mobile device, the app automatically configures just those sensors selected by the author of the mission and present the sampling rate. The mission author can also select a chain of transformations for the data, including; selecting one of the sensor streams, finding the maximum, minimum or average value, and integrating the data (e.g. to compute velocity from acceleration). Figure 6 shows the authoring tool, with processing to select the 'tilt' stream from the orientation sensor, then to record its maximum value.

Data produced by all the contributors to a Sense-it mission can be saved as a spreadsheet for further processing, comparison or display. This ability to export all the data for a mission is an extension of the facility under the Record tab to save the data produced by the single user.

6 Evaluation

The Sense-it app and nQuire-it platform were developed through a process of design-based research (Barab and Squire 2004) involving an iterative sequence of design, implementation and testing. Early testing was carried out at The Open University and included heuristic usability evaluation (Nielsen and Molich 1990) of the interfaces with experts in human-computer interaction. Later testing involved usability trials with students from Sheffield UTC. Participants in the missions have mostly been adult volunteers, recruited for a study of crowd-sourced meteorology (reported in Aristeidou et al. 2015).

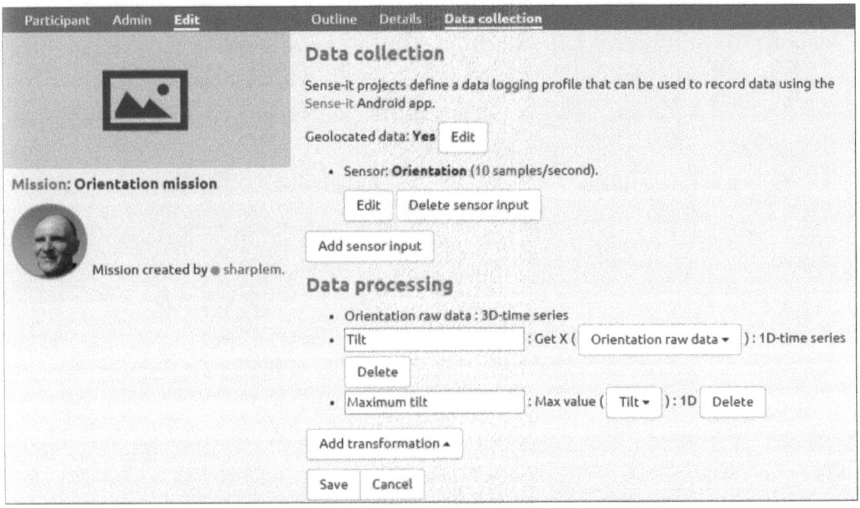

Fig. 6. The authoring tool for Sense-it missions.

6.1 Evidence of Learning

It is not possible to carry out an evaluation of learning outcomes, since setting pre- and post-tests of domain knowledge would not be appropriate for this informal mobile learning activity. Instead, we report issues arising from mission comments and discussions on the nQuire-it forums. A social network analysis of user engagement are reported elsewhere (Aristeidou et al. 2015). Comments from the adult users posted on the forum and to missions included general responses to the app and mobile phone sensors, including:

"I was very pleasantly surprised about the sense-it application used for the experiments. I had no clue the little device in my pocket had so many sensors (I had an idea about some, but not all) and that the output of the sensors could be so easily recorded. I keep using the mobile application for things of my own."

They also showed evidence of learning about the process of collecting data and from the results of the investigation:

"I tried measuring through the window and with the window open, I got a big difference (and yes, the windows were just washed :-). I knew windows absorb some light but the difference was really big." (Belgium, Record the Sunlight)

"Belgrade has a good average. I wouldn't expect this!" ('Germany, Record the Sunlight)

"I wasn't aware of how a noisy neighbourhood I live!!!;-)" (Argentina, Noise Map)

6.2 Calibration of Devices

An important issue was calibration of the sensors. Prior to the creation of 'Record the sunlight' project, trials took place to test whether the light sensors on mobile phones were correctly calibrated. A first step involved measuring the light of a halogen 42 watt bulb with plain glass, bought new and suspended on a wire with no shade and no other ambient light in the room. Eight mobile devices were placed flat, directly under the light bulb and about 1 metre away, and recorded the 20 samples of light, repeating the measurement three times. An approximation to the theoretical Lux of the particular light bulb in that distance was calculated with the inverse-square law ($Lux = \frac{Lumens}{4\pi d^2}$) to be equal to 66.85. The results showed a wide divergence of measurements ranging from 33 to 1000 Lux. The conclusions from this experiment were that there was large discrepancy between the theoretical Lux and the measurements. Furthermore, there were differences among the mobile devices of the same brand and model. These led to a more thorough investigation involving the help of experts.

First, advice was sought from a calibration expert. One method proposed for calibrating the application, was to add a scaling feature to the software, allowing the user to increase or decrease the level by reference to a calibrated professional light level meter. Shortcomings for using this method were the absence of such a scaling feature on Sense-it app and the use of the application by people without access to a professional meter. Yet, a professional light meter was used to calculate the difference between the measurements by mobile devices and a calibrated sensor.

Then, a camera expert was contacted for further investigation. As scaling between devices was one of the possible options, device datasheets were studied in order to provide information such as integration time and wavelength response. Some of the mobile devices used in the experiment had linear sensors in them, which means that if the light input doubles, the output will also double (in some other cases when the input doubles the output quadruples). For such linear sensors, a scaling relation may work as long as the scaling is done for the same light source between devices and not between a halogen bulb and sunlight. This inability is due to the possible difference in wavelength responses.

However, the light sensors on some phones only output a limited number of levels since they are used primarily for dimming the screen in sunlight rather than giving accurate Lux readings. Moreover, some sensors have 'max' values, beyond which they will not be sensitive to any increase in Lux, and this may be an issue when measuring bright sunlight. Another important factor affecting the measurements is the tolerance associated to particular sensors which may relate to the uncertainty of the output of the chip for a given light input; for example a device sensor may have a tolerance of ± 15 % varying the results compared to other devices. Finally, hardware damages (e.g. scratched/dirty monitor) may also affect the measurement values. The need for calibration scaling will occur for other sensors, such as atmospheric pressure and magnetic field. Though they give continuous readings, not restricted to pre-set levels, they can be poorly calibrated (for example, the air pressure sensor on the lead author's Samsung Galaxy Nexus phone consistently gives an atmospheric pressure reading of 19-21mb lower than that recorded by a local weather monitoring station).

6.3 Facilitation and Measurements

An examination of the learner interactions for each of these missions shows important differences in facilitation, process and outcome. Record the Sunlight was intended to be short duration and was facilitated by Aristeidou, with 146 contributions. Within the data, there were eight invalid measurements which were removed from the analysis. The measurements were from eleven different places in Europe (Milton Keynes, Oxford, Stockholm, Athens, Belgrade, Liege, Lausanne, Barcelona, Limassol, Central Greece and Great Missenden) ranging from 2 to 37 readings and 1 to 5 people measuring in each place. Graphs were produced for the measurements in every location indicating the variation in readings for the period and the average Lux. According to the final results, Limassol had the highest average sunlight for that time interval and Stockholm the lowest (Fig. 7).

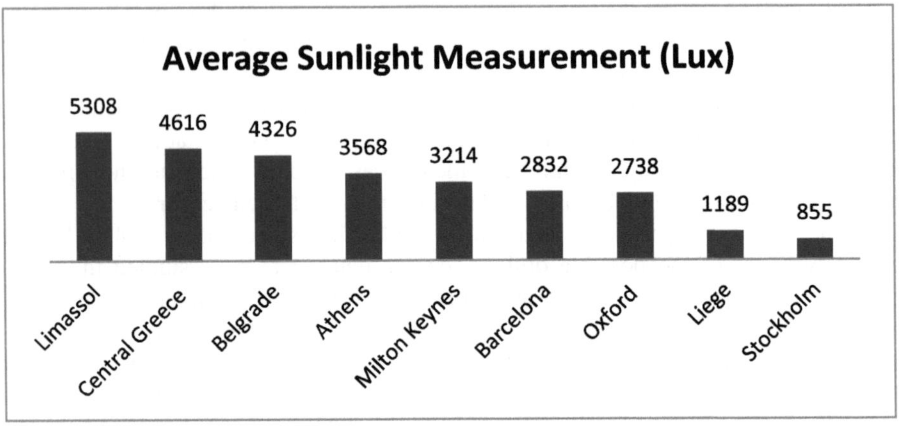

Fig. 7. Average light levels for cities measured on the Record the Sunlight mission

Air Pressure and Rainfall recorded 34 contributions. The contributions were made mainly in Milton Keynes, London and Bilbao. The analysis showed no clear relation between air pressure and rainfall, but it did identify calibration issues with air pressure sensors, and also produced a lively discussion on the complexities of relating rainfall and air pressure. Although this mission was available for as long as the 'Record the sunlight' mission, it was less popular as not many mobile devices supported an air pressure sensor.

Noise map recorded 92 items. Fastest Lift, requiring a more complex set of actions to record the velocity of a lift (elevator), has had 25 contributions over a period of 5 months. The relations between intentions, guidelines, complexity, and facilitation of sensor missions all appear to have influence on their popularity, persistence and outcomes.

7 Conclusions

Sense-it is an innovative application that makes data streams from all the sensors on an Android mobile device available for examination, play, and inquiry-based learning. Linked to the nQuire-it platform, Sense-it provides a means to enact 'citizen inquiry' that involves members of the public in initiating and facilitating collaborative science learning missions, based on data collected in the wild.

The nQuire-it platform can be accessed at www.nquire-it.org. The Sense-it app can be downloaded free, from https://play.google.com/store/apps/details?id=org.greengin.sciencetoolkit&hl=en_GB. The nQuire-it platform is open source. Code is available at https://github.com/IET-OU/nquire-web-source.

Acknowledgements. We wish to thank Nominet Trust for funding this project, and Sheffield UTC for the support of teachers and students as collaborators in the design of nQuire-it and Sense-it.

References

Anastopoulou, A., Sharples, M., Ainsworth, S., Crook, C., O'Malley, C., Wright, M.: Creating personal meaning through technology-supported science learning across formal and informal settings. Int. J. Sci. Edu. **34**(2), 251–273 (2012)

Aristeidou, M., Scanlon, E., Sharples, M.: Weather-it missions: a social network analysis perspective of an online citizen inquiry community. In: Conole, G., et al. (eds.) EC-TEL 2015. LNCS, vol. 9307, pp. 3–16. Springer, Heidelberg (2015)

Barab, S., Squire, K.: Design based research: putting a stake in the ground. J. Learn. Sci. **13**(1), 1–14 (2004)

Brossard, D., Lewenstein, B., Bonney, R.: Scientific knowledge and attitude change: the impact of a citizen science project. Int. J. Sci. Edu. **27**(9), 1099–1121 (2005)

Cohn, J.P.: Citizen science: can volunteers do real research? BioSci. **58**(3), 192–197 (2008)

Silvertown, J.: A new dawn for citizen science. Trends Ecol. Evol. **24**(9), 467–471 (2009)

Herodotou, C., Villasclaras-Fernández, E., Sharples, M.: Scaffolding citizen inquiry science learning through the nQuire toolkit. In: Proceedings of EARLI SIG 2014: Computer Supported Inquiry Learning, 18–20 August, Malmö, Sweden, p.5 (2014)

Lintott, C.J., Schawinski, K., Slosar, A., Land, K., Bamford, S., Thomas, D., Vandenberg, J.: Galaxy zoo: morphologies derived from visual inspection of galaxies from the sloan digital sky survey. Mon. Not. Roy. Astron. Soc. **389**(3), 1179–1189 (2008)

Nielsen, J., Molich, R.: Heuristic evaluation of user interfaces. In: Proceedings of the ACM CHI 1990 Conference, Seattle, 1–5 April, pp. 249–256 (1990)

Raddick, M.J., Bracey, G., Carney, K., Gyuk, G., Borne, K., Wallin, J., Jacoby, S.: Citizen Science: Status and Research Directions for the Coming Decade. Astro 2010: The Astronomy and Astrophysics Decadal Survey, Position Papers, no. 46 (2009). http://www8.nationalacademies.org/astro2010/DetailFileDisplay.aspx?id=454. Accessed 29th June 2015

Sharples, M., Scanlon, E., Ainsworth, S., Anastopoulou, S., Collins, T., Crook, C., Jones, A., Kerawalla, L., Littleton, K., Mulholland, P., O'Malley, C.: Personal inquiry: orchestrating science investigations within and beyond the classroom. J. Learn. Sci. **24**(2), 308–341 (2014)

Alternative Assessments: The Journey from Venue-Based Examinations to Take-Home and Online Timed Assessments

Odette Swart(✉)

College of Accounting Sciences,
University of South Africa, Pretoria, South Africa
swarto@unisa.ac.za

Abstract. Limited venues and the astronomic costs of securing venues all over the world to assess students at the University of South Africa (Unisa), South Africa's biggest open distance learning institution, forced the university to embark on a journey exploring different possibilities to move away from the traditional venue-based examinations. Alternative assessment types were identified and thus the focus was placed on available technology-enhanced options. One of these options included take-home assessments (including timed assessments and multiple-choice questions that could be completed on personal computers as well as mobile devices). The Unisa systems did not make provision for alternative assessments and had to be reconfigured by way of action research to accommodate different forms of technology-enhanced assessments. The process proved to be quite complex, as various parties had to be consulted. Various other issues, such as exploring the system requirements for the new business processes; the needs of the academics, including quality assurance of these assessments; and the requirements of the Examinations department had to be addressed. Feedback was also provided by the module lecturers and students who participated in the pilot. The need to document the progress of the project since inception thus arose to provide a clear understanding of the lessons learned by a mega-university.

Keywords: Action research · Alternative assessment · Open distance learning institution · Take-home assessments

1 Introduction

The University of South Africa (Unisa) is Africa's largest open distance learning (ODL) institution, with more than 350,000 registered students from 130 countries in Africa and globally every year (Unisa 2015a).

Unisa has seven academic colleges, namely the:

- College of Accounting Sciences (CAS)
- College of Agriculture and Environmental Sciences (CAES)
- College of Economic and Management Sciences (CEMS)
- College of Education (CEDU)
- College of Human Sciences (CHS)

T.H. Brown and H.J. van der Merwe (Eds.): mLearn 2015, CCIS 560, pp. 378–390, 2015.
DOI: 10.1007/978-3-319-25684-9_28

- College of Law (CLAW)
- College of Science, Engineering and Technology (CSET).

In 2013, a total of 839 formal qualifications were offered by Unisa. In the same year, 355 240 students were enrolled. The student profile indicated that 90,4 % of these students were part-time students – thus studying while employed – and only 9,6 % were full-time students. Also interesting is that in 2013, 62,9 % of the students were female and 37,1 % were male. In the same year, 58,6 % of the students fell in the 25–39 age group, while 24,1 % of Unisa students were 24 years and younger. Only 14 % of the students were in the 40–49 age group and 3,4 % were 50 years and older. Of all the registered Unisa students, 8,5 % were not South African residents (Unisa 2014).

As Unisa has registered students all over the world, study material is provided via couriers or the postal service and/or online access. Online access is possible through myUnisa – Unisa's online platform (learning management system [LMS]) and used to communicate with registered students. Limited venues and the astronomical costs of securing venues all over the world to assess students at Unisa forced the university to embark on a journey exploring different possibilities to move away from the traditional venue-based examinations.

In addition to the high cost of the venues, a ministerial compact between Unisa and the Minister of Higher Education and Training followed from an audit undertaken by the Higher Education Quality Committee of the Council on Higher Education in South Africa. As a result, in September 2013, the Principal and Vice-Chancellor of Unisa initiated the review and reconfiguration of Unisa's assessment systems and practices project. A steering committee in the form of a task team was established and the project was approved by the Senate Teaching and Learning Committee (STLC) and Senate. One of the objectives of the review and reconfiguration (R&R) task team was to review and reconfigure existing systems and practices in general. The other objective was the approval and implementation of alternative assessments, thereby increasing non-venue-based technology-driven summative assessments.

The approach followed was to involve all the different stakeholders in the project, which included the academics from the colleges as well as the support departments at the university. All the colleges were requested to identify a number of modules to take part in the alternative assessment project according to certain criteria. Emphasis was placed on the fact that only modules with limited numbers of students had to be nominated to take part in the pilot project. In addition, postgraduate modules were preferable, which would allow for flexibility in the implementation phase. This request was not necessarily adhered to, as undergraduate and postgraduate modules and even modules with over a thousand registered students were identified. The most important criterion was that lecturers had to be willing to be innovative and prepared to experiment.

After the identification of modules in every college, they had to go through the normal approval processes, namely via college boards, the STLC and Senate. The following types of alternative assessment were approved by Senate:

- Take-home examinations
- Timed examinations
- Portfolios

- E-portfolios
- Research portfolios
- Webinars
- Peer review
- Continuous assessment
- Multiple-choice questions (MCQs) generated by random selection.

After the above assessment methods and modules were approved by Senate, a workshop was held with all the academics (primary/module lecturers of each approved module) involved to define and develop the processes. Academics involved in similar types of alternative assessment were grouped together with representatives of various support departments, which included business analysts and personnel from the Information Communication and Technology (ICT) section, representatives from the Directorate: Student Assessment and Administration and other stakeholders. Take-home examinations and timed examinations were grouped together, while portfolios, e-portfolios and research portfolios were grouped together. The remainder of alternative assessments consisted of webinars, peer review, continuous assessment and MCQs generated by random selection.

Each group was tasked with the instruction to define and develop the processes for the specific group and a team leader (R&R task team member) was assigned to each group to drive the process in collaboration with the academic and support departments. Only later in the experimental phase did the team realise that MCQs generated by random selection fitted in better with the first group and was actually a type of timed examination. It was therefore incorporated into the take-home and timed examinations group.

The aim of the action research was to determine a process whereby alternative non-venue-based assessments could be performed. The focus of the remainder of the paper will be on the action research performed on the take-home and timed examinations (including the MCQs generated by random selection). Conclusions were drawn from the findings and finally, based on the literature review and findings, the research conclusions and recommendations are summarised.

2 Literature Review

In the literature review, the related aspects relevant to alternative assessments in an ODL environment are discussed. Students in an ODL environment have to study through self-instruction, as they do not have the benefit of a full-time lecturer. At Unisa a blended approach is followed. According to the Unisa ODL policy, blended learning is accomplished by using multiple teaching and learning strategies as well as a range of technologies in combination with face-to-face interaction and deploying both physical and virtual resources (Unisa 2008). Study material is provided online on myUnisa by way of official study material, additional resources, discussion forums, announcements, and so forth, in addition to printed material delivered via postal service and/or couriers.

Students are encouraged to think and build knowledge at their own pace (Goolamally et al. 2010). Unisa's ODL Research Framework and Plan describes open distance learning as follows (Unisa 2015b):

> ODL is a multi-dimensional concept aimed at bridging the time, geographical, economic, social, educational and communication distance between student and institution, student and academics, student and courseware and student and peers. Open distance learning focuses on removing barriers to access learning, flexibility of learning provision, student-centeredness, supporting students and constructing learning programmes with the expectation that students can succeed.

Even though only 8,5 % of registered students did not reside in South Africa in 2013, it amounted to 30,434 students who had to write their examinations outside South African borders. Limited venues and the astronomic costs of securing venues all over the world to assess students at Unisa forced the university to embark on a journey exploring different possibilities to move away from the traditional venue-based examinations. According to a guideline compiled by the LSE Teaching and Learning Centre (2013), take-home examinations can be very useful in testing certain skills, for example in law and management qualifications. In addition, it may even allow for more 'authentic' assessments due to assessments over a longer time period (e.g. 48 or 72 h) to replicate the environment in which the students' knowledge and skills would be used. In a study by Norcini et al. (1996) it was found that candidates who completed a take-home examination for recertification purposes appeared to take modules more seriously and preferred this alternative assessment. In addition, the scores they obtained compared similarly to many closed-book (venue-based) examinations. Kim et al. (2008) found that the nature of every module (e.g. the history, purpose and student characteristics) determined the impact on assessment methods used. Therefore, not all types of alternative assessment are suitable for all modules, and careful consideration should be given in the selection of the type of assessment.

In September 2013, the Principal and Vice Chancellor of Unisa initiated the review and reconfiguration of Unisa's assessment systems and practices. A steering committee in the form of a task team was established and the project was approved by the STLC and Senate. One of the objectives of the R&R task team was to increase non-venue-based technology-driven summative assessments. The research design and methods used are discussed in the next section.

3 Research Design and Method

As little was known about alternative assessments at the stage the project originated, and as the pilot project occurred in an experimental environment, it was decided to make use of action research. Mouton (2001) states that action research usually has exploratory, descriptive or action-related purposes. McNiff (2002) confirms that action research combines diagnosis, action and reflection. A number of characteristics of action research were identified by Denscombe (2003) and Ponte et al. (2004), namely that action research is:

- practical – thus developing solutions to practical problems which will in turn inform practice (Creswell 2005);
- focussed on change;
- an interactive cyclical process of planning, implementation and reflection;
- driven by participation; and
- an inherently interactive form of knowledge development.

Meetings were held with academics, representatives from ICT (which is responsible for the analysis, development and implementation of the systems), representatives from the Academy of Applied Technology in Teaching and eLearning (AATTeL) (which is responsible for research, training, testing and support) and the business analyst to try to establish the requirements of the academics involved in the project. This 'wish list' included information on the module code and the specific college involved, contact details of the lecturer involved, the number of students registered, the type of module (year module or semester module), details of the formative assessments, what will be required for the summative assessments, the latest date for system changes required, the type of verification required, additional software used in the specific module and required for the summative assessment and the capabilities the required software should have that would have to feed into myUnisa.

MyUnisa is the platform used to interact online with registered Unisa students via mobile devices and desktops. They log onto myUnisa to get access to their official study material, additional resources, announcements, discussion forums, and so forth. Registered students can also be contacted by the lecturers via email by posting announcements on myUnisa. Lecturers involved in this pilot project were requested to contact their students and inform them of the fact that the module was part of the project and all the effects it would have on them. They were also informed that there would be a mock examination to test whether all systems worked and to assist the students where they experienced problems. It was decided to make use of myUnisa for the alternative assessment, as students were used to it and they can access it simply with a username and password.

Access was one of the main concerns, as even though Unisa is an ODL university with a blended (online and paper-based) mode of delivery, lecturers expressed the concern that not all students will necessarily have access to a computer and the internet to complete the online timed examinations, as continuous power supply (South Africa is currently experiencing load shedding on a frequent basis) and functioning uninterrupted internet connections are crucial factors. Load shedding is defined in Wikipedia (2015) as where electricity delivery is intentionally stopped for non-overlapping periods of time over different parts of the distribution region, where the demand for electricity exceeds the power supply capability of the network. We realised that we needed a backup plan. It was decided to provide for an alternative option in cases where students were having a problem with access to a computer. One of the options was to book computer laboratories at the Unisa regional centres.

In addition, another major concern regarding access was how we would be able to verify the identity of the students that completed the assessment. Research was done to examine online proctoring as an option. Proctoring allows students to take an online examination at home or at the office while being monitored online by an offsite proctor. However, the student must have a webcam and microphone, and we could not expect our students to incur additional costs. In addition, we were uncertain whether employers would allow us to 'take control' over their computers in cases where students would prefer to use their employer's computers. We also looked at the option of making screenshots while students are busy completing the assessment. Key stroke recognition also sounded like an excellent idea, and even a 'lock-down mode', but it did not seem to assist with our objective to verify that the student writing the examination is actually the one that is supposed to write it. We also looked at options of a one-time password, similar to that used by the banks for online banking, but the system could not accommodate it for the pilot phase. A confirmation by email was also an option, but it might be that the email may not reach the student in time due to high traffic on the internet. In the end it was decided to make use of an honesty declaration and to make the terms and conditions of myUnisa stricter and more explicit by warning students about disciplinary action.

All these issues were taken into account by incorporating them into a standard operating procedure (SOP). The SOP addressed the following issues:

- The process to be performed by a student
- The assessment routing process
- The assessment marking process
- The assessment mark-capturing process
- Archiving of assessment
- Verification of marks for quality assurance purposes
- The mark sign-off request sent to chairs of departments, directors or deans.

The business analyst made use of this SOP to compile the business requirement specification. The decision was made to do the project in two phases.

Phase 1 would be the pilot phase and will continue until the end of 2015. Amendments had to be made to the assessment plans (combination of formative and summative assessments and percentage contribution of year mark to final mark) to include the various alternative assessments, but no major system changes or major developments would be done on the student system or on myUnisa during this phase. The student system incorporates all the student information and includes records of all marks attained during the formative and summative assessment periods. Phase 2 will commence after the pilot phase and will include all the requirements that could not be implemented during the pilot phase. These will hopefully include a plagiarism tool to be identified and implemented, the one-time pin security feature and improvements and changes regarding lessons learned from Phase 1.

The specific modules that were involved in the May/June examination period were identified. Of the five modules identified to take part in the pilot during this period, two were from CEMS, one from CSET, one from CHS and one from CAES. Therefore, the pilot involved four of the seven academic colleges at Unisa. These modules were all undergraduate modules and on different levels (first, second and third year). The South African Qualifications Authority (SAQA 2012) provides level descriptors for the South African National Qualifications Framework (NQF) to contribute to coherence in learning achievement and facilitate evaluation for comparability between qualifications and thus articulation within the NQF. The modules selected were from different NQF levels and included one module on NQF Level 5 and two modules each on NQF levels 6 and 7. Therefore, there was a relatively even distribution of modules in the academic colleges as well as on the NQF levels. The lecturers involved with these modules were invited to training sessions to assist them with setting up the assessments. Three of the modules involved in the May/June 2015 examination period made use of dynamically generated MCQs (SAmigo, one of the Sakai tools, was used). The other two modules made use of the Sakai e-Assessment tools to upload the assessment questions.

All students registered for the specific modules writing in the May/June examination period were requested to take part in a mock examination beforehand to ensure that all systems worked and that students could familiarise themselves with the new method of assessment. The mock examination was very important, as supplementary students also had to write the alternative assessment and were not previously assessed in this way. The system settings would thus be tested and adjusted after the mock examination to ensure that the actual examination would run as smoothly as possible. One of the challenges identified was that myUnisa times out after 40 min and lecturers were advised to take this into account. Colleagues from ICT and AATTeL were notified of the planned assessment dates of the modules involved and placed on standby for assistance. An email address was also provided to students to assist with any technical problems they experienced with the system.

After the students completed the assessments, the myUnisa Gradebook (a tool used to record and store marks for assessments completed in the LMS) was used to capture the marks from the e-Assessment tool and also served as validation and archiving method at the same time. The ICT colleagues compiled a document to provide guidelines for marking online summative assessments with Gradebook, as the Gradebook tool is not linked directly to the student system (a system that includes all student information for summative assessments), the XMO (a system used to manage workflow processes for summative assessment marks online) or the assessment plan (used for the planning of the assessments and to record the weight or contribution ratio of year marks and examination marks towards the student's final mark). The existing XMO was used to capture the final assessment marks and to transfer it to the Unisa student system for sign-off and release to the students. Feedback was requested from lecturers in the form of detailed reports per module regarding their own experiences as well as the experiences of students communicated per email, discussion forums or module evaluations. The feedback from students and lecturers that were involved in the action research are discussed in the next section.

4 Discussion of Results

The objective of the action research was to develop a process to perform non-venue-based technology-enhanced alternative assessments. After these assessments were completed in the pilot phase, interesting observations were made by students and lecturers, which are discussed below.

4.1 Feedback from Students

Students were requested by the lecturers of all the modules that were involved in the pilot to provide feedback regarding their experiences per email or on the discussion forums of myUnisa. From the replies received it was clear that students experienced some anxiety about the change in assessment, and this resulted in more queries from students. The mock examinations alleviated a lot of these fears. The lecturer of INV3703 also performed a module evaluation and received responses from 50 students.

From the feedback received from students via email, discussion forums on myUnisa and module evaluation after the assessments it seems they were very positive about the experience and also preferred the venue-based assessment. Students requested some form of proof that they are writing an examination in order to apply for study leave. The system could not accommodate this for the May/June pilot. Lecturers provided an email to these students stating the fact that students were required to complete the online alternative assessment at a certain date. Surprisingly, few complaints (only six) were received from students that they did not have access to a computer or the internet. The applicable Unisa regional centres were contacted by the lecturer to assist the students with a timeslot in a computer laboratory.

Load shedding did not present a problem, as students had more than one opportunity to complete the assessment. Some students experienced connectivity problems and complained about system failures and timeouts, but the problem was overcome by allowing students more than one attempt. The MCQs could be completed on personal computers as well as on mobile devices. Students complained, however, regarding some of the browsers they used on the mobile devices. Students who made use of Mac computers, tablets, iPhones and iPads experienced problems with the Safari browser. It appears that this browser is not compatible with the myUnisa tools.

In general, students strongly supported the online assessment. Students were reminded during the semester that they have to answer the assessments independently and may not solicit or obtain assistance from anyone or provide assistance to other students for any specific content on the examination. One of the students alerted the lecturer of INV3703 on the discussion forum regarding a certain college that made contact with students to offer possible examination assistance. Identity verification remains an area of concern and therefore students are continuously made aware of possible disciplinary action that may be taken against them, which resulted in the inclusion of the honesty declaration that had to be completed by all students.

4.2 Feedback from Lecturers

The lecturers involved in the specific modules provided detailed reports on their experiences. All the modules involved in the pilot were online modules. This means that all study material and communication with students occurred through the myUnisa website. All the module lecturers made use of mock examinations that were made available to students on myUnisa before the actual assessment. This was to ensure that the students understood how it worked and to test the system. A summary of the feedback from the module lecturers is provided per module below and the module codes of the modules that took part in the pilot are used as headers. The respective colleges are indicated in brackets.

4.2.1 CAD161S – Computer-Aided Draughting (CSET)

CAD161S is a computer-aided draughting module in the Department of Mechanical and Industrial Engineering, which uses Autodesk Inventor Professional to design mechanical components and produce engineer's drawings. In addition to Autodesk, the module lecturer made use of the e-Assessment tool on myUnisa to design the assessment. Students were required to upload the completed assessment that consisted of drawings via e-Assessment on myUnisa. The module had 116 registered students with examination admission, of which 82 completed and submitted the assessment. Therefore, 71 % of students attempted the online assessment and the pass rate was 95 %.

4.2.2 CAD161S – Computer-Aided Draughting (CSET)

This module is one of the modules in the Department of Industrial and Organisational Psychology and focuses on personality and related individual differences in the work context. The assessment tested theory and insight into the subject matter. The module lecturer made use of dynamically generated MCQs (SAmigo) from an extensive question bank as part of a timed online assessment. However, as myUnisa has a time-out period of 40 min, the module lecturer decided to split the 75 questions into three sections of 25 questions each. The online assessment was opened two days before the due date to allow the students enough time to submit the assignments and to allow for possible system failures. Each student had two chances to submit and the highest mark of the two was allocated as the final mark. Of all the students who attempted the assessment, 875 completed Section A, 869 completed Section B and 865 completed Section C. Therefore, of the 900 students registered for IOP1601, 865 (96 % of all registered students) completed all sections of the assessment and the module pass rate was 70 %.

4.2.3 PYC2606 – Basic Measurement and Questionnaire Design (CHS)

PYC2606 is one of the modules of the Department of Psychology and aims to introduce leaners to the field of psychometrics in psychology as well as the basic skills to construct and develop a questionnaire. The lecturers involved in the module had been working on more advanced forms of MCQs for some time, and had incorporated it into assignments. Unfortunately, the current MCQ system does not provide for advanced types of MCQs, and the lecturers had to adjust their assessment accordingly. Students had a timed online assessment and received the scenario information 30 min before the examination commenced. SAmigo and the additional resources folder on myUnisa were used for this purpose. Students had 2 h and 30 min to complete the 50 MCQs. They were given two examination opportunities, and of the expected 1,068 registered students, 839 (789 current and 50 supplementary students) completed the assessment. Therefore, 79 % of the registered students attempted the online assessment. The pass rate was 56 %.

4.2.4 CEC3701 – Conservation Ecology (CAES)

CEC3701 is a module in the Department of Environmental Sciences that enables students to critically assess different habitats (i.e. marine, estuarine, freshwater and terrestrial) in the southern African context as well as the influence humans have on each habitat. Only supplementary students were assessed during this period and therefore the decision was made to make use of a similar format to the paper that was written in October 2014. Only six students indicated that they did not have access to a computer and the internet and were informed that they may use the facilities at any Unisa regional centre. The examination question paper was uploaded on myUnisa using the e-Assessment tool. Of the possible 28 students eligible to do the assessment, 26 (93 %) made use of the opportunity. Of these, 22 students typed the answers and four submitted handwritten answers. The pass rate was 84,6 %.

4.2.5 INV3703 – Investments: Derivatives (CEMS)

INV3703 is one of the modules in the Department of Finance, Risk Management and Banking. This assessment consisted of various types of questions, namely MCQs and matching and numerical response questions. As the module primarily consisted of calculations and the interpretation of those calculations, the majority of the questions were numerical response questions. Potentially, the nature of the module could pose a risk in terms of students working together, but as the questions were randomly delivered with SAmigo, it made it very difficult for a group of students to attempt the examination at the same time while working together on it, as students received the same type of questions with different information at different stages of the examination. In the case where MCQs, numerical responses or fill-in questions are used, it is the responsibility of lecturers to maintain a large database of a variety of questions in order to ensure the validity of the assessment. The alternative assessment of this module stretched over a two-week period. There were a total of 311 current and supplementary students registered, of which 288 students completed the assessment over the two-week period. The majority of students attempted the assessment on the date the assessment was released to students for assessment and again on the last date on which submission was available. Only a few students attempted the assessment during the period between the release and submission dates.

4.3 Additional Comments

One of the module lecturers indicated that one student blatantly plagiarised the answer despite the honesty declaration that was included in the system. Students could not complete the upload of their answers before ticking a box to confirm that it was their own work. The specific lecturer did not mark any of the plagiarised questions, as students were warned several times before the assessment that plagiarised answers would not be marked. Another lecturer was notified by a student that a 'private college' offered students a 'tutored' service to assist with the examination. Lecturers also expressed concern regarding the quality assurance of the assessments, as this new delivery method added some complexity in this area.

4.4 Summary of Results

A summary of the results from the modules as indicated in the previous paragraphs is presented in Table 1 below. It was interesting to note that this pilot included large student numbers even though only five modules participated in this examination period. These modules from four different colleges were also on different NQF levels. The participation rate of students who completed these online assessments was very high and in the case of three of the modules exceeded 93 %.

Table 1. Summary of results of modules who took part in the pilot during the May/June 2015 examination period

NQF level	NQF 5	NQF 6		NQF 7		Total
Module code	**CAD161S**	**IOP1601**	**PYC2606**	**CEC3701**	**INV3703**	
Registered students with examination admission	116	900	1 068	28	311	2 423
Completed assessments	82	865	839	26	288	2 100
• Current semester	68	783	789	0	258	1 898
• Supplementary	14	82	50	26	30	202
% attempted assessment	71%	96%	79%	93%	93%	87%
Module pass rate (passed/written %)	95%	70%	56%	85%	57%	-

A total of 2,423 registered students with examination admission were requested to take part in the pilot and 2,100 students completed the assessments. Of these students, 1,898 were current registered students and 202 were supplementary students. The percentage of total students who participated in the pilot project amounted to 87 % of total registered students of the modules.

5 Conclusion

Of the 2,423 students who took part in the pilot, 87 % attempted the technology-enhanced alternative assessment. The aim of the action research was to make provision for the increase in technology-enhanced summative assessments. The lecturers and students that took part in the pilot for the five modules that were used for the timed and take-home alternative assessments did not experience major challenges during the May/June 2015 examination period. The MCQs (SAmigo) tool proved to be sufficient in most cases to assess students with a range of question types. In the other cases the e-Assessment tool was used for the assessment. In the case of two of the modules that formed part of the pilot, myUnisa was capable of dealing with nearly 1 000 students per module.

This paper focused on the development of technology-enhanced summative assessments specifically for timed and take-home examinations. The high participation rate of students expresses the readiness of students for online alternative assessments. Identity verification of students completing online assessments remains an area of concern to lecturers and further effort should be made to find a suitable solution to this problem. In addition, with the change of the examination delivery method Unisa should rethink the way of doing quality assurance of assessments, as the delivery method added some complexity in this process. Except for the issue of identity verification of students and the quality assurance of assessments, the module lecturers who took part in this pilot found the experience to be very positive and would like to continue with online technology-enhanced alternative assessments in the future.

Even though only five modules were involved in the pilot project, more modules will make use of alternative assessments in the October/November 2015 examination period and will include semester modules as well as year modules. In addition, online questionnaires should be sent to students for feedback after the October/November 2015 examination, as the feedback from the May/June 2015 examination period was mainly summarised by the module lecturers from emails received from students and discussion forums. This project provides a huge opportunity for further research on alternative assessments and the effect on the way we teach by incorporating mobile learning to a much greater extent. In future it may result in more and more modules making use of alternative assessments for formative as well as summative purposes, as this maiden voyage with its rippling effect may result in many cruises on the massive open waters.

Acknowledgements.
Prof PH Havenga
Prof IJ Kroeze
Ms B Brand
Mr CF Erasmus
Ms LA Louw
Mr FJ Masithulela
Ms F Myburgh
Mr CJ Opperman
Dr P van der Merwe

References

Creswell, J.W.: Educational research: planning, conducting and evaluating quantitative and qualitative research. Pearson Prentice Hall, Upper Saddle River (2005)

Denscombe, M.: The Good Research Guide for Small-Scale Social Research Projects. Open University Press, England (2003)

Goolamally, N., Yusoff, Y., Subramaniam, T., Latif, S.: Teaching and learning of technical subject in an ODL environment. In: Proceedings of Global Learn Asia Pacific, pp. 3927–3932 (2010). http://eprints.oum.edu.my/407/. Accessed 22 June 2015

Kim, N., Smith, M.J., Maeng, K.: Assessment in online distance education: a comparison of three online programs at a university. Online J. Distance Learn. Adm. XI(1) (2008). http://www.westga.edu/~distance/ojdla/spring111/kim111.html. Accessed 24 August 2015

LSE Teaching and Learning Centre. Take home examination papers: guidance for tutors and course conveners (2013). http://blogs.lse.ac.uk/lseteachingblog/files/2013/05/Note-of-guidance-on-take-home-exams-FINAL-May-2013.pdf. Accessed 24 August 2015

McNiff, J.: Action research for professional development: concise advice for new action researchers (2002). http://www.jeanmcniff.com/ar-booklet.asp. Accessed 25 July 2015

Mouton, J.: How to Succeed in Your Master's and Doctoral Studies. Van Schaik, Bellville (2001)

Norcini, J.J., Lipner, R., Downing, S.M.: How meaningful are scores on a take-home recertification examination? Acad. Med. **71**(10), S71–S73 (1996). October, Supplementary

Ponte, P., Beijard, D., Ax, J.: Don't wait until the cows come home: action research and initial teacher education in three different countries. Teacher. Teach. Theory Pract. **10**(6), 591–621 (2004)

SAQA: The South African Qualifications Authority: level descriptors for the South African National Qualifications Framework (2012). http://www.saqa.org.za/docs/misc/2012/level_descriptors.pdf. Accessed 23 July 2015

Unisa: Unisa Open Distance Learning Policy, approved by Council 3 October 2008 (2008). http://staffcmsys.unisa.ac.za/cmsys/staff/contents/departments/tuition_policies/docs/OpenDistanceLearning_Council3Oct08.pdf. Accessed 24 August 2015

Unisa. An institutional profile: Unisa facts and figures, HEMIS 2009–2013 (2014)

Unisa: Facts and figures: student enrolments (2015a). http://www.unisa.ac.za/Default.asp?Cmd=ViewContent&ContentID=15888. Accessed 23 July 2015

Unisa: Unisa's Open Distance Learning Research Framework and Plan 2012–2015, approved by Senate 14 March 2012 (2015b). http://www.unisa.ac.za/contents/faculties/service_dept/ice/docs/Final%20Proposal%20ODL%20Research%20Framework%20and%20Plan%202012%20(edited)%20(Submitted%20to%20SENRIC%206%20February%202012).pdf. Accessed 23 July 2015

Wikipedia. Rolling blackout (2015). https://en.wikipedia.org/wiki/Rolling_blackout. Accessed 24 August 2015

Socio-Technical Factors that Influence Learning Management Systems' Adoption in Developing Countries

Mpaphi Molebatsi(✉)

School of Computing, University of South Africa, Pretoria, South Africa
Mpaphi@gmail.com

Abstract. The advent of information technology has brought major developments in the way institutions harness, store and distribute information. This paper draws a lot of insight from already identified socio-technical factors and information system theories to measure and test their influence towards learning management system adoption. These factors are used to stress the give-and-take interrelationship between humans and technology and in the process promoting usage which in turn promotes efficiency. Course instructors, system administrators and content developers need to be aware of such factors in order to maximize utilization of the tools that are employed by institutions to improve education.

Keywords: Learning management systems · System adoption · m-Learning · Institutions of higher learning · Developing countries

1 Introduction

Different universities in developing countries have begun to realise the importance of using technological tools such as learning management systems (LMSs) to enhance learning and the running of the day to day activities of the organization. However, these LMSs have proven to be very costly in terms of acquisition and operation. In addition to the cost of purchasing, there are costs related to consulting, technical configuration, administrator training and maintenance. According to Monarch Media (2010), software vendors have devised pricing models to make their products more look like they are affordable to possible client institutions. These models include, firstly, the *direct purchase model* where the software is purchased, installed, and managed in-house. The vendor takes all the responsibility for the appropriate functioning of the product to the buyers including the handling of future upgrades. Secondly, is the *third-party maintenance model*, where an institution buys the software and installs it on its own data platform, but the maintenance and upgrades are managed by the vendor or another third party. In this case the responsibility that comes with maintenance remains with the vendor. Lastly, is the *Software as a Service (SaaS) model* where the company buys the software, but it is housed by the provider and managed remotely by a third party (generally the vendor). In this model, administrators, content builders, instructors, and learners access the system over the Internet. At first glance this may seem to be cost reducing but in essence increases the cost of the whole initiative.

T.H. Brown and H.J. van der Merwe (Eds.): mLearn 2015, CCIS 560, pp. 391–404, 2015.
DOI: 10.1007/978-3-319-25684-9_29

However, the significance and benefits of all these systems remain to be in question. This is because they are designed to fit the environment of the developed countries, not taking in consideration the obvious fact that the developed countries are very different in every aspect to the developing countries. Let alone the fact that they face different challenges, both socially and economically (OECD 2003). In developing countries there are more pressing issues like poverty alleviation, diseases, clean water supply, HIV pandemic, good governance than halving a fully-fledged functional system and technological infrastructure. With growing inequality between communities in developing countries, it is very difficult to consolidate the level of knowledge and needs of these communities. In some areas there are competent computer users who can browse and search the internet, whilst in others to most, the functioning of computers remains a mystery. They have not heard of or seen modern technological tools such as laptops and smart phones and do not know how to operate them or how they can use them to improve their lives.

By the same token, institutions face the daunting task of selecting the best choice for their use as there is a plethora of different learning management systems (LMSs) available (McLoughlin and Lee 2007). The best choice depends on what the institution intends to address by acquiring the LMS. Institutions of higher learning may want to address pedagogical issues such as enhancing the quality of virtual learning, mobile learning, improving access to learning content, embrace more learner centred education and individualized learning, while corporations may want to address knowledge sharing, just-in-time remediation and knowledge reuse (Nayak and Poonphon 2007). However, these institutions may find that the level of usage of LMSs is just not satisfactory because the people who are supposed to be using these systems do not find them useful in addressing their needs (Molebatsi and Kekwaletswe, 2011). This is perpetuated by both management and system administrators as they tend to not involve the intended users in decisions making regarding acquisition and content (Molebatsi and Kekwaletswe, 2011).

Much as new technological systems are needed, there are many factors that affect the rate of adoption of such systems (Butler and Sellbom 2002). These factors include but are not limited to, reliability, learning to use new technology, institutional support, sociological, psychological and security variables (Bacow et al. (2012); Bhati et al. (2010); Lopes (2008)). Under the right circumstances, system's adoption should be easy and accepted and put to use as soon as possible. Rycus et al. (2006) classified the systematic barriers into fiscal, barriers as well as legal and judicial barriers. They put it that the fiscal environment is critical in any analysis of the adequacy of multi-system efforts to promote successful adoptions. This may depend on state funding, planning and support. While the legal and judicial barriers in the legal system may include inconsistencies in the policies of the country, which are in most cases the procedures followed to giving the green light have lengthy delays and the failure by various parties to realise the urgency to eliminate these barriers.

Technologies make us want to do things differently. In the present landscape of technological and social change, where there is a whole lot of tasks to do with a lot of different technologies, there is need to find means to fuse these two in order to perform tasks effectively (McLoughlin and Lee 2007). Institutions tailor these technologies for their users in order to fit the objectives of the intended use. The latest developments of technology in the information age put more emphasis on the need to enable and support, not only the acquisition of knowledge and information, but also to develop the skills and resources necessary to engage with social and technological change, and to continue learning throughout life (Owen et al. 2006). Such initiatives allow institutions to track and monitor usage in the process giving management the bird's eye view of the organisation.

2 Research Problem

Institutions of higher learning in developing countries continue to invest in LMS with a variety of course management software to support their day to day work activities (Marchewk et al. (2007). However, the value and full benefits of such systems are generally not fully realized as many struggle to address the socio-technical aspects during adoption (Molebatsi and Kekwaletswe 2011). Just to note, there are many other factors that need to be addressed that also contribute to little or no usage of such systems such as technical factors, quality factors and economical factors, but this study is only concerned with socio-technical factors. Socio-technical factors are those factors that recognise people and technology. Other factors may relate to policies, governance and infrastructure are also not discussed.

3 Research Question

1. What are the socio-technical factors that influence adoption of learning management systems in developing countries?
2. To what extent do these factors influence the adoption of learning management systems in developing countries?
3. To what extent is age related to socio-technical factors that influence the adoption of a learning management system in developing countries?

4 Justification of the Study

Learning management systems are systems that can be accessed by different devices such as computers, laptops, tables and cellular phones. Most of these devices are portable and easy to carry with. However, this study does not view the prospect of using mobile devices in accessing LMSs as a sole reason to classify them under mobile learning. This study adopts a more pragmatic and cognitive view of what mobile learning is. Laouris and Eteokleous (2005) argue that a socially and educationally responsible definition must view the learner as the one being mobile and not his/her devices. They point out that the learning environment needs to move with the learner and not the device, but his/her whole learning environment. This definition therefore views mobile devices as aiding the learning environment. Therefore, this study sees this definition more logical than others that define this concept from the point of mobile devices and not the learner as articulated by Laouris and Eteokleous (2005).

5 Literature Review

Meaningful discussion on significance of the LMSs and socio-technical aspects requires a basic consensus on definitions. In this section, learning management systems, socio-technical components, adoption and full utilisation are defined and briefly described.

6 Learning Management Systems

Besides the term learning management system, numerous other terms exist with similar meaning, such as course management system or e-learning platform.There are several definitions of LMSs (Watson and Watson 2012; Szabo and Flesher 2002; Oakes, K. 2002; Bailey, G.D. 1993). According to Ellis, (Ellis R 2009), a learning management system can be described as a software application that automates the administration, tracking, and reporting of training events and they should be able to do a number of activities such as support for blended learning, administration tools, content integration, adherence to standards, assessment capabilities, skills management the following (TrainCentre 2013).

1. **Support for Blended Learning:** The fact that different people learn in different ways, an LMS should present a programme of study that allows mixing classroom and virtual courses easily. Collective, these two features enable dogmatic and personalized learning.
2. **Administration Tools:** It is important for LMSs to allow administrators to manage user registrations and profiles, chart certification paths, allocate tutors, define individual roles, set curricula, author courses, manage content, and administer internal budgets and user payments if applicable especially in a mobile learning environment. A complete access to the training database system by system administrators enables them to generate standard and customized reports on individual and group performance.
3. **Content Integration:** It is significant for LMSs to provide native support to a wide range of third-party courseware. In the quest to select the best choice for use, decision makers must keep in mind that some LMSs are often compatible only with the vendor's own courseware and others do little more than pay hypocrisy to learning content standards. LMS vendors ought to be able to confirm that third-party content will work within their system.
4. **Adherence to Standards:** LMSs should try to support standards such as Sharable Content Object Reference Model (SCORM) and Aviation Industry [Computer Based Training] Committee. Support for standards means that the LMS can bring in and manage content from other applications and courseware that complies with the same standards regardless of the authoring system that produced it.
5. **Assessment Capabilities:** Evaluation, testing, and assessment engines help developers build a program that becomes more valuable over time. It is a good idea to have an assessment feature that enables authoring within the product and includes assessments as part of each course.

6. **Skills Management:** A skills management constituent enables organizations to measure training needs and identify improvement areas based on worker's collective competence in specified areas. Skills assessments can be culled from numerous sources, including peer reviews and 360-feedback tools.
7. **Centralize and Automate Administration:** Applications must be used to create the reusable learning objects that are accessible through a central location, such as the repository. The application automates development by providing authors such as learners and instructors with templates and storyboarding capabilities that incorporate instructional design principles. Using these templates, authors may develop an entire course by using existing learning objects in the repository, creating new learning objects, or using a combination of old and new objects enabling more interaction with learning content.
8. **Assemble and Deliver Learning Content Rapidly:** LMSs must allow users to decompose learning objects into reusable content units and must allow dynamic assembly of such units into personalized learning content. The term 'rapidly' here stresses that one of the system goals is to bring into being a courseware that is versatile and yet very simple to use with minimum effort and time required. This takes note of the different competence levels of the LMS user.
9. **Use Self-service and Self-guided Services:** An LMS should allow the learners to use the self-service and self-guided services to set up and view learner's centre information, view learner's general information, view a learner's admissions information, view a learner's transfer credit information, and view a learner's academic information. In addition, it must allow instructors to view their teaching schedule, their exam schedule, their textbook summary, their grade rosters, enter grades, and post grades, view their class rosters, access the Grade Book and class assignments, link to personal data summaries, search for classes, browse the course catalogue, locate a faculty member, and access the advisor centre.

But most importantly LMSs should integrate with other enterprise application solutions used by Human Resource and Accounting, enabling management to measure the impact, effectiveness, and overall cost of training initiatives. In addition, when systems are integrated, HR can capture new employee's information into the HR system and the employee is automatically signed up for training tailored to his or her role within the organization. Researchers such as Laster 2005; Mullinix and McCurry 2003; Simpson and Payne 1999, posit that an LMS provides access to student-centred teaching approaches, increased accessibility, assessment and evaluation features, and improved management of course content and administrative tasks. All these should be possible in a mobile learning environment and through the use of mobile devices.

7 Types of Learning Management Systems

There are different types of LMS that are on the market and they include the following:

1. **Proprietary LMS:** Horton and Horton (2003) posit that proprietary LMSs are moving towards the end of their lifetime. This is because they are based entirely on the heritage of Computer Based Training (CBT) systems which were popular before

the emergence of the e-Learning and m-Learning standards era and before adoption of SCORM. These systems cannot function in a simple way with other m-Learning and e-Learning components such as Sharable Content Object components (SCO's) as defined by SCORM, neither there is a modest technique of establishing their interoperability with other m-Learning and e-Learning systems (Fertalj et al. 2006). Exporting and importing objects of knowledge and exchange of raw materials is very cumbersome with these systems. In addition, the process of integration of a proprietary with other LMS components end-to end with adjustment of the contents can sometimes take a very long time, in the process, increasing the cost of maintaining these systems (Campbell 2004).
2. **Standards Based LMS:** The term 'Standards based LMSs' refers to the type of LMSs that follows certain standards during their design phase. The fact that most companies that produced proprietary LMSs are now producing standards based LMSs makes them the most trending category. Fertalj et al. (2006) claim that conformity with standards, especially with widely accepted standards like SCORM, guarantees satisfactory levels of interoperability, not only for LMS, but for the m-Learning and e-Learning material as well. However, systems that are based on standards can be only as good as the standard itself. From literature, it is clear that most companies have adopted SCORM. That being said, these companies continue to face problems because SCORM is constantly changing due to technological advances and new possibilities, especially in communications (Campbell 2004).
3. **Open Architecture LMS:** Campbell (2004) postulates that open architecture LMSs need just a slight effort to set up, integration with contents and establishment of communication with other systems. Exchange of the contents with other systems should be easy, because m-Learning and e-Learning standards are decided about common tasks and expectations from LMSs. Therefore, truly open systems will need only minor adjustments to fulfil all requirements imposed by those standards (Campbell 2004).

8 Examples of Learning Management Systems

There is a wide range of LMSs among which institutions in developing countries need to select their best choice from. The options differ in terms of capabilities and other features. According to Bersin and Associates (2004), the main LMSs on the market at the moment are:

- Blackboard
- Desire2Learn
- Moodle (Open source)
- Instructure Canvas

There are now dozens of different types of LMS used by organizations and institutions of higher learning to manage-learning and deliver course materials to employees and learners. These systems characteristically share a common feature.

9 Benefits of LMSs

According to Jong and Wang (2009), e-Learning has become one of the most important developments in the information systems industry. To systematically manage learning and development of staff, institutions employ LMSs because of the following: ability to deliver engaging and motivating training, reliability, streamlined training and learning processes, control, scalability and wider reach, tracking and simple reporting, easy and secure exchange of learning data, technology leverage, multifunctional, flexible access to training resources, reduced learning costs, multiple learning channels and multiple media formats, reduced dependency, increased interaction between learners and instructors, twin benefits– traditional and innovative tools, and consolidation of learning information into one platform (White and Larusson 2010).

10 Theoretical Framework

Different theories have been used in Information Systems research to explain the different needs and requirements for different tools that aid teaching and learning in mobile learning, online learning and distance learning setting. Moreover, these theories are again used to explain learner's preferences that result in usage of these tools. This study applies the socio-technical theory to explain and validate the factors that influence LMS's adoption in developing countries.

Walker, et al. (2007), posit that socio (referring to people and society) and technical (referring to machines and technology) elements are combined to become 'sociotechnical' (all one word) and/or 'socio-technical' (with a hyphen). Both variations mean the same thing. According to Emery and Trist (1960), the concept of a socio-technical system was created in the context of labour studies by the Tavistock Institute in London at the end of the fifties, when labour studies were for the most part concerned with the adaptation of humans to the organizational and technical framework of production. The concept of the socio-technical system was established to stress the reciprocal interrelationship between humans and machines and to foster the program of shaping both the technical and the social conditions of work, in such a way that efficiency and humanity would not contradict each other any longer Ropohl, G. (1999). Institutions of higher learning are intricate and multifarious organizations, composed of interdependent and interrelated social and technical aspects, where changes in one aspect can impinge on the others. Therefore, the introduction of any new technology such as LMS into such a setting will necessitate reassessing changes in pedagogical principles, delivery of modules, test taking, assignment submission and work processes, and cultural change. Coiera (2004) claims that because attitudes and utility of technology are simultaneously socially shaped, socio-technical aspects should be taken into cognisance in adoption of any tools.

Therefore, socio-technical theory provides a paradigm against which workflow and perfusion of LMSs in teaching and learning could be better explored and understood. Bostrom, and Heinen (1977), presented a socio-technical model (Fig. 1) to illustrate MIS problems and failures.

As illustrated above, there are several factors one can deduce from the model. They include people (learners, instructors and system administrators), technology (learning

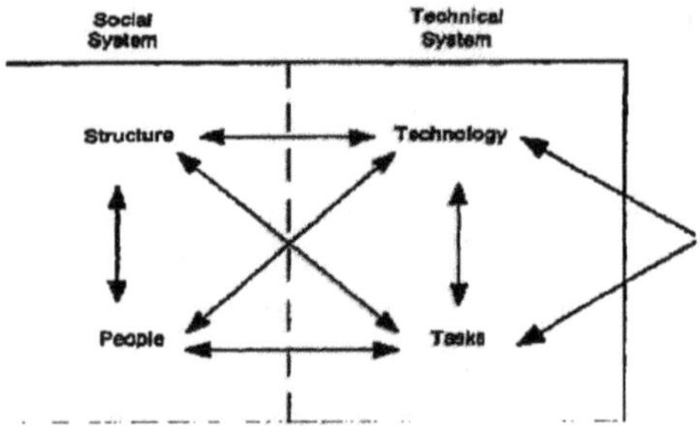

Fig. 1. MIS Problems and Failures: Bostrom and Heinen (1977)

management systems), task (assignments, tests, evaluation) and lastly, this study introduces another factor which is communication tools as there is need for learners and instructors to communicate.

11 Socio-Technical Constructs

Researchers MacKenzie and Wajcman 1999, posit that a socio-technical perspective can provide a stronger framework than any other approach because of its integrative and holistic nature. By emphasizing the complex relations between social and technical aspects of a technology, Sawyer et al.'s (2003) study shows how a socio-technical approach can be used to predict emerging technologies and to provide useful insight into them. To put this to context, this perspective will assist in giving insight on LMSs in the context of developing countries. The socio-technical constructs include the following":

12 The Type of Students Using the System (People)

There is a disparity among university learners who are accepted at these institutions. Some have been exposed to LMSs while some have not. Some are first time users of both computers and LMS, while others are experienced users as they can download materials from different sites on the Internet. They are also account holders of networking sites such as Facebook, Twitter, Skype and others. It was also noted by Robbie (2005), that university learners will only make use of an LMS if the instructors make use of it. Otherwise it is as good as useless as it will not play any role in their studies. Considering the fact that many of the developing countries are still struggling to have infrastructure that enables easy access to technology and availability, most learners in such countries therefore are likely to be first time users of these technologies.

13 Technology Fit (Technology)

Technology fit refers to the degree to which a particular technology can be applied to a task and achieve better results as compared to when it has not been employed (Goodhue and Thompson 1995). According to Zigurs and Buckland (1998), technology fit refers to a set of communication, structuring and information processing tools that are designed to work together to support the accomplishment of group tasks. However, not all technologies fit the tasks for which it is being used for. Certain tasks may require certain technologies and vice-versa. Even in the same group of technologies that are designed for that particular task, there is usually one that best suits that task. Technology fit means that a technology is more likely to have a positive impact on individual performance and that it should be used if the capabilities of that technology matches the tasks that the user must perform (Goodhue and Thompson 1995), i.e., the correspondence between task requirements, individual abilities, and the functionality of the technology ('interactions' between task, technology, and individual). As noted by Benbasat et al. 1986; Dickson et al. 1986; Zigurs and Buckland 1998), technology will be used only if its functions are available to the user through the technology support or the learner's undertakings. According to Goodhue and Thompson (1995), there are eight dimensions one can use to measure task-technology fit and they include the following: quality, compatibility, ease of use, systems reliability, and relationship with users. However, this study selects only those that are applicable in the context of teaching and learning.

14 Task Fit (Task)

Gebaue and Shaw (2002) posit that tasks have been analysed and ranked according to different characteristics, such as structure, repetitiveness, complexity of cognitive processes, and ambiguity. As Anthony (1965) put it, these tasks have different functions within the organization such as management tasks, leadership tasks, operational or administrative tasks, and learning tasks. The characteristics of a task determine the technology that is to be employed for it to be carried out effectively. According to Davenport et al. 1996, information and knowledge tasks have received particular attention. This refers to all activities of an individual organised with the intention to improve his or her knowledge, skills and competence (European Communities 2006). Acting upon this task must be intentional and with a predetermined purpose and organised in some way, including being organised by the learner himself or herself. In the context to learning tasks, this would require that a learner undertakes using the available learning resources, such as LMSs, to improve his or her knowledge of a specific topic. It happens usually in the form of writing assignments, doing research, presentations, tests and participating in discussions. For this study, the task characteristics identified include time criticality, task-non-routineness and task interdependence.

15 Communication Tools

Learning Management Systems are learning tools that can be used for a varying range of purposes (Ellis 2009). These contain communication tools such as asynchronous discussion tools, that allow-creating topics relevant to the unit where learners and staff can post and reply to messages, announcements, where you can create and send text announcements to learners and staff involved in a unit, chart tools, that allows you to communicate in real time with other people involved in the unit, mail tools, that allow you to communicate with learners and staff involved in your unit, in text- or HTML format and file attachments and one can use the Who's Online tool to chat in real time with students and staff users who are enrolled in any of the units with which you have an involvement and who are logged in to the LMS at the same time you are logged in (LMS Support Team 2010).

16 Methodology

This study takes a positivist approach by formulating empirical and testable constructs to be validated. A needs assessment evaluation methodology was applied in this study. The needs assessment was used to identify specific socio-technical factors that motivate institutions of higher learning to adopt an LMS as part of their teaching and learning strategies. To get a deeper understanding of the LMS phenomenon, this study employed a quantitative approach to measure and tests the identified constructs. Age was used as a control variable to measure the extent at which it influences adoption of these systems. The demographics analysed are (a) program of study, (b) level of study, (c) age group and (d) gender. This study was conducted by using a survey approach in which a structured closed-ended questionnaire was designed, based on a 5 point-Likert scale, probing the respondents to give their views about the importance of each of the constructs. This was self-administered to learners in institutions of higher learning in developing countries. The participants for this study were selected from different institutions in developing countries and had registered for courses in Information and Communication Technology, Engineering, Arts, Business, Sciences and Finance. This study employed simple random sampling. As claimed by Statisticsbyrachel.com (2012) simple random is an example of probability sampling where a list comprising of all of the population is created and used to obtain participants by random selection. It assures that each individual has an independent and equal chance of being selected. Guided by the research question, the identified constructs were used to design the measuring instrument that was used for the study. Out of the 300 questionnaires distributed, only 255 questionnaires were used and 45 questionnaires were discarded because not all the sections of the questionnaire were completed. The remaining 255 questionnaires were recorded in the Statistical package for social scientists (SPSS) v22 for analysis.

17 Data Analysis and Findings

Saunders et al. (2007) posit that reliability is the degree to which a measuring instrument is steady and consistent in measuring what it is envisioned to measure. Internal consistency reliabilities of identified constructs were tried with Cronbach's alpha coefficient, which is prescribed to be no less than 0.7 for it to be satisfactory (Pallant 2005). The measuring instrument was tested for reliability and was found to be conforming to the Cronbach's alpha of 0.831 for People construct (Peo), 0.874 for the Task Tit construct (TaskF), 0.831 for the Technology Fit construct (TechF) and 0.776 for Communication Tools construct (ComT). These are illustrated in table below.

Item-Total Statistics						
	Scale Mean if Item Deleted	Scale Variance if Item Deleted	Corrected Item-Total Correlation	Squared Multiple Correlation	Cronbach's Alpha if Item Deleted	Cronbach's Alpha
Peo1	40.80	63.737	.585	.	.883	0.831
Peo2	41.50	57.610	.926	.	.862	
Peo3	41.70	58.172	.731	.	.875	
TaskF1	41.40	73.645	.125	.	.901	0.874
TaskF2	41.40	73.645	.125	.	.901	
TaskF3	41.80	70.957	.248	.	.899	
TechF1	40.90	64.068	.845	.	.873	0.831
TechF2	41.10	63.867	.745	.	.875	
TechF3	40.40	68.831	.611	.	.884	
ComT1	40.80	63.737	.585	.	.883	0.776
ComT2	41.50	57.610	.926	.	.862	
ComT3	41.70	58.172	.731	.	.875	

18 Influence of Age on Socio-Technical Constructs

The model summary is significant because the significance level was found to be less than 5 % as illustrated in Table 1.1. This then means that age does influence socio-technical constructs. The analysis of variance was also found to be significant as it was also less than 5 % as illustrated on Table 1.2. However, it was found that age (which remained a constant value for all the constructs) has a significance value as it remained less that 5 % on all the constructs except for task fit. This means that age does not influence task fit.

Model Summary[b]										
Model	R	R Square	Adjusted R Square	Std. Error of the Estimate	Change Statistics					Durbin-Watson
					R Square Change	F Change	df1	df2	Sig. F Change	
1	.670[a]	.449	.443	.669	.449	72.353	4	355	.000	2.179

a. Predictors: (Constant), TaskFit, People, TechnologyFit, CommunicationTools
b. Dependent Variable: Age

ANOVA[a]						
Model		Sum of Squares	df	Mean Square	F	Sig.
1	Regression	129.344	4	32.336	72.353	.000[b]
	Residual	158.656	355	.447		
	Total	288.000	359			

a. Dependent Variable: Age
b. Predictors: (Constant), TaskFit, People, TechnologyFit, CommunicationTools

Coefficients[a]										
Model		Unstandardized Coefficients		Standardized Coefficients	t	Sig.	95.0 % Confidence Interval for B		Collinearity Statistics	
		B	Std. Error	Beta			Lower Bound	Upper Bound	Tolerance	VIF
1	(Constant)	2.810	.234		12.020	.000	2.351	3.270		
	TechnologyFit	-.214	.077	-.176	-2.773	.006	-.366	-.062	.387	2.582
	People	1.494	.339	1.830	4.411	.000	.828	2.160	.009	110.886
	CommunicationTools	-.877	.339	-1.065	-2.582	.010	-1.544	-.209	.009	109.655
	TaskFit	-.053	.056	-.043	-.954	.341	-.164	.057	.767	1.303

a. Dependent Variable: Age

19 Discussion

This study identified the socio-technical factors namely type of people using the system, task-fit, technology-fit and communication tools. With these in mind, institutions of higher learning in developing countries can realize the value and full benefits of using LMS should they address the socio-technical factors. From analysis, it is clear that these factors affect adoption greatly than previously thought. The responses shows that participants are keen to know what the technology brings to them, and if this is not identified and addressed leads to failures in both organizational goals and mobile learning initiatives.

20 Conclusion

This study notes that LMSs are very important for institutions in the developing world. These may assist them to cater for large numbers of students in different parts of the world. Considering the fact that developing countries usually have a challenge to build more universities, they can adopt new technologies that will allow them to have more learners enrolling in these institutions in the process solving problems of crowded classrooms and inadequate skilled personnel. The identified socio-technical factors in this study were tested and from the results it is clear that technology-fit, task-fit, communication tools and people using the system do influence system adoption. There is still much that need to be done so that these barriers could be understood better enabling easy adoption of LMSs.

References

Anthony, R.N.: Planning and Control Systems: A framework for Analysis. Harvard University Graduate School of Business, Cambridge (1965)

Bailey, G.D.: Wanted: A road map for understanding integrated learning systems. In: Bailey, G.D. (ed.) Cmoputer-based Integrated Learning Systems, Educational Technology Publications, Englewwod Cliffs, NJ, pp. 3–9 (1993)

Bacow, L.S., Bowen, W.G., Guthrie, K.M., Lack, K.A., Long, M.P.: Barriers to adoption of online learning systems in U.S. Higher Education. ITHAK (2012)

Benbasat, I., Dexter, A.S., Todd, P.: An experimental program investigating colour-enhanced and graphical information presentation: An integration of the findings. Commun. ACM **29**(11), 1094–1105 (1986)

Bersin and Associates. Learning management systems: The six challenges in implementation. What works. Research and Consulting in e-Learning (2004)

Bhati, N., Mercer, S., Rankin, K., Thomas, B.: Bariers and fascilitators to the adoption of tolls for online pedagogy. Int. J. Pedagogies Learn. **5**(3), 5–19 (2010). eContent management

Butler, D.L., Sellbom, M.: Barriers to adopting technology for teaching and learning. EDUCAUSE Quately **25**(2), 22–28 (2002)

Campbell, K.: Effective writing for e-Learning Environments. Idea Group Publishing, Hershey (2004)

Coiera, E.: Four rules for the reinvention of health care. BMJ **328**(7449), 1197–1199 (2004)

Dickson, G.W., DeSanctis, G., McBride, D.J.: Understanding the effectiveness of computer graphics for decision support: A cumulative experimental approach. Commun. ACM **29**(1), 40–47 (1986)

Ellis, R.K.: (2009). Learning Circuits: FieldGuide to learning management systems. American Society for Training &Development (ASTD). ASTD Inc

Emery, F.E., Trist, E.L.: Socio-technical systems. In: Management Sciences Models and Techniques, vol. 2. London (1960)

European Communities (2006). Classification of learning activities. ISSN 1725-0056

Fertalj, K., Jerković, H., Hlupić, N.: Comparison of e-learning management systems. In: Proceedings of the 5th WSEAS International Conference on E-ACTIVITIES, Venice, Italy (2006)

Gebauer, J., Shaw, M.J., Gribbins, M.L.: Task − Technology fit for mobile information systems. Int. J. Electronic Commerce (2006)

Goodhue, D.L., Thompson, R.L.: Task-Technology fit and individual performance. MIS Q. **19**(2), 213–236 (1995)

Jong, D., Wang, T.S.: Students acceptance of web-based learning system. Academy Publisher, Oulu, vol. 45, Issue 3 pp. 194-201 (2009). ISSN:0378-7206

Horton, W., Horton, K.: E-learning tools and techniques. Wiley Publishing Inc, New York (2003)

Laouris, Y., Eteokoeous, N.: (2005). We need an educationally relevant definition of mobile learning. In: Proceedings of the 4th World Conference on mLearning (mLearn 2005), pp. 1–13. Cape Town. www.mlearn.org.za/CD/papers/Laouris%20&%20Eteokleous.pdf 25 October 2014

Laster, S.: Model-driven design: systematically building integrated blended learning experiences. J. Asynchronous Learn. Netw. **8**(5), 23–40 (2005)

Lopes, V.: Course management systems and campus-based learning. Higher Education Quality Council of Ontario. Cabadian Society for the study of higher education (2008). www.csshe-scees.ca/pf/PF_29_Lopes.pdf. Accessed 1 September 2014

MacKenzie, D., Wajcman, J.: (1999). The Social Shaping of Technology, 2nd edn. Open University Press, Buckingham and Philadelphia, vol. 57, pp. 459–460 (1999, 2000)

Marchewk, J.T., Liu, C., Kostiwa, K.: An Application of the UTAUT model for understanding student perceptions using course management software. Commun. IIMA **7**(2), 93–104 (2007)

McLoughlin, C., Lee, M.J.W.: Social software and participatory learning: pedagogical choices with technology affordances in the web 2.0 era school of education. In: Proceedings Ascilite Singapore (2007)

Monarch Media (2010). Open-Source learning management systems: Sakai and Moodle. Business White Paper. At www.monarchmedia.com/enewsletter_2010-3/open-source-lms-sakai-and-moodle.pdf. 2 December 2014

Mullinix, B.B., McCurry, D.: (2003). Balancing the learning equation: Exploring effective mixtures of technology, teaching and learning. At www.technologysource.org/article/balancing_the_learning_equation, 1 November 2014
Nayak, K., Poonphon, S.: Advantages and disadvantages of learning management systems. In: Fourth International Conference on eLearning for Knowledge-Based Society. School of Information Technology. Assumption University Bangkok, Thailand (2007)
Oakes, K.: E-learning: LCMS, LMS- They're not just acronyms but powerful systems for learning. Training Dev. **56**(3), 73–75 (2002)
Organisation for Economic Co-operation and Development (2003). Poverty and health in developing countries: Key Actions. OECD policy brief. At www.oecd.org/health/18514159.pdf. 23 January 2015
Owen, M., Grant, L., Sayers, S., Facer, K.: (2006). Social software and learning. Futurelab, Bristol, England. www.futurelab.org.uk/download/pdfs/research/opening_education/Social_Software_report.pdf. Accessed 6 February 2015
Robbie, D.: Students use and experiences of Bb at Swinburne - A longitudinal study 2001 – 2005. In: Paper presented at the Blackboard Asia Pacific Users Conference, Melbourne (2005). www.ascilite.org.au/conferences/singapore07/procs/steel.pdf. Accessed 27 September 2014
Ropohl, G.: Philosophy of socio-technical systems. Soc. Philos. Technol. **4**, 186–194 (1999)
Bostrom, R.P., Heinen, J.S.: MIS problems and failures: A socio-technical perspective. MIS Q. **1**(3), 17–32 (1977)
Rycus, J.S., Freundlich, M., Hughes, R.C., Keefer, B., Oakes, E.J.: Confronting barriers to adoption success. J. Fam. Court Rev. 44(2) (2006). www.ihs-trainet.com/assets/BarriersArtic.pdf. Accessed 3 October 2014
Szabo, M., Flesher, K.: CMI theory and practice: Historical roots of learning managment systems. In: Paper presented at the E-Learn 2002 World Conference on E-Learning in Corporate, Government, Healthcare, & Higher Education, Montreal, Canada (2002)
Simpson, M., Payne, F.: Using information and communications technology as a pedagogical tool: Who educates the educators? J. Educ. Teach. **25**(3), 248–262 (1999)
Watson, W.R., Watson, S.L.: An argument for clarity: What are learning management systems, What are they not, and what should they become? TechTrends **51**(2), 28–34 (2012)
TrainCentre. LMS and LCMS: What is the difference? (2013). www.etraincenter.com/lms-lcms-compare.aspx. Accessed 11 August 2014
Walker, G., Stanton, N., Salmon, P., Jenkins, D.: A review of sociotechnical systems theory: A classic concept for new command and control Paradigms. Human Factors Integration Defence Technology Centre. HFIDTC/2/WP1.1.1/2 (2007)
White, B., Larusson, J.A.: Strategic directives for learning management system planning ECAR. Research Bulletin. Educause. Statisticsbyrachel (2010). www.statisticsbyrachel.wordpress.com/2015/02/29/sampling-techniques/. Accessed 4 October 2014
Zigurs, I., Buckland, B.K.: A theory of task/technology fit and group support systems effectiveness. MIS Q. **22**(3), 313–334 (1998)

Author Index

MIX
Papier aus verantwortungsvollen Quellen
Paper from responsible sources
FSC® C105338

If you have any concerns about our products,
you can contact us on
ProductSafety@springernature.com

In case Publisher is established outside the EU,
the EU authorized representative is:
Springer Nature Customer Service Center GmbH
Europaplatz 3, 69115 Heidelberg, Germany

Printed by Libri Plureos GmbH
in Hamburg, Germany